14

DISCARD

‖‖‖‖‖‖‖‖‖‖‖‖‖‖‖
D0890144

DATE DUE

	PRINTED IN U.S.A.

Toleration in Conflict
Past and Present

The concept of toleration plays a central role in pluralistic societies. It designates a stance which permits conflicts over beliefs and practices to persist while at the same time defusing them, because it is based on reasons for coexistence in conflict – that is, in continuing dissension. A critical examination of the concept makes clear, however, that its content and evaluation are profoundly contested matters and thus that the concept itself stands in conflict. For some, toleration was and is an expression of mutual respect in spite of far-reaching differences, but for others, it is a condescending, potentially repressive attitude and practice. Rainer Forst analyses these conflicts by reconstructing the philosophical and political discourse of toleration since antiquity. He demonstrates the diversity of the justifications and practices of toleration from the Stoics and early Christians to the present day and develops a systematic theory which he tests in discussions of contemporary conflicts over toleration.

RAINER FORST is Professor of Political Theory and Philosophy at the Goethe University in Frankfurt am Main, Germany. In addition, he is Co-Director of the interdisciplinary Research Cluster 'Formation of Normative Orders' at the Goethe University. His books include *Contexts of Justice*, *The Right to Justification* and *Justification and Critique*. In 2012, he received the Gottfried Wilhelm Leibniz Prize, the highest honour awarded to German researchers.

IDEAS IN CONTEXT

Edited by David Armitage, Jennifer Pitts, Quentin Skinner and
James Tully

The books in this series will discuss the emergence of intellectual traditions and of
related new disciplines. The procedures, aims and vocabularies that were generated will
be set in the context of the alternatives available within the contemporary frameworks
of ideas and institutions. Through detailed studies of the evolution of such traditions,
and their modification by different audiences, it is hoped that a new picture will form of
the development of ideas in their concrete contexts. By this means, artificial distinctions
between the history of philosophy, of the various sciences, of society and politics, and of
literature may be seen to dissolve.

The series is published with the support of the Exxon Foundation.

A list of books in the series will be found at the end of the volume.

Toleration in Conflict

Past and Present

RAINER FORST

Translated by CIARAN CRONIN

CAMBRIDGE
UNIVERSITY PRESS

CAMBRIDGE UNIVERSITY PRESS
Cambridge, New York, Melbourne, Madrid, Cape Town,
Singapore, São Paulo, Delhi, Mexico City

Cambridge University Press
The Edinburgh Building, Cambridge CB2 8RU, UK

Published in the United States of America by Cambridge University Press, New York

www.cambridge.org
Information on this title: www.cambridge.org/9780521885775

First published 2013

Printed and bound in the United Kingdom by the MPG Books Group

A catalogue record for this publication is available from the British Library

Library of Congress Cataloguing in Publication data
Forst, Rainer, 1964– author.
Toleration in conflict : past and present / Rainer Forst.
    pages   cm. – (Ideas in context)
Includes bibliographical references and index.
ISBN 978-0-521-88577-5 (hardback)
1. Toleration – History.   2. Religious tolerance.   3. Toleration – Political aspects.   I. Title.
HM1271.F6962   2012
201'.723 – dc23   2012019060

ISBN 978-0-521-88577-5 Hardback

For Sophie and Jonathan

Contents

Preface

'The problem of tolerance, my dear Engineer, is rather too large for you to tackle.' During work on the present book these words, which Thomas Mann's Settembrini hurled at Hans Castorp, occasionally rang in my ears. This was not only because the matter in dispute between the two characters is important for the problem of toleration, for Castorp had taken the liberty of criticising as intolerant Settembrini's plans for an enlightened world government of freethinkers who would 'strike out' metaphysics and God in order finally to overcome intolerance. Nor was it because engineers actually have an easier time with tolerance than do philosophers, for engineers use the concept in the sense of the permissible deviation from predefined norms compatible with the function of a technical system. In engineering, in contrast with philosophy, not only are these reference norms fixed but even the inaccuracies of measuring instruments, which necessitate a 'dimensional tolerance', are regarded as measurable. No, the main reason was because, as I increasingly immersed myself in the topic, the goal I had set myself – namely, to write a systematic treatise on toleration against the background of a history of the arguments offered for it and of practices of toleration which would help us to orient ourselves in our present-day conflicts – at times seemed to recede ever further into the distance. At a certain point, however, after having explored the (virtually boundless) expanse of the historical and contemporary discourse concerning toleration, I got the impression that I could present a reconstruction of this discourse and a freestanding theoretical proposal – which I do here in the hope that the result may to some extent measure up to the problem.

Without the assistance of a whole series of persons, it would not have been possible for me either to begin or to complete this project, for which reason I would like to express my sincere gratitude to them here without wanting to make them responsible for the result as well. In the first place, I would like to thank Axel Honneth for a more than ten-year rewarding and productive collaboration in Berlin, New York and Frankfurt. The countless discussions that we conducted during this time, also in the relevant research seminars, enriched and shaped my thinking in decisive ways. To Jürgen Habermas, who showed unfailing support and interest in this project and offered me valuable advice, I am grateful for remaining a conversation partner for me from the time of my studies and my doctorate. Over the years, Charles Larmore has helped me with numerous comments and, importantly, critical queries on a whole series of my writings.

During the years of work on this book, I was able to present and discuss my ideas on many occasions. I received valuable suggestions from so many colleagues and friends on these occasions that it is impossible to do justice to them in detail here. I would like to thank expressly those who took the time to send me written comments or who in constructive conversations helped me to clarify my ideas – although some of them will think that I may not have done so sufficiently: Joel Anderson, Richard J. Bernstein, Bert van den Brink, Dario Castiglione, Ingrid Creppell, Richard Dees, Günter Frankenberg, Elisabetta Galeotti, Stefan Gosepath, Klaus Günther, Rahel Jaeggi, Otto Kallscheuer, the late Andreas Kuhlmann, Matthias Lutz-Bachmann, Catriona McKinnon, Stephen Macedo, Donald Moon, Glen Newey, Peter Niesen, Werner Plumpe, Henry Richardson, Thomas M. Schmidt, Marcus Willaschek and Melissa Williams. Martin Saar undertook to subject the entire work to a critical reading and to provide comments on it, for which I am deeply grateful to him.

My most profound debt of gratitude is to Mechthild Gross-Forst, not only for the first critical reading but also for her never-flagging support and encouragement, without which I would not have been able to manage this project. My work on it coincided with the first five years in the lives of our children, Sophie and Jonathan, who time and again had to allow their father to go to his office so that he could work on 'his book' – even though there were so many other books, even ones with pictures, from which he could have read to them during that time. I dedicate this book to them in the hope that one day they will say that it was worth it.

Addendum to the English edition

It is a source of great joy for me to be able to present my book to English-speaking readers in translation, something the author of an (originally)

eight-hundred-page work can scarcely dare to hope for. It makes me all
the more happy because not only the history of English and American political theory and practice but also contemporary Anglo-American political
philosophy plays a major role in this book. My English-speaking colleagues,
with whom I have been discussing these issues over many years, can now
assess the work as a whole (and examine more closely whether the errors lie
where they suspected). Since the present publication is an abridged version,
I'm tempted to say that anything they could still find wanting is covered
in the longer version; but I will resist this temptation. The book contains
everything essential. I have also refrained from addressing important recent
contributions on the past and present of toleration which have appeared
since the German publication (2003) in order not to extend the treatise once
again.

The credit for making the improbability, and also in a certain sense
the impossibility, of a translation of this book overflowing with historical
references possible is due to a series of people. In the first place I would like
to extend my sincere gratitude to my outstanding translator Ciaran Cronin.
Himself a proven political philosopher, he has worked over several years to
produce an English version which leaves nothing to be desired. I cannot
thank him enough for this. In addition, Erin Cooper provided indispensable
assistance in the search for innumerable English references and also offered
many helpful comments.

I would like to extend my sincere thanks to Cambridge University Press
for taking the risk of publishing this hefty tome in English. That this risk was
taken is due in the first instance to Jim Tully who supported this undertaking
unstintingly from the beginning and who, together with Quentin Skinner,
Jennifer Pitts and David Armitage, to whom I am also extremely grateful,
adopted the book into the prestigious series 'Ideas in Context' – even though
its particular methodological approach, in connecting the history of ideas,
the analysis of political practice and past and present political philosophy, is
a quite uncommon one, not least in its attempt to encompass two thousand
years of a history of ourselves. As I conceive it, arguments which arose in
specific contexts migrate into others and become transformed, but in the
process acquire and preserve a distinctive systematic force that reaches into
our contemporary world. This idea of a 'critical history of argumentation'
also involves a risk if it is viewed purely from the perspective of the history of
ideas or from a systematic perspective alone. However, we will not get very
far in political theory if we fail to explore productive connections between
these perspectives, an approach which I am confident is true to the spirit of

the series. In this connection, thanks are also due to two anonymous readers for the Press who made a number of helpful suggestions for producing an English version.

On the part of Cambridge University Press, special thanks are due to Richard Fisher for persisting with and promoting this demanding undertaking. Elizabeth Friend-Smith, Lucy Rhymer, Joanna Breeze and Frances Brown have made outstanding contributions to its realisation, for which I am very grateful. That this publisher appreciates its authors above all else is something I have experienced throughout the entire process – up to the realisation of the cover whose image, Paul Klee's painting *Carpet of memory*, reflects the artist's impressions of his travels through Tunisia in 1914. This book also weaves such a carpet extending across cultures and eras and I hope that it is useful in opening up new paths of reflection. Were it also to be judged beautiful, that would be high praise indeed.

Introduction: toleration in conflict

The title *Toleration in Conflict* has a range of meanings. First, toleration is an attitude or practice which is only called for within social conflicts of a certain kind. The distinctive feature is that tolerance does *not* resolve, but merely contains and defuses, the dispute in which it is invoked; the clash of convictions, interests or practices remains, though certain considerations mean that it loses its destructiveness. 'Toleration in conflict' means that the parties to the conflict adopt an attitude of tolerance[1] because they recognise that the reasons for mutual objection are counterbalanced by reasons for mutual acceptance which do not annul the former but nevertheless speak for toleration, or even require it. The promise of toleration is that coexistence in disagreement is possible.

This raises a series of questions to be answered in the present study: What kind of conflicts call for or permit toleration? Who are the subjects and who or what are the objects of tolerance? What kinds of reasons are there for objecting to what is tolerated and how should the opposed reasons for acceptance be understood? What are the limits of toleration in different cases?

Any philosophy which seeks to understand social reality must come to terms with this concept. For conflicts which prove to be irresoluble are clearly as much a part of human existence as is the desire that they should not exist. The problem of toleration was familiar even before the concept acquired its enduring, post-Reformation form, if one thinks, for example, of Herodotus' description of differences among cultures; to put it somewhat

---

1. In the following, I do not want to make a strong conceptual distinction between 'toleration' and 'tolerance'. The former term will be used in a more general sense, whereas the latter will be used in a narrower sense primarily to refer to the personal attitude (or virtue) of tolerating the beliefs or practices of others.

1

grandly, toleration is a general human concern and is not confined to any particular epoch or culture. For as long as there has been religion, the problem of people of different beliefs and the problems of heretics and of nonbelievers have existed. Even more generally, wherever convictions concerning values have taken shape among human beings, the confrontation with others who have opposing convictions presents a challenge which may not admit of a straightforward response in terms of the values in question. If this challenge is to lead to the development of a tolerant attitude, therefore, people first have to perform a complex form of labour on their own convictions. Hence, the struggle against what at a certain point came to be called 'intolerance' has a long history; it seems to be the more original phenomenon and it calls for a pacifying, conciliatory or moral response.

Consequently, 'toleration in conflict' also means, second, that the demand for toleration is not situated above or beyond social disputes but emerges within them, so that its concrete shape is always tied to a particular social and historical context. Toleration is itself involved in the conflict, it is an *interested party*, even if, structurally speaking, its normative foundations should be as impartial as possible in order to render mutual toleration possible. Although it seeks to strike a balance, the demand for toleration is not 'neutral' in the sense that it is not also a practical demand of the parties to a conflict – and this in very different ways, for example, as partisanship for impartiality, but also as the attempt to maintain existing relations of power by granting freedom. Thus, as will transpire, the history and the present of toleration are always at the same time a history and a present of social struggles. This history is inscribed in the concept of toleration and we must reconstruct it if we want to understand the latter in its full complexity. It is a mistake to believe that systematic conceptual analysis and reflection on the history of a concept are two different theoretical enterprises, as I hope this book will show.

The third meaning is connected with the second. For tolerance is not only called for in conflicts of a particular kind and it not only represents a specific requirement of parties engaged in social controversies, but it is also itself the *object* of conflicts. The meaning of toleration is not only unclear but also profoundly controversial, both in the history of the concept and in the present day. It can happen, for example, that one and the same policy or isolated action is regarded as an expression of toleration by one person and as an act of intolerance by another. But, still worse, it is even contested whether toleration is *something good at all*. Whereas for some tolerance is a virtue demanded by God, morality, reason or at least by prudence, for others it is a condescending and paternalistic, potentially repressive gesture; for one person it is an expression of self-confidence and strength of character, for another an attitude of insecurity, permissiveness and weakness; for some it is a sign of respect for others, or even of esteem for what is alien or foreign, for others it is an attitude of indifference, ignorance and isolation. Examples of these conflicting views are legion; one need only think of Voltaire's or Lessing's praise of toleration as a sign of true humanity and supreme culture, whereas Kant speaks of the 'arrogant name of tolerance';[2] finally, arguably the most famous quotation for a critique of toleration is to be found in Goethe: 'Tolerance should be a temporary attitude only; it must lead to recognition. To tolerate means to insult.'[3]

The fourth meaning of 'toleration in conflict', finally, is that disagreements over the use and evaluation of the concept such as these are due to the fact that, although there is only one *concept* of toleration, different *conceptions* of toleration have developed over history which are in conflict with one another in past and present social controversies. Thus, there is a conflict *within* the concept of toleration itself which I will subsume under the broad headings of 'power' and 'morality'. But, in addition, not only do different conflicting conceptions of toleration exist; there is also a wide variety of extremely different *justifications of toleration*, ranging from religious, through pragmatic political, from primarily epistemological, through specifically ethical justifications, to deontological moral ones. These, too, as is only to be expected, are in conflict with one another. In what follows, I will undertake a systematic reconstruction of these conceptions and justifications and examine which of them is the most viable given the social conflicts we face.

The four meanings of the title 'toleration in conflict' mentioned above provide the point of departure for a philosophical analysis of this concept. Our current situation is marked to a high degree by conflicts to which toleration alone seems to provide an answer. The problem of toleration is a live issue in a variety of ways, not only within societies which are increasingly marked by a plurality of religions, cultural forms of life and particular communities.[4] Civil wars in which the conflicting parties define themselves in ethnic or religious terms confirm this in a drastic way; but profound controversies over where the limits of toleration should be drawn also arise within democratic societies. Especially at the international, global level the

---

2. Kant, 'What Is Enlightenment?', 21.
3. Goethe, *Maxims and Reflections*, 116 (translation amended).
4. The ubiquitousness of this problem is shown by the depiction of the situation in sixty countries on all continents in Boyle and Sheen (eds.), *Freedom of Religion and Belief.*

demand for toleration is a consequence of a multiplicity of conflicts and practical constraints to act cooperatively – contrary to the scenario of a 'clash of civilisations'.[5] Given this situation, the call for toleration is, of course, as unanimous as it is multi-voiced, so that there is an urgent need for clarification. What is the precise meaning of the concept and what value should we attach to it?

These brief reflections suggest that a wide-ranging examination of the concept must take three essential aspects into consideration. First, it must acquire a firm grasp of the history of the concept in order to gain a contextual understanding of the conflict constellations and social meanings encountered there; only an awareness of the complexity of the history of toleration as an 'idea in context' can lead to a more acute awareness of its present complexity. In this way it not only becomes possible (and necessary) to revise one-sided interpretations of this history and certain (pre-)judgements concerning toleration – for instance concerning Christian, humanist and sceptical toleration and that of the sovereign state, of liberalism and of the Enlightenment; it also becomes apparent how rich the spectrum of justifications for toleration is, in what contexts they arose and what context-transcending systematic force they possess. In my view, to understand the history of a concept also means to understand to what extent we are still part of it. Finally, the view of history will also have to be a genealogical one which reveals how, in this 'history of the present', toleration had (and has) an ambivalent relation to power.

Second, the study should examine the key dimensions of the concept, in particular the normative and the epistemological dimensions. Its goal is to develop a unified systematic theory of toleration from an analysis of the plurality of existing justifications of toleration, one capable of avoiding the dead ends of alternative approaches. And, third, it should situate the concept thus explained in current political conflicts and examine its content in a concrete way, that is, not only ask what constitutes a tolerant person but also what constitutes a tolerant society. The present book accepts this challenge, though this calls for qualification, because a truly 'comprehensive' study which would reconstruct the potential for toleration of *all* existing religions, also taking historical perspectives into account for example, cannot be undertaken here. Since reflection on the finitude of human reason plays an important role in my argument, it is advisable to keep it in mind at this point as well. Thus, in what follows my primary concern is to understand

5. See the debate triggered by Samuel Huntington's book of the same name.

and discuss in a systematic way in their respective contexts the arguments for toleration developed in the European discourse on toleration since the Stoics, with the aim of drawing on this background to formulate my own systematic proposal which must be able to demonstrate its claim to validity in other contexts.

The extensive literature on these problems reflects the analytic and normative vagueness and contextuality of the concept of toleration alluded to above, so that there are good reasons for dubbing it a 'philosophically elusive concept'.[6] I myself speak of a 'controversial' concept but take the view that the reasons for the controversy over the concept are open to historical explanation and systematic clarification. Beyond the alternative between a one-dimensional justification of a specific understanding of toleration to the exclusion of all others and merely providing an inventory of all of these meanings, the path to a complex, normative conception of toleration remains open. A study of this kind fills a gap in the literature not merely in this respect, however, but also in a methodological sense. For treatments of toleration can be categorised, in general, as historical, normative (for the most part excluding epistemology and the psychological dimension) or as 'applied' or 'practical' (in concrete political or legal theory). My aim has been to combine these perspectives.

It may be useful at this point to mention briefly the central ideas of the two parts of the book. First, I would like to counter the suspicion, inspired by the abundance of historical and contemporary understandings and appraisals of toleration, that we are dealing not with a single but with multiple concepts of toleration. In my view, as I have already indicated, we should start from the assumption that there is a single concept of toleration and a plurality of conceptions (or notions) of it. I distinguish four such conceptions. These are associated in turn with different justifications of toleration, though each conception does not necessarily have just one corresponding justification. The goal of the first part of the study is to develop a systematic account of justifications of toleration. The history I construct is thus principally a history of justifications.

The in many respects paradoxical structure of the concept of toleration set forth in the first chapter already indicates the aim of the investigation, namely, to resolve these paradoxes. The central thesis also follows from this, namely, that my proposed conception and justification of toleration is superior to the others in this respect.

6. Heyd, 'Introduction', 3.

It will also emerge in the first part that the discourse of toleration, viewed in historical terms, is characterised by two general overriding perspectives: one grounded mainly in the theory of the state, which can also be called 'vertical', and a 'horizontal', intersubjective perspective. In the former, toleration is understood chiefly as a political practice, a form of state policy, whose purpose is to maintain freedom, public order, stability, the law or the constitution – and thus always also power. From the second perspective, tolerance is understood as an attitude or virtue of persons in their behaviour towards one another. Toleration appears to them to be the right and appropriate response to the conflicts rooted in their incompatible ethical convictions. These perspectives cannot always be clearly separated and in certain authors they are present simultaneously; but distinguishing them goes a long way towards illuminating the complex discourse of toleration.

This distinction helps to establish an at once parallel and conflictual development within this discourse, namely, on the one hand, a *rationalisation of political power* and, on the other, a *rationalisation of morality*.[7] The first means that, over the course of history, state power became increasingly independent and autonomous vis-à-vis the authority of the Church and (gradually) freed itself from religious legitimation, with the result that the perspective of the theory of the state leads, on the one hand, to a primarily political justification of toleration as a measure taken by the sovereign state, though one which, on the other, is prompted by critical demands for legitimation and liberation on the part of the citizens. Hence, to say, in the context of the rationalisation of power, that toleration policy is always also power policy means not only that demanding toleration is a form of criticism of intolerant rule (and hence also a form of power), but that the ruling political power itself seeks to make use of toleration and regards toleration policy as a more rational continuation of government by other means. In the process it changes its character from a 'repressive' to a 'caring' and 'productive power', as one might say following Michel Foucault, a power which stipulates what is 'normal' and 'deviant', where the latter is differentiated in turn into what is tolerable and what is intolerable. This form of power rules not by restricting freedom directly but by granting

---

7. Here I take my orientation from the thesis of the contradictory process of social rationalisation developed by Jürgen Habermas in *The Theory of Communicative Action*. However, I confine myself to the relation between power and morality insofar as it is important for the development of toleration and do not adopt the concepts of system and lifeworld which are central for Habermas's comprehensive social analysis. There are also important differences in our respective understandings of the 'rationalisation' or 'autonomisation' of power and morality; I have commented on these in my book *The Right to Justification*, chs. 3 and 4.

freedom for specific, restricted purposes, not through exclusions but through forms of inclusion which simultaneously discipline and liberate.[8]

Closely associated with this rationalisation of power, and yet from a normative perspective in conflict with it, is the rationalisation of normative arguments for toleration. Here an increasingly independent moral justification of the demand for toleration in the name of justice emerges – in a polemical stance chiefly against religious, state and civil intolerance, of course, but also against one-sided, hierarchical practices of toleration. Furthermore, from the perspective of moral philosophy, moral arguments for toleration have a tendency to become autonomous not only vis-à-vis religious justifications, but also vis-à-vis justifications which rest on particular conceptions of what constitutes the 'good life'. The development of the idea of toleration goes hand-in-hand not only with an awareness of the diversity of such conceptions of the good but also with an awareness of the legitimacy of this plurality. In this way, talk of the 'discourse of toleration' becomes reflexive and refers, following Jürgen Habermas's concept of discourse, to a discourse of the justification of tolerance. In that discourse, normative arguments, which have both a *superordinate* and a *binding* normative character in relation to the convictions and evaluative attitudes involved in the conflict, must speak for toleration. Hence, the history of toleration is also the history of the development of a new understanding of morality and of a new outlook on the ethical, legal, political and moral identity of persons, a conflictual history of normative demands, struggles and continual redefinitions of human beings' understanding of themselves.[9]

The presentation of the historical discourse of toleration in the first part is guided by a twofold dialectical intention, if I may venture to use this term. First, it is a question of situating the discourse of toleration in the field of tension *between power and morality* in order to highlight the social and normative dynamics of the development of toleration and to show that, in the opposition between power and morality, the demand for toleration is

8. In 'What Is Critique?' Foucault situates his understanding of power and government, and of critique itself, in the context of the history of the countervailing rationalisation of subjectivisation and 'de-subjection' (32). Yet, however much he criticised the model of juridical or repressive power, Foucault remained fixated on forms of disciplining and controlling (bio-)power, so that he largely failed to take into consideration this way of exercising power through toleration and granting freedom. It also represents a special practice of power in virtue of the fact that it divides the space of what deviates from the norm once again into two parts.

9. In this sense, the history of toleration is also a history of the struggles for (and the emergence of different forms of) recognition – parallel to Axel Honneth, *The Struggle for Recognition*. However, I attempt to reconstruct its basic 'normative logic' between power and morality with the help of the principle of justification.

driven by a persistent questioning of the legitimacy of the existing relations of toleration. The history of the twofold rationalisation reveals a logic of the appeal to a *right to justification* that, in its historically situated form as concrete criticism of intolerance or false toleration, provided the foundation of emancipatory demands and, in normative terms, at the same time represents the ground of justification of what I consider to be the most consistent, reflexive-critical conception of toleration. As a consequence, this foundation is as much a 'historical truth' as it is a 'truth of reason'.

Second, the systematic presentation of historical conceptions and justifications of toleration developed in the first part (and summarised in chapter 8) provides the basis for an examination of their respective strengths and weaknesses with the aim of constructing a theory which points beyond them. Elaborating this theory will be the task of the second part. Here it becomes apparent that – not only in view of the diversity of incompatible ethical conceptions of the good, but also because of the diversity of toleration justifications which, contrary to what they claim, are particular or, in a dialectical inversion, are in danger of drawing too narrow limits – a higher-level and normatively autonomous conception of toleration is necessary which builds upon the very basic right which is the motor of the dynamics of the historical discourse of toleration. In this way, a reflexive moral theory of toleration becomes possible in which *the higher-level principle of justification itself is the sole normative ground invoked in justifying toleration*. This is the systematic point of the proposed theory: in both respects, historical and systematic, the principle of or right to justification proves to be at the core of the concept of toleration, because toleration turns essentially on the justifying reasons for specific freedoms or restrictions on freedom. Achieving reflexive and recursive clarity about this means taking a decisive step towards answering the question concerning the basis of toleration.

With the idea of a theory of toleration which is independent of controversial ethical doctrines and yet is compatible with them, and hence is in a certain sense 'tolerant', I draw upon a central idea of John Rawls[10] which he developed in the context of his theory of justice. Herein also resides the greatest difference from Rawls, however; for this leads me not to a 'political' conception of toleration which would represent the intersection of an *overlapping consensus* of ethical doctrines, but to a Kantian conception of toleration which has an *autonomous moral* foundation, and is ultimately founded

10. Rawls, *Political Liberalism*, 10: 'political liberalism applies the principle of toleration to philosophy itself'.

on a particular conception of *practical (justifying) reason* and *moral autonomy* –
yet which is not a 'comprehensive doctrine' in Rawls's sense of the term.

The kernel of the proposed conception of toleration will be presented
in the second part, initially in the form of a theory of practical justification
according to which norms must be reciprocally and generally justifiable in a
context in which they claim reciprocal and general validity – more precisely,
it must not be possible to reject them in a reciprocal and general manner.
This principle of practical reason and the criteria of reciprocity and generality make it possible to distinguish between *morally* binding norms which
are non-rejectable in this sense and *ethical* values which one can reasonably
affirm or reject (or towards which one is indifferent) independently of moral
considerations. This in turn provides the basis for the differentiation, which
is constitutive for the issue of toleration, between (1) one's own ethical conceptions of the good which one affirms without reservation, (2) universally
valid moral norms, (3) other conceptions of the good which one criticises
or rejects but can (and must) tolerate because they are not immoral and
(4) those conceptions which one condemns not primarily on ethical but on
moral grounds because they violate the criteria of reciprocity and generality.
It will become apparent, however, that the distinction between moral norms
and ethical values *itself* becomes a focus of conflict and must be redefined in
the light of particular conflicts over toleration; nevertheless, if reciprocally
justified toleration is to be possible, the basic distinction cannot be placed in
question.

In this way, it becomes clear to what extent the fundamental respect
for others as morally autonomous persons represents the basis of toleration
and to what extent tolerance is a moral virtue of *justice* – and a discursive
virtue of practical reason. Finally, this conception must prove itself in the
controversy with the alternative classical and contemporary notions and
justifications of toleration and show to what extent it goes beyond the latter
without undercutting them, that is, to what extent it justifiably claims to be
an autonomous and higher-level theory.

In a further step, the epistemological implications of my preferred
'respect conception' of toleration will be thematised. Here the conception of
practical reason invoked above must exhibit its theoretical side. What conception of ethical 'truth' – with respect to one's own convictions and those
of others – corresponds to the normative theory? A sceptical, a relativistic,
a fallibilistic, a pluralistic or a monistic one, to name just a few? As in the
normative discussion, here too an attempt will be made to defend a higher-
level, epistemological conception of the self-relativisation of ethical claims to

truth which does not lead to relativism and does not rest on any of the other particular theories of truth. As long as reason recognises its own finitude in questions of ethical truth, a space of 'reasonable' yet profound differences opens up which makes it possible to communicate about the boundaries of mutual understanding. The moral constructivism presupposed is a *practical*, not a *metaphysical* one.

Finally, we must ask what kind of relation to self and which emotional and volitional qualities and abilities are characteristic of the tolerant person. The result will reveal that the virtue of tolerance does not imply any specific ethical ideal of the person, though it does involve specific 'firm' convictions and a certain capacity for distancing oneself from oneself – and hence for tolerating oneself.

In the final chapter of the study, the proposed conception will be given a practical-political interpretation and it will be shown, not only that it involves a conception of democracy which lends the principle of justification political substance, but that the proposed approach makes possible a *critical theory of toleration* which is capable of critically analysing not only forms of intolerance but also forms of *repressive* and *disciplining* toleration. The question of a 'tolerant society' will be posed and discussed against this backdrop, drawing on a series of examples. The latter will comprise conflicts from different countries over the status of religious and ethno-cultural minorities, toleration of same-sex relationships, though also the relation to extremist political groups. These analyses will show how contested the concept of tolerance remains in the present day. For not only are the limits of toleration up for discussion but also the general understanding and justification of toleration.

This is a study of toleration; but, because of the complexity of the concept, it is also more than that. It deals simultaneously with the complex dynamic between power and morality, with the relation between religion, ethics and politics, with the capability and limits of practical reason in the face of profound ethical conflicts and, finally, with the need for a conception of morality which is situated at a higher level than this controversy and is independent of the contended evaluations (without being completely detached from them). This is perhaps the central lesson to be drawn from an examination of the issue: seeing oneself and the world with tolerant eyes means being able to distinguish between what human beings can require of one another morally and what is perhaps much more important for them, namely, their conceptions of what makes a life worth living and good. And it means seeing that the latter is a topic of endless dispute, but one which need not place in question the validity of morality, the truth of one's own convictions or the integration of a society. This insight is the accomplishment of reason for which the concept of toleration stands. Put in more abstract philosophical terms, it means correctly understanding the identity and difference of human beings.

PART I

Between power and morality: the historical discourse of toleration

A history of toleration can be many things. It can be a conceptual history and trace the changes in the use of the concept; it can be a history of ideas and situate these changes within the intellectual horizon of the period in question; or it can be a social history and present the social and political conflicts associated with the demand for toleration – and all of these approaches can pursue quite different methodological paths and provide very different normative interpretations of this history (for example, as a history of the progress of reason or as a history of the increase in power). What I attempt in the following takes up aspects of the approaches mentioned and fits them into what might be called a *critical history of argumentation*. Its goal is to analyse the central arguments which were offered for an attitude or a policy of toleration in their sociohistorical and philosophical contexts and to examine them critically, primarily with reference to their systematic content but also with regard to their role in the conflicts of their time.

The philosophical *and* political discourse of toleration must be reconstructed and in the process the social struggles and power relations within this discourse must be borne in mind no less than the corresponding contexts of argumentation; this is why I always link the systematic analysis of the justifications of toleration with a genealogical analysis of the practices of toleration (as practices of power). Contrary to the frequently advocated but jejune distinction between a 'historical' and a 'systematic' approach,

13

I hope to be able to show that the context-transcending systematic force and the contemporary relevance of the various theories of toleration become apparent precisely when they are understood against the background of their specific historical context of argumentation and conflict. A vivid representation of the historical conflicts over toleration should serve to show how much this history lives on in the present without attempting to update it in an unhistorical way in the process.

My general aim is neither to present a linear history in the sense of a series of theories building upon one another and culminating in a comprehensive synthesis – still less one which appeals to historical necessities – nor to present a no less heroic history of radical breaks and contingencies or a history of past options intended to revive memory of them. The history I relate is, however, intended to make the complexity of the concept of toleration so clear that some of our deeply ingrained judgements (and prejudices) concerning it are shaken. Even though the ambivalences exhibited by the concept of toleration will not thereby be overcome – if anything, they will become more acute – nevertheless they will become more transparent. This may not mark the grand liberation from our captivity to a one-sided history but it may throw a little more light on how multi-layered the concept and practice of toleration are, how many different paths lead to toleration and which of them are dead ends.

Regardless of its orientation, a history of toleration always presupposes one thing: a preconception of its subject matter. This is a hermeneutic insight[1] which must be taken to heart, all the more so with a concept whose meaning and evaluation fluctuate so widely. Therefore, in order to clarify the issues to be discussed and to avoid misunderstandings, I offer a preliminary definition of the concept which specifies the paradoxes of toleration to be resolved. Following that I will introduce, initially in a highly general, heuristic way, a distinction between four conceptions of toleration. In the historical survey, this distinction will help us to understand how the concept of toleration can stand for two things: for the struggle against power and against intolerance and yet at the same time also for a practice of power, for a demand for recognition and yet also for the restriction of this recognition,

---

1. 'A person who is trying to understand a text is always projecting. He projects a meaning for the text as a whole as soon as some initial meaning emerges in the text. Again, the initial meaning emerges only because he is reading the text with particular expectations in regard to a certain meaning. Working out this fore-projection, which is constantly revised in terms of what emerges as he penetrates into the meaning, is understanding what is there.' Gadamer, *Truth and Method*, 267.

at times even for a form of contempt (as Goethe thought). The goal of the first part of the study is to outline a systematic account of justifications of toleration with the aid of these four conceptions. Finally, I will indicate what I mean when I understand toleration as a 'normativity dependent concept', namely, that it has to rely on justifications of a certain kind.

1

Toleration: concept and conceptions

§1 The concept of toleration and its paradoxes

In view of the diverse and conflicting understandings and usages of the concept of toleration mentioned in the introduction, one might be led to assume that there is not just one, but many, conflicting concepts of toleration, much in the sense that Isaiah Berlin spoke of 'two concepts of liberty'.[1] However, this assumption is mistaken. For, if these usages are to count as intelligible understandings of toleration, they must share a core meaning, and this core is the *concept* of toleration. They differ in how they elaborate this core and thus constitute different *conceptions* (or ideas or notions) of toleration.[2] It is contradictory to speak of a divergence among 'concepts' of toleration, for this very way of speaking presupposes that there is no such divergence.[3] This is why I follow John Rawls's proposal (apropos the concept of justice) in distinguishing between concept and conception. The 'concept' includes the central semantic contents of the concept, whereas 'conceptions' are specific interpretations of the elements contained within the concept.[4] These central elements, of which there are six, will be set forth in what follows.

(1) First, it is important to specify the *context of toleration* in greater detail. By this is meant in the first place the relation between the tolerators and

---

1. Berlin, 'Two Concepts of Liberty'.
2. I argue that this is also the actual thesis of Berlin's discussion of freedom in Forst, 'Political Liberty'.
3. Putnam, *Reason, Truth and History*, 116–19, offers a transcendental argument for the claim that shared concepts are necessary preconditions for understanding different *conceptions* of something – which are therefore *not* fundamentally incommensurable. This is particularly relevant for the question of the sense in which one can or must speak of a cross-cultural concept of toleration.
4. See Rawls, *A Theory of Justice*, 5. The idea of this distinction, though not the terminology, can be found in Hart, *The Concept of Law*, 156.

17

the tolerated, for example between parents and children, between friends, colleagues, members of a religious community or citizens, or even between 'world citizens' who do not share any of these specific contexts. The reasons for or against toleration will shift according to context; in one, toleration may be exercised out of love, in another, for pragmatic reasons or based on mutual respect.

Furthermore, there is the question concerning the subjects of toleration. Is it exercised by persons, by groups, by 'society' or by the 'state'? And what are the objects of toleration? Convictions, systems of convictions, worldviews, personal qualities, even persons themselves, individual actions, practices, etc.? And, finally, which actions are required or forbidden by toleration? Does it merely call for a negative 'putting up with' (*Duldung*) or for a positive, active recognition, or even promotion, of others? What form of letting be (*Gewährenlassen*) and nonintervention is advisable? Is attempting to persuade through speech also one of the inadmissible forms of influence?

In what follows, I will limit myself to the context which played the central role in the history of toleration and which is also the most important in contemporary discussions, namely, that of a religiously and culturally pluralistic society or political community. Answers to the questions posed will be offered within this framework; thus, apropos the question of the subjects of toleration, it is of considerable importance whether one is thinking of the state or the government or of the citizens themselves. As regards the question of the objects of toleration, in this chapter I will first speak in general terms of 'convictions' and 'practices'.

(2) Of primary importance for the concept of toleration is the fact that the tolerated convictions or practices are regarded as false or condemned as bad in a substantive normative sense; drawing upon Preston King, this can be described as the *objection component*.[5] Without this component one would not speak of toleration but either of indifference (the absence of a negative or positive valuation) or of affirmation (the presence of a positive valuation). Although these two attitudes are often confused with toleration, in fact they are incompatible with it.[6]

For there to be a genuine occasion for toleration the objects to be tolerated must be convictions and practices which are regarded as sufficiently important for it to be worthwhile to form a negative judgement about them. To understand 'normatively substantive objection' only as implying 'moral'

5. Here I follow King, *Toleration*, 44–51, who calls this the 'objection component'.
6. Thus, Walzer, *On Toleration*, 10–11, uses too broad a concept of toleration since he includes both attitudes.

objection would represent an unnecessary restriction of the general concept of toleration, however, for this would exclude criticism on aesthetic grounds, for instance. The reasons for objecting to particular practices may be of very different kinds and moral reasons represent just one possible category.[7]

A very important problem concerning the objection component is broached by the formulation 'normatively substantive' when tolerance is regarded as an individual virtue (and *only* in this case, which already involves a specification of the general concept of toleration). For although it would be an exaggeration to demand that the reasons for objection should be 'objective' or 'capable of being generally shared', nevertheless certain criteria for a 'rational' critique are indispensable. This becomes clear once one asks why the expression that someone should 'tolerate other races' or the call to tolerate 'people who look different' are problematic. The reason is that the objection component is preserved and reinforced in toleration to the extent that, as will soon become apparent, positive reasons for acceptance are juxtaposed with it without the negative valuation being revoked. If the objection were to rest on mere prejudices, however, such as the inferiority of certain 'races' (or even on blind hatred) and no reasons existed which were in a basic sense intersubjectively defensible, then the call for tolerance would accept such objections and prejudices as valid judgements to a certain extent. This could lead to the *paradox of the 'tolerant racist'* according to which someone with extreme racist antipathies would be described as tolerant (in the sense of a virtue) provided only he showed restraint in his actions (without changing his way of thinking). And the more such prejudices he had, the greater would be his scope for tolerance.[8] To call on a racist to be tolerant, therefore, is a mistake; what is required is instead that one should repudiate this prejudice and attempt to convince him of its groundlessness.[9] Otherwise the

7. Thus, Warnock, 'The Limits of Toleration'.
8. On this paradox, see Horton, 'Three (Apparent) Paradoxes of Toleration', 17–18, and (drawing on Horton) Newey, *Virtue, Reason and Toleration*, 107–8. Neither author makes altogether clear whether the paradox results from the fact that someone becomes even more tolerant the more negative judgements she makes without acting accordingly (so that the problem is primarily a matter of quantity), or whether it results from the fact that someone would be described as tolerant even if she were to base her rejection on racist prejudices (so that the problem is primarily a qualitative one). In my view, only the latter leads to a paradox, whereas it is not problematic to say that someone is required to show more tolerance the more (minimally justified) negative judgements she makes. Horton, 'Toleration as a Virtue', is clearer on this point. He points out that this problem was the motivation for Nicholson, 'Toleration as a Moral Ideal', 160, to demand a moral justification of the rejection and not to admit mere 'tastes or inclinations'. Although the former is rightly criticised by Warnock, 'The Limits of Toleration', she herself fails to offer a criterion for when a rejection based on 'dislike' is sufficiently justified.
9. Crick, 'Toleration and Tolerance in Theory and Practice', is clear on this point.

demand for toleration would be in danger of exerting repressive effects by perpetuating social discrimination and baseless condemnations.

Resolving this paradox regarding the virtue of tolerance, however, cannot come down to the global demand to eliminate the problem of toleration altogether by promoting the cause of 'enlightenment' and the abolition of all relevant negative judgements. It must be a matter of formulating minimal conditions for objection judgements, which, to put it in negative terms, exclude grossly irrational and immoral prejudices. The reasons for objection must be sufficiently 'defensible' that it remains comprehensible why the convictions and practices of others are condemned; the bare reference to 'differences in appearance' or 'coming from elsewhere' cannot serve as a substantive criticism. Reasons for objection will be drawn from particular ethical belief systems; yet they must also be recognisable and intelligible as reasons where the reasons in question are not shared. The key point is that they must not fall below a certain moral threshold below which one cannot speak of tolerance as a virtue. The resolution of this first paradox is thus an indication that the virtue of tolerance needs a moral justification through which this threshold can be determined.

This shows that, on the one hand, it is wrong to regard the concept of toleration as a contrasting concept to that of prejudice, for the dissolution of prejudices may remove the objection judgement and with it also the precondition for toleration. Although someone who combats prejudices also combats intolerance, she also promotes tolerance in the process only if she is convinced that meaningful negative judgements remain valid even when the prejudices are overcome. On the other hand, it is correct to regard the virtue of tolerance as being in conflict with prejudices insofar as it only comes on the scene when the latter have been 'purified' into judgements.

(3) In addition to the objection component, toleration, as already indicated, also has an *acceptance component*[10] which specifies that the tolerated convictions and practices are condemned as false or bad, yet not so false or bad that other, positive reasons do not speak for tolerating them. The important point here is that the positive reasons do not cancel out the negative reasons but are set against them in such a way that, although they trump the negative reasons (in the respect relevant in the corresponding context), and in this sense are higher-order reasons,[11] the objection nevertheless retains

10. King, *Toleration*, 51–4.
11. Heyd, 'Introduction', speaks aptly of 'second-order reasons' (13); however, in his theory of a gestalt switch from the criticised convictions and practices to the human personality of the tolerated other, he incorrectly assumes that the negative reasons are disabled in the process:

its force. The practical reflection of those who exercise tolerance consists in this balancing of reasons and the various justifications of toleration differ primarily in how they reconstruct these reasons and the corresponding forms of reflection.

The nature of the reasons for objection or acceptance remains open at the level of the general definition of the concept. Thus, a negative aesthetic valuation can be offset by a positive ethical or moral evaluation or a religiously grounded objection by other religiously grounded considerations. In the case in which both the objection and the acceptance components involve reasons of the same kind, a paradox results which leads directly to the heart of the problematic of toleration, namely, that such reasons seem to call for both objection as well as acceptance. This paradox can be resolved in such a way that, within a religious framework of justification, for example, orders of reasons are constructed such that it is regarded, for instance, as God's will to tolerate those who have a false faith and to try to persuade them instead of oppressing them or trying to force the true faith upon them.[12]

But if the reasons for objection as well as those for acceptance are identified as moral, the paradox is exacerbated into the question of *how it can be morally right or even obligatory to tolerate what is morally wrong or bad.* This paradox, which I call the *paradox of moral toleration*, has been exhaustively discussed in the recent literature on toleration and has inspired very different proposals. Preston King proposes to resolve it by prioritising objections according to which acting on the first objection would lead to consequences to which one objects even more strongly.[13] D. D. Raphael attempts to specify the second objection in terms of the criterion of the violation of rights.[14]

According to John Horton, resolutions of the paradox are possible if either pragmatic reasons speak for toleration or it becomes clear that lack of toleration would jeopardise a higher-level value like freedom or autonomy as a matter of principle.[15] Other authors are more sceptical concerning

'The virtue of tolerance consists in a switch of perspective, a transformation of attitude, based not on the assessment of which reasons are overriding but on ignoring one type of reason altogether by focusing on the other' (11).

12. Thus, Garzón Valdés, '"Nimm deine dreckigen Pfoten von meinem Mozart!"', 484, is mistaken in his general assertion that the 'system of norms' underlying the negative valuation must always be of a different kind than the 'justifying system of norms' which provides positive reasons, and hence that 'intra-systemic tolerance' is not possible.

13. King, *Toleration*, 31.

14. Raphael, 'The Intolerable', 147.

15. Horton, 'Three (Apparent) Paradoxes of Toleration', 13. See Raz, 'Autonomy, Toleration and the Harm Principle', for a similar view.

such resolutions of the paradox.[16] According to Susan Mendus, we must go beyond liberal justifications and appeal to the communitarian-socialist idea that tolerating something which one objects to, but which nevertheless is part of people's identities, is imperative if we are to create an inclusive society to which all can feel they belong.[17] Glen Newey comes to the conclusion that tolerance must be regarded as a supererogatory attitude on the grounds that the reasons for objections are morally sufficient to repudiate a conviction or practice *pro tanto*, and hence that there cannot be an obligation to tolerate.[18]

This is not the place to examine these (and other) proposals since that would mean examining the full spectrum of justifications for toleration. It becomes clear, however, that resolving the paradox of moral toleration depends on a more precise clarification of how the reasons for objection must be constituted in order to admit a morally grounded, higher-level acceptance component without contradiction; and this necessitates falling back on the distinction between *ethical* and *moral* reasons, and the corresponding judgements concerning 'wrong' or 'bad' convictions and practices (though this distinction will itself become questionable in the light of certain toleration conflicts). Hence, resolving this second paradox represents a second reason for a specifically moral justification of toleration.

The paradox in question is reflected at the epistemological level. For, if the objection to 'wrong' convictions is understood as a function of being convinced of the truth of one's own system of values, then the *paradox of the relativisation of truth* follows. According to this, the person who exercises toleration seems to be compelled, on the one hand, to regard her convictions as true if she is to arrive at a negative judgement but, on the other, to assume that the convictions objected to could also be true if she is to arrive at a judgement of acceptance.[19] This paradox represents a serious encumbrance for the concept of toleration for it amounts to the demand for a kind of relativisation

16. Thus, also Halberstam, 'The Paradox of Tolerance', for whom only placing limits on one's own convictions promises a solution, and (for a moderate view) Becker, 'Toleranz', 419, for whom tolerance always has 'something irrational' because it involves making concessions to a position to which one believes one is justified in objecting.

17. Mendus, *Toleration and the Limits of Liberalism*, 161–2.

18. Newey, *Virtue, Reason and Toleration*, 73–4.

19. Julius Ebbinghaus formulated this point clearly: 'How can … someone who is convinced of the need to accept certain assertions as true be tolerant? Doesn't that mean requiring him to concede in the same breath that he could also regard these very same assertions as false? This is all the more problematic when the assertions concern conditions of his eternal well-being, which lose their entire value for a human being when he cannot be sure that all contrary statements are false. Can one conceive of anything more paradoxical?' Ebbinghaus, 'Über die Idee der Toleranz', 1–2.

and restriction of one's own convictions which does not fundamentally place in question one's conviction concerning their truth – a *relativisation without relativism*, as it were. I will try to argue that this is possible.

(4) The concept of toleration implies the need to specify the *limits of toleration*, the boundary separating it from what cannot be tolerated. This is a conceptual matter, for toleration involves a precarious balance between negative and positive reasons and presupposes the willingness to suspend toleration when the tolerated convictions and practices are judged so negatively that the positive reasons are no longer sufficient. The space of toleration is intrinsically limited. Wanting to tolerate 'everything' is contradictory, for in that case one would have to tolerate a practice and at the same time also tolerate its not being tolerated. But unlimited toleration is also impossible for practical reasons, for, according to Popper, it would entail the paradox that toleration would disappear altogether: if toleration extends to the enemies of toleration, it leads to its own destruction (this could be called the *paradox of self-destruction*).[20] This paradox is overcome when it becomes clear that toleration is justifiably restricted and when it is understood as a matter of reciprocity, so that intolerance does not have to be tolerated (and under certain conditions should not be tolerated either).

But how is the limit of toleration drawn? Here it is important to recognise that, in addition to the reasons for objection and reasons for acceptance, we need a third category of reasons, namely, those for rejecting convictions and practices, where the rejection can no longer be offset by reasons for acceptance. Hence one can speak of a *rejection component*.[21] The nature of the reasons for rejection is not laid down in advance: they can be of the same kind as the reasons for objection or the reasons for acceptance, but they can also be of a different kind.[22] These are real possibilities and in the case of morally grounded toleration, for instance, it is true, notwithstanding initial appearances, that there is a homology, not between the reasons for objection and those for rejection, but rather between the (moral) reasons which call for a conditional acceptance and the (moral) reasons which under other circumstances call for the rejection. The reasons for acceptance thus already contain a determination of their limits.

20. Cf. Popper, *The Open Society and Its Enemies*, vol. 1, 292–3, n. 4; Popper, 'Toleration and Intellectual Responsibility', 17–20. On this, see the discussion of Horton, 'Three (Apparent) Paradoxes of Toleration', 14–16.
21. King, *Toleration*, 55, also speaks here of 'rejection'; however, he does not offer any further specification of objection and acceptance and hence only describes intolerance, not the legitimate limits of toleration.
22. Newey, *Virtue, Reason and Toleration*, 32–4, correctly points this out.

Against this background it becomes clear that we should make a distinction between two boundaries. First, the boundary between (a) the normative domain of that with which one agrees completely, in which there is affirmation and no objection – the domain of what is truly 'one's own', as it were – and (b) the domain of what can be tolerated in which there is normative objection and yet also an acceptance which leads to toleration. The second boundary, the true limit of toleration, runs between the latter domain and (c) the domain of what cannot be tolerated, of what is strictly rejected and repudiated. As regards toleration, therefore, we must distinguish three normative domains, not just two.

In light of the foregoing, however, the above-mentioned resolution of the paradox of self-destruction seems to lead to a new paradox, this time one not easily overcome. If the concept of toleration implies the necessity of drawing a boundary, then every concretisation of the concept leads to the drawing of a boundary which places the tolerant on the 'good' side in contrast to those who are labelled as 'intolerable' or 'intolerant' by this act. But then there is no true toleration because this one-sided act seems itself to be an act of intolerance and of arbitrary exclusion. That which lays claim to the name of toleration merely serves to protect and strengthen one's own evaluative convictions and practices and to claim a higher form of legitimacy for them. Neither side can fall back on such a claim to legitimacy, however. Therefore, the *paradox of drawing the limits* states that toleration must always flip over into its opposite, intolerance, once it traces the inevitable boundary between what can and cannot be tolerated.[23]

This paradox points to central difficulties with the concept of toleration. For it can indeed be shown that where the maxim 'No toleration towards the intolerant!' was filled with content, intolerance all too often crept in and made its presence felt, for example when the adherents of a particular religion were – and are – distrusted and condemned as a group; this is especially apparent in the treatment of Jews or atheists. There are very good reasons for mistrusting the way in which the boundaries separating the 'tolerant' from the 'intolerant' were drawn historically and continue to be drawn today. Here we should not forget that toleration is always also a matter of power.

However, the all-embracing, deconstructivist-sceptical rhetoric must itself be treated with scepticism, for it conflates two meanings of 'intolerance' which should be kept apart. For to describe both the attitude and

---

23. Thus, in particular, Fish in his critique of liberalism (though he does not use these words), 'Mission Impossible'; cf. also (in a weaker form) Minow, 'Putting Up and Putting Down'.

behaviour of those who roundly reject the norm of toleration and the attitude and conduct of those who do not tolerate this as 'intolerance' presupposes a relativism and scepticism concerning values which fundamentally doubt the possibility not only of drawing the limits of toleration in a non-arbitrary way, but also of drawing them *impartially* in the light of higher-order considerations. It also makes it incomprehensible how one could still take an independent ethical or moral stance founded on anything more than purely arbitrary, particular and perspectival reasons.[24] Then the problem of toleration also disappears, of course, for the objection component gets lost.

This answer does not resolve the paradox in question, however. Rather, this presupposes the possibility of a non-arbitrary but reciprocal form of justification of the limits of toleration, so that the identification and critique of intolerance cannot itself be designated as 'intolerance'. Not every rejection could then be criticised as intolerance, but only a rejection which lacks good reasons.[25] The concept of toleration can be rescued only if we succeed in placing it on a higher-level, generally justifiable foundation which cannot be deconstructed as one-sided and arbitrary. Thus, in the demand for a resolution of this paradox and for a reflexive determination of its limits, we find a further, third pointer to the need for a certain moral justification of toleration.

(5) The concept of toleration is further characterised by the fact that tolerance must be exercised *of one's own free will* and may not be coerced to such an extent that the tolerating party has no possibility of expressing their objection or acting accordingly. For in that case one would speak instead of 'putting up with' or 'enduring' practices against which one is powerless.[26] However, to conclude that the tolerating party must be in a position of power from which it could effectively prevent the practices in question is unfounded.[27] For a minority which is not equipped with such power can also adopt an attitude of tolerance and be of the (uncoerced) conviction that,

24. Fish's recommendation at the end of his essay ('Mission Impossible', 2332), which casts doubt on the existence of a higher-level morality of equal respect – 'Figure out what you think is right and then look around for ways to be true to it' – thereby becomes unintelligible, for then neither what can still be called 'right' nor what motivates someone to remain true to it is clear.
25. Correspondingly, by way of definition, a prejudice would be an objection without good reasons and false tolerance would consist in unjustified acceptance.
26. Cf. Garzón Valdés, "'Nimm deine dreckigen Pfoten von meinem Mozart!'", 471. However, this played an important role in the early Stoic and Christian meaning of the word. Cf. §4.
27. Thus, for example, Crick, 'Toleration and Tolerance in Theory and Practice', 147; King, *Toleration*, 21; Mendus, *Toleration and the Limits of Liberalism*, 9. Nicholson, 'Toleration as a Moral Ideal', 161, expresses tentative doubt concerning this dominant position, though he is not consistent. The outstanding exception is Williams, 'Toleration: An Impossible Virtue?', 19.

were it to have sufficient means of power at its disposal, it would not use them to the disadvantage of others.

(6) Finally, something which has already proved to be important several times must be borne in mind, namely, that the concept of toleration can signify both a *practice* and an individual *attitude* or (given a corresponding justification) a virtue – for example, the legal-political practice within a state of according minorities certain liberties, on the one hand, and the personal attitude of tolerating practices with which one does not agree, on the other.[28] The former can certainly occur without the latter, for in a state there can be a 'policy of toleration', and hence particular rights for minorities, even though the majority of citizens reject this and the government which accords these rights does not have a tolerant attitude but instead pursues a completely different power-political calculation. Thus, an analysis of toleration which focuses primarily on the political-structural, practical level of producing a peaceful coexistence among cultural groups, such as that presented by Michael Walzer in his instructive description of different regimes of toleration, ranging from multinational empires to multicultural immigrant countries,[29] remains normatively indeterminate not only with respect to the question of which conception of toleration is appropriate for a country in which controversy reigns over whether it conforms to the model of the nation-state or to that of a society of immigrants. In addition, such a conception does not address the crucial question of which virtue of tolerance it is that the citizens of a tolerant society can expect of one another in a given case.

§2 Four conceptions of toleration

In light of this characterisation of the central elements of the concept of toleration, in what follows I will outline four conceptions which provide specific interpretations of these elements. All of them refer to the political context of a state in which the citizens (as members of particular communities) exhibit important, profound differences. These conceptions of toleration are not construed as different regimes of toleration, whether in the sense of a historical series or in Walzer's sense. For, as current discussions of the problem of toleration show, these conceptions exist *simultaneously* in present-day

28. Some authors propose reserving the term 'toleration' for the former and the term 'tolerance' for the latter. See Lukes, 'Toleration and Recognition', 214, n. 2; Newey, *Virtue, Reason and Toleration*, 5. This distinction (which is also disputed in English) does not exist in German. For my use of these terms see note 1 in the introduction.
29. Walzer, *On Toleration*, in particular chs. 1 and 2.

societies. Moreover, many of these heated discussions about what toleration means in concrete terms can be understood as conflicts between these
conceptions.[30] To begin with, the four conceptions will be presented in a
language of relations of recognition which remains substantially neutral as
regards the question of justification and permits a differentiated view of
these interpersonal relations.[31] Although particular dimensions of justification will already be broached, only in the course of the first part of the
study will it become apparent which justifications are compatible with these
conceptions.

(1) On the first conception, which I call the *permission conception*, toleration
designates the relation between an authority or a majority and a minority
(or several minorities) which does not subscribe to the dominant system
of values. Toleration here means that the authority (or majority) grants the
minority the permission to live in accordance with its convictions so long as
it – and this is the crucial condition – does not question the predominance of
the authority (or majority). The Edict of Nantes of 1598, which was supposed
to put an end to the conflicts between Catholics and Huguenots in France,
can serve as a historical example. In it Henry IV declared: '[N]ot to leave any
occasion of trouble and difference among our Subjects, we have permitted
and do permit to those of the Reformed Religion, to live and dwell in all the
Cities and places of this our Kingdom and Countreys under our obedience,
without being inquired after, vexed, molested, or compelled to do any thing
in Religion, contrary to their Conscience, nor by reason of the same be
searched after in houses or places where they live.'[32] The more than four
centuries separating us from this edict (which was revoked in 1685) should
not mislead us into thinking that this form of toleration has lost its relevance,
however; on the contrary, it is often raised as a minimal demand by oppressed
minorities and plays an important role in the interest calculations of states
and majority populations.[33]

As long as the difference between the minority and the majority remains
within limits and a 'private matter' so that no demand is made for a public

---

30. I analyse this in §38.
31. This leaves open the possibility of identifying a normative dynamic of conflicts of recognition
     within and between these conceptions. This draws on Honneth, *The Struggle for Recognition*,
     though without adopting a teleological developmental perspective extrapolated out of the
     concept of recognition.
32. The Edict of Nantes, quoted from Mousnier, *The Assassination of Henry IV*, 316-47.
33. A further, informative historical example, which reveals the diversity within the permission
     conception, is the millet system of the Ottoman Empire; cf. Kymlicka, 'Two Models of
     Pluralism and Tolerance'.

political status based on equal rights, the minority can be tolerated on this conception primarily on pragmatic grounds, though also for reasons of normative principle. The minority can be tolerated on pragmatic grounds because it does not disturb law and order, whereas, on the contrary, combating it would entail significant costs; and for principled reasons because, for instance, it is regarded – in the light of a certain notion of conscience – as illegitimate (and not just as impossible, though possibly that too) to force people to renounce their deepest convictions, especially their religious ones, as long as the latter do not have politically and ethically 'unacceptable' consequences. According to the permission conception, therefore, toleration means that the authority or majority which has the power and opportunity to intervene and to coerce the minority into (at least external) conformity, 'puts up with' their difference and refrains from intervening, while the minority is forced to accept the authority's position of power. Therefore, the toleration situation is not reciprocal: one side permits the other certain deviations provided that the political dominance of the permission-granting side is not infringed upon.[34] Toleration is understood accordingly as *permissio mali*, as putting up with a conviction or practice which is regarded as neither worthy nor deserving of equal treatment, even though it does not exceed the 'limits of the bearable'. It is this conception which Goethe had in mind in his (already quoted) dictum concerning toleration as an insult.[35]

(2) The second conception of toleration, the *coexistence conception*, resembles the first in that, according to it, tolerance likewise counts as an appropriate means of avoiding conflict and pursuing one's own ends and does not itself represent a value or rest on strong values. Toleration is justified primarily in pragmatic and instrumental terms. What changes, however, is the constellation formed by the subjects and objects of toleration. For now an authority or majority and a minority or minorities do not confront one another but groups of approximately equal strengths who recognise that they must practise tolerance for the sake of social peace and in their own interests. They prefer peaceful coexistence to conflict and consent to the rules of a modus vivendi in the shape of a mutual compromise. The toleration relation is thus no longer a vertical one, as in the permission conception, but a horizontal one: those who exercise tolerance are at the same time also

---

34. Yovel, 'Tolerance as Grace and as Rightful Recognition', 897–8, calls this form of tolerance 'tolerance as grace', with which he correctly describes, on the one hand, the one-sided and despotic granting of liberties though, on the other, he imputes a particular motive ('beneficence') that is merely one among many others.
35. Goethe, *Maxims and Reflections*, 116.

tolerated.[36] Of course, here the insight into the preferability of a condition of toleration does not have a normative character but is rather an insight into practical necessities. Hence, it does not lead to a stable social condition, for once the relations of social power shift in favour of one or the other group, the essential reason for toleration no longer exists for this group.[37]

The coexistence conception admits of a weaker and a stronger reading. According to the first, toleration is merely a result of the fatigue induced by intense and unsuccessful conflicts and struggles and is seen as a kind of truce which holds up only as long as one party has not recovered more quickly and believes itself to be in a position to pursue aggressively its continuing goal of achieving social dominance. Such a situation of toleration is extremely unstable and marked by mutual distrust. The stronger reading takes its cue from a modified version of Hobbes's *Leviathan*. According to this, the subordination of the various parties to a maximally neutral and moreover (contrary to Hobbes's argument) evaluatively and religiously restrained supreme power makes possible the development of stable structures of coexistence, and possibly also of cooperation, because a legal condition accepted by all sides exists.[38] Although all those concerned continue to act overall on the basis of strategic calculation, the advantages of the state of coexistence in the situation seem to be much more attractive than the other alternatives. Toleration can – in conformity with a 'liberalism of fear'[39] – be guided by a pragmatic insight into the excessively high costs of confrontation and by insight into the horrors and cruelty of religious conflicts[40] and hence have a rational, normative core in the shape of the principle of avoiding the *summum malum*. However, this does not lead to a form of mutual recognition which goes beyond the sufferance of others and rests on farther-reaching moral or ethical considerations.

(3) By contrast, the *respect conception* of toleration proceeds from a morally grounded form of mutual respect on the part of the individuals or groups who exercise toleration. The tolerating parties respect one another as autonomous persons or as equally entitled members of a political community constituted under the rule of law.[41] Although their ethical convictions about the good

36. Cf. Garzón Valdés, "'Nimm deine dreckigen Pfoten von meinem Mozart!'", 474–7.
37. See Rawls, 'The Idea of an Overlapping Consensus', 433; Fletcher, 'The Instability of Tolerance'.
38. On the idea of such a development, see Dees, 'The Justification of Tolerance'.
39. See Shklar, 'The Liberalism of Fear'; Williams, 'Toleration, a Political or Moral Question?'
40. See Margalit, *The Decent Society*, 176–80; also Becker, 'Nachdenken über Toleranz'.
41. Compare the (contrasting) notions of respect of Scanlon, 'The Difficulty of Tolerance', Yovel, 'Tolerance as Grace and as Rightful Recognition' and Bobbio, 'Tolerance and Truth', 134.

and worthwhile life and their cultural practices differ profoundly and are in important respects incompatible, they recognise one another – and here an alternative with far-reaching consequences presents itself – as ethically autonomous authors of their own lives[42] *or* as moral and legal equals in the sense that, in their view, the basic structure of political and social life common to all, which concerns the basic questions of the ascription of rights and the allocation of social resources,[43] should be governed by norms which can be accepted by all citizens alike without privileging any single 'ethical community' (e.g. a religious community). This is based on respect for the moral autonomy of the individual and her 'right to justification' of norms which claim to be reciprocally and generally valid. Notwithstanding the (important but here not further thematised)[44] alternative between justifications based upon a theory that – following classical liberalism – treats the right to be the autonomous author of one's life as central and justifications based upon an approach which emphasises the principle of the impartial justification of universal norms of justice, the respect conception does not require that the tolerating parties must regard and value the others' conceptions of the good as equally (or in part) true and ethically good but that they should be able to view them (and here the alternative again comes into play) as the results of autonomous choices or as not immoral. The person of the other is *respected*; her convictions and actions are *tolerated*.

Two models of the respect conception can be distinguished, that of *formal equality* and that of *qualitative equality*. The former assumes a strict separation between the private and public domains according to which ethical differences between citizens should be confined to the private domain and must not lead to conflicts within the public political sphere. All citizens are equal and, as equals, they stand 'outside' or 'above' their private convictions. This model can be found in liberal and republican versions depending on whether individual, private liberty or the political equality of the *citoyens*

---

42. Weale, 'Toleration, Individual Differences, and Respect for Persons'; for a specific, 'perfectionistic' version, see Raz, 'Autonomy, Toleration and the Harm Principle'.
43. See Rawls, 'The Basic Structure as Subject', *Political Liberalism*, Lecture 7.
44. The extent to which the second justification alternative should be preferred will emerge in the course of the study, for the first rests on non-generalisable, liberal conceptions of the good life and the autonomous individual and, in addition, leads to contradictions in justifications of toleration – for example, where too narrow boundaries are set to respect by limiting it exclusively to 'autonomously chosen' convictions and forms of life; by contrast, the proposal to tolerate convictions whenever they can be traced back to autonomously made decisions would set very wide limits to respect. However, it is important in this context to recognise how wide the spectrum of ethical justifications of respect is and that they are far from being centred exclusively on respect for 'freely chosen' convictions; on this, see §30.4.

is accorded central importance; an example of the latter is the view of the French authorities that headscarves as a religious symbol have no place in a public school.[45] The model of formal equality, therefore, turns essentially on defending classical liberty rights of citizens and avoiding discrimination on ethical grounds.

The model of qualitative equality, by contrast, is a reaction to the fact that certain strict regulations of formal equality are in danger of giving preference to ethical-cultural forms of life whose convictions and practices can be more easily reconciled with such a separation between 'private' and 'public' or correspond to the received understanding of this separation. Viewed in this light, the model of formal equality is itself potentially intolerant and discriminatory towards forms of life which lay claim to a kind of public presence that contradicts customary practice and conventional institutions. According to the alternative model, persons respect one another as legal and political equals who nevertheless have different, politically relevant ethical and cultural identities with a special claim to consideration and toleration because the values and convictions constitutive of these identities have a special existential meaning for persons. This demand for respect in the sense of fairness calls, finally, for particular exceptions to or changes in traditional rules and structures.[46] On this understanding, mutual toleration implies recognising the claim of others to full membership in the political community without demanding that in the process they must renounce their ethical-cultural identity in ways that cannot be reciprocally required.

(4) In discussions of the relation between multiculturalism and toleration, a fourth conception is occasionally encountered which can be called the *esteem conception*. It involves a more demanding form of mutual recognition than the respect conception for, according to it, toleration means not only respecting the members of other cultural or religious communities as legal and political equals but also esteeming their convictions and practices as ethically valuable.[47] However, if this is to remain a conception of toleration

45. See Galeotti, 'Citizenship and Equality' and below §38.
46. On this, see below §§37 and 38.
47. Thus, for example, Bauman, *Modernity and Ambivalence*, 234–8. Bauman traces this mutual attachment back to the shared consciousness of contingency. See also Kristeva, *Strangers to Ourselves*. Apel, 'Plurality of the Good?' offers a differently situated example. He thinks that all members of a solidary, all-encompassing argumentation community have a duty of 'affirmative tolerance' which is an implication of esteem for the plurality of cultural traditions and involves its active promotion. Only in this way can we do justice to the principle of taking the interests of all participants in discourse into consideration. A further example is the religious-pluralistic conception of Mensching, *Tolerance and Truth in Religion*, who argues for a 'substantive tolerance' of esteem.

and the objection component is not to be lost, the esteem in question must be limited or 'with reservations', such that the other form of life does not count as equally as good as, or even better than, one's own – at least not in the respects which matter. One values certain aspects of this form of life while objecting to others; however, the domain of what can be tolerated is defined by the values which one affirms in an ethical sense. Thus, from a liberal perspective, this conception of toleration corresponds, for example, to a version of value pluralism which holds that a rivalry exists within a society between intrinsically worthwhile yet incompatible forms of life[48] or, from the communitarian perspective, to the view that there are particular, socially shared notions of the good life whose partial variations can be tolerated.[49]

§3 Toleration as a normatively dependent concept

These four conceptions of toleration invite the question of how it is to be decided which of them is the most appropriate and best-justified conception in a particular context, such as that of an ethically pluralistic society. To put it in terms of recognition: should we favour the 'thinnest' conception, or instead the one which implies the most demanding form of mutual recognition, ranging from the hierarchical or strategic-reciprocal form in the permission or the coexistence conception, through the egalitarian form in the respect conception, up to the ethically 'thick' form in the esteem conception? It seems as though the concept of recognition initially introduced in a descriptive sense is not sufficient to decide this question without further ancillary assumptions.

Even more important, however, is the fact that, based on what has been said until now about the concept of toleration, the latter *cannot* itself answer the question concerning the best conception, since each of these conceptions can justifiably claim to be an interpretation of the concept. Moreover, it even turns out that this concept leaves open the question of which of the various justifications of toleration broached in the various conceptions is the correct one. Hence, in order to acquire a normative content and to lead to a justified conception, it needs to be filled out with other principles or values. And although the above-mentioned six characteristics of the concept set the limits to what can qualify here as filling, nevertheless the concept of toleration itself remains a *normatively dependent concept* which is indeterminate without other normative principles.

48. Thus, Raz, 'Autonomy, Toleration and the Harm Principle'.
49. Cf. Sandel, 'Moral Argument and Liberal Toleration'.

The history of toleration can then be understood as the history of the justifications used to fill the three components of objection, acceptance and rejection with content. These extend from religious, through liberal, to utilitarian or communitarian justifications; analysing these will be the task of the first part of the book. The issue here is, on the one hand, to recognise the normative dependency of the concept but also, on the other, to define the criteria for normative justifications arising out of the concept itself. An important implication of the former is that, contrary to a widely held view, toleration is not itself a value but first acquires value – in particular, becomes a virtue – if and only if the corresponding components are well grounded. Thus, there is also such a thing as 'false toleration', especially where unacceptable moral offences are passively tolerated; as Thomas Mann's character Settembrini states, toleration can become a crime 'when applied to evil'.[50] Hence, toleration is a positive attitude or practice when it subserves something good, that is, when it is required for the sake of realising higher-level principles or values and is justified accordingly.

Important criteria for the normative foundations we are seeking follow from the concept of toleration itself, however, because it is normatively, not conceptually, dependent, and certainly not conceptually amorphous. First, these foundations (principles or values) themselves must be *normatively freestanding* and not depend on further foundations, which would lead to conceptual fuzziness and to the danger of an infinite regress. And, second, these foundations must be *higher-level* ones, so that they are capable of mediating practical conflicts and, in particular, of making toleration mutually *binding* in spite of ethical conflict and of drawing the limits of toleration *impartially*. It is part of the logic of the concept of toleration that it depends on such higher-order justifications, for otherwise the acceptance and rejection components could not develop the normative power they need in order to be able to bind persons with *different* systems of values and to facilitate mutual tolerance. This demand ultimately makes it possible not only to single out just one of the conceptions of toleration as preferable in the context of a pluralistic society, which is the ultimate concern of this study. In addition, it also suggests a specific justification for toleration which corresponds best to the criteria of normative self-sufficiency, moral obligatoriness and impartiality and is superior to all other justifications. It proves to be the conception which is capable of resolving the paradoxes besetting the concept.

50. Mann, *The Magic Mountain*, 506.

Hence, the concept of toleration is not, as one might assume, an *essentially* contested concept. By 'essentially contested concepts', W. B. Gallie meant concepts – he mentions art, democracy, social justice – not only whose use is deeply contested but for which no clear standards of use of the concept can be discerned. '[I]t is quite impossible to find a general principle for deciding which of two contestant uses of an essentially contested concept really "uses it best".'[51] Consequently, transitions between such – in more recent terminology, 'incommensurable' – uses of a concept are possible only in the form of conversions, that is, the acquisition of entirely new ways of seeing through a radical turn.

First it must be recognised, as already indicated above, that Gallie's thesis cannot mean that the core of a concept such as democracy, justice or toleration is completely contested, for then it would no longer be clear whether such rival interpretations – Gallie calls them 'uses' – really refer to the same thing. Only the interpretations of a concept – the conceptions – can be contested, not the concept itself in its core meaning.[52] And, as we have seen in the case of the concept of toleration, this central content can contain specific criteria for possible ways of employing the concept. From this follow general rules for the correct use.[53] Hence, the concept of toleration is 'contested' not in its 'essence' and in the standards governing its use, but in its interpretations, for it is compatible with a range of conceptions which conflict over individual issues and which, because the concept of toleration is normatively dependent, are associated with different justifications.

But then the question of whether – as Gallie doubts – the principles governing the correct use of the concept could be used to single out the 'best' conception must be answered in a differentiated way. On the one hand, not all of the resources necessary to single out the 'best' conception of toleration can be drawn from the formal concept of toleration, for this would contradict the normative dependency thesis. On the other hand, essential criteria for judging the quality of a conception and justification of toleration can be gleaned from the paradoxes of the concept outlined above, depending on whether and how they can contribute to resolving these paradoxes. Even if other normative resources may be necessary, nevertheless these criteria are

51. Gallie, 'Essentially Contested Concepts', 189 (the aforementioned description can be found on 169: '[T]here are concepts which are essentially contested, concepts the proper use of which inevitably involves endless disputes about their proper uses on the part of their users').

52. Thus, also Lukes, 'Relativism', 187; for a different view, see Swanton, 'On the "Essential Contestedness" of Political Concepts', 816.

53. Gallie implicitly makes this assumption when he stresses that the opponents must have a shared point of reference – an 'exemplar' (176).

specific to the concept of toleration and represent formal specifications for the preferable conception.

However, regarding the concept of toleration, which Gallie does not explicitly discuss, it is in addition unclear whether it falls under his own verdict of being an essentially contested concept. For, when Gallie considers what significance the higher-level insight into the fact of the essential contestability of concepts has as a logical possibility and human probability, he entertains the possibility that this could lead to a spirit of toleration, of esteem for the rival conceptions in an open conflict of opinions.[54] Toleration would then rest on a higher-order insight which would possibly remove it from the endless conflict of opinions. However, Gallie himself recognises that this is not only a practically vain hope, for this higher-order insight seems to be irreconcilable with the assumption constitutive for the theory that the participants in such conflicts are convinced from their respective perspectives that their use of a concept is the only correct one. Therefore, this elegant path to toleration seems to be blocked off if conflicts are reconstructed from the *participant perspective* rather than from a higher-level *observer perspective*. Such a 'sublation' (*Aufhebung*) of the conflict – even of the conflict between conceptions and justifications of toleration itself – has been repeatedly attempted in the history of toleration; however, these attempts all too often prove to rest on a particular participant perspective. And thus I will not attempt such a sublation in what follows, though I will attempt a different one which is aware of the tension between these perspectives.

54. Gallie, 'Essentially Contested Concepts', 193. On this, see the critique of Vernon and LaSelva, 'Justifying Tolerance', 17–18.

2

More than a prehistory: antiquity and the Middle Ages

§4 *Tolerantia* in antiquity: the Stoics and early Christianity

1. Greek and Roman antiquity was acquainted with the phenomenon of intolerance and with certain practices of toleration, but not, prior to Cicero, with the term. The history of the practice of toleration in the ancient world is too extensive to be recounted here. It includes, among other things, the history of the treatment of dissenters in Athens and an explanation of why even there, within a polytheistic culture, 'corrupters of youth' and advocates of alien deities were condemned to death as was Socrates for the sake of the gods who guarded over the polis.[1] It would also include a history of imperial rule in the empires of Alexander, the Ptolemies and the Seleucids and, finally, in the Roman Empire, a complex history of the annexation of foreign territories and the assimilation of alien deities,[2] but also of the (always calculated and limited) toleration of the beliefs and rites of conquered peoples in order to be better able to rule them. Here, and especially in the Roman Empire, toleration was chiefly a function of insight into the limits of imperial power, and at the same time into the strategic possibility of maintaining it.[3] Not only could this toleration be revoked at any time; it was also granted to different religious groups in different degrees depending on whether they

---

1. On this, see Nestle, 'Asebieprozesse'. On the demarcation of the Greeks towards the outside see Detel, 'Griechen und Barbaren'.
2. Here polytheism and the possible translatability of deities play an important role; see Assmann, 'Praktiken des Übersetzens und Konzepte von Toleranz im Alten Orient und in der hellenistisch-römischen Antike'. Cancik and Cancik-Lindemaier, 'Moralische *tolerantia* – wissenschaftliche Wahrnehmung des Fremden – religiöse Freiheit und Repression', 273, call the Roman practice of assimilation of gods 'additive universalisation'. On the parallel, equally prevalent intolerance in the Roman Empire see *ibid.* 275–9. See also Kötting, *Religionsfreiheit und Toleranz im Altertum*, 20–8.
3. See Garnsey, 'Religious Toleration in Classical Antiquity', 9.

were classified as dangerous or there was a prospect of useful alliances. Such constellations reveal, on the one hand, that granting liberties in accordance with the permission conception generally rests on strategic considerations, but also, on the other, that in such contexts the essential arguments for more extensive toleration are developed by the victims of persecution and oppression who oppose the existing social order. They are the ones who present the reasons for toleration. This is made clear by an examination of the evolution of early Christian arguments for state and religious toleration.

However, these arguments could not draw upon the contemporary meaning of the word *tolerantia* which we encounter for the first time around 46 BCE. Cicero employs it in his work *Paradoxa stoicorum* to designate the virtue, characteristic of the wise man, of 'enduring fate, contempt for human affairs' (*tolerantia fortunae, rerum humanarum contemptione*), be it pain, misfortune or injustice.[4] Cicero (in *De finibus bonorum et malorum*) places particular emphasis on the dignified endurance of pain.[5] This Stoic virtue is discussed in greater detail by Seneca. He speaks of 'brave endurance' (*fortis tolerantia*) of torture, for example, as a 'branch of bravery', one of the cardinal virtues.[6] On this understanding, tolerance as a virtue does not refer primarily to the relation to others or to the relation between subject and authority, but to the relation *to oneself* as a precondition of dignified behaviour. It is a matter of forbearance, endurance and steadfastness, and is an indication of inner strength. The virtue of tolerance presupposes, if you will, a labour on oneself, an ethics of self-control which leads to ethical perfection. This is an important point that always features in the discourse over toleration however much it distances itself from this origin of the concept, namely, the question of the attitude towards oneself expressed in tolerance.

2. The word *tolerantia* finds its way into translations of the Bible in the sense of patient endurance of suffering; the corresponding Greek term is *hypo-moné*. By this is meant the patience of the believers who, trusting in the kingdom of God, 'with a noble and good heart . . . hear the word, retain it, and by persevering produce a crop', as Luke 8:15 puts it. In the First Letter to the Corinthians, Paul speaks of the love which is rooted in hope and lends the believer the strength to tolerate both the injustice and the weaknesses of others. Although here the attitude of tolerance continues to be interpreted as

---

4. Cicero, *Paradoxa stoicorum*, vol. IV, 278. On the etymology in antiquity see especially Besier and Schreiner, 'Toleranz', 450–1.

5. Cicero, *On Moral Ends*, Bk 2, §94.

6. Seneca, *Seneca's Letters to Lucilius*, vol. LXI, 5 and 10 ('ceterum illic est fortitudo, cuius patientia et perpessio et tolerantia rami sunt').

inner steadfastness and *patience*, it is transferred to behaviour towards others in the sense of *indulgence*: 'Love is patient, love is kind. It does not envy, it does not boast, it is not proud . . . it keeps no record of wrongs . . . It always protects, always trusts, always hopes, always perseveres' (1 Corinthians 13:4–7).

These two meanings of *tolerantia* can likewise be found among the apologists and Church Fathers, namely, the patient acceptance of what cannot be changed in the assurance of the kingdom of God and indulgence towards others. These thoughts mirror the social reality of the time in a complex manner. For Christianity, in contrast to other cults, was not tolerated in the Roman Empire during the first three centuries of the Common Era, as it was spreading and the Church was forming and developing. Its exclusive character and its refusal to worship the emperor as godlike were, in the opinion of both sides,[7] incompatible with the Roman order. Thus, the following dimensions of the connection between patience and indulgence are encountered in the patristics.

First Tertullian, continuing the Christian appropriation of Stoic thought, speaks of the virtue of tolerance (*virtus tolerantiae*) through which God endows the believers with the ability to endure persecution and evil.[8] This patient tolerance is an exercise in humility which follows the (unattainable) example set by Jesus, whose patience in the face of humiliation and suffering on the Way of the Cross are seen as a true sign of his divinity. To follow his example is an exercise in earthly self-overcoming and is at the same time founded on confidence in the kingdom of God. Enduring pain, oppression and humiliation is regarded as a test of the believer to hold fast to the gospel in spite of despair and, as Augustine writes, to believe and love *unconditionally*. In the words of Cyprian, who speaks of the *tolerantia passionis*[9] and of the *tolerantia mortis*:[10]

> We must endure and persevere, beloved brethren, in order that, being admitted to the hope of truth and liberty, we may attain to the truth and liberty itself; for that very fact that we are Christians is the substance of faith and hope. But that hope and faith may attain to their result, there is need of patience.[11]

Enduring pain and injustice, a sign of inner strength and self-control for the Stoics, is now a sign of unconditional trust, a sign of the strength of faith.

---

7. See Garnsey, 'Religious Toleration in Classical Antiquity', 9–10; Speyer, 'Toleranz und Intoleranz in der alten Kirche', 92.
8. Tertullian, *De fuga in persecutione*, §§2, 7.   9. Cyprian, *De mortalitate*, §§10, 17.
10. Cyprian, *De lapsis*, §2.   11. Cyprian, *De bono patientiae*, §13.

Thus, Augustine speaks in *The City of God* of 'pious endurance of temporal ills' for which God reserves an 'eternal reward'.[12]

Second, this attitude *to oneself*, which is in essence an attitude *to God*, is transferred to relations *to others*, which leads to the problem of toleration proper and to important justifications of toleration. Thus, Cyprian writes: '[F]or as long as this body endures, it must needs have a common lot with others, and its bodily constitution must be common. Nor is it given to any of the human race to be separated from one another, except by withdrawal from this present life. In the meantime, we are all, good and evil, contained in *one* household.'[13] From this follow two types of intersubjective toleration: the 'good' tolerate one another in their weaknesses in the spirit of love and form a 'bond of harmony'. Cyprian calls this *mutua tolerantia*.[14] That gives them the fortitude to endure those who are 'evil', which is required as part of God's test – to endure what is bad because human beings are not authorised to judge upon earth. In addition, calm indulgence – as shown for example in 'enduring the Jews' (*in Iudaeis tolerandis*)[15] – can make the true faith appear attractive in the eyes of unbelievers and people of other faiths.

Tertullian presents another argument for toleration. He recalls Jesus who (according to Matthew 12:18–20) follows the exhortation to 'proclaim justice to the nations' in a peaceful way: 'He will not quarrel or cry out; no-one will hear his voice in the streets. A bruised reed he will not break, and a smouldering wick he will not snuff out, till he leads justice to victory.' This is one of the passages in the Bible which was often cited as an argument for toleration, and it was interpreted in such a way that the deluded sinner ('the bruised reed') will likewise enjoy the grace and mercy of Christ.[16]

Excursus: This is an appropriate juncture to examine the relevant statements in the Bible, in particular those in the New Testament,[17] for they are of central importance not only for the Church Fathers but also for the entire European discourse of toleration. A salient feature of the latter is that, well into the modern period, it is also a discourse about Christian tolerance (and Christian intolerance), and many of the arguments draw their support from biblical sources.[18] Two points are especially important in this regard, namely, the role of conscience and the two-kingdoms doctrine.

12. Augustine, *The City of God against the Pagans*, vol. I, §29 (44).
13. Cyprian, *Ad Demetrianum*, §19.   14. Cyprian, *De bono patientiae*, §15.
15. *Ibid.* §6.   16. See Kamen, *The Rise of Toleration*, 12.
17. For the Old Testament see Fabry, 'Toleranz im Alten Testament?'
18. On what follows, see in particular (in spite of its apologetic leanings) the informative account of Lecler, *Toleration and the Reformation*, vol. I, ch. 2. In addition, especially concerning Paul, Broer, 'Toleranz im Neuen Testament?'

(1) *Conscience*. The New Testament attaches particular importance to the individual conscience. The pure conscience or 'pure heart' (Matthew 5:8) as a 'light within you' (Matthew 6:23) 'testifies' (cf. 2 Corinthians 1:12; Romans 2:15; 1 Timothy 1:5) to the earnestness and sincerity with which the individual follows God. It is still a long way from here until the 'errant' but well-meaning conscience will be accorded binding power, and hence until the sincerity of the conscience will be completely separated from its contents. Nevertheless, already in the First Letter of Paul to the Corinthians there is a passage about respect towards the weak and erring conscience which is exercised out of love and can even overrule the truth. For it is true that eating meat which was sacrificed to idols is not a sin because the idols do not exist. Yet out of love for those who continue to adhere to this belief through a 'weak conscience', they should not be induced or compelled to eat such meat (1 Corinthians 8:1–12).

In the Letter to the Romans there is a corresponding discussion of whether the Jewish distinction between pure and impure food should be respected (Romans 14:1–23):

> Accept him whose faith is weak, without passing judgment on disputable matters . . . Who are you to judge someone else's servant? To his own master he stands or falls . . . You, then, why do you judge your brother? . . . For we will all stand before God's judgment seat . . . So then, each of us will give an account of himself to God. Therefore let us stop passing judgment on one another. Instead, make up your mind not to put any stumbling-block or obstacle in your brother's way . . . Let us therefore make every effort to do what leads to peace and to mutual edification. Do not destroy the work of God for the sake of food. All food is clean, but it is wrong for a man to eat anything that causes someone else to stumble. It is better not to eat meat or drink wine or to do anything else that will cause your brother to fall. So whatever you believe about these things keep between yourself and God. Blessed is the man who does not condemn himself by what he approves. But the man who has doubts is condemned if he eats, because his eating is not from faith; and everything that does not come from faith is sin.

This final sentence in particular expresses the crux of this argument. Since everyone will appear before God with his own conscience and give an account of his deeds, it is not a matter for others to deflect him from the path dictated by his conscience, even if they happen to be in possession of the truth. An important feature of this argument, however, is that it is concerned with a difference of a rather incidental kind, with *adiaphora* (to use the later terminology), not with a difference in central articles of faith.[19] In addition, it should be noted that the conviction concerning the truth is unequivocal. Thus, inner faith does not become true faith in virtue of the fact that one is profoundly convinced of its truth. The weak individual is protected out of a spirit of love so as not to coerce his conscience; the truth itself is not relativised. Therefore, if the individual in question were inclined to act in a way which impinged on 'justice' or on the 'service' owed to Christ, the argument might no longer apply. The precondition for the brotherly love which sustains tolerance is that there is a fundamental unity in God. Therefore, the universalism of love is one which includes others in *one's own truth*: 'There is neither Jew nor Greek, slave nor free, male nor female, for you are all *one* in Christ Jesus' (Galatians 3:28).

Hence there is no room for toleration when it is a question of the sanctity of the Temple and Jesus drives those out who turn the Temple into a 'den of robbers' (Matthew 21:13). Even more, there are numerous unambiguous passages in the New Testament condemning unbelievers, heretics and schismatics to which the persecution and extermination of dissenters in later centuries could appeal. To cite just a few: 'I am the Alpha and the Omega, the First and the Last, the Beginning and the End. Blessed are those who wash their robes, that they may have the right to the tree of life and may go through the gates into the city. Outside are the dogs, those who practise magic arts, the sexually immoral, the murderers, the idolaters and everyone who loves and practises falsehood' (Revelation 22:13–15). False prophets are cursed (Galatians 1:8), heretics are condemned in the sharpest terms (Titus 3:10), blasphemers are 'handed over to Satan' (1 Timothy 1:20), and Paul proclaims: 'God will judge those outside. Expel the wicked man from among you' (1 Corinthians 5:13).[20]

When it comes to spreading the true faith, Jesus tells his disciples:

> If anyone will not welcome you or listen to your words, shake the dust off your feet when you leave that home or town. I tell you the truth, it will be more bearable for Sodom and Gomorrah on the day of judgment than for that town . . . Whoever acknowledges me before

19. 'For the kingdom of God is not a matter of eating and drinking, but of righteousness, peace and joy in the Holy Spirit, because anyone who serves Christ in this way is pleasing to God and approved by men' (Romans 14:17–18).
20. Compare in this sense also his admonition in Galatians: 'If anybody is preaching to you a gospel other than what you accepted, let him be eternally condemned! Am I now trying to win the approval of men, or of God?' (Galatians 1:9–10).

men, I will also acknowledge him before my Father in heaven. But whoever disowns me before men, I will disown him before my Father in heaven.   (Matthew 10:14–33)

And he continues with the famous saying: 'Do not suppose that I have come to bring peace to the earth. I did not come to bring peace, but a sword' (*ibid.* 34).

(2) *Two kingdoms.* But what kind of sword is this? In spite of the physical expulsion of the traders from the Temple, numerous passages stress that it is a question of 'the sword of the Spirit, which is the word of God' (Ephesians 6:17), not of an earthly sword. 'The weapons we fight with are not the weapons of the world. On the contrary, they have divine power to demolish strongholds' (2 Corinthians 10:4). The implication is that the word is the sole weapon of the Christians, not earthly coercion or violence. For as Jesus responds to Pontius Pilate: 'My kingdom is not of this world' (John 18:36).

With this a key justification for vertical toleration, i.e. toleration of religion by the state, is obtained. Just as the true religion is not justified in exercising earthly coercion and earthly power, because it should convince through the word alone and does not aspire to political authority, temporal power is not authorised to arrogate power with regard to this kingdom and to influence it through coercion or violence. The state has no right to coerce in religious matters, religion no right to coerce in political matters. However, this should not be understood as a kind of 'contract' between temporal and spiritual power, for in Christian thought there can be only one truth *in faith* and the priority is fixed. Thus, Jesus informs Pilate: 'You would have no power over me if it were not given to you from above' (John 19:11). Hence: 'We must obey God rather than men!' (Acts 5:29). Accordingly Paul writes to the Romans: 'Everyone must submit himself to the governing authorities, for there is no authority except that which God has established' (Romans 13:1). This is open to different interpretations. One leads to the idea of the Christian empire as advocated by Lactantius and Eusebius of Caesarea at the time of Constantine.[21] But another interpretation is that the power of religion – later, of the pope – is superior to that of the emperor. (*End of the excursus*)

In the opinion of the Church Fathers – and here the third dimension of their understanding of toleration, which concerns the relation *to political authority*, comes into play – the arguments of religious conscience and of the two kingdoms must be combined into a fundamental justification of freedom

21. On Eusebius see Rilinger, 'Das politische Denken der Römer', 565–8.

of religion. They address the latter as a demand to the Roman emperor and it already involves important reasons for toleration destined to be revived centuries later. The word *tolerantia* is employed not in this context, however, but in a different one, namely, *libertas religionis*. In Tertullian we first encounter an argument from fairness which he addresses to the emperor and in which he denounces the unequal treatment of the Christians in comparison to the other religions and cults tolerated by Rome: 'Every province even, and every city, has its god . . . we alone are prevented having a religion of our own.'[22] Yet he also cites more fundamental reasons: 'For see that you do not give a further ground for the charge of irreligion, by taking away religious liberty, and forbidding free choice of deity [*optio divinitatis*], so that I may no longer worship according to my inclination, but am compelled to worship against it. Not even a human being would care to have unwilling homage rendered him'.[23] He explains this in greater detail in a letter to the African proconsul Scapula from 212 CE:

> However, it is a fundamental human right, a privilege of nature
> [*humani iuris et naturalis potestatis est*], that every man should worship
> according to his own convictions: one man's religion neither harms
> nor helps another man. It is assuredly no part of religion to compel
> religion – to which free-will and not force should lead us – the
> sacrificial victims being required of a willing mind. You will render no
> real service to your gods by compelling us to sacrifice.[24]

Around a century later, at the time of the persecution of Christians by the emperor Diocletian, Lactantius also stresses that a coerced sacrifice is not a true sacrifice: 'For unless it is offered spontaneously, and from the soul, it is a curse, as when men sacrifice, compelled by proscription, by injuries, by prison, by tortures . . . But we, on the contrary, do not require that any one should be compelled, whether he is willing or unwilling, to worship our God, who is the God of all men.' For 'nothing is so much a matter of free-will as religion; in which, if the mind of the worshipper is disinclined to it, religion is at once taken away, and ceases to exist'.[25] Here we encounter central arguments of ground-breaking significance for the future of the discourse of toleration, which are presented in the present context initially as arguments for permission toleration, though they can also be used (and were used) for conceptions of toleration which go beyond this:

---

22. Tertullian, *Apologeticus adversus gentes pro christianis*, §24.   23. *Ibid.*
24. Tertullian, *Ad Scapulam*, §2.   25. Lactantius, *The Divine Institutes*, vol. v, 21 and 20.

First: The two-kingdoms doctrine means that temporal power does not have any authority in religious matters.

Second: Coercion is illegitimate in religious affairs because it leads to a merely enforced and hypocritical faith which cannot be pleasing to God.

Third: Compulsion is useless in religious matters because belief cannot be coerced but must come about and be adhered to voluntarily.

Fourth: Universal toleration is possible because religions which confine themselves to inner convictions and to forms of worship cannot harm one another.

These are the most important reasons advanced by the Christian apologists and Church Fathers in defence of their faith and their church against persecution and discrimination in the Roman Empire, and hence for *vertical* toleration by the state. Nevertheless, let me briefly reiterate here the arguments already discussed for a *horizontal*, intersubjective toleration towards 'brothers' or people of different faiths:

First, there is the *mutua tolerantia* inspired by love designed to create a 'bond of concord' within the community, as Cyprian puts it. However, this love can also be extended to people of different faiths, as Tertullian intimates when he speaks of not breaking the 'bruised reed'.

Second, in addition to love as a positive motive for tolerance, a further reason for tolerance towards others can reside in the fact that the conflict is a test imposed by God as a proof of the strength of inner faith which renounces earthly success and exhibits humility.

Third, the reference to faith which is grounded in inner conviction, and hence follows one's own conscience, also speaks for horizontal toleration. For a false, coerced faith is not pleasing to God.

Fourth, this is especially required if such compulsion turns out to be fruitless in any case because genuine convictions cannot be brought about in this way.

Fifth and finally, Paul not only calls for respect for the inner, even the weak, conscience but also warns against making oneself into a judge over others, for a judgement of merit or blame will first be made 'before God's judgement seat' (see above). Thus, Jesus also preaches: 'Do not judge, or you too will be judged' (Matthew 7:1). This is central to Christian thought concerning toleration: here on earth no human being should presume to make a judgement which is God's privilege alone.[26] This is shown, for example, in the parable of the weeds, perhaps the most prominent passage for justifying Christian tolerance:

> The kingdom of heaven is like a man who sowed good seed in his field. But while everyone was sleeping, his enemy came and sowed weeds among the wheat, and went away. When the wheat sprouted and formed ears, then the weeds also appeared. The owner's servants came to him and said, 'Sir, didn't you sow good seed in your field? Where then did the weeds come from?' 'An enemy did this,' he replied. The servants asked him, 'Do you want us to go and pull them up?' 'No,' he answered, 'because while you are pulling the weeds, you may root up the wheat with them. Let both grow together until the harvest. At that time I will tell the harvesters: First collect the weeds and tie them in bundles to be burned; then gather the wheat and bring it into my barn.'   (Matthew 13:24–30)

Jesus explains the parable to his disciples:

> The one who sowed the good seed is the Son of Man. The field is the world, and the good seed stands for the sons of the kingdom. The weeds are the sons of the evil one, and the enemy who sows them is the devil. The harvest is the end of the age, and the harvesters are angels. As the weeds are pulled up and burned in the fire, so it will be at the end of the age. The Son of Man will send out his angels, and they will weed out of his kingdom everything that causes sin and all who do evil. They will throw them into the fiery furnace, where there will be weeping and gnashing of teeth.   (*Ibid.* 37–42)

At the same time this passage shows the ambivalence of this justification of toleration. For all of the reasons presented in support of horizontal toleration presuppose that there is no more doubt concerning knowledge of the truth of God than there is concerning his authority and his final justice to come. Toleration is contingent upon this knowledge of a higher truth and justice, a justice which may demand tolerance here on earth but which will not show *any* tolerance at the 'end of all days'. Toleration among mortals is due to

---

26. This is also the teaching of another passage which is important in the context of toleration. When the Apostles were accused before the High Council, the legal scholar Gamaliel stood up and declared: 'Leave these men alone! Let them go! For if their purpose or activity is of human origin, it will fail. But if it is from God, you will not be able to stop these men; you will only find yourselves fighting against God' (Acts 5:38–9).

their confidence in ultimate and just divine intolerance, in its 'fiery furnace'. The connection between earthly tolerance and divine intolerance can also be seen in Cyprian (whose refusal to recognise the ceremonies of the Romans cost him his life). For as much as he enjoins the Christians to the patience which bears evil 'mildly and gently and imperturbably', he specifies where the strength for this patience comes from: '[W]e must not withhold the fact in the furthest particular, that placed as we are in the midst of these storms of a jarring world, and, moreover, the persecutions both of Jews or Gentiles, we may patiently wait for the day of (God's) vengeance, and not hurry to revenge our suffering with a querulous haste.'[27]

It is also in Cyprian that we first encounter the famous maxim that 'outside the Church nobody can be saved', even though he thinks that this truth, which calls for the exclusion of unbelievers from the Church, should be imposed only with the 'spiritual sword'.[28] Later, however, this became a fatal argument when combined with a famous Bible passage. The passage in question is the one which contains the dictum *compelle intrare*:

> A certain man was preparing a great banquet and invited many guests. At the time of the banquet he sent his servant to tell those who had been invited, 'Come, for everything is now ready'. But they all alike began to make excuses. The first said, 'I have just bought a field, and I must go and see it. Please excuse me'. Another said, 'I have just bought five yoke of oxen, and I'm on my way to try them out. Please excuse me'. Still another said, 'I have just got married, so I can't come'. The servant came back and reported this to his master. Then the owner of the house became angry and ordered his servant, 'Go out quickly into the streets and alleys of the town and bring in the poor, the crippled, the blind and the lame'. 'Sir', the servant said, 'what you ordered has been done, but there is still room'. Then the master told his servant, 'Go out to the roads and country lanes and make them come in, so that my house will be full.'   (Luke 14:16–23)

As we shall see, this parable was often cited to legitimise enforced conversion and, in particular, the persecution of heretics. Therefore, the initial conclusion to be drawn is that the early Christian message of toleration is ambiguous. The reasons for toleration simultaneously cast over this tolerance a shadow which is an implication of the claim to universal and absolute truth and retributive justice.

---

27. Cyprian, *De bono patientiae*, §21.   28. Cyprian, Epistle IV, §4.

Structurally speaking, the analysis of the early Christian toleration discourse shows not only that many of the later especially important justifications of toleration are already at work here, albeit in a rough form. It also shows that the twofold perspective on toleration as state practice (chiefly in accordance with the permission conception) and intersubjective attitude was an early development (to which the Stoics contributed a third dimension, that of the scrutinising relation to self).

What these Christian arguments demanded as regards religious freedom was soon destined to be realised; indeed these demands were surpassed. In the famous Edict of Milan of 313, the emperors Constantine and Licinius granted the Christians and the pagan cults extensive freedom of religion:

> We . . . are of the opinion that among the various things that would profit men, or which should be set in order first, was to be found the cultivation of religion; we should therefore give to both Christians and all others free facility to follow the religion which each may desire [*libera potestas sequendi religionem quam quisque voluisset*], so that by this means whatever Divinity is enthroned in heaven may be gracious and favourable to us and to all who have been placed under our authority.[29]

However, this not only marked the transition to a toleration of the Christians. For in the end Constantine officially embraced Christianity. Especially after his defeat of Licinius in 324 when he became the sole emperor, Christianity rapidly rose to become the state religion and Caesaropapism became established (as also subsequently under his sons Constantinus and Constans). Now the situation was reversed. The Edict of Milan was annulled in the Edicts of Thessalonica (380) and Constantinople (392), Christianity was elevated to the state religion and pagan cults were prohibited even in private.[30]

§5 The Janus face of Christian toleration

1. In a relatively short time, the Christian Church changed from being a persecuted into being a tolerated church, then into a recognised church and the official church. Finally, it itself became a persecuting church which not only wielded the 'spiritual sword' but, now that it was possible, also the temporal sword. In a Christian state, there is a correspondence between obedience to God and obedience to the emperor. The power of the emperor

---

29. Edict of Milan, in Ehler and Morrall (eds.), *Church and State through the Centuries*, 5.
30. See Lecler, *Toleration and the Reformation*, vol. 1, 44–5; Cancik and Cancik-Lindemaier, 'Moralische *tolerantia*', 275–6; Kötting, *Religionsfreiheit und Toleranz im Altertum*, 29–33.

originates from God, and when it is wielded against the unbelievers it is in the service of the truth. In the course of the fourth century, heresy became a crime of *lèse-majesté* and could be punished with death as well as with imprisonment or banishment.

This new situation represents a decisive turning point in the history of Christian toleration, which is marked by the work of St Augustine. His importance resides not only in the fact that he developed important arguments for toleration but also that under certain conditions they become inverted into justifications for intolerance. An altered, more institutionally oriented and authoritative understanding of the Church and a redefinition of its relations to the state played a role in this process. The definition of this relation is a complex matter and evolved through different phases. Although Augustine was originally guarded concerning the use of state force on behalf of the Church (as *corpus Christi*) and of the true faith, as the bishop of the North African city Hippo (from 395 CE onwards) he abandoned this position as the conflicts with the Donatists became more intense and violent and he legitimised the employment of force against the schismatics. When he set about writing his book on the city of God (*The City of God against the Pagans*) following the conquest of Rome by the Visigoths in 410, the situation changed once again. Thus, on the one hand he makes a sharp division between the eternal kingdom of God and the secular state in order to safeguard the purity of the eschatological teaching and to detach the destiny of the Church from that of the secular empire. On the other hand, the earthly State at the same time not only remains necessary for creating order and peace but is also subordinated to the heavenly State. In what follows, I will outline the essential Augustinian arguments for toleration and then show how they can mutate into their opposite. The considerations presented relate in essence to the *horizontal* level of toleration between adherents of different religious faiths, in particular of different interpretations of the Christian faith. For two reasons, however, this becomes amalgamated with a *vertical* relation between polity and minority: first, because Augustine also speaks from the perspective of the institution of the Church and, second, because the latter can fall back on state force as its – to anticipate a later usage – 'temporal arm'.

(1) The argument for toleration *from love* plays a special role in Augustine. By this is meant a complex relation to oneself, to God and to others. The relation to oneself here should not be understood as self-love, unless it is in the sense that 'no one . . . can love himself except by loving God'.[31] The

---

31. Augustine, Letter 155, §15, *Political Writings*, 98. See also *The City of God*, vol. XIX, 14 (940–2).

unconditional love of God is the basis of the relation to oneself and to others as creatures of God, to self insofar as it leads to faith and to humility bordering on 'contempt of self',[32] to others insofar as it leads to love of one's neighbour whose weaknesses and sins must be endured. Since nobody in the human world branded by original sin is without weakness and sin, human beings need the patient tolerance of others and owe it to one another.[33] Hence, the virtue of tolerance is understood here in accordance with the ancient use of the concept as patient endurance, though it is now connected with the teaching of the sinfulness of human nature, the unattainability of happiness here on earth and the hope in a merciful God. God tests the strength of faith by inflicting suffering; and the only reward for the earthly pilgrimage, which must be absolved in patience and confidence, is that which God will confer on the citizens of his eternal state on the Day of Judgement: 'For patience itself will not be eternal, since it is only necessary where there are evils to be borne; rather, it is the goal attained through patience that will be eternal.'[34]

Hence, tolerance is grounded in the supreme virtue of love which is nourished by the love of God and it exercises compassion and patience towards the failings of others. Augustine often cites Jesus, who tolerated and endured even his most bitter adversaries, as an example of this attitude.[35] The test represented by the exercise of toleration reinforces the believer, as Augustine explains:

> Indeed, all the enemies of the Church, however blinded by error or depraved by malice, train the Church in patience if they are given the power of inflicting bodily harm; whereas, if they oppose her only by their wicked beliefs, they train her in wisdom. Moreover, they train her in benevolence, or even beneficence, so that she may show love even to the enemies by persuading them either through teaching or by stern discipline.[36]

However, this final remark already alludes to the possible inversion of this love into 'discipline' (see below).

---

32. Augustine, *The City of God*, vol. xiv, §28 (632). 'Two cities, then, have been created by two loves: that is, the earthly by love of self extending even to contempt of God, and the heavenly by love of God extending to contempt of self.'
33. 'Sive patientia, sive sustinentia, sive tolerantia nominetur, pluribus vocabulis eadem rem significat'; Augustine, *Sermo Lambot*, 4 ('whether it be called patience, restraint, or tolerance, all of these words signify the same thing').
34. Augustine, *The City of God*, vol. xiv, 9 (601).
35. See Letter 43, §23 and Letter 44, §11.
36. Augustine, *The City of God*, vol. xviii, 51 (898).

(2) The argument from love is supplemented by a second argument, a specific interpretation of the doctrine of the *two kingdoms*. Given their limited faculty of judgement, human beings are neither able nor permitted to set themselves up as the final judge over other human beings and their sins. For here on earth the two kingdoms are 'entangled' and 'mingled with one another', and even among the 'most declared enemies' there may be some who are 'predestined to become our friends'.[37] It is the privilege of God alone to disentangle these threads at the Last Judgement; his judgement must not be anticipated. Augustine frequently cites the parable of the wheat and the weeds to clarify this conception: the weeds should not be pulled up too soon so as not to pull up the wheat along with them. Only at the harvest will this be announced, at 'the end of the world'.[38]

(3) Another important argument is the *preservation of unity* through toleration. This holds for the heretics and schismatics. The good of the unity of Christians in God – and in the Church – is such a supreme good that peaceful efforts to convince are called for towards the apostates, not violence. During his time as bishop, Augustine repeatedly sought out conversations with the Donatists in order to show them what evil they were committing and how incorrectly they were interpreting scripture. So as not to aggravate the divisions and conflicts which split families in two,[39] 'those who are of a different opinion from us must be corrected with meekness'.[40] The tolerant who condone the 'wicked' in their error deserve praise and honour because 'they tolerate in the interest of unity that which in the interest of righteousness they hate'.[41]

(4) The argument from *freedom* and the *non-coercibility of conscience* is also to be found in Augustine. Not only is genuine, non-hypocritical faith alone pleasing to God; in addition faith can be stable and enduring only as something freely embraced and wanted: *Credere non potest homo nisi volens*.[42] Genuine faith should be accepted on the basis of insight, not through coercion or other motives; it should be independent. Therefore, Augustine declares that he desires that nobody 'should against his will be coerced into the Catholic communion, but that to all who are in error the truth may be openly declared, and being by God's help clearly exhibited through my ministry, may so

37. Augustine, *The City of God*, vol. i, 35 (49).
38. Augustine, Letter 53, §6; see also Letter 43, §21. Also *The City of God*, vol. xx, 5 (971ff.).
39. See Augustine, Letter 33.
40. Augustine, Letter 43, §1.   41. Augustine, Letter 43, §21.
42. Augustine, *In Johannis Evangelium*, vol. xxvi, §2: 'A man . . . cannot believe unless he is willing.'

commend itself as to make them embrace and follow it'.[43] Therefore, here there should be no 'enforced conversion'.

(5) Most of Augustine's discussions address the issue of toleration towards heretics within the Christian faith and are not applied in the same degree to pagans and Jews.[44] The relationship between the Christians and the Jews, in particular, who, in Augustine's eyes, 'slew and rejected the Giver of true glory and of the Eternal City',[45] poses a problem of enmity and oppression which stretches from the origin of Christianity up to the present day and has repeatedly led to specific attempts to justify toleration. In Augustine we find in this connection the (later influential) argument of 'involuntary testimony'.[46] The Jews who have been expelled from their country and henceforth live in exile 'bear witness for us that we have not invented the prophecies concerning Christ'.[47] In this way, they testify against their will to the truth of the Christian faith and aid indirectly in spreading this faith. For this reason they should be tolerated; God will pass judgement on them himself at the end of all days.

It was the protracted, intense conflicts with the Donatists in particular which led Augustine to change his position on toleration towards heretics and schismatics. The Donatists were particularly widespread in North Africa, and in certain regions they even formed a majority. They got their name from the bishop Donatus, who, during the reign of Constantine, developed a conception of the sacraments which deviated from Catholic teaching, and in particular opposed the association between the Catholic Church and the state. Towards the end of the fourth century, the intensity of the conflicts increased and there were enforced baptisms and attacks on churches, and priests were murdered. Moreover, the theological conflict was bound up with social antagonisms. On the Donatist side, the 'circumcellions' (migrant workers) and Berber-Punic peasants were in conflict with the landowners and the state, which enjoyed the support of the Catholic Church.[48] Augustine found himself confronted not only with a real schism but with a large-scale social protest with revolutionary tendencies: 'Unity is shunned, and

43. Augustine, Letter 34, §1.
44. According to Augustine, the mission to the pagans should also be peaceful. In *The City of God*, vol. v, §26, however, he praises the emperor Theodosius for having destroyed the pagan idols. And in Letter 93, §10 he endorses capital punishment for violations of the official prohibition on sacrifices.
45. Augustine, *The City of God*, vol. v, §18 (223).
46. On this argument and its historical reception see Schreiner, '"Tolerantia"', 367–81.
47. Augustine, *The City of God*, vol. XVIII, §46 (891).
48. On this, see Grasmück, *Coercitio: Staat und Kirche im Donatistenstreit*.

the peasants are emboldened to rise against their landlords; runaway slaves, in defiance of apostolic discipline, are not only encouraged to desert their masters but even to threaten their masters, and not only to threaten but to plunder them by violent raids.'[49]

In the light of this situation his stance changes and the same reasons which previously spoke for toleration are now reinterpreted as calling for intolerance.

(1') Love of one's neighbour, which is founded on the unconditional love of God, now calls no longer for condoning sins and errors, but for action to be taken against them; to condone them now appears itself to be sinful:

> For if any one saw his enemy running headlong to destroy himself when he had become delirious through a dangerous fever, would he not in that case be much more truly rendering evil for evil if he permitted him to run on thus, than if he took measures to have him seized and bound? And yet he would at that moment appear to the other to be most vexatious, and most like an enemy, when, in truth, he had proved himself most useful and most compassionate; although, doubtless, when health was recovered, would he express to him his gratitude with a warmth proportioned to the measure in which he had felt his refusal to indulge him in his time of frenzy.[50]

Augustine goes on to cite examples of individuals converted in this way who, once cured of their illness, expressed gratitude for the bondage and protection against self-destruction. 'Paternal care', 'the love which seeks to heal' of a mother who is solely concerned with the salvation of her children, is what motivates the Church to lead its errant children back onto the correct path.[51] If this necessitates a temporary 'castigation', then this is done out of love and not out of hate, which for Augustine is the crucial distinction.[52] The love of one's neighbour, which is rooted in the love of God, demands that the soul be saved from eternal damnation, even against its blinded will. To fail to observe this precept would be *evil tolerance*, 'a useless and unprofitable patience'.[53]

(2') Following this precept, Augustine develops the doctrine of 'good coercion', according to which 'the thing to be considered when any one is coerced, is not the mere fact of the coercion, but the nature of that to which he is coerced'.[54] This, of course, presupposes a twofold retraction

---

49. Augustine, Letter 108, §18. Augustine, *Letters*, vol. II, 235–6.
50. Letter 93, §2.   51. Letter 93, §6.   52. Letter 93, §3.
53. Letter 93, §1. Augustine, *Letters*, vol. II, 57.   54. Letter 93, §16.

of the two-kingdoms argument for toleration. First, it must be possible to disentangle the threads of the righteous and the sinners already here on earth in order to arrive at a sufficiently well-grounded judgement; then, second, it also becomes a matter for the secular justice of the state to assist in imposing the truth. In the first place, therefore, the parable of the wheat and the weeds must be reinterpreted. When the master warned against pulling up the weeds, he justified this on the grounds that the wheat might also be destroyed in the process. Then Augustine proceeds:

> This shows sufficiently that rigorous discipline flourishes when fear of pulling up the grain does not exist, that is, when the sin of each is so known and appears so despicable to all that there are absolutely no defenders of the sin . . . then the stringency of discipline must not rest, for the more carefully brotherly love is protected, the more effective is the punishment of corruption.[55]

Then the parable of the weeds permits 'good coercion' once it becomes possible to distinguish sufficiently between good and evil. Thus, Augustine writes to the Donatists that, by separating themselves from the Church, they have proved themselves 'to be weeds; and what is worse, you have prematurely separated yourselves from the wheat'.[56]

Second, Augustine counts heresy and schism among the crimes which by their very nature fall under the jurisdiction of temporal justice, and this not only on account of the social unrest they foment. Appealing to Paul, who counts idolatry among the reprehensible 'works of the flesh' (Galatians 5:19), Augustine writes:

> Why then do the Donatists think it right that the severity of the law is applied to poisoners, and wrong when applied to heresies and unholy dissensions, since the Apostle puts these last crimes on the same level with other fruits of iniquity? Would human power by chance be forbidden to deal with those crimes?[57]

Since the earthly powers have true power only through God, they can and should intervene on behalf of the truth: 'whenever they [i.e., the emperors] command something good, none other than Christ commands it through

---

55. Augustine, *Contra epistulam Parmeniani*, vol. III, II, §13 (quoted from Aquinas, *On Law, Morality, and Politics*, 192).
56. Augustine, Letter 76, §2.
57. Augustine, *Contra epistulam Parmeniani*, vol. I, X, §16 (quoted from Lecler, *Toleration and the Reformation*, vol. I, 55).

them'.[58] This does not contradict the doctrine of the two cities, for there, too, Augustine regards it as the duty of the emperors to 'make their power the handmaid of His majesty by using it to spread His worship to the greatest possible extent', and the 'Christian emperor' Constantine serves him as a shining example.[59] With this the two-kingdoms doctrine loses its validity as an argument for toleration.

(3') Even though toleration was required towards people of different faiths as a means of preserving Christian unity, in the case of a widespread schism this unity calls for intolerance and combating heresy. Although the sacraments of the Donatists are recognised for the sake of Catholic unity, they must nevertheless be forcibly converted to the true Church. Here Augustine cites the passage from the Bible regarding *compelle intrare* (or *cogite intrare*) and legitimises enforced conversion:

> Wherefore, if the power which the Church has received by divine appointment in its due season, through the religious character and the faith of kings, be the instrument by which those who are found in the highways and hedges – that is, in heresies and schisms – are compelled to come in, then let them not find fault with being compelled, but consider whither they be so compelled.[60]

(4') As regards freedom of conscience, Augustine does not retract the position that faith must rest on one's own insight and conviction; nevertheless, he now takes the view that coercion can be decisive in bringing about this insight. This refutes the non-coercibility of conscience. The 'alarm' (*terror*) that the heretics suffer through violence has 'directed their minds earnestly to the study of the truth'; 'the admonition which He so gently gave and His paternal correction' have opened their eyes to the truth, so that they have subsequently expressed gratitude for their liberation from delusion and illness.[61]

> [N]ot that any one can be good in spite of his own will, but that, through fear of suffering what he does not desire, he either renounces his hostile prejudices, or is compelled to examine the truth of which he had been contentedly ignorant; and under the influence of this fear repudiates the error which he was wont to defend, or seeks the truth of

58. Augustine, Letter 105, §11 (quoted from Augustine, *Political Writings*, 168); see also Letter 93, §20.
59. Augustine, *The City of God*, vol. v, §§24 and 25 (232); also *ibid.* vol. xix, §17 (945–7).
60. Augustine, Letter 185, §24; see also Letter 93, §5, Letter 173, §10 and Letter 208, §8.
61. Letter 93, §§1 and 2. see also Letter 105, §5.

which he formerly knew nothing, and now willingly holds what he formerly rejected. Perhaps it would be utterly useless to assert this in words, if it were not demonstrated by so many examples. We see not a few men here and there, but many cities, once Donatist, now Catholic, vehemently detesting the diabolical schism, and ardently loving the unity of the Church.[62]

This is how Augustine justifies the especially severe laws against the Donatists from 405 onwards which finally stripped them of their churches and possessions. He continues in explaining his change in position:

> For originally my opinion was, that no one should be coerced into the unity of Christ, that we must act only by words, fight only by arguments, and prevail by force of reason, lest we should have those whom we knew as avowed heretics feigning themselves to be Catholics. But this opinion of mine was overcome not by the words of those who controverted it, but by the conclusive instances to which they could point.[63]

He lists a whole range of testimonies by Donatists who had abandoned their beliefs out of fear of political repression and now showed themselves to be happy at having been liberated from evil and having adopted the path of truth. Consequently, 'freedom of conscience' resides in the freedom to adopt the *true* faith; there is no freedom with regard to false doctrines: 'For what is more deadly to the soul than freedom for error?'[64] Conscience is not an independent authority which must be respected in its own right; it is in the service of truth and salvation. It is the latter that ultimately commands the complete attention of the caring shepherd.

The fact that Augustine rejects capital punishment for heretics is bound up with the importance attached to the need to embrace the faith on the basis of one's own insight. Thus, he implores the tribune Marcellinus not even to put the Donatists who have killed Catholic priests to death, but instead to treat them with 'paternal care' and not to deprive them of the opportunity to repent and convert.[65] Nevertheless, the Augustinian justifications of intolerance were repeatedly cited during the Middle Ages to justify the violent suppression of dissenters, and the legitimation of force against heretics duly became a principle of canon law with the Decree of Gratian (1140).[66]

62. Letter 93, §16.   63. Letter 93, §17.
64. Letter 105, §10 (quoted from Augustine, *Political Writings*, 168).
65. Letter 133, §§1 and 2.
66. On this, see Schreiner, '"Duldsamkeit" (tolerantia) oder "Schrecken" (terror)'.

2. This brief account of the Janus face of Christian toleration, using Augustine as an example, suffices to reveal a number of structural aspects of the justification of intolerance.

(1) The first point concerns the above-mentioned argument from love. The central point here is that brotherly love (a) is mediated *through God* and (b) is concerned exclusively with the other person's *salvation*. Salvation in this sense is an objectively definable matter and has nothing to do with the individual's 'carnal' preferences and desires or 'false' convictions. Hence, the other person is loved 'in God', that is, for the sake of her salvation as laid down by the true religion. This constitutes a paternalistic form of *ethical perfectionism*, an ethics of self-perfection in striving for independently definable, supreme human goods and ends. It includes the imperative to support others in this striving and to open their eyes for these goods and ends – on the paternalistic variant, this holds even when they have a different conception of what is good for them.[67] On the Christian understanding, this may imply that the 'spiritual welfare' of an individual must be secured even *against* her express will, in short, that one must use force to liberate others from falsehood and to attain the truth. Arguments such as these involve a structural division of the individual into the existing and the 'true' self and the duty to enable the latter to prevail over the former. At the extreme this can even mean tormenting the body and letting it die in order to save the soul. Although Augustine explicitly rejects the latter implication, he nevertheless speaks of two kinds of deaths, the death of the body and the death of the soul. The first is unavoidable and 'good for good men' because it is followed – through God's mercy – by eternal bliss; the second, the death of the soul, occurs when God abandons a soul to damnation, which can precede or follow the death of the body.[68] Hence, the salvation of a soul is beyond human control and depends on mercy; at the same time it is also independent of the human body and its sensations. Therefore, the danger of this division resides in the 'inauthentic self' being neglected, or even instrumentalised and destroyed, in favour of the 'true self'[69] and in this ultimately being seen as an ethical duty towards those concerned – though also of course a duty

---

67. On the theory of perfectionism – though not of a religious kind – see Rawls, *A Theory of Justice*, §50; also Raz, *The Morality of Freedom*, and the more recent approaches of Hurka, *Perfectionism*, and Sher, *Beyond Neutrality*. I will repeatedly return to the different forms of ethical and political perfectionism.

68. Augustine, *City of God*, vol. XIII, §2 (542).

69. In a deliberate anachronism Brown, *Augustine of Hippo*, 136, also calls Augustine the 'first theorist of the Inquisition'. On this, see the next section.

towards God. For the central point is that the 'true self' must also show itself to be worthy of His mercy.

Isaiah Berlin has this danger of a division of self in mind in his essay on two concepts of liberty when he argues that theories of positive liberty conceive of a 'dominant' or 'true' self which must be affirmed against a 'lower' self, and coercion can be justified in the process. The 'true' self is related to a more inclusive entity and power, be it a church or a 'race', though 'reason' can also serve to legitimate its claim to domination.

> Once I take this view, I am in a position to ignore the actual wishes of men or societies, to bully, oppress, torture them in the name, and on behalf, of their 'real' selves, in the secure knowledge that whatever is the true goal of man (happiness, performance of duty, wisdom, a just society, self-fulfilment) must be identical with his freedom – the free choice of his 'true', albeit often submerged and inarticulate, self.[70]

Berlin highlights the fact, and this is of more general significance for the question of toleration, that this argumentative structure by no means applies only to religious self-definitions. This raises the reflexive question of whether, when apparently ethically innocent, 'secular' concepts of self are employed to justify freedom and toleration, such a division, with the attendant dangers, also creeps in, for example in the ideal of an 'autonomous' as opposed to a 'heteronomous' self.

However, the inversion of the argument from love has a further aspect.[71] For even if the primary aim of coercion is the salvation of those who are to be cured of their heresy, the coercion can be legitimate even when it proves to be pointless and does not lead to a change in heart on the part of the heretics. For in such cases checking their harmful influence *on others* can constitute a duty to the latter and their salvation. Since coercion out of love is beholden to the salvation of all individuals, the duty to stem the evil is inclusive; brotherly love is universal. It is not for nothing that Augustine describes the heretic as a 'poisoner', and later the heretic will be regarded as a dangerous pathogen capable of infecting others: *haeresis est infectivum vitium*, as Thomas Aquinas will say.[72]

In both dimensions, therefore, the double-edged character of a love becomes apparent which is unconditional only as love of God and only

70. Berlin, 'Two Concepts of Liberty', 133.
71. For an exhaustive analysis of these two dimensions see Schmidt-Leukel, 'Ist das Christentum notwendig intolerant?', 182–3.
72. Thomas Aquinas, *Commentum in quartum librum sententiarum*, dist. 13, q. 2, a. 3, 330 ('heresy is an infectious disease').

from there extends to human beings. Hence, it is *qualified* in a particular sense – its object is not the human being as such in her pure 'worldly' self-determination.

(2) The inversion of the Augustinian arguments also reveals how precarious toleration becomes when it rests on parables such as that of the wheat and the weeds or on the assumption of the non-coercibility of the conscience. The former comes unstuck once the asserted uncertainty of judgement in relation to the transgressions and sins of individuals is called into doubt and no normative reasons speak *in principle* against the presumption to make such a judgement. Later justifications of toleration will attempt to do this. Moreover, even though non-coercibility features prominently in the toleration discourse of the modern period, for example in Locke, it turns out to be empirically untenable once it is shown that 'milder' and effective force can bring about a change in convictions which is retrospectively regarded and accepted by those affected as an advance in knowledge. Augustine was convinced that this is possible and in this way sowed an important seed of doubt concerning one of the most prominent justifications of freedom of conscience.

(3) Finally, arguments that toleration promotes unity are also ambivalent. For, since they are teleologically structured, they too depend in the final analysis on the realisation of the sought-for goals; hence, toleration is also merely a conditional requirement. Should it turn out that the desired unity cannot be achieved in this way, other routes must be pursued. Hence, this kind of justification of toleration both includes and excludes: it includes in that tolerance is exercised only in order to lead others to the truth, and it excludes in that it excepts those with whom this does not work (irredeemable heretics), or with whom it is hopeless from the beginning (obstinate unbelievers), from the scope of this justification of toleration. Here, too, the fragility of Christian toleration becomes apparent, which is ultimately due to the fact that all Christian justifications of toleration not only rest, as goes without saying, upon the Christian faith, but are aimed exclusively at furthering the true faith, and this for the sake of the salvation of every human being. This is the reason for its Janus face, for toleration may at times be the correct means along the path to this goal, but sometimes instead force and violence, or what Augustine calls *terror*.

3. Here it is not possible to trace the history of toleration, as an idea and as a practice, during the Middle Ages. A couple of remarks which are limited to the most important points for what follows must suffice. As regards the arguments for toleration, it should be noted that they do not go beyond

what was worked out by Augustine but merely apply and embellish it. Only with Thomas Aquinas do new viewpoints come into play, which also applies to the legitimation of intolerance and the use of violence. Especially as the political dominance of the Church increased, institutions and practices for imposing the true faith developed which pursued the goal of subordinating temporal to spiritual power on the one hand, while subsuming human beings under a fully inclusive intellectual and practical framework on the other. To this end human beings were divided into different categories, ranging from the true believers, through the heathens (including the Muslims), the Jews, the errant (those still trapped in superstition), to the 'heretics'. Both are aspects of a mode of exercise of power that can be called, following Foucault, 'pastoral power' or 'power of the shepherd'. Power is exercised on the model of a shepherd to whom a flock is entrusted, who knows what is best for them and is solely responsible for them.[73] This calls for an 'individualising power', a power which does not lose sight of any of the sheep, which must have knowledge of all of their sins and must itself account for them before God. Therefore, the exercise of power on the part of the shepherd involves unconditional devotion to his task, and on the side of the flock unconditional obedience and heart-searching, direction of conscience and openness towards a shepherd. Thus, Augustine speaks of those who are forced to convert by the 'fatherly diligence' of the Church as the 'sheep of Christ' who 'wander off' and must be led back to the flock.[74]

The first component of this specifically Christian form of domination – the subordination of temporal power under the domination of the Church – exercised a pervasive influence over the political dynamics of the medieval period. In the late fifth century Pope Gelasius developed his 'two-powers doctrine' according to which there are two powers which rule the world: the consecrated *auctoritas* of the bishops and the temporal *potestas*.[75] Although each of these, like the two kingdoms in Augustine, has its own task, they do not have equal status, for in the end the priests will also have to account for the deeds of the kings and emperors. Hence, they are also the latters' shepherds. Although the Church needs the 'temporal arm' of the state in

---

73. See Foucault, 'Omnes et singulatim', especially 307–9. However, Foucault assumes that this form of power, which originated with Christianity, was less politically important in the Middle Ages and that only in the early modern period did a new form of pastoral-political rationality emerge that went hand-in-hand with specific forms of knowledge, power and control. Although this is true, the political forms of pastoral power in the Middle Ages should not be overlooked.
74. Augustine, Letter 93, §10. Augustine, *Letters*, vol. II, 65.
75. Gelasius, Letter I, §§2–3 (quoted from Robinson, *Readings in European History*, 72–3).

order to secure peace upon earth, the king or emperor, although appointed by God, does not have any power over the pope but is, on the contrary, subjected to his supreme spiritual authority. The temporal *regnum*, itself a result of the Fall of Man, is necessary in order to protect human beings from evil; the spiritual power, the *sacerdotium*, on the other hand, is the true soul of the state (in contrast to its earthly body).

According to this doctrine, the Church, especially in the empire of Charlemagne, was not understood as one institution within the political whole; rather temporal and spiritual power were regarded as (hierarchically ordered) parts of the all-encompassing Church, of the *ecclesia* as the 'body of Christ', its leader. This constellation exerted a pervasive influence over the political and social order of medieval society. It also explains why the imposition of the Christian religion and the interests of the Church were also interests of the state, which led under Charlemagne, for example, to the forcible conversion of conquered peoples, such as the Slavs and the Saxons, to Christianity. Moreover, it explains why heresy became a *crimen publicum*, a twofold *lèse-majesté*. The stability of the faith determined the stability of the state, and conversely: *ecclesiam et Imperium esse unum et idem*.[76]

However, this involves a certain tension, for it was not always clear how the legitimate spheres of power of the emperor and of the Church should be defined in relation to one another, that is, when the one or the other 'sword' was required. If the emperor himself was appointed by the grace of God and exercised power in temporal matters, wasn't he the embodiment of the social order? Shouldn't the Church have the function of enjoining the subjects to obey the emperor, who, after all, was ultimately the protector of Christendom? The conflict thus broached exploded with full force in the so-called Investiture Controversy between Henry IV and Pope Gregory VII, which marked the beginning of a long process of separation of *regnum* and *sacerdotium*. Gregory VII claimed not only the sole right (until then the preserve of the king) to appoint or dismiss bishops (who exercised considerable 'temporal' power), but also the right to dismiss emperors who, after all, owed their office to the priesthood alone. The fundamental question of the status of temporal vis-à-vis spiritual power was at stake in this conflict, which began in 1075 and was fiercely fought (one need only think of Henry's Walk to Canossa in 1077 or his coronation by an antipope in 1084) and was resolved only in 1122 with the Concordat of Worms in which a modus vivendi was

---

76. As stated in a thirteenth-century German document, quoted in Lecler, *Toleration and the Reformation*, vol. 1, 70 ('Church and Empire being one and the same').

agreed.[77] Although the path leading to a complete separation between temporal and spiritual power was destined to be a long one, nevertheless the Investiture Controversy can be seen as the beginning of this separation and the development of a 'secular' political order which requires a justification of its own.[78]

The second component mentioned above, the integration of human beings in the spiritual and institutional framework of power, is particularly important for the problem of toleration. For as long as the above-mentioned temporal–spiritual unity is preserved, the question of toleration – and of intolerance – is always posed from the perspective of the Church; there is no independent dimension of state toleration that supersedes this. Thus, even where we encounter arguments for or practices of toleration, the permission conception provides the yardstick according to which wickedness – unbelief, false belief, immorality – can only be endured when intervening would lead to even greater evil: *minus malum toleratur ut maius tollatur* was the judgement of the contemporary jurisprudential literature (especially in the commentary of Johannes Teutonicus on the Decree of Gratian, *Glossa ordinaria*, 1215).[79] Moreover, in this context it was always emphasised that what was involved were temporary permissions and by no means approval of the relevant convictions and practices: *ecclesia non approbat, sed permittit.*[80] This made it clear that those who were tolerated were condemned, outcasts of the political order, of society and of the Church – an evil to be endured. Hence, to belong to these groups was a stigma which went hand-in-hand with ostracism, a position which could all too often tip over into defencelessness against outbreaks of violence. Being tolerated was not merely an 'insult', to recall Goethe's term, but also a precarious, fragile condition. Even worse, it was a distinctive form of being subject to domination, control and disciplining. For, since it could be revoked at any time, this kind of permission toleration had to be 'earned' through good conduct. Therefore *being excluded* and stigmatisation are just one side of toleration as a practice of power; the other side is *being included or secluded*. The bestowal of toleration renders those who are tolerated dependent and prisoners of their situation; they are under observation and rely on

77. On this, see Struve, 'Regnum und Sacerdotium', 232–5. Hartmann, 'Toleranz im Investiturstreit', shows how temporary constellations of toleration, in the sense of the coexistence conception, arose within these conflicts.
78. Thus, Böckenförde, 'The Rise of the State as a Process of Secularisation', 28–33. Berman, *Law and Revolution*, emphasises the significance of this conflict for the emergence of independent systems of canon and secular law which underlie the Western legal tradition.
79. See Bejczy, 'Tolerantia', 370 ('the lesser evil is tolerated in order to remove the greater').
80. *Ibid.* ('the Church does not approve, but merely permits').

the protection of the stronger, the prince, against other, aggressive groups among the population. Exclusion and inclusion as seclusion coexist here, and this connection constitutes the distinctive feature of this form of power as toleration since the tolerated subjects are already 'outside' and 'inside' and no other option seems open to them.[81] Here one can speak of *disciplining through toleration*: power disciplines through a strategic interplay of permission and prohibition.

A further dimension of this disciplining can be established by drawing on another aspect of Foucault's conception of power. The 'practice of division' implied by toleration – between the true believers and the different groups who adhere to false beliefs – gives rise to a social image of these 'subjects' as 'subjected' which is part of the practices governing their 'treatment', whether the latter be designed to improve them through instruction or to ensure their good conduct. Nevertheless, Foucault's dichotomous image must be differentiated, for the aforementioned division runs not only between the 'normal' and the 'non-normal', between those in the right and those in error or in the wrong, but also *within* the group of those who deviate from the norm, provided that some of them are ascribed a kernel which makes toleration and salvation possible. This complicates the notion that subjects are 'produced' through effects of power, for although these subjects deviate from the norm, they are nevertheless accorded a certain social status, albeit a strictly regulated one.[82] 'Production' in this context merely expresses the fact that a social discourse which draws such a sharp distinction between the 'correct' and the 'false' or 'tolerable' as does religiously justified permission toleration, and gives rise to corresponding practices and institutions of improvement or control, produces ascriptions of identity which develop a dynamic of their own and shape the self-understanding of subjects. We must not, of course, assume a *uniform* process of such formation; societies and identities are too complex to bring about one-dimensional identities – something which also holds for medieval society. This is all the more true because those who were tolerated were only too well aware of the precariousness and humiliating

---

81. In *Madness and Civilisation* (38ff.) Foucault describes a specific constellation of such inclusion and exclusion, using the treatment of madness in the Middle Ages as an example.

82. See Foucault, 'The Subject and Power', especially 214–16, on pastoral power. Since Foucault's research was primarily oriented to disciplinary institutions, such as the insane asylum, the school or criminal justice, whose immediate aim is to produce 'subjected subjects' (albeit with 'humane' means), he failed to recognise the specificity of permission toleration as a form of power (though its analysis conforms to the logic of his later investigations on 'government'). In what follows, I will attempt to show how this form of power continues and develops through history.

nature of this form of toleration. This 'sense' was and is the motor of social resistance and social struggles, and understanding it calls for knowledge of the 'readiness to resist' of subjects in situations in which the exercise of power mutates into domination (or is experienced as such), and for insight into the claim 'not to be governed like that' and to question power as to its *reasons* which arises in particular situations of subjection.[83]

The situation of the Jews in medieval society is the clearest example of disciplining through toleration.[84] Profoundly despised and hated for religious reasons, they were in constant danger of becoming victims of the frequent pogroms and expulsions for which a pretext, such as the accusation of host desecration or ritual murder, could readily be found. They were 'tolerated' exclusively through the granting of safety guarantees by the Church and by princes, but then chiefly for pragmatic reasons, as a useful evil. They were only permitted to engage in certain activities, in particular trade and finance, which were advantageous for the institutions which granted the permissions, resulting in social antipathies and increased hostility in response.[85] At the theological level, Augustine's argument concerning the 'involuntary testimony' of the Jews to the truth of Christianity was an important argument, as was the assurance that they would receive their ultimate, deserved punishment from God himself. Forced baptism, which in practice was a frequent occurrence (especially at the time of the crusades), was in theory generally rejected and Jewish religious observance was often tolerated, albeit in a restricted form. Yet it was imperative that condoning should not be mistaken for approval, and thus toleration was always a precarious matter also on the side of the Church (in the thirteenth century both Pope Innocent IV and Pope Alexander IV ordered the burning of the 'blasphemous' Talmud). Cardinal Nicholas of Cusa represents an example of the ambivalence of toleration towards the Jews. In 1451 he granted them toleration in Hildesheim on the condition that they not practise usury, not blaspheme against God and wear a yellow circle on their chests as a mark of identification.[86]

Another group – besides the 'Gypsies', beggars and lepers[87] – to whom the relation between toleration which includes and toleration which excludes

---

83. Thus, also Foucault, *What Is Critique?*, 29 and 31.
84. On what follows see the wide-ranging discussion in Stow, *Alienated Minority*; also Lohrmann, 'Fürstenschutz als Grundlage jüdischer Existenz im Mittelalter', and Besier and Schreiner, 'Toleranz', 462–5.
85. See Stow, *Alienated Minority*, ch. 10.
86. Besier and Schreiner, 'Toleranz', 464.   87. See *ibid.* 471–2.

applies, albeit in a different way, is prostitutes.[88] Augustine already pled for condoning this evil in order to avoid greater evil, where adultery, rape and sodomy were sometimes mentioned (though not by Augustine).[89] A sin is tolerated in order to prevent a greater sin; in late medieval France, brothels were called *maisons de tolerance*. However, there were also fundamental (not merely pragmatic) limits to toleration towards 'sinful' individuals. Homosexuality, for example, could not be tolerated under any circumstances because it was seen to jeopardise the basic rules of social coexistence.

However, not only the internal social relation to such groups was in need of clarification but also the external relation to the 'heathens', the idolaters, in particular the Muslims, who were increasingly regarded as a religious and political challenge. The dictum of the non-coercibility of conscience – in both its empirical and normative forms: that it cannot be coerced and that it ought not to be coerced – also held in principle towards those groups; yet this was placed in question especially in times of crisis. Forced conversions of conquered peoples were thus a frequent occurrence – war was the preparation for the mission. In 1008, for example, Bishop Bruno of Querfurt called upon Henry II to use the sword so that a Slavic people, the Liutitians, might be 'compelled to enter'.[90] Hence, the dictum *compelle intrare* was also extended to heathens and no longer applied exclusively to heretics, as in Augustine.

In this context the crusades are the most important historical manifestation of the self-assertion and expansion of Christianity, in particular in the struggle with Islam. At first, the missionary idea was not foremost in this enterprise but the reconquest of the holy sites following the occupation of Jerusalem by the Seljuks in 1071. However, not only did bloody massacres of 'unbelievers' take place during the seven crusades (extending into the thirteenth century), especially after the conquest of Jerusalem in 1099;[91] in addition, their subjugation through war was regarded as a precondition for their religious instruction. Bernard of Clairvaux, the driving force behind the Second Crusade (1147–49), who already in 1128 characterised killing in the name of Christ as killing 'with a clear conscience'[92] in a pamphlet supporting

---

88. See Schuster, *Das Frauenhaus*, especially 212. In addition Graus, 'Randgruppen der städtischen Gesellschaft im Spätmittelalter', especially 404–11.
89. Augustine, *De ordine*, 2, 4, 12.
90. Bruno of Querfurt, quoted in Lecler, *Toleration and the Reformation*, vol. 1, 74.
91. See Möhring, 'Die Kreuzfahrer, ihre muslimischen Untertanen und die heiligen Stätten des Islam'.
92. 'The knight of Christ, I say, may strike with confidence and die yet more confidently, for he serves Christ when he strikes, and serves himself when he falls.' Clairvaux, *In Praise of the New Knighthood*, 132.

the Order of Knights Templar, wrote to Pope Eugene III in 1147: 'At some point the whole host of the heathens must reach it [the Christian truth]! Are we to wait for the faith to occur to them of itself? Whoever arrived at the faith by accident?'[93] The force of arms was not supposed to banish false belief directly but only to create the political conditions for conversion to the true faith; thus, Clairvaux could reject conversion through force while simultaneously advocating subjugation through force. Ramon Llull, an advocate of conversation between religions, still defended this dual strategy.

Among all groups, however, one posed by far the greatest challenge to the spiritual and temporal power of the Church, namely the heretics who questioned the truth of the faith 'from within'. It comes as no surprise, therefore, that there was no room for toleration towards them either in theory or in practice – except as a result of a balance of forces. Their treatment, in particular, earned medieval society the moniker of a 'persecuting society'.[94] The 'heretics' were regarded as weeds which had to be destroyed where they could be clearly identified. Following the Decree of Gratian, capital punishment, in particular burning at the stake, became increasingly common as a punitive measure and was legally established in 1224. The full force of clerical and temporal suppression was mobilised against heretical movements when they posed a serious threat, as the crusades against the Albigensians (1209–29) demonstrate.[95] Such movements posed multiple challenges to medieval society, as regards both its spiritual foundation and the social order (especially that of property) and political and clerical rule. Accordingly, the duty to contain such movements was justified in multiple ways: as a duty towards God, towards the emperor or princes, towards the Church and the rest of the faithful who had to be protected against the dangerous and infectious 'virus' of unbelief, and finally towards those affected themselves whose souls had to be saved. And thus an institution to combat dangerous heresies emerged at the end of the twelfth century, at first decentrally and later as a papal institution, which was placed (largely) under the control of the Dominicans and Franciscans, namely, the Inquisition.

The Inquisition was a kind of 'tribunal of conscience'. Since its primary concern was to expose spiritual crimes, on the one hand it depended on clues to such crimes which often consisted of mere suppositions and insinuations, and on the other it had to find ways of penetrating into the depths of the soul.

93. Clairvaux, *The Letters of St. Bernard of Clairvaux*.
94. Moore, *The Formation of the Persecuting Society*, especially 11–27.
95. See Bosl, 'Reformorden, Ketzer und religiöse Bewegungen in der hochmittelalterlichen Gesellschaft', 282–9.

Interrogation, deception and torture were regarded as such means should the truth fail to come to light in any other way.[96] The inquisitor was at once prosecutor and judge and confessor. Once accused, only those who confessed and repented their sins could avoid the punishment which threatened the convicted or obdurate heretic: the stake. Penitential punishments of the most varied kinds (such as public flagellation) were imposed on repentant heretics. The aim of the process was the destruction not of the heretic but of the heresy; the declared goal was the salvation of the soul of the accused who had to be led back to the correct path. If the heresy could not be eliminated in any other way than through the death of the heretic, however, the latter was deprived of the protection of the Church and was delivered over to the temporal authority which then performed the corresponding punishment, burning alive at the stake. The Inquisition remained an effective instrument for suppressing heresy over many centuries, as is shown by the example of Spain in the fifteenth and sixteenth centuries. It is the extreme expression of the logic of the distinction between a 'true' and an 'inauthentic' self, so that the latter had to be destroyed in order to save the former, chiefly through repentance (sometimes enforced through torture), though possibly also through its physical destruction. Even at the stake, immediately before he was put to death, the condemned could still save his soul and receive the Eucharist.[97] A cruel logic: to suffer physical death in order to escape eternal death.

4. The, for its time, representative, most comprehensive and, for later theology, authoritative discussion of toleration towards the above-mentioned groups is to be found in the *Summa Theologiae* of Thomas Aquinas.[98] Thomas leaves no doubt that all forms of unbelief are sinful, that unbelief is even a 'mortal sin' (10, 4), and thus that the question of toleration must always take the form of what reasons there could be for condoning such sins. In this context Thomas distinguishes between three kinds of unbelief. The pagans oppose the true faith which they have not (yet) accepted; the Jews oppose the faith which was already prefigured in their own; and, finally, the heretics oppose the faith which they had already accepted and distort it (10, 5). The latter sin is the most serious because it amounts to a violation of a promise one has given; the sin of the Jews is less serious, and that of the pagans even less so, since they do not break any promise (10, 6).

---

96. See the detailed account in Lea, *A History of the Inquisition in the Middle Ages*, vol. I, especially chs. 5 and 6.
97. *Ibid.* 546.
98. Thomas Aquinas, *Summa Theologiae*, vol. XVIII, 1a2ae, 19, 5. In what follows, the *Summa Theologiae* will be quoted according to the question and article number of the relevant part.

The answer to the question 'Whether unbelievers should be compelled to the faith?' (10, 8) reflects these differences. Pagans and Jews 'are by no means to be compelled to the faith, in order that they may believe [*ut ipsi credant*], because to believe depends on the will' (10, 8). Nevertheless they should not hinder or blaspheme against the true faith, and thus waging 'war with unbelievers' can be justified, not in order to convert them by force, but in order to prevent them from blocking the path to the true faith for others. Associations with Jews and pagans are not forbidden unless it is to be feared that 'simple people' could thereby be led away from the true faith (10, 9). To the question of whether the rites of the unbelievers ought to be tolerated (10, 11), Thomas answers that, although they have no inherent value and are sinful, they can nevertheless be condoned in order to avoid a greater evil (10, 11). Here Thomas cites Augustine's argument for toleration of 'harlots'.

He offers some more specific directives concerning behaviour towards the Jews: 'Thus, from the fact that the Jews observe their rites, which, of old, foreshadowed the truth of the faith which we hold, there follows this good – that our very enemies bear witness to our faith, and that our faith is represented in a figure, so to speak' (10, 11). With this Thomas takes up the Augustinian argument of involuntary witness; at the same time he nevertheless makes clear that there is a fundamental enmity towards the Jews and that tolerance towards them is at the discretion of the Church, that they are 'subjected to the Church' (10, 10) and the latter can dispose of their possessions.

The justifications for toleration discussed thus far (always within the framework of the permission conception) did not go beyond Augustine. However, in the discussion of the question of whether it is permissible to baptise Jewish children against their parents' will, Thomas introduces a new argument, that of 'natural justice' (*justitia naturalis*) (10, 12). This states that a child as long as it has not attained the use of reason remains under the guardianship of its father, for it is by nature part of its father. To violate this natural order through an enforced baptism would contradict the custom of the Church and is not right (something reinforced by the further argument that it is not desirable either, for children baptised in this way might easily be led to renounce the faith).

None of these arguments for toleration applies in the case of heretics, however. Thus, although accepting the faith is a matter of free will, 'keeping the faith, when once one has received it, is a matter of obligation' (10, 8); and thus heretics and apostates 'should be submitted even to bodily compulsion, that they may fulfil what they have promised, and hold what they, at the time, received' (10, 8). Nor does the parable of the weeds contradict this use of force, for here Thomas appeals to the late Augustine who does not see any reason for toleration when it is clear who belongs among the weeds and there is a danger of infection. Thomas appeals in addition to the *compelle intrare* dictum, which is now interpreted as a 'compulsion to remain' or 'return'. The association with heretics is also a punishable sin (10, 9); they are in effect excommunicated.

Thomas goes even further in his affirmative stance on the persecution of heretics:

> On their own [i.e. the heretics'] side there is the sin, whereby they deserve not only to be separated from the Church by excommunication, but also to be severed from the world by death. For it is a much graver matter to corrupt the faith which quickens the soul, than to forge money, which supports temporal life. Wherefore if forgers of money and other evil-doers are forthwith condemned to death by the secular authority, much more reason is there for heretics, as soon as they are convicted of heresy, to be not only excommunicated but even put to death. (11, 3)

The Church is merciful and issues two warnings to those concerned; yet if the latter prove to be obstinate they are delivered over to the secular tribunal and hence to their death. The eradication of heresy is a multiple duty – towards God, those affected and those who may be threatened with infection – and thus no mercy is to be shown where no conversion is possible. Repentant sinners, by contrast, are again admitted to penance, although this must not give rise to the impression that they are escaping their just punishment (11, 4). Above all stands the loving concern for the 'eternal salvation' of human beings and this is far more important than the 'temporal good', for example the 'life of the body' (11, 4). Here, too, the division of the self leads to a logic of destruction of what stands in the way of true salvation, even if that be the human being himself whose salvation is in question. '[O]ne is more bound to succour a man who is in danger of everlasting death, than one who is in danger of temporal death' (10, 12). To this way of thinking there is no 'human being' who should be respected in abstraction from the condition and future of his soul as regards its eternal salvation. According to this Christian-perfectionist way of thinking, such respect and toleration would be sinful.

5. In the meantime, medieval theology had raised a problem which would be of some importance for the future of the idea of toleration, that of the *errant conscience*. The question is, if a person follows his conscience, and if

following one's conscience – supposedly in observance of God's instruction – with complete inner conviction is itself an imperative and something good, how can someone who in good faith follows an error commit a sin, even though he believes he is doing right and following God's will? Yet, on the other hand, how can failing to observe God's true commands fail to be a sin?

Peter Abelard, the twelfth-century thinker who was innovative in more than just this point, vigorously defended the former position. Although, as noted above (§4, Excursus), Paul already preached forbearance vis-à-vis the errant and weak conscience, nevertheless this remained confined to minor differences in religious observances, to *adiaphora*. In his treatise on morality, *Nosce te ipsum*, Abelard offers a more exhaustive treatment of the problem. Since the sin does not reside in the act but in the will, a sincere act in the consciousness of obeying God does not constitute a sin, even if it errs in relation to the true calling of man, an area in which error is in any case a frequent occurrence, according to Abelard. Therefore, someone who rejects the true faith in the erring conviction that the latter is displeasing to God does not sin.[99] For finite human beings, it would be more sinful not to obey their conscience which shows them the correct path according to their convictions; and thus even Christ's persecutors were bound to follow their profoundly mistaken conviction and to act accordingly.[100] Abelard thereby contradicts the thesis that the Jews 'murdered God', one of the essential foundations of Christian anti-Judaism.

Abelard's theses were condemned as heresy by the Synod of Sens in 1140, not least due to the interventions of Bernard of Clairvaux. Nevertheless the problem which he discussed remained, and Abelard's theory was taken up by some of his disciples. Opposed to this was another school for which conscience could not claim any force or priority over the objective divine order, so that there could be no question of heretics appealing to their (erring) conscience. Thomas Aquinas attempted to synthesise these two schools. First he opposes the latter school and accords a binding force to the errant conscience, since an act of will which opposes what reason asserts is bad.[101] Conscience must follow the 'dictate of the reason', which may be in error; nevertheless, in case of an error this is not conscious and thus to act against it would be an action against what appears to be right and commanded by God. However, this does not as yet answer the question of whether and in what case an erring conscience excuses an action for Thomas; and in addressing this

---

99. Abelard, *Ethics*, 24.   100. *Ibid.* 29.
101. Thomas Aquinas, *Summa Theologiae*, vol. I/II, 19, 5.

question he again shuts the door for freedom of conscience which previously seemed to be open. For he accepts only involuntary ignorance as an excuse, but not wilful ignorance. Ignorance is involuntary when it is mistaken about certain facts – he gives the example of the man who does not know that the woman who is lying beside him is not his wife.[102] However, ignorance should be traced back to the will when it is directly intended or when someone does not know something he ought to know due to carelessness; Thomas calls the latter an indirect (or mediate) voluntary ignorance. The latter includes all cases where someone violates divine law which he or she should know, for example an adulterer. Hence, ignorance is not a reason for exculpation with regard to divine laws and the errant conscience cannot provide any reasons for justifying toleration in this domain.[103] It is permissible to follow one's conscience only when it does not conflict with divine truth; one has a duty to overrule a conscience which errs in this regard.

Only at the end of the seventeenth century will Pierre Bayle take this up and defend the 'rights' of the erring conscience; nevertheless, this demonstrates the latent effect of the problem which Abelard introduced into theoretical reflection.

§6 Truth in discourse: unity in plurality

1. The growing plurality of Christian convictions in a society undergoing increasing economic and cultural change during the twelfth century,[104] coupled with the confrontation with the other monotheistic religions, called for a fundamental process of self-reflection within Christianity which often took a specific literary form, namely, the religious conversation in which representatives of different religions or persuasions meet in order to determine the correct path to the true faith through argument. However, there is still a long way to a Lessing-style theory of the agreement among the religions as equal beneficiaries of divine truth (here on earth). For these discourses did not in the first instance serve the goal of an open discussion about the truth to be sought or about the routes to God. They were not *truth-seeking* discourses but *truth-imposing* discourses in which it was shown, through confrontations with one's adversaries, how the latter run out of arguments and are forced

---

102. *Ibid.* 19, 6. This example is also found in Abelard, *Ethics*, 10–11.
103. In another work, *Quaestiones Quodlibetales*, vol. I, Art. 19, he goes as far as to assert that even ignorance of a papal decree is inexcusable because there exists a duty of general knowledge.
104. Bosl, 'Reformorden, Ketzer und religiöse Bewegungen in der hochmittelalterlichen Gesellschaft', 245, speaks with A. Dempf of the 'first European Enlightenment'.

to acknowledge this. The Jews, in particular, when they featured as conversation partners, served to demonstrate the superiority of Christianity.[105] Hence, here dialogue aimed not at mutual understanding concerning commonalities and differences, but at refuting one's opponent.[106]

It is Abelard who again represents a clear break with this tradition, even though in this respect he remained part of an ostracised minority in his own time, and irenism, the doctrine of religious reconciliation leading ultimately to unification, would become an influential position only much later within humanism. Abelard marks the beginning of the idea of the deeper religious and ethical unity within, and in spite of, the multiplicity of religious beliefs, a unity which is nevertheless clearly Christian in nature and grounded in the Christian God. After his condemnation in 1140, he wrote the *Dialogus inter Philosophum, Judaeum et Christianum* in the monastic prison in Cluny, though it remained unfinished on account of his death in 1142. Therefore, although it cannot be ascertained without doubt how the judgement, which he reserved for himself as judge over the three adversaries, would have turned out, it can be reconstructed from the direction taken by the conversation. The aim of the dialogue is to demonstrate on the basis of rational considerations – hence at the level laid down by the philosopher at the beginning of the dialogue as the level for the discussion – that the Christian faith, in contrast to the Jewish belief in the law and the philosophical doctrine of the natural moral law, is the *true ethic*. It is a philosophical Christianity which he espouses and in this way he grants himself the freedom from the theological doctrine of this time which in his view autonomous, self-governing reason demands.

It is already established as an uncontroversial presupposition at the opening that all three of them, the philosopher, the Jew and the Christian, see themselves as worshipping one and the same God; therefore, there can be no dispute about this. The philosopher wants to exclude arguments over the issue of the true faith which would not be valid for a religiously impartial reason; according to him, the essential source of intolerance is the uncertainty of those who blindly follow their hereditary faith and thus fear challenges to and queries of their convictions. In the conversation between the philosopher and the representative of the Jewish faith which follows, this accusation is levelled at the latter; his belief in the law is rejected as insufficiently justified and criticised as a strict and authoritarian, and ultimately irrational, form of ethics which is inferior to the natural moral law. Therefore, the Jew,

105. Wieland, 'Das Eigene und das Andere', 13, offers the examples of the dialogues of Peter Damian, Petrus Alfonsi, Odo of Cambrai, Gilbert Crispin and Rupert of Deutz.
106. On this, see also Nederman, *Worlds of Difference*, ch. 2.

as depicted by Abelard, has no chance of satisfying the requirements of the discourse; he is by no means granted equal status with the two other adversaries. The Jew himself complains of being unbearably 'afflicted ... by the Law's yoke', and thus already makes the key criticism of his own faith.[107]

Although Christian prejudices against Judaism are introduced into the conversation in this way, not only is the Jew represented as a rational conversation partner but his faith also contains the kernel of the natural moral law which points the way to the true ethics. Hence, he does not stand in glaring contradiction to the truth. Moreover, in the passage mentioned, Abelard has the Jew make a complaint against unjust treatment in Christian societies, something very unusual in Christian writings of this time. Although the Jew is thus not an equal in the conversation, he is not an 'enemy' either; he is someone who partakes in an incomplete and faulty way in the truth, but does not deserve to be subjugated for this reason.[108]

This situation is different in the conversation between the philosopher and the Christian. Now it is the former who is often on the defensive and must ultimately agree with the Christian that the highest good, which they are both attempting to define, resides in the contemplation of God which constitutes true blessedness.[109] Without the confident expectation of this eternal bliss as a reward for the virtuous, the central argument goes, the idea of the *summum bonum* remains indeterminate and as a result the virtues and the moral law – the *lex naturale* – remain ineffectual. Morality is not observed for its own sake, it is not autonomous; the goal of just conduct is eternal happiness, which can only lie in a future life free from sorrows.[110]

In this way, Abelard attempts to vindicate the Christian faith as the true ethics, which means that the path of morality and reason, regardless of the original faith in which it was initially pursued, will be the route to salvation, provided that heritage, prejudices or blind acceptance of authority do not deflect one from this path. This is an important message for toleration, though also an ambivalent one. On the one hand, it forbids discrimination against, or attempts to convert, anyone who observes the natural moral law – of 'love for God and neighbour'[111] – since this already is the kernel of true faith. This represents a decisive step in the discourse of toleration. The foundation of mutual toleration is the natural moral law which, although grounded in God, can be grasped by all who can use their reason properly. On the other hand, however, morality remains dependent on the true faith for

107. Abelard, *Dialogue*, 68.
108. On this, see Wieland, 'Das Eigene und das Andere', 15–18.
109. Abelard, *Dialogue*, 119, 123, 219, 235.   110. See *ibid.* 104.   111. *Ibid.* 69.

its perfection and in order to unfold a motivational power through the hope of eternal happiness, with the result that there is a 'rationally grounded' requirement to pursue the path consistently and not to stop at an earlier stage. It remains the case that the question of morality cannot be answered in the context of the Christian doctrine of salvation without appealing to the human good, and the reason for toleration remains bound to the truth of God, the supreme good. Nevertheless, a new space has been won for tolerance and respect towards others, as opposed to merely putting up with them for pragmatic reasons. The moral law is the link, and the routes to truth and salvation are no longer laid down dogmatically, in accordance with the teachings of the Church, though it is still assumed that they must lead to the true faith.

2. Ramon Llull's *Liber de gentili et tribus sapientibus* (c. 1276) represents a further stage in the development of the interreligious discourse of toleration. Here, too, different religions – in this case, Islam in addition to Judaism and Christianity – appear before the tribunal of philosophical knowledge, so that rational grounds alone are supposed to speak for the truth of one of these routes to salvation. However, in this case ethics does not provide the primary basis of the considerations, but each of the conceptions of God and the world must prove its worth as a whole and show itself to be superior to the others.

Llull was influenced by the experience of the coexistence of Christians, Jews and Muslims on his native island of Mallorca. He was convinced that he possessed the science – an *Ars inveniendi veritatem* – that enabled him to demonstrate the superiority of the Christian doctrine of the Trinity and the Incarnation in peaceful discursive exchanges with the other two religions. This science is based on shared truths which *cannot be reasonably disputed* concerning God's essence and creation which need only be combined in the correct way to arrive at true knowledge. The *Liber de gentili* is a typical example of this method.

The framing narrative of the conversation, which takes the form of a succession of extended self-presentations of the religions, is Llull's description of a 'Gentile' (i.e. a pagan) – 'very learned in philosophy'[112] – who knows nothing about God and the resurrection and is cast into deep despair by the thought of death. In a forest he encounters three wise men – a Jew, a Christian and a Saracen – who stand at a well with five trees whose meaning is explained to them by the charming figure of 'Intelligence'. The flowers on the first tree consist of combinations of pairs of the seven virtues of God which characterise him in equal measure and without contradiction. The

---

112. Llull, *Book of the Gentile and the Three Wise Men*, quoted from Llull, *Doctor Illuminatus*, 86.

second tree has combinations of uncreated and the created virtues (with corresponding specifications of the relations and order of priority among them), the third combinations of the uncreated virtues and the seven deadly sins, the fourth combinations of the created virtues, and finally the fifth combinations of these virtues and the mortal sins. These trees and their flowers are *not* themselves a matter of dispute among the three wise men, so that one of them expresses the wish for all: 'Ah! What a great good fortune it would be if, by means of these trees, we could all – every man on earth – be under one religion and belief.'[113]

Thus, they decide to sit down under the trees and to conduct an argument in order to determine *which* of their religions could bring about such a unity. At this point the pagan joins them and *together* they rescue him from his despair by 'proving' the existence of God and the resurrection. Once they have succeeded in doing this and the pagan breaks out in praise of God, however, they thrust him into despair once again with the demand that he should now convert to the true faith, which each of the three wise men claims to embody.

Here I cannot discuss the self-presentations which now follow in detail. It is striking that, in spite of all the differences, mutual condemnations and deprecations are seldom, and a speaker often expresses agreement with the previous speaker in presenting his own proof. However, even though this is not explicitly emphasised, the pagan at times interjects critical questions concerning the Jewish and Islamic faiths which either remain unanswered or are given clearly inadequate answers.[114] This does not occur in this form in the confrontation with Christianity. It is also important that, although each of the three wise men raises an exclusive claim to salvation for his religion, nevertheless the Christian impresses upon the pagan that the Christian religion includes what is true in the other two and in addition offers the best explanation of the flowers because the other two religions do not contain the ideas of the Trinity and of the Incarnation of God.

Nevertheless, the outcome of the book remains open. After all three have spoken, the pagan commences a prayer whose intensity deeply impresses the three wise men, although its content is neutral towards them. When, following the prayer, he wishes to inform them of his choice they hastily take leave with the remark that each of them wishes to regard himself as the winner, and in addition they want to continue the debate over who has

113. *Ibid.* 90.
114. On Judaism see, for example, *ibid.* 106, 113–14; on the 'faith of the Saracens', where this is even clearer, see 142–3, 148–9, 154–5.

presented the better arguments. Thus, the pagan's choice remains unknown. Having excused themselves for possibly harsh words, the three wise men take leave of one another resolving to continue their discussion with the goal of establishing the true faith.

Not only on account of this unusual ending – also judged by the course of the conversation – does Llull's *Liber de gentili* mark an important stage in the discourse of toleration which reveals new aspects of the question of religious truth. For it should be noted what Llull presupposes as beyond dispute, namely belief in a deity, a shared form of discursive reason and agreement over the virtues of the good and moral life. Even if a closer examination of the five trees shows that their content is by no means neutral because based on Christian religious convictions, here Llull provides the foundation for a form of religious toleration which is *itself* based on a religious core. Viewed retrospectively, however, different routes to toleration branch out from here.

(1) The path of *reductive unity* according to which this common core alone constitutes the truth of religion and everything that goes beyond is an incidental matter – *adiaphora* – derived from the particular traditions. This is the position defended by Christian humanism and remained influential until its culmination in the idea of a 'rational religion'.

(2) The path of *unity through amalgamation* according to which a new form of religion incorporating the old ones will emerge from the exchange among the different religious persuasions. This is a variant of humanist irenism.

(3) The path of *competitive unity* which states that the competition of words and actions will reveal which is the true religion, though only at the Last Judgement. Until then there is an equality in the competition owing to a shared origin. This position will find its clearest expression in Lessing's parable of the rings.

(4) The path of *inclusive unity* according to which one religion incorporates the truth of the others, so that the latter have a certain justification, though the former represents the consummate path to salvation.[115]

(5) The path of *pluralist unity* according to which the different religions can claim to participate in the single, infinite divine reality and to represent one of the possible paths to salvation.[116] Each religion interprets this

---

115. Compare the concept of 'inclusivism' in Schmidt-Leukel, 'Zur Klassifikation religionstheologischer Modelle'.
116. This comes close to the conception of Hick, 'The Pluralistic Hypothesis', and Mensching, *Tolerance and Truth in Religion*.

reality in its own way and regards its own path from its perspective as most in harmony with this reality.

(6) Finally, the path which Llull himself pursues can be called that of *unity through refutation*. Starting from shared convictions, one of the religions manages to refute the others, so that they are converted to the truth. This is the point of toleration towards them. The *concordantia* over essential matters which makes the discourse possible leads to a *unitas* in faith.

These six paths will feature prominently in the modern discourse of toleration. Differentiating them is important in order to avoid over-generalisations concerning a unitary religious thinking which 'recognises' difference and leads to toleration; for such thinking and such recognition assume many forms. Some of the models mentioned take an unqualified affirmative stance towards their own truth, others by contrast presuppose a greater cognitive distance from it. Some recognise the truth of other religions, others do not. Yet common to all of these models is the fact that they are themselves based upon *religious* foundations and thus suppress the question concerning the toleration of convictions which do *not* belong to the religious unity which is supposed to be created or affirmed.

The *Book of the Gentile and the Three Wise Men* represents an exception in Llull's own work. For although in the end it advocates the path of unity through refutation, the fact that the outcome of the dispute is left open means that this refutation is not explicitly carried out (though it is implicit in certain passages).[117] In the *Liber Tartari et Christiani* (1285), however, he himself takes a stance in support of Christianity following a disputation; the book ends with the baptism of the Tartar whose salvation was the concern of the three learned men. In the *Liber de quinque sapientibus* (1294), Ramon presents an apology for the Catholic faith as compared to Islam and the Eastern churches; and, finally, in the autobiographical *Disputatio Raymundi christiani et Hamar sarraceni* (1308), Ramon, an imprisoned Christian, conducts a debate with the learned Muslim Homer who is supposed to convert him. In this discussion Ramon emphatically rejects the Muslim faith as 'diabolical law'.[118] In his *Vita coaetanea* (1311) he insists that it is possible to prove on purely rational grounds why Christianity is the true religion. In addition, after 1292 his plea for a peaceful mission changes into clear support of the crusades.[119] Where

---

117. On Llull's work see Colomer, 'Die Vorgeschichte des Motivs vom Frieden im Glauben bei Raimund Llull'.

118. *Disputatio*, 12 (442).

119. Colomer, 'Die Vorgeschichte des Motivs vom Frieden im Glauben bei Raimund Llull', 103.

the 'spiritual sword' of the Church is not sufficient to impose the truth, the temporal sword must be employed.[120]

3. The third major work in the medieval tradition of religious conversations of importance for the justification of toleration is *De pace fidei* (1453) by Nicholas of Cusa, which at the same time marks the transition to early modern, humanist thought. This work is situated at the juncture between a conventional and a novel understanding of religious plurality, between an apologetics of Catholic dogma and a negative theology of an ineffable God whose true being remains unknown (*incognitus et ineffabilis*)[121] and discloses itself to finite minds only through conjectures, as Nicholas explains in his central works *De docta ignorantia* and *De coniecturis*. Whereas, for Abelard, the unity of the religions is grounded in the moral law and he defends Christianity as the true ethic which cannot be reasonably rejected, and whereas Llull wants to promote religious unity through rational insight into the religion which is superior as a whole, Nicholas aspires to a 'peace of faith' based upon agreement – *concordantia* – over a single true religion which allows for a variety of usages and forms of worship: *una religio in rituum varietate.*[122]

This formula was supposed to help in overcoming the religious conflicts with which Nicholas wrestled throughout his life both in theology and philosophy and in church politics, whether as a member of the Council of Basel (from 1431 onwards) in the conflict between the Council and the pope[123] and in the (related) conflict between Rome and the Eastern Church,[124] in the conflict with the Hussite movement (1450–52)[125] or, and especially, regarding the challenge posed by Islam. The latter was the immediate occasion for writing the work on peace.[126] In May 1453 Christian Europe was shocked by news of the conquest of Constantinople by Turkish troops – as was the cardinal of the bishopric of Brixen who recounts at the beginning of his work his vision, under the impression of the horrific news, that 'of a few wise men familiar from their own experience with all such differences which are observed in religions throughout the world, a single easy harmony could

---

120. As it is put in the *Disputatio clerici et Raymundi phantastici* (1311), quoted in Lecler, *Toleration and the Reformation*, vol. I, 77.
121. Nicholas of Cusa, *On the Peace of Faith*, ch. 1 (§5).
122. *Ibid.* ch. 1 (§6) ('one religion in a variety of rites').
123. On this, see Meuthen, 'Nikolaus von Kues in der Entscheidung zwischen Konzil und Papst'.
124. Cf. Krämer, 'Der Beitrag des Nikolaus von Kues zum Unionskonzil mit der Ostkirche'.
125. Cf. Hallauer, 'Das Glaubensgespräch mit den Hussiten'.
126. Cf. Meuthen, 'Der Fall von Konstantinopel und der lateinische Westen'.

be found and through it a lasting peace established by appropriate and true means'.[127]

In this vision the author finds himself before God's throne and is privy to the latter's regret concerning the religious disputes on earth. Two explanations are offered for this: on the one hand (as the archangel indicates), the different interpretations of the single truth defended by different prophets and teachers which are a consequence of the incomprehensibility of God's infinitude; and, on the other, the free will of human beings which is led astray by the 'Prince of Darkness'. The archangel appeals to God to reveal himself to those endowed with reason through his Word so that they can recognise

> that there is only one religion in the variety of rites. But if perhaps this difference of rites cannot be removed or if it is not expedient to do so in order that the diversity may contribute to devotion, as when any religion expends a more attentive effort in performing its ceremonies as if they would become the more pleasing to you, the King: at any rate, just as you are one, there should be one religion and one veneration of worship.[128]

This passage already reveals that Nicholas's chief concern is to promote religious peace through religious unity and unification and that he regards the toleration of a plurality of different forms of worship in largely pragmatic terms as a means to this end. For God also instructs his Word, who has 'become flesh', to assemble the wisest representatives of the different nations and languages so that 'all diversity of religions will be led to one orthodox faith' (*una fides orthodoxa*).[129]

In this way, seventeen envoys from the different nations and religions are assembled who are first instructed in the true religion by the Word of God, then by the Apostle Peter and finally by the Apostle Paul. Nicholas makes clear from the beginning that this is the Catholic religion alone. Accordingly, in the seventeen short dialogues which follow, the fundamental truths of Catholic Christianity are presented in such a way that in the end the envoys of polytheistic religions, Judaism, Islam and other Christian denominations are convinced of this truth. Whether it be the Trinity, the doctrine of the Word of God become flesh in Jesus Christ, the virgin birth, the crucifixion and resurrection of Jesus, baptism, the Eucharist and the other sacraments: the Catholic faith always provides the basis for defining the truth in matters

127. Nicholas of Cusa, *On the Peace of Faith*, ch. 1 (§1).
128. *Ibid.* ch. 1 (§6).   129. *Ibid.* ch. 3 (§8).

of dogma and rites, and only on this basis are the possible ritual deviations and their limits addressed.[130] Thus, ritual variations with respect to Holy Communion, the practice of circumcision or the organisation of the religious service, for instance, are regarded as tolerable as long as they do not affect the kernel of the truth. Here, too, Nicholas chiefly adduces pragmatic considerations; at no point do the other religions contain a truth that is not contained in Christianity. In addition, the alternatives are depicted as religious forms derived from one-sided, traditional interpretations of the truth and are tolerated only for the sake of general peace.[131]

The conversation 'in the heaven of reason' (*in caelo rationis*) ends with the conclusion of a concord of religions (*concordia religionum*) by the wise representatives of the nations and God assigns them the task of spreading this truth in their countries and ensuring the unity of 'true worship'.[132] Then they should come together once again in Jerusalem and establish an everlasting peace in the faith.

The dream of the 'peace of faith', therefore, is the dream of a Catholic peace, albeit one which leaves room for differences in rites. The argument which initially follows the humanist path of *reductive unity* – that is, the unity achieved by tracing religious differences back to a religious core common to all human beings, as opposed to the *adiaphora* – ultimately leads to the path of *inclusive unity* according to which the Christian-Catholic religion contains the truths of all other religions and thus represents the perfect religion, even though it can also tolerate other observances. Moreover, certain conversations even lend the treatise the character of the path of *unity through refutation*. Because no concessions are made in the core religious domain, the doctrines of the other religions which go beyond it appear as false doctrines which are refuted.[133] This makes it apparent how far removed the ideas of Nicholas of Cusa are from a 'pluralistic' understanding of religion or from that of a Lessing, which envisages an equality among the routes to salvation at least here on earth – an understanding of religion alien to the Christian Middle Ages.

In the position defended in *De pace fidei* Nicholas is thinking in more traditional terms than Abelard in that he does not ground the unity which

---

130. Thus also de Gandillac, 'Das Ziel der una religio in varietate rituum', especially 202, and Wieland, 'Das Eigene und das Andere', 23–4.

131. Thus, in the closing conversation Paul asserts: 'It is very often necessary to condescend to human weakness if it does not offend against eternal salvation. For to seek exact conformity in all things is rather to disturb the peace' (*On the Peace of Faith*, ch. 19 (§67)).

132. *Ibid.* ch. 19 (§68).

133. On this, see also Nicholas's critique of Islam in *Cribratio Alchorani*.

facilitates religious peace in rational insight into (Christian) ethics but in the more inclusive Christian faith itself. At the same time, in so doing he recoils before the radicality of his own negative theology which crops up at the beginning of the religious conversation in the reference to God's incomprehensibility. For as long as God can be conceived only in an awareness of our ignorance of him (hence the *docta ignorantia*), and as long as religions are based upon the conjectures of finite minds and the one religion 'is partaken of variously... by the inhabitants of this world', as he puts it in *De coniecturis*,[134] different forms of religious expression can be interpreted in a pluralistic manner. However, Nicholas did not make this idea of the finitude of reason the basis of his conception of toleration;[135] the true religion does not condone the presumptuous claim to human knowability nor does it allow its validity to be relativised through insight into the limits of human reason.

4. This brief survey of the dynamic of medieval religious discourses suffices to reconstruct the most important approaches to a religious justification of toleration (and its limits) developed within this context. However, its focus on Christianity should not give the impression that such self-reflexive discourses and discourses concerning toleration did not also take place within and between the other religions.[136] Although I cannot explore the wealth of these debates in detail here, I should mention the two most important representatives of twelfth-century philosophical reflection within Judaism and Islam in which we encounter important arguments for toleration within and between religions, namely, Maimonides and Averroes.

These two thinkers were contemporaries and both grew up in an Islamic-dominated Cordoba marked by a coexistence among religions. Both were influenced by the reception of Aristotle in the Arab world, which led to the emergence of a multifaceted scientific and philosophical culture which posed a major challenge for the theologians of all three religions. Thus, it is no accident that Abelard depicts his philosopher who questions the truth of the religions as a representative of this Islamic culture.[137] In fact,

134. Nicholas of Cusa, *De coniecturis*, 239.
135. Thus, Popper, 'Toleration and Intellectual Responsibility', 192, is also wrong when he situates Nicholas of Cusa within a 'sceptical tradition' which placed the accent on human ignorance as the basis for inclusive toleration. On the transitional position of Nicholas's theology, see Weischedel, *Der Gott der Philosophen*, vol. 1, 157–64.
136. On Judaism and Islam, in addition to Christianity, see the collection of Lewis and Niewöhner (eds.), *Religionsgespräche im Mittelalter*, and the instructive comparison in Niewöhner, 'Dialoge, die nicht stattgefunden haben'.
137. A clear indication of this can be found in Abelard, *Dialogue*, 79.

a general comparison between Abelard, Maimonides and Averroes suggests itself. The latter two thinkers, like the former, sought to interpret their faith in the light of reason and philosophy (which in Maimonides' and Averroes' case chiefly meant Aristotelian philosophy) and to go beyond contradictory readings of the Word of God – in this sense all three were working towards an 'Enlightenment'; still, common to all three is that they did not arrive at a 'rational religion'. The role of reason was to cognise (one's own) faith as the true faith and to confirm it in its core beliefs; reason, in spite of its freedom, remained tied to the antecedent truth of revelation. Philosophy not only has the freedom but also the duty to provide a rational interpretation of scripture in order to promote true knowledge.

This is a central idea of Maimonides, also known as Rabbi Moses Ben Maimon (acronym: Rambam), in particular of his most important work *The Guide for the Perplexed* (1190; originally *Dalâlat al-Hâ'irin* or *Môreh Nebûkim*). In this book, which is addressed to a philosophically educated disciple who doubts the truth of the Jewish religion, Maimonides, the head of the Jewish community in Old Cairo, sets himself the task of bringing Aristotelian philosophy into harmony with the Jewish faith in the Law. The Law not only permits philosophical questioning but even demands it along the path to human perfection, and philosophy in turn confirms the truth of the Law in its supreme perfection – albeit in an esoteric form which goes beyond the (necessary and correct) faith in the Law of the mass of human beings.[138] Some of Maimonides' most important writings, such as the important *Mishneh Torah* (1180), are devoted to the correct interpretation of the Law; however, the *Guide for the Perplexed*, written in Arabic, is addressed to the philosophically educated reader who is capable of understanding the 'profound mysteries'[139] of scripture which are not accessible to all and are not supposed to be, lest the faith in the Law be undermined. Should it succeed, the book will provide 'the solution of those important problems of religion, which are a source of anxiety to all intelligent men' (Introduction, 80).

138. Leo Strauss emphasises these two components, the 'philosophical foundation of the law' in Maimonides and the distinction between exoteric and esoteric interpretation (also very important for his own thought), in *Philosophy and Law*, 101ff.

139. Maimonides, *Guide for the Perplexed*, Introduction, 81; see also the remarks on the two meanings of the word, the one silver and the other gold: 'The same is the case with the figures employed by the prophets. Taken literally, such expressions contain wisdom useful for many purposes, among others, for the amelioration of the condition of society; e.g., the Proverbs (of Solomon), and similar sayings in their literal sense. Their hidden meaning, however, is profound wisdom, conducive to the recognition of real truth' (77). (In the following this work will be cited according to book, chapter and page number.)

The Law revealed by Moses is the undisputed, repeatedly confirmed presupposition of thought and action. Thus, for Maimonides the first task is to liberate the Law from contradictions and absurdities, in particular from ideas concerning the corporeality of God. The 'negative attributes of God' alone 'are the true attributes' (I, 58, p. 204) and all anthropomorphisms must be rejected. Maimonides attempts at all times to reconcile the biblical view of the world with the Aristotelian, but he departs from Aristotle at one point (which is central for the theological-philosophical discussions of the time), namely, in the issue of whether the universe is eternal or created. Since this question cannot be decided by philosophical and scientific reflection, Maimonides argues that one can accept the idea that the universe was created 'on the authority of Prophecy, which can teach things beyond the reach of speculation' (II, 16, p. 346). In case of doubt, revealed truth should be accorded priority where reason runs up against the limits of its finitude (cf. I, 31) and where the contrary view would imply that 'we should necessarily be in opposition to the foundations of our religion, we should disbelieve all miracles and signs, and certainly reject all hopes and fears derived from Scripture' (II, 25, p. 378). Hence, religious belief must be rationally tenable, yet it is neither necessary nor feasible that everything which is believed be rationally demonstrable.

The 613 precepts and prohibitions of the Law have three purposes according to Maimonides: the ethical purpose of promoting good morals, the political purpose of erecting a just social order and the philosophical purpose of achieving true knowledge and overcoming false doctrines (III, 31, p. 563). The first two goals are concerned with the state of the body and its perfection, its protection and security, the latter with the supreme perfection of the soul, the mind, and hence of the faith. This is the true meaning of the Law (III, 27, p. 550). The last-mentioned path is not open to everyone, whereas the ethical-political precepts are universally binding and represent a stage along the path to achieving the philosophical life (III, 28). Maimonides clarifies his doctrine of the good life by means of a parable. The king is in his palace surrounded by a city. The country dwellers do not have access to the city, and in the city some have turned their back to the palace and some face it. A few have advanced as far as the walls of the palace, of whom some have reached the ante-chamber and others have entered the house; and a very few of the latter are granted the privilege of speaking with the king. Maimonides explicates the parable as follows: The people outside the city have no religion; they are like 'irrational beings' (III, 51, p. 656). Those who have turned away and embraced false doctrines are the heretics, 'and under certain circumstances it may become necessary to slay them, and to extirpate their doctrines, in order that others should not be misled' (p. 657).[140] Those who have not yet seen the house but who wish to approach it are 'the multitude that observe the divine commandments, but are ignorant' (p. 657), whereas those who have reached the external walls of the palace are the scholars of the Talmud. Those who have been admitted into the ante-chamber are the ones who have followed the path of true knowledge and have advanced as far as natural science and metaphysics. Beyond these wise men, finally, are the ones in the house of the king who have attained the highest stage of perfection and whose entire thought is devoted to God. The highest worship of God is the privilege of the Prophets to whom God has revealed himself. The reason or intellect which emanates from God onto them constitutes the bond between them and God; they are entirely filled by God (p. 659). This meditative *Vita contemplativa* alone constitutes the perfection of the rejection of the world and devotion to God attainable for a few human beings, which makes insight into the effective properties of God, into divine mercy, justice and virtue possible. Thus, the divine Law is confirmed through an insight situated at a level beyond mere obedience to the Law. The Law points beyond itself to its source (III, 54) from which emanates the call to the enlightened to exercise loving-kindness, judgement and righteousness and thereby 'to imitate the ways of God' here on earth (p. 675). This is the highest level attainable by human beings, the union of the active and the contemplative life in God.

Maimonides' doctrine is ambivalent when it comes to toleration within and between religions. On the one hand, the conception of the agreement between faith and reason creates room for divergent interpretations and turns its back on a tradition-bound understanding of scripture; on the other hand, this freedom is bound up with the primacy of the Law, so that deviations from the Law are condemned emphatically, even to the point of calling for heretics to be put to death. The problem is that it remains unclear how the distinction between reasonable interpretive differences and heresy is to be made. Even more important, however, is the doctrine of the philosophical-religious life which forms the core of *The Guide for the Perplexed*. The rudiments of a justification of toleration can be discerned in this book insofar as the philosophical life and the *imitatio dei* go beyond the positive faith in the Law in a twofold sense, namely as an existential condition beyond

---

140. On capital punishment for idolaters see also III, 29, III, 33, III, 37, III, 40. In the *Mishneh Tora* (13), too, Maimonides defends the death penalty for a voluntary and deliberate transgression of the Law if it is witnessed and a warning had been given. On the death penalty for blasphemy and worshipping idols, see also 77 and 80.

the merely ethical life of obedience to the Law outside the royal palace and as action in accordance with the precepts of mercy, justice and virtue – three precepts with a normative content *common* to the Jewish, Christian and Islamic faiths. However, only in combination with the idea that, not only the observance of the Jewish Law, but different paths of the religious life, can lead to the highest condition would this constitute an argument from *pluralist unity* on which the three monotheistic religions could equally claim to represent paths to God.[141] However, Maimonides' emphasis on the constitutive role of the precepts of the Torah for the ascent to the truth and the attainment of the supreme good speaks against this interpretation; Moses was the only one who advanced into the presence of God in the heart of the palace (III, 51, p. 661). Still, there can be no doubt that a conception of religious unity can be found in Maimonides insofar as he represents the messianic kingdom as one in which the conflict between the different religious outlooks will be replaced by the knowledge of the truth, so that, in the words of Isaiah 11:6, 'the wolf shall dwell with the lamb' (III, 11, p. 483). If the supreme insight into the truth leads to a comprehensive point of view which includes all of the positive religions, then Maimonides can be interpreted as defending an argument of *inclusive unity*. According to this argument the Jewish religion contains the complete truth, yet it incorporates the truth of the two other religions, so that the latter acquire a certain justification, even though without the necessary correction they lead away from the true path (and like Christianity are in danger of becoming idolatry and following false prophets).[142] However, as long as the idea that transcending the Law presupposes the Law implies an exclusive claim for this path, even this interpretation would remain questionable. For, in that case, paths not strictly in conformity with the Law would lead away from the palace rather than towards its outer walls (to remain with the picture evoked by the parable). The path of *unity through refutation* of the false teachings would then be the only remaining route to the production of the *unitas* in faith. Maimonides' texts are not univocal as regards these three different interpretations.

Maimonides' *Guide for the Perplexed* can be read as a response to Abelard's religious conversation even though it was not intended as such. In Abelard, reason proves that the Christian faith is the superior ethic and opposes a traditionalistic understanding of faith, whereas the Jewish belief in the Law is criticised as authoritarian. Maimonides, on the other hand, tries to prove that this faith in the Law is the superior, rationally confirmed path to the true life and to the apprehension of God (as Abelard would say). However, the true faith is not singled out chiefly by its ethical character; Maimonides accords greater prominence to the revealed Law. It makes striving for the supreme good a duty and does not promise the latter as a reward for virtuous conduct.

Like Maimonides, Ibn Rushd – or, to give him his Latinised name, Averroes – the most important Aristotelian among the Islamic philosophers of his time, is also concerned with the reconcilability of faith and reason, and like Maimonides he defends the view that the Law, the Shari'a, not only permits, but even requires, the philosophical search for truth, though of course only for those who are capable of ascending to such elevated questioning. Thus, here, too, we encounter the distinction between a philosophical-esoteric study and an exoteric exegesis of scripture and of the belief in the Law. This leads Averroes, on the one hand, to defend the freedom of philosophy (and the rational examination of scripture) even more emphatically than Maimonides and, on the other, to a rational defence of the religious laws. The former grounds a certain toleration 'towards the inside', that is, within Islamic theological disputes, the latter a certain toleration 'towards the outside', that is, towards other religions. They both run up against their limits, however, when, in the former case, philosophically untrained and unqualified individuals express doubts about the divine truth and when, in the latter, the fundamental principles of religion are called into question.

The primary sources for the relevant reflections of Averroes are to be found less in his famous commentaries on Aristotle and Plato than in his works (both from around 1180) 'On the Harmony of Religion and Philosophy' (or 'The Decisive Treatise': *Kitab fasl al-maqal*) and the *Tahafut al-Tahafut*, 'The Incoherence of the Incoherence' (or 'The Refutation of the Refutation'). Both works, though especially the latter, are direct answers to the challenge posed to the philosophers, the *falasifa*, by the orthodox Islamic theologian al-Gazali, who in his *Tahafut al-falasifa* presented a detailed refutation of the philosophical conceptions of his time, in particular those of Avicenna, intended to convict them of heresy in fundamental questions such as the creation of the universe and eternal life. Hence, Averroes' defence is concerned with toleration towards philosophical doubt, indeed with its indispensability.

In the 'Decisive Treatise' he undertakes to justify the philosophical questioning schooled in Aristotelian thought as the 'study of existing things and reflection on them as indications of the Artisan'.[143] Since this form of speculation, as he seeks to demonstrate through an interpretation of corresponding passages from the Qur'an, is required by the divine Law, and since it must proceed in accordance with the best rules of the art of inference and demonstration, regardless of who developed these instruments of thought, it is an error of the 'gross literalists' (I) to see a danger for the faith in the philosophical search for truth, 'for truth does not oppose truth' (II). The philosophy which seeks demonstrative knowledge based on proven principles is, however, reserved for a select few who are permitted to explore the areas in which the religious Law is in need of interpretation. All others must confine themselves to the 'apparent meaning' (II) which must be understood literally, and to confuse them in this regard is to summon them to unbelief (II) and must be punished. There is no room for interpretation with regard to basic truths of religion ('acknowledgement of God, Blessed and Exalted, of the prophetic missions, and of happiness and misery in the next life'; II); here error is inexcusable. In the 'internal' domain where interpretation is called for, however, strict unanimity among the learned should not be expected but instead a kind of reasonable difference of opinion, and hence 'no one should be definitely called an unbeliever for violating unanimity on a point of interpretation in matters like these' (II). He who errs here errs in good faith and conscience and hence this cannot constitute a sin. However, Averroes applies this argument, which is also found in Abelard, exclusively to the philosophers who reflect, for instance, on the question of whether the world is eternal or created:

> It seems that those who disagree on the interpretation of these difficult questions earn merit if they are in the right and will be excused [by God] if they are in error. For assent to a thing as a result of an indication [of it] arising in the soul is something compulsory, not voluntary: i.e. it is not for us [to choose] not to assent or to assent, as it is to stand up or not to stand up. And since free choice is a condition of obligation, a man who assents to an error as a result of a consideration that has occurred to him is excused, if he is a scholar. (II)

With this kind of excusable error Averroes contrasts that of the unlearned who doubt things which they are not authorised to doubt. The domain of

---

143. Averroes, *On the Harmony of Religion and Philosophy*, vol. I. In what follows this work will be cited according to chapter number.

permissible differences of interpretation is restricted in a twofold sense: by that which cannot be doubted and by the barrier to access for non-scholars. In his counter-attack Averroes goes so far as to pin the blame for misleading those who are unqualified to engage in demonstration on theologians like al-Gazali and not on the philosophers, since in his view it is the theologians who introduce interpretive differences into their texts which are not destined for the mass of the believers (111). Thus, they are the true unbelievers who mislead the people into unbelief (111).

Whereas Averroes creates space for different interpretations of central metaphysical questions, and in this sense for the autonomy of reason not directed by authority – albeit in a restricted, esoteric sense – with such arguments, the final twenty sections of the *Tahafut al-Tahafut* contain an even more radical relativisation of the purely religiously grounded truth. Against al-Gazali's assertion that the philosophers defend heretical positions on the question of the resurrection, Averroes objects that they accept the doctrine of the resurrection of the body (in a certain form) in common with the other religions, not just Islam. The reason Averroes offers for this is important. For, he argues, this doctrine cannot be proven by reason, even though it does not seem to be irrational either. Rather, it is enjoined for rational and ethical reasons, for without such a belief in the highest good a flourishing social order of virtuous human beings who abide by the laws would be impossible. In other words, religion is ethically and politically *useful* and the doctrine in question should be affirmed for this reason.[144] Moreover, the religions of Islam, Christianity and Judaism are equivalent in this respect according to Averroes. Thus, each religion is obligatory for the masses in the form in which it was taught to them, whatever its specific content, provided that it (a) leads to an ethical-political social order and (b) provides room and a breeding ground for philosophical speculation. The learned man is the one who leaves the particularity of his religion behind him without denying it and seeks the best religion 'of his period',[145] which for Averroes means the Islamic faith. Hence, the learned men, as Maimonides also asserts, are the successors of the Prophets; they recognise the truth of the Law revealed to

144. Averroes, *Tahafut al-Tahafut*, 359: 'But the philosophers in particular, as is only natural, regard this doctrine as most important and believe in it most, and the reason is that it is conducive to an order amongst men on which man's being, as man, depends and through which he can attain the greatest happiness proper for him, for it is a necessity for the existence of the moral and speculative virtues and of the practical sciences in men . . . [T]he practical virtues can only become strong through the knowledge and adoration of God by the services prescribed by the laws of the different religions.'
145. *Ibid.* 360.

them without being able to regard it as purely rationally grounded. Heresy in the guise of doubt in a 'higher order', by contrast, is disruptive of religion and virtue and cannot be tolerated. If those who proclaim such doctrines represent a genuine danger, the theologians as well as the philosophers must call for their execution, but otherwise merely for their refutation.[146]

Although the toleration of Averroes also has definite limits, his arguments nevertheless go beyond Abelard and Maimonides when he acknowledges more clearly than they do the validity of the other religions as compatible with both the ethical and the philosophical life, and thereby adopts a differentiated stance on the truth content of religion: as an ethical content shared by each of the three religions he is examining, as a rational content which can be developed out of the different religions and as a transcendent content which nevertheless has a 'temporal core', as we might say. This restores speculation to its rightful place, whereas an equivalence among religions pertains from an ethical perspective. Hence, ideas can be found in Averroes that can point to various of the above-mentioned paths to religious unity, and thereby justify toleration: a notion of reductive unity in the reference to ethical and speculative commonalities and a notion of competitive unity in the reference to the most advanced religion at a certain time. It is ideas such as these – in particular that of an autonomous philosophical truth alongside the religious truth that poses a challenge to every religious orthodoxy – which underlay the enduring influence of Averroes under the guise of 'Averroism' into modern times, especially during the Renaissance.[147] Averroes was often misinterpreted within this reception as a radical critic of religion. Thus, the mistaken belief persisted that he was the author of the treatise on the 'three imposters' Moses, Jesus and Muhammad, probably a product of the Islamic cultural sphere during the tenth century which found its way by different paths (via the court of the Hohenstaufen emperor Frederick II in Sicily) into Boccaccio's *Decameron* and continued to circulate into the eighteenth century.[148] It is, as it were, the negative variant of the 'parable of the rings'.

These brief remarks cannot claim, any more than the foregoing, to trace in detail the complex philosophical and theological theories of the late Middle Ages which contributed to the discourse of toleration within and between the various religions. However, they should suffice to highlight certain

---

146. *Ibid.* 362.
147. On this, see Leaman, *Averroes and his Philosophy*, 163–78, and Renan's classic study, *Averroès et l'Averroïsme*.
148. See Minois, *Histoire de l'athéisme*, 73–4; see also Niewöhner, *Veritas sive varietas*, and Lowell and Anderson (eds.), *The Treatise of the Three Impostors and the Problem of Enlightenment*.

structural features of important arguments for toleration. The predominance of Christian reflections is to some extent unavoidable here, however, for the modern discourse is clearly shaped by Christianity, as regards the reasons both for tolerance and for intolerance. Yet it would be a mistake to fail to appreciate the discussions of toleration in the other religions (and only Judaism and Islam could be briefly mentioned here) and their influence on later thinkers, both Christian and secular. As is shown by the example of Averroes in particular, innovative and courageous ideas are to be found here which in certain respects go beyond the Christian dissident Abelard, for instance. In all of these efforts a central feature must be kept in mind, namely the search for a form of faith, of discursive reason and of universal morality situated at a higher level than the dispute. The modern justifications of toleration will in different ways take this as their starting point.

§7 The defender of peace

1. The texts discussed thus far document changes in the self-understanding of religion which began to take shape in particular from the twelfth century onwards and (as outlined in §5.3) placed in question the incorporation of individuals into an all-embracing, religiously defined form of society typical for the Middle Ages and revealed possible new forms of horizontal, intersubjective toleration. Something similar holds for the discourse of toleration at the level of the theory of the state. Its development following the Investiture Controversy is marked by an increasing autonomy of secular vis-à-vis church power, in particular vis-à-vis the claim to universal political authority of the papacy.[149] A central work in this regard, which paved the way for a secular justification of the state, is Marsilius of Padua's *Defensor pacis* (1324).

Marsilius' thought was shaped by the Averroist reception of Aristotle of his time. This was especially prevalent at the University of Paris where Marsilius was rector for a short time before seeking protection against religious persecution from the Holy Roman Emperor Louis IV, whom he supported in the latter's conflict with the popes in Avignon. In sharp opposition to the subordination of the *regnum* to the *sacerdotium*, Marsilius defends a secular, rational justification of the role of the state. The latter's task is the 'life and the good life' (*vivere et bene vivere*)[150] of the citizens who have entered the

---

149. On this, see Miethke, 'Der Weltanspruch des Papstes im späteren Mittelalter'.
150. Marsilius of Padua, *Defensor pacis*, Part I, ch. 3, §5 (the following citations in the text refer to this work).

political community for this sole purpose. The state as the *perfecta communitas* is a self-sufficient institution which in the first instance secures the basic conditions for a good life, most importantly civil order and peace. This peace, according to Marsilius, is jeopardised by one main cause which must be counteracted, namely the claim to temporal political power of the papacy or the Church which is without political or theological foundation. Marsilius acknowledges the role of the Catholic Church in the corporative state of his time as the institution that enunciates the truth regarding the eternal and blessed life; nevertheless, it is clearly subordinate to the political authority not only in all secular matters but also in central ecclesiastical matters. The state is not 'neutral' with regard to religion, for Marsilius leaves no doubt that the political community has a religious foundation – albeit with the pragmatic justification, reminiscent of Averroes, that religion promotes the obedience to the law necessary for the stability of the state (I, 5, 10–11).

Good government is established for the 'common advantage' and can rule only 'according to the will or consent of those subject' (I, 8, 3); the ruler who is appointed by election is bound by the laws enacted by the lawmaker, which is composed of the 'whole body of citizens' (I, 12, 3) and enacts the laws by majority decision ('[taking] into consideration the quantity and the quality of the persons'). Here Marsilius defends what was for his time a very broad interpretation of the legal principle *Quod omnes similiter tangit, ab omnibus comprobetur* ('what concerns all must be approved by all'), whose upshot was an early, still corporatively structured form of popular sovereignty and democratic self-legislation. It is the citizens themselves who define the public good 'because no one knowingly harms himself' (I, 12, 5) and no law is as well observed as that which free citizens have imposed upon themselves (I, 12, 6); the citizen body can not only criticise the government but can also depose it (I, 15, 2).

This logic of the autonomous state implies that the latter has far-reaching powers regarding religion. It appoints the priests who profess God's teaching and administer the sacraments, and all priests, including the pope, are subjected to its jurisdiction. The Church and the pope do not have any temporal power whatsoever, not even over priests; priests are merely doctors who can diagnose aberrations and illnesses of the soul but are not permitted to cure them by coercive means (II, 9, 3). Christ alone is the supreme judge in matters of the divine Law, and since his kingdom is 'not of this world', as Marsilius explains in detail in the second part of the *Defensor pacis*, this cannot be a temporal jurisdiction. Questions of excommunication can be decided only by a general council, which is convened in turn by the 'faithful human legislator' (II, 18, 8), and an excommunication ruling requires the consent of the legislator. This is because, in the kind of Christian society which Marsilius has in mind, excommunication represents a comprehensive social exclusion (II, 6, 12; III, 16) – not to mention the implications of excommunication in the case of rulers. By means of all of these expedients – and others concerning the internal organisation of the Church – Marsilius seeks to avoid what he regards as the most important cause of the political unrest and weakness of states (anticipating Machiavelli, he often mentions the weakness of the Italian system of states), the 'pestilence of civil regimes' (I, 1, 5): the usurpation of power by the pope which not only is politically pernicious but is also a perversion of the original Christian intention.

A variety of very important arguments against the imposition of religion by force can be found in Marsilius of immediate relevance for the question of toleration. First, the Church does not have any legitimate means of exercising such compulsion, for this would be a form of exercise of temporal power which is not open to it. Its means are confined to the word, and its court is not of this world (II, 1, 4; II, 4; II, 9). Second, religious compulsion is pointless because a coerced faith is not pleasing to God and is not a genuine faith (II, 5, 6; II, 9, 5 and 7). These two arguments still leave room for a certain form of religious compulsion, namely, that which the secular lawmaker exercises against heretics, though not in order to convert them but to suppress them for political reasons. And thus in an important passage Marsilius argues: 'By these considerations, however, we do not wish to say that it is inappropriate that heretics or those who are otherwise infidel be coerced, but that the authority for this, if it be lawful to do so, belongs only to the human legislator' (II, 5, 7). It is difficult to judge how strong a qualification is expressed by the reference to lawfulness and permissibility – *si liceat hoc fieri* – here. However, it can be inferred from the rest of the argument that the reasons justifying the punishment of heretics or infidels are not to be taken from divine law (which falls within Christ's jurisdiction; II, 10, 2), but can only be political in nature, such as the incitement to revolt – which could apply to a religious minority as much as to a pope condemned by the secular courts. This amounts to a third – albeit, in Marsilius' formulation, ambivalent – argument against the suppression of religion: in a state which is beholden to human laws enacted by the citizens themselves, the exercise of legal coercion must be *justified in universal political terms*, that is, in terms of reasons which demonstrate a political offence of relevance for the well-being of the citizens. This argument is ambivalent in presenting the possibility of suppressing a religious minority with flimsy political arguments; nevertheless, it represents an important, forward-looking argument insofar as it emphasises that political coercion is in need of general justification and furthermore uncouples this justification in the first instance from the religious law. Precisely this ambivalence can be found in Marsilius:

> Now if human law were to prohibit heretics or other infidels from dwelling in the region, and yet such a person were found there, he must be corrected in this world as a transgressor of human law, and the penalty fixed by that law for such transgression must be inflicted on him by the judge who is the guardian of human law by the authority of the legislator . . . But if human law did not prohibit the heretic or other infidel from dwelling among the faithful in the same province, as heretics and Jews are now permitted to do by human laws even in these times of Christian peoples, rulers, and pontiffs, then I say that no one is allowed to judge or coerce a heretic or other infidel by any penalty in property or in person for the status of the present life. And the general reason for this is as follows: no one is punished in this world for sinning against theoretic or practical disciplines precisely as such, however much he may sin against them, but only for sinning against a command of human law.
>
> (II, 10, 3)

Hence, for a secular condemnation it is not sufficient to identify some-one as a heretic (which is a matter for the priests); it has to be shown to what extent a legal offence exists, for 'there are many mortal sins even against divine law, such as fornication, which the human legislator knowingly permits . . . and should not prohibit by coercive force' (II, 10, 7). Notwith-standing the ambivalence of Marsilius' argument from a formal point of view, there is much to be said for the fact that the strict separation between human and divine law places limits on the scope for legitimate reasons for suppressing religion, and thus that there is a major difference between it and the medieval practice of identifying secular and spiritual offences. Taken together, therefore, all three arguments – (a) that the exercise of spiritual power should be restricted, (b) that religious belief is a voluntary matter and (c) that political force is in need of justification – amount to an argument for toleration and freedom of religion which was very far-reaching for its time; on the other hand, however, they cannot disguise the fact that the state on Marsilius' conception is one in which Catholic priests are assigned by the lawmaker to preach the true doctrine, and thereby to stabilise the political community. The distance to a 'secular' state is still great, though decisive rudiments of it can be found in this work. As still needs to be shown, there is a direct line leading from here to the later modern attempts to establish the state as a neutral peacemaker in religious conflicts, and thus to promote human well-being.

2. I should not bring the chapter on antiquity and the Middle Ages to a close without offering a brief résumé of its results. The first conclusion should be to contradict the widespread notion that toleration is a child of modernity, whereas antiquity and the Middle Ages represent nothing more than a prehistory of minor importance.[151] The idea of toleration was reinterpreted and radicalised during the modern period, especially following the Reformation, and the spectrum of toleration justifications was greatly extended; nevertheless, a large proportion of the new justifications proposed took their inspiration from existing arguments, arguments which, as we have seen, were always developed *in conflict*, that is, in the context of particular social and philosophical controversies, to mention only the most important:

- the separation between temporal and spiritual power
- the call for fair treatment without arbitrary distinctions
- the demand for a specifically 'human', political justification for the exercise of secular-political force
- the idea of the non-coercible conscience and of faith founded on free conviction
- the notion that the real sinner cannot be distinguished by the human eye (as in the parable of the weeds)
- considerations relating to natural law
- pragmatic and strategic considerations
- religious motives of love and compassion
- the idea of a deeper religious unity

In addition, the analysis of these arguments should have made clear that, even where human beings were not understood as autonomous moral beings, they were nevertheless participants in conflicts in which those affected were very much aware that they had *not* been given any sufficient reasons for the exercise of power or domination. For this is what is ultimately at stake at the core of conflicts over toleration, namely the *reasons* which the parties to the conflict could provide for their claims to respect and freedom or, conversely,

151. See also Nederman, *Worlds of Difference*, who underscores the importance of medieval arguments for toleration. However, greater attention must be paid to the limits of their transferability and their competitive position vis-à-vis modern justifications than Nederman does.

to political power. The demand for justifying reasons is in the first instance a phenomenon of political practice and any normative theory must take this into account.

Thus, the analysis of the inversion of the Christian arguments for toleration into arguments for intolerance demonstrates not only the danger of such a dialectic of religious toleration justifications, but also that those in power were always concerned to legitimise their domination. Of all the arguments which were presented to this end, however, we encountered one which is structurally the most complex and will often crop up, namely the perfectionist argument which justifies the suppression of heresy, not just by appeal to internal peace, and the duties towards God and towards others who could be infected, but by appeal to the well-being of the suppressed *themselves* – even to the extreme that they must die for the sake of the salvation of their souls. This represents a major challenge for all justifications of toleration, but especially for the attempts to ground toleration itself in a theory of the 'good life'.

Finally, it has become apparent that the opposition 'power versus toleration' is too simplistic, for all too often the granting of toleration was (and is) itself a practice of power and domination. As long as it was a matter of political or ecclesiastical toleration, hence of vertical, institutional toleration, the permission conception was the dominant form, and in this form spaces of toleration are often likewise spaces of disciplining and stigmatisation.

Furthermore, the complexity of the question of religious toleration has become apparent. On the one hand, it is clear how closely an exclusive claim to religious truth is associated with the non-toleration of errors and 'blasphemers'; on the other hand, however, it is also clear what a high price those demand who can conceive of toleration only in such a way that it involves abandoning the religious claim to truth. One misunderstands the history – and perhaps also the concept – of toleration if one sees it as a learning process leading up to this sceptical goal. For the difficulty of toleration, which so many authors have wrestled with, is precisely to justify toleration *without* calling for the abandonment of ethical and religious claims to truth. The history of toleration is also the history of these attempts.

Ultimately, these efforts begin at different levels. At the theological-philosophical level, it was and is a matter of conceptualising the above-mentioned paths towards unity and of seeking toleration on a religious basis; at the moral level, of justifying respect for human autonomy itself in an autonomous manner; at the ethical level, of developing a doctrine of the good which excludes intolerance; at the epistemological level, of clarifying the question of the necessary relativisation of the truth; and at the level of the theory of the state, of securing peace through toleration. Although many modern authors combine these levels in their justifications of toleration, it is helpful to keep these differences in mind if we want to understand the reasons for their success or failure.

3

Reconciliation, schism, peace: humanism and the Reformation

§8 Human dignity and religious harmony: humanist justifications of toleration

1. The essential hallmark of the 'new era', which, with humanism and ultimately the Reformation, fundamentally transformed the cultural conditions of the discourse over toleration, is the problematisation and gradual dissolution of the two main components of the medieval spiritual-political order, namely, its subsumption of the human being into religious-ecclesiastical structures of thought and action and its subordination of secular to spiritual power (see above §5.3). This order had undergone a series of conflicts and trends towards opening since the Investiture Controversy and the social transformations of the twelfth century. However, it was only with the cultural upheavals which began with the Italian Renaissance and then spread progressively to other regions of Europe that a new consciousness of subjectivity and of politics developed which lent the question of toleration a new urgency and called for new answers. In the words of Jacob Burckhardt, with the waning of the Middle Ages in the Italian city-states 'an *objective* treatment and consideration of the state and of all things of this world became possible. The *subjective* side at the same time asserted itself with corresponding emphasis; man became a spiritual *individual*, and recognised himself as such.'[1]

This comprehensive transformation in human life and thought presents too many aspects to be dealt with exhaustively in the present context. What is striking, however, is the emergence of a new understanding of individuality, even though it developed in two very different directions: in humanism, taking its cue from the idea of self-perfection through one's own efforts as both a task and an opportunity (drawing on ancient ideals of virtue and

---

1. Burckhardt, *The Civilization of the Renaissance in Italy*, 70 (emphasis in the original).

cultivation), and later in Protestantism, by contrast, in the individualisation of faith and the radical idea of individual responsibility before God. The latter idea took critical aim at the humanistic ideal of the self-creating, free human being who, in Luther's view, denies his own finitude and sinfulness. Notwithstanding these differences, both movements led to an advance in individualisation in the religious domain, the former through a new consciousness of human freedom and dignity, the latter through the emphasis on religious immediacy and inwardness. Correspondingly, the fifteenth and sixteenth centuries are marked by a multiplication of forms of religious life and by a heightening of religious conflicts over the contents and institutions of the true faith. The latter led, after the split of the Reformation, to long and bloody wars of religion which profoundly shaped modern history. In this way, the issue of toleration became one of the central questions, if not *the* central question, of this epoch.

A new consciousness of historical and political plasticity gradually gained the upper hand. History and political institutions came to be regarded as the work of human beings, social life as in principle predictable and plannable and as a challenge for technical thought. A new economic order and dynamic emerged and, with the collapse of the Holy Roman Empire, nation-states (in England, France, Spain) or smaller political units (in Germany and Italy) took shape and gave rise to new political challenges. Although, according to 'civic humanism', meeting these challenges called for virtuous human beings who were capable of putting themselves at the service of *fortuna*, it was but a short step from this autonomous notion of the political to that of Machiavelli's *Il principe*. The latter view accorded priority to the imperative to preserve the state and regarded it as the supreme virtue of the prince to use all the necessary means to this end, even if this clashed with classical conceptions of virtue.[2] The conception of the autonomy of the political which this prefigures – for which the concept of 'reason of state'[3] coined in the sixteenth century is characteristic – henceforth attaches merely instrumental significance to religion. This is an extreme example of the priority of *self-assertion* which for Blumenberg is the hallmark of modernity – where by 'self-assertion' is meant not only physical and political self-preservation but a new understanding of self and the world which goes hand-in-hand with a general 'disappearance of order'. Stripped of their religious-metaphysical confidence in a comprehensive order created for humans, including time, the

2. See Skinner, *The Foundations of Modern Political Thought*, vol. 1, ch. 5; Münkler, *Machiavelli*, pt 3.
3. See Meinecke, *Machiavellism*; Münkler, *Im Namen des Staates*.

world, society and one's own life, independent human thought and action were confronted with new tasks of self-justification through one's rational faculty in many areas, extending from economics through politics to science.[4]

Two aspects of the 'disappearance of order' alluded to were especially important for the discourse over toleration and raise the following questions. First, to what extent did the increasing pluralisation and individualisation of religion lead to new justifications of toleration at a 'horizontal' level? And, second, how was the relation between religion and politics understood from the 'vertical' perspective of the theory of the state once the link between *regnum* and *sacerdotium* was definitively broken? In short, what implications do the increasing autonomy of the religious subject and of the sphere of political power have for the justification of toleration?

To take the former issue first, characteristic of humanist thought is the argument of *reductive unity* previously discussed (see §6.2), that is, the attempt to single out a universal religion which includes all human beings and makes possible an agreement on essential articles of faith. It forms a consensus in which the different positive religions intersect and thus banishes their differences into the domain of what is legitimate but inessential, that is, of the *adiaphora*. This irenic tendency, which also marked Nicholas of Cusa's writing on peace (though to a lesser extent), can be found among important representatives of Italian humanism, for instance in Ficino and Pico, but most of all in Erasmus of Rotterdam and, with a specifically political twist, in Thomas More. The essential humanist justification of toleration is not primarily that toleration is required for the sake of religious unity, but that toleration is enjoined as an expression of an already *existing* unity among human beings through God's will.

In the Italian culture of the Renaissance, the trend towards the increasing autonomy of religious life from the Church and dogma was far developed for the time. Not only was the parable of the rings, as found in Boccaccio,[5] an expression of a relation to the other religions marked by peaceful coexistence; in addition, the history of the 'three imposters' Moses, Christ and Muhammad, whose author is unknown, made the rounds in circles critical

---

4. See in particular Blumenberg, *Säkularisierung und Selbstbehauptung*, 158–66; see also Horkheimer, 'The End of Reason', which highlights the concept of 'self-preservation' in a variety of ways; Henrich, 'Die Grundstruktur der modernen Philosophie' and 'Selbsterhaltung und Geschichtlichkeit'; Spaemann, 'Bürgerliche Ethik und nichtteleologische Ontologie'; Blumenberg, 'Selbsterhaltung und Beharrung'.

5. Boccaccio, *The Decameron*, First Day, third story. However, this story has its origins as far back as the thirteenth century.

of religion[6] (parallel to the ubiquitous criticism of the conduct of ecclesiastical dignitaries). Although such an extensive critique of religion is not to be found among the humanists, the idea of a universal human religion – a 'religious-universalist theism', as Dilthey puts it – is.[7] Such an idea is to be found in a Neoplatonist version in Marsilio Ficino, the head of the 'Platonic Academy of Florence', in particular in his most important works *Theologia platonica* and *De Christiana religione* (both 1474). By means of a theological interpretation of the idea of the 'One and First', the doctrine of the Ideas and the idea of the immortality of the soul, Ficino aspires to a 'philosophical religion' which proves the identity of genuine philosophy and true religion. Here religion is understood as an authentically human, natural striving of the soul towards God; in spite of all formal differences, at its core is the subjective relationship to God and it represents the highest form of love: 'And anyone who surrenders himself to God with love in this life will recover himself in God in the next life. Such a man will certainly return to his own Idea, the idea by which he was created.'[8] Based on this universal human, quasi-'natural' religion, Ficino argues for the legitimacy of religious differences beyond this core content:

> Nothing displeases God so much as being scorned; nothing is more
> acceptable to him than adoration . . . That is why divine Providence
> never allowed any regions of the world at any time to be totally
> deprived of religion, although there has been in various places and at
> various times some diversity in the rites of worship. It is even possible
> that such a variety through God's own disposition gives birth to a
> certain beauty in the universe, worthy of admiration. The Most High is
> more concerned with being worshipped in truth, than with being
> worshipped through this or that particular gesture . . . He is rather
> adored anyhow, even clumsily but humanly, than not adored in any
> way because of pride.[9]

This quotation reveals that for Ficino (more so than for Nicholas of Cusa) the plurality of religious forms is not just an evil to be accepted, but is willed by God and has a value of its own. Nevertheless, this does not mean, as in the pluralistic understanding of religion, that all of these forms of worship are of

6. See Burckhardt, *The Civilization of the Renaissance in Italy*, 222ff.; Lowell and Anderson (eds.), *The Treatise of the Three Impostors and the Problem of Enlightenment*.
7. Dilthey, 'Auffassung und Analyse des Menschen im 15. und 16. Jahrhundert', 45.
8. Ficino, *Commentary on Plato's Symposium on Love*, 145.
9. Ficino, *De Christiana religionis*, ch. 4 (quoted from Lecler, *Toleration and Reformation*, vol. 1, 111). See in this sense also *Platonic Theology*, 14, 9 and 10.

equal worth, for some of them are 'clumsy'. Thus, they first become objects of toleration by those who are certain of the superiority of their own, namely the Christian, faith. Ficino, who was ordained to the priesthood in 1473, was convinced that the kernel of the true religion was a Christian one; and he regarded his own work as an instrument of Providence which demonstrated this through philosophical reflection.[10]

It was Giovanni Pico della Mirandola, an outstanding younger member of the Academy in Florence and a pupil of Ficino, who finally set about translating the humanist dream of an all-inclusive synthesis, founded upon human dignity and transcending all of the philosophical and religious differences of his time, into action. Taking his inspiration from Christian Neoplatonism, though in a version more receptive to the philosophy of Aristotle, scholasticism[11] and Avicenna and Averroes, in 1485–86 he composed 900 theses, ranging from ethics through the philosophy of nature to theology, and invited scholars from all parts of Europe to Rome to conduct a debate on them. He wanted to show that all philosophical and theological teachings are essentially in agreement on these theses: Christian doctrine and the Christian theologians and philosophers from the Church Fathers to Ockham, Greek philosophy before and after Plato and Aristotle and their ideas themselves, the teaching of the Qur'an and the medieval Arab philosophers, the teachings of the Jewish religion including the Cabala, and, finally, ancient mythology, hermeticism and the teachings of Zarathustra. However, the discussion to which Pico aspired never took place; Pope Innocent VIII took issue with thirteen of his theses (e.g. regarding magic as perfected natural philosophy), and, when Pico responded by defending them, the pope ended by condemning all 900 theses as heretical and excommunicated Pico, who was forced to flee.

The most important document of Pico's attempted philosophical-religious synthesis is the (later so-called) *Oratio de hominis dignitate* (1486), which was intended to serve as the opening address to the discussion of his theses. In the first part Pico outlines his understanding of human dignity, in the second his universal programme of reconciliation (and its sources). According to Pico, we misunderstand the place of human beings in the cosmos when we regard them as mediators between God and nature, and assign them a fixed place in the eternal order. Human beings owe their existence instead to God's wish to find an observer and admirer of his creation, so that they cannot have a fixed place within this creation. Instead, God spoke:

10. See Kristeller, *The Philosophy of Marsilio Ficino*, 320.
11. On his high regard for scholasticism, see his *Letter to Ermolao Barbaro* (3 June 1485).

We have given to thee, Adam, no fixed seat, no form of thy very own, no gift particularly thine, that thou mayest feel as thine own, have as thine own, possess as thine own the seat, the form, the gifts which thou thyself shalt desire. A limited nature in other creatures is confined within the laws written down by Us. In conformity with thy free judgement, in whose hands I have placed thee, thou art confined by no bounds; and thou wilt fix limits of nature for thyself. I have placed thee at the centre of the world, that from there thou mayest more conveniently look around and see whatsoever is in the world. Neither heavenly nor earthly, neither mortal nor immortal have We made thee. Thou, like a judge appointed for being honourable, art the molder and maker of thyself; thou mayest sculpt thyself into whatever shape thou dost prefer. Thou canst grow downward into the lower natures which are brutes. Thou canst again grow upward from thy soul's reason into the higher natures which are divine.[12]

The human being is indeterminate, a 'chameleon', who can become a plant or an animal as much as a 'heavenly animal' (5), and specifically by his own efforts; he is a sculptor of himself. In addition to this self-perfection, however, Pico leaves no doubt that human beings have a vocation on which all philosophies and religions agree. Their 'holy ambition' must consist in aspiring 'to the highest things' and in the process spurning 'all earthly things' and striving towards God (7), more precisely striving through love of God to become one with him ('we shall not now be ourselves, but He himself who made us'; 14). The soul should become a 'house of God' (12) by means of philosophy, which leads through morals, dialectics and natural philosophy to theology: 'that after she has, through morals and dialectics, cast off her meanness and has adorned herself with manifold philosophy as with a princely garment, and has crowned with garlands of theology the summits of the gates, the King of Glory may descend, and, coming with the Father, may make his residence in her' (12). Then human beings are in a position to fulfil the vocation of their indeterminacy (*die Bestimmung seiner Unbestimmtheit*), namely to be the 'lovers' (14) of creation.

Pico's *Oratio* is not only typical of the humanist understanding of the dignity of the human being as the 'middle of creation', which has the power of shaping reality and of self-creation;[13] it is also characteristic of *Christian* humanism which connects this freedom and (in Nietzsche's term)

---

12. Pico della Mirandola, *On the Dignity of Man*, 4–5. The following citations in the text refer to this edition.

13. On this, see Gerhardt, *Selbstbestimmung*, 131–5.

'unfinishedness' back to a supreme striving of the soul towards God. The 'deification of man' has not yet progressed so far that he can aspire to be the ruler over a universe purged of any trace of the divine will; he is still oriented to achieving the highest perfection through 'most holy theology' (11).

Pico's justification of toleration is correspondingly ambivalent. On the one hand, he follows the path of reductive unity – combined with the path of unity through amalgamation. He claims that the different teachings he presents, however pagan they may have appeared to the Christianity of his time, all make an *independent* contribution to the truth of the inclusive synthesis of all doctrines; it follows that all of the *particular* teachings that contribute to the synthesis must be tolerated for the sake of the truth of the *whole*. On the other hand, however, he leaves no doubt that the supreme form of truth is a Christian-Neoplatonist theology on the basis of which the contribution of the other teachings must be assessed. This is shown by the revealing passage in which he deals with Judaism. Although it is one of Pico's great merits in the context of his time that he presents Judaic writings, in particular the Cabala, as an autonomous source of divine wisdom, he nevertheless regards his view as necessary 'for defending religion against the rude slanders of the Hebrews' (29); for on a closer reading he 'saw in them (God is my witness) a religion not so much Mosaic as Christian' (32). In support he cites the doctrine of the Trinity, the becoming flesh of the Word, original sin, etc. Thus, as regards doubt about Christianity on the part of Judaism, 'there is no corner left in which they may hide' (32).[14] This not only reveals the limits which a defence of the truth of Judaism in a Christian-dominated society ran up against at this time if it was not to be summarily condemned as heresy; it also reveals an immanent problem of a Christian-humanist reduction argument: regardless of the esteem in which the contribution of 'others' to the reconciliatory truth

14. A similar ambivalence of humanist toleration towards the Jews can also be found in the German humanist and pioneering Hebraist Johannes Reuchlin who was deeply influenced by Pico. In 1510, Reuchlin wrote a recommendation opposing the position of the converted Jew Pfefferkorn who had demanded that all Jewish writings directed against the Christian faith be burnt. This led to a major controversy between the two men and other scholastic and humanist thinkers. Reuchlin took the position that only the obvious 'diatribes' should be burnt, but not other writings such as the Talmud, for the following reasons: (a) although there is much bad and untrue in it, it is advantageous to know it in order to be able to form a judgement of one's own about it and to refute it clearly; (b) there is also much that is good in it, even though not in pure form; nevertheless, the wise man can make gold out of 'dross'; (c) one should not risk pulling out the wheat with the weeds; (d) prohibition of the writings would only lead to a hardening of positions; toleration, by contrast, offers the prospect of convincing the Jews through the word of the truth: 'That one should not burn the books of the Jews and that one should convert them gently and amicably to our faith, with God's help, through rational disputation.' Reuchlin, *Augenspiegel*, vol. xx.

is held, they are nevertheless inferior when it comes to the supreme truth. This can mean two things for toleration: either toleration of these doctrines as contributions to the truth, as in Pico, or, for the critics of this position, their non-toleration on account of their obstinate insistence on 'half-truths', and hence also un-truths. Which of these proves to be decisive cannot be determined apart from additional assumptions; in any case, there is no question in these humanist views of a stronger justification of toleration which accords the exercise of the other faith an independent right.

2. The justification of toleration which is most typical of Christian humanism as a whole is to be found in the work of Erasmus of Rotterdam, the most highly regarded scholar of his time – Dilthey calls him the 'Voltaire of the sixteenth century'[15] – although it is scattered throughout his writings. Like all comprehensive justifications of toleration it exhibits the dual thrust of, first, toleration among Christians who argue over the true form of Christianity and, second, toleration between Christians and (the different categories of) non-Christians; nevertheless, both point back to the shared, central idea of a unity in Christ. Thus, he writes in *Enchiridion* (1503), which is intended to equip the 'Christian soldier' with the weapon of the word and the truth concerning the Christian life:

> [For] unto what purpose pertain words of dissension where so great unity is, it savoureth not of christian faith that commonly a courtier to a town dweller, one of the country to an inhabiter of the city, a man of high degree to another of low degree, an officer, to him that is officeless, the rich to the poor, a man of honour, to a vile person, the mighty to the weak, the Italian to the German, the Frenchman to the Englishman, the English to the Scot, the grammarian to the divine, the logician to the grammarian, the physician to the man of law, the learned to the unlearned, the eloquent to him that is not eloquent and lacketh utterance, the single to the married, the young to the old, the clerk to the layman, the priest to the monk, the Carmelites to the Jocobites, and that (lest I reherse all diversities) in a very trifle unlike to unlike, is somewhat partial and unkind. Where is charity that loveth even his enemy, when the surname changed, when the colour of the vesture a little altered, when the girdle and the shoe and like fantasies of men make me hated unto thee? Why rather leave we not these childish trifles, and accustom to have before our eyes that which pertaineth to the very thing? . . . [F]or in one spirit we be all baptised to make one body, whether we be Jews or gentiles, whether we be bound

15. Dilthey, 'Auffassung und Analyse des Menschen im 15. und 16. Jahrhundert', 42.

or free, and all we have drunk of one spirit, for the body (saith Paul) is not one member but many.[16]

In this quotation we encounter the most important elements of Erasmus's thinking on toleration:

(a) The notion that all Christians share a central religious doctrine, a *Christiana philosophia*, whereas over the course of time they have quarrelled over inessential matters which are now taken to be so important that the suspicion of heresy has become ubiquitous. By contrast, in order to overcome the religious conflicts it is necessary to go back to the sources of the Gospels and to the original teaching of Christ, which are essentially concerned with the *ethical* conduct of life.[17]

(b) The concomitant of this reduction to the essentials is a very broad conception of the inessential for its time – the 'childish trifles' in the above quotation, the *adiaphora*. Among them Erasmus counts not only the 'ceremonies' or rules of the Sabbath, which only lead to schisms, but also Catholic dogmas such as the understanding of the Trinity which at his time led to heated theological debates:

> On what pretext will we ask pardon for ourselves . . . who formulate so many definitions about matters which could have either been ignored without loss of salvation or left in doubt? Or is he not destined to have fellowship with the Father, Son, and Holy Spirit who cannot disentangle according to the method of philosophy what distinguishes the Father from the Son or the Holy Spirit from both or what the difference is between the generation of the Son from the Father and the procession of the Spirit? You will not be damned if you should not know whether the Spirit proceed from the Father and the Son as a single or a double principle, but you will not escape perdition unless you see to it in the meantime that you have the fruits of the Spirit, which are charity, joy, peace, patience, kindness, goodness, forbearance, gentleness, faith, moderation, self-control, and chastity . . . The sum and substance of our religion is peace and concord. This can hardly remain the case unless we define as few matters as possible and leave each individual's judgement free on many questions. This is because the obscurity of most questions is great and the malady is for the most part intrinsic to our human nature: we do not know how to yield once a question has been made a subject of

16. Erasmus, *The Manual of the Christian Knight*, 208–10 (translation selectively modernised).
17. See especially Erasmus, 'Letter to Paul Volz', 113; *Vorreden zum Neuen Testament*, 59–60; *Theologische Methodenlehre*, 303–43.

contention. And after the debate has warmed up each one thinks that
the side he has rashly undertaken to defend is absolute truth . . . Many
puzzling questions are now referred to an Ecumenical Council. It
would be much more fitting to defer such questions to that time when
we shall see God face to face without the mirror and without the
mystery.[18]

Erasmus emphatically condemns the scholastic debates over such matters
and – especially in his famous work *Praise of Folly* (1511) – with bitter scorn;
in his opinion they disguise either stupidity or lust for power; at any rate
they always lead away from the true teaching of Christ and to unnecessary
strife and schisms.

(c) An important implication of this broad conception of the *adiaphora* is
the narrowing of the definition of heresy. According to Erasmus, the concomitant of the escalation of the theological debates and definitions is an
absurd and dangerous pursuit of heretics: 'Once he counted as a heretic who
diverged from the Gospels, the articles of faith or from precepts of equal
authority to them. Today anyone who diverges in any way from Thomas
Aquinas is called a heretic, indeed anyone who diverges from a fictive argument that some sophist or other in the schools thought up yesterday.'[19]

This position is especially important in the context of the controversies between Luther and the Church.[20] Luther did not look like a heretic
in the light of Erasmus's tracing of the central articles of faith back to an
ethical teaching of Christ. Erasmus initially sympathised with Luther, since
the latter not only criticised the sale of indulgences as he did, but also the
ecclesiastical and papal abuse of power (which Erasmus had denounced in
the most forceful terms in the dialogue *Julius Exclusus*, in which Peter refuses
Pope Julius II entry into heaven) and the self-perpetuating character of theological debates; but, notwithstanding his defence of Luther, he was at pains
not to be identified with him and his views. He consistently exhorted both
sides to the dispute to moderation, to conduct the conflict peacefully and to
tolerate different interpretations of scripture, though, as the confrontations
became more acute, both sides pressed him to make a declaration of loyalty.
Erasmus defended a thoroughgoing reform of the Church but rejected the
Reformation because it was incompatible with his ideal of the *concordia* of
Christians and a unified Church – he also believed that there could be no
salvation outside of the Church (that is, the universal Church which takes its

18. Erasmus, 'Erasmus' Letter to Carondolet', 99–101.
19. See Erasmus, 'Brief an Albrecht von Mainz' (19 October 1519), in *Briefe*, 267.
20. On this, see Bainton, *Erasmus of Christendom*, 151–200.

cue from the old Church)[21] – and it was becoming increasingly radicalised. Finally, he abandoned his neutrality and distanced himself from Luther in his work *De libero arbitrio* (1524). There he uncovered contradictions in Luther's rejection of freedom of the will, while at the same time defending the conception of salvation through God's mercy. Luther responded in his work *De servo arbitrio* (1525) with fierce attacks on Erasmus, which cemented the break between them.[22] The difference between the humanist and reformational conceptions of the human being emerges clearly in this controversy: the free and responsible being who nevertheless depends on God's support, on the one hand, the sinful being with his presumptuous notion of his own freedom, on the other.

(d) Love and peace were central to Erasmus's 'philosophy of Christ'; he reserved his sharpest criticism for the armed conflicts between human beings, whether of the same or of different faiths, especially in his work *Querela pacis* (1516). Charity for Erasmus is the supreme commandment which trumps all others and calls for leniency towards those of other faiths; it tolerates their difference while at the same time trying to lead them to the truth with patience and mildness.

> The greater the disease is, the greater cure will pure charity put thereto. He is an adulterer, he hath committed sacrilege, he is a Turk: let a christian man defy the adulterer, not the man; let him despise the committer of sacrilege, not the man; let him kill the Turk, not the man. Let him find the means that the evil man perish such as he hath made himself to be, but let the man be saved whom God made. Let him will well, wish well, and do well, to all men unfeignedly.[23]

For Erasmus the goal of love is to overcome the differences between human beings which foster discord and to lead them to unity in God's truth. It is the 'human being' as God's creature who is the object of this love, not the human being as he is and has made himself. He is respected not as an 'autonomous individual' but as a member in the fellowship in Christ. Love and mildness alone can move the 'weak' to repent, not war or force.[24]

---

21. Erasmus, *Concio in Psalmum LXXXV*, 507–8.
22. See Erasmus, 'Letter to Luther' (11 April 1526), *The Correspondence of Erasmus: Letters 1658–1801 (1526–1527)*, vol. XII, 135–8.
23. Erasmus, *The Manual of the Christian Knight*, 206–7 (translation selectively modernised).
24. See, in particular, Erasmus, *Theologische Methodenlehre*, especially 257–343. 'As Christ, too, preached to all, he never lured anyone to himself with flattery or promises, nor did he compel anyone by force even though he was all-powerful. He solicited through good deeds, through the example of his life, and the Apostles did the same. Thus, one must examine whether those

(e) A further important element of Erasmus's justification of toleration is freedom of conscience, traditionally understood in terms of the goal of a 'love from a pure heart, a clear conscience and a sincere faith'.[25] Christ preaches the true, not a hypocritical, faith, and thus force is ruled out as a means of conversion. For Erasmus this is bound up with the humanist emphasis on rhetoric, the power of the word, which must be able to convince without resorting to force or violence.[26]

Taken together, these components yield Erasmus's doctrine of toleration. The theology of reduction provides the essential justification for tolerating different interpretations of scripture by Christians, and the doctrines of love and of conviction through the word enjoin toleration towards people of different faiths. At the same time, however, these arguments also mark the *limits* of Erasmus's toleration. For, even though he defines heresy narrowly, he nevertheless leaves room for it. Those who repudiate the basic teachings of Christ and permanently jeopardise the possibility of achieving harmony among Christians must be condemned as heretics. They can be expelled from the Church and, in addition, the secular rulers have the right to use force against heretics who cause schism and rebellion. In extreme cases they can even impose the death penalty.[27] This reveals, in turn, an ambivalence in the justification of toleration which appeals to an underlying unity. Since toleration is the means whereby this unity is generated and reinforced, it runs up against its limits where heresy poses a fundamental threat to this undertaking. Erasmus himself argued for a very generous interpretation of this limit; but it remains in principle a matter of discretion when the threat of schism or rebellion becomes too great.[28]

A limit of Erasmus's argument for toleration also becomes evident in the relations between Christians and members of different religions. The supreme duty is to guide them to the truth by the means enjoined by Christ, through love and meekness; but the theological reduction by no means goes so far as to accord to them a share in the truth. They are called upon to see themselves instead as members of the body of which they have always been a part. It is a Christian duty to bring this about. On the other hand, the

are of the correct opinion who want to make the Turks into Christians with the machines of war alone. Rather should the theologians adopt a similar tone to the Apostles in this matter. Should the purity of their lives shine through, then they truly could become Christians' (343).

25. *Ibid.* 317.

26. On this, see Remer, *Humanism and the Rhetoric of Toleration*, esp. ch. 1.

27. See Erasmus, *Supputatio errorum in censuris Beddae*, 581. See also *Theologische Methodenlehre*, 451.

28. Erasmus regarded this condition as fulfilled by the revolt caused by the Anabaptists, with whom he at first sympathised. See Lecler, *Toleration and the Reformation*, vol. 1, 124.

relationship to the Jews reveals the problematic character of this argumentation. They are subjected to an especially sharp attack: they, to whom the Messiah was promised and who then turned against him, are 'excluded from the covenant' and are 'an exceedingly devious race', 'avaricious', a 'criminal, stubborn and seditious people'.[29] Although they may not be forced to convert, in contrast to the pagans they nevertheless rightfully remain excluded from the communion of the Lord.[30]

Consequently, Erasmus's Christian-humanist justification of toleration contains a 'dogmatic core', notwithstanding his ideal of a largely non-dogmatic religiosity. For although many conflicts are defused through the theological reduction, there nevertheless remains an all the more resilient kernel which leads to new exclusions and the risk of arbitrary demarcations. Yet there is a further problem whose seriousness becomes fully apparent in the conflicts of the Reformation. For, when an acrimonious dispute breaks out over the articles of faith which Erasmus counts among the *adiaphora*, then the only hope held out by the project of reducing the kernel of the faith to a handful of assertions is the recognition that until now the dispute was only over 'inessential matters'. However, such a position cannot fail to meet with the resistance of more comprehensive interpretations of the faith precisely where toleration is most urgently required. Its reduced religion is then no longer capable of mediating between the positions which it hopes to bridge. Therefore, humanist toleration finds itself in a *dilemma*: either it contains too many doctrinal religious contents and gives rise to new demarcations, or it contains too few and remains ineffective and vague concerning controversial religious questions. This was indeed the fate of humanist toleration during the Reformation era; it condemned irenism to becoming a utopia of reconciliation. This does not mean, however, that the humanist attempt to trace faith back to a non-dogmatic, universally shared foundation was not influential. It crops up again in many authors during the Reformation as an objection against intolerance, for example in Castellio, and it leads from post-Reformation ideas of reconciliation to recent attempts to achieve unity in central questions of faith.

3. Characteristic of Erasmus's political philosophy is that he does not regard the sphere of the political as being governed by independent laws. In contrast to his contemporary Machiavelli, and following Plato's *Republic*, the political ruler for Erasmus should be both a Christian and a philosopher and his political legitimation is a function of his virtuous conduct of life, his

---

29. Erasmus, *Theologische Methodenlehre*, 237–53.   30. *Ibid.* 245.

selfless efforts to promote the common good and his concern for the Christian character of the polity. In order to 'correct the morals of the people', Erasmus writes in *Institutio principis Christiani* (1515), the prince must lead a 'blameless life'.[31] Only in this way, and not by governing through fear, can the ruler bind the souls of the citizens to himself; his laws should 'conform to the ideals of justice and honour'.[32] The task of politics is to instruct in the good, to create a virtuous and Christian people; and the most important precondition for this is the correct formation and education of the prince. It is his attachment to the teaching of Christ which first makes a legitimate bond between the people and their ruler possible.[33]

The insight that such a conception of the good ruler of a virtuous society is a utopia is to be found not in Erasmus but in his friend Thomas More. The latter's work *Utopia* (1516) combines in its two parts – the critique of social conditions in England and the description of the society of Utopia by the seaman Hythloday – the caustic social criticism of the Erasmus of *Moriae encomium* (*Praise of Folly*), which was dedicated to More, with the vision of the *Institutio*. To be sure, More sprinkles both the social criticism and the depiction of life in Utopia with subtle irony; he was aware of the unbridgeable gulf between reality and the ideal of 'Nowhere', from which he draws the power to distance himself from both (something which has led to highly contentious readings of the book).[34] The spirit of humanism enables More to distance himself radically from his time and to imagine an entirely different world – the idea of a 'New World' was topical following the discovery of America – as a desirable goal of human striving; at the same time it enables him to adopt a sceptical posture towards the feasibility of such a goal.[35] Here modern consciousness shows itself to be creative, utopian and at the same time critical and realistic; precisely in the openness and indeterminacy of this book resides its innovative power.

More's work occupies an intermediate position in many respects. On the one hand, it contains a novel perspective on society as an institutional framework which can be constructed and shaped by human beings.

31. Erasmus, *The Education of a Christian Prince*, 21.   32. *Ibid.* 79.
33. On this, see also the image of the concentric circles with Christ as the centre, around him the Church, the secular ruler and finally the people. Christ remains in this image the guiding principle of the other circles: 'Each of the elements has its own place. Fire, however, which occupies the highest place, little by little draws all the others to it and, as far as it can, transforms them into its own nature.' Erasmus, 'Letter to Paul Volz', 119.
34. See Nipperdey, 'Thomas Morus'; Jäckel, 'Nachwort'; Skinner, *The Foundations of Modern Political Thought*, vol. I, 255–62. For a more detailed analysis, see Forst, 'Utopia and Irony'.
35. See the closing remark in More, *Utopia*, 110–11.

Habermas speaks in this connection of a 'revolution in approach' which unites Machiavelli and More. *Survival* rather than *the good life* becomes the primary focus of political thought. Technical possibilities of a beneficial and stable social order are sought, with an emphasis in More on the economic structure, in Machiavelli on the art of government.[36] On the other hand, we should bear in mind, against this reading, that the new 'technical' order of society is framed normatively by traditional conceptions of virtue and a comprehensive idea of justice, leading to the quasi-communist version of Plato's *Republic* which More presents. Moreover, the vision of society as capable of being constructed remains split in a double sense: first, in addition to the altogether positive depiction of how material inequality and the striving for gain are overcome in Utopia, More also depicts the prevailing conformism in drastic terms, which induces a sense of alienation both from one's own social context and from this utopia; and, second, More speaks of a 'utopia', an ideal Platonic conception, which must first be mediated with reality and cannot be simply realised by human action.

More's conception of toleration exhibits the same intermediate character. Whereas in the first part he criticises the Church under the negative influence of scholasticism in terms similar to Erasmus, in the second part he describes the tolerance of the Utopians. Although a multiplicity of different religious conceptions of the true Deity are to be found in Utopia, all Utopians share the same fundamental principles concerning the worship of the one God who is conceived in different ways. These 'different roads' leading 'to a single destination'[37] make possible a shared form of worship and shared priests. Moreover, there is a discernible trend towards religious unification, towards a form of the pagan religion based on natural reason which comes close to Christianity. Thus, when the Utopians first come in contact with Christians the latter manage to make this religion accessible to them, especially since, according to More, the teachings of Christ correspond to the strongly egalitarian and anti-materialist character of the Utopian social order. More presents three reasons why toleration prevails in Utopia at both the political-constitutional and the social-intersubjective level:

(a) The founder of the state, Utopus, was able to seize power because of the religious divisions in Utopia, which meant that it was unable to defend

36. Habermas, 'The Classical Doctrine of Politics in Relation to Social Philosophy', 41–62.
37. 'Though there are various religions in Utopia . . . all of them, even the most diverse, agree in the main point, which is worship of the divine nature; they are like travellers going to a single destination by different roads.' More, *Utopia*, 104.

itself against external enemies. From this he concluded that the peaceful coexistence of religions under a regime of toleration strengthened rather than weakened the state (in which he anticipated the argument of the French *politiques*). As a result, intolerance, the disparagement of the beliefs of others and the use of violence in religious affairs, is met with the most severe punishment – a fate which Christian fanatics can also suffer. Atheists, however, cannot be tolerated, 'since [a citizen] would openly despise all the laws and customs of society, if not prevented by fear' of being punished by God for his crime against the state.[38]

(b) In addition to this practical political justification of toleration 'for the sake of peace', More identifies two further justifications on the horizontal level. According to the first, finite beings are not in a position to judge whether God might will that there should be different ways of worshipping him and hence whether it is presumptuous to make an exclusive claim to the truth.

(c) Second, where only one belief is true, the 'natural strength' of the truth will prevail of its own accord without any need of additional support.[39]

The latter two arguments were already prefigured by Nicholas of Cusa and are sketched out in the parable of the rings; they represent variants of a religious justification of toleration already mentioned (§6.2). In addition, they must be seen against the background of a very broad agreement in religious questions among the Utopians. Striking, and of major importance for the modern understanding of toleration, however, is, first, the fact that More makes explicit the separation between the vertical, pragmatic political perspective and a horizontal, intersubjective-religious justification and, second, that the former is introduced in purely political terms. This radicalises the stance of Marsilius, who defended the autonomy of the state vis-à-vis the Church in institutional and (to a limited extent) normative terms, and it represents an important bridge to the thought of Machiavelli. Still, in contrast to Machiavelli, this political autonomy is not yet so extensive that the state can make completely free use of religion. Here More still adopts an intermediate position insofar as the state and social order continue to be seen as founded upon religion. Religion remains a fundamental, independent force in the thought and action of human beings and towards the institutions of the state; they cannot dispose over it at will. This is even more true of More the statesman who became Speaker of the House of Commons in 1523 and Lord Chancellor in 1529 and strongly opposed the Reformation. In his

38. *Ibid.* 98.   39. *Ibid.*

Dialogue concerning Heretics (1528) he asserts that, although it is not within the power of the Church, it is within the power of the state to condemn and execute heretics who are not willing to recant and who cause violent public turmoil.[40] He himself paid with his life for his refusal to acknowledge the royal supremacy in religious matters and to grant Henry VIII the Oath of Supremacy. He died in 1535 on the scaffold.

4. In Machiavelli, as I have indicated, we encounter another face of political humanism. He understands the state as a human construction which calls for a corresponding art and virtue. However, this virtue – *virtù* – is detached from the religious ethics of Christian humanism and is given a normative formulation in terms of autonomous political concepts. The preservation of the state and the preservation of the power necessary to this end become the supreme principles of political action. In contrast to Erasmus and More, in his *Principe* (1513) Machiavelli emphasises the theoretical and practical necessity of a sober consideration and exploitation of the inherent laws of the political domain:

> However, how men live is so different from how they should live that a ruler who does not do what is generally done, but persists in doing what ought to be done, will undermine his power rather than maintain it. If a ruler who wants always to act honourably is surrounded by many unscrupulous men his downfall is inevitable. Therefore, a ruler who wishes to maintain his power must be prepared to act immorally when this becomes necessary.[41]

A prince who sought to emulate Erasmus's ideal of the good ruler would act in a highly irresponsible manner according to Machiavelli. His virtues would inevitably mutate into vices in the political domain; and thus the prudent statesman is forced to adopt certain vices if he wants to act in a politically virtuous manner and not to deliver the polity over to its enemies. For ultimately only a stable state can suppress the evil in human beings and compel them to act virtuously.[42] This end justifies setting aside the requirements of morality and religion; more than that, it permits and requires that religion be employed as a political instrument. Thus, the prince may act 'treacherously, ruthlessly or inhumanely, and disregard the precepts of religion' when necessary, but in doing so he must maintain the appearance of piety so as not to forfeit the allegiance of his citizens.[43] In the *Discorsi* (1522) Machiavelli stresses even more forcefully the political utility of religion. Whereas in the

40. More, *Dialogue concerning Heretics*, chs. 13, 14.
41. Machiavelli, *The Prince*, ch. xv, 54–5.   42. *Ibid.* xxiii.   43. *Ibid.* xviii.

Principe he defends the view that the depravity and unreliability of human beings are such that it is better for the prince to be feared than to be loved,[44] in the later work on the free republic he adds that this is too insecure and hence that the indispensable fear of violating the law must be fear of God. Taking the example of the Roman republic, he tries to show that religion is 'the instrument necessary above all others for the maintenance of a civilised state',[45] because it leads to obedience and harmony both in the army and among the citizenry. Thus, he continues:

> The rulers of a republic or of a kingdom, therefore, should uphold the basic principles of the religion which they practise in, and, if this be done, it will be easy for them to keep their commonwealth religious, and, in consequence, good and united. They should also foster and encourage everything likely to be of help to this end, *even though they be convinced that it is quite fallacious*.[46]

According to Machiavelli, however, the Christian religion, as it developed within the Catholic Church and moved away from its origins, is not suited to this purpose. Apart from the wickedness and corruption of the priesthood and the decisive contribution of papal policy to the political fragmentation of Italy, the Christian religion is unworldly and feeble by comparison with ancient religion. It contains only 'principles of idle effeminacy rather than those of heroic courage', where Machiavelli counts tolerance among the former.[47]

The specifically modern spirit of Machiavelli's political philosophy comes clearly to the fore in these reflections. The political sphere is an autonomous sphere of action, not just in an institutional but also in a normative sense; it has its own laws and is emancipated from the previously valid religious principles. However, this sphere is not an ethical vacuum but has its own ethos, its own values and virtues, which can be traced back to ancient republican ideals and interpret the latter in a 'realistic' way.[48] It is autonomous but not value-free. In this way, Machiavelli opens up political space for *independent* justifications of political power and political action, a space which is occupied by the art of preserving the state or 'reason of state' (as it is later called).[49] The Prince derives the justification of his actions in the first

---

44. *Ibid.* xvii.   45. Machiavelli, *Discourses*, bk i, ch. 11, 139.
46. *Ibid.* i, 12, 143 (emphasis added).   47. *Ibid.* ii, 2.
48. Berlin places special emphasis on this in 'The Originality of Machiavelli' (drawing on Meinecke, *Machiavellism*, 38–48, and in contrast to, for example, Münkler, *Machiavelli*, 281–99).
49. On this, see Meinecke's classic study, *Machiavellism*, and especially Münkler, *Im Namen des Staates*.

instance from the imperatives of defending the state against internal and external enemies, which for Machiavelli implies that, from the perspective of its subjects, the legitimacy of the state continues to be based on religion. Nevertheless, this 'rationalisation' of state action (as the emancipation from traditional guidelines) contains within itself the seeds of a further, countervailing 'rationalisation' which was already prefigured in Marsilius but is neglected by Machiavelli. The space of *political justification* becomes receptive to questions of legitimation on the part of the subjects themselves. Whether these questions are formulated in terms of the concept of the common good or of the legal principle *Quod omnes tangit*, this always instigates a dynamic of justification which would ultimately subject the 'rational' exercise of power, no longer to the prudent judgement of the Prince, but to a more extensive legitimation, as subsequently in social contract theories. As this dynamic unfolds, the question of political power always remains linked to questions of religious truth or moral norms; however, with the decline of the theological-political order of the Middle Ages, this would still be possible only in the form of comprehensive, independent attempts at political legitimation.

Consequently, the autonomisation and rationalisation of political power in the early modern era has a complex, multi-layered significance for the question of toleration. First, religion becomes an instrument for preserving power and is employed rationally in accordance with the yardstick of 'raison d'état'. This can speak *for* (limited) toleration in accordance with the *permission conception* in some cases (as in More's and Machiavelli's examples of upholding existing religious conceptions for the sake of securing power), but in other cases it can speak *against* it (if in this way political rule or harmony among the citizens cannot be generated – for example, where deep divisions and heresies exist which lead to rebellion).[50] Toleration is justified and applied chiefly in a strategic manner as part of a calculus of power or art of rulership. Thus, raison d'état exhibits a specific, 'rational' form of politics – in Foucault's terms, a specifically modern 'rationality of the state' – which is concerned with the complete government and direction of the citizens. Even though it depends on the autonomy of the state vis-à-vis religion, it nevertheless is prepared to adopt the heritage of 'pastoral power' in that it seeks to control the social life of the subjects.[51] Foucault sees a

50. On this, see Scheuner's rich study, 'Staatsräson und religiöse Einheit des Staates'. In addition Münkler, *Im Namen des Staates*, 109-26, 217-32.
51. Foucault, 'Omnes et singulatim', esp. 315-25. Here, however, the following qualifications should be emphasised. In the first place, Foucault excludes Machiavelli from this line of thought within raison d'état, because according to Foucault he is only concerned with reinforcing the power of the prince who remains external to the totality of the state (Foucault,

'rationalisation' of power in the methods used to achieve this control, and in this sense granting toleration for strategic purposes (a topic he does not address explicitly) constitutes such a 'patient' instrument of government.[52] Power has the task of making life as secure as possible and of averting harm; and for this purpose it requires the necessary knowledge and advanced technical means. Machiavelli and (at least in part) More stand for this new understanding of politics, as Habermas emphasises: Machiavelli with his emphasis on the technique of acquiring power and the 'art of governing men',[53] More with his emphasis on the socio-economically optimal way of 'organising society by the techniques of a legal order',[54] extending to the regulation of the working day, clothing, marriage and child rearing.

Therefore, with the increasing emancipation of politics from religion in the early modern period, new techniques and strategies of state power emerge which at the same time bring into play the other side of this development, namely, the increased need of justification in the political domain. With this we broach the second, equally important aspect of the rationalisation of power, namely the rationalisation of normative arguments for its exercise.[55] The space of legitimation of power cannot be filled indefinitely by techniques of power. Comprehensive and accepted legitimations are needed which establish a bond between ruler and ruled. In the context of the question of toleration, this means that both policies of intolerance and policies of toleration stand in need of public justification; a reflexive imperative encroaches into the political domain, leading to a new dynamic of social conflicts over the practices and justifications of toleration. The normative arguments, the legitimations as well as the challenges to power, abandon the inherited political-theological frame of reference; the (primarily instrumental-strategic) rationalisation of power goes hand-in-hand with

'Governmentality'). However, this interpretation of Machiavelli's reflections is too one-sided, as is shown not only by his remarks on the integrative power of religion but also by his frequent remarks on the importance and promotion of virtue and on demographic policy (e.g. in *Discorsi* II, 3). Second, Foucault sees only initial intimations of such a form of politics in the sixteenth and seventeenth centuries, and in his view it becomes established only during the eighteenth century (cf. Foucault, 'Governmentality', 99).

52. On government and patience see Foucault, 'Governmentality', 96.

53. Habermas, 'The Classical Doctrine of Politics in Relation to Social Philosophy', 59.

54. *Ibid.* 50.

55. The following account of the interrelation between the strategic-technical and the legitimatory rationalisation of political power draws upon Habermas's theory of rationalisation (in *Theory of Communicative Action*, esp. vol. II, 153–97), though it does not adopt the structure of the division into 'system' and 'lifeworld'. Instead it locates an internal, dynamic and conflictual form of rationalisation already within the domain of political power (see Habermas's discussion of the rationalisation of law and his critique of Weber in *ibid.* vol. I, 243–71, and *Between Facts and Norms*, 66–81).

a rationalisation of the normative 'space of reasons', as it were – in short, with a rationalisation of political morality which is linked, in turn, with a more comprehensive moral rationalisation. For horizontal relations between human beings also come under reflexive and justificatory pressure. Not only does the question of how to deal with profound (primarily religious) differences at the state level become an open problem, but also the question of how one can coexist with members of different religions within a single society.[56] The conflicts surrounding the Reformation will bring the challenges at both of these levels out into the open. They call for new strategies as well as new justifications of vertical political, and of horizontal intersubjective, toleration – though it must be emphasised that the associated attempts to find a universally shareable moral basis of reciprocal recognition and tolerance were destined to remain founded on religious premises until well into the Enlightenment period. Here it should be noted that the modern discourse of toleration is marked by the conscious separation between these two perspectives, the perspective of the theory of the state and the intersubjective social perspective. Moreover, the modern discourse of toleration, which begins at this time, is marked, following the collapse of the ecclesiastical-political order, by the increasing autonomy of these two domains vis-à-vis traditional religious guidelines and by the tension between them.

§9 The conscience of the believer and the separation between the spiritual and secular domains: the Reformation

1. The Reformation marked a decisive turning point in the modern development towards an autonomisation of religious individuality vis-à-vis ecclesiastical-doctrinal authority and towards the formation of a secular conception of the state – in particular, the separation between secular and spiritual or ecclesiastical authority. Yet however much this fostered trends implicit in humanism, the gulf between the humanist and Lutheran views of human beings could hardly have been greater. Whereas the former emphasised human dignity and freedom, the latter emphasised the worthlessness of human beings before God, their sinfulness, fallenness and contingency on God's mercy. Moreover, whereas in Erasmus the temporal ruler was called upon to rule by means of Christian virtues, Luther's conception of the state

---

56. Rawls, *Lectures on the History of Moral Philosophy*, 7–8, sees this question posed by the Reformation as marking the beginning of modern moral philosophy.

was closer to Machiavelli for whom secular power was grounded in the need to suppress human wickedness. These differences found clear expression in the controversy between Erasmus and Luther already alluded to. Whereas Erasmus was willing to make a concession to Luther to the extent that Luther attributed 'something' to the free will as regards salvation but 'the most' to mercy, he insisted that the doctrine of the reward of the virtuous and the punishment of the wicked by God would become invalid, and God himself would become responsible for wickedness, if the free will were something vain, with the result that human beings would be cast into deep despair.[57] Luther, by contrast, regarded this very despair, and the insight into the impossibility of human beings withstanding God's judgement and counting as just, as the necessary condition of the true faith, which can hope to be vindicated only through God's mercy, not through the works of the will. As Luther retrospectively described his formative 'Tower Experience', in which he recognised that God's justice is an undeserved gift to the believer who acknowledges his own inadequacy, one attains the true faith only through insight into one's subjective unworthiness and the freedom from works and things external to oneself.[58]

Insofar as the Reformation can be seen as a move towards the increasing independence of religious subjectivity and the emergence of freedom of conscience, therefore, it can be so only indirectly by dint of an almost paradoxical dialectic in which the radical, anti-humanist problematisation of the subjective will and its autonomy places human beings directly before God, and thus makes them independent of the traditional mediating role of the Church and its authority. Subjectivity proceeds from the critique of subjectivity. The significance of this dialectic for the problematic of toleration becomes clear when one considers how Luther takes up and interprets the two central topoi of toleration in the New Testament, namely respect for conscience and the two-kingdoms doctrine (see the Excursus in §4). In both cases he shows himself to be a radical pupil of Augustine. Luther is far from understanding what he terms 'freedom of conscience' as the freedom to follow one's subjective ethical convictions; instead he views freedom of conscience negatively as the freedom from false doctrines and authorities, which – the

57. Erasmus, *On the Freedom of the Will*, 95–6.
58. Luther, 'Preface to the Complete Edition of Luther's Latin Works (1545)'. On the discussion concerning this experience see Lohse (ed.), *Der Durchbruch der reformatorischen Erkenntnis bei Luther*; also Luther, *Concerning Christian Liberty*, and *On the Bondage of the Will*, esp. 309–34. This is also clear in the *Heidelberg Disputation*, 65: 'It is certain that man must utterly despair of his own ability before he is prepared to receive the grace of Christ.'

extreme case being the sale of indulgences – establish false hierarchies among the in principle equal believers and give the false impression of a justification through external works.[59] Only the rejection of these doctrines of the Roman Church makes possible the true *freedom* of conscience in its reliance upon, indeed utter *subjection* to, God. Conscience is the locus of unqualified faith, of recognition of one's own sinfulness and imperfection and of receptiveness to the message of the word, whose authority here alone counts. Hence, the conscience is liberated from its 'imprisonment' by the Church so that it comes to see itself as bound to and directed by God – self-appropriation (*Selbstaneignung*) leads to self-assignment (*Selbstübereignung*) in the faith. Thus, at the end of his speech at the Diet of Worms in 1521, in which he refuses to recant his condemned writings, Luther says: 'if my judgment is not in this way brought into subjection to God's word, I neither can nor will retract anything; for it cannot be right for a Christian to speak against his conscience'.[60] Consequently, conscience is not an expression of religious subjectivism but the *work of God*. This provides the basis for Luther's central argument for toleration, which leads at the same time to the heart of the two-kingdoms doctrine:

> Each must decide at his own peril what he is to believe, and must see to it that he believes rightly. Other people cannot go to heaven or hell on my behalf, or open or close [the gates to either] for me. And just as little can they believe or not believe on my behalf, or force my faith or unbelief. How he believes is a matter for each individual's conscience, and this does not diminish [the authority of] secular governments. They ought therefore to content themselves with attending to their own business, and allow people to believe what they can, and what they want, and they must use no coercion in this matter against anyone. Faith is free, and no one can be compelled to believe. More precisely, so far from being something secular authority ought to create and enforce, faith is something that God works in the spirit. Hence, that common saying which also occurs in Augustine: no one can or ought to be forced to believe anything against his will.[61]

Through his word, God reveals himself to the individual in his faith, and thus it is part of the latter's freedom and vocation to open himself up to this truth. Freedom of conscience is the freedom to receive this message. With this Luther defends (following Augustine) the view not only that

59. Luther, *The Babylonian Captivity of the Church*.
60. Luther, 'Before the Diet at Worms (18 April 1521)'.
61. Luther, *On Secular Authority*, 25–6.

conscience *cannot* be coerced, but also that it *should not* be coerced, since otherwise human beings presume to do God's work, namely wanting to lead someone to the truth and to salvation.

Luther's appropriation of the two-kingdoms doctrine as he presents it in *On Secular Authority* (1523) takes up this point. All true believers belong to the kingdom of God which is purely spiritual; here no temporal law or sword is needed since God's word alone holds sway. The members of this kingdom, the true Christians, are pious through their faith and will be saved through God's mercy. They are, as Luther stresses in *Concerning Christian Liberty* (1520), free from secular requirements insofar as they lack nothing for salvation; rather the believer becomes a priest who may appeal to God on behalf of others. As a corporeal being and member of the secular kingdom, on the other hand, the human being is required to do good works from his faith – though not in order to become pious – and that means in the first place 'to chasten his own body' and to humble his will.[62] Thus, Christians make themselves the servants of others, 'obeying their will out of gratuitous love' (*umbsonst*).[63] This involves becoming part of the secular kingdom and subordinating oneself to the secular authorities. The true Christians do this voluntarily, however, for they do not fall under the law of the secular kingdom, which includes all those who do not live as Christians, in order to hold their wickedness in check. Since according to Luther 'all the world is evil and . . . scarcely one human being in a thousand is a true Christian', so that it is impossible to govern a people with the Gospel, 'God has ordained the two governments, the spiritual [government] which fashions true Christians and just persons through the Holy Spirit under Christ, and the secular [*weltlich*] government which holds the Unchristian and wicked in check and forces them to keep the peace outwardly and be still.'[64] Although the (few) true Christians have no need of the secular kingdom, they nevertheless recognise that it has been ordained by God to curb evil and protect the weak, as St Paul says (Romans 13:1–2): 'Everyone must submit himself to the governing authorities, for there is no authority except that which God has established. The authorities that exist have been established by God. Consequently, he who rebels against the authority is rebelling against what God has instituted.' In Luther's interpretation of this passage, the relation between the two kingdoms and the two 'governments' has special importance: In the kingdom of God the word alone rules, because the goal is to create 'a free,

---

62. Luther, *Concerning Christian Liberty*, ¶55.
63. *Ibid.* ¶86.   64. *On Secular Authority*, 10–11.

willing people' of Christ 'without coercion or constraint' through the inner conviction of conscience alone.[65] In addition to this 'spiritual government' in his own kingdom, God has ordained the 'government of the sword' for the kingdom of the world. God does not exercise this directly; rather it is conducted by the secular authority, which thereby performs God's work as external work – not in order to make human beings pious but to preserve external freedom. This construction has far-reaching implications for the problematic of toleration. On the one hand, the secular authority is to be obeyed, since it also performs God's work on earth; on the other hand, it must be extremely careful not to go so far as to infringe upon the tasks of the spiritual government. Luther places particular emphasis on this point:

> Secular government has laws that extend no further than the body, goods and outward, earthly matters. But where the soul is concerned, God neither can nor will allow anyone but himself to rule. And so, whether secular authority takes it upon itself to legislate for the soul, it trespasses on [what belongs to] God's government, and merely seduces and ruins souls.[66]

'Freedom of conscience' must be respected by secular authority, therefore, not because there is a 'subjective right' to decide ethical questions in accordance with one's conscience; rather, respect for freedom of conscience is required by respect for God's spiritual government, for only faith which is justified by the word is pleasing to God. What is to be respected is not the subjective freedom of conscience but its being *bound* by God. God alone can show the soul the path to heaven; he alone, not the emperors, can govern souls. Insofar as the emperors try to do this and prohibit the distribution of Luther's translation of the New Testament – as, for example, in Meissen, Bavaria and Brandenburg – then civil disobedience is mandatory: not rebellion but disobedience of iniquitous laws and acceptance of the resulting punishment.[67]

The Church, as an institution whose sole task is to pronounce God's word and administer the sacraments, is answerable to temporal power, according to Luther, and should be organised internally along democratic lines; it does not possess divinely ordained authority.[68] Should it take it upon itself to offer authoritative interpretations of the word and, as in the sale of indulgences, to falsify the faith by doing God's work, it must be criticised just as much

---

65. *Ibid.* 13.   66. *Ibid.* 23.   67. *Ibid.* 29.   68. Luther, *Address to the Nobility*, 16.

as when it regards itself as authorised to exercise temporal power and to challenge the secular authorities. Heretics should be fought with the word, for 'heresy is a spiritual thing; it cannot be struck down with steel, burned with fire or drowned in water'.[69] The truth of the Gospel is sullied by attempts to impose it with violence. At the same time, however, the revealed truth does not permit any toleration in doctrinal matters or any relativisation of the word: 'the Gospel can tolerate no other teaching besides its own'.[70]

The two-kingdoms doctrine combined with his particular understanding of the conscience, therefore, leads Luther to a justification of toleration which excludes any deviation from the absolute claim to truth of the Gospels, but whose core claim is that the work of the faith is God's work (and not that of the individual). Correspondingly clear limits must be set: to temporal power regarding the government of souls, to the Church regarding its spiritual and temporal power and, finally, to the believers regarding obedience to the secular authorities. This justification of toleration has been very influential in the modern discourse, as we shall see in John Locke for example (though in connection with a different understanding of political legitimacy). It is the result of an appropriation of the two-kingdoms doctrine, in particular in the form of Augustine's distinction between the *civitas Dei* and the *civitas terrena*, with the important difference that Augustine subordinated the secular kingdom founded upon sin more emphatically to the heavenly, something which later served to legitimate the theocratic system of the Middle Ages. Luther, who opposed this blending of secular and spiritual power, traces a sharper boundary between the two kingdoms or 'governments', although he is in no doubt that the secular government is also God's government. 'God himself is the founder, lord, master, protector, and rewarder of both kinds of righteousness. There is no human ordinance or authority in either, but each is a divine thing entirely.'[71] This has two kinds of implications, because, on the one hand, the state remains anchored in the overarching divine order (in which it meets its limits), but, on the other hand, it becomes an independent institution which is indirectly furnished with divine authority (in its own domain).

This becomes apparent where the reformational opposition to the privileges of the Church led to social revolts against the reigning feudal order, in particular during the peasant revolts of 1524–25, in which the Anabaptist

---

69. Luther, *On Secular Authority*, 30.
70. Luther, *Sermons of Martin Luther*, vol. I, 148. On this, see Kühn, *Toleranz und Offenbarung*, ch. 2.
71. Luther, 'Whether Soldiers, Too, Can Be Saved', 100.

Thomas Müntzer interpreted Christianity in socially revolutionary terms.[72] For Luther this represented an illicit confusion of the two kingdoms which entailed the additional risk that the princes would react more strongly against the Reformation, and thus he opposed these revolts with increasing severity. Luther's strict stance against these revolts is even more important for the problem of toleration because the uprising itself was legitimated using Protestant-Christian arguments. In order to demarcate his position, Luther emphasised that the agitators not only were sinning against the commandment to respect secular authority but that they were also heretics who merited punishment for spreading dangerous and false views. Therefore, in 1531 he sided with Melanchthon, who demanded the death penalty not only for rebellious Anabaptists but also for those who, even though they remained peaceful, nevertheless disrupted the 'ecclesiastical order'. This placed in question the original toleration towards heresy as a 'spiritual thing' and brought the temporal and the spiritual – more precisely, the ecclesiastical – order closer together: heresy and rebellion were all but identified, as already in earlier times, in order to legitimate secular punishment.

This becomes even more apparent in Luther's redoubled efforts to institutionalise the Reformation with the aid of the sovereign princes, a process in which he relativised some of the central claims of his doctrine of toleration. Here, too, we find the picture familiar from the Church Fathers, especially Augustine: as soon as one's own doctrine becomes dominant, challenges are no longer met with the tolerance which previously, from the perspective of a minority, was assumed to be required. The formerly invisible, hidden Church of the faithful was becoming transformed into an institution, for which purpose Luther required the princes, who in his view were supposed to guarantee the possibility of promulgating God's word. Although he initially opposed the suppression of the Catholic Mass in the Lutheran countries, in 1525 he defended it.[73] To the objection against this practice – based on his own doctrine – that the secular authority has no power over worship and religion, he replies: 'Our government does not force belief in the Evangelic faith, but only suppresses external abominations.'[74] *Freedom of conscience* is now interpreted as freedom from direct compulsion to believe, it no longer includes *freedom of worship*; religious differences can be tolerated, if at all,

---

72. Cf. Münkler, 'Politisches Denken in der Zeit der Reformation', 648–55; Skinner, *The Foundations of Modern Political Thought*, vol. II, 73–80; Kamen, *The Rise of Toleration*, 30–42.
73. Luther, *Vom Greuel der Stillmesse*.
74. Luther, Letter to George Spalatin (11 November 1525), 146.

inwardly and in private. Elsewhere Luther emphasises that 'in a given place a single sermon should be delivered'.[75] This principle, which anticipates the principle of the Religious Peace of Augsburg of 1555, *cuius regio, eius religio*, also played a leading role in the foundation of the Lutheran national churches. The latter were subordinated to the sovereign prince who made regular 'visitations'. His *cura religionis* was supposed to ensure that the subjects heard the word of God – including the duty to attend church service: 'And even if they do not believe, for the sake of the Tenth Commandment they should be compelled to attend the sermon so that they learn at least external exercises of obedience.'[76] In this way, a system of state churches was erected which blurred the boundary between secular and spiritual power, so that the highest office of the prince was 'to promote God's honor and to avert blasphemy and idolatry'.[77] Thus it happened that Luther's first use of the word 'toleration' in German in 1541 occurred in a negative semantic context, namely the rejection of a 'perpetual tolerance' (*ewige tollerantz*) in the sense of a stable coexistence of the reformed and the Catholic teaching.[78] In addition, he defended expulsions of members of other religions, whether members of other Protestant movements or Jews, towards whom, in view of their insistence on their faith, Luther adopted an increasingly hostile stance – to the point where in his writing *Von den Juden und ihren Lügen* (*Of the Jews and Their Lies*) (1543) he calls for the suppression of the Jewish faith and the expulsion of the Jews.[79]

2. Therefore, while Luther – and even more clearly Zwingli and Calvin[80] – took the route of an increasing instrumentalisation of secular power for the purposes of institutionalising the Church and promulgating of the truth, others took as their starting point the Lutheran 'liberation' of conscience from its 'bondage' by the Church and its dogmas and interpreted Christian belief in an undogmatic, spiritual-individualist, almost mystical way.[81] Thus,

75. Luther, Brief an Johann von Sachsen (Letter to Elector John of Saxony) (9 February 1526), 28.
76. Luther, Brief an J. L. Metzsch (Letter to J. L. Metzsch) (26 August 1529), 136–7.
77. Luther *et al.*, *Ob Christliche Fürsten schuldig sind.*
78. Luther, Brief an die Fürsten Johann und Georg von Anhalt (Letter to the Princes Johann and Georg of Anhalt) (12 June 1541), 441.
79. On this, see Bienert, *Martin Luther und die Juden.*
80. Cf. Calvin, *Institutes of the Christian Religion* [*Institutio christianae religionis*], bk IV, ch. 20.3 (635): '[The civil polity] not only tends to secure . . . that men may breathe, eat, drink, and be sustained in life, though it comprehends all these things when it causes them to live together; yet, I say, this is not its only tendency; its objects also are, that idolatry, sacrileges against the name of God, blasphemies against his truth, and other offences against religion, may not openly appear and be disseminated amongst the people.' On this, see also Walzer, *The Revolution of the Saints*, ch. 2.
81. Cf. Troeltsch, *The Social Teaching of the Christian Churches*, vol. II, 691–799.

'spiritualists' such as Hans Denck, Sebastian Franck and Caspar Schwenck-feld developed justifications of toleration and freedom of conscience which, in contrast to Luther, emphasise the idea of doctrinal toleration. Particularly noteworthy in this context is Franck's original and important work.[82] Franck, who, aside from Luther's influence, was deeply influenced by Denck's teaching of an inner, undogmatic Christianity[83] and by Erasmus's irenism, advocates what was for his time a very far-reaching, inclusive position on toleration. It is based on a form of religious individualism which separates faith completely from any concrete authority, be it that of the Church or even that of scripture, and traces it back exclusively to the 'inner light' of the Holy Spirit. According to Franck, all determinate forms of religion not only deflect attention away from this inner purity and truth, but lead to endless disputes between religions, denominations and sects – disputes over 'pigeon droppings',[84] as he put it in one place; and he is equally clear in his important work *Paradoxa* (1534): 'Scripture kills... But the spirit makes alive.'[85] The true Church is an invisible Church, and history, in Franck's view, shows that its members are always persecuted as heretics by those who press the faith into rules, laws and ordinances which are in reality unchristian. In his heresy chronicle *Chronica, Zeitbuch und Geschichtbibell* (1531), Franck attempts to show using a range of examples how many 'loyal, godly' people became victims of persecutions of heretics (especially by the Roman Church). As a result, the doctrinal toleration implied by Franck's Christianity is very far-reaching. Since 'the New Testament is nothing other than the Holy Spirit, a good conscience, untainted love, a pure heart, a blameless life, righteousness of the heart which is grounded in an uncorrupted faith', God is concerned solely with this purity and is, beyond all determinateness of religion, an 'impartial God', who 'loves everyone deeply' – 'with no regard to person, name or nation'.[86] For intersubjective, horizontal toleration, this implies that all who truly seek God are brothers and should treat one another as such; God's impartiality radiates onto relations between human beings. Moreover, the remarkable thing about Franck is that he interprets this in universal terms:

> To me, anyone who wishes my good and can bear with me by his side, is a good brother, whether papist, Lutheran, Zwinglian, Anabaptist, or

82. See the detailed account in Barbers, *Toleranz bei Sebastian Franck*; in addition Blaschke, 'Der Toleranzgedanke bei Sebastian Franck'; Furcha, '"Turks and Heathen Are Our Kin"'.
83. See especially Denck, 'Wer die Wahrheit wahrlich lieb hat' (1526) and 'Divine Order and the Work of His Creatures' (1527).
84. Quoted from Blaschke, 'Der Toleranzgedanke bei Sebastian Franck', 55.
85. Franck, *280 Paradoxes or Wondrous Sayings*, 6.   86. *Ibid.* 158, 132, 134–5.

even Turk, even though we do not feel the same way, until God gathers us in his own school and unites us in the same faith . . . Let no one try to be master of my faith and to force me to follow his belief; he must be my neighbour, and become my well-beloved brother; even if he is Jew or Samaritan, I want to love him and do him good as much as in me lies. I reject no one who does not reject me. As a human being, I treat all other human beings justly.[87]

According to this humanist-spiritualist conception, believers of very different persuasions share a universal 'inner truth'. It is not the place of human beings, who are trapped in their finitude, to presume to anticipate God's judgement concerning error or orthodoxy; God in his impartiality demands equally individual piety and mutual, impartial tolerance among those who believe in him.

For vertical state toleration, this implies that no human authority can legitimately prescribe or promulgate a positive form of faith; God's people is a 'free people' and God wishes neither a faith pressed into rules nor a coerced, hypocritical faith.[88] Faith, as in Luther, is God's work and the temporal power has no authority in this domain: 'For thoughts are scot-free and no one is able to coerce, capture, or stop the will.'[89] And, finally, a secular or an ecclesiastical authority would not have sufficient dogmatic reasons for condemning heretics either. Here it becomes apparent how the doctrinal conception of toleration reinforces the state requirement of toleration and attempts to pull the ground out from under the persecution of heretics.

However, such a position of 'universal toleration' also has definite limits. For it tends to be as intolerant towards those who interpret the word 'externally and carnally' as towards those who think certain positive forms of religion are indispensable and part of the truth,[90] and especially towards those who, like the revolutionary Anabaptists, want to found God's kingdom on earth. In Franck's view, they are genuinely harmful sects which must be combated with force.[91]

In spite of these limits, it must be acknowledged that Franck develops what was for his time a very far-reaching argument which contains very important elements for the subsequent discourse over toleration. In the first place, there is the separation between authentic, individual religiosity and the ecclesiastical order and even the authority of scripture; furthermore,

---

87. Franck, *Das verbüthschiert mit siben Sigeln verschlossen Buch* (1539), quoted (with alterations) from Lecler, *Toleration and the Reformation*, vol. 1, 175.

88. Franck, *280 Paradoxes or Wondrous Sayings*, 162, 480.   89. *Ibid.* 72–3.

90. Cf., for example, Franck, *Chronica* 2, CC–CCI.   91. Franck, *Chronica* 1, CCXCI–CCXCII.

and even more important, there is the doctrinal toleration which views even non-Christians as 'children' of an impartial God who must be tolerated in their otherness – a line of argument which implies a relativisation, if not a complete rejection, of the concept of heresy without resting upon a form of religious scepticism. With this Franck takes up a strand of the unitary religious thought which is already found in the medieval religious conversations (cf. above §6) and will continue as far as Lessing. Finally, in Franck we encounter a very important legacy of humanism, in addition to irenism, which henceforth acquires steadily increasing weight in the discourse over toleration: in addition to the believer, the 'human being' features as a human being and not merely as a religious being – in Franck's words, 'As a human being, I treat all other human beings justly.'[92] This lays the groundwork for a distinction between the person, who should be respected 'as a human being', and the person as a representative of particular religious beliefs which one rejects but nevertheless tolerates because one regards the other as a fellow human being to whom one owes a certain respect. To be sure, in Franck, as in Christian humanism, this distinction remains entirely within the religious sphere, for respect is owed to the person as a 'child of God'.

3. These components can also be found in the argument concerning toleration of Sebastian Castellio, which marks a new stage in the modern discourse on toleration. In Castellio, humanist and Protestant ideas combine to produce a conception of toleration which exhibits 'modern' characteristics far ahead of its time.

Castellio's line of argument is typical of many writings on toleration in that it was a response to an immediate occurrence.[93] In October 1553, the physician Michel Servet, who had rejected the doctrine of the Trinity in some of his writings, was executed at the instigation of Calvin in Geneva which was under Calvin's rule. Fleeing the Inquisition in France, Servet had sought refuge in Geneva where he was imprisoned, condemned and burned at the stake. These proceedings led to a wide-ranging debate which climaxed in the controversy between Castellio and Calvin. In his work *Declaratio orthodoxae fidei* (1554), the latter defended the execution as necessary in order to vindicate God's honour and to prevent the dissemination of the 'heretical poison' being spread by Servet. Castellio, who was initially a collaborator of Calvin in

92. See also a representative of the 'radical reformation', Balthasar Hubmaier, *Heretics and Those Who Burn Them*, 61, who says with reference to the parable of the weeds: 'The result of these words will not be negligence but a struggle because we combat without interruption, not against human beings, but against their godless teachings' (translation amended).
93. On the prevailing circumstances, see Lecler, *Toleration and the Reformation*, vol. 1, 325–60; in addition Guggisberg, *Sebastian Castellio*, chs. 5 and 6.

Geneva but later distanced himself from him and moved to Basel, responded to Calvin directly in his work *Contra libellum Calvini* (1554), though he had already responded in the collection of texts on toleration towards heretics, *De Haereticis, an sint persequendi* (1554), which appeared under the pseudonym Martinus Bellius. Castellio follows the model of Sebastian Franck who likewise presented texts from the Bible, the Church Fathers and the reformers in defence of toleration in the appendix to this *Chronica* with the aim of denouncing the arbitrariness of the definition of heretics and their persecution. In Castellio we likewise find passages by contemporary authors such as Erasmus, Luther, Franck, Brenz and even Calvin, including two texts of his own under other pseudonyms. The most important piece, however, is the preface addressed to the Duke of Württemberg in which Castellio presents his central idea.

(a) Castellio's primary concern is the separation between a universally valid and intelligible morality of life conduct and of behaviour towards others, on the one hand, and, on the other, the sphere of dogmatic religious questions which lead to disputes even though they are *adiaphora*, that is, things which do 'not need to be known for salvation by faith'.[94] Whereas transgressions of the basic principles of the universal morality which forms the core of Christianity, but which is nevertheless 'written in the hearts of all men from the foundation of the world',[95] are generally easy to judge and condemn, transgressions in spiritual matters are sources of inexhaustible disputes.

(b) Accordingly, Castellio distinguishes between two types of heretics: first, those who 'stubbornly' violate the universal moral norms, 'idlers' as much as 'persecutors' or atheists, and second those who deviate in spiritual matters. With reference to the latter, Castellio, like Franck, points out that there is an inflation of completely arbitrary mutual accusations of heresy and persecution: 'When I reflect on what a heretic really is, I can find no other criterion than that we are all heretics in the eyes of those who do not share our views.'[96]

(c) This division within the normative domain involves a further, decisive step. In order to criticise the arbitrariness of human definitions of heresy while nevertheless leaving intact the kernel of the Christian conception of morality, Castellio has to make an epistemological distinction between those truths which are manifest and universally accessible and

94. Castellio, *Concerning Heretics*, 122.   95. *Ibid*. 131.
96. *Ibid*. quoted from Marshall, *John Locke, Toleration and Early Enlightenment Culture*, 321.

those handed down only in an 'obscure' and 'puzzling' form even in scripture (thereby taking up the problem of legitimate religious differences extending from Abelard through Averroes to Nicholas of Cusa discussed in §6). The humanist distinction between the essential and the inessential does not play the guiding role here, therefore, but the distinction between 'evident', chiefly ethical-moral, truths, and those which are the focus of *legitimate* and *irresolvable* controversies and interpretive differences because of the *finitude* of the human cognitive faculty: 'These dissentions arise solely from ignorance of the truth, for if these matters were so obvious and evident as that there is but one God, all Christians would agree among themselves on these points as readily as all nations confess that God is one.'[97] The central religious truths are a 'gold coin' which has value and is accepted everywhere; by contrast, the many religions and confessions merely represent 'impressions and images' which should be viewed with indulgence.

In many respects, Castellio is not the religious sceptic he is often assumed to be.[98] First, he holds that the core content of faith and morality – that which is necessary to achieve salvation – is revealed clearly to human beings, is 'written in the heart' by God. Second, he assumes, following the parable of the weeds, that an ultimate truth also exists in the incidental yet hotly contested matters, though only God knows it. Thus, it is arrogant of human beings to anticipate the judgement of the 'righteous judge' by presuming to judge this matter before the time is ripe; at the same time this does not entail any fundamental scepticism concerning one's own religion. Moreover, third, Christ, whose tolerance we should take as an example, enjoins us to be humble and lenient in our dealings with one another. However, this is not to relativise one's own religious outlook:

> Let not the Jews or Turks condemn the Christians, nor let the Christians condemn the Jews or Turks, but rather teach and win them by true religion and justice, and let us, who are Christians, not condemn one another, but, if we are wiser than they, let us also be better and more merciful. This is certain that the better a man knows the truth, the less is he inclined to condemn.[99]

---

97. *Ibid.* 132.
98. This view is defended, for example, by Skinner, *The Foundations of Modern Political Thought*, vol. II, 248.
99. Castellio, *Concerning Heretics*, 132–3.

Both the inclusive morality and the epistemological uncertainty in controversial religious questions are justified in *religious* terms in Castellio and not in terms of an autonomous reason or in a sceptical manner. An autonomous morality distinct from religion does not yet provide the basis for mutual toleration; this morality still has a religious character and is bound up with ethical rules of conduct ('persecutors' and 'gluttons' are mentioned in the same breath as heretics of the first order), and thus 'godlessness' constitutes the indispensable limit of Castellio's toleration, as he explains in his writing against Calvin:

> In my opinion we must distinguish between the godless and those that err . . . If they deny God, blaspheme, and openly offend Christian doctrine, if they detest the saintly life of pious men, I admit that they should be handed over to prosecution by the magistrate, not because of religion, which in their case does not exist, but because of their lack of it.[100]

Nevertheless, his distinction between two normative domains – (1) the sphere of *universally valid morality* accessible to human reason prior to all positive religion which can be reduced to the formula of *reciprocity* (that is, not to do anything to another person which one would not wish done to oneself), and which according to Castellio is 'so true, so just, so natural, and so written by the finger of God in the hearts of all men that there is no one so degenerate, so estranged from discipline and enlightenment, but that he will confess this rule to be right and reasonable the moment it is proposed to him',[101] and (2) the sphere of *religious differences of opinion* which, because of the finitude of the human cognitive faculty, are as legitimate as they are unavoidable and irresolvable – anticipates a difference between two types of normative 'truth' which is crucial for the discourse on toleration, namely, between *moral* truth and *religious-ethical* truth. This is only structurally prefigured in Castellio, for he does not distinguish questions of the morally right, the ethical good and religious truth sufficiently to differentiate between an autonomous morality and a domain of rational, ethical-religious differences of opinion. Nevertheless, Castellio takes a major step in the direction of this normative and epistemological distinction.

Therefore, Castellio's argument, in spite of its limitations, represents an important stage in the process of a 'rationalisation of morality' within the

---

100. Castellio, *Contra libellum Calvini*, quoted from Lecler, *Toleration and the Reformation*, vol. 1, 354.
101. Castellio, *Counsel to France in Her Distress* (1562), 261.

intersubjective discourse over toleration. As in Franck, the moment of doctrinal toleration comes to the fore, though Castellio is not as hostile as Franck to all forms of positive religion; and, above all, the human being emerges as a moral person *beyond* doctrinal, confessional commitments and identities. This becomes especially clear in Castellio's response to Calvin's argument that 'one should forget all mankind when [God's] glory is in question'.[102] Castellio contradicts Calvin in the most forceful terms: '*To kill a man is not to protect a doctrine, but it is to kill a man.*'[103] This sentence, in its simplicity and conciseness, represents one of the most important results of the humanist and Protestant discussions of toleration: the human being appears as a person to be respected beyond doctrinal disputes and beyond religious authorities – though, of course, as an immediate subject of God.

Thus, we can conclude that, although the *humanist argument* that religious conflicts can be overcome through reduction to essential articles of faith[104] and the *Protestant argument* of the freedom of conscience before God and of the two kingdoms are to be found in Castellio, here a further, *third way* of justifying a respect conception of toleration is opened up which henceforth, from Bodin through Coornhert to Bayle, represents an important alternative, namely, the appeal to a universal human morality of mutual respect and of the need to justify actions which restrict the freedom of others accordingly, while simultaneously pointing to the unavoidability and legitimacy of religious controversy, so that controversial doctrines cannot provide justification for restricting liberty.

§10 *Cuius regio, eius religio*: toleration as modus vivendi and as an instrument of social discipline

1. The analysis of the discourse concerning toleration in the Reformation era and the attendant conflicts would remain incomplete were we to overlook the realities of political toleration, as reflected in particular in the Religious Peace of Augsburg of 1555. Rather than offering an exhaustive treatment of these complex historical processes,[105] my main concern here will be to

102. Calvin, *Declaratio orthodoxae fidei*, quoted in Lecler, *Toleration and the Reformation*, vol. I, 333.
103. Castellio, *Contra libellum Calvini*, quoted in Wilbur's translation, *A History of Unitarianism*, 203.
104. A further interesting example of such a line of argument is Jacobus Acontius' work *Stratagemata Satanae* (1565). By tracing faith back to a few central fundamental truths accessible to reason – destined to prevail in the free conflict of opinions – he believes that, combined with a Christian morality of brotherly love, he can combat the activity of the Devil who sows the seeds of religious strife and hatred everywhere.
105. Compare the accounts of Heckel, *Deutschland im konfessionellen Zeitalter*, and Schulze, *Deutsche Geschichte im 16. Jahrhundert*, esp. ch. 2.

examine a particular constellation of toleration which exhibits an instructive combination of the coexistence and permission conceptions of toleration. In addition, a further aspect of the rationalisation of political power in the era of confessionalisation will become apparent here, namely the strengthening of political authority through various policies of internal and external toleration and intolerance.

The spread of the Lutheran doctrine went hand-in-hand with the formation of regional churches, which were directly subject to the sovereign princes according to the *ius reformandi*. The policy of Charles V, the emperor of the 'Holy Roman Empire of the German Nation', sought to counter this development by promoting the 'unity' – *concordia* – of the empire, not only in political but also in religious matters, and by preserving the supremacy of the Catholic faith.[106] In particular, Charles's attempt, in the Edict of Worms of 1521, to impose the imperial ban on Luther and his followers gave rise to conflicts in the Diets of Speyer (1529) and Augsburg (1530). In the latter, the Lutherans' profession of faith as set forth in the 'Augsburg Confession' met with rejection. Following this, the Lutheran Imperial Estates, now called 'Protestants', formed the 'Schmalkaldic League', which marked the beginning of a period of armed conflicts. Once it became clear that no side would be able to achieve a clear or permanent victory, Ferdinand, the brother of Charles (who abdicated in 1556), convened the Imperial Diet in Augsburg in 1555 in which the so-called Religious Peace of Augsburg between the 'old religion' and the 'Augsburg Confession' was concluded. Its central points were the following:

(1) Out of the 'exigency' of the empire and for the sake of peace in view of the 'division in religion', as the text states explicitly, freedom of conscience was to be recognised – but *only* for the Electors, not for their subjects.[107] The right of the sovereign princes to determine the religion within their territories was recognised in accordance with the principle *cuius regio, eius religio*. Hence, the religious-political unity lost by the empire in the process was restored at the level of the individual territories and strengthened the position of the sovereign princes.

(2) The Peace held only between the adherents of the Catholic faith and those of the Lutheran Augsburg Confession. Other denominations (such as the

106. Cf. Schulze, 'Concordia, Discordia, Tolerantia'.
107. Religious Peace of Augsburg (1555), in Ehler and Morrall (eds.), *Church and State through the Centuries*, 164–72.

Calvinists) or groups (such as the Anabaptists) were expressly excluded and could continue to be treated and punished as heretics.

(3) The only option for those subjects who did not want to follow the profession of faith of their sovereign prince was emigration, a possibility – the *beneficium emigrandi* – envisaged by the treaty.

(4) The only exception to the political-religious unity within the territories was the imperial cities with populations of mixed denominations. For them, the modus vivendi, which entailed separation at the level of the empire, was interpreted as prescribing peaceful coexistence inside the city walls.

(5) In order to prevent the secularisation of the ecclesiastical principalities, the 'ecclesiastical reservation' stated that church dignitaries who converted to the new Confession would lose their offices and incomes, and thus their bishoprics.

The conclusion of the Religious Peace made clear how profoundly the religious-political landscape had changed. The empire had become a mosaic of different denominations and the goal of religious harmony was transferred to the individual territories, while the empire was henceforth only a legal-political unity, even though the peace settlement remained committed to the goal of creating a confessional unity.[108] In reality the idea of an ecclesiastical-political unity, the *respublica christiana*, was abandoned in order to bring the armed conflicts to an end. Hence, toleration in the sense of a strategically and pragmatically motivated coexistence conception reigned between the principalities, whereas within the political units only a toleration in accordance with the permission conception was possible (a toleration of difference as long as it remained silent: *haereticus quietus*); here the principle of one faith in one country officially held sway.

The peace compromise was seen by both sides as the lesser evil by comparison with open conflict, and it was assumed to hold merely *ad tempus*, for the time being.[109] Features such as the 'ecclesiastical reservation' favoured the old religion and the demand of the Protestant Imperial Estates for individual freedom of conscience was rejected, so that there can be no question of a genuine 'parity' among the denominations.[110] Nevertheless, the Protestants voted for the peace settlement in the hope not only that it would

---

108. On this, see the detailed account in Heckel, *Staat und Kirche*.
109. Cf. Besier and Schreiner, 'Toleranz', 482; Heckel, *Deutschland im konfessionellen Zeitalter*, 45–63.
110. On this, see Conrad, 'Religionsbann, Toleranz und Parität am Ende des alten Reiches'; Dickmann, 'Das Problem der Gleichberechtigung der Konfessionen im Reich im 16. und 17. Jahrhundert'.

solidify their own position but also that they would thereby create the pre-conditions for a wider expansion.[111] Both sides continued to see themselves as the true representatives of Christianity and were far from granting the other denomination – much less any others[112] – an intrinsic entitlement. The situation of peaceful coexistence and toleration duly turned out to be unstable. The 'ecclesiastical reservation' was attacked by the Protestants and the disputes in the Imperial Diet were marked by the Protestants' attempts to improve their own position vis-à-vis the privileges of the Catholic majority, while the Catholics sought to suppress the Protestant faith in the course of the Counter-Reformation. Finally, the growing strength of Calvinism also played an important role in the German territories.[113] The conflicts became more acute and finally came to a head in the Thirty Years War. Only the Peace of Westphalia of 1648 brought about a legal regulation of the denominations which, although it built upon the Augsburg compromise, nevertheless (a) improved the legal status of tolerated members of different faiths (regarding the *exercitium religionis privatum*), (b) granted the reformed (Calvinist) confession equal status with the Augsburg Confession and (c) provided for an equitable resolution of the ecclesiastical reservation.[114] These represented important steps towards assuring the equal status of the (dominant) denominations while upholding the principle of 'one territory, one faith'.

2. Just as important as the origin and fate of toleration between the territories in accordance with the coexistence conception in the Religious Peace of Augsburg, however, is the structure within the territories. The reverse side of external toleration was internal intolerance, which served to stabilise internal political authority.[115] Religious peace towards the outside went hand-in-hand with internal religious pacification, interconfessional

---

111. Cf. Paulus, 'Religionsfreiheit und Augsburger Religionsfriede'.
112. The contrast to this is offered by Poland during the second half of the sixteenth century, especially under the rule of Stephen Bathory (1576–86), where a whole variety of confessions and sects, e.g. the Unitarian 'Socinians', were tolerated. See Lecler, *Toleration and the Reformation*, vol. 1, 383–423.
113. For this period, see Heckel, *Deutschland im konfessionellen Zeitalter*, 67–127.
114. Cf. Conrad, 'Religionsbann, Toleranz und Parität am Ende des alten Reiches', 164–96; Dickmann, 'Das Problem der Gleichberechtigung der Konfessionen', 243–51; Heckel, *Deutschland im konfessionellen Zeitalter*, 198–207.
115. A historical parallel to this system of tolerance and intolerance is offered by the millet system of the Ottoman Empire, albeit within the framework of a permission conception. The Muslim ruler of the empire granted certain Christian and Jewish communities a limited right of autonomous organisation of their religious and social life, without individual freedom of religion being granted within the millets and without the (bureaucratically governed) millets themselves having a claim to equal rights with the Muslim authority. On this, see Kymlicka, 'Two Models of Pluralism and Tolerance'; Walzer, *On Toleration*, 17–18.

toleration with intraconfessional consolidation. This interrelation between increasing 'confessionalisation' and the strengthening of political authority by combining religion with princely power has been analysed as a process of 'social disciplining'.[116] This describes the comprehensive political-legal regulation of conduct in accordance with confessional guidelines under state and ecclesiastical supervision which developed in both the Catholic and the Lutheran and reformed Imperial Estates. A political-confessional order – extending from the economic domain (of a society increasingly organised in corporations) to the religious domain, from the school system to the organisation of the military, from public administration to family and sexual life – developed which was concerned with integrating the individual as a 'conscientious',[117] 'subjected' subject. Police ordinances, guild ordinances, begging ordinances, hospital ordinances, marriage ordinances, etc., were issued.[118] Here we encounter a form of 'pastoral power' in which traditional theocratic elements intermingle with those of early modern absolutism in the evolving society.[119] An instructive phenomenon in this regard is the increase in witch-hunting during this period, a practice which would continue deep into the seventeenth and even into the eighteenth century. This involved a confluence of different motives, but in general these formal-bureaucratic processes tended to support social disciplining and the consolidation of political authority by combating the 'diabolical' evil in society which emanated from marginal individuals and was an enemy beyond confessional divisions, so that the good, pastoral-political order could prove itself by combating this enemy.[120]

116. This concept was coined by Gerhard Oestreich in his study 'Strukturprobleme des europäischen Absolutismus', though he was more concerned with the formation of absolute rule and transformations in the administration, army and school system and (drawing on Weber) in the economy, and less with processes of confessionalisation. However, elsewhere he emphasises the intermeshing of religious and social disciplining; see Schulze, 'Gerhard Oestreichs Begriff "Sozialdisziplinierung in der frühen Neuzeit"', esp. 279. Analyses of confessionalisation as a procedure of social disciplining in the context of state formation in particular can be found in Reinhard, 'Zwang zur Konfessionalisierung?', and Schilling, 'Die Konfessionalisierung im Reich'. For a comprehensive treatment, see Hsia, *Social Discipline in the Reformation*.

117. The role of the formation of conscience as an 'inner mission' is analysed by Kittsteiner, *Die Entstehung des modernen Gewissens*, esp. Pt C, though it makes (too strong) a distinction between 'inner mission' and 'social disciplining'. On this, see also Tully, 'Governing Conduct'.

118. Oestreich, 'Strukturprobleme des europäischen Absolutismus', 193, speaks of a 'police and ordering state' which was supposed to train the lower social strata in particular to lead a 'disciplined life'. See also van Dülmen, *Entstehung des frühneuzeitlichen Europa*, 360–7.

119. Cf. Foucault, 'Governmentality', on the emergence of reflection on government in the sixteenth century, though again the religious aspects are neglected.

120. On this, see Honegger (ed.), *Die Hexen der Neuzeit*.

However, it is not enough to view internal intolerance alone as the reverse side of inter-territorial toleration and confessionalisation. For policies of *toleration* were also implemented as a further strategy of enhancing power: toleration, too, as we have frequently remarked, can be an effective instrument of power and disciplining. Moreover, here, at the beginning of the modern period, it was the same groups as in medieval society who were exposed to an interplay of toleration and persecution which is integral to a complete picture of their domination (see above §5.3).[121] In the first place, these were once again the Jews.[122] We have already pointed out that they were treated in hostile terms in Erasmus's humanist writings and in Luther and only seldom found advocates like Franck and Castellio.[123] In practice, their toleration was set down in 'Jewish ordinances' enacted by the sovereign prince – whether Catholic or Protestant – whose aim was to differentiate 'Christian freedom' from 'Jewish servitude'[124] and which extended from the particulars of political, economic and religious life to those of private life. The Jewish ordinance of the city of Frankfurt, for example, stipulated that Jews were not allowed on the street on Sunday and that they were not permitted to handle food and vegetables offered for sale to Christians.[125] Furthermore, such ordinances, for instance the Jewish ordinance of Hessen, forbade the erection of any new synagogues, stipulated that Jews should refrain from making religious utterances, laid down with whom and when they could engage in trade and, finally, forbade sexual relations with Christian women on pain of death.[126]

Nevertheless, these Jewish ordinances were also 'toleration ordinances'. They permitted the Jews a strictly regulated social and economic life, for which they had to pay 'protection money' and the price of discrimination and stigmatisation (in many places they had to wear clear signs such as yellow rings, stars or distinctive hats). In return they received a certain, always revocable, protection against attacks and expulsions, which were frequent occurrences. Occasions for such infringements were easily found by drawing upon a traditional palette of Jewish 'crimes', extending from the ritual

---

121. For a survey of these groups see Roeck, *Außenseiter, Randgruppen, Minderheiten*. In addition Scribner, 'Preconditions of Tolerance and Intolerance in Sixteenth-Century Germany'.
122. Cf. Haverkamp (ed.), *Zur Geschichte der Juden im Deutschland des späten Mittelalters und der frühen Neuzeit*; Battenberg, *Das europäische Zeitalter der Juden*, vol. I; Hsia and Lehmann (eds.), *In and Out of the Ghetto*.
123. On this, see Oberman, *Wurzeln des Antisemitismus*, esp. on Reuchlin, Erasmus and Luther.
124. Battenberg, 'Jews in Ecclesiastical Territories', 249, quoting from a Cologne ordinance concerning Jews.
125. Friedrichs, 'Jews in Imperial Cities', 286.   126. Besier and Schreiner, 'Toleranz', 487.

murder of Christian children, through host desecration and well-poisoning, to usury.[127] For protection against such pogroms, the Jews depended on the territorial sovereign and city authorities granting them a restricted and secure social space in which they could live and work. The Jewish ghettos had already developed during the Middle Ages and were maintained in the early modern period or were relocated to the city walls or to villages outside the city. The sovereign princes, in turn, could in this way ensure the loyalty and services of the Jews, of which they could make good use in a developing mercantile society.[128]

This example, which could only be mentioned briefly here, not only shows how the exclusionary tendencies and stigmatising practices of medieval society continued into the early modern period (as is also testified to by other groups, such as 'vagrants', 'lepers' and prostitutes); in addition, it reveals the complex interrelation between inclusion and exclusion, recognition and disrespect, permission and prohibition, toleration and disciplining. The Jews were stigmatised as a separate group and were excluded from society, while at the same time also being partially included (and confined) within it and were 'tolerated' – a form of toleration which is indeed, as Goethe put it, an 'insult'. Here we encounter a form of the permission conception of toleration which employs toleration as a rationalised form of the exercise of power and the 'production' of subjects.

3. To conclude this chapter on humanism and the Reformation with a brief remark, with this the Janus-faced character of toleration typical of the modern discourse comes to the fore. On the one hand, the politics of toleration (in accordance with the permission or the coexistence conception) is an expression of the *rationalisation of power* and the consolidation of political authority vis-à-vis the claim to power of the Church; and whereas it is characteristic of the confessional era that the two sides are intimately interrelated, nevertheless the weights have clearly shifted in favour of the secular authority and the primacy of preserving social peace. On the other hand, this increased the justification pressure on the state toleration policies. An intersubjective conception of toleration emerges – through a kind of *rationalisation of morality* – which leads to far-reaching demands more in accordance with a respect conception, in relation not only to state, but also to

127. On this, see Schöndorf, 'Judenhaß und Toleranz im Spiegel von Flugschriften und Einblattdrucken des 16. Jahrhunderts'; Roeck, *Außenseiter, Randgruppen, Minderheiten*, 24–36; Hsia, 'The Usurious Jew'. Balthasar Hubmaier, who as an Anabaptist later argued for toleration (see above n. 92), played a prominent role as chief prosecutor and agitator in the expulsion of the Jews from Regensburg in 1519.
128. Cf. Ries, 'German Territorial Princes and the Jews'.

interpersonal, civil toleration. In this connection, *three* key lines of argument have emerged: the humanist route of defusing religious strife by appealing to a religious foundation shared by all parties; the reformational route which stresses individual responsibility before God and the inviolability of conscience as 'God's work' in connection with the two-kingdoms doctrine; and, finally, the route which emphasises an overarching morality of reciprocity in the light of irresolvable religious differences among finite rational beings. Although all of these approaches represent important advances towards a 'subjectivisation' of faith and the dissociation from dogmatic, ecclesiastical authorities, they remain situated within Christian-theological terrain. It will become apparent in what follows, however, how they change against this background and in part emancipate themselves from it – though it remains to be seen whether they do so completely, so that they overcome the specific demarcations from non-Christians and non-religious groups.

In view of the emergence of the two major perspectives of toleration – that is, state toleration in accordance with the permission conception and intersubjective toleration informed by the respect conception, notwithstanding the internal differences between these two perspectives – the subsequent discourse of toleration in the modern period is marked by the dynamics and conflicts within, and in particular between, these perspectives, sometimes even within the thought of a single theorist, such as Bodin. The counterpart of the autonomisation of political power, as the emancipation from religious authorities, is an autonomisation of morality. Henceforth these perspectives become differentiated and enter into an antagonistic relation: toleration is situated within the conflict between power and morality.

4

Toleration and sovereignty: political and individual

§11 The primacy of politics over religious truth

1. Sixteenth-century France provides the backdrop for the decisive further development in the discourse of toleration as political thought and action became increasingly independent of religious authorities. This development was triggered by fierce religious wars leading to a secular understanding of the state, whose counterpart was the increasing autonomy of individuals and their revised self-understanding. 'Sovereignty' is the key term in this context, for which in particular the work of Jean Bodin is emblematic at the political level and that of Michel de Montaigne at the level of individual ethics.

Let us first consider the political context. Here we find the continuation of what was highlighted above with reference to Machiavelli's freestanding conception of the political and to the Religious Peace of Augsburg concerning the primacy of political over religious unity. With increasing religious plurality, followed by the Reformation and the ensuing conflicts, the traditional constellation of church and state collapsed and the *political* question of how to uphold the unity of the state and, most importantly, to preserve peace acquired central importance. The state – or, more precisely, the sovereign – understood as an increasingly neutral authority situated above the religious denominations, was proposed as an answer to this question. Thus, out of the crisis of the Wars of Religion there developed a discourse of sovereignty and toleration in which the latter features as the only rational option for securing peace, a discourse in which a 'secular' legitimation of the state, which enjoys sovereign authority above the parties to the religious conflict[1] (even though it remains bound to the dominant religious denomination), took shape. This

1. In his article 'The Rise of the State as a Process of Secularisation', 33–8, Böckenförde represents this, with particular reference to the French development, as the decisive 'second stage of the

idea was first developed by the *politiques*, a heterogeneous group of politically minded lawyers in France during the second half of the sixteenth century, and in particular by Bodin, and it would acquire a distinctive expression in the seventeenth century in the political philosophy of Hobbes. However, we should bear in mind in this context that the legitimation of the supreme status of the sovereign – for example in Bodin, though also still in Hobbes – continued to be justified in religious terms, and the fear of God continued to be seen as the main prop of obedience to the law. Therefore, the modern sovereign state also remained contingent upon a superordinate, transcendent normativity which each side in the ensuing conflict between the Crown and the forces of democracy would claim for itself.[2] This conception of sovereignty and toleration found paradigmatic expression in the Edict of Nantes of 1598, which represented an attempt to permit two religions in a single state. This experiment can be understood on the model of the permission conception of toleration: the Catholic side granted the Protestant side certain liberties on terms which it itself dictated.

However, a historically informed analysis of these developments should relativise the thesis that the sovereign, and in certain respects absolutist, state that emerged from the civil wars as the unrivalled decision-making authority made religious toleration possible at the political level.[3] In the first place, it was solely a matter of toleration in accordance with the permission conception based primarily on strategic considerations which could just as easily become inverted into intolerance under new circumstances, as can be seen from the historical developments during the sixteenth and seventeenth centuries leading up to the revocation of the Edict of Nantes by Louis XIV in 1685. The sovereign ruler can with equal ease grant or revoke toleration for reasons of state;[4] to be more precise, the sovereign who grants

secularisation process' (34) of the state, following the first stage marked by the Investiture Controversy.

2. Thus, it is incorrect to assert that the concept of sovereignty in the modern theory of the state transformed the all-powerful God into the omnipotent lawgiver, as Schmitt claims in *Political Theology* (36); instead there was an attempt to connect the higher-level religious normativity with political sovereignty, though always in opposition to those who saw a contradiction between the two. The concept of sovereignty remained inextricably bound up with the thematisation of its limitations in natural law – and with the justification of the exercise of political power (see below §14).

3. See Schnur, *Die französischen Juristen im konfessionellen Bürgerkrieg des 16. Jahrhunderts*, 9–11, 67, and Koselleck, *Critique and Crisis*, ch. 1, drawing on Schmitt, *The Leviathan in the State Theory of Thomas Hobbes*, chs. 4 and 5. According to Schmitt, however, this also contained the 'seed of death' (*ibid.* 57) of the Leviathan (see below §16.1).

4. Cf. Scheuner, 'Staatsräson und religiöse Einheit des Staates', 394–5; Münkler, *Im Namen des Staates*, 228; Dreitzel, 'Gewissensfreiheit und soziale Ordnung', 6–7.

toleration at a moment of danger can later withdraw it once his position has been strengthened by this measure. When he grants toleration, it must be *wrested* from him because often it represents the second-best solution from his perspective. Thus, the radical theories of resistance based on natural law, such as those developed by the Huguenot monarchomachs, represented the reverse side of the political constellation which rendered toleration opportune primarily as a policy of power geared towards reinforcing political authority and securing peace as opposed to any farther-reaching demands for equal rights – and hence also a second-best solution from the perspective of the minority. Therefore, a more comprehensive analysis of the discourse of toleration reveals the simultaneity and conflictual character of two perspectives, namely the conception of toleration as a permission of the sovereign based on the theory of the state in contrast to an intersubjective, interreligious conception which looks for different, reciprocally justifiable forms of coexistence. On a political interpretation, this second perspective in turn represents a challenge for the first, as will become apparent in particular in the case of the political conflicts in the Netherlands which reveal the possibility of an alternative political conception of toleration. With this a central conflict emerges within the discourse over toleration based on the theory of the state and the problem of toleration shifts into the broad context of the question of political *justice* that goes beyond the solution based on the theory of sovereignty.

2. In order to do justice to the French conflicts over toleration, the year 1560 must be regarded as a watershed between a period in which the monarchy was resolved to impose by any means possible the principle *une foi, une loi, un roi* against Protestantism – that is, against the Calvinist Huguenots (as they were called) – whose strength was nevertheless continually increasing (especially in the south), and the period in which the latter had formed a political party which offered resistance and struggled successfully for the granting of toleration.[5] Under the regimes of Francis I (1520–47) and Henry II (1547–59), the Huguenots were persecuted as heretics in order to preserve or restore the absolute unity of the faith. The crisis came to a head in 1559, the year of the death of Henry II, the author of the plan 'to extirpate heresy',[6] when the Huguenots, under the leadership of prominent figures from among the nobility, switched to a strategy of counter-attack. Catherine de Medici, the mother of the new king Francis II, who was still under age, took control

---

5. On the historical context and the history of ideas, see especially Lecler, *Tolerance and the Reformation*, vol. II, part 6, and Bermbach, 'Widerstandsrecht, Souveränität, Kirche und Staat'.
6. See Lecler, *Toleration and the Reformation*, vol. II, 30.

of the government following his death in the same year and initiated the 'merciful' Edict of Amboise (March 1560) which was supposed to put an end to the violent persecution of the Huguenots provided that they 'would be good enough to live henceforth as good Catholics'.[7] At the same time the historic plan was formed to convene a national council to remove the sources of conflict between the denominations, at which point the attempts to restore political and religious unity began to drift apart.

In the same year the new chancellor, Michel de L'Hôpital, took office. Although in his address to the Estates-General in December 1560 he expressed his unequivocal support of the principle 'one faith, one law, one king', he referred the efforts to achieve religious unity to a 'holy council' (*sainct concile*) which would 'confer a good order' (*donner quelque bon ordre*), as this was understood by the Catholic Church.[8] And however much he insists that the duty of the true believer is to guide the errant back onto the correct path, he nevertheless employs the classical argument of the non-coercibility of conscience and non-violent conversion in his political justification of toleration in addition to the humanist argument of the deeper underlying unity of all Christians – 'luthériens, huguenots, papistes: ne changeons le nom de chrestien'.[9] Yet he immediately adds the pragmatic argument that violence merely gives rise to opposing violence and revolt, and thus jeopardises the survival of the state and leads to civil war, the greatest of all evils. The Estates-General duly adopted a policy of toleration towards the Huguenots, coupled with a strict prohibition on the propagation of Protestant teaching and on disputes in religious questions.

L'Hôpital's attitude changed when, on the one hand, the religious conflicts became more acute, bringing with them the threat of civil war and hence also of a weakening towards the outside and, on the other, the planned attempt at religious reconciliation, the Colloquium of Poissy in 1561, failed. He now adopted the argument defended in a pamphlet attributed to the Catholic lawyer Étienne Pasquier which appeared in the same year and which for the first time anticipates the position of the party later referred to (pejoratively) as the *politiques*.[10] The author is in no doubt that one true religion exists, but asserts that this is a matter for the Judgement Seat of God. It is not God's will to impose the truth by force here on earth. At the political

7. *Ibid.* 41.

8. L'Hôpital, [Speech to the Estates-General of Orléans (13 December 1560)], 399.

9. *Ibid.* 402: 'Lutherans, Huguenots, Papists – let us not abandon the single name "Christian".'

10. The title of the work is *Exhortation aux Princes et Seigneurs du Conseil privé du Roy, pour obvier aux seditions qui semblent nous menacer pour le fait de la Religion*, in Pasquier, *Écrits politiques*, 35–90.

level, it follows that it is legitimate to grant toleration; but the author goes even further in arguing that at this level the acceptance of two churches in one state represents the only way of achieving peace. Anything else would be self-destructive; it must be recognised

> that we could not ruin the Protestants without bringing about our own ruin, given their number and quantity. Just as when some member of the human body is rotten it must be amputated promptly before it causes greater harm; but to wish to amputate it when the infection has spread to some of our more noble parts is, in good French, to kill and destroy the part which has not yet been infected in trying to amputate the infected part.[11]

In his address to parliament in January 1562, L'Hôpital adopts this image of the body in conflict with itself and the position of the 'politicians' who want to preserve or create political unity and peace within the state at the cost of a religious split. This group of (predominantly Catholic) lawyers would unite into a party only in the 1570s,[12] but its mode of argumentation is already prefigured here. Given that civil war is the greatest political evil of all, peace must be secured by the monarch standing as far as possible above the various denominations – not in the sense that he does not belong to any denomination, but that he does not feature as a party to religious conflicts. Therefore, to employ force against the Protestant confession would be to wage war against a part of his own body. Here L'Hôpital makes a distinction between *constituenda religione* and *constituenda republica*, between religious affairs and affairs of state: political rule and the existence of the nation as a political unit become problems in their own right, and their destiny – insofar as this concerns the temporal realm – has priority over religious truth. Taking this distinction as his point of departure, L'Hôpital highlights a difference between the citizen as a subject of rights, and thus as a legal person, and the citizen as a member of a confession or a religion, an ethical-religious person as it were, and he concludes that even someone who has been excommunicated does not forfeit his civil rights.[13] In this way, shared membership in

---

11. *Ibid.* 51: 'que nous ne sçaurions ruiner les Protestans sans nostre generale ruine, veu leur grand nombre et quantité. Tout ainsi comme au corps humain, lors que quelque membre est pourry, il le fault desmembrer de bonne heure avant qu'il ayt jetté son mal plus hault; mais quand il a penetré jusques aux parties nobles de nous, de le vouloir couper, c'est, en bon langage François, en cuidant oster la partie istiomenee, tuer et amortir celle qui n'estoit encores offensee.'
12. See especially Schnur, *Die französischen Juristen im konfessionellen Bürgerkrieg des 16. Jahrhunderts*.
13. L'Hôpital, 'Speech to the Assembly of Parliamentary Delegates in Saint-Germain, January 3, 1562', 452–3.

the national political body acquires a new independence from the religious community, even though shared Christianity remains the basis of political membership.[14]

In practice, of course, this did not mean that the observance of the Protestant religion was granted freedom as a civil right. The 'January Edict' of 1562 only permitted the Huguenots to hold religious services outside of the cities, although this went much further than earlier regulations. However, the violent conflicts between the confessions continued, and in the same year there began a succession of wars which were merely interrupted by precarious peace agreements and permissive edicts. The date of the 'St Bartholomew's Day massacre' on 24 August 1572 marked the most extreme outbreak of violence. Abandoning a strategic policy of toleration, Catherine de Medici used the wedding of her daughter with the Protestant Henry of Navarre as an opportunity to have the leaders of the Huguenots murdered, which led to a bloodbath with 3,000 Huguenots slain in Paris and 20,000 in the provinces. There followed a further series of armed conflicts and temporary compromises, where the latter were supported in particular by the *politiques*, who managed to impose their view under Henry III in 1576 with the Edict of Beaulieu which accorded the Protestants freedom of worship in all cities outside Paris.

3. In the same year Jean Bodin's *Six livres de la République*, a paradigmatic work for the thought of the *politiques*, appeared in which the new doctrine of political sovereignty is formulated. In the preface Bodin writes that he understands his book as a contribution to overcoming the 'raging storm' which is shaking the French 'ship of state', and he goes to considerable lengths to set his doctrine of sovereignty apart from that of Machiavelli. The latter's name had become a term of abuse which was also used against the *politiques*, who were accused of instrumentalising religion for political purposes, a charge which this group turned back against those who claimed power under the banner of religion.

Bodin's treatment of toleration is completely informed by the standpoint of the theory of the state, that is, by the question of how sovereignty, 'the absolute and perpetual power vested in a commonwealth',[15] can be maintained under the conditions of 'internal disorder' which call for

14. The distinction (discussed by Franck and Castellio) between the person as 'Christian' and as 'human being', which points to an even deeper commonality among human beings, also features in L'Hôpital. Cf. Schnur, *Die französischen Juristen im konfessionellen Bürgerkrieg des 16. Jahrhunderts*, 20.
15. Bodin, *The Six Books of a Commonwealth*, Book I, ch. 8, 1.

intervention. Bodin starts from the premises that 'factions and parties' of all kinds constitute a danger for the state against which it must defend itself[16] and that religion is 'the force that at once secures the authority of kings and governors, the execution of the laws',[17] which precludes toleration towards atheists. He goes on to argue that the sovereign, who for Bodin is God's representative on earth,[18] must prevent doubt being cast on the established state religion. In support of this he cites a reason bound up with the essence of religion: since the latter rests on a belief which cannot be proven with certainty, it is both futile and dangerous to question it and to call for rational arguments and evidence.[19] In order to avert this danger, he regards banning new religious orientations which sow seeds of doubt and the legal prohibition of discussions of religion as justified.[20]

The case is different if several religious orientations have already achieved a foothold within a state. In that case the sovereign should not use force to convert the subjects to the true faith. Indulgence alone represents a possible path to conversion. Finally, Bodin stresses the idea, which was central to the political context of his time, that in such situations the sovereign must try to maintain a position of power above the parties in order to be able to resolve conflicts; at any rate he must avoid becoming involved in a conflict whose outcome is uncertain.

Hence, Bodin's argument for toleration from the theory of the state combines considerations of different kinds; the decisive point, however, is the pragmatic political calculation in which religion becomes an object of prudent action rather than a factor determining policy. Following this logic, in the same year he supported toleration of the Huguenots as a deputy to the Estates-General.

4. The year 1576 also marked the foundation of the 'Catholic League', which conducted a fierce campaign against the Huguenots with the support of Spain. The conflict was aggravated by the fact that, on the death of the brother of Henry III in 1584, the Protestant Henry of Navarre became the heir to the throne according to the *loi salique*. In 1585 the League imposed an edict which forced the Huguenots to choose between conversion and exile, again resulting in years of military conflicts. In 1589 Henry III was murdered and Henry of Navarre was crowned King Henry IV. Given the persistent opposition, including that of the pope, who issued a deposition

16. *Ibid.* IV, 7, 138.   17. *Ibid.* 141.   18. *Ibid.* I, 10, 40.   19. I will return to this in §12.
20. Cf. Bodin, *Six Books*, vol. III, 7, 105; vol. IV, 7, 140. A marginal note in the Latin version of *Six livres* from 1586 is especially clear on this point: 'It is dangerous to discuss religion.' On the politics of non-discussion, see also Holmes, 'Jean Bodin'.

proclamation in 1591, Henry renounced the Protestant faith and converted to Catholicism in 1593.

Finally, in 1598 Henry IV proclaimed the Edict of Nantes, which granted the Huguenots freedom of conscience and limited freedom of worship and which, even in its terminology, is a classical document of the permission conception of toleration. Thus, it states:

> [N]ot to leave any occasion of trouble and difference among our Subjects, we have permitted and do permit to those of the Reformed Religion, to live and dwell in all the Cities and places of this our Kingdom and Countreys under our obedience, without being inquired after, vexed, molested, or compelled to do any thing in Religion, contrary to their Conscience, nor by reason of the same be searched after in houses or places where they live.[21]

Freedom of worship was granted in certain places subject to strict regulations, while the exercise of the reformed religion continued to be prohibited in Paris and within a radius of five miles around the capital. Where religious services were permitted, however, churches could also be built; Huguenots could assume public office, they could found schools and universities, and they were granted – though only in an appendix to the ninety-five primary and fifty-six secondary articles – 'secure places' with fortified garrisons. In many respects, therefore, this marked the end of the persecution of the Huguenots, though not of their status as a merely 'tolerated' minority religion. Although the king who now confronted them was willing to grant them recognition in this position, he nevertheless stipulated the dominant position of the Catholic Church in many details and made it his goal to contain and 'depoliticise' Protestantism, since the existing Huguenot political organisations were dissolved.[22]

The Edict exhibits characteristic features of a permission conception. It is motivated by pragmatic and strategic considerations and it aims to promote internal peace in order to safeguard the political authority of the sovereign and the dominant position of the majority religion. At the same time it includes measures to protect the position of the minority, which as a result continues to depend on the goodwill of the political authority and is forced to exercise discipline in its own interest. Thus, here too the result is a complex relation between permission and constraint, between toleration

---

21. The Edict of Nantes 1598, in Lindberg (ed.), *The European Reformations Sourcebook*, 306.
22. Compare the analysis of the Edict in Hinrichs, *Fürstenlehre und politisches Handeln im Frankreich Heinrichs IV*, 258–9 and 299–308.

and domination, which, exactly as the *politiques* anticipated, led to a strengthening of sovereign power and to a reduction in conflicts. However, the subsequent development during the seventeenth century up to the revocation of the Edict in 1685, by which time it had long since been reduced to an empty shell, shows that the sovereign power by no means continues to uphold the toleration granted in a particular situation under changed circumstances. Thus, toleration in accordance with the permission conception not only remains unstable and susceptible to revocation, but also represents a particular form of the rational exercise of power, a particular practice of imposing discipline through restrictions on freedom. In this sense, Goethe's dictum that a toleration of this kind represents an 'insult' remains valid – which is not to imply that in certain situations it may not represent an important advance over violent intolerance.

§12 Truth in discourse: plurality and harmony without unity

1. The importance of the late sixteenth-century French context is not confined to a new perspective and practice of toleration based on the theory of the state which drew a specific lesson from the religious civil war. New answers also emerged in the other dimension of the discourse on toleration, at the intersubjective or horizontal level on which human beings as citizens and believers – two roles which, as we have seen, were increasingly separated – must ask themselves on what basis they can live with adherents of a different religion. Two documents which testify to the disillusionment at the failure of the hopes of religious reconciliation are important in this regard, namely Jean Bodin's *Colloquium heptaplomeres* and the *Essais* of Michel de Montaigne (see below §13) in which the problem of toleration was formulated against the background of a new conception of subjectivity that went beyond traditional ties and conceptions.

   Whereas in the *Six livres*, which is completely indebted to the perspective of the theory of the state, Bodin arrived at a conception of toleration dominated by the imperative of upholding sovereignty, in the *Colloquium heptaplomeres de rerum sublimium arcanis abditis* – which circulated in manuscript form after its presumed completion in 1588 and was published in its entirety only in 1857[23] – he changes his perspective. The main issue is no longer how

---

23. Here it should be noted that it is controversial whether Bodin should be regarded as the author of the *Colloquium*. On this, see Faltenbacher, *Das Colloquium Heptaplomeres* and (ed.), *Magie,*

'the state' – that is, the sovereign ruler – should deal with religious difference, but how individuals, as reflecting religious subjects, should respond
to the plurality of religions and to what extent they must examine their
own convictions. Here Bodin arrives at an incomparably more radical and
more comprehensive conception of toleration than in his theory of the state,
although they share a specific conception of the essence of religion. Only
both works taken together, that on the *one-sided* toleration of the state and
that on the *mutual* toleration of individuals, constitute Bodin's doctrine of
toleration – and reveal the tensions between a conception of toleration based
on a theory of sovereignty and a conception geared towards intersubjective
reciprocity. Bodin's work is an early, very clear example of the cleavage
between two distinct perspectives in political philosophy in general, and in
the discourse over toleration in particular; others (for example Montesquieu
and Rousseau) would follow.

In the *Colloquium*, Bodin takes up the traditional form of the religious
conversation, as this was found in Abelard, Llull and Nicholas of Cusa (see
above §6), while simultaneously breaking radically with this tradition. As
with these predecessors, the conversation takes place in a neutral location
in which the representatives of different religions meet. In Bodin, however,
it is the house of a liberal-minded Catholic, Paulus Coronaeus, in Venice, a
city in which many religions coexisted, and no longer a space of unspoilt,
philosophical nature as in Llull, let alone the 'heaven of reason' of Nicholas
of Cusa. Already in Abelard, Llull and Nicholas the conversations were no
longer merely intended to impose the truth with the interlocutors playing the
role of mouthpieces who facilitate the victory of certain positions; rather they
sought to promote a certain kind of discursive ascertainment of the truth.
Notwithstanding their differences, however, in all of them the Christian
religion proved in different ways – through ethical reflection in Abelard,
through the *ars inveniendi veritatem* in Llull, through the *concordantia* in central
issues of faith in Nicholas – to be superior before the judgement seat of
reason. In spite of the clauses about religious toleration, they left no doubt
that proving this was their goal. The assumption was that the truth had to
be discursively demonstrable and that it had to point the way to religious
unity in spite of difference and plurality. It was this goal which Bodin tried

Religion und Wissenschaft im Colloquium heptaplomeres, and the contrasting view of Häfner (ed.),
Bodinus Polymeres. Without being able to address historical questions in greater detail here, in
what follows I accept the dominant view that a comparison of the conversation on religion with
Bodin's other works supports his authorship, and that the important differences are (in part) a
result of, and throw an important light on, the nature of the subject matter.

to show to be no longer tenable. The presuppositions which continued to be shared by all, he argued, no longer enabled one faith to emerge as superior to all others; given the comprehensive and profound nature of the theological differences, the kind of reconciliation envisaged by Christian humanism was no longer viable.[24] The time for conceptualising toleration in *this* way was past. The point of Bodin's religious conversation, therefore, was different, namely to demonstrate the *futility* of such conversations, to show that hope for reconciliation *and* the controversy over the true religion were equally futile. This is the important message that the *Colloquium* conveys about toleration.[25]

In the house of the Catholic Coronaeus, representatives of the most diverse religions and confessions from different countries have come together: the Lutheran Fridericus Podamicus, the Calvinist Antonius Curtius, the Jew Salomon Barcassius, the Muslim convert Octavius Fagnola, the syncretist (and occasionally sceptical) Hieronymus Senamus and the representative of the idea of a natural religion Diego Toralba. In the *Colloquium*, Bodin describes how these seven learned men succeed in the first three books in conducting an open discussion, in spite of religious differences over questions of ethics, natural philosophy and metaphysics; in the remaining three books, by contrast, the situation changes once the host, after reaching the point at which religious conflicts could no longer be denied, raises the prior question of whether it is 'seemly' or 'permissible' for a 'good man' to discuss religion at all.[26] This question plays the leading role in the discussions which follow, and is ultimately answered in the negative.

The fourth book opens with an issue which also played an important role in other writings of Bodin and points forward to the end of the sixth book, that of harmony in and through opposites. As in the sixth book of the *Six livres*, where Bodin already elucidates his idea of 'harmonious justice' in a state centred around the sovereign,[27] in the *Colloquium* he also employs

---

24. An example from the French context is the irenist Guillaume Postel, who tried to show in *De orbis terrae concordia* (1544) that a universal religious harmony based on a reduced Christianity was possible. On this, see Lecler, *Toleration and the Reformation*, vol. II, 32–9.
25. Cf. Roellenbleck, 'Der Schluß des "Heptaplomeres" und die Begründung der Toleranz bei Bodin'.
26. '[W]e must consider the question that was presented yesterday: namely is it proper for a good man to discuss religion'; Bodin, *Colloquium of the Seven*, 163 (the page numbers in the text refer to this translation).
27. Bodin, *Six Books*, vol. IV, 6: 'Just as conflicting voices and tones combine into a smooth, natural harmony, so, too, vices and virtues, which are in essence different elements, contrary motions, sympathies and antipathies, can be connected with each other by an indissoluble linking element lying midway between the extremes, giving rise to the harmony of this world and its parts' (this passage does not appear in the abridged English translation).

the theory of musical harmony to represent the plurality and diversity of religions as *concordia discors*, as a harmony among *irreducible opposites*.[28]

It would be a mistake to regard this 'theory of musical harmonies' as a kind of humanist argument for religious unity which asserts that reciprocal toleration is based on the fact that each position is justified as a 'part' of the inclusive divine and cosmic truth, and hence must be recognised, and even valued, as such.[29] For this harmony is *not* apparent to the individuals, but only from a divine perspective which is not that of the believers with their finite cognitive faculties. They are convinced that their *particular* faith is the true one, and hence that it is *not* particular; however, they recognise that the others have different religious convictions which are not patently irrational or immoral either, and hence that they have reached the limits of mutual understanding and of their persuasive abilities.

The path leading the participants to this insight is long and arduous. First they traverse the pro and contra of some classical arguments for toleration, specifically at the religious level and the level of the theory of the state. Although the latter do not play a dominant role, here, too, it is pointed out that atheism must be avoided at all costs, that the sovereign should not question established religions, that religious plurality can lead to dissension and conflict, but that this danger diminishes as the number of sects in a given state increases because they neutralise one another. The example of the Ottoman Empire is cited as proof of the possibility of tolerating a plurality of religions (151–3). More important than these considerations, which are often not pursued to their conclusion, are those situated at the level of intersubjective, interreligious toleration. The argument for freedom of conscience, together with that about the erroneous conscience, proposed by Octavius is criticised on the grounds that it does not make sense to regard all convictions or actions which spring from conscience as good (157–8). Moreover, Toralba's humanist argument that one should be content with a stripped down natural religion is rejected by appeal to the importance of rites and ceremonies, which cannot be dismissed as mere *adiaphora* (225–7), as is Senamus's attempt to embrace all religions as parts of the truth. To this Salomon responds: 'I would prefer that you were hot or cold rather than lukewarm in religion, Senamus' (465). This places in question justifications of toleration which are of central importance for humanism and for the Reformation. On what can toleration be founded instead?

---

28. See Kuntz, 'The Concept of Toleration in the Colloquium Heptaplomeres of Jean Bodin'.
29. Remer, however, defends this view in *Humanism and the Rhetoric of Toleration*, 223.

The key to this resides in the specific conception of the essence of religion itself which Bodin presents in response to Coronaeus's reiterated question of whether it is permissible and good to discuss religion at all (163). Both Toralba and Salomon, though also Fridericus and Curtius, answer this question in the negative. One reason is that the 'common' people, the mass (*vulgus*), do not understand such complicated matters, so that discussions of this kind foster doubt and discord rather than progress in faith.

Senamus goes so far as to assert that, even when a new faith is better or closer to the truth than the old, the former should not be introduced in order to avoid causing disturbances. According to Fridericus, at most a private discussion among learned men could be appropriate and advantageous (164). However, Toralba and Salomon express even more fundamental reservations concerning why this is problematic. The true reason resides in the essence of religion itself, which is neither a mere opinion (*opinio*) nor founded upon knowledge (*scientia*). Rather, it is entirely a matter of a belief (*fides*) which does not rest on proofs and arguments, and hence it is destroyed by attempts to judge it in accordance with the standards of proofs and secure knowledge (168). Faith is a 'pure assent without proof': *fidem in assensione pura, sine demonstratione* (169); it is acquired and practised in trust in the correct doctrine and it is itself a kind of trust, a 'gift of God' which cannot be demonstrated like a proof and does not lead to certain 'knowledge'. Therefore, if faith rests upon such free assent, Toralba argues, to place it in question using human arguments or by demanding such arguments is an ungodly act; hence one should not engage in discussions about religion (170).

This point is reinforced by Senamus's assertion that in religious disputes there is no neutral judge and there are no impartial witnesses; for at the heart of the dispute is precisely *who* could function as a judge or as a witness in such matters (131). To prove this, Bodin shows how, as the conversation among the seven progresses, all efforts to reach agreement are thwarted and how great are the divergences over questions such as the essence of God, salvation, immortality, fasting, etc., questions which cannot be dismissed as incidental matters. And in all of these disputes, Bodin continues to show that none of the interlocutors is inferior to any of the others. No matter how severe the accusations may be, the interlocutor always has a ready answer and a new challenge. Each is able to make his own position as plausible as possible through explanations or counter-attacks. Nevertheless, a common point emerges in spite of all of the differences: the moral laws laid down in the Decalogue can also be regarded as laws of nature (according to Toralba;

192–3) which are shared by all. And all of the interlocutors agree in rejecting atheism (307–11).

Thus, it is no surprise that, at the end of the final book, the individual professions of faith make the irreconcilable religious differences clear (460–5). In the final chorus intoned by Coronaeus, the aphorism 'Lo, how good and pleasing it is for brothers to live in unity, arranged not in common diatonics or chromatics, but in enharmonics with a certain, more divine modulation' (471) expresses the view that the enharmonic form of coexistence arrived at must be regarded in the light of the differences as good and pleasant, as a 'higher' form of unity – albeit a unity that must renounce the goal of religious reconciliation. And thus the interlocutors agree to regard their differences as – to use an apposite Rawlsian expression, though one foreign to this era[30] – reasonable disagreements, that is, as differences which cannot be overcome through the use of human cognitive faculties to ascertain the ultimate truth, though ones which cannot be attributed to patent irrationality or to the others' errors either (which Bodin makes clear through the high level at which the dispute is conducted and by the fact that the positions are not refuted) and they do not represent a moral mistake (since here there is no disagreement). Hence, they embrace each other in brotherly love and remain obliged to one another, each remaining true to his religion and defending it, though from now on they refrain from any further discussion of religion. They respect one another as human beings with whom they share important things, and on this basis they tolerate one another in the diversity of their beliefs, convinced of the truth of their own and of the falsehood of the others' beliefs. They agree on the limits of agreement.

With this justification of toleration, Bodin develops the approach already expounded by Castellio, which goes beyond both the approach based on the idea of freedom of conscience and the reductionist humanist justification, but without falling back on religious scepticism in the process; the insight into the limits of agreement and demonstration in matters of faith developed by Bodin does not place one's own faith in question.[31] It merely stresses that it is a matter of *faith*. In this way, special emphasis is put on the epistemological component of the conception of toleration, whereas in Castellio it

30. On this, see §33 below. *Note added to the English edition*: At the time I wrote this, I did not know the late Rawls piece 'On My Religion' (published in Rawls, *A Brief Inquiry into the Meaning of Sin and Faith*). But I regard it as an important confirmation of my view that Rawls cites Bodin's *Colloquium of the Seven* and its conception of toleration based on the insights of insurmountable religious pluralism as being of special relevance for his own views.
31. Here, too, I disagree with Skinner, *The Foundations of Modern Political Thought*, vol. II, 248, who attributes a sceptical argument to Bodin and Castellio.

was the normative component. The key innovation for the individual's self-understanding is that, although he continues to regard himself as beholden to a religious truth, he can nevertheless respect others as moral persons or fellow citizens without sharing or esteeming their ethical-religious identity. With this Bodin takes an important step towards a respect conception of mutual toleration which would later also be relevant for approaches within the theory of the state, although Bodin does not draw this conclusion. As we have seen, it is not the insight into the mutuality and equality of the tolerance situation which he transposes to the political level but the anxiety that religious conflict leads to unrest and civil war. In this way, as regards the political perspective, he remains captive to the permission conception as what was politically possible and necessary at the time.[32]

§13 Plurality and particularity of values and of the self or: scepticism and toleration

1. In both form and content, Michel de Montaigne's *Essais* (1580–88) represent a unique document of the evolution of a new form of subjective relation to self at a time of social and political upheaval.[33] Montaigne not only withdrew from his active political life as, among other things, mayor of Bordeaux to his country estate but also withdrew into himself in order to undertake a radical ethical-existential self-questioning. In this way, he sought to gain a foothold which would enable him to become 'a witness of this noteworthy spectacle and seeing our society's death' while in the process preserving 'peace and life's repose' – in other words, an inner sovereignty.[34] His thought involves an interplay between different moments which are central to the problem of toleration: theoretical and practical scepticism, an ethical doctrine of virtue (derived from the Stoics) and a specific conception of the essence of religion and of the state.

In this Montaigne takes his cue from Bodin in several respects, though he radicalises the latter's theories. In Montaigne we also encounter the idea

---

32. This is not the only split in Bodin's thought. For he is also the author of the *Démonomanie des sorciers* of 1580, a wide-ranging treatise justifying the witch trials. It represents entering into a pact with the devil as a disruption of the divine *concordio discors* that must be prevented. Bodin remains a thinker of the sixteenth century, however much his writings point beyond it.

33. Compare Horkheimer, 'Montaigne and the Function of Skepticism'; Starobinski, *Montaigne in Motion*, ch. 1.

34. Montaigne, *Essays*, Book III, ch. 12, 323 (cited in the following according to book, chapter and page number of the English edition).

of a harmony of opposites and of 'different tones' (iii/13, 835), though for him this goes hand-in-hand with decidedly sceptical conclusions about the finitude and limits of human reason. Similar to Bodin, Montaigne stresses the unavoidability of religious disagreement among reasonable persons and thus he disapproves of discussions about the 'true faith'. Yet this does not lead him to adopt a hostile or indifferent stance towards religion either. Rather, based on an even clearer distinction between faith and knowledge than that to be found in the *Colloquium heptaplomeres*, Montaigne sees no inconsistency in affirming the traditional – in his case, Catholic – faith and rejects not only religious strife but also religious innovations. In a final parallel to Bodin, this is connected with the warning, issued against the backdrop of the civil war, against the political consequences of such strife. Obedience to the king and adherence to the established political-religious framework are of paramount importance for Montaigne.

In what follows, I will present a brief account of these aspects of Montaigne's thought. It should be noted in advance, however, that Montaigne's philosophy may be characterised as a *philosophy of ambiguity* in more than one respect, not only because he emphasises the ambiguity of the phenomena and the narrowness of our perspectives on the world, but also because he himself is ambiguous – in part because the individual essays were written at different times – and one can find very different, at times contradictory, statements in his writings, as he says himself (iii/2, 610). Thus, the point cannot be to present an unequivocal interpretation of Montaigne's entire thought but to explore its relevance for the problem of toleration.

Fundamental for this exploration is, in the first place, his perspectivism and his scepticism concerning the possibility of reaching agreements in opinions and judgements. '[T]here were never in the world two opinions alike, any more than two hairs or two grains. The most universal quality is diversity' (ii/37, 598). A human being is incapable of having a single thought or sense experience or of making a single perception or judgement from an objective, neutral perspective; he is always led to one or another standpoint by contingent experiences or by moods and interests. However, not only do these differences exist *between* human beings, according to Montaigne, but we ourselves often alter opinions of which we were nevertheless initially firmly convinced (ii/12, 423). All of this is proof of the finitude of the human mind and its inability to arrive at certain knowledge. Therefore, following the sceptic Pyrrho, Montaigne thinks it appropriate to refrain from all judgements of truth and aspire to a form of ataraxia, a peaceful and sedate condition of life, exempt from the agitations we receive through the impression of the opinion and the knowledge we think we have of things. Whence are born fear, avarice, envy, immoderate desires, ambition, pride, superstition, love of novelty, rebellion, disobedience, obstinacy, and most bodily ills.   (II/12, 372)

The thesis of the perspectival character of knowledge is related to ethics in two ways: first, by the fact that a certain attitude of ataraxia represents an appropriate way of life for the sceptic and, second, by the fact that the multiplicity of opinions and judgements also leads to a multiplicity of values, to ethical pluralism. Montaigne defends the latter in an extremely radical form for his time:

Some say that our good lies in virtue, others in sensual pleasure, others in conforming to nature; one man in knowledge, one in having no pain, one in not letting ourselves be carried away by appearances . . . There is nothing in which the world is so varied as in customs and laws. A given thing is abominable here which brings commendation elsewhere: as in Lacedaemon cleverness in stealing.   (II/12, 435, 437)

Montaigne is so keenly aware of the plurality of values, which count as 'laws of conscience' in the contexts in which they are accepted according to 'custom' (I/23, 83), that he can 'believe in and conceive a thousand contrary ways of life' (I/37, 169). Both at a particular moment and over time, both within individual societies and between societies and eras, a bewildering diversity of ethical convictions exists, according to Montaigne, a fact which leads him to speak of a 'plurality of worlds' (II/12, 390).[35]

Finally, another multiplicity must be borne in mind over and above the multiplicity of opinions and of values, namely the *multiplicity of the self*. The differences between human beings alluded to are also encountered within the subject: 'Never did two men judge alike about the same thing, and it is impossible to find two opinions exactly alike, not only in different men, but in the same man at different times' (III/13, 817). Montaigne heightens this even further into a basic anthropological thesis about the fickleness and inconstancy of human nature; the self for Montaigne is full of contradictions, the soul has many faces (II/1, 243-4), human beings do not live according to any fixed plan: 'We are all patchwork, and so shapeless and diverse in composition that each bit, each moment, plays its own game. And there is as

---

35. See Stierle, 'Montaigne und die Erfahrung der Vielheit', §2.

much difference between us and ourselves as between us and others' (244). With this, the three components of epistemic, ethical and inner-subjective plurality and difference are identified which could serve as the basis for a very far-reaching reflection on toleration. However, they do so only in part because three further countervailing components of Montaigne's philosophy must be considered: the above-mentioned ethical component, a religion-theoretical component and a political component.

First, as regards the ethical component, it is clear that the two ethical implications of Montaigne's doctrine of multiplicity, namely, ataraxia and heeding value pluralism, can be reconciled only if, in spite of the plurality of values, the person who recognises this truth – which does not hold for the general mass of people, according to Montaigne – himself turns it into a virtue, specifically the virtue of restraint in judgement. The latter has two aspects: 'The wise man should withdraw his soul within, out of the crowd, and keep it in freedom and power to judge things freely; but as for externals, he should wholly follow the accepted fashions and norms' (1/23, 86). Therefore, Montaigne's ethics has three dimensions: first, an awareness of the historical and cultural relativity of conceptions of value and forms of life; second, the individual ethical conclusion to strive for an unprejudiced frame of mind and to withhold judgement, though this always remains an aspiration which can never be fully realised (due to the tendency to inner turmoil); and, third, external conformity, refraining from giving external expression to one's scepticism and from opposing the customs and laws. The second dimension points to what might be called a 'disenchanted Stoicism' typical of Montaigne. Bearing in mind the fickleness and inconstancy and the to a considerable extent physically conditioned limits of possible self-restraint, the supreme goal in life is to achieve a state of constancy (1/12, 30) and of *sovereignty*. The latter consists in regarding death dispassionately (1/20), courageously accepting one's own 'nullity' (11/7, 275) and attempting to achieve a kind of freedom from the vicissitudes of life which is self-sufficient, is no longer dependent on social recognition and is in harmony with 'nature' (111/13, 885), as he puts it at the very end of the *Essays*. Here the idea of a higher way of life suggests itself which not only is one among many ethical options but is itself sustained by a higher-level insight into the truth of the plurality of values and of human fallibility and fickleness. This would represent a philosophical mode of life, even though Montaigne qualifies this with frequent allusions to the unattainability of the Stoic ideal of mastery of the self and its bodily sensations under the sole guidance of reason (cf. 11/37, 575; 111/3, 621).

In this way Montaigne overcomes the danger, to which he frequently alludes, of losing one's orientation in the multiplicity of values. However, even more important is the fact that he thereby links reflection on the problem of toleration back to its starting point in the Stoics (see §4.1), that is to the tolerating subject's relation *to himself*, to the sense of inner strength which consists in recognising one's own fallibility and weakness and in transforming it into tolerance, and which as a result also includes tolerance towards oneself.[36] In Montaigne it is both the recognition of one's own fallibility as a finite, bodily and imperfect being[37] and the attempt to perfect oneself through ataraxia as 'immobility of the judgement' (II/12, 435) that lead to toleration. The awareness of internal difference leads to toleration of external difference; one's own particularity and imperfection leads to tolerance of the same thing in others as part of a Pyrrhonian, perfectionist ethics.

But how do things stand with religion? Isn't religion, like the other values and laws of conscience, also merely a matter of habit, so that we must assume a multiplicity of religions and confessions to be tolerated in accordance with the ataraxia of withholding judgement? The answer to this question is to be found in the 'Apology for Raymond Sebond' (II/12), the longest text among the *Essais*, and it proves to be a complex one. For Montaigne leaves no doubt, on the one hand, that the many forms of religion we encounter are historically evolved forms of life which have become habitual through custom (399, 433), and are thus products of the human mind and of contingent circumstances. However, he gives *this* insight into the finitude of the human mind and its products a particular twist, for his scepticism is levelled exclusively against the attempts of human beings to demonstrate the true religion by rational means and to believe they could achieve knowledge of God (a conviction also ultimately held by Sebond, whom Montaigne tries to 'defend' by refuting the doubters who called for further proofs). Faith is just a *faith*, a gift founded on an 'extraordinary infusion' (321), and ultimately on *God's grace*, which is to be accepted without any rational demonstration.

> The knot that should bind our judgment and our will, that should
> clasp and join our soul to our creator, should be a knot taking its twists

36. On this, see Nussbaum's interpretation of Seneca in 'Toleration, Compassion, and Mercy', 37–54, though she associates this with the motive of compassion.
37. Creppell, 'Montaigne', underscores the importance of the awareness of one's own particularity and embodiment for Montaigne's reflection on toleration. For Creppell, however, Montaigne's conception of toleration is based on the conviction of the 'value of particularity', which, if it were true, would cast doubt on whether it should be regarded as a conception of toleration at all rather than as one of esteem for others.

and its strength not from our considerations, our reasons and passions, but from a divine and supernatural clasp, having only one form, one face, and one aspect, which is the authority of God and his grace.   (326)

For Montaigne, the fact that religion is accepted in the manner of custom is no reason to raise the sceptical question of whether it is the 'true' faith, provided that religion is understood as faith. To pose this question in the quest for proofs or evidence is already a form of atheism, a 'proposition as it were unnatural and monstrous' (325). With an acerbity in no way inferior to Luther's in form or content, Montaigne attacks human beings' humanist 'presumption' – as, for example, in Pico – to be 'observers' of the creation, but also the Protestant 'arrogance' of believing that they had a better understanding of God. Faith is understood, following Augustine, as an unfathomable work of God, as a mystery and a sign of his mercy: 'Our faith is not of our own acquiring, it is a pure present of another's liberality. It is not by reasoning or by our understanding that we have received our religion; it is by external authority and command' (369). Thus, the Pyrrhonian sceptics, who question a religion made (or reformed) by human beings *and* the meaningfulness of strife over the true religion, are those best equipped to resist 'superstition and love of novelty' (372), those who suppress knowledge and in the process first open up the necessary space for faith: 'The more we cast ourselves back on God and commit ourselves to him, and renounce ourselves, the better we are' (375). With this mixture of scepticism about knowledge and confidence in faith, or 'Pyrrhonian fideism',[38] Montaigne's thought takes an unexpected turn towards the affirmation of religion. For however much, on the one hand, it undercuts dogmatic disputes about religion, it equally undercuts doubt concerning the established Christian religion as 'coming from the hand of God direct' (383). Although Montaigne's fideism is not so extreme as to preclude rational considerations in support of faith (326), the latter do not provide conclusive reasons either for or against it. The decisive thing is not to want to 'enslave' (389) God to human reason and to recognise that 'our religion . . . as by a common and supernatural inspiration' is also gaining acceptance among pagan peoples; and most important of all is not to presume to cast doubt on the established religion, for that surpasses human intellectual capacities from the beginning:

---

38. In the appropriate expression of Brush, *Montaigne and Bayle*, 109, in contrast to Gessmann, *Montaigne und die Moderne*, 53–6, and Levine, 'Skepticism, Self, and Toleration in Montaigne's Political Thought', who also attribute religious scepticism to Montaigne.

> The first law that God ever gave to man was a law of pure obedience; it
> was a naked and simple commandment about which man had nothing
> to know or discuss; since to obey is the principal function of a
> reasonable soul, recognizing a heavenly superior and benefactor . . .
> The plague of man is the opinion of knowledge.   (359)

Montaigne is accordingly opposed to all innovation in religion (II/12, 429)
and even to the attempts to demonstrate the superiority of a new faith (455):
precisely in virtue of human fallibility and finitude, he argues, the desire to
fathom the 'true faith' is arrogant and blasphemous. Here Montaigne radicalises Bodin's argument for toleration based on 'reasonable disagreement'
into an idea (more reminiscent of the Bodin of the *Six livres*) which contains
the seeds of intolerance. Because the dispute over the true religion is not only
not decidable, but beyond all human capacities, it is *forbidden* to conduct such
a dispute. Thus, he advises the Catholics not to be drawn into theological discussions, and especially not to make compromises: 'We must either submit
completely to the authority of our ecclesiastical government, or do without
it completely' (I/27, 134) – where the latter, in his view, amounts to crass
disobedience. Disputes over religious questions only lead to schisms and
'stir up heresies' (I/56, 233); Montaigne even goes so far as to entertain a
prohibition on writing on religious matters (234) and placing the 'dangerous
blade' of the intellect 'in tutelage' (II/12, 420).

In this way, he extends the Pyrrhonian, perfectionist ethics in important
ways, specifically such that now the external conformism to which the wise
man and sceptic is enjoined is justified not only by the fact that it enables one
to live one's life in peace, but also by the fact that complete scepticism, complete withholding of judgement, cannot be lived out.[39] Faith now provides
an additional reason for not following scepticism in the religious domain:
scepticism does not have any relevance in this domain since it only examines
the constructs of the human intellect. God's doings are purely a matter of
faith, not of *knowledge* or of *doubt*.

On the other hand, this argument also militates against a dogmatic *religious certainty* which is convinced of being in possession of the single true
religion which everyone must recognise on rational grounds. In many places
Montaigne attacks such a form of religious zealotry, whether on the Catholic
or the Protestant side (II/12, 323; III/8, 716); this neutrality, which led him to
esteem Henry of Navarre in particular, whom he knew personally, is likewise

---

39. Schneewind, *The Invention of Autonomy*, 47, calls this test of the practicableness of a morality
    'Montaigne's test'.

part of the ethos of Montaigne.[40] Still, it does not lead him to doubt that the 'best and soundest side' of his time is the one 'which maintains both the old religion and the old government of the country' (II/19, 506).

In conclusion, the final aspect to be considered, i.e. the political, makes this religious argument into one particularly susceptible to intolerance; for now it is political and not religious reasons which speak against religious discussions and innovations – and accordingly political interventions can also be legitimated on these grounds. Against the background of the civil war, whose horrors he frequently cites, Montaigne calls not only for religious obedience from the Catholics but also for unconditional obedience by all citizens towards the king and the established institutions. And since calls for innovations in religion are inseparable from political innovations, it follows that the principle *une foi, une loi, un roi* should not be impugned. Here, too, we encounter a demand for obedience reminiscent of Luther, only that now it is addressed to the Protestants:

> I am disgusted with innovation, in whatever guise, and with reason,
> for I have seen very harmful effects of it . . . Thus, it seems to me, to
> speak frankly, that it takes a lot of self-love and presumption to have
> such esteem for one's own opinions that to establish them one must
> overthrow the public peace and introduce so many inevitable evils, and
> such a horrible corruption of morals, as civil wars and political changes
> bring with them in a matter of such weight – and introduce them into
> one's own country . . . The Christian religion has all the marks of the
> utmost justice and utility, but none more apparent than the precise
> recommendation of obedience to the magistrate and maintenance of
> the government.   (I/23, 86–8)

A form of permission toleration, as envisaged by the Edicts, can serve at best as an expedient to prevent greater evil (90), and it is not even certain whether the strategies of the *politiques* lead to success instead of to greater strife, something confirmed, according to Montaigne, by historical examples (II/20, 510).[41]

Once again, to conclude this analysis of Montaigne, a conception of toleration proves to be highly ambivalent. On the one hand, the *Essais* advance further than any previous theory towards the idea of a fundamental difference between perspectives and evaluations as something unavoidable within the

40. On this, see Schultz, *Die Erfindung der Toleranz.*
41. See also Skinner, *The Foundations of Modern Political Thought*, vol. II, 280–1, on Montaigne's
    critique of the Tolerance Edict of January 1562 and his support of the opposition to it by the
    Parlement of Paris.

context of finite reason. On the other hand, this finitude of knowledge is interpreted in such a way that it highlights not only the pointlessness, but also the illegitimacy and dangerousness, of religious discussions. This can lead not only to the intolerance of believers towards 'innovators' but also to that of the state towards such 'seditious doctrines' – provided that they do not confine themselves to an *exercitium privatum*. In this way, the eminently important distinction between knowledge and faith becomes inverted into potential intolerance.

2. The connection which Montaigne typically makes between a neo-Stoic ethics of individual sovereignty and a theory of political sovereignty which, at the level of the theory of the state, admits toleration as a second-best solution only in accordance with the permission conception can also be found in other important late sixteenth-century authors. Foremost among them is Justus Lipsius, though Guillaume du Vair should also be mentioned. In his work *De la constance* (1594), the latter transposes to the French context a combination of a Stoic ethics of ataraxia, steadfastness in the face of the operations of Fortuna, and a political conservatism that accords priority to obedience towards the established religious-political order. This combination was developed by Lipsius, following Montaigne, in his books *De constantia in publicis malis* (1584) and *Politicorum sive civilis doctrinae libri sex* (1589) against the background of the Dutch civil war and struggle for independence (to which I will return in §14).[42] Although born a Catholic, Lipsius became a professor for rhetoric and history at the Lutheran university in Jena, later at the Calvinist university in Leiden and, finally, at the Catholic university in Louvain, which led him to convert back to Catholicism in 1591. His two books, which circulated much more widely than those of his contemporaries Bodin and Althusius, exerted a profound influence on his European contemporaries. As in Montaigne, his recourse to Stoic ethics is bound up with scepticism concerning human cognitive abilities in science and morality; and he, too, defends obedience to custom and law in religious and political matters for the sake of internal and external peace. Therefore, in *Politicorum* he adopts a clear stance in support of upholding *one* dominant religion as a means of guaranteeing peace, with the result that another religion could be tolerated at most *privatim*. Here we

42. On Lipsius's and du Vair's political neo-Stoicism, see Schnur, *Die französischen Juristen im konfessionellen Bürgerkrieg des 16. Jahrhunderts*; on conservatism in Lipsius, du Vair and Montaigne, see Skinner, *The Foundations of Modern Political Thought*, vol. II, 277–83; on Lipsius's and Montaigne's scepticism, see Tuck, 'Scepticism and Toleration in the Seventeenth Century'; on Lipsius's life, work and influence, see Oestreich's exhaustive study, *Antiker Geist und moderner Staat bei Justus Lipsius (1547–1606)*, and his essay 'Justus Lipsius als Theoretiker des neuzeitlichen Machtstaates'.

encounter an early version of the distinction between public *confessio* and private *fides* to which Hobbes would later attach so much importance. By contrast, insofar as adherents of other religions publicly advocate their faith and thereby provoke the threat of sedition – *publice peccare in religione* – they must be combated with maximum severity: 'There is no place for clemency here. Burn, cut, in order that some member perishes rather than the whole body.'[43] Only when the illness has spread to such an extent that amputation is no longer possible does Lipsius plead for a conditional, pragmatic toleration (as previously did L'Hôpital, who employed the same image).

This is a further illustration of the fact that a sceptical position does *not* automatically lead to a tolerant one, as is often assumed.[44] For scepticism can mutate, for the sake of individual and political peace, not only into a policy of non-discussion but also into a policy of suppression of discussion and dissent as such. This follows from a specific connection with a certain theory of religious belief and political unity, with the result that scepticism does *not* refer to the religious domain, as becomes especially apparent in Montaigne.[45] However, even when scepticism is extended to religion, this is not the *via regia* to toleration, for it can of course lead to intolerance towards all those who are *not* sceptics.

3. Especially Lipsius's call to 'burn' the members of other religions who jeopardise the peace elicited the emphatic objection, leading to a heated controversy, of a figure who defended a conception of toleration that for the first time included atheists, namely Dirck Volckertszoon Coornhert. Although a Catholic, Coornhert embraced an individualistic, spiritualist conception of religious faith profoundly influenced by Sebastian Franck that enabled him to appeal to both sides in the Dutch conflict to exercise tolerance – something which duly earned him the enmity of both.[46] In his conception of toleration, which he presents in his works *Synodus van der Conscientien vryheyt* (1582) and the Lipsius critique *Proces van 't ketter-dooden* (1590), he connects a variety of well-known arguments: freedom of religious belief as a gift from God, doctrinal uncertainty here on earth where no human being should be the judge of the true faith, moral reciprocity and the strict separation between the two kingdoms, which he interprets in a way that already comes close to that of Locke, since Coornhert no longer wants to entrust the state with the task of protecting religion either. At most the state

43. Lipsius, *Politica* IV.3 (393), referring to Cicero.
44. Tuck emphasises this in 'Scepticism and Toleration in the Seventeenth Century'.
45. Tuck overlooks this important aspect.
46. See Lecler, *Toleration and the Reformation*, vol. II, 32–9.

should be given the task of protecting citizens against violence in religious matters.

In his book on the trial of the killing of heretics, composed as a dialogue, Coornhert argues against Lipsius's thesis that only religious unity can guarantee the unity of the state on the grounds that it would mean ignoring the question of the true religion entirely and granting the state the right to impose a 'false freedom' (*valsche vrede*)[47] on the citizens. On this view, it would also have been justified to suppress the rise of Christianity. Here it becomes apparent that Coornhert turns the argument of religious truth against Lipsius, while at the same time reserving for God (but not the state) the right to judge the truth by appeal to human finitude, a non-sceptical argument for toleration which nevertheless incorporates scepticism to some extent.

It will not be possible to discuss this and the ensuing controversy further here. However, it should be stressed that Coornhert was the first to extend toleration to atheists as well, specifically employing the same argument concerning faith as a sign of God's grace as employed by Montaigne and Luther following Augustine. Coornhert makes the point that an atheist should be regarded as someone who has not yet received this gift from God and that it cannot be a task for human beings to remedy this or to punish the godless person who has not yet received divine illumination for following his conscience.[48] This, for its time, unusually courageous argument shows how a moral impulse can lead to a radical reinterpretation of traditional articles of faith.

§14 Resistance and toleration

1. The controversy between Lipsius and Coornhert is not the only reason for examining the religious conflicts in the Netherlands. For the rebellion of the Dutch provinces against Spanish domination revealed a connection between the issue of religious toleration and the legitimacy of political resistance which extended the political discourse over toleration in important respects. Here, too, we encounter for the first time a modern individual justification of toleration founded on natural law, and the possibility of a connection between vertical, state-based reflection and horizontal, intersubjective reflection on toleration becomes apparent. Together, these perspectives clearly mark the transition to the seventeenth-century discourse concerning toleration.

47. Coornhert, *Proces van 't ketter-dooden ende dwangh der conscientien* (Trial of the Killing of Heretics), 252.
48. 'Zijnse heel ongheloovigh, soo en heeft heur Godt des gheloofs gave noch niet gegheven'. Coornhert, *Proces van 't ketter-dooden*, §533.

In the sixteenth century, the seventeen Dutch provinces were under a foreign rule as a part of the Spanish branch of Charles V's empire. Based on a kind of 'Magna Charta' (the *Blijde Inkomst* of Brabant), this regime accorded the provinces a status of relative political and economic autonomy and the parliaments of the estates political consultation rights, which repeatedly led to conflicts between the king or his governors and the representatives of the provinces. At the same time, Protestantism, and increasingly Calvinism, was spreading in the northern provinces, particularly in Holland and Zeeland. Following his accession to the Spanish throne in 1555, Philip II attempted to put a stop to this and to suppress heresy through the Inquisition.[49] This provoked not only fierce opposition on the part of the Calvinists, which discharged in the iconoclastic riots of 1566, but also on the part of the moderate Catholic representatives of the aristocracy such as William of Orange (who would later convert to Calvinism). Their primary concern was to defend the liberties and the unity of the Dutch provinces, if necessary at the cost of tolerating the other denomination (though not the Anabaptists, who were persecuted by both sides as religious and social radicals). Economic arguments played an important role in this context, as can be seen from William's memorandum of 1566 in which he supports a religious settlement as a means of preserving peace, national unity and economic development. Religious violence, he argued, not only was fruitless but drove foreign and native businessmen out of the Dutch 'market of all Christianity'[50] and in the end led only to revolt and to the ruin of the country.

Philip II responded by rejecting this proposal in its entirety; on his instructions, the Duke of Alba instituted a military dictatorship between 1567 and 1573 which was aimed at eliminating religious difference and political rebellion – and it achieved the exact opposite. William of Orange became the leader of the revolt against foreign domination by Spain, and in the 'Pacification of Gent' (1576) the Estates-General agreed in a peace treaty between the warring provinces to support one another in the battle against the Spanish troops, but without challenging the sovereignty of the king. Freedom of conscience was to be universally recognised, though the Protestants were granted freedom of worship only in the provinces of Holland and Zeeland.

49. On the Dutch political-religious context at this time in general see Saage, *Herrschaft, Toleranz, Widerstand*, Part I, and Lecler, *Toleration and the Reformation*, vol. II, part 7.
50. Von Oranien, 'Denkschrift über den kritischen Zustand der Niederlande und über die Maßnahmen zu seiner Verbesserung [Memorandum on the Critical State of the Netherlands and on the Measures Necessary for its Improvement]', 127. Hassinger underlines the particular importance of economic arguments for toleration in the Dutch context in 'Wirtschaftliche Motive und Argumente für religiöse Duldsamkeit im 16. und 17. Jahrhundert'.

This agreement formed the basis of the more wide-ranging 'Religionsfrid' of 1578 whose central article was a reciprocal agreement among the provinces to grant freedom of conscience *and* worship to Catholics and Calvinists in all of the provinces. In William of Orange's view, only such a horizontal toleration between the denominations, modelled on the coexistence conception, could generate the necessary support to achieve national independence – hence a form of mutual toleration directed *against* foreign domination (and also against Catholic and Calvinist radicals in their respective provinces). In this way, Calvinist monarchomachs like Duplessis-Mornay associated the issue of toleration intimately with resistance. In a defence of the 'Religionsfrid', he pointed out the need for *reciprocal* toleration: one must also grant the freedom one claims for oneself to the other side.[51] Finally, an anonymous pamphlet of 1579[52] brought together the most important arguments for religious peace (from the perspective of the Calvinists): the importance of toleration for achieving or defending political autonomy, the inseparability of freedom of conscience and freedom of observance, the resulting separation between Church and State with their distinct tasks of securing eternal salvation as opposed to securing public peace and – a key innovation – the defence of religious freedom as an *individual natural right*:

> Liberty of conscience consists of two parts, *viz.*, the inward and outward cultivation of God: the inward concerns the heart, the outward consists of worship and also has two parts, *viz.*, the vocal confession of faith and the exercise of ceremonies ... The main benefit given to us by the recovery of liberty is that everyone may satisfy his conscience, practise religion freely and serve God as he thinks he should. This liberty belongs to us according to natural right. And nobody may deprive us of it, nor forcibly convert us to a different religion than that which our conscience prescribes to us. If he nevertheless attempts to do so, he is a tyrant and we need not obey him.[53]

Here, for the first time in the history of toleration, freedom of conscience is demanded as an individual *basic right*, an argument which points forward to the seventeenth-century, natural law-based discourse concerning toleration, which found its paradigmatic expression in Locke in particular – a parallel

---

51. Duplessis-Mornay, 'Discours sur la permission de liberté de religion dicte Religionsvrede au Pais-Bas' (1578), quoted in Lecler, *Toleration and the Reformation*, vol. II, 214–15.
52. 'Discours contenant le vray entendement de la pacification de Gand', quoted in Lecler, *Toleration and the Reformation*, vol. II, 215–18.
53. *Ibid.* (quoted from De Roover, *A Kingdom of Another World*, 174).

also relevant as regards the question of legitimate resistance stressed by the author of the pamphlet. This also holds for Duplessis-Mornay who supported the religious peace and is regarded (along with Hubert Languet) as the author of the central work of the monarchomachs, *Vindiciae contra tyrannos* of 1579, which appeared under the pseudonym Stephanus Junius Brutus. Combining arguments based on traditional feudal law with arguments based on modern natural law, it offers a comprehensive justification of the right of resistance of the 'people' – though the latter is still conceived in traditional terms as an organic unity represented by the estates – against the king, who becomes a tyrant not only by breaking the covenant (*foedus*) with God to follow the divine laws, but also the contract (*pactum*) with the people to promote its welfare. On this conception, kings are appointed by the people; the people who are 'free by nature'[54] have agreed to obey him only in return for certain benefits, in particular the protection of property.

Therefore, the monarchomachs appealed to different principles to justify resistance against the king: his responsibility before God, traditional contracts and ancestral 'liberties' of the provinces and the estates and the natural right of individuals prior to the relationship between ruler and subjects.[55] In this way, the resistance also had a 'conservative' component – the return to the old liberties – and it could be exercised only by the legitimate representatives of the people and not in a 'disorderly' fashion. However, individual political units could also exercise legitimate resistance, and not only the majority of the highest officeholders, as in Calvin. Finally, this doctrine of resistance, which transformed a religious justification into a political justification based on natural law, provided the legitimation for the secession of the northern provinces in the 'Union of Utrecht' (1579) after the breakdown of the religious peace and the decision of southern provinces to submit to Spanish rule in the 'Union of Arras'. In 1581, the 'United Provinces' of the north declared their independence from Spanish 'tyranny' (but only achieved recognition as a republic in 1640 following protracted conflicts). This sealed the division of the Netherlands. Different toleration regimes developed within the different provinces; whereas the Catholic side was unwilling to accept the validity of the argument for freedom of conscience, the northern provinces were committed to rejecting religious persecution.

The split put an end to the brief period during which reciprocal toleration (albeit based on the coexistence conception) combined with resistance

---

54. Brutus, *Vindiciae contra tyrannos*, 92.
55. On this, see Saage, *Herrschaft, Toleranz, Widerstand*, ch. 1; Skinner, *The Foundations of Modern Political Thought*, vol. II, part 3, esp. ch. 9.

against an unjust and intolerant government, a form of toleration which first emerged at the *social* level and later developed into a demand for *political justice*.[56] This possibility of linking horizontal with vertical toleration, as well as the contractualist justification based on natural law and the argument that freedom of conscience and freedom of worship go hand-in-hand, though also economic perspectives, were destined to play an important role, especially in seventeenth-century England. The important point is that this approach draws attention to a conflict within the perspective of toleration founded on the theory of the state. At the political level, an individualistic, natural law-based argument comes into conflict with the formerly dominant permission conception which adheres to the new concept of sovereignty, thereby underlining what was already intimated by Marsilius of Padua, namely, the intrusion of demands for justification into the political domain, which represented the reverse side of political 'rationalisation'.

2. In this way, the issue of mutual toleration remained virulent, both within and between the separate camps, in the henceforth divided Netherlands. The internal conflicts were aggravated by the fact that, with the rise of Arminianism and the doctrinal conflict over predestination, a schism occurred within Calvinism itself. In the course of the debate, the 'Remonstrants', as the followers of Arminius were known, appealed to the secular magistrates to enjoin the Calvinist churches to practise toleration, which the latter duly did in isolated cases – for example, the estates of Holland and West Friesland imposed toleration on both sides by ordinance in 1614. The author of the text was the lawyer Hugo Grotius, himself an Arminian, who, in his defence of the prohibition on discussion in the Bodinian tradition, emphasised the power of the state over ecclesiastical affairs on the one hand and the doctrinal agreements among the reformed churches on the other.[57] This brought the priority of political sovereignty to the fore once again, only this time in a clearly 'Erastian'[58] form which also accorded the temporal power supreme authority in ecclesiastical affairs. The Calvinist Johann Althusius, who was critical of Arminianism, and Grotius agreed on this point. In his *Politica methodice digesta* (1603, revised 1614), Althusius linked the idea of God's covenant with the people with a doctrine of the inalienable sovereignty of the people who appoint the government through

---

56. Saage, *Herrschaft, Toleranz, Widerstand*, 252, emphasises this in contrast to the Hobbesian thesis that the power of the sovereign is constitutive for toleration.

57. On this, see Lecler, *Toleration and the Reformation*, vol. II, 306.

58. This refers to the position of the eponymous Thomas Erastus that the secular jurisdiction has priority over the ecclesiastical even when it comes to upholding the ecclesiastic order.

a mutually binding contract. The political order, whose purpose it is to realise the good life on the basis of God's commandments, is framed by the eternal natural law which has a divine origin and is accessible to human reason. Within this order, the secular *majestas* also has the task of securing the religious and ecclesiastical order; therefore, toleration cannot be shown to heretics who challenge the foundation of the faith.[59] Freedom of conscience (though not freedom of worship) can be granted at most to those who uphold the basic principles of the faith, for example peaceful Catholics; however, in situations in which there is no other way to preserve the peace, toleration of other religious denominations and their observances is also possible. Of course, this in no way impinges upon the right of the secular ruler to put an end to theological controversies, something to which Althusius attaches particular importance.

Grotius concurs with this position in his work *De imperio summarum potestatum circa sacra* (1614–17), though with a different, religiously undogmatic twist. Although the secular ruler has the right to determine the religion within his own territory, 'to suppress the false [religions], either by lenient means or by force'[60] and to put an end to theological disputes, he will exercise this right prudently and thus avoid inciting the churches to intolerance. He will ensure that the basic truths are observed and his official state religion will not impose additional constraints on the conscience of the individual.[61]

In his most important work, *De iure belli ac pacis* (1625), Grotius turned his attention once again to the question of toleration. In 1619 he had managed to escape lifelong imprisonment in the Netherlands, where the Remonstrants were persecuted by the secular authority which supported the opposing side, only by fleeing. In general, his work represents an attempt to found the modern doctrine of internal and external sovereignty on natural law, and thus at the same time to subject it to normative constraints, through a version of natural law which occupies a middle ground between partially Aristotelian and partially Christian and modern-individualist premises.[62] Natural law, according to Grotius, springs from 'care of maintaining society in a manner conformable to the light of human understanding',[63] and its precepts of moral justice 'would take place, though we should even grant, what without the greatest wickedness cannot be granted, that there is no God, or that he

59. See Althusius, *Politica methodice digesta*, ch. 28, in particular §56.
60. Grotius, *De imperio summarum potestatum circa sacra*, cited in Lecler, *Toleration and the Reformation*, vol. II, 313.
61. See Kühn, *Toleranz und Offenbarung*, 374–89.
62. On this, see Tuck, *Natural Rights Theories*, ch. 3.
63. Grotius, *The Rights of War and Peace*, Preliminary Discourse, §8, 85–6.

takes no care of human affairs'.[64] Hence, reason is sufficiently autonomous to be capable of moral insight, yet it thereby simultaneously submits itself to God's will. Natural law, which according to Grotius is the foundation of both civil law and the law of nations, is 'a command of reason' and, as such, must be regarded as a divine commandment; yet it has an independent status: '[T]he law of nature is so unalterable, that God himself cannot change it.'[65]

Against this background, Grotius asks to what extent 'offences that are committed against' God are punishable. In his view, there is a 'true religion, which has been common to all ages' which rests on four propositions: God exists and there is only one God, he is a spiritual being, he directs human affairs and he is the creator of all things.[66] These propositions are reflected in the ten commandments. Of the four propositions, the first and third are of absolutely fundamental significance for *every* religion. Hence, disputing them must be punished in the name of the state as well as of human society as a whole.[67] The other two propositions, by contrast, are more contentious, 'not so manifest', and hence those who succumb to error in this regard should not be punished because God has not revealed the truth to them. They err in good conscience no less than those peoples who do not adopt the Christian teaching because they lack the 'assistance of God's grace' and hence the correct insight.[68] According to Christ's teaching, they should not be forced to convert because faith should arise voluntarily. Thus, here, an argument based on natural law is combined with a humanist argument. According to the former, it is 'contrary to reason' and at variance with the nature of (Christian) faith to employ force; according to the latter, the religiosity to be promoted universally can be reduced to a handful of principles. Finally, there is the further idea of the limitations of human beings' cognitive capacities in religious matters, so that each side is forbidden to impose its truth upon others.[69]

With this Grotius combines different arguments for toleration which set limits to the right of the sovereign to protect and defend the religious foundations of the state, though without disputing his right to do so in principle. This reveals the ambivalence of a conception of natural law that continues to be conceived as a law of divine creation. The toleration of the state is justified and restricted *simultaneously* in the name of this very law, for questioning the grounds of legal principles themselves cannot be tolerated. And however much this ambivalence recurs in many seventeenth-century

64. *Ibid.* §11, 89.   65. *Ibid.* book I, ch. 1, §10.5, 155.   66. *Ibid.* book II, ch. 20, §45.1, 1032.
67. *Ibid.* §46.4, 1037–8.   68. *Ibid.* §48.1, 1041.   69. *Ibid.* §50.3, 1046–8.

natural law theorists, the individualistic argument for freedom of conscience based on natural law nevertheless had a critical force which would later lead to a more radical separation between the state and the Church and to a further secularisation of the state.

It should be noted here that the transition to a discussion of toleration based on natural law once again opens up a broader discursive space which introduces a new dynamic into debates concerning toleration. As a result, within the discourse on the theory of the state an important locus of controversy developed in which demands for justification were increasingly raised at the political level against the dominance of the sovereign and the focus of the issue of toleration shifted to the fundamental question of political *justice*. The sovereign who seeks to neutralise religious conflicts through toleration became the problem for those who developed a new understanding of themselves, of religion and of the state during the religious controversies. The discourse of political *and* individual sovereignty pressed for new forms of social and political life. This would become the central problem of the seventeenth century during which the spectrum of justifications for toleration – ranging from Hobbes's solution based on a strict theory of sovereignty and its further development in Spinoza, to Locke's and finally Bayle's conception, which in turn goes beyond the limits of Locke's thought – took shape which informs reflection on toleration to the present day. However, the sixteenth century remains the decisive juncture in the discourse on toleration. At the political level it marks the emancipation of the sovereign state from religion and the beginning of the natural law argument combined with the two-kingdoms doctrine; at the intersubjective level it marks the emergence of the three paradigmatic justifications of toleration, the humanist justification, that of the Reformation and the combination of a morality of reciprocity and the insight into the finitude of reason, as found in particular in Castellio and Bodin.

5

Natural law, toleration and revolution: the rise of liberalism and the aporias of freedom of conscience

§15 Political and religious freedom as a birthright

1. The seventeenth-century religious and political conflicts led to an amplification of the modern discourse concerning toleration which reached its political-philosophical culmination in the works of Spinoza, Locke and Bayle. In order to reconstruct the various strands of argument leading to this culmination, we must first turn to the English historical context. For the latter involved a particular set of conflicts which resulted in a combination of demands for toleration and for more far-reaching political and social emancipation. It entailed a new and, as we shall see, revolutionary concept of politics. For what had already announced itself in the French and Dutch debates was now openly demanded, namely an individual natural right to freedom of religion (i.e. freedom of conscience and of worship) which precedes the state and, as a personal possession or birthright, cannot be alienated. Moreover, it was counted among those rights for whose protection individuals first established the state. On this conception, individual rights, which are conferred by God, are natural (and 'sacred'), whereas the authority of the state is artificial; the concomitant of the right to religious freedom, and in this sense to a form of toleration which can no longer be understood on the permission model, is the right to democratic self-determination. This idea played an important role in the revolution of the 1640s and Locke would lend it a paradigmatic form, albeit one in certain respects less radical than the thought of certain theorists of toleration prior to Locke.

Hence, *liberalism*, according to which individual rights exist prior to the state and political authority is established through a contract subject to conditions, appears at the forefront of the discourse concerning toleration. This doctrine (to which the concept 'liberalism' was not yet attached) incorporated a series of prior, in particular Protestant, arguments for toleration – especially the two-kingdoms doctrine and the idea of freedom of conscience (as bound to God alone) – in such an ingenious way that the still-widespread view that toleration is a child of liberalism, a notion shared by many advocates as well as many critics of liberalism, took root.[1] However, this image – which is as one-sided as the conflicting view already criticised that it was the modern, absolute sovereign who made toleration possible by bringing civil war to an end – stands in need of correction. For it is evident that the discourse concerning toleration and many of the 'liberal' arguments, not to mention many important arguments not taken up by liberalism, already existed before liberalism, even though liberalism led to the development of an innovative, theoretically and politically extremely influential argument concerning toleration. On the contrary, liberalism, which has many parents – one need only think of its political-economic component – should be regarded as a child of toleration,[2] as an important stage in the ongoing discourse of toleration. Liberalism is a late arrival in this discourse, though an extremely successful one. However, it by no means represents the culmination of this discourse, for its justification of toleration – for example, in the form presented by Locke – is neither the only nor the most consistent one, as I will try to show.

We should note further that early liberalism relies to a large extent on religious premises precisely where it argues for religious toleration – a prime example being the above-mentioned conception of conscience and its freedom, whose reverse side is dependence on God. Here it is not yet a question of the complete ethical autonomy to discover and live in accordance with one's own 'conception of the good life'. Rather, it is freedom of conscience itself as the 'work of God' which supports the demand that this moral authority should be granted political freedom – and this entails important limits to this justification of toleration, as is evident in many authors.

The natural rights of individuals are also understood in such a way that they are conferred upon them as free and equal creatures of God by his authority, and it is by appeal to his laws and commandments that the right and the duty of political resistance are grounded. Political freedom and obedience to God here go hand-in-hand. The fact that the state is confined to

1. See for example Macedo, 'Toleration and Fundamentalism', and Mendus, *Toleration and the Limits of Liberalism*, where Locke is referred to as the first theorist of toleration (or at least the first worthy of discussion).
2. Rawls, *Political Liberalism*, xxiv, expresses this cautiously as follows: 'Thus, the historical origin of political liberalism (and of liberalism more generally) is the Reformation and its aftermath, with the long controversies over religious toleration in the sixteenth and seventeenth centuries.'

secular tasks, therefore, does not mean that it is justified primarily in secular terms. However, a work such as Hobbes's *Leviathan* (1651), which belongs in this context, pointed to opposing trends which are likewise typical of the seventeenth century. An example of the latter is the spirit of the emerging new science which seeks to replace the appeal to divine natural right, also to be found in Hobbes, with the power of 'natural reason' and the political sovereignty founded upon it, and in this sense develops further Grotius's argument that the laws of nature would be knowable and valid even if God did not exist (see above §14.2).

Finally, it should be borne in mind that the widespread view that the social and legal philosophy of liberalism remains captive to a form of 'atomism' because of its individualistic premises, which do in fact represent a break with the older conception of the organic unity of the 'people',[3] is already in need of correction in view of the fact that, although it is the freedom of the conscience of the individual that is defended, this is supposed to open up the social space for the *communal* exercise of religious worship and for a plurality of ecclesiastical organisations. This is also an important implication of the interdependence of freedom of conscience and freedom of worship, and it is further proof that a historically informed examination of what is meant by 'liberalism' is worthwhile and has the potential to challenge positive as well as negative preconceptions.

2. Characteristic of the conflicts in seventeenth-century England was that socio-economic disputes associated with the implementation of an early capitalist economic order, the political struggle between the Crown and Parliament and the religious tensions between the Anglican state church, Catholicism and the various Protestant groups, in particular the Calvinist Puritans, were interconnected in a complex way. Although all of these aspects are important for the question of toleration, it will not be possible to do full justice to this complexity here, but only to trace the essential lines of conflict in the political-religious domain.[4]

Crucial for understanding the conflicts over toleration in England is the existence of the Anglican state church. Henry VIII had appointed himself head of the Church in the place of the pope in 1533, thus sealing the break with Rome, and demanded that his secular and ecclesiastical

---

3. I have discussed this problematic in Forst, *Contexts of Justice*, chs. 1 and 2.
4. The most exhaustive treatment of this conflict situation (up to 1660) is provided by the four-volume study by Jordan, *The Development of Religious Toleration in England*. See also Saage, *Herrschaft, Toleranz, Widerstand*, pt II; Goldie, 'Absolutismus, Parlamentarismus und Revolution in England'; and Lecler, *Toleration and the Reformation*, vol. II, pt 8.

officeholders take the Oath of Supremacy (Thomas More, among others, refused to do so and was duly beheaded). This schism marked the beginning of the protracted conflicts with Catholicism, whose adherents were no longer suspected in the first instance of being heretics but instead of being traitors. This schism became even more pronounced during the reign of Elizabeth I (1558–1603) following the brief Catholic restoration (and a policy of suppression and persecution of Protestantism) under Mary Tudor, with the re-establishment of Anglicanism as the state church and its consolidation in the statute of 1562, which represented a compromise between Protestant theology and Catholic rites and ecclesiastical organisation. In a Papal Bull of 1570, Pope Pius V excommunicated Elizabeth, declaring her to be deposed and freeing her subjects from the duty of allegiance to the heretic, which meant in turn that observant Catholics in England were from now on regarded as traitors and were persecuted. The situation was aggravated even further by the fact that, following the execution of Mary Stuart in 1587, Catholic Spain attempted (unsuccessfully) to conquer England and various conspiracies to murder the queen came to light. Catholics would henceforth be open to the suspicion of being in league with foreign powers, which explains why Locke continued to exclude them from toleration. On the Catholic side, on the other hand, one finds a range of arguments towards the end of the sixteenth century whose mirror images were to be found in France on the Protestant side: on the one hand, theories of resistance against godless rulers, on the other, arguments against an official church and for the separation of Church and State.[5]

However, the Anglican state church had to deal not only with Catholicism but also with the Protestant groups for whom this church did not advance far enough along the path of the Reformation, as well as a variety of persecuted sects, such as the Quakers, the Anabaptists and the Antitrinitarians. Still, the Calvinist dissidents, the so-called Puritans, posed the greatest challenge. They demanded that Anglicanism be purified of all forms and contents that could not be justified on the basis of scripture; Presbyterianism, in particular, criticised the established system of bishops and called for an elected ecclesiastical hierarchy. For these critics, the Church of England, at least in many respects, still seemed to be a continuation of Catholicism by other means. The state church responded to this criticism in turn with severity and under the leadership of the Archbishop of Canterbury, John Whitgift, with new forms of suppression and of the Inquisition.

---

5. See Lecler, *Toleration and the Reformation*, vol. II, 365–75.

However, enforcing external conformity was just one side of the state church, the other being an internal toleration in doctrinal matters due to the fact that it was composed of different religious elements. Richard Hooker's *Laws of Ecclesiastical Polity* (1593ff.) is characteristic of this mixture of external intolerance and internal toleration and openness, a product of the irenic attempt to reconcile the different conflicting Christian denominations. In this apology for the Church of England, Hooker defends religious conformism as part of the citizens' duty of obedience, but is mainly interested in *outward* conformity. He employs an important reinterpretation of the doctrine of the *adiaphora*, the 'arbitrary matters' and inessential aspects of faith, to justify this conformity, which according to the underlying Erastian understanding of religious organisation was laid down by the state. Whereas on Erasmus's humanist understanding the *adiaphora* were to be left up to the individual's conscience, Hooker argues that questions of the liturgy, for example, which counted as such incidental matters, should be regulated by the state authority in order to avoid unnecessary conflicts. According to this view, as long as the official church safeguards the essential articles of faith and certain freedoms of interpretation, issues such as the external constitution of the Church and religious ceremonies are matters for the ruler to decide.[6] As for the essentials of the faith, Hooker argues that the Catholic religion, although misguided, does not destroy the foundations of the faith necessary for salvation, which indicates that Hooker understood the Anglican creed as a conciliatory doctrine that could incorporate Catholicism and hence could put an end to religious strife.[7] As the religious conflicts intensified in the ensuing period, this idea of reconciliation was frequently cited in support of Anglicanism, whose doctrinal openness was emphasised. This is especially true of the liberal theology of John Haies and the 'Latitudinarianism' of William Chillingworth. In *The Religion of Protestants a safe way to Salvation* (1638), the latter argues that religious peace is preserved by the different religious denominations recognising the central importance of the belief in scripture, whereas there can be reasonable disagreement over its detailed interpretation in the common search for truth. Hence, the universal dogmas should remain aloof from such controversies.[8]

6. Hooker, *Laws of Ecclesiastical Polity*, vol. I, 14; II, 1; V, 71.
7. Edwin Sandys also defends the Anglican Church in this irenic spirit in his 1605 work *Europae speculum, or A View or Survey of the State of Religion in the Westerne Parts of the World*.
8. On Chillingworth, see Lecler, *Toleration and the Reformation*, vol. II, 430–3; Kühn, *Toleranz und Offenbarung*, 397–426; Remer, *Humanism and the Rhetoric of Toleration*, ch. 3.

Under the reign of James I (1603–25), who insisted on the absolutist claim to rule by divine right, the religious tensions between the Church and Catholicism, on the one side, and radical Protestantism, on the other, increased in intensity. However, the conflicts between the king and Parliament, primarily over the right of approval of taxation and the limits of the royal prerogatives, also became more acute. The conflict erupted into the open under Charles I (1625–49) when Parliament proposed a Petition of Rights in 1628, with the result that the king ruled alone without Parliament for eleven years until 1640. During this time he also took measures against his Protestant critics, especially the Puritans, because he feared that the latter wanted to do away with the monarchy as well as the bishops. This earned him the accusation of 'papism' from the Protestant side.

The situation escalated in 1640 when the rebellion of the Scottish Presbyterians, on whom the Anglican Church was to be imposed, forced Charles I to convene the parliament which, being dominated by Puritans, made a series of demands on the Crown. This marked the beginning of the 'Long Parliament' (which would be dissolved only in 1660). Finally, in 1642, the parliament created its own army to oppose the power of the king, the trigger being provided by a Catholic rebellion in Ireland and the fear of a 'papist conspiracy'. The parliament now no longer saw itself merely as an institution which petitioned the ancient rights of Englishmen since Magna Carta against the king, but increasingly as the representative of the sovereign people and the bearer of legislative sovereignty. Authors such as William Prynne and Henry Parker regarded the right of self-government as a rationally evident basic law of justice that did not require any historical precedents. As the *Remonstrance of Many Thousand Citizens* (1646) of the Levellers, who were particularly radical in this respect, put it: 'For whatever our forefathers were, or whatever they did or suffered or were enforced to yield unto, we are the men of the present age and ought to be absolutely free from all kinds of exorbitances, molestations or arbitrary power.'[9] Human beings, on this view, were not by nature part of a social order but free, and the state was not a natural or an organic formation but a purely artificial one which was the result of a contract of the citizens among themselves and with the appointed government. Here an idea played a major role which Locke would later formulate thus: life, liberty and estate belong to the natural property of men to which they have an inalienable right that pre-exists the state. This idea also played a major role among the Levellers, who stressed the birthright to property,

9. Quoted from Sharp, *The English Levellers*, 35.

liberty and freedom (Richard Overton) and in this connection called for an extension of political participation rights. Liberty was a property conferred by God which no one had the right to dispose of or to steal from others. The economic rhetoric of natural law which comes to light here even went so far as to assert (as, for instance, in John Goodwin) that the social contract between the people and the king is an employment contract stipulating that the king is the wage earner who should perform his work for the well-being of the people within the framework of the laws enacted by Parliament and is afforded the necessary means to do this, but who can be dismissed at any time if he does not perform his duties to the satisfaction of his employers.[10] Such arguments ultimately served to justify the execution of the king (and the abolition of the House of Lords) in 1649.

This was the work of the so-called Rump Parliament under the leadership of the party of the Independents of Oliver Cromwell, who shortly thereafter assumed power as Lord Protector. The 'Rump' is what remained after the parliamentary army, which had defeated the king, rebelled against the Presbyterian majority in Parliament in 1648 and expelled this group, which was leaning towards reinstating the Crown. The Independents had formed themselves into a party prior to this when the Presbyterians in Parliament had secured the assistance of the Scots in the conflict against the Crown in 1643 by promising to establish a Presbyterian ecclesiastical regime in England. However, the latter quickly turned out to be a new, in this instance Calvinist, form of the official Church, which sought to use state power to suppress dissent, especially on the part of the independent Protestant groups.[11] This met with fierce resistance from the Independents and the Levellers, who regarded it as just a new, even worse 'papist' system following the Anglican one, although a majority of the Independents were not opposed to a state church as such, provided that it was open and decentralised.

Now it became apparent that the birthright argument applied equally to political and religious liberty. The liberties of conscience and worship were also regarded as inalienable and prior to the state. This was asserted in its most radical form by the Levellers, for example by John Lilburne, who, in *Englands Birth-Right Justified* (1645), defended a strict doctrine of popular sovereignty and presented every form of authority, whether political or religious, as having to justify itself in principle. Thus, the authority of the king, as well as that of the presbyters and their parliamentary majority, was

10. Goodwin, *The Obstructors of Justice or A defence of the Honourable Sentence passed upon the late King by the High Court of Justice* (1649), quoted in Saage, *Herrschaft, Toleranz, Widerstand*, 158–9.
11. Cf. Houston, 'Monopolizing Faith', 158.

seen as mere tyranny which robbed the 'well-affected' (Lilburne's restrictive qualification), free-born Englishmen of their natural claim to liberty. Enforced religion, like political despotism, is illegitimate, Lilburne argued, and serves only the self-interests of the ruler, and hence must be met with resistance: 'O cruell, pitifull, lamentable and intollerable Bondage, no longer to be indured, suffered, nor undergone, the burdens being far heavier than the poore labourers can bear.'[12] This shows how much the language of toleration in this debate, which was of major importance for the development of modern toleration discourse, was one of *emancipation*. Both political and religious liberty were understood as a basic claim within a just polity in which every form of power is established by the citizens themselves and must justify itself towards them.

This was stressed by a whole range of authors in their tracts. In his works *The Compassionate Samaritane* (1644), *A Helpe to the Right Understanding of a Discourse Concerning Independency* (1644/45) and *Tolleration Justified, and Persecution Condemned* (1645/46), the Leveller William Walwyn presented a series of arguments for toleration which were directed against the attempts of the Presbyterians to enforce conformity. He first points out that, on the Protestant understanding, every individual has a duty to form and live out his faith with the help of the truth revealed in scripture, which is in need of interpretation. To follow any directives other than those thus recognised as justified by one's conscience is a sin, and so, too, is religious indoctrination which can lead only to hypocrisy or atheism. Here, too, it is the specific idea of a free conscience that is at the same time bound by God which is added to the notion that this freedom cannot be transferred to the political power, or usurped by it (or another power), without sin:

> That which a man may not voluntarily binde himselfe to doe, or to forbear to doe, without sinne: That he cannot entrust or refer unto the ordering of any other: Whatsoever (be it Parliament, Generall Councels, or Nationall Assemblies): But all things concerning the worship and service of God, and of that nature; that a man cannot without wilfull sin, either binde himselfe to doe any thing therein contrary to his understanding and conscience: not to forbeare to doe that which his understanding and conscience bindes him to performe: therefore no man can refer matters of Religion to any others regulation. And what cannot be given, cannot be received: and then as

12. Lilburne, *Englands Birth-Right Justified*, 303.

a particular man cannot be robbed of that which he never had; so neither can a Parliament, or any other just Authority be violated in, or deprived of a power which cannot be entrusted unto them.[13]

Once again it becomes apparent how much the argument concerning the *unfree free conscience* is based on faith and at the same time frees the latter from political constraints – a connection between the Protestant concept of conscience and the idea of the natural right of the individual which became paradigmatic for this time. Walwyn accordingly rejects all attempts to distinguish between external and internal conformity in his work on toleration and demands strict adherence on the part of the state to the principle of the individual freedom of conscience as a divine commandment.

The epistemological argument that the truth requires interpretation and that the finitude of human beings' rational faculties – '[t]he uncertainty of knowledge in this life: no man, nor no sort of men can presume of an unerring spirit'[14] – inevitably leads to different interpretations, coupled with the notion that faith must rest on justified conviction, means that in Walwyn's view, as in Castellio's, the golden rule of reciprocity calls for mutual toleration in Christian brotherly love:

> God being all Love, and having so communicated himselfe unto us, and gave us commands to be like him, mercifull, as he our heavenly Father is mercifull; to bear with one anothers infirmities: neither does reason and true wisdome dictate any other to us, then that we should do unto others, as we would be done unto our selves; that spirit therefore which is contrary to God, to reason, to the well-being of States, as the spirit of Persecution evidently is; is most especially to be watcht, and warily to be circumscribed, and tied up by the wisdome of the supream power in Common-wealths.[15]

It is apparent how strongly Walwyn's epistemological, moral and political justifications of toleration remain captive to a religious conceptual framework; yet it is also clear that he, like many of his predecessors, is looking for definitions of finite reason, of reciprocal morality and of the tasks of the state which are above the confessional conflicts, as indicated by the enumeration 'contrary to God, to reason, to the well-being of States'.

A further argument – in this case one which points forward not to Locke but to Lessing and Mill – can also be found in Walwyn, namely that of the productive conflict between competing interpretations of the truth. Given

13. Walwyn, *A Helpe to the Right Understanding*, 136–7.
14. Walwyn, *The Compassionate Samaritane*, 104.   15. Walwyn, *Tolleration Justified*, 162–3.

that fallible human beings are capable of approaching the truth only by trial
and error, the plurality of interpretations, according to Walwyn, can have
the positive effect that the truth comes to light and becomes established
through the interplay of arguments and counter-arguments. Thus, he argues
against the censorship of opinion as follows:

> Besides, a Toleration being allowed, and every Sect labouring to make
> it appear that they are in the truth, wherof a good life, or the power of
> godlinesse being the best badge or symptome; hence will necessarily
> follow, a noble contestation in all sorts of men to exceed in godlinesse,
> to the great improvement of vertue and piety amongst us. From
> whence it will be concluded too, that that Sect will be supposed to
> have least truth in them, that are least vertuous, and godlike in their
> lives and conversations.[16]

Expressed in economic terms, Levellers like Walwyn (or Lilburne) argue
against a 'monopoly on knowledge' by one sect or authority and for a 'mar-
ketplace' of interpretations, an argument which can also be found around
the same time in Milton.[17]

What is striking about Walwyn's argument is, finally, that it transcends
a boundary which was insurmountable for many of the liberal Protestant
thinkers, that of toleration of non-Protestants. Admittedly he is thinking primarily of toleration towards all variants of Protestantism (ranging from the
Presbyterians through the Independents to the Anabaptists); and although
he is not altogether clear when it comes to toleration of Catholics and Jews,
he nevertheless also dares to advocate toleration of blasphemy, and even of
atheism. The former will be easily identified in the public forum as erroneous,
he argues, and the latter can be overcome only through the force of good
arguments (through the 'efficacy and convincing power of sound reason and
argument').[18] Here, too, Walwyn's toleration is not only historically ahead
of Locke's.

Typical for the mixture of traditional Christian and individualistic, natural law points of view, as found in Walwyn, but without the strong emphasis on the social-emancipatory moment privileged by the Levellers, are the
influential writings on toleration of John Goodwin, *Theomachia, or the Grand
Imprudence of Men Running the Hazard of Fighting Against God* (1644), and
of Henry Robinson, *Liberty of Conscience, or the Sole Means to Obtaine Peace
and Truth* (1644). For both writers the Bible serves almost exclusively as

16. *Ibid.* 167.   17. Cf. Houston, 'Monopolizing Faith', 152–3.
18. Walwyn, *Tolleration Justified*, 164.

their basis of argument, with Goodwin placing greater emphasis on tolerance and humility as virtues of finite, limited creatures, following Gamaliel's
advice (Acts 5:38–9) not to condemn heretics over-hastily since they may be
performing the work of God who alone has the right to judge. Therefore,
intolerance is a crime, a struggle against God: 'Observe, That for any man, or
men, to attempt the suppression of any Doctrine, way, or practice that is from
God, is to fight against God himselfe.'[19] Robinson places less emphasis on the
limits of human knowledge in matters of faith than on the biblical arguments
against religious indoctrination, which is a sin – and is in any case futile.[20]
The conversion of people of other faiths, i.e. of non-Protestants, remains
the goal of Christian policy, but it cannot be achieved by force. Moreover,
such practices are detrimental to the economy and to foreign trade, according to Robinson, who was involved in international trade.[21] Concerning the
critical issue of the toleration of Catholics, Robinson pleads for a graduated
regime of toleration in which they are not granted the same liberties as the
Protestants, but are tolerated 'in a qualified and more moderate manner'.[22]

A particular aspect of this debate concerning toleration is the importance
of the idea of public political debates itself, an early example of the demand
for a civic public sphere which was justified in part politically by appeal to the
need for political power to justify itself, and in part religiously, with reference to the necessity and productiveness of public debate over the truth. The
writings of John Milton, one of the most prominent representatives of
the Independents and a confidant of Cromwell, are particularly representative of this position. In his *Areopagitica* (1644), he pillories the censorship
of the press introduced by Parliament, which he regards as both political and
religious tyranny; only through free and open discussion can one learn to
distinguish between truth and falsehood, and between virtue and sin.[23] God
granted human beings the imperfect faculty of judging for themselves and of
learning from mistakes, and neither a state nor a group of ministers should
presume to reduce the wealth and diversity of the world, as God created it,
for human beings. The truth will ultimately triumph of its own accord: 'For
who knows not that Truth is strong, next to the Almighty. She needs no
policies, nor stratagems, nor licensings to make her victorious – those are
the shifts and the defenses that error uses against her power.'[24] As in other
writings, Milton is correspondingly critical of the Presbyterians.[25]

19. Goodwin, *Theomachia*, 17.   20. Robinson, *Liberty of Conscience*, 119–22.
21. See *ibid.* 123, 163.   22. *Ibid.* 114.   23. Milton, *Areopagitica*, 729.   24. *Ibid.* 747.
25. As, for example, in *The Reason of Church Government Urged against Prelaty* (1642).

In Milton, this defence of freedom of religion and freedom of the press is also part of a more comprehensive conception of the 'natural' liberties of citizens and their political rights. In *The Tenure of Kings and Magistrates* (1649), he legitimises political resistance (and tyrannicide) by appeal to the birthright of self-government, specifically also in religious matters.[26] Milton's thesis is 'that the civil power hath neither right, nor can do right, by forcing religious things; I will now show the wrong it doth by violating the fundamental privilege of the gospel, the new birthright of every true believer, Christian liberty'.[27] The true Christians are born free and their conscience is sacrosanct; this is at once a Christian and a political birthright.

Still, Milton does not overcome the above-mentioned limitation of Protestant arguments for toleration, namely intolerance towards 'papists'.[28] Already in the *Areopagitica*[29] he excludes them (as well as superstition) from toleration, and in another passage, having argued for toleration of the Protestant sects, Milton explains:

> But as for popery and idolatry, why they also may not hence plead to be tolerated, I have much less to say. Their religion the more considered, the less can be acknowledged a religion, but a Roman principality rather, endeavoring to keep up her old universal dominion under a new name, and mere shadow of a catholic religion; being indeed more rightly named a catholic heresy against the scripture, supported mainly by a civil and, except in Rome, by a foreign power: justly therefore to be suspected, not tolerated, by the magistrate of another country. Besides, of an implicit faith which they profess, the conscience also becomes implicit, and so by voluntary servitude to man's law, forfeits her Christian liberty. Who then can plead for such a conscience, as being implicitly enthralled to man instead of God, almost becomes no conscience, as the will not free, becomes no will. Nevertheless, if they ought not to be tolerated, it is for just reason of state more than of religion; which they who force, though professing to be protestants, deserve as little to be tolerated themselves, being no less guilty of popery in the most popish point.[30]

26. 'I question not the lawfulness of raising war against a tyrant in defense of religion or civil liberty', Milton, *The Tenure of Kings and Magistrates*, 766. Or in *The Second Defense of the People of England* (1654): 'And what can conduce more to the beauty or glory of one's country than the recovery, not only of its civil, but its religious liberty?' (818)

27. *Ibid.* 850.   28. See Carlin, 'Toleration for Catholics in the Puritan Revolution'.

29. Milton, *Areopagitica*, 747: 'I mean not tolerated popery and open superstition.'

30. Milton, *A Treatise of Civil Power*, 846.

This quotation illustrates the complexity and limitations of Milton's argument for toleration. First, freedom of conscience, understood in Protestant terms as independence from human laws in the orientation to scripture alone, becomes the true hallmark of religion as such, so that the Catholic faith, which binds individuals to the authority of the pope, clearly robs the conscience of this liberty, and hence cannot lay claim to freedom of conscience either. In addition, however, Milton points out that Catholics obey not only the authority of the pope but also that of foreign powers, which is ultimately the decisive point for excluding them from toleration for political reasons – here the prejudice against Catholics as traitors, which had particularly deep historical roots in England, becomes apparent. Finally, Milton underscores that the coercion of conscience on religious grounds must be rejected as a typically 'papist' practice, so that only the political government has the authority to impose limits on toleration in practice. It may also do this, Milton adds, towards blasphemers, who cannot lay claim to freedom of conscience for themselves either.[31] Again the ambivalence of religious justifications of toleration becomes apparent. Once it becomes a question of the religious assumptions and implications of the basis of one's own faith, limits are placed on toleration, even though the concept of 'freedom of conscience' at first sight seems to be intended universally.[32] At the same time the example of Walwyn shows that the combination of natural law with freedom of conscience can also make this boundary more permeable.

This is also made apparent by one of the most famous writings on toleration of the era, namely *The Bloudy Tenent of Persecution* (1644) by Roger Williams. Williams began his career as an Anglican chaplain but later embraced Puritan Separatism and Baptism, only finally to distance himself from all forms of organised religion. He emigrated to New England, but religious and political disputes with the authorities there forced him to leave, whereupon he founded the colony of Rhode Island in which he established a comprehensive regime of freedom of conscience. In order to acquire the charters for the colony he had to make frequent visits to London where his writings, which were the fruit of a controversy with the leading Puritan theologian of Massachusetts, John Cotton, appeared. The most important work among them, *The Bloudy Tenent*,[33] caused a sensation not only in the

31. *Ibid.* 843.
32. This ambivalence is also abundantly clear in Milton's late work *Of True Religion, Haeresie, Schism, and Toleration*, whose subtitle is: *And what best means may be us'd against the growth of Popery* (1673), albeit already in the context of the debates on toleration following the Restoration.
33. In 1652 Williams follows this with a sequel with the title *The Bloudy Tenent yet More Bloody by Mr Cottons endeavor to wash it white in the Blood of the Lambe.*

new colonies but also in England and was condemned to be burnt by the (Presbyterian dominated) Lower House of Parliament.

Williams's work, which takes the form of a dialogue between Truth and Peace, is a summation of many of the arguments for toleration developed up to this time and represents a particular example of the *religious* justification of a purely *secular* state. Almost every sentence of this extensive book contains a reference to the Old or the New Testament and to the history of Christianity; yet its import is a more radical separation between Church and State than is to be found in any author before him. All of the arguments which would later be found in Locke are also to be found in Williams. Yet, paradoxically, they are more beholden to a religious argumentative framework than Locke's theory while clearly going beyond Locke's restrictions on toleration and making a clear separation between religion and politics, i.e. between '*spirituall*' and '*civill matters*'. Of central importance for Williams is the doctrine of the two kingdoms, the political and the spiritual, where the political remains willed by God so that peace should reign upon earth. However, for Williams neither the ruler nor the citizens need be Christians. Secular justice is a purely temporal matter; the state is established by the consensus of the citizens and the government is assigned the task of securing the common good – 'the *defence* of *Persons, Estates, Families, Liberties* of a *City* or *Civill State*, and the *suppressing* of *uncivill* or injurious persons or actions by such *civill punishment*'[34] – but not with regulating spiritual and religious matters.

Williams develops this natural law-based argument primarily in terms of the biblical doctrine of the two kingdoms and links it with the doctrine of the necessity of free, uncoerced belief in God: 'But *Faith* is that *gift* which proceeds alone from the *Father* of Lights.'[35] Furthermore, he points out, especially with reference to the parable of the weeds, that God alone is the ultimate judge concerning the true faith and human beings are not permitted to make any judgement about this which would justify force, as opposed to expulsion from the Church. As a consequence, what is required is not doctrinal or ecclesiastical toleration but a form of official and civic toleration that distinguishes between the *civill weapons of justice* and the *spirituall weapons* of the Church, including excommunication.[36] In so arguing, Williams assumes not only that the coercion of conscience is *ineffective* and futile but also that it is *illegitimate*. For the citizens have conferred coercive power over conscience

---

34. Williams, *The Bloudy Tenent*, 160 (emphasis, also in the following quotation, in the original).
35. *Ibid.* 138.   36. *Ibid.* 147.

neither on the state nor on the Church, nor could they have done so because conscience is answerable to God alone. Thus, intolerance is the greatest sin of all because it usurps God's judgement and curtails the freedom of the faithful. Today's *soul-killers* could be the *soul-savers* of tomorrow.[37]

Williams leaves no doubt that he is convinced of the existence of the true faith and of the true Church and he stresses the legitimacy of 'Spirituall *killing* by the most sharpe two-edged Sword of the Spirit, in delivering up the person excommunicate to *Sathan*'.[38] Yet he stresses in no less drastic terms not only that the weapons of the secular power of the state do not serve this purpose, but also that they should not be made to serve this purpose. Even though God's church has room only for the true believers, all of those who obey the purely secular laws must be admitted into the 'world or civil state', be they 'papists', Jews, Turks, blasphemers or heathens – Williams also unequivocally supports toleration of the religious ceremonies of the North American Indians (whose land rights he defended).[39]

> And I aske whether or no such as may hold forth other *Worships* or *Religions (Iewes, Turkes,* or *Antichristians)* may not be peaceable and quiet *Subjects*, loving and helpfull *neighbours*, faire and just *dealers*, true and loyall to the *civill government?* It is cleare they may from all *Reason* and *Experience* in many flourishing *Cities* and *Kingdomes* of the World, and so offend not against the *civill State* and *Peace*; nor incurre the punishment of the *civill sword*, notwithstanding that in *spirituall* and *mysticall account* they are ravenous and greedy *Wolves*.[40]

This shows to what extent for Williams the religious-ethical identity of a person is distinct from her identity as a citizen and legal person and as a moral person: non-Christians, and even 'anti-Christians', are capable of respecting the laws of the state and the basic rules of morality.

Consistent with this, Williams also attacks the Anglican doctrine of 'outward conformity' insofar as he rejects the *adiaphora* doctrine underlying it. It is not possible to define the fundamental truths necessary for salvation unambiguously, he argues, nor can they be distinguished clearly from the inessential issues. What falls under the one category or the other cannot be laid down by a universal authority which sets itself up as a state church.[41]

Therefore, with Williams the debate concerning toleration reaches a point in the middle of the seventeenth century at which, at the interface

---

37. *Ibid.* 209.   38. *Ibid.* 192.   39. *Ibid.* 3–4, 9, 30, 63, 95, 196–7, 252–72.
40. *Ibid.* 142.   41. *Ibid.* 64–71.

between traditional religious arguments stemming mainly from Protestant thought and the modern, individualistic doctrine of natural law, a theory of the separation between Church and State and of freedom of conscience emerges which is far more radical as regards the limits of toleration than its predecessors and many of its successors. Only Bayle would venture similar theses towards the end of the century. At the same time, however, Williams's theory is typical of its time in being a transitional theory. For its arguments remain firmly rooted in Christian soil, and on that basis it arrives at a secular conception of the state and of the demand for unlimited toleration, both of which he argues are 'the will and command of *God*',[42] as he states at the outset. This is due in part to the concrete situation of conflict from which this work emerged, namely the refutation of Cotton's political theology; yet it also provides evidence of what 'toleration in conflict' means in a specific historical context. The call for toleration represents a partisan position in a concrete political controversy which seeks to channel the religious conflicts in such a way that different reasons speak for toleration, reasons which can in turn conflict with one another, for example religious with independent political considerations. And thus this also constitutes the limit of such an argument, though a different one than in Milton, namely not the inability to tolerate other religious orientations but the impossibility of *sharing* the arguments for toleration with *non*-Protestants. How toleration is supposed to be justified from their perspective, be they 'papists', Jews, Turks or 'anti-Christians', if not by adopting the particular religious framework of justification remains an open question in Williams in spite of his quest for impartiality.[43] Here it becomes apparent that a theory of *reciprocal* toleration calls for independent normative arguments capable of convincing members of different religious persuasions.

However, it should be noted that the above-mentioned theories,[44] especially those of Walwyn and Williams, continue what was prefigured in the Dutch Revolt, namely the combination of the dimensions of vertical and horizontal toleration. For they trace the legitimation of the state back to a consensus among the citizens who, rather than surrendering certain liberties to the state, regard the latter as an instrument for preserving these liberties.

---

42. *Ibid.* 3.   43. Thus, *ibid.* 205–6.
44. Given the copiousness of the debate, a whole series of others could be added, for example Richard Overton's *The Araignment of Mr. Persecution* (1645). Deeply influenced both in form and content by Williams, Overton presents the court case against 'Mr. Persecution' as a drama in which the latter has to defend himself against the accusations and testimony of, among others, 'Mr. Soveraignty of Christ', 'Mr. Nationall Strength' and 'Mr. Humaine Society', and in the end is sentenced to death.

As a consequence, they confer the liberties in question on each other mutually as fundamental liberties – they are *not* 'granted', but secured, by the state. From being a *good* granted to the individual by the state in accordance with the permission conception, toleration has become a *right* which the citizens accord each other reciprocally. As a result the theoretical discourse concerning the state moves into a new phase which would culminate in the declarations of individual rights in the American and French revolutions. This is the real meaning of the *birthright* to freedom.

    3. To be sure, political practice did not accord with the radicality of the demands for political and religious freedom. Following the defeat of the king and the assumption of power by the Rump Parliament under the leadership of Cromwell's Independents, new lines of conflict emerged within the victorious coalition which in turn exhibited political and religious aspects. This became evident, on the one hand, in the famous Putney Debates in 1647 over the extension of suffrage, which turned on the precise meaning of the 'birthright' to political participation and what kind of economic independence was required if one was to count as 'well-affected'. Here different conceptions emerged between the more conservative Independents around Cromwell, who argued in favour of land ownership, and the Levellers.[45] A similar conflict arose in the Whitehall Debates of 1648–49, which dealt with the boundaries of religious toleration.[46] Whereas Independents such as Ireton stressed the right of the magistrate to intervene in cases of blasphemy, rejected freedom of worship for Catholics and Anglicans and warned against unrestricted religious individualism, other Independents such as Goodwin and the Levellers argued against such curtailments of freedom of conscience and worship. The former prevailed politically (and militarily) and while radicals such as Lilburne, Overton and Walwyn ended up in prison, others such as Milton rose to political office. Under Cromwell's rule as Lord Protector (from 1653 onwards) until the restoration of the monarchy and the supremacy of the Church of England in 1660, general religious freedom was not granted, though sects such as the Quakers and even the Unitarians were tolerated and the Jews, who had been banished from England since 1290, were (unofficially) readmitted.

---

45. However, opinions diverge over how radical the demands of the Levellers were. On this, see Macpherson, *The Political Theory of Possessive Individualism*, 3; Saage, *Herrschaft, Toleranz, Widerstand*, 190–208; Goldie, 'Absolutismus, Parlamentarismus und Revolution in England', 321–5.
46. The debates can be found in Woodhouse (ed.), *Puritanism and Liberty*, 125–78.

Among the writings on toleration during this period, apart from James Harrington's *The Commonwealth of Oceana* (1656),[47] which argues in Erastian terms for a national religion, albeit one which respects freedom of conscience, one in particular stands out. Its author draws on the modern doctrine of natural law to develop a political science modelled on the new sciences according to which the state established by contract does *not* involve a separation between Church and State, but is a *Common-Wealth Ecclesiasticall and Civill* which is supposed to put an end to the religious dispute. The work in question is the *Leviathan* of Thomas Hobbes.

§16 The mortal god and freedom of thought

1. Several of the strands of argument reconstructed thus far come together in Thomas Hobbes's political work to form a theory of sovereignty which understood itself as the culmination of theological and political thought and as overcoming the conflicts of its time. A new kind of scientific treatment of the question of the origin and preservation of the state was supposed to enable those human beings who were sufficiently prudent to establish a commonwealth in which the causes of the illnesses under which, in Hobbes's view, a state such as England was suffering would be eliminated. First and foremost among them was the evil of religious strife, which Hobbes dealt with at length in his writings. Whereas the topic merited only a couple of chapters (albeit central ones) in the *Elements of Law Natural and Politic* (1640), it already commanded an entire section of its own in *De cive* (1642), until fully half of *Leviathan* (1651) was devoted to issues concerning religion; finally, the analysis of the English civil war in *Behemoth* (1668) leaves no doubt that the religious parties, whether 'papists', Presbyterians or Independents, were all to blame for the ruin of the state.[48] Hobbes understood these works explicitly as political interventions. This explains, for example, why he brought forward the publication of the book *On the Citizen*, which was supposed to form the third part of his philosophical system, while he was in exile in France, where he had fled in 1640 out of fear of being prosecuted by Parliament as an ally of the king. After his return to Cromwell's England in 1651 and following the Restoration of the monarchy under Charles II, whose tutor he had been in France, in 1660, he remained involved in the political,

---

47. See Harrington, *The Commonwealth of Oceana*, 38–42, 82–3, 202–3.
48. See especially the first dialogue in Hobbes, *Behemoth or The Long Parliament*.

philosophical and theological debates of his time. However, in contrast to the 1640s, his doctrine could no longer be clearly associated with the royalist party (in combination with Anglicanism), a fact which made him a target of a whole variety of criticisms.

Hobbes's contribution to the modern discourse on toleration was for a long time underestimated,[49] yet it occupies a unique position within this discourse. Although it opposes the intolerance of the churches or of religious groups as one of the chief ills, it regards toleration not as something good in itself but as a possible source of further ills. Therefore, both intolerance in the state and the appeal to conscience and the idea of a right of religious freedom must be avoided. The citizens should be able to live without fear, and for this it is necessary to eliminate the causes of possible conflicts entirely and to establish a sovereign who unites all power on earth and is itself without fear, like the Leviathan described in the Book of Job (41:1–26):

> Any hope of capturing it will be disappointed; were not even the gods overwhelmed at the sight of it? No one is so fierce as to dare to stir it up. Who can stand before it? Who can confront it and be safe? – under the whole heaven, who? . . . When it raises itself up the gods are afraid; at the crashing they are beside themselves . . . On earth it has no equal, a creature without fear.

The motive of fear is of central importance for deciphering the logic of Hobbes's *Leviathan*. The fear of an invisible power is the source of religion[50] and the fear of death is the most powerful passion of human beings (90), whose basic instinct is self-preservation. Thus, the foundation of the state as an artificial being must exploit this fear of *earthly death* in order to establish an enduring condition of peace. To this end it must banish the fear of *eternal death* which, according to Hobbes, is the sole reason, in addition to the fear of an earthly death, not to obey the sovereign (403). In order to lend adequate weight to the principle 'The Passion to be reckoned upon, is Fear' (99) in constructing the machine of state, therefore, it is not sufficient to guarantee security on earth; one must also ensure that the laws of the sovereign do not come into conflict with the preservation of eternal life, for Hobbes regards this conflict as even more serious than the purely 'secular' one. The fact that Hobbes devotes two extended sections of *Leviathan* to this question,

---

49. This situation has undergone a change in recent times; see for example (the in detail very different treatments in) Ryan, 'A More Tolerant Hobbes?'; Tuck, *Hobbes*, 76–91; Sommerville, *Thomas Hobbes*, chs. 5 and 6; Burgess, 'Thomas Hobbes'; Münkler, *Thomas Hobbes*, 138–56; Großheim, 'Religion und Politik'.
50. Hobbes, *Leviathan*, 42 and 76–7 (in what follows, this edition will be cited in the text).

therefore, is not merely a reflection of the discussions of his time but is central to his whole undertaking.

In what follows, I will limit myself to reconstructing the central steps in Hobbes's definition of the relationship between politics and religion in order to show how he tries to neutralise religion politically – not, as for example in Locke, by 'privatising' it by granting freedom of religion but, precisely the opposite, by the fact that the sovereign, as the embodiment of the unity of state and church, overcomes religious conflict and employs toleration exclusively as a means to preserving peace. In this way, Hobbes attempts to recreate the unity of state and church which was in danger of collapsing entirely; yet he does so by means of modern law itself. Exaggerating somewhat, his proposal is to re-establish a *doctrine of divine right without God*, for although the sovereign is God's representative on earth, he owes his life entirely to the prudent contract among the citizens. This argument, whose essential points are prefigured in *Elements* and *De cive*, is first developed fully (with certain alterations) in *Leviathan*.

Hobbes sees human beings as endowed with the natural right to take whatever measures they judge necessary, whether preventative or punitive, to preserve their lives. The laws of nature, by contrast, are rules of reason which specify the means conducive to this end, in the first instance, peace (91–2). The precepts of a morality of reciprocity find their way into these laws, which bind human beings *in foro interno*; in order to enforce them *in foro externo*, however, a sovereign power is needed to ensure that the imperative of self-preservation calls for nothing other than the observance of these laws (110). Therefore, only the 'mortal God' of the state can give rise to the certainty on earth which is necessary for the natural laws – which are laws of God (192)[51] – to become positive laws and thereby acquire binding force (185). Thus, the latter do not dictate merely that a sovereign should be established, but also that one should submit entirely to his power of judgement. In order to achieve this it is indispensable that the natural right to act in accordance with one's own judgement, which in the state of nature leads to the latent or open war of all against all, be transferred through a contract involving all of the citizens to the sovereign who is not a partner to the contract (120).

51. See also Hobbes, *Elements*, 95: 'The laws mentioned . . . as they are called the laws of nature, for that they are the dictates of natural reason; and also moral laws, because they concern men's manners and conversation one towards another; so are they also divine laws in respect of the author thereof, God Almighty; and ought therefore to agree, or at least, not to be repugnant to the word of God revealed in Holy Scripture.'

This is how, according to Hobbes, the Leviathan originates as a mortal god who is subject only to the immortal God and is without rival on earth because he represents the citizens completely. The decisive point is that they have transferred their individual power of judgement to him and henceforth no one any longer has the right to oppose his own judgement to that of the sovereign, unless his self-preservation is at stake (151). What counts is the sovereign's 'absolute and ultimate authority'.[52] In concluding the contract, the citizens have obligated themselves to recognise him as the supreme judge in all matters, for anything less would mean a regression to the state of war. Moreover, the Hobbesian theory of absolute representation assumes that the citizens regard the sovereign as the embodiment of their own judgement and will – an identity argument which will later reappear in Rousseau.

If this identification is to succeed, for Hobbes it is absolutely crucial to show that neither self-interest or certain passions, nor imperatives of morality or those of God, can come into conflict with the laws of the sovereign. As regards self-interest, this is justified by appeal to the interest in security and effective law, as regards the passions, above all by exploiting fear. In virtue of the fact that the citizens only have to fear the Leviathan, who by contrast does not need to fear them, they are secure from one another and also from him as long as they do not threaten him.

Hobbes introduces the doctrine of the laws of natural to demonstrate the compatibility, even the unity, of morality and law – i.e. the command of the sovereign. Natural laws contain the kernel of morality so that preserving peace, mutually renouncing freedom and upholding the contract count as supreme laws. Hence, there are no remaining moral contents over and above the sovereign laws and their interpretation to which individuals could appeal (see chs. 14, 15 and 26).

Even more difficult is the issue of God's commands and whether they can come into conflict with the commands of the sovereign – and if so, what should be done. In order to solve this problem which he regards as central, Hobbes attempts nothing less than to justify in theological and political terms the religious unity of God, sovereign and subject, using the following arguments.

(a) Without being able to discuss the controversial issue of Hobbes's religiosity and his understanding of religion in detail here,[53] it is important

---

52. Kersting, *Die politische Philosophie des Gesellschaftsvertrages*, 100–3.
53. On this, see (in addition to the texts cited in n. 49) the essays in King (ed.), *Thomas Hobbes: Critical Assessments*, vol. IV: *Religion*; also Springborg, 'Hobbes on Religion'. The (exaggerated) thesis that Hobbes's political theory has a pronounced Christian background is defended by Hood, *The Divine Politics of Thomas Hobbes*, and Martinich, *The Two Gods of Leviathan*.

for an understanding of his political philosophy to recognise that for him only one conception of religion is acceptable, the one which can be reconciled with the science of nature and of politics adjudged by him to be correct. The rational kernel of all religion, according to Hobbes, resides in the assumption of a first cause, a first mover of things (77). But reason is incapable of knowing more than that God is unique, infinite and all-powerful; therefore, in addition it regards God as unfathomable. Different positive religions have developed out of this kernel of 'natural piety'.[54] They can be traced back to a divine revelation and they can be *believed* by those to whom such a revelation has not been granted only on the basis of trust, with nothing more than merely historical evidence (198). Reason remains a corrective in the sense that, although faith can surpass reason, it cannot contradict it (255–6) – which leads Hobbes to criticise the idea of 'incorporeal spirits', for example.

(b) This raises the issue of the interpretation of the Word, to which Hobbes responds with a combination of theological and political considerations. Evidently it requires an authority empowered by God to make this interpretation and this can only be the sovereign, according to the laws of nature which are 'undoubtedly' (198) divine in origin. It is incumbent on the sovereign to lend these laws force and their chief requirement is that he should be obeyed. According to Hobbes, it is neither knowable nor rationally possible that God could have empowered another authority to perform this function. Hence, in the 'naturall Kingdome of God' (278), in which, in contrast to a prophetic realm, God does not rule directly but 'by the naturall Dictates of Right Reason' (246), there is no public religious authority apart from the sovereign.

(c) The political authority of the sovereign in religious matters is virtually unbounded. Because the divine natural laws dictate strict obedience to the sovereign, he also has the power to declare that his laws are divine, from which it follows that nobody who refuses to obey the sovereign can appeal to divine commandments (198–9). Since the law is the 'publique Conscience' (223), nobody may refuse to obey the sovereign by appealing to his 'private conscience', which is merely private opinion. An erroneous conscience, according to Hobbes, is not an excuse and cannot be tolerated, for anyone who knows that his conscience can err must obey the will of the sovereign all the more. Hence, there is no privilege of freedom of conscience. In Hobbes's view, the idea that such a privilege exists is as pernicious a principle as that of the two kingdoms, assuming that the latter means that one must obey two masters on earth, or even that the authority of the state is subordinate

54. Hobbes, *Man and Citizen*, 72.

to ecclesiastical authority (227). '*Temporall* and *Spirituall* Government, are but two words brought into the world, to make men see double, and mistake their *Lawfull Soveraign*' (322). Hobbes even envisages a kind of political and religious service in which the people 'may assemble together, and (after prayers and praises given to God, the Soveraign of Soveraigns) hear those their Duties told them, and the Positive Lawes, such as generally concern them all, read and expounded, and be put in mind of the Authority that maketh them Lawes' (235).

Finally, the sovereign also has the power and the authority to guide the opinions of the citizens, because they have direct relevance for civic peace: 'For Doctrine repugnant to Peace, can no more be True, than Peace and Concord can be against the Law of Nature' (125).

(d) Not only is the sovereign absolute in the domain of civil laws, he is also the supreme head of the Church itself. He prescribes the public worship which becomes necessary because the state 'is but one Person' (252) and hence can worship God in only one way too. Here the extent of the idea of the unity of the citizens in the person of the sovereign becomes apparent, for the latter also has just one (public) religion which is simultaneously that of the citizens. The sovereign is also the final authority concerning the always very difficult and controversial question of whether a miracle has occurred. Since the citizens have subordinated their judgement to him 'in all doubtfull cases', it is up to him as 'God's Lieutenant' (305) to judge whether God has performed a miracle or not; Hobbes describes the sovereign as 'Publique Reason' (306) to which private reason must submit.

For, in the final analysis, the sovereign not only prescribes and interprets scripture,[55] but also appoints priests and can even exercise the priestly office in person, by preaching, baptising, administering the sacrament of communion and ordaining priests (372-4). Moreover, judgements concerning what constitutes heresy are also his responsibility (399). In this way, Hobbes strips the Church of any power of its own and subordinates it entirely to the state, as he stresses in particular in the controversy with Cardinal Bellarmine in the central chapter 42 on ecclesiastical power. In the fourth part of *Leviathan* on the 'Kingdome of Darknesse', his rejection of the Catholic Church, in particular, and its claim to have the authority to interpret scripture becomes fully apparent. Hobbes summarises his position as follows:

55. This involves a radicalisation of his position by comparison with *Elements* and *De cive*; for although in those works the sovereign is also invested with power over the Church, nevertheless the latter enjoys a spiritual authority in the interpretation of scripture; see *Elements*, 59, and *De cive*, 245.

> From this consolidation of the Right Politique, and Ecclesiastique in Christian Soveraigns, it is evident, they have all manner of Power over their Subjects, that can be given to man, for the government of mens externall actions, both in Policy, and Religion; and may make such Laws, as themselves shall judge fittest, for the government of their own Subjects, both as they are the Common-wealth, and as they are the Church: For both State, and Church are the same men.   (377–8)

However, this leaves two questions open. Is there a point at which obedience to the sovereign ends for a Christian? And what is meant by specifying the 'externall actions' to which the laws of the sovereign refer?

(e) The first question concerns the problem which is central for Hobbes, namely, that the citizen's fear of the sovereign could come to an end where he must fear that, by obeying the laws, he may avoid earthly death only to suffer eternal death. This is the theme of chapter 43 on 'what is necessary for a man's reception into the kingdom of heaven'. Here Hobbes is not content to show that obedience to the sovereign is dictated by the divine natural laws; rather he seeks an answer based on a dogmatic theological foundation that takes the following form: 'All that is Necessary *to Salvation* is contained in two Vertues, *Faith in Christ*, and *Obedience to Laws*' (403). The *unum necessarium* to achieve eternal life is the proposition 'Jesus is the Christ' (407); everything else is incidental by comparison and it is up to the sovereign to regulate it. With this Hobbes adopts an extreme position which is structurally equivalent to Chillingworth's Anglican-humanist position, but which places such radical restrictions on the basic content of faith that the domain of the *adiaphora* includes all of the things over which the confessions of his time quarrelled. Therefore, Hobbes's message is that as long as the sovereign does not command anything which challenges this article of faith, he is to be obeyed; anything else, i.e. obeying a command which leads to eternal death, would be 'madnesse' (403).

Nevertheless, the two virtues specified can conflict when an irreligious sovereign commands a Christian to repudiate Christ. To this Hobbes offers a very important answer: the Christian cannot be obliged to abjure his faith inwardly; but he does not do this by obeying such a command either. For in that case he merely follows an externally enjoined action, which is really the action of his sovereign and does not impinge on his inner faith, and hence is not a sin (343). Here Hobbes underlines that a prohibition of one's own faith 'is of no effect; because Beleef, and Unbeleef never follow mens Commands' (*ibid.*). And when he returns (in a later passage) to the duty to obey a sovereign who is an infidel, he again stresses that faith is unaffected by this because it is 'internall, and invisible' (414).

(f) This also points to the answer to the above-mentioned second question concerning the restriction on 'external actions'. For in many contexts Hobbes states that faith is a work of God and cannot be brought about through external force – and that the laws of the sovereign only refer to actions, not to inner convictions. Already in chapter 26, where Hobbes accords the sovereign the right to represent his laws as God's will, he qualifies this by stating that, although the subjects are bound to follow these laws, they cannot be obliged to believe this as well. 'For mens beliefe and interiour cogitations, are not subject to the commands, but only to the operation of God, ordinary, or extraordinary' (198). Faith, according to Hobbes, is 'free' in a sense reminiscent of Luther, because it is a gift 'which God freely giveth to whom he pleaseth' (*ibid.*). Therefore, the sovereign cannot determine inner faith (*fides*) by regulating its external profession (*confessio*) (223); he is only the 'public' conscience. His body includes the bodies of the citizens, but not their souls. He determines their actions entirely, but not their thoughts.[56] 'It is true, that if he be my Soveraign, he may oblige me to obedience, so, as not by act or word to declare I beleeve him not; but not to think any otherwise then my person perswades me' (256). And in another passage: 'Faith is a gift of God, which Man can neither give, nor take away by promise of rewards, or menaces of torture' (343). Reason and faith obey laws of their own, the citizen's body the laws of the state.[57]

Thus, freedom of conscience returns in *Leviathan*, but only as inner freedom which cannot claim any practical right for itself. In his criticism of Catholicism, Hobbes observes that the sovereign can question someone he employs in an official position about their opinions, but that this has certain limits:

> But to force him to accuse himselfe of Opinions, when his Actions are not by Law forbidden, is against the Law of Nature; and especially in them, who teach, that a man shall bee damned to Eternall and extream

56. Kersting, *Thomas Hobbes zur Einführung*, 165, remarks in this connection that the sovereign is 'a teacher of behaviour, not of convictions'.

57. Schmitt, *The Leviathan in the State Theory of Thomas Hobbes*, 56–7, considers the difference between inner belief and external profession as the key fault line in the Hobbesian unity of religion and politics, which in his opinion (an anachronistic one, as was shown, for example, by the discussion of the Levellers) became the 'barely visible crack' through which modern liberalism entered after 'a liberal Jew' (57), Spinoza, focused his attention on it. Koselleck, *Critique and Crisis*, 31–3, likewise regards it as the point of entry for a private morality that critically undermines the state.

torments, if he die in a false opinion concerning an Article of the Christian Faith. For who is there, that knowing there is so great danger in an error, whom the naturall care of himself, compelleth not to hazard his Soule upon his own judgement, rather than that of any other man that is unconcerned in his damnation?   (471–2)

This opens up the prospect of toleration in Hobbes. The sovereign protects the citizens against the illegitimate suppression of conscience by the churches and limits his own religious authority to extremely basic teachings and to what is politically necessary.[58] Otherwise, freedom of belief reigns, though not freedom of worship. Although the space of freedom granted is not protected in principle or by law, pragmatic considerations and the limitation of the laws to external conduct together provide a political justification for condoning nonconformist thoughts – for example in the field of science (a case in point being Galileo, whom Hobbes defends in *Leviathan* (473–4), but also in religion.[59] The fact that the framework of toleration is defined primarily in terms of policy and public order precludes a narrow religious demarcation; the sovereign will eliminate politically harmful dogmas as a matter of prudence, but he himself does not have any religious ambitions.[60] This is the other side of the metaphor of the body: the sovereign will not injure himself unnecessarily.

However, these implications of steps (e) and (f) of the argument for toleration should not blind us to the fact that the foregoing steps and the argument as a whole leave it entirely within the power of the sovereign to revoke this toleration at a single stroke, not to mention the fact that freedom of conscience without the freedom to express oneself does not seem especially attractive. Moreover, even if the sovereign can exercise his right to control opinion only through external laws, the notions of a political religious service developed by Hobbes tend to support extensive recourse to 'spiritual' – not to mention pastoral – means of domination. For the path to the domination of the body leads through the soul, as Hobbes is well aware. The skilful manipulator of behaviour will begin by training convictions; and even if this were not successful, the sovereign would have complete external power to punish nonconformist behaviour.

Thus, the doctrine of toleration in *Leviathan*, if one can even speak of such, is precarious to say the least. However much Hobbes wants to combat

58. Münkler, *Thomas Hobbes*, 152–3.
59. See Ryan, 'A More Tolerant Hobbes?', 38, who regards Hobbes as defending an 'unusual degree of intellectual or moral or religious *laissez-faire*'.
60. Tuck, *Hobbes*, 73–4, 88.

religious extremism and to create space for the new, enlightened spirit (against 'superstition'), he can imagine a political order only as a religious-political unity, as *a single* body. Yet he fails in his ambitious project of enlisting the 'new' science and individualistic natural law to construct an 'old' political order which would overcome the conflicts of the new era by seamlessly uniting the sword and the crosier. The attempt to rationalise the expansion of sovereign power on the grounds that the sovereign, as 'public reason', has control and authority over all justifications, be they moral, political or religious, founders on the justification imperatives which arise in these three domains: the independent moral reflection of individuals on their 'natural' rights and duties which lead in the political domain to the demand for political emancipation and (as regards religious policy) for freedom of conscience and worship, as was shown by the debates during the Civil War. Hobbes resists these trends of his time with all his force; yet the guarantee of freedom from fear concerning earthly or eternal life which the Leviathan grants his subjects cannot suffice at any of these levels. The legal situation remains too insecure, the guarantee of freedom too modest, the stripped-down public religion too empty.

Nevertheless, Hobbes's apotheosis of the state, in virtue of its attempt to banish intolerance and to overcome or neutralise the individual reservations of citizens concerning the peace- and decision-making power of the sovereign, represents a consistent development within the discourse of toleration founded on the theory of sovereignty. The state elevated above all conflicts seeks to absorb the normative substance of religion and morality into itself to such an extent that it has the last word, inasmuch as politically relevant conflicts still occur at all. Its will alone decides, and this is ultimately also the will of all individuals. This idea of a political identity logic was one of the reasons for Hobbes's strong enduring influence, as can be seen, for example, from Rousseau's idea of a 'common will'. Rousseau, in particular, who undertook to found the state on the democratic demand for justification, would agree with Hobbes not only that the body politic needs a single, united political will, but also that a reduced political religion in the form of a 'civil religion' is necessary to maintain sovereignty.

2. Hobbes's influence on the modern discourse concerning toleration was already made apparent during his lifetime by an extremely important text, the *Tractatus theologico-politicus* (1670) of Benedict de Spinoza. However, in this plea for free thought and speech, the doctrine of absolute temporal and spiritual sovereignty generated by a contract is transformed into an argument that culminates in the thesis: 'In fact, the true aim of government

is liberty.'[61] Its aim is not only to guarantee a life without fear; drawing on the metaphysical doctrine of freedom and happiness which Spinoza developed in his major work *Ethica ordine geometrico demonstrata* and which also forms the basis of the theological-political treatise, he argues 'that the best government will allow freedom of philosophical speculation no less than of religious belief' (261). This already points to the controversies with which Spinoza – in this also similar to Hobbes – has to contend, namely those in theology and political theory.

Both Spinoza's thought and his life were shaped by the quest for 'freedom of philosophical speculation' and by the struggle against intolerance. Spinoza received a Jewish education as the son of Portuguese Jews, the so-called 'Marranos', who were forcibly baptised Catholic and had left Portugal for Amsterdam via Spain so that they could live in accordance with their faith and escape the threat of the Inquisition. However, his further studies estranged him from this context. In 1656 he was excommunicated by the Jewish community and banned from the synagogue[62] and in 1660 he was forced to leave Amsterdam. He enjoyed the support of the Regents' party of Jan de Witt, under whose leadership the Netherlands had developed into a successful trading nation (and a colonial power) in which a variety of ethnic and religious minorities were granted a level of social toleration which was generous by comparison with other countries. Spinoza wrote his treatise at the request of the Regents, though this exposed him to criticism from many sides and in particular to the accusation of atheism. With the accession to power of the 'Stadtholders' under William III of Orange, the circulation of Spinoza's works was forbidden.

As early as 1665, in a letter to Heinrich Oldenburg, Spinoza describes his motives for writing the *Tractatus*.

> I am now writing a Treatise about my interpretation of Scripture. This I am driven to do by the following reasons: 1. The Prejudices of the Theologians; for I know that these are among the chief obstacles which prevent men from directing their mind to philosophy; and therefore I do all I can to expose them, and to remove them from the minds of the more prudent. 2. The opinion which the common people have of me, who do not cease to accuse me falsely of atheism; I am also obliged to avert this accusation as far as it is possible to do so. 3. The freedom of philosophizing, and of saying what we think; this I desire to vindicate

---

61. Spinoza, *A Theological-Political Treatise*, 259. (Page references in the text are to this edition.)
62. On this, see Yovel, *Spinoza and Other Heretics*, vol. 1: *The Marrano of Reason*, chs. 1 and 2.

in every way, for here it is always suppressed through the excessive authority and influence of the preachers.[63]

These motivations explain why Spinoza devotes three-quarters of his work to theological questions before turning to the theory of the state proper. He is convinced that the struggle for free thought must first be conducted on theological terrain and that the principal evil is not the state but the churches and popular religious prejudices – and the state only insofar as it becomes the instrument of power-hungry religious politics. Thus, Spinoza undertakes to show, as the subtitle of the *Tractatus* puts it, 'that freedom of thought and speech not only may, without prejudice to piety and the public peace, be granted; but also may not, without danger to piety and the public peace, be withheld' (1).

The arguments for toleration which Spinoza presents to this end can be divided into three categories: (a) theological justifications, (b) political justifications founded on natural law and (c) perfectionist justifications. However, a complete reconstruction of his arguments must take into consideration how Spinoza's fundamental philosophy, as presented in the *Ethica*, shapes each of them.

(a) In order to understand Spinoza's attitude towards religion, three things must be distinguished: first his own philosophical conception of the essence of God and of the corresponding form of worship; second, his criticism of positive religion and scripture; and, third, his conception of a minimal religion conducive to peaceful social coexistence.

The first goes to the heart of his thought, the philosophical knowledge independent of faith that God is the 'unconditional infinite' substance of all being, an unlimited power which brings forth the individual things as modes of itself, so that these things are equipped with different attributes all of which are united in this power. Spinoza's God loses all transcendence and becomes pure immanence. Apart from God there is no substance, and 'whatsoever is, is in God, and without God nothing can be, or be conceived'.[64] Thus, all knowledge of existence is also knowledge of God;[65] and accordingly the very first chapter of the *Tractatus*, where Spinoza launches his critique of 'prophetic knowledge', states that: 'Nevertheless [natural knowledge] has as much right as any other to be called Divine, for God's nature, insofar as we share therein, and God's laws, dictate it to us' (13–14). This already contains the kernel of his critique of all further speculative religion and of his defence

63. Spinoza, *The Correspondence*, 206.   64. Spinoza, *Ethics*, Part i, Prop. xv (55).
65. Cf. *ibid*. Part ii, Prop. xliv (116).

against the accusation that his pantheism is a disguised form of atheism. It also contains the kernel of his idea of human perfection as striving towards knowledge *sub specie aeternitatis*, the highest form of knowledge attainable by human beings.[66]

Second, Spinoza's critique of positive religion – and, in particular, his historical-critical method of studying scripture, which was far ahead of his time – must be understood against this background.[67] In combating theological prejudices, which in combination with the churches' claim to political authority and popular superstition give rise to the chief evil of intolerance, Spinoza subjects scripture to an examination 'in a careful, impartial, and unfettered spirit' (8), as he puts it, and concludes that scripture is not a 'message sent down by God from Heaven to men' (165), but a historical document which becomes sacred through its use alone and contains in essence some truths beyond the reach of all speculative theological disputes (186). The method of interpreting scripture, according to Spinoza, 'does not widely differ from the method of interpreting nature' (99). Although it will not be possible to present Spinoza's historical-philological analysis of the Bible here, it is worth mentioning that, en route to his plea for such a residual religion, he subjects the declarations of the prophets concerning divine revelation to a radical critique and concludes that their views are subjective and historically coloured, contradictory, and hence unreliable (27–30, 35). Further contents of scripture are also exposed as mere 'histories' (78–9), for instance stories of miracles, and the authorship of large parts of the Bible, in the first instance that of Moses, is placed in question.

Interesting in this connection is a comparison with the teaching of Maimonides (see above §6.4), from which Spinoza expressly seeks to distance his critique, though the commonalities go further than he is willing to acknowledge. Both thinkers seek to interpret scripture in rational terms and to overcome its anthropomorphisms and inconsistencies, and both of them want to create a space of freedom within theology for philosophical questioning. Both also agree that the freedom in question should be reserved exclusively for those who go beyond the merely conventional belief in the law of the mass of the people and aspire to philosophical knowledge of divine truth, and thus to the supreme spiritual perfection (and blessedness). In Maimonides, however, this highest form of knowledge of God is the prophetic, a view Spinoza rejects entirely (114ff.); and for Maimonides reason remains bound to scripture in such a way that its task is to interpret scripture in rational terms and

66. Cf. *ibid*. Part v, Prop. xxix (267).   67. On this, see Strauss, *Spinoza's Critique of Religion*.

thus to confirm it. Spinoza calls this a 'dogmatic' position which attempts to make scripture conform to reason in order to derive philosophical truths from it (114–17; 190–1). In contrast to this, he argues for a radical separation between philosophy and theology, between reason and faith: scripture 'does not teach philosophy' (190), nor any speculative truths; still more, reason alone is supreme in the philosophical domain of 'truth and wisdom', whereas 'the sphere of theology is piety and obedience' (194). Neither sphere is subservient to the other, yet theology must be 'in accordance with reason' (195). The belief in revealed religion rests on a 'moral certainty' like that which the prophets also possessed; nothing more is necessary for a pious life. Faith, which in essence demands obedience to God's commandments, promises most mortals, who cannot achieve an ethical life through reason alone, 'very great consolation' (199) and a blessedness in which they may believe, even if reason views it with scepticism.

This already points to the third moment of Spinoza's conception of religion alluded to above, namely the minimal religion founded on scripture alone which is conducive to peaceful social relations for those who cannot approach God by way of reason but only through belief in 'histories' or 'narratives' (79, 175). Spinoza reduces this core content, not unlike Hobbes, to the basic imperative of obedience to God, which consists in love of one's neighbour (176, 183). Hence, faith does not involve any speculative dogmas but only those which are necessary for obedience to God; and Spinoza adds that this leaves no room for ecclesiastical disputes. Spinoza lists seven dogmas – that there exists a God or supreme being who is one, omnipresent, rules over all things, promotes justice and charity, redeems, and forgives sinners (186–7) – which represent the indispensable minimum for obedience. It is up to the individuals themselves how they adapt these dogmas to their intellectual capacities and interpret them; furthermore, works alone, not speculative discussions, will reveal who has the best faith (188).

Hence, the theological argument for toleration has different facets. First, the content of faith is reduced radically to an ethical-moral kernel which calls for love of one's neighbour and, in particular, toleration: '[W]hosoever persecutes the faithful, is an enemy to Christ' (185). Second, it is up to individual believers how they make these dogmas fit with their more comprehensive doctrines; in this Spinoza anticipates Rawls's idea of an overlapping consensus in the theological context:

> As, then, each man's faith must be judged pious or impious only in respect of its producing obedience or disobedience, and not in respect of its truth; and as no one will dispute that men's dispositions are

exceedingly varied, that all do not acquiesce in the same things, but are
ruled some by one opinion some by another, so that what moves one to
devotion moves another to laughter and contempt, it follows that
there can be no doctrines in the catholic, or universal, religion, which
can give rise to controversy among good men . . . To the universal
religion, then, belong only such dogmas as are absolutely required in
order to attain obedience to God, and without which such obedience
would be impossible; as for the rest, each man – seeing that he is the
best judge of his own character – should adopt whatever he thinks best
adapted to strengthen his love of justice.   (186)

In addition to this argument for freedom of thought in the religious domain,
Spinoza provides another argument for freedom of philosophical thought
which is central to his concerns – he refers to it as the main point of his
treatise (189). A space is opened up for it by the fact that philosophical truth,
as long as it does not undermine obedience, cannot come into conflict with
a religious faith which is only concerned with obedience:

> Faith, therefore, allows the greatest latitude in philosophic
> speculation, allowing us without blame to think what we like about
> anything, and only condemning, as heretics and schismatics, those
> who teach opinions which tend to produce disobedience, hatred,
> strife, and anger; while, on the other hand, only considering as faithful
> those who persuade us, as far as their reason and faculties will permit,
> to follow justice and charity.   (189)

This completes the theological argument and the justification of the freedom
to philosophise. Spinoza now turns his attention to the state in order to
show how far freedom is its purpose, and how obedience towards God can
be brought into line with obedience towards the temporal sovereign.

(b) At the level of the theory of the state, the agreements between
Spinoza's arguments and those of Hobbes are as conspicuous as are their
differences. An important parallel is the construction of a conflict-riven
state of nature in which individuals make unhindered use of their right
of self-preservation and then, through a contractual agreement to transfer this right, constitute a state which formulates and at the same time
enforces positive laws, and thereby gives rise to a condition of general peace.
However, there are already major differences in their underlying premises
concerning natural freedom and individual rights. Spinoza derives the striving for self-preservation from his notion that everything created by God
strives to preserve its being (*in suo esse perseverare conatur*). It is God's power
that endows them with this striving against anything which could destroy

their being and towards extending their own effective power.[68] This leads Spinoza not only to the assertion that individual human beings have a right of nature that 'is coextensive with their power' and that this is 'the power of God' (200); in addition, he places even greater stress than Hobbes on the fact that in the state of nature there is no real 'right' in the normative sense, only the power of persistence or of augmenting one's effective power. Here there are no 'laws of nature' in Hobbes's sense; the state of nature, according to Spinoza, is prior to religion (and to God's commandments) (210).

In order to be able to live 'securely and well' (202), individuals enter into a strictly reciprocal contract in which they renounce the individual exercise of their rights (or powers) and transfer them to the collectivity, so that its will is dominant. Although, as in Hobbes, the resulting sovereign is not bound by the contract himself, Spinoza thinks that Hobbes is also inconsistent on this point because he makes everything depend on fear as the motive for obedience and fails to emphasise the idea of obeying the laws from freedom as a logical consequence of entering into the contract. Democracy is 'a general union of human beings which, taken together, has the supreme right to everything of which it is capable' (205). Because here the subjects themselves constitute the sovereign, the latter will make decisions in accordance with reason so as not to harm itself; hence, reason holds sway in a democracy and the individual members are free (206). Here Spinoza anticipates Rousseau's central idea that, in a democracy, personal and political freedom are guaranteed by the rule of the general will:

> [A]s obedience consists in acting at the bidding of external authority, it would have no place in a state where the government is vested in the whole people, and where laws are made by common consent. In such a society the people would remain free, whether the laws were added to or diminished, inasmuch as it would not be done on external authority, but their own free consent.
>
> (74)[69]

Therefore, democracy is the 'most natural', though not the only legitimate, form of government, because it preserves natural freedom to the greatest extent.

However, here, as in Hobbes, the question also arises of how the laws of the state can be brought into harmony with divine commandments. This

---

68. Spinoza, *Ethics*, Part III, Prop. VI (175).
69. The same argument can be found in *ibid*. Part IV, Prop. LXXIII (235–6).

broaches two problems, first that of a possible justification of resistance and, second, that of toleration of religious difference. Spinoza, like Hobbes, responds to the first problem by appealing to an immanent connection between the minimal religion and obedience to the sovereign as the supreme temporal and spiritual authority; he responds to the second – in contrast to Hobbes, though in accordance with a certain logic of the latter's theory – by appealing to a residual right to free thought which was not renounced in the contract.

The former reveals the political implications of Spinoza's criticism of religion. Not only is it impossible for epistemic reasons to appeal directly to the word of God against the laws of the state, it is also illegitimate because no universal norms exist prior to the state and what just action means is first determined in the state. Thus, the obedience that God demands towards his ethical precepts is transformed into obedience towards the sovereign who posits normativity:

> Justice, therefore, and absolutely all the precepts of reason, including love towards one's neighbour, receive the force of laws and ordinances solely through the rights of dominion, that is . . . solely on the decree of those who possess the right to rule. Inasmuch as the kingdom of God consists entirely in rights applied to justice and charity or to true religion, it follows that . . . the kingdom of God can only exist among men through the means of the sovereign powers.   (247)

With this the content of the admissible religion has migrated from the ethical into the political domain. It is not possible to appeal to God's will beyond the will of the political collectivity. Temporal law has clear priority, and therefore the temporal power also has the right to make 'any laws about religion which it thinks fit' (212), for otherwise it would not enjoy complete sovereignty. Those in possession of sovereign power are 'the interpreters and the champions' of ecclesiastical law (245), they prescribe 'the rites of religion and the outward observances of piety', for this belongs to the domain of earthly justice, which is that of the state. The 'love of one's country' (249) then counts as 'the highest form of piety', and the obedience which the faithful owe God they owe (on earth) entirely to the state.

This is the one side of the coin: the centralisation of religious power in the power of the state in order, in combination with a dogmatic reduction, to undercut religious strife between the confessions in the public domain. The other side consists in turn in setting a limit to the power of the state in order to prevent this power from becoming intolerant. Here Spinoza brings his natural law-based argument into play once again in setting a *factual* limit to the transfer of rights to the state which, in virtue of the identification of natural law and natural power, itself becomes a limit founded on natural law. Since 'no one the whole world over can be forced or legislated into a state of blessedness' (118), nobody *can* relinquish his right to freedom of thought and belief to the sovereign, even if he wanted to (257). The sovereign cannot sensibly require this either – not only, it should be noted, out of consideration for inner conviction as a necessary condition of the spiritual welfare of the individual, but in an awareness of the limitations of his own power. Free thought is the most original freedom of the individual and it cannot be relinquished. Accordingly, the sovereign can regulate only external religious observances (*externo cultu*), not piety itself or inward worship (*interno cultu*), because these 'are within the sphere of everyone's private rights, and cannot be alienated' (*quod in alium transferri non potest*) (245). For this reason any state which attempts to exercise political control over thoughts is bound to fail; it will act against nature and bring about its own destruction. The state exists for the sake of this freedom (259), according to Spinoza, and it includes the freedom to express one's opinions in word and print, though *not* to act on them. The realm of truth is distinct from the realm of justice. Freedom of thought and speech reaches its limit, in turn, where 'seditious' opinions (260) are defended which not only jeopardise public justice, and hence the state itself, but are also not mere opinions, but actions. This completes the argument from the theory of the state.

(c) In addition to the theological argument and the natural law-based political argument, in Spinoza there is also a perfectionist justification of toleration which is important in the context of his ethics, as already indicated. For his ethics, in spite of its distinctiveness, remains a doctrine of blessedness which states that the highest good of the mind consists in knowledge of God,[70] and that its chief satisfaction consists in regarding things *sub specie aeternitatis*; such perfection of the mind constitutes the true blessedness.[71] It is 'mental love of God' for which Spinoza wants to create room in his discussion of theology and the theory of the state; it constitutes the real ethical purpose of the state, even though this path to blessedness is open to only a few, and ultimately only to the 'wise' (175–6, 216).[72] It is not the task of the state to lead human beings actively to the good; however, insofar as

---

70. *Ibid.* Part IV, Prop. XXVIII (205).   71. *Ibid.* Part V, Prop. XXXIII (263–4).
72. *Ibid.* Part V, Prop. XLII (270–1). In 'Die Autonomie des Denkens', 288, Dilthey points out the Stoic roots of this ethics.

it suppresses intolerance on the part of the churches and of the people[73] it makes possible the form of existence in which this perfection can be achieved (257). This telos marks the culmination of Spinoza's doctrine of toleration, which treats the justifications of toleration on the first two levels as 'steps' leading to the possibility of the intellectual perfection of the few.

To summarise, one can say that Spinoza develops the 'doctrine of toleration', which is merely hinted at in Hobbes, in a consistent manner. However, in the process he tends to exacerbate the conflict between, on the one side, a secular political power which has the right not only to stipulate the external forms of worship but also to govern the 'hearts' of the subjects as a spiritual power and to subordinate the political role of religion entirely to its own purposes, and, on the other, the claim of individuals to freedom of religion, thought and speech. The very means which, according to Spinoza, the secular sovereign requires to prevail against the churches, confessions and other religious extremists also jeopardises the toleration which is his main concern. On the one hand, this is supposed to create the space of freedom but, on the other, the latter is simultaneously shut down. In this way, the powerful sovereign can banish intolerance from society, but he himself is able to employ toleration as well as intolerance for practical purposes. These difficulties remain even in the case of a democracy, for then minorities would confront a majority which can view itself as a kind of ecclesiastical power, as the 'interpreters and champions' of scripture.

Moreover, the dogmas from which no deviation can be permitted have the potential to lead to exclusions based on appeals to articles of faith, for example if a group were to cast doubt on the dogma of God's singularity. Since Spinoza regards this as indispensable for obedience – both to God and to the state – this could entail narrow, religiously based restrictions on toleration (not only towards the atheists).

In this context it is also important to recognise how difficult it is to draw the boundary between the harmful, 'seditious' opinions, which Spinoza wants to exclude on the grounds that they constitute actions, and the unorthodox opinions that the citizens are permitted to express.[74] As long as the state is also the supreme political and religious power, disagreement and nonconformity can easily be construed as a challenge to the public order.

In addition, Spinoza's reference to the natural 'legal' limits to the extent of the political power to coerce the mind and thought is dubious, given

73. On the 'civilising' role of religion and the state, see Strauss, *Spinoza's Critique of Religion*, 224–50; Yovel, *Spinoza and Other Heretics*, vol. 1, ch. 5.
74. See also Hampshire, *Spinoza*, 149.

Spinoza's own conception of government as 'rule over hearts', all the more so in the light of 'rationalised' methods of indoctrination[75] and 'thought control', i.e. the production of compliant or 'reformed' subjects of which Augustine already spoke.

Thus, the price which Spinoza is ultimately willing to pay for the freedom to philosophise is a high one, specifically an absolute sovereign, a reduction of religious faith to ethical, and ultimately political, obedience, and restrictions on freedom of worship and action in general at the sole discretion of the sovereign. Spinoza wants guarantees of political freedom as much as of freedom of thought; however, in the process he jeopardises individual freedom of action. Measured by the connection between individual freedom of conscience and worship and political freedom as demands of justice discussed in §15, Spinoza's theory fails to live up to its claim to privilege freedom as the purpose of the state. In the final analysis, it is the perfectionist argument within the framework of an 'elitist' ethics[76] and the complete transfer of the domain of justice to sovereign legislation that prevents him from exploiting the potential of his own argument to safeguard the natural freedom of individuals. The right to justification, which he emphasises in his grounding of democracy, is subordinated in Spinoza's theory of the state, which ultimately remains beholden to Hobbes, to the task of securing the authority of a sovereign who should be strong enough to guarantee free thought. The guiding perspective thereby shifts from a horizontal to a vertical conception of toleration which must be viewed as a modified permission conception.

3. A brief comparison with a text which, like Spinoza's *Tractatus*, appeared in 1670 (in England) and which represents the concrete objection of someone who suffered religious persecution, may serve to clarify how much more radical and more 'enlightened' Spinoza's conception of religion is than the one presented there, though also how far Spinoza's political theory lags behind the 'birthright' argument. The text in question is William Penn's *The Great Case of Liberty of Conscience once more briefly debated and defended*. I will discuss the situation in England after the restoration of the Stuarts under Charles II and the reinstatement of the Anglican ecclesiastical regime in 1660 in greater detail later; here it suffices to note that this led to a period of persecution and repression of religious nonconformists and *Dissenters* under which groups like the Quakers, to which Penn belonged, also suffered. Penn was imprisoned a number of times (*The Great Case* was also

75. See Smith, 'Toleration and the Skepticism of Religion in Spinoza's *Tractatus Theologico-Politicus*', 137.
76. Bartuschat, 'Einleitung', xvii, describes Spinoza's ethics in these terms.

written in prison). Nevertheless, having regained his freedom, he managed to found the North American colony of Pennsylvania in 1681, which under his leadership undertook the 'Holy Experiment' of a peaceful coexistence of different religious confessions (though one in which non-Christians enjoyed only limited rights).[77]

In his short text, Penn attacks the persecution by the Church of England in a series of arguments which connect up with the discourse of religious and political freedom sketched in §15 and present the latter in an especially vivid way, in particular the connection between a Protestant conception of conscience and a contractualist democratic justification of the state. On the very first page Penn makes clear that, although he is speaking for a persecuted minority, he is not making a plea for special consideration but is stating a claim to freedoms 'to which we are entitled by English birth-right'.[78] The spectrum of arguments he goes on to present ranges from specifically Christian-theological considerations, through considerations founded on a reason-based conception of rational law, to normative democratic considerations. I would like to mention the latter here briefly in order to show how strongly Penn, on the one hand, connects the question of toleration more closely than Spinoza with that of the correct religion, yet the extent to which, on the other, he defends a stronger egalitarian understanding of reciprocal justice. He also makes clear from the outset that there can be no question of separating freedom of thought from freedom of worship (134).

Penn's central theological argument is the doctrine of the two kingdoms in the version which emphasises that God is 'the object as well as the author, both of our faith, worship, and service' (135), and hence that any human enforcement of worship of God is a direct violation of divine 'prerogatives'; it represents an illegitimate usurpation of divine power which is in the first instance a crime *against God*. God, according to Penn, has equipped all human beings with a faculty of reason which comprises an 'instinct of a Deity' (140) within it that develops in an autonomous way into a veneration of God through the individual's exercise of discursive judgement. Penn rejects the attempt to steer this process from the outside with reference to human fallibility as *contrary to reason*.

At the level of political morality, Penn argues that intolerance is *unjust* as well as *imprudent*. The basic rule of justice to treat others only as one wants to be treated oneself states that it is unjust to claim for oneself the privilege

---

77. See Kamen, *The Rise of Toleration*, 205–11.
78. Penn, *The Great Case of Liberty of Conscience*, 128 (cited in the text in what follows).

of coercing others according to one's own conception of truth, a right which one would never grant them (143). Penn attempts to show that religious persecution is imprudent by citing a range of factors, for instance that this could have negative economic effects, that the 'papists' could employ this as a pretext for their own repressions in their countries, and that this only foments sedition and hatred. Besides – and here we once again encounter the classical argument which also plays an important role in Spinoza – this is completely *futile*, for conscience simply cannot be coerced (146; see also 130: 'neither can any external coercive power convince the understanding of the poorest ideot').

Finally, Penn rounds off his argument with the contractualist point that the right to freedom of religion is such a fundamental right and 'property' (147) of English citizens that it constitutes the foundation of the state, not something at the disposal of the state. Were the state to weaken it, it would undermine itself.

This brief examination of one of the many texts which, apart from the well-known writings of a Spinoza or a Locke, present comprehensive and important justifications of toleration shows, first, that although Spinoza was more sceptical towards religious justifications of toleration than, for instance, Penn – in the latter they also entail that the 'papists' and non-Christians are not included in the argument from the beginning (in contrast to Roger Williams, for example) – nevertheless, second, that Penn has a clearer conception of toleration as a question of reciprocal justice between citizens, and hence does not regress to a permission conception and the idea of a religion imposed by the state. Neither in Spinoza nor in Penn do religious scepticism and scepticism towards absolute power go hand-in-hand; rather, in both respects the two authors proceed in opposite directions.

Penn's text, as we have seen, takes up the threads of the toleration debate in the context of the English Civil War and points forward to post-Restoration England, that is to the context in which John Locke's reflections on toleration developed, extending from the beginning of the Restoration to the Glorious Revolution.

§17 Letters on toleration

1. In Locke's case, as in that of other authors discussed thus far, it is important to emphasise that his ideas and arguments arose under specific conditions of political and cultural conflict, while also insisting that their content transcends this context and continues to shape contemporary discourse

concerning toleration – in Locke's case, profoundly so. And, as with some of the theories already discussed, his theory of toleration is also marked by a mixture of an individualistic concept of conscience originating in Protestantism and an understanding of natural law which leads to the demand for political emancipation – in combination with an empiricist theory of knowledge. It is not an exaggeration to say that this liberal justification of toleration reaches its culmination in Locke's work. As we shall see, although there are no entirely new normative arguments in Locke by comparison with Walwyn, Milton and Williams, his most famous work on toleration, the (first) *Letter Concerning Toleration*, can claim originality primarily in liberating the familiar arguments more fully than previously (though not entirely) from their religious garb and lending them systematic form. However, the comparison with Walwyn or Williams will reveal that Locke draws the limits of toleration, for example towards Catholics and atheists, more narrowly than they do.

First some observations on the historical context are in order. In 1660, Stuart rule was restored under Charles II who enjoyed the support of a compliant parliament. The Anglican state church was also re-established and immediately set about implementing a range of legal measures, the so-called Clarendon Code, to impose uniformity on the religious nonconformists or Dissenters (for instance, through the Uniformity Act of 1662). Aside from the Catholics, the Presbyterians and Independents, but also the Quakers, Baptists and Unitarians, were the victims of these laws and persecutions.[79] The king himself, who sympathised with Catholicism and had promised religious toleration in 1660, at times sought to alleviate these harsh laws in collaboration with the Dissenters and moderate Anglicans, in particular through the Declaration of Indulgence of 1672, though he revoked this a year later in order to buttress his power through an alliance of Anglicans and gentry. This provoked the opposition of the Dissenters who formed the Whig party under the leadership of the Earl of Shaftesbury, who was at various times Lord Chancellor. The Whig party sought on the one hand to achieve legal toleration, but also on the other to thwart the danger of a Catholic assumption of power, which ultimately developed into the main point of conflict with the Tories – especially as it became known that the heir to the throne, the later James II, was a Catholic. The so-called Exclusion Crisis (1679–81), the attempt to obtain a law excluding Catholics from the line of succession, ultimately ended in defeat and Shaftesbury fled to Holland in 1682. James II,

79. On this, see Goldie, 'The Theory of Religious Intolerance in Restoration England'.

who became king in 1685 and advocated freedom of conscience,[80] attempted to push through a new Declaration of Indulgence against the opposition of the Anglicans in 1687, but had to flee in 1688 following the invasion of England by William of Orange. The Glorious Revolution brought William to the throne in 1689, though his power was tied to Parliament. In the same year he enacted the Toleration Act which granted nonconformist Protestants freedom of worship, though it left in place a series of restrictions and exclusions for Catholics, Unitarians and other groups (see section 6 below).

These events formed the background for Locke's work on politics and religion, which can be divided into four phases.[81] The first phase, during which he taught at Oxford and practised medicine, covers the *Two Tracts on Government* (1660–2), in which Locke, perturbed by the religious turmoil of his time, takes up the theory of external conformity defended by Hooker and radicalised by Hobbes. In these writings, therefore, we encounter an apparently completely 'un-Lockean' Locke. This changed when he made the acquaintance of the later Earl of Shaftesbury in 1666, into whose service he entered in 1667 and for whom he wrote the 'Essay on Toleration' (1667) as an aid to argument against the king. In this work Locke retracts the thesis that the sovereign is authorised to regulate 'indifferent' religious matters and places greater emphasis on the limits of the authority of the state in religious questions. During the Exclusion Crisis, Locke began work on the later *Two Treatises of Government*, in which he refutes Filmer's influential theory, which the Tories used to justify absolutism, and defends the right to resistance. In the third phase, which began with his exile in Holland in 1683 where he followed Shaftesbury, Locke wrote the *Epistola de tolerantia* (1685), in which he adopted the position of the Dissenters and developed a systematic theory of toleration against the background of the revocation of the Edict of Nantes and James II's accession to the throne. The final phase began in 1689 with his return to England and the publication of his most important works in the same year, the *Two Treatises*, the *Letter Concerning Toleration* (first published in Latin in Holland, then in the same year in a translation by William Popple, both anonymously) and the *Essay Concerning Human Understanding*. These were followed in later years (1690, 1692, 1704) by three further letters on toleration which Locke wrote mainly to refute the objections of Jonas Proast. Finally, in 1695 Locke's study *The Reasonableness of Christianity* appeared in which he defended a deistic position.

80. On this, see Kamen, *The Rise of Toleration*, 207–8.
81. See Goldie, 'Introduction', 15; In addition Tully, 'An Introduction to Locke's Political Philosophy'.

In what follows, the most important stages and arguments in Locke's reflection on toleration will be outlined: first the *Two Tracts*, then the *Essay*, the first *Letter Concerning Toleration* (in connection with his mature political theory and epistemology), and finally the controversy with Proast, which leads to a discussion of Locke's approach as a whole. This will be followed by a critical examination of the practice of toleration on the basis of an analysis of the Toleration Act.

2. The two *Tracts on Government*, which were written between 1660 and 1662 and remained unpublished, provide additional evidence of the influence exercised by Hobbes's *Leviathan* on the discourse concerning toleration of his time, even though Locke situates important elements of Hobbes's theory within a religious framework more deeply indebted to Hooker.[82] Moreover, in Locke's argument, which is infused with the spirit of the Restoration, he diplomatically leaves open the question of whether the absolute sovereign (be it a person or a citizen assembly) is appointed directly by God or through a contract among the citizens; he draws on both premises in an attempt to demonstrate that the civil magistrate has the authority to regulate civilly *and* ecclesiastically indifferent matters by law. In this, Locke (especially in the first, so-called *English Tract*) contradicts Edward Bagshaw's 1660 work, *The Great Question Concerning Things Indifferent in Religious Worship*, which had attacked precisely this regulatory authority of the state as an interference with freedom of conscience. Among such *adiaphora* – that is, to repeat, things which God has not prescribed in scripture as necessary for achieving salvation – are, for example, as Locke specifies, the place and time of religious services, kneeling for the sacraments and certain forms of prayer. According to Locke, it was essentially disputes over such matters that plunged England into war and revolt – though now, with the return of the king, this was fortunately a thing of the past. Therefore, Locke's chief anxiety here is not, as in Hobbes and Spinoza, the abuse of temporal power but the intolerance among the Christian confessions, the 'tyranny of a religious rage', which makes necessary a strong sovereign as *conservator pacis*.[83] He alone can banish the threat of religious civil war and of false appeals to conscience which bring about the destruction of the state.

At the core of the argument in this text is Locke's view of the secular authority as the custodian of earthly justice, that is, of the regulation of external actions. In matters concerning natural and divine law, the role of the

---

82. Locke, in contrast to Hobbes, makes several positive references to Hooker.
83. Locke, *First Tract*, 7 and 41.

secular legislator is confined to proclaiming and implementing such law;[84] in matters which are indifferent, however, individuals have transferred their natural freedom to regulate them in accordance with their own judgement to the sovereign. For at stake here are matters in which human beings are no longer directly subjected to God, but which must nevertheless also be regulated in the general interest of peace, which only the legitimate legislator may do. If the sovereign did not issue any rules, according to Locke, dissension would immediately break out over the proper form of worship, since human beings are not naturally disposed to tolerance in the absence of legal coercion;[85] even worse, individuals could appeal to freedom of conscience at will as a pretext to shield themselves from the laws:

> I grant all agree that conscience is tenderly to be dealt with, and not to be imposed on, but if the determining any indifferent outward action contrary to a man's persuasion . . . be imposing on conscience and so unlawful, I know not how a Quaker should be compelled by hat or leg to pay a due respect to the magistrate or an Anabaptist be forced to pay tithes . . . Imposing on conscience seems to me to be, the pressing of doctrines or laws upon the belief or practice of men as of divine original, as necessary to salvation and in themselves obliging the conscience, when indeed they are no other but the ordinances of men and the products of their authority; otherwise, if you take it in our author's [i.e. Bagshaw's] sense every lawful command of the magistrate, since we are to obey them for conscience sake, would be an imposing on conscience and so according to his way of arguing unlawful.[86]

Locke goes on to point out that the boundary between questions to be decided in a 'civil' versus a 'spiritual' way cannot be clearly drawn; his fear is that virtually any refusal to obey could be justified in religious terms, if only strategically:

> Let the people (whose ears are always open to complaints against their governors, who greedily swallow all pleas for liberty) but once hear that the magistrate hath no authority to enjoin things indifferent in matters of religion, they will all of an instant be converts, conscience and religion shall presently mingle itself with all their actions and be spread over their whole lives to protect them from the reach of the magistrate . . . Do but once arm their consciences against the magistrate and their hands will not be long idle or innocent.[87]

84. Locke, *Second Tract*, 63–71.   85. Locke, *First Tract*, 41.   86. *Ibid.* 22–3.   87. *Ibid.* 36.

From this Locke concludes that the sovereign has 'an absolute and arbitrary power' in the domain of indifferent, external actions.[88] In this he relies on the fact that the secular power will use this right prudently so as not to provoke internal disorder itself. The sovereign is, of course, answerable only to God.

These arguments have earned the early Locke the reputation of an authoritarian thinker[89] who rejects toleration and who only later became an advocate of toleration when he began to work for Shaftesbury.[90] This view is not entirely unfounded given Locke's rejection of an inclusive freedom of worship and his thesis that the rights to act freely are transferred to the sovereign. However, it overlooks the fact that Locke explicitly confines his argument to 'exterior, indifferent actions',[91] to actions and *not* convictions, and also *only* to such actions as fall within this domain of state regulation in general and not into that of divine natural law. For the latter specifies what constitutes the God-given freedom of individuals as beings bound to God, and where the limits of the authority of the state lie, namely in the 'internal worship of hearts' which is beyond the reach of any positive law and in the essential external acts of worship, such as prayer or receiving the sacraments, that do not fall under the category of the *adiaphora*.[92] As Locke stresses at the opening of the second treatise, the Latin Tract, the magistrate does not have any power of command here, only God himself. All that the magistrate can regulate is the external conformity of the religious service. Here Locke sets much narrower limits to sovereignty than does Hobbes because his conception of the *adiaphora* is far more restricted than Hobbes's; hence the claim that the sovereign is only answerable to God has a different substance than it does in Hobbes. Locke agrees with Hobbes, however, in emphasising that, in indifferent matters, the sovereign can in any case only oblige 'formally' but not 'materially', 'obliging men to act but not to judge', thereby preserving the inner freedom of conscience.[93] The state only governs the body; God alone governs the soul.[94] Moreover, the sovereign can even fall afoul of this limitation if he tries to make the regulation of *adiaphora* internally binding. For he then commits a sin, according to Locke.

88. *Ibid.* 9.
89. Dunn, *The Political Thought of John Locke*, 30; Cranston, 'John Locke and the Case for Toleration', 80.
90. Tully, 'An Introduction to Locke's Political Philosophy', 50; Creppell, 'Locke on Toleration', 215; also already Gough, 'The Development of Locke's Belief in Toleration', 63.
91. Locke, *First Tract*, 15.   92. Locke, *Second Tract*, 57–8.   93. *Ibid.* 76–7.
94. Locke, *First Tract*, 29: 'the heart may be lift up to heaven, while the body bows'.

The references to freedom of conscience in the above quotations should be borne in mind in this context. For Locke attaches great importance to the fact that the state should in no way interfere with the matters that do not belong among the *adiaphora*. The internal conscience remains free, and not only, as Locke already states here (and not first in later works), because it cannot be coerced, but also because it *may not* be coerced, since this is a matter for God alone:

> But the understanding and assent (whereof God hath reserved the disposure to himself, and not so much as entrusted man with a liberty at pleasure to believe or reject) being not to be wrought upon by force, a magistrate would in vain assault that part of man which owes no homage to his authority, or endeavor to establish his religion by those ways which would only increase an aversion and make enemies rather than proselytes.[95]

Religion, according to Locke, 'cannot be wrought into the hearts of men by any other power but that of its first author'. Moreover, Locke, like Walwyn, stresses that human beings *cannot* transfer their freedom of conscience to the sovereign under any circumstances, because, unlike indifferent matters, they are not at liberty to determine their faith.[96]

Hence, taken together, these two early treatises seem to represent neither an absolutist rejection of toleration nor an early version of the later letter on toleration. Here motifs and arguments clearly overlap which, on the one hand, highlight the sovereign as the external pacifying power who puts an end to confessional intolerance, though in the process he restricts individual freedom; but, on the other hand, these arguments imply that the sovereign runs up against an absolute barrier in the shape of individual faith and conscience and certain guidelines for their external forms of worship (prayer, sacraments). This is not yet the barrier of natural freedom leading to the justification of resistance; but it is already clear that it is the individual's allegiance to God that places limits on the sovereign. *Liberal freedom* springs in Locke's thought from the immediate *bond between individuals and God* which endows them with a certain political inviolability.

3. The 'Essay on Toleration', written in 1667 to support Lord Ashley's (the later Earl of Shaftesbury) calls for toleration, marks a turning point in Locke's thinking concerning toleration and prefigures the arguments of the later letter on toleration. Locke begins by defining the role of the state which

95. *Ibid.* 13.   96. *Ibid.* 15.

is founded, whether by God or by contract, in order to promote the public good and above all to preserve the peace, whereas the concern for spiritual welfare is not its task: 'The magistrate as magistrate hath nothing to do with the good of men's souls or their concernments in another life, but is ordained and entrusted with his power only for the quiet and comfortable living of men in society.'[97] Against this background, the decisive change vis-à-vis the *Two Tracts* resides in the fact that Locke now differentiates three categories of opinions and actions in regard to which the question of toleration arises for the state: first, speculative opinions and acts in the religious service which, in Locke's (revised) opinion, are of no concern to society or the state; second, social opinions and actions which are politically indifferent; and, third, virtues which are important for society. Locke now calls for an 'absolute and universal right of toleration' for the first category, for the following reasons.[98] As regards purely speculative opinions (for example concerning the Trinity), they are not a concern of the secular power because they in no way affect the question of civil and political conduct: whether one is a good citizen or not does not depend on correct belief in such matters. In addition, Locke employs the well-known argument that no one has power over things which explicitly concern the relation between the individual and God, and hence no one can transfer such power to the sovereign either. Finally, he gives the argument an epistemological twist, for he thinks that it is essential to human understanding that it is not subjected to commands or coercion, whether they come from oneself or from others.

In contrast to the position of the *Tract*, Locke now extends this freedom to the religious service as well, specifically to matters such as the time, place and detail of the form of worship, which he previously regarded as indifferent and in need of political regulation. 'Because this is a thing wholly between God and me, and of an eternal concernment, above the reach and extent of polities and government, which are but for my well-being in this world.'[99] Locke now rejects the distinction between essential contents of the religious service and *adiaphora* – 'in religious worship nothing is indifferent'[100] – and regards the external mode of worshipping God as inseparable from inner faith.

Here the ethical-religious core of Locke's doctrine of toleration becomes apparent, for he stresses the limits of the authority of the state in questions of salvation and of spiritual well-being in general, observing that here it is a matter of the 'private interest' to pursue one's *own* good, a good whose

97. Locke, 'An Essay on Toleration', 144.   98. *Ibid.* 136.   99. *Ibid.* 137.   100. *Ibid.* 139.

pursuit is exclusively a matter for the person whose life is concerned. He likewise connects this with an epistemological argument, namely that of the fallibility both of the state and of the individual, so that it is rational to pursue one's own path. The state

> ought not to proscribe me the way, or require my diligence, in the prosecution of that good which is of a far higher concernment to me than anything within his power, having no more certain or true infallible knowledge of the way to attain it than I myself, where we are both equally enquirers, both equally subjects, and wherein he can give me no security that I shall not, nor make me any recompense if I do, miscarry.[101]

How one seeks and describes one's own good and the path to God is, according to Locke, a 'voluntary and secret choice of the mind' – an expression which refracts like a prism the religious, ethical, epistemological and natural legal components of his argument. According to this argument religious coercion is contrary to the will of God who wants to produce a free belief by his own means, and hence it cannot lead to salvation; moreover, it is neither possible, because convictions cannot be coerced, nor justifiable on account of reciprocal fallibility; therefore, no human being or state is authorised to use such coercion. It is no accident, then, that Locke also employs the striking formulation of a 'right of toleration'.

Locke treats the two above-mentioned categories of opinions and actions accordingly. As in the *Tracts*, he regards a basic regulatory competence of the state in matters which are 'indifferent' in a civil sense, such as the education of children or the use of property, as given, though only when this is required by the public good. Then the citizens may not appeal to their conscience when they reject such regulations. Finally, when it comes to the virtues, the state should not ordain anything opposed to them, but neither should it undertake to lead people to virtue, which remains the preserve of the individual conscience.[102]

In the second part of the essay, in which Locke rhetorically addresses the king, he recommends, for the sake of the preservation and stability of the kingdom, that the king should grant toleration to the Protestant Dissenters and also to the sects (which, in Locke's opinion, would then neutralise each other), but deny it to the 'papists'. For the latter defend opinions which are 'absolutely destructive' for the government because of their loyalty to the pope and possibly to foreign Catholic powers;[103] they use toleration only

101. *Ibid.*   102. *Ibid.* 144–5.   103. *Ibid.* 151–2.

for their own purposes but do not accept it as a claim on themselves; and, in contrast to Protestant groups, they cannot be integrated through toleration but would remain 'irreconcilable enemies'. Locke would continue to defend this, for his time typical, anti-Catholic position in the *Epistola de tolerantia*, though he insists that in doing so he is guided not by dogmatic religious considerations, but by political ones.

4. As already noted, Locke wrote his *Letter Concerning Toleration* in 1685 during his exile in Holland under the impression of the revocation of the Edict of Nantes, and the resulting persecution of the Huguenots in France, and of the accession of the Catholic James II to the throne in England. Although the letter is less outstanding for its originality than for the systematic and synthetic thrust of its arguments, it counts as the most important modern text on toleration, one which raises the arguments for toleration offered up to that point to a new philosophical level. His argument can be fully reconstructed, however, only in the context of his two major contemporary works, the *Two Treatises of Government* and the *Essay Concerning Human Understanding*.

The former, especially the *Second Treatise*, contain Locke's mature contractualist theory of the state and mark the complete breakthrough of a liberal conception of natural law. Individuals are presented as by nature completely free and equal and as not subjected to any government but only to the law of nature. 'And Reason, which is that Law, teaches all Mankind, who will but consult it, that being all equal and independent, no one ought to harm another in his Life, Health, Liberty, or Possessions.' Locke continues with the following important remarks:

> For Men being all the Workmanship of one Omnipotent, and infinitely wise Maker; All the Servants of one Sovereign Master, sent into the World by his order and about his business, *They are his Property*, whose Workmanship they are, made to last during his, not one another's Pleasure.[104]

Thus, individuals have a duty towards God to preserve themselves, and towards each other and towards the state they have a natural right to their preservation, that is, to be more precise, to the preservation of their property, among which Locke counts life, freedom and possessions.[105] Since they belong to God, individuals have a natural freedom to such property, but they do not have the freedom to destroy it themselves or to enslave themselves:

---

104. Locke, *Two Treatises of Government*, II, §6, 271 (emphasis R.F.).   105. *Ibid.* §87, 323–4.

'No body can give more Power than he has himself.'[106] Thus, in order to escape the insecurity and dangers of the state of nature and gain legal assurance of their freedom (property), individuals unite through a contract into a commonwealth and entrust legislative authority to a government and its agencies; however, they retain their natural claims, which are prior to the state, and reserve the highest power (on earth) for themselves, which justifies a right of resistance. Hence, the argument of the (as it might be called) 'twofold property' is of central importance in Locke: because individuals are God's property, the property (in the broad, Lockean sense) which God confers upon them is beyond the reach of the state; even if they wanted to they could not renounce their natural freedom. This is central for early liberalism: human beings stand directly before or under God and as such confront the earthly institutions of the state and the Church; their *freedom* is rooted in the fact that they are *servants* of God. They belong completely to themselves, because they belong entirely to God. In other words, individual human beings assume the place formerly occupied by the Church or the state as institutions authorised and instituted directly by God; and the individual liberties are justified by this figure of thought. This also holds for freedom of religion, as the letter on toleration will show.

To be sure, this argument also draws its sustenance from another source in addition to natural law, a primarily epistemological one. It consists in the doctrine developed in *An Essay Concerning Human Understanding* that the entire material of knowledge has its origin in experience and is acquired either through sense perception or through 'the *Perception of the Operations of our own Minds*'.[107] This also holds for the idea of faith, and ultimately also for the idea of God as an eternal, all-powerful and all-knowing being.[108] According to Locke, therefore, reason remains the critical authority in questions of religion and revelation in order to set limits to religious fanaticism.[109]

Therefore, faith, in order to justify its conviction that it is true, can arise in no other way than through the individual's own examination and insight.[110] Thus, Locke states in the section that immediately follows that those who do not grant others such freedom of religious belief, but who seek to impose it through authority, must already have a corrupt, false faith themselves, for they think that it is possible to arrive at certainty of faith in this way; but there is no faith without consent and no consent without rational examination.

---

106. *Ibid.* §23, 284.   107. Locke, *An Essay Concerning Human Understanding*, Book II, Ch. 1, §4, 105.
108. *Ibid.* IV, 10, 6, 621.
109. See *ibid.* IV, 28 and 29. See also Locke's later arguments in *The Reasonableness of Christianity*.
110. Locke, *An Essay Concerning Human Understanding*, IV, 19, 1, 697.

Therefore, enforced faith cannot lead to a *genuine* and *examined* faith, and thus not to the *true* faith.

However, not only is coercion an inappropriate means of persuasion in matters of understanding and faith, but in general the attempt to bring about certain convictions deliberately: 'But they being employed, *our Will hath no power to determine the Knowledge of the Mind* one way or other; that is done only by the Objects themselves, as far as they are clearly discovered.'[111] An additional (apparent) paradox: the autonomy of the understanding follows from its heteronomous determination by the objects of perception or reflection. This also holds, Locke adds, for the idea of God.

It is against this background that the doctrine of toleration which Locke defends in his *Epistola de tolerantia* must be understood.[112] In analysing its argument, it makes sense first to clarify Locke's *ideé force*.

(1) Locke's central idea is that the supreme aspiration and interest of a human being is to ensure his eternal salvation and that the path thereto does not lie open to the finite mind; rather each must choose for himself and take responsibility before his own conscience in order to be able to face God one day.

> Every man has an Immortal Soul, capable of Eternal Happiness or
> Misery; whose Happiness depending upon his believing and doing
> those things in this Life, which are necessary to the obtaining of Gods
> Favour, and are prescribed by God to that end; It follows from thence,
> *1st*, That the observance of these things is the highest Obligation that
> lies upon Mankind, and that our utmost Care, Application, and
> Diligence, ought to be exercised in the Search and Performance of
> them; Because there is nothing in this world that is of any
> consideration in comparison with Eternity.   (47)

This supreme concern, according to Locke, is the highest obligation of a human being towards himself as a creature of God, and hence ultimately a duty towards God. Because of its significance for the individual it cannot

---

111. *Ibid.* IV, 13, 2, 650–1 (emphasis in original).
112. A note on the text: although the English translation of the *Epistola* prepared by Popple deviates from the original in a couple of places and at times uses more colourful language, these marginal differences do not falsify the meaning. Thus, what Locke meant when he stated in his instruction concerning his literary estate that Popple prepared the translation 'without my privity' remains open: 'without my knowledge', 'without my permission' or 'without my cooperation'. There is a fair amount of evidence that Locke knew of the translation and also that he inspected it. The decisive point, however, is that he defended it without qualification in the debates with Proast, for example, as Tully points out in his edition of the 'Letter' on which I draw in what follows.

be relinquished to anyone else; to put it graphically, as one subject to such an obligation, the human being already towers above the concerns of the world as a radically individualised being. Moreover, since the faith which is supposed to justify the individual before God must be professed by him in good conscience, it must rest upon the most profound personal conviction concerning its truth. Thus, apropos this faith Locke holds that 'Every man, in that, has the supreme and absolute Authority of judging for himself' (*ibid.*).

(2) Only against the background of this basic idea can the remaining arguments and their respective justifications be reconstructed. The most important is the separation of the above-mentioned 'supreme' interest from the 'civic interests', which are the only ones that fall under the competence of the state. From the very beginning, the argument proceeds from the interests of the individuals who entrust the state with certain tasks; it is no longer the interests of the state which are determining for the question of toleration. In order to fix the 'just Bounds' (26) between the state and religion, Locke takes up the two-kingdoms doctrine and distinguishes between the two types of interests mentioned, where those described as 'civil' concern 'Life, Liberty, Health, and Indolency of Body; and the Possession of outward things such as Money, Lands' (*ibid.*), etc. The secular authority is entrusted only with the care of these interests but *not* with the concern for spiritual welfare. The reasons for this are the following:

(a) The individual *cannot* transfer authority over matters of faith to other persons or to the state (or to the Church), because it is reserved for God alone; only he has the power to bring about true faith (26–7). Although Locke's position here (as in his earlier writings) is clearly situated within the Protestant tradition of the 'unfree free conscience', that is of a conception of conscience as bound to God and as answerable to him alone, nevertheless a shift in emphasis is already discernible from a conscience *directed* by God (in accordance with the Puritan view) to a conscience which *seeks* God for itself.

(b) Furthermore, the individual *cannot* relinquish the care of his salvation to others who dictate to him what he should believe: 'For no Man can, if he would, conform his Faith to the Dictates of another' (26), and: 'All the Life and Power of true Religion consists in the inward and full perswasion of the mind; and Faith is not Faith without believing' (*ibid.*). The secular authority only has 'outward force' at its disposal, which, according to Locke, can never give rise to an 'inward persuasion' such as faith requires: 'And as such is the nature of the Understanding, that it cannot be compell'd to the belief of any thing by outward force' (27). Only inner insight based on reasons can lead to faith, but not coercion or violence of any kind. Locke regards this point, which he derives from his epistemology, as absolutely essential; it leads him to assert in various places that external pressure can achieve nothing in the domain of faith, and hence that intolerance is condemned to failure already for this purely empirical reason: its means are 'not proper to convince the mind'.[113]

(c) Furthermore, the individual *ought not* to relinquish his freedom of conscience and adopt a religion other than the one of which he is convinced, for that would be to commit the sin of hypocrisy and compromise his eternal salvation (*ibid.*).

(d) In addition, even if reason (b) were not valid, it would be very *imprudent* of individuals to entrust their spiritual welfare to the state, for that would be to exchange the 'Light of their own Reason' (*ibid.*) for the arbitrary preferences of the ruler or the customs of a particular place. For, assuming that there is 'but one truth, one way to heaven' (*ibid.*) but that this is *not* evident to finite minds here on earth (37), it would be much too risky to entrust the fate of *one's own* salvation to people who do not have any superior knowledge of the truth and who cannot be trusted not to pursue other ends of their own in their choice of my religion, and no rational person would do this. 'The one only narrow way which leads to Heaven is not better known to the Magistrate than to private Persons, and therefore I cannot safely take him for my Guide, who may properly be as ignorant of the way as myself, and who is certainly less concerned for my Salvation than I myself am' (*ibid.*). When the state has abused its trust and made a wrong decision, it can compensate the citizens for many losses, according to Locke, but not for the loss of eternal life. 'What Security can be given for the Kingdom of Heaven?' (36).

The epistemological argument of the finitude of the human mind with regard to religious truth also serves Locke in addressing the question of horizontal toleration, that is, of toleration between citizens and also between their associations, the churches. Here the notion that the churches do not possess any kind of coercive power apart from the means of ecclesiastical discipline (including excommunication), and that there are no earthly judges of the true faith or the true Church, necessitates strict reciprocity: 'For every Church is Orthodox to itself; to others, Erroneous or Heretical' (32). Thus, Locke not only pleads for equal treatment of the Christian churches, but also

---

113. Locke, *A Letter Concerning Toleration*, 27.

at the intersubjective level for a strict separation between the roles of the ethical-religious person and the citizen: a citizen may be 'Christian or Pagan' (31), but he may not suffer any loss of his basic rights on religious grounds.

(3) In addition to the main argument outlined and its various justifications, Locke's letter contains a series of other arguments for toleration. Addressing Christians, he asserts that toleration is the 'Characteristical Mark of the True Church' (23) which follows the spirit of Jesus and his meekness and compassion. Accordingly, toleration is an immediate demand of the Gospels (25). Finally, the Christians should also recognise that their most bitter conflicts were in any case only over incidental matters of the faith, while there is agreement on essential matters (35) – an irenic trait in Locke's theory that appears at times.

(4) Furthermore, he argues, like others before him, and in particular Mill after him, that in the interest of truth it is best to allow toleration to operate, for the truth, 'once left to shift for her self' (46), will most easily prevail. Those who want to assist its victory by inappropriate means merely harm it.

(5) Finally, Locke presents a (well-known) pragmatic political argument which recommends toleration as the best policy for promoting and securing peace (51).

Locke's letter contains a whole range of further discussions which were very important for the discourse concerning toleration and proved to be highly influential, for example his definition of the Church as a purely voluntary association for the purpose of divine worship which must subordinate itself to the civil laws, even though it enjoys freedom in its articles of faith and its forms of worship (31) – thereby retracting his argument in the *Two Tracts*. However, he continues to emphasise that the appeal to freedom of conscience must not serve people to claim 'impunity for their Libertinism and Licentiousness' (25–6), for example to sacrifice infants or 'lustfully pollute themselves in promiscuous Uncleanliness' (42).

Especially important in this context is his discussion of the limits of toleration. It follows from what has been said that these cannot be justified in religious terms but must be justified instead on the basis of the normative political principles of the polity. Accordingly, those sects cannot be tolerated which claim a prerogative for themselves that they are unwilling to grant to others, and thereby except themselves from the reciprocity among citizens and religious communities (50). Among these are, for example, groups which teach that contracts with certain citizens who are judged to be heretics are not binding, that the Church has the right to excommunicate kings who thereby forfeit their claim to political authority, that the Church can claim no temporal power at all and that there is no universal duty of toleration (51). And there can be no question of tolerating those groups who show loyalty to political authorities other than their own for religious reasons and who harbour the threat of treason (*ibid.*). Even though Locke does not say so explicitly, these remarks are clearly aimed at the Catholics or 'papists' who, in his view, have no claim to toleration. In this way, he remains faithful to the sweeping condemnation of Catholics as potential subversives and representatives of an intolerant religion which was prevalent in the England of his time. Jews (40) and pagans, by contrast, can be tolerated.

Finally, Locke adds: 'Those are not at all to be tolerated who deny the Being of God. Promises, Covenants, and Oaths, which are the bonds of Human Society, can have no hold upon an Atheist. The taking away of God, tho but even in thought, dissolves all' (51). This confirms that, although Locke in his theory arrived at a separation between the *religious-ethical* and the *political-legal* person, he did not make a separation between the religious-ethical and the *moral* person. The laws of morality are accessible to the 'light of Nature' only as divine laws; without God they lose their binding character.[114] In the discourse of toleration, morality had not yet been 'rationalised' to such an extent that it had liberated itself from particular religious foundations – Bayle, who was writing at the same time, would be the first to attempt this; nevertheless, in Locke (and this sets him apart from Bayle) the moment of political-moral rationalisation – that is, the demand for justification addressed to the secular power – reached a new level. It is perfectly clear that political authority is determined by the basic interests of individuals who reserve the power of political justification for themselves – while the ultimate normative power of justification remains, of course, with God. This is characteristic of Locke's liberalism and lends it, on the one hand, its political force, though at the same time a strong religious component: 'for Obedience is due in the first place to God, and afterwards to the Laws' (48). The latter leads him to set narrower limits in his doctrine of toleration than are to be found in some of his immediate predecessors, for example the Levellers. It leads to his fear – which could be called *Locke's fear*, for, although he was by no means the only one who had it, he lent it particular emphasis – that morality and a state are impossible in the final analysis without a shared foundation in God. Locke is far from calling for a general freedom of conscience which would also extend to the conscience of atheists, as does Bayle; thus, he remarks against the atheists that, apart from the destructive

114. Thus, also Locke, *An Essay Concerning Human Understaning*, II, 28, 8, 352.

influence that they exercise, they 'can have no pretence of Religion where-upon to challenge the Privilege of a Toleration' (51). The freedom that Locke calls for is only a freedom of religion, not a general freedom of conscience.[115] He regards the latter as too politically dangerous, for it would leave too much scope for disobedience of the law – on this point Locke remained true to the position of the *Two Tracts*. He calls for freedom only for the forms of 'reasonable' religion which can be reconciled with his guidelines and accept the boundary between secular and spiritual power. Thus, his fear concerns not only the destructive force of atheism but also the irrational forces of 'enthusiasm' and excessive religiosity.[116] In this sense, his citizens are not only subjects with a conscience but also 'conscientious subjects' who accept the rule of law and integrate this into their behaviour both as ethical-religious persons and as legal persons.[117] In this light, Lockean liberalism is at once a programme of liberation and of social pacification – all for the sake of safeguarding 'property' in the broad sense.

5. However, this does not complete the analysis of Locke's letter on toleration. For the four justifications in the main argument that the concern for salvation cannot and ought not to be transferred to any authority besides one's own conscience raise the questions of (A) which justification is the most important for Locke and (B) which is the most coherent.

(A) Locke addresses the question of the relative weights of the justifications in three parts of the text. The first discussion is designed to support freedom of conscience by appeal to the epistemological thesis of the finitude of reason in matters of faith and the resulting self-relativisation of one's own claim to truth:

> The care of the salvation of men's souls cannot belong to the magistrate; because, though the rigour of laws and the force of penalties were capable to convince and change men's minds, yet would not that help at all to the salvation of their souls. For, there being but one truth, one way to heaven; what hope is there that more men would

115. See Dunn, 'The Claim to Freedom of Conscience'.
116. This is underlined in different ways by McClure, 'Difference, Diversity, and the Limits of Toleration', who interprets Locke's doctrine of toleration as an attempt to make an epistemologically and politically regulatable 'diversity' out of profound religious 'differences', and by Creppell, 'Locke on Toleration', who emphasises the connection between external constraint though the law and internal self-restraint.
117. That this involves a particular form of 'subjectivisation' connected with a new form of 'juridical government' is emphasised by Tully (drawing on Foucault) in 'Governing Conduct'.

be led into it, if they had no other rule to follow but the religion of the court . . . ?   (16–17)

Here Locke grants, counterfactually, that the ruling authorities could after all succeed in changing 'inward' convictions by certain means, and invokes the idea of epistemological relativisation in an attempt to rescue the non-transferability argument. Here this seems to be the more fundamental reason.

In another place, however, he takes precisely the opposite tack. There he addresses the question of toleration between churches each of which claims to represent the sole truth:

> [I]f it could be manifest which of these two dissenting churches were in the right way, there would not accrue thereby unto the orthodoxy any right of destroying the other. For churches have neither any jurisdiction in worldly matters, nor are fire and sword any proper instruments wherewith to convince men's minds of error, and inform them of the truth.   (32)

This argument neutralises the above-mentioned one, as it were: it is now the epistemic self-relativisation that is bracketed and (disregarding the reference, aimed specifically at churches, to their purely spiritual means) the main burden of argument is borne by the thesis of the non-coercibility of convictions.

Therefore, we must consult a third passage in order to establish where Locke sees the primary thrust of his argument. He does this in the context of a further fundamental discussion of the question of whether it is within the competence of the ruling authority, whether at the advice of a church or not, to prescribe a religion to the citizens:

> But after all, the principal consideration, and which absolutely determines this controversy, is this: although the magistrate's opinion in religion be sound, and the way that he appoints be truly evangelical, yet if I be not thoroughly persuaded thereof in my own mind, there will be no safety for me in following it. No way whatsoever that I shall walk in against the dictates of my conscience, will ever bring me to the mansions of the blessed . . . Faith only, and inward sincerity, are the things that procure acceptance with God.   (52–3)

Hence, it is a combination of justifications 2(b) and 2(c), the non-coercibility of conscience, or the impossibility of deliberately influencing it, and the avoidance of hypocrisy – in sum, the emphasis on the authenticity of faith – that shoulder the main burden of the Lockean justification. The faith that leads to God can come only from within, and it cannot gain access through the human will, whether one's own or someone else's.[118]

Clearly, therefore, Locke's letter on toleration rests primarily on a justification whose essentials – though now within the context of an empiricist epistemology and a contractualist theory of the state – can already be found in Augustine (cf. §5.1 above), though the Augustine *before* he reversed his position in the dispute with the Donatists. He also regarded conscience not only as not coercible, since true faith springs from insight alone: *credere non potest homo nisi volens*; he was also convinced that anything else merely leads to hypocrisy and hence is offensive to God.

(B) Therefore, the non-coercibility argument also stood and still stands at the centre of the controversies surrounding Locke's justification of toleration, and already the reference to Augustine prefigures the direction taken by this debate. For it was the latter who, during his time as bishop of Hippo, stood his argument for toleration on its head and developed the doctrine of 'good coercion': given the great numbers of errant individuals who oppose the true Church, it is a Christian duty to lead them to repent (for their own good and that of others whom they might carry with them) and to force them to enter. Force, according to Augustine, had proved very helpful in bringing the errant to see reason, as many former Donatists, who were pressured to convert to the true faith, had happily assured him. Of course, the *terror* itself does not bring about the saving insight; it merely dissolves the delusion and opens the eyes for the 'consideration of the truth'.[119] As a result, the thesis that true faith, as inner faith, cannot be coerced is refuted, assuming that the pressure is exerted in the right way.

It was to precisely this argument (though not with reference to Augustine) that Jonas Proast appealed in his critique of Locke, which has lost none of its relevance. It involved the two thinkers – under the pseudonyms 'Philanthropus' and 'Philochristus' – in a long-drawn-out controversy which lasted

---

118. This is the position which can also be found in the important fragment 'Toleration D' of 1679: '[Y]et the power of using force to bring men to believe in faith and opinions and uniformity in worship could not serve to secure men's salvation, even though that power were in itself infallible, because no compulsion can make a man believe against his present light and persuasion, be it what it will, though it may make him profess indeed. But profession without sincerity will little set a man forwards in his way to any place but that where he is to have his share with hypocrites, and to do anything in the worship of God which a man judges in his own conscience not to be that worship he requires and will accept, is so far from serving or pleasing God in it, that such a worshipper affronts God only to please men' (276).
119. See §5.1 above.

until Locke's death and which he took very seriously.[120] Proast, a minister who taught at Oxford, published his work *The Argument of the Letter Concerning Toleration Briefly Consider'd and Answer'd* in 1690. In it he first makes clear that he regards Locke's argument that faith cannot be brought about through external pressure or violence as central and proceeds to refute it in a sophisticated way. He agrees with Locke that force may not be used instead of reasons and arguments, but asserts that it can be useful in an *indirect* way:

> But notwithstanding this, if Force be used, not in stead of Reason and Arguments, i.e. not to convince by its own proper Efficacy (which it cannot do), but onely to bring men to consider those Reasons and Arguments which are proper and sufficient to convince them, but which, without being forced, they would not consider: who can deny, but that indirectly and at a distance, it does some service toward the bringing men to embrace that Truth, which otherwise, either through Carelesness and Negligence they would never acquaint themselves with, or through Prejudice they would reject and condemn unheard, under the notion of Errour?[121]

Since men are often careless, sluggish and weighed down by prejudices in their duty to care for their souls, not the least sign of which is the many sects and aberrations, it is a genuine Christian duty to lay 'Thorns and Briars' across their path to error, and hence to employ a certain force – though this force should not be too extreme, a point to which Proast attaches great importance. '[W]hat human method can be used . . . to make a wiser and more rational Choice, but that of laying such Penalties upon them, as may balance the weight of those Prejudices which enclined them to prefer a false Way before the True . . . ?'[122] This method had repeatedly proved its worth, according to Proast, which showed, contrary to Locke, that external force is both necessary and helpful in promoting the true faith; for only in this way can the fetters be cast off from the soul so that it can acquire the freedom to listen to and understand the truth. The care of the truth is entrusted to the secular sovereign who is duly authorised in the best interest of the citizens; for what interest could be more important than one's own salvation? As a result, his coercive power cannot be said to be one of enforcing the true religion but of suppressing false religion and liberating from it.

120. Instructive analyses of the debates can be found in Nicholson, 'John Locke's Later Letters on Toleration', and Vernon, *The Career of Toleration*.
121. Proast, *The Argument*, 5.   122. *Ibid.* 11.

Two things become apparent in Locke's answer to Proast, the *Second Letter Concerning Toleration* (1690): on the one hand, the weakness of his 'principal consideration' (2(b) and 2(c)) of non-coercibility which Proast correctly points out and which has led some commentators to declare that it represents a complete defeat for Locke;[123] on the other hand, however, that Locke's *Letter* contains additional arguments through which he can rebut Proast, in particular the argument of epistemic self-relativisation combined with the reciprocal claim to justification (i.e. 2(d)). His answer accordingly involves two components, the (vain) attempt to rescue the non-coercibility argument and the rebuttal of Proast by challenging his central premise, the assumption that the 'true faith' is on the side of the secular authority.

Concerning the former, Locke is forced to concede the possibility of what he referred to at one point in his first letter as a thought experiment, namely that internal convictions could be produced through external force. The enforcement of external conformity and refraining from certain practices, in combination with the prohibition of certain utterances, could, according to Locke, indeed 'do some service indirectly and by accident'.[124] For a range of primarily empirical and pragmatic reasons, however, Locke argues that Proast should not be followed. In the first place, these are at most exceptional cases, whereas the normal case would be to produce hypocrisy or complete disorientation. Moreover, Locke doubts whether the distinction between 'direct' and 'indirect' force could be maintained in practice; Proast's argument would instead lead to the use of direct force. Still more, it is entirely unclear how one could distinguish between those who are engaging in serious reflection and are seeking the truth and those who are not and need to be admonished. In the final analysis, this would lead to coercion and punishment being employed against all those who did not conform to the national church. But what about those who are members of the national church merely out of prejudice? Should they also be forced to reflect? According to Locke, this would ultimately boil down to a general and 'plain persecution for differing in religion',[125] a despotic persecution of all dissent.

Even though these counter-arguments capture problems with Proast's position, they cannot rebut his essential argument on an empirical level: it could very well be that certain forms of pressure or force could lead people to abandon their (wrong) faith and, albeit over time, adopt new, 'inwardly' affirmed convictions. Even regulating what can be expressed in word and print and which doctrines are socially permitted can influence this, not

---

123. Thus, Waldron, 'Locke', 119.   124. Locke, *A Second Letter*, 77, also 69.   125. *Ibid.* 97.

to mention other educational mechanisms including specific methods of psychological manipulation and mind control. If one considers that there is no epistemic criterion to distinguish between convictions which arise in this way and 'genuine' convictions – where it is open to question whether any such 'genuine', inward convictions which are produced entirely without external influences exist – then the argument that the coercion of conscience is *irrational* because *impossible* collapses.[126]

However, this does not exhaust the potential of Locke's argument, even though in his answer to Proast he is now forced to shift the emphasis from the refuted points 2(b) and (c) to 2(d): the epistemological self-relativisation argument coupled with the argument of the reciprocal justification of norms and of the use of social power. With this Locke provides the normative argument which is necessary after the collapse of the argument of non-coercibility.[127] Locke underlines that the argument in question, which Proast highlights and criticises, is just one argument and *not* the central one, thereby correcting the statement in the first *Letter* about the 'principal consideration'; for even if it were dropped (which he tacitly concedes), 'either of the other would be a strong proof for toleration'.[128] Locke now launches a direct attack on Proast's central assumption, 'this lurking presupposition, that the national religion now in England, backed by the public authority of the law, is the only true religion',[129] in order to undercut his argument. For, as Proast says, the latter in fact rests on the assumption that only a magistrate who represents the *true* religion is authorised to employ limited coercion in matters of faith.[130] But Locke refuses to concede this point to Proast; his opponent should instead present an argument 'without supposing all along your church in the right, and your religion the true; which can no more be allowed to you in this case, whatever your church or religion be, than it can to a papist or a Lutheran, a presbyterian or anabaptist; nay, no more to you, than it can be allowed to a Jew or a Mahometan'.[131] Appealing to

---

126. This is Waldron's conclusion in 'Locke', 116–19. Mendus's attempt in 'Locke: Toleration, Morality, and Rationality' (drawing on Williams, 'Deciding to Believe') to appeal to the non-influenceability of 'genuine' in contrast to 'sincere' convictions fails for lack of a clear distinguishing criterion. See also Geuss's criticism of the argument to be found in Locke in *History and Illusion in Politics*, 74–5.

127. Waldron, 'Locke', 120, calls for such a moral argument, but mentions neither Locke's alternative justification nor the associated necessary epistemological component. Nicholson, 'John Locke's Later Letters on Toleration', refers to this component but neglects the normative side. The converse holds for Vernon, *The Career of Toleration*, who emphasises the element of 'public reason' and does not attach sufficient importance to its epistemological side.

128. Locke, *A Second Letter*, 67.   129. *Ibid.* 65.   130. Proast, *The Argument*, 26.

131. Locke, *A Second Letter*, 111.

the epistemological point which challenges the possibility of proving the path of the true religion beyond doubt, Locke calls for a conception of the relationship between politics and religion which does not operate with such a manifestly unjustified assumption that it possesses the absolute truth. For the assumption that one's own church is the true one is characteristic of all churches and must be granted to all of them. Moreover, if one were to grant a right to enforce conformity, this would also hold for the Jews and Muslims against the Christians, it would hold in the Catholic countries against the Protestants, and in England, should the power relations change, it would likewise authorise the current Dissenters to coerce the members of the national church.[132] 'What is true and good in England, will be true and good at Rome, too, in China, or Geneva.'[133] Arguing for the need to relativise what it means to speak of religious truth, Locke calls for a reversal of roles and a *universalisable* justification of toleration, which he goes on to present: according to this argument *all force is in principle in need of justification, and there are no good, demonstrable reasons for imposing religious belief by force.*

In his answer to Locke – *A Third Letter Concerning Toleration* (1691) – Proast recognises that Locke is not able to provide a fundamental counter-argument to the non-coercibility argument, but points out other problems with this position; and he readily concedes that the result which Locke fears, namely a general suspicion against Dissenters, would arise: 'For the *Dissenters* . . . whom I am *for punishing*, are onely such as *reject* the *true Religion*, proposed to them with Reasons and Arguments sufficient to convince them of the truth of it . . . For if they did so consider them, they would not continue *Dissenters*.'[134] That this simple logic presupposes that the Church of England possesses the truth, and that this is now the central focus of Locke's critique, Proast regards as the real challenge. Thus, he exhorts Locke:

> But as to my *supposing* that the *National Religion now in* England, *back'd by the Publick Authority of the Law*, is the *onely true Religion*; if you own, with our Author, that there is but *one* true Religion, I cannot see how you your self can avoid *supposing* the same. For you own your self to the Church *of England*; and consequently you own the *National Religion now in* England, to be the true Religion.[135]

Otherwise, Proast argues, Locke would have to repudiate his own religion and assert that all religions are true or that none of them is, with the result

---

132. *Ibid.* 65, 77, 85.   133. *Ibid.* 95.   134. Proast, *A Third Letter*, 24 (emphasis in original).
135. *Ibid.* 11 (emphasis in original).

that he would not be able to privilege his own religion. For 'the *National Religion* is either true, or not true'.[136]

Locke responded to Proast's new treatise in turn with a text of more than 330 pages, the *Third Letter for Toleration to the Author of the Third Letter Concerning Toleration* (1692), in which he attempts to refute Proast word for word, having understood the challenge contained in the latter's accusation of apostasy. And thus he addresses the essential point:

> To you and me the Christian religion is the true, and that is built, to mention no other articles of it, on this, that Jesus Christ was put to death at Jerusalem, and rose again from the dead. Now do you or I know this? I do not ask with what assurance we believe it, for that in the highest degree not being knowledge, is not what we now inquire after . . . For whatever is not capable of demonstration, as such remote matters of fact are not, is not, unless it be self evident, capable to produce knowledge, how well grounded and great soever the assurance of faith may be wherewith it is received; but faith it is still, and not knowledge; persuasion, and not certainty . . . Knowledge then, properly so called, not being to be had of the truths necessary to salvation, the magistrate must be content with faith and persuasion for the rule of that truth he will recommend and enforce upon others.[137]

With this the main burden of Locke's justification of toleration has clearly shifted. The epistemological-empirical, religiously tinged thesis of the non-coercibility of genuine and authentic faith is no longer central, but instead the *normative thesis* that the exercise of political power is in need of justification and the *epistemological thesis* that reasons of faith are not sufficient to justify the use of coercion. It is the connection between these two theses that enables Locke to contradict Proast and to ground the *right* to toleration: 'For force from a stronger hand, to bring a man to a religion which another thinks the true, being an injury which in the state of nature every one would avoid; protection from such injury is one of the ends of a commonwealth, and so *every man has a right to toleration*.'[138] At the same time, however, this is a Pyrrhic victory for Locke, for, in order to achieve it, he must abandon the main argument of his first *Letter*. Therefore, in a certain sense it is true that in this point he is defeated by Proast; however, in another sense it is also true that he defeats Proast. He only needed to change and radicalise the main thrust of his justification of toleration, in fact in precisely the

136. *Ibid*. 20 (emphasis in original).   137. Locke, *A Third Letter*, 144.
138. *Ibid*. 212 (emphasis R.F.).

normative-epistemological direction that Pierre Bayle took in the same year in which Locke wrote his first letter on toleration (cf. the following §18). This path – the normative thesis that power or rule is in need of justification and the epistemological thesis of the relativisation of the claims to truth of a religious faith which recognises that it is faith – which is intimated in Castellio, as well as in Bodin and others, will prove to be the superior one, as will become apparent in what follows.

As regards Locke, it is obvious that the strength of his justification of toleration only becomes evident through a revision, which shows once again that it is crucial to evaluate texts systematically in their historical context and in doing so to acknowledge writings that are frequently ignored.[139] However, it must be added that his theory constitutes the main point of intersection of *different* modern justifications of toleration, all of which can be found in his complex texts. Apart from the aforementioned normative-epistemological twofold thesis, Locke provides a whole series of other justifications which, although they still depend heavily on religious premises, nevertheless have the potential to liberate themselves from the latter. This is made apparent, for example, by the extent to which an *ethical liberalism*, which, as we shall see, represents an alternative to the approach to the justification of toleration which I highlight, can appeal to Locke, namely on the assumption that the argument concerning freedom of conscience can be understood in such a way *that political freedom of conscience is the precondition for the formation of a faith based on inward conviction, and thus for achieving eternal salvation*. If we reformulate this – as the development of morality, especially since the eighteenth century, will make possible – in such a way that freedom of conscience becomes *the necessary condition for the autonomous formation, and the pursuit and realisation, of convictions and conceptions of the good, and that this autonomy alone can lead to a good life*, the result is an ethically based connection between political liberty, personal autonomy and the conditions of the good life. This connection has shaped a powerful tradition of thought concerning toleration within liberalism – initially founded on Christian assumptions, but later independent of these – leading from Locke through Humboldt and Mill to contemporary thinkers like Raz and Kymlicka.[140] Within this

---

139. To complete the story: following a long silence, Proast took up the debate once again in 1704 with the well-known arguments (*A Second Letter to the Author of the Three Letters for Toleration*), whereupon Locke (who had the upper hand as regards titles) began his *Fourth Letter for Toleration*, though he was not able to complete it before his death in the same year.

140. See for example Raz, *The Morality of Freedom*, chs. 14 and 15; Kymlicka, *Multicultural Citizenship*, 81: 'So we have two preconditions for leading a good life. The first is that we lead our life from the inside, in accordance with our beliefs about what gives value to life . . . The

conceptual framework, freedom of religion and conscience becomes a necessary precondition for an autonomous life, and the latter in turn for a good life based on an individual conception of the good. As a result, respect for the autonomy of a person, and the corresponding demand for toleration, are justified on the basis of a specific liberal conception of the good life. I will return to this neo-Lockean justification of toleration in the systematic part of my argument (see Chapter 9) – and I will favour a neo-Baylean alternative over it.

6. At this point, let us first briefly review the 'materiality' of the discourse concerning toleration from the perspective of the genealogist who is aware of the interrelations between toleration and domination or 'domestication'. For, as we have seen, in 1689, thus in the year in which Locke's *Letter* appeared, William III and his wife Mary issued the famous Toleration Act, which provides a further example of the attempts to stabilise a precarious political power by granting certain liberties to individual dissenting minorities in order to *liberate* them from certain repressions while at the same time *pacifying* them, i.e. rendering them governable. The Act reveals, in turn, the Janus face of the permission conception for which it clearly stands and which, with it, enters a new phase of the politics of power. For the rationalisation of power kept pace with the rationalisation of political morality, as presented in Locke's letters, inasmuch as the toleration (and at the same time the disciplining) of minorities in accordance with the new level of legitimation of monarchical authority represents itself as an action 'by and with the Advice and Consent of the Lords Spiritual and Temporal and the Commons in this present Parliament Assembled'.[141]

It is interesting that Locke, for whom this toleration policy could not go far enough, nevertheless supported it as a step in the right direction. Although the Act excluded more groups than he thought appropriate, it observed the strict exclusions of Catholics and atheists which he advocated. Thus, Locke wrote to Limborch, an Arminian theologian with whom he was in close contact in the Netherlands (and who regarded himself as the addressee of the first letter on toleration):

> No doubt you will have heard before this that Toleration has now at
> last been established by law in our country. Not perhaps so wide in
> scope as might be wished for by you and those like you who are true
> Christians and free from ambition or envy. Still, it is something to have

second precondition is that we be free to question those beliefs, to examine them in light of whatever information, examples, and arguments our culture can provide.'
141. Toleration Act, 303, facsimile in Grell, Israel and Tyacke (eds.), *From Persecution to Toleration*.

progressed so far. I hope that with these beginnings the foundations have been laid of that liberty and peace in which the church of Christ is one day to be established. None is entirely debarred from his own form of worship or made liable to penalties except the Romans, provided only that he is willing to take the oath of allegiance and to renounce transubstantiation and certain dogmas of the Roman church.[142]

In order to establish what was meant by saying that 'none' apart from the Catholics is 'entirely' restricted in their freedom of religion and worship, we need to examine the Toleration Act more closely. From the beginning it is clear from the rhetoric that it is a decree of very specific exceptions for clearly circumscribed groups from laws specified in detail the content of which is conformity to the Church of England. Hence, in contrast to a horizontal conception of toleration, it clearly involves a relation between a norm-setting power and subjects who, as 'nonconformists', are being granted certain liberties. Thus, the Toleration Act (in which the word 'toleration' never appears) is also called 'an Act for Exempting Their Majesties Protestant Subjects, Dissenting from the Church *of England*, from the Penalties of certain Laws'.[143] Hence, it was only Protestant Dissenters, thus Presbyterians, Independents, Baptists and Quakers, who were supposed to enjoy these rules of exception, not any other religious communities – not even Unitarian Protestants like the Socinians or Deists, to whom Locke himself was close. This becomes evident from the formula of the oath and the profession of faith mentioned by Locke which the Act treats as indispensable. They had to be sworn before certain institutions in order to acquire the status of an 'officially recognised Dissenter' as it were. The oath of allegiance to William contains the 'anti-papist' formula that excommunications decreed by the pope against kings are to be ignored and that one is not beholden to any other sovereign, whereas the official profession of faith essentially emphasises belief in the Christian Trinity. The Protestants who accepted this enjoyed exemptions from certain conformity laws and were granted freedom of religious worship, subject to clear and detailed regulations. However, they were not released from the duty to pay taxes to the Anglican Church.

Therefore, the Act did not annul the existing uniformity and conformity laws; instead it specified exactly who was exempted from which of these requirements under which circumstances – in the sense of a concession, *not* of a right. The motivation for this is stated clearly at the beginning: 'Forasmuch

---

142. Locke, letter to Limborch, 6 June 1689, 633.
143. Toleration Act, 303 (emphasis in original).

as some Ease to Scrupulous Consciences in the Exercise of Religion may be an effectual means to unite Their Majesties Protestant Subjects in Interest and Affection.'[144] There is no attempt to conceal that it is a question of a pragmatically based legislation intended to benefit only 'conscientious' subjects who do not question the prerogative of the Church of England and show themselves to be loyal citizens. This corresponds to the religious policy of William of Orange which is identical with the position of the *politiques*: the issue of enforcing religious truth is subordinated to the imperatives of political stability, a position which in the Netherlands led him to side with Calvinist orthodoxy and in England with the Church of England.[145] On the other hand, William himself, again for domestic and foreign policy reasons, strove for a broader toleration of Catholics and also implemented this to an extent in practice, though not in the form of decrees, so that 'King William's Toleration' was regarded as more extensive than the legally decreed toleration.[146]

The result is a complex picture of inclusion and exclusion. Alongside the official church there were a series of Protestant minorities who now enjoyed certain liberties (and as a result spread rapidly), yet who had to accept the supremacy of the Anglicans and counted as 'second-class citizens' not only with regard to religion.[147] They were subject to the ambivalences of per-mission toleration (to which we have frequently alluded): it liberates on the one hand, while disciplining on the other; it annuls certain punishments and impositions, but in return exacts a price in the form of a heightened expectation of good conduct, loyalty and submission to the peace-making sovereignty, which holds the opposing, official church in check. At the same time these groups are stigmatised as deviant. This amounts to a situation of *exclusion through inclusion*, of being trapped in a situation of freedom and con-straint at the same time. Toleration *permits and forbids*, with the ruling power in the state, which presents itself as the supreme judge, laying down the rules, even though it is at the same time compelled to respond in a flexible manner to shifts in social relations of power. In this respect, here the moment of the rationalisation of the exercise of power through toleration also points to the rationalisation of political morality, to the increased demand for justification on the part of the citizens, albeit in a very attenuated form. As a result the constellation of power becomes even more complex. It is not just a matter of a one-dimensional 'subjectivisation' and disciplining of the citizens who

144. *Ibid.*   145. On this, see especially Israel, 'William III and Toleration'.
146. See Bossy, 'English Catholics after 1688'.
147. See White, 'The Twilight of Puritanism in the Years before and after 1688', 314–15.

have internalised their nonconforming identity; there is also a countervailing tendency to resist this form of the exercise of power – especially when its 'benevolent' character mutates into the direct exercise of domination.[148]

On the other hand, the case is different with groups which are excluded in principle from the toleration granted. These are the already mentioned 'papists', although many Protestants insisted, like Locke, that they were denounced exclusively for political, not for religious reasons. Something similar also held for atheists and Unitarians who were supposedly refused toleration on moral grounds. For it was assumed that atheists, as Locke said, where incapable of moral convictions, and the denial of the divinity of Christ, as was found among the Socinians, as much as the denial of a deity who intervenes in the course of the world, as encountered among the Deists, was regarded as leading directly to atheism. As a consequence, these groups could not be tolerated because they were not seen as morally trustworthy.[149]

As was so often the case if one considers the various 'tolerance groups', the Jews represented a special case of disciplining and 'confinement' through toleration. Although they had been 'tolerated' once again in England only since 1656, they were in a particularly precarious situation and had to 'earn' their toleration through especially good conduct, which James II made clear in 1685 in a toleration decree granting them certain liberties: 'His Majesties Intention being that they should not be troubled, upon this account, but quietly enjoy the free exercise of their Religion, whilst they behave themselves dutifully and obediently to his Government.'[150] Their social and legal status remained ambivalent; they were regarded neither as aliens nor as fellow citizens, but were treated as the one or the other according to the situation.[151] Although the London Jews, along with the Amsterdam Jews, supported the Glorious Revolution, they were nevertheless excluded from the Toleration Act. Even under William III, the policy of extracting extreme taxes from the Jews in return for toleration remained in force. The Earl of Shrewsbury justified one of these special taxation measures in the name of the king in terms

---

148. Here I will draw in turn on Foucault's analysis of power, though in the version developed only in his later writings – for example, 'What is Critique?' – which accords a more central role to the moment of resistance as opposed to the disciplinary moment (highlighted especially in *Discipline and Punish*). Furthermore, I have already alluded in a variety of historical constellations to the moment of exclusion through inclusion and to the affinity between permission/freedom and prohibition/unfreedom, and hence do not follow Foucault's strict historical periodisation in relation to this practice of exercising power though toleration. It is true, however, that this structure assumes different forms in different historical epochs, as I have suggested in each case.
149. On this, see Dees, *Trust and Toleration*, ch. 5.
150. Quoted in Katz, 'The Jews of England and 1688', 223.   151. *Ibid.* 238.

which scarcely disguise the implicit threat: '[T]o let them understand what obligations they have to his Majesty for the Liberty & Privildges they enjoy by his Protection & Indulgence, & how much it is their advantage as well as it is becoming them not to be wanting in all sutable retours of affection & Gratitude for the kindness they have received & may expect.'[152] Once again permission toleration reveals its Janus face: on the one hand freedom from persecution is granted but, on the other, it has to be 'purchased' – also literally – through a quid pro quo which the state stipulates arbitrarily, since the group is marked out as deviating from the norm. It continues to depend for protection against worse treatment directly on the sovereign, who takes advantage of this.

Recognising this connection between toleration, freedom and discipline necessitates taking a critical view of the history of toleration, acknowledging the 'twofold rationalisation' of power and morality and avoiding the error of wanting to write a progressive linear history of freedom by focusing exclusively on the theoretical discourse of toleration (and even that in a one-sided manner). But it also means recognising the moment of freedom, not only in reflection upon toleration, but also in the politics of toleration. For, in spite of practices of domination, the Toleration Act, and the development it set in motion, also shows that in certain situations political authority cannot avoid paying the price of toleration itself. How high this price is is not fixed by one side only, though it is rarely fixed by both sides equally.

§18 The society of atheists, the struggle between faith and reason and the aporias of freedom of conscience

1. While toleration, albeit in a restricted sense, gradually became established in England in the course of the Glorious Revolution, it was on the retreat in the France of Louis XIV. There the Edict of Nantes had ensured the Huguenots a certain level of social security and religious freedom without making them into citizens with equal rights. Once the 'Sun King' assumed the reins of government in 1661, however, he intensified his attempts to sub-ject his kingdom to the principle *un roi, une foi, une loi*. This led to a series of discriminatory social measures in the years which followed, including direct suppression and violence, culminating from 1681 onwards in the billeting of soldiers in Protestant homes in order to force the occupants to abjure. This triggered a major wave of emigration, which the king prohibited on

---

152. Quoted in *ibid.* 241–2.

pain of severe punishment since he did not want to lose these subjects. In spite of this, many succeeded in fleeing to countries such as the Netherlands, England and Brandenburg which did not apply the *ius reformandi* strictly and accepted Huguenots; in the Edict of Potsdam of 1685, the Great Elector officially opened his territory to the French emigrants, a policy which brought substantial economic benefits. In France, by contrast, in the same year, after all of the persecutions, Louis XIV officially revoked the Edict of Nantes in the Edict of Fontainebleau on the grounds that there were no longer any Protestants in his realm who needed protection.[153] This goal of achieving a religiously united kingdom won the support of political theologians like Bossuet who connected the divine right of kings in their writings with the duty to assist in imposing the true religion also by coercive means.[154] Thus, although Pierre Bayle shared the fate of many other philosophers of toleration whose lives were marked by the intolerance of their time, this was especially true in his case (as it was in a different way of Spinoza), since he became the victim of intolerance both at the hands of the Catholics in France and at those of the Calvinists in his place of refuge, Rotterdam.[155] Born in 1647 in southern France as the son of a Huguenot pastor, he acquired a higher education only at the age of twenty-two by visiting a Jesuit seminary in Toulouse and converting to the Catholic faith. Only a year later he recanted, something which was forbidden on pain of severe punishment, and fled to Geneva. From 1675 onwards he taught at the Protestant Academy of Sedan until this was shut down in 1681 and he fled to Rotterdam, where a large community of the *refuge* had formed and he, like his former colleague and mentor in Sedan, the theologian Pierre Jurieu, was appointed professor (of philosophy and history) at the École Illustre.

During this phase Bayle began to publish a series of writings all of which turn on the problem of toleration, in particular on the complex questions concerning the relationship between morality, reason and faith. With the exception of his famous philosophical-historical dictionary, all of these writings had to be published anonymously. Since his authorship did not long remain a secret, they not only made him into a target of hatred in France but also met with opposition within his own Huguenot community and earned him the bitter enmity of Jurieu, who ultimately succeeded in having Bayle dismissed from his professorship in 1693.

153. On this, see Labrousse, *Bayle*, ch. 1.
154. See Bossuet, *Politics Drawn from the Very Words of Holy Scripture*.
155. The most comprehensive study of Bayle's life and work is Labrousse, *Pierre Bayle*, vol. I: *Du pays de foix à la cité d'Érasme*; vol. II: *Heterodoxie et rigorisme*.

The most important writings of this 'masked philosopher' will be discussed in detail in the following sections. Therefore, I will confine myself here to briefly situating them in the context of the conflicts of his time. He published his *Lettre sur la comète* in 1682, and a year later in an extended version as *Pensées diverses sur la comète*,[156] in which he denies that the appearance of a comet over Europe in 1680 (later known as Kirch's Comet) can be regarded as a sign from God; it is, he argues, nothing more than a natural occurrence that should be regarded in scientific terms. However, what makes this work so important for the question of toleration, and into one of the most daring works of modern political philosophy, is a long passage in which Bayle discusses the question of atheism. There he defends not only the thesis that superstition and religious fanaticism are worse evils than atheism but also the thesis, which was unheard of at the time, that it is not fear of God that motivates people to act morally but other motivations, and hence that atheists are also capable of moral action, and that even a state composed of atheists could exist. Just as heathens and Christians are capable of committing serious crimes, Bayle argues, so too are atheists capable of doing good. For the first time an author contradicted what I above called 'Locke's fear' in such clear terms and advocated a conception of morality as a freestanding human capability independent of religion. The assertion that even unbelievers are capable of acting morally has found its way into the literature as 'Bayle's Paradox' (he himself described it as a paradox).[157]

Yet, more than any other work it was the next, the *Critique générale de l'histoire du calvinisme de M. Maimbourg* (1682), which made him into a persecuted author. There he criticises the historical presentation and condemnation of Calvinism by the Jesuit Maimbourg as biased pseudo-historiography. He already expresses the idea which would later acquire major importance, namely that the assertion that one is undoubtedly on the side of the true religion, and hence has the right to suppress others, is inconsistent with the Christian religion, that it cannot be upheld on the basis of common human reason and the universal morality of reciprocity and that it is the source of all evil in existing societies.[158] In the works which followed he elaborated on this conception of an epistemic and moral relativisation of the absolute claims to truth of religion, which struck many contemporaries as an

---

156. An English translation by R. C. Bartlett has been published under the title *Various Thoughts on the Occasion of a Comet* and will be cited in what follows as *Various Thoughts*.
157. See *Nouvelles lettres de l'auteur de la Critique générale* (1685), 9.2 and 9.3, and the *Historical and Critical Dictionary*, 'First Clarification'.
158. See *Critique générale*, 13.6 (56–7) and 23.4 (105).

expression of atheism or of sceptical indifference, by trying to establish that this did not place the claim to truth of faith in question but instead restored it to its true domain, that of religious belief rather than of knowledge.[159] In questions of faith, Bayle argued, it is conscience which is the decisive court of appeal, not the faculty of reason which relies upon clear evidence; thus, religious disputes cannot be resolved unanimously by rational means nor can faith arise in any other way than through inward conviction.[160] Moreover, here Bayle already formulates the idea which would play an important role in later writings, namely the *right* of the erroneous conscience to freedom, because it follows what it regards as God's commandments.

When it became known that Bayle was the author of the *Critique générale* and he could not be apprehended, his brother was arrested and imprisoned in 1685 and subjected to incessant pressure to convert. He died after a couple of months in prison, just a few days after the revocation of the Edict of Nantes. In response Bayle wrote his short work *Ce que c'est que la France toute catholique générale sous le régne de Louis Le Grand* (1686), in which, on the one hand, a Protestant presents a bitter indictment of the developments in France, though, on the other, a Huguenot emigrant makes an appeal for moderation. There he already announced a work which would deal with the question of toleration in greater detail, which duly appeared in the same year: the *Commentaire philosophique sur ces paroles de Jésus-Christ 'Contrain-les d'entrer'; Où l'on prouve, par plusieurs raisons démonstratives qu'il n'y a rien de plus abominable que de faire des conversions par la contrainte, et où l'on réfute tous les sophismes des convertisseurs à contrainte, et l'apologie que St. Augustin a faite des persécutions.*[161] This work can be regarded, alongside Locke's *Epistola de tolerantia*, as the most important contribution to the modern philosophy of toleration. Moreover, as we shall see, it is superior to Locke's contemporaneous work in a variety of respects because it anticipates the problems with arguments for toleration which became clear to Locke only in the course of the debate with Proast and from the outset places the main emphasis on the normative-epistemological justification at which Locke arrived only later.

---

159. See *Nouvelles lettres*, especially letters 8–13.
160. Under Bayle's influence, Henri Basnage de Beauval published his work *Tolérance des religions* in 1684 in which he emphasises these points, in particular the primacy of justice and reciprocity over the non-redeemable claim to indubitable truth.
161. A complete English translation of this important text appeared in 1708 under the title *A Philosophical Commentary on These Words of the Gospel, Luke 14:23, 'Compel Them to Come In, That My House May Be Full'*. A modern translation of the first two parts by A. Godman Tannenbaum has appeared under the title *Philosophical Commentary on these Words of Jesus Christ, Compel Them to Come In* and will be cited in what follows.

Bayle's key insight is that only a generally valid justification of toleration which rests on higher-level conceptions of reason and morality could lead to a generally intelligible, binding and fair form of toleration. At the same time, as the long title reveals, Bayle goes back to the most important source of the (Christian-perfectionist) justification of the coercion of conscience, namely, the parable of *compelle intrare*, and to Augustine's position in the controversy with the Donatists, to which thinkers like Bossuet[162] appealed in order to legitimise the persecution of the Protestants. In 1687 Bayle added a third part to the *Commentaire* which attempts to refute Augustine's argument word for word. In my view, the *Commentaire* can be regarded as the culmination of the modern controversy concerning toleration not only because it returns to Augustine but also because of the carefulness and radicality with which Bayle contrasts and discusses the most diverse arguments for intolerance and toleration. In no other work is the drama of toleration, the arguments for and against freedom of conscience, presented in such a fundamental fashion. It contains in essence the justification of toleration which would prove to be the most systematically fruitful and it avoids the problems of the early liberal as well as the purely religious justifications: the combination of an autonomous morality of reciprocal justification and the theory of the separation of faith and knowledge which, based on an epistemological conception of the finitude of reason, undercuts dogmatic disputes over religion without questioning those religious claims to truth which confine themselves to the domain of faith. As a result, it contains the presuppositions for a theory of toleration which will be able to overcome the paradoxes of toleration sketched at the outset of this study.

The rational moral principle of impartiality and the idea that religious claims to truth are so constituted that they cannot appeal to clear evidence and rational grounds set Bayle at odds not only with the Catholic Church but also, as we have seen, with his Calvinist fellow-believers who suspected him of Socinianism and even of atheism. Pierre Jurieu was especially prominent among the latter, with the result that a bitter controversy and enmity broke out between him and Bayle.[163] Jurieu defended in certain respects the

---

162. Shortly after the revocation of the Edict of Nantes in 1685, Bossuet is reported to have delivered a widely noted sermon on the saying *compelle intrare* in the presence of the king in which he defended the royal policy; it may have provided the motivation for Bayle's thematic starting point in his work on toleration. Kilkullen, *Sincerity and Truth*, 89 n. 146, refers to Bossuet's sermon (which is no longer extant); Mendus, *Toleration and the Limits of Liberalism*, 7, quotes Bossuet as asserting that 'I have the right to persecute you because I am right and you are wrong.'

163. On this, see Labrousse, 'The Political Ideas of the Huguenot Diaspora (Bayle and Jurieu)'.

diametrically opposed position to Bayle. On the one hand, it viewed it as heresy to question the assertion of the true religion on earth while, on the other, accusing Bayle of political quietism. For Bayle, in contrast to Jurieu, followed the *politiques* in viewing a strong ruler like Henry IV as necessary in order to guarantee civic toleration, whereas Jurieu followed the tradition of the Calvinist monarchomachs in defending a right of resistance against illegitimate political authority (although he himself had in mind not the ideal of a democratic commonwealth but one which connects true religion with political government).[164] Bayle responded in various writings, among them the *Avis important aux réfugiez sur leur prochain retour en France* (1690), in which he attacks the political radicalism of the Huguenots as well as their religious intolerance.

A series of political attacks on Jurieu can also be found in Bayle's most influential and important work, the voluminous *Dictionnaire historique et critique*, published in 1696, in which he attempts to write a critical history of all of the philosophical and theological errors which humanity had accumulated since antiquity.[165] To this end he writes a multiplicity of articles devoted to the authors and historical figures whom he regards as the most important, each article comprising a short main text confined to the available facts and a series of footnotes commenting upon it. The most important error attacked by Bayle is the failure to differentiate between faith and reason, between theology and philosophy, both on the part of those who regard religious truth as demonstrable and believe that religious disputes can be settled conclusively by rational means, as well as on the part of those who think that religion must confine itself to what can be shown by rational means, and thereby arrive either at a deistic or a sceptical position. Neither should philosophy be annexed to faith nor faith to philosophy; instead, according to Bayle, they represent different answers to different human questions. Thus, faith does not appear as *irrational* but rather as *super-rational*, an idea with whose help Bayle, as we shall see, attempts to defuse dogmatic religious conflicts without placing the possibility of faith as such in question.

---

164. See, for example, Jurieu's 1687 work attacking Bayle with the revealing title *Traité des droits des deux souverains en matière de religion: la conscience et le prince. Pour détruire le dogme de l'indifférence des religions et de la tolérance universelle.*

165. A complete English translation of the *Dictionnaire* by Desmaizeaux appeared in London in 1732 under the title *The Dictionary Historical and Critical of Mr Peter Bayle*. A recent English translation of selections from the most important philosophical sections of the *Dictionnaire* by R. Popkin has appeared under the title *Historical and Critical Dictionary: Selections*, and will be cited in what follows.

Bayle's *Dictionnaire* became one of the most important points of reference for the French Enlightenment and had a profound influence on its conceptions of toleration and its definition of the relation between faith and reason, even though there are important differences in this respect between authors like Montesquieu, Rousseau, Voltaire and Diderot. Bayle is the first modern author in whom the spirit of the Enlightenment finds a clear and differentiated expression in a critique of religious dogmatism and in the emphasis on a 'natural' rational morality.[166] However, Bayle not only established a high level of discussion of the problem for later theorists of toleration and critics of religion, but also presented them with a riddle. Especially the manner in which he demolished philosophical and theological positions in the *Dictionnaire* and reduced icons of religion and philosophy to human proportions (often also with references to their sexual lives, which earned Bayle harsh criticism) earned him the reputation of being a radical sceptic, even a materialist atheist, in metaphysical and religious questions. In his monograph on Bayle, Ludwig Feuerbach calls him 'the footloose, unattached sceptic, the dialectical guerrilla leader of all anti-dogmatic polemicists'[167] and particularly emphasises his critique of religion and his notion of the 'independence of ethical reason', which Feuerbach rightly regards as anticipating Kant's moral philosophy and describes as a 'salutary lightning strike out of the blue against the prevailing theories of happiness'.[168] But at the same time he regards Bayle's justification of the possibility of faith as an 'act of self-denial' and testily characterises him as an 'intellectual flagellant'.[169] This ambivalence persists in contemporary interpretations which veer between a view of Bayle as an atheistic libertine[170] and presenting him as a good Calvinist.[171] But Bayle is neither the one nor the other. He is a radical critic of a dogmatic religion which challenges the validity of the precepts of reason; yet his doctrine of the finitude of human reason also prepares the ground for a faith which *knows* that it is faith. He underscored this in the clarifications which he appended to the *Dictionnaire* in 1701 at the insistence of his Rotterdam community, as well as in other writings up to the time of his death in 1706.[172]

2. In analysing his writings let us first return to Bayle's paradox, which directly contradicts what I above called Locke's fear. Both concern the question of whether an atheist can be a trustworthy member of society who

166. Cassirer, who describes Bayle's *Dictionnaire* as the founding work of the French Enlightenment, makes this point in *The Philosophy of the Enlightenment*, 167.
167. Feuerbach, *Pierre Bayle*, 3.   168. *Ibid.* 103.   169. *Ibid.* 160, 163.
170. Wootton, 'Pierre Bayle, Libertine?'.   171. Labrousse, *Pierre Bayle*.
172. See, for instance, Bayle, *Entretiens de Maxime et de Themiste*, 5.

is capable of acting morally. Locke had denied this, thereby setting a clear limit to toleration. For Locke, anyone who doubts the existence of God also doubts his norms of justice on earth and their binding character, for one is ultimately accountable to God for their observance. Without a foundation in God neither morality nor the state is possible – a fear which, to be sure, neither originates with Locke nor is confined to his time but continues to shape the discussion of the limits of toleration up to the present day.

Bayle's *Pensées diverses sur la comète* attacks this conception with a vehemence which was disconcerting for his contemporaries. The context in which he develops these ideas is his critique of superstition, which leads him to question whether idolatry is not a worse transgression than atheism (§129).[173] Bayle answers in the affirmative because idolaters offend God by using him for human purposes and create new gods tailored to human interests, whereas atheists simply lack faith (§132). Bayle then addresses what I call 'Locke's fear'. The reason why atheism is regarded as the worst crime is 'the false prejudice concerning the lights of the conscience [*lumières de la conscience*], which are imagined to be the rule of our actions in the absence of a proper examination of the true springs that make us act' (§133). It is assumed that a conscience which believes in providence and in divine reward for virtue and punishment of vice is motivated to act morally out of fear of God. 'It is all well and good to say this' (§134), according to Bayle, but it is quite at variance with experience. For although in a perfectly ideal world one would have to assume that the Christians would be the most virtuous human beings, in the real world it is precisely those who profess their faith most vigorously who prove to be capable of the worst crimes. In support of this argument he cites the examples of fanatical soldiers who are willing to commit crimes for religious reasons (§139) and of the Crusades (§140). These examples demonstrate, among other things, that it is not true that the Christian religion makes people meek since it can lead to extreme violence (§141). Therefore, a 'corruption of morals' is never proof of atheism, according to Bayle, and not only is atheism not a greater evil than fanaticism but, on the contrary, excessive religion and superstition are the worst things of all (§159) – a judgement of Bayle's which Voltaire would later repeat approvingly.[174]

From a philosophical point of view, this proves, according to Bayle, that human beings do not as a general rule act in accordance with the

---

173. In what follows, I will quote *Various Thoughts* from the English translation followed by the relevant French expressions in brackets where this seems necessary to facilitate better comprehension.
174. Voltaire, *A Philosophical Dictionary*, article 'Atheism'.

principles of 'natural justice' (§136) which they all share regardless of their religion – a thesis he introduces here as it were in passing – but in accordance with other motives, specifically under the negative influence of passions and habits (§135) and under the positive influence of countervailing considerations, such as the fear of legal punishment and the concern with forfeiting social recognition. And precisely these positive considerations, according to Bayle, also hold for atheists, which means that, as regards morals, a society of atheists is as enduring as any other. Both negatively and positively, atheists and religious believers are equals – 'Jew and Mohammedan, Turk and Moor, Christian and Infidel, Indian and Tartar, the inhabitant of the firm earth and the inhabitant of the isles, nobleman and commoner' (§136; also 144). This leads him to the revolutionary idea of a society of atheists:

> There are no annals that inform us of the morals and customs of a nation steeped in atheism. Therefore, one cannot refute by experience the conjecture one makes to begin with on this subject; namely, that the atheists are not capable of any moral virtue and that they are ferocious beasts among whom there is more reason to fear for one's life than among tigers and lions. But it is not difficult to show that this conjecture is very uncertain. For since experience shows us that those who believe in a paradise and a hell are capable of committing every sort of crime, it is evident that the inclination to act badly does not stem from the fact that one is ignorant of the existence of God and that it is not corrected by the knowledge one acquires of a God who punishes and rewards. It follows manifestly from this that the inclination to act badly is not found in a soul destitute of the knowledge of God any more than in a soul that knows God; and that a soul destitute of the knowledge of God is no freer of the brake that represses the malignity of the heart than is a soul that has this knowledge. It follows from this in addition that the inclination to act badly comes from the ground of man's nature and that it is strengthened by the passions, which coming from the temperament as their source, are subsequently modified in many ways according to the various accidents of life. Finally, it follows from this that the inclination to pity, to sobriety, to good-natured conduct, and so forth, does not stem from the fact that one knows that there is a God . . . but from a certain disposition of the temperament, fortified by education, by personal interest, by the desire to be praised, by the instinct of reason [*instinct de la Raison*] or by similar motives that are met with in an atheist as well as in other men.   (§145)

As for the motivations that lead to morality, Bayle cites a series of motives which an atheistic society could integrate (§172), the most important among them being, as mentioned, the fear of the law (§161) and above all the striving for recognition, i.e. social esteem and honour (§§146, 162–3): 'For it is to the inward esteem of other men [*l'estime interieure des autres hommes*] that we aspire above all' (§179). Viewed in this light, 'Locke's fear' is unfounded, since human beings live in any case not according to their principles of conscience but to other passions and considerations shared by all human beings.

However, this is just one aspect of Bayle's reflections. For atheists and religious believers are alike not only in their negative and positive passions but also in their autonomous faculty of moral insight (which Bayle understands in virtually Kantian terms).[175]

> Reason dictated to the ancient sages: that it was necessary to do what is good for the love of the good itself, that virtue was its own reward, and that it belonged only to a vicious man to abstain from evil for fear of punishment... This makes me believe that reason without the knowledge of God can sometimes persuade a man that there are decent things which it is fine and laudable to do, not on account of the utility of doing so, but because this is in conformity with reason... For one must know that although God does not reveal himself fully to an atheist, he does not fail to act upon the latter's mind and to preserve for him that reason and intelligence by means of which all men understand the truth of the first principles of metaphysics and morals [*tous les hommes comprenent la vérité des premiers principes de Métaphysique & de Morale*].
>
> (§178)

With this Bayle takes the decisive step towards his justification of toleration. For if atheists and religious believers of all kinds not only are capable of positive passions of moral conformity and of self-interest but are also able to comprehend the basic principles of theoretical and practical reason and to act in conformity with them, this opens the way for a conception of toleration based on mutual respect and the justification of one's own claims on a common rational basis which is no longer tied to particular religious assumptions and goes beyond the narrow limits of toleration stemming from 'Locke's fear'. This is what Bayle attempts in the *Commentaire philosophique*.

---

175. In addition to Feuerbach, *Pierre Bayle*, 103, Labrousse also emphasises this in *Pierre Bayle*, vol. II, ch. 9.

Hence, Bayle's thought renders entirely intelligible what became increasingly clear in the course of the discourse concerning toleration, namely that the conflicts over toleration provide the context for the development of an *autonomous conception of morality* which rests on a freestanding faculty of practical reason to act in a justifiable way – i.e. on the basis of justifications independent of particular religious views.

3. In composing his *Commentaire*, Bayle adopts the persona of an Englishman who has been requested by the author of the book on the 'very Catholic France' to refute the reading of the parable of the *compelle intrare* to which the contemporary French 'converters' (*Convertisseurs*) appealed to compel the Huguenots to abjure their faith. He connects this with a fierce indictment of the 'papist' practice which is legitimated by the assumption that one possesses the true Church and is duty-bound to God, society and not least the 'converted' themselves to assist in imposing it. Already in the preface Bayle objects that this is a 'childish' argument, for the crux of the controversy between Protestants and Catholics is precisely which church is the true one and 'nothing is more ridiculous than reasoning by always assuming the thing in question'.[176] This question cannot be decided unilaterally by the Protestant side either, he argues, but only on the basis of 'shared principles'. And what holds for the question concerning the true Church, according to Bayle, also holds, when it *cannot* be decided on the basis of such principles, for resulting arguments concerning reciprocal toleration: that there is no right to persecute those who think differently from us must be demonstrated on generally intelligible grounds which *universally* challenge the claim of any religion to this right. Moreover, those who, like the 'papists', reject such reasons pose a threat to peaceful social relations because of this intolerant attitude and cannot be tolerated, especially not in political offices. However, with Henry IV in mind, he makes an exception to this for the king, who as a person must be free to profess a religion of his choosing. This already points to central features of Bayle's justification of toleration. On the one hand, it aims at a fundamental normative and epistemological refutation of the right of religious coercion and it seeks strictly reciprocally and generally valid arguments for toleration; on the other hand, in its search for a universal form of civil toleration, it sets itself apart from toleration in the vertical, political dimension. The latter continues to be conceived in accordance with the permission conception, even though the sovereign is entrusted with the task of adopting as neutral a stance as possible in religious questions.

176. Bayle, *Philosophical Commentary*, Preface, 13–14 (cited in what follows by section and page number).

The argument for universal toleration and the rejection of the 'convertist' reading of the parable of the *compelle intrare* in the first part of the *Commentaire* takes as its starting point the reflection with which the treatment of morality in the *Pensées diverses* concluded, namely that the 'natural light' of reason 'reveals' to all human beings the most general and infallible principles of metaphysics and morality, in particular principles of a 'universal reason [*raison universelle*] which enlightens all spirits and which is never lacking to those who attentively consult it' (1.1, p. 31). They constitute the foundation which God has imbued in all human beings, including the pagans. Therefore, they represent the first 'natural religion' which is 'strengthened and perfected by the Gospels' (*ibid.*) which were revealed only *after* this 'inner light'. From this it follows for Bayle that every interpretation of scripture must measure up to the principles of this original light, of this independent reason.

Finite human reason, which leads to rationally intractable disputes in the domain of 'speculative truths', does *not* lead to such differences in questions of morality, of the 'idea of natural equity' (1.1, p. 30): here there are 'moral laws without exception' which 'enlighten every man coming into the world'. Bayle adds, in almost Kantian terms: 'But since passions and prejudices only too often obscure the ideas of natural equity, I would advise a person who intends to know them well to consider these ideas in general and as abstracted from all private interest and from the customs of his country' (*ibid.*). Then one should ask oneself whether a certain practice could meet with universal agreement in a particular society: 'Is such a practice just in itself? If it were a question of introducing it in a country where it would not be in use and where he would be free to take it up or not, would one see, upon examining it impartially that it is reasonable enough to merit being adopted?' (*ibid.*). This dispassionate examination must be demanded in questions of justice, according to Bayle, and it is possible in principle for every human being to do so who follows the 'primitive universal ray of light' (*lumière primitive & universelle*) with which God enlightens all human beings. Every individual must follow this light (*ses propres lumières*) against the authority of custom or the Church according to Bayle; and no interpretation of scripture, from whatever authority, can overrule this 'natural revelation' of the golden rule of reciprocity (1.1, p. 32).

With this Bayle has established crucial presuppositions for the argument that the literal interpretation of the *compelle intrare* proverb must be mistaken because it contradicts the justice corresponding to the natural light. However, he first makes a detour following a classical line of argument.

Presupposing the idea of God as an idea of reason, Bayle argues that only a faith based on inward conviction can be pleasing to God who judges everything in accordance with its true worth; but such a faith cannot be elicited by force, only its opposite or even hypocrisy (1.2, p. 36), a grave violation of conscience. Only as free, therefore, can faith be pleasing to God. However, Bayle immediately presents the (Augustinian) counter-argument, which Proast also cited against Locke and which led the latter to revise his argument – namely, that the 'Convertists' need not exercise any direct coercion on conscience but could seek to induce the latter to return to the 'true path' merely by shielding them from bad teachings and through suitable instruction, for which a certain amount of pressure may also on occasion be necessary. Bayle recognises the force of this objection, which boils down to the claim that methods of indoctrination and the suppression of false doctrines from the public arena can also lead to 'serious' and inward convictions; and thus he recognises the flaws in the classical argument for freedom of conscience. Against the 'specious chicanery' (1.2, p. 37) of this objection he proposes a different, stronger argument. In this way, he situates his approach from the outset on a terrain which Locke would reach only with great difficulty, namely the normative-epistemological thesis that the enforcement of religious faith is not reciprocally justifiable.

This thesis presupposes two things: first, the higher-level normative principle that practices which set general restrictions on faith and action must be justified in a reciprocal manner and, second, the epistemological relativisation of the claim to speak for the true Church, so that the claim to reciprocity cannot be contravened by appeal to this exclusive truth. As regards the former, in the third chapter of the first part Bayle emphasises that Christian moral teaching is in complete harmony with the 'natural religion' of the rational moral principles and, that being the case, there is no normative disagreement between his argument and the teaching of scripture (1.3, p. 39). These kinds of reassurances concerning dogma repeatedly crop up in Bayle's work (which, it should be borne in mind, is essentially concerned with the legitimacy of a certain interpretation of scripture). In the fourth chapter he goes on to deliver the 'crushing blow' (1.4, p. 45) by accusing the literal interpretation of the 'Convertists' of turning precisely this natural morality on its head and of turning patent crimes into virtues. The reason for this is the presumption that one has the right to impose the true religion by force, so that violence suddenly becomes 'good' or 'salutary'. According to Bayle, this is 'the most abominable doctrine that has ever been imagined' (1.4, p. 47), for with this argument *anyone* can twist *anything* into its opposite. After all, every religion and church claims that it is the true one, and hence according to this argument every church and religion would also claim the right to use force. With this the two components of this argument – the normative component of the independent morality of reciprocity and the epistemological component of the non-demonstrability of the true faith – become apparent. For, according to 'natural' moral concepts (and contrary to dogmatic distortions), violence remains nothing but violence, and the claim to speak for the unquestionably true religion cannot be redeemed by means of 'natural' reason. Only when both components are considered together is Bayle's resulting argument tenable, because it demonstrates how the groundless claim to be authorised to use force in the name of truth involves violations of reciprocity. Thus, the emperor of China would be well advised not to tolerate any Christians in his kingdom, for the latter are merely intent on propagating their religion by force (1.5); and nowhere could Christians or any other religion deplore intolerance, for this would then be the fundamental right of all religions (1.7 and 1.9). In arguing thus, Bayle consistently appeals to the overriding normative principle that one must accord all others the same rights as those which one claims for oneself.

Bayle clearly recognises the extent to which this reciprocity argument presupposes that the claim to represent the true religion (and hence, if necessary, also to legitimise 'mild force' in Proast's sense) cannot be supported with reasons *which cannot be reasonably rejected*, at least not here 'on earth' among finite rational beings. Therefore, at the end of the first part of the *Commentaire* he states that:

> If one would say, 'it is very true, Jesus Christ has commanded His Disciples to persecute, but that is none of your business, you who are heretics. Executing this commandment belongs only to us who are the true Church,' they would answer that they are agreed on the principle but not in the application and that they alone have the right to persecute since truth is on their side . . . One never sees the end of such a dispute, so that like waiting for the final sentence in a trial, one is not able to pronounce anything upon these violences; they will stay sequestered at the very least, and this will always be to the advantage of the victorious party. The suffering party would only make itself fret by reviewing its controversies one by one and would never be able to have the pleasure of saying, 'I'm unjustly treated,' except by assuming it is in the right and saying, I am the true Church. But the others would presently reply, 'You are not the true Church, therefore you are justly treated. You have not proved your claim as yet. We will dispute it.

Forbear your complaints then until the trial is decided'... When one reflects on all this impartially, one is reduced necessarily to this rare principle, *I have truth on my side, therefore my violences are good works. So and so errs: therefore his violences are criminal.* To what purpose, pray, are all these reasonings? Do they heal the evils which prosecutors commit, or are they capable of making them reconsider? Is it not absolutely necessary in order to cure the furore of a zealot who ravages a whole country or to make him comprehend his doings, to draw him out of his particular controversies and remind him of principles which are common to both parties such as the maxims of morality, the precepts of the Decalogue, of Jesus Christ and of His Apostles, concerning justice, charity, abstinence from theft, murder, injuries to our neighbour, etc.?   (1.10, pp. 84–5)

Here Bayle makes clear that the issue is not just a matter of appealing to an independent, rational sense of morality *as morality*, free from fanatical notions, shared by all human beings in order to be able to rectify moral and religious truth; it is also a matter of undercutting religious disputes insofar as they come to be seen, not as completely pointless, but nevertheless as ultimately irresolvable by rational means. This calls for a conception of the *finitude of reason* according to which disagreements among finite rational beings in questions of faith are unavoidable. The reason for this is that human beings form their convictions in a particular environment which leads them onto a particular path to faith, but that over time they learn that they are fallible and prone to error and are capable of learning and recognising that, in matters of faith, they believe in a kind of 'moral certainty'. From the former insight it follows that one should remain open to the possibility of further learning especially in religious questions (1.5, p. 52), from the latter that there are answers to questions of which one is convinced without having more than 'probable reasons' for them (*ibid.*). It is especially, though not only, true of questions of religion that 'evidence is a relative quality' (II.1, p. 93), that habit, training or other factors are such that rational individuals arrive at very different assessments and judgements, and that differences can arise which cannot be resolved on the basis of an unambiguous rational judgement. Therefore, a rational human being is aware of the 'burdens of reason' (to use a term of Rawls)[177] and knows, according to Bayle, that 'it is humanly inevitable that men in different ages and countries should have very different sentiments in religion, and interpret some one way, some

177. I will return to this point in §33.

another, whatever is susceptible to various interpretations' (II.6, p. 140). From this Bayle concludes that 'difference in opinion seems to be man's inherent infelicity, as long as his understanding is so limited and his heart so inordinate' (II.6, p. 141). Therefore, the desire that all human beings should unite in one religion will remain unfulfilled, and the best response to this is to espouse toleration. Bayle's key insight boils down to the fact that rational human beings should recognise their own finitude of reason and the unavoidability of religious differences, but that they should also recognise that this is not a reason to mistrust their own faith, for this is in no way refuted or reduced to something subjective by this insight. This is the major topic of the *Dictionnaire*, to which I will turn in the next section.

With this argument, Bayle succeeds in presenting a justification of toleration that enables him to refute comprehensively the literal interpretation of the *compelle intrare* parable – as irrational, immoral and unchristian, as well as being imprudent in a pragmatic sense, for example concerning peace in the state. At the limits of his conception of the state oriented to sovereignty, and in a certain proximity to the monarchomachs whom he elsewhere criticises, Bayle argues in this context that the 'Convertists' could not appeal to a royal edict (such as the Fontainebleau revocation edict) either, because even edicts must be based on a 'good reason' (I.4, p. 46) and an edict prohibiting a religion cannot be legitimate (I.6, p. 66). Like Hobbes, Spinoza and Locke, Bayle argues that, independently of whether the sovereign is appointed by God or by a contract, he has no right to coerce in matters of conscience, for, given that conscience, 'with regard to each particular man, is the voice and law of God in him' (*ibid.*), nobody could have surrendered this voice to the authority of a temporal power. To follow one's conscience in religious matters is not only an inalienable right of the individual, it is also one's duty towards God.

At the beginning of the second part of the *Commentaire*, which takes up a series of objections against the justification of toleration elaborated in the first part, Bayle once again addresses the above-mentioned objection, familiar from Augustine (and Proast), that a form of indirect force can have the effect of liberating conscience from false convictions, thereby opening one's eyes for the truth. Like Locke, Bayle first attempts to present immanent objections, arguing that reflection under the impression of fear cannot lead to an impartial assessment of the truth and that the Convertists could not intend their objection seriously, for they are not willing to acknowledge every serious decision, but only those in agreement with their own position (II.1, pp. 90–1). However, here the line of argument from the first part is repeated insofar as Bayle, going beyond these immanent arguments and appealing to the relativity of religious evidence, questions the basic presupposition of this objection, namely that of possessing knowledge of the true religion and Church. This sets a pattern for how the argument unfolds in the second part of the *Commentaire* as a whole: only the above-mentioned, normative-epistemological position offers a way out of the difficulties in which the liberal-Protestant justification of freedom of conscience becomes entangled.

This is most evident in the passage in which Bayle presents the objection that his argument for freedom of conscience is powerless against the claim that what is ultimately at stake is enforcing the *true* religion (II.8). At this point, Bayle initially responds not with his conception that religious force cannot be reciprocally justified but by appealing to the rights of the 'erroneous conscience'. Assuming the principle that the greatest sin of all is to act against what the 'light' of one's conscience prescribes (II.8, pp. 151–2) because that would be to act against what one believes God requires, Bayle argues in the tradition extending back to Abelard that an 'erroneous conscience' which has carefully pondered a question and then acts in good faith should not be morally condemned. Bayle concludes that 'the first and most indispensable of all our obligations, is that of never acting against the promptings of conscience' (II.8, p. 156).

However, at this point Bayle sees what other readers of his work, for instance Jurieu,[178] also immediately recognised, namely that this argument can be turned on its head. For, assuming that a serious conscience includes the belief that God commands a person to enforce the recognised truth with fire and the sword, then that would be the supreme duty of such a 'conscientious persecutor' and all attempts to dissuade him from this would be open to criticism as illegitimate, intolerant interferences in his freedom of conscience (II.8, 156–7). Thus, the call for toleration would prove, paradoxically, to be the most extreme form of intolerance.[179] Bayle is frank enough to acknowledge this problem:

> The . . . difficulty proposed is that my doctrine, in its consequences, destroys what I would like to establish. My design is to show that persecution is an abominable thing, and yet everyone who believes himself obliged by conscience to persecute would, by my doctrine be required to persecute and would be sinning if he did not.   (II.9, p. 166)

---

178. See Jurieu, *Traité des droits des deux souverains*, 69.
179. This represents a particular form of the 'paradox of drawing the limits' discussed in section 1.

Moreover, he concedes that for the present he cannot rebut this,[180] but he nevertheless insists that the practice of persecution should be morally condemned:

> I do not deny that those who are actually persuaded that it is necessary to extirpate sects in order to obey God are obliged to follow the motions of this false conscience and that, in not doing so, they are guilty of disobedience to God since they do a thing they believe to be in disobedience to God. But, (1) it does not follow that they do without crime what they do by conscience. (2) This does not hinder our crying out loudly against their false maxims and endeavouring to enlighten their understandings.   (II.9, p. 167, translation amended)

By subjectivising conscience, which is now acknowledged to be as much a religious as a moral conscience,[181] Bayle has manoeuvred himself into an impasse, for he absolutises the right of the erroneous conscience to follow its voice as much as its duty to do precisely this. But this has the paradoxical consequence that one has a moral right – and even a duty – to do something immoral. The mistake is that Bayle has here substituted the 'light of conscience' for the 'natural light' of morality and reason and has subjectivised it to such an extent that the standards of reciprocal justification and of the self-imposed modesty of finite reason, which he elsewhere regards as hallmarks of reason, recede into the background. But Bayle must appeal to precisely these two elements if he is to avoid this impasse of absolutising subjective conscience, which inadvertently pursues the logic of the argument for freedom of conscience *ad absurdum*. Otherwise he would not have any standard for identifying the error of the 'conscientious persecutor', in contrast to the other, legitimate errors in the domain of religion, as a 'crime' and declaring the prohibition of such crimes to be a duty of the state (II.9, p. 167). Furthermore, the only way to rescue his argument for toleration resides in modifying the thesis of the unconditional right or supreme duty of the erroneous conscience to such an extent that the 'conscientious persecutor' has the prior duty to ask himself what would follow if he really had such a right; and it must be clear to him to what extent this would lead to a hopeless

---

180. This is also emphasised by Rex, *Essays on Pierre Bayle and Religious Controversy*, 181–5, and Kilkullen, *Sincerity and Truth*, 89–105. However, whereas Rex thinks that this paradox undermines Bayle's argument entirely, Kilkullen correctly points to the resources on which Bayle can draw to avoid it, in particular the reciprocity argument, though he does not place sufficient emphasis on the moral importance of this argument and he fails to take the epistemological component into consideration.

181. Mori, 'Pierre Bayle, the Rights of the Conscience, the "Remedy" of Toleration', 52, draws attention to the conflation of these two conceptions of conscience.

moral chaos which God could not have willed, because everyone could claim this right according to the standard of reciprocity (II.8, p. 159). Therefore, it is only the insistence on a morality of reciprocal justification, including the epistemic relativisation of claims to irrefutable religious truth, that leads Bayle back onto the path of the argument for toleration. Accordingly, there cannot be a 'right' to persecute others. Bayle must presuppose that rational human beings who are endowed with a conscience have this insight, and an error on this point cannot have any morally legitimising force – there cannot be freedom of conscience for murder or other crimes (II.9, p. 168). For '[i]n this regard, namely, in respect to the knowledge of our duties to moral standards, revealed light is so clear that few people can mistake it, when in good faith they are seeking out what it is' (II.10, p. 183).

But given this justification of toleration, how do things stand as regards its limits? According to what has been said and in the light of Bayle's book on the comet and his assessment of the moral capabilities of the atheist, these limits must be very broad and must be geared to the principle of reciprocity itself. In fact, Bayle courageously accepts the objection that his argument is in danger of leading to a *tolérance générale* and questions the supposedly disastrous consequences that follow from this (II.7, p. 145). Against the *Demi-Tolérans* of his time, he defends a universal, impartial toleration arrangement which, in addition to toleration among Christians, also includes toleration towards Jews, Muslims (who may also undertake missions), pagans and even the Socinians (who at the time were targets of extreme hostility): 'There can be no solid reason for tolerating any one sect which does not equally hold for every other' (*ibid.*). Therefore, the only possible reason for defining the limits of toleration is the 'maxim' '*that a religion which forces conscience has no right to be tolerated*' (II.7, p. 147). This includes, as already remarked at the outset, not only the 'papists' but also intolerant Protestants like Jurieu (or those who condemned Servet in Geneva; II.5, pp. 133–4), who are beyond the scope of toleration not for religious reason but for reasons of political morality: 'A party which, if it were the strongest, would tolerate no other and would force the other's conscience ought not to be tolerated. Now such is the Church of Rome' (II.5, p. 130).[182] Yet, notwithstanding the restrictions on their dangerous activities, Catholics should not suffer any ill treatment either to their persons or to their property, and the 'private' practice of their religion, including rearing their children in their own faith, should also be permitted (II.5, p. 129). They should be free from religious

182. Thus, also in the *Dictionary*, article 'Milton', remark O.

indoctrination. Bayle sees in this an advantage of fair, Protestant toleration (II.5), even though it does not mean complete freedom of worship for
everyone (II.5, pp. 130–1).

However, with regard to toleration towards atheists a further difficulty
with the religious concept of conscience which could also be found in Locke
becomes apparent – and the drawback of Bayle's attempt to identify the
independent morality of the 'natural light' with the morality of the Gospels,
even though the former has priority over the latter. For in the *Commentaire*, in
contrast to the *Pensées diverses*, Bayle's chief concern is to promote toleration
among Christians and in this context he distances himself from the atheists,
to whom he was often accused of belonging. Those who deny the existence
of God, according to Bayle, could not appeal to the religious justification for
freedom of conscience and could not lay claim to the 'asylum of conscience'
(II.9, p. 167) which is bound to God and hence may not be interfered with
by the state. Still, even though they have forfeited this special protection,
they should be treated in accordance with the law, and the fact that they
do not recognise any laws above the human is cause for concern only if
they behave as 'insurgents' and continue, in violation of the prohibition
of the sovereign, to propagate their views in such a way that the laws are
infringed. These formulations remain extremely vague and open to a more
rigid or a more tolerant reading, depending on how the talk of a 'threat'
to the law or to public peace by the atheists is understood. Yet even if
we regard these remarks by Bayle as a pragmatic concession to his time,
and even if we set the threshold mentioned high, this remains a regression
behind the position arrived at in the *Pensées diverses*, even though he does
not fully revert to what I called Locke's fear. Nevertheless, it reveals the
arduousness of the path leading to a genuinely freestanding conception of
morality and to the corresponding definition of the limits of toleration,
which, on Bayle's essential conception, could be measured solely in terms of
whether a group recognises the requirement of reciprocal justification and
of relativising one's own claims to absoluteness. Bayle succeeded in taking a
major step along the path to such a conception which overcomes the aporias
of freedom of conscience.

4. We have not yet sufficiently clarified the important relationship
between faith and reason which arises in connection with the topos of the
finitude of reason. Bayle's *Dictionnaire* is devoted to this issue; it can be traced
through a multiplicity of the entries, culminating in the clarifications which
he appended to a later edition.

His main concern in this connection is not, as many of his readers in the age of the Enlightenment assumed, to reject faith as 'irrational' – but neither is it to affirm faith even against reason, following the tradition of Montaigne and Pascal, in an extreme form of fideism.[183] He is concerned to create room for religious answers to metaphysical questions by placing limits on the negative, destructive force of reason which must recognise its own limits – answers which can neither be provided by reason nor demanded of it, though they cannot be prohibited by it either. In this way – and this is Bayle's real concern – dogmatic disputes concerning the 'true faith' and proofs of it are undercut without faith, which remains within the boundaries of what can be rationally debated but cannot ultimately be resolved by reason, thereby becoming empty. Both sides, reason and faith, must heed their respective limits: reason recognises its limitations in speculative matters which can find further answers only in the mode of faith; and faith does not try to represent and enforce its 'truths' as conclusively justified truths which cannot be reasonably disputed. Neither of the two sides has authority over the other as long as each remains within its own sphere. Faith lies *beyond reason*, but it is not *irrational*; at the same time (theoretical and practical) reason remains the faculty which is common to all human beings and unites them in spite of religious differences, and also remains a corrective to superstition and irrational religion. The key issue here is that 'rational faith' does not seek irrefutable evidence for its convictions; although it rests on proven considerations, it always knows that it is a *faith*. Therefore, the inevitable consequence is religious *strife*, but not religious *conflict* in the name of the 'true religion'. Reason includes religious disagreement not in such a way that it can resolve this disagreement but that the adversaries recognise that they are located on a terrain marked by 'reasonable differences'. Bayle was the first thinker to develop this notion of 'reasonable faith' in such a consistent way.

Reason, according to Bayle, has a salutary effect in uncovering the errors which human beings have accumulated in their dogmatic systems; however, it is equally capable of exercising a destructive influence leading to complete scepticism if it lacks 'divine support'; for without the latter

---

183. Thus, Popkin, 'Pierre Bayle's Place in 17th Century Scepticism', 1, who qualifies this only in relation to Bayle's later work. By contrast, Brush, *Montaigne and Bayle*, 300, describes Bayle correctly as a 'semi-fideist' insofar as he understands the truth of faith as non-demonstrable, but at the same time not as irrational. One could speak, in a somewhat strained neologism, of 'rational fideism'.

it [reason] is a guide that leads one astray; and philosophy can be
compared to some powders that are so corrosive that, after they have
eaten away the infected flesh of a wound, they then devour the living
flesh, rot the bones, and penetrate to the very marrow. Philosophy at
first refutes errors. But if it is not stopped at this point, it goes on to
attack truths.[184]

In his article on the sceptic 'Pyrrho', in particular – which can also be read as a
commentary on Montaigne – Bayle walks a fine line between emphasising the
legitimacy of the sceptic's reservation of judgement concerning unresolved
metaphysical-religious questions and warning against pushing this too far
into an excess of reason. The crucial thing is to recognise the 'infirmity of
reason' which can never find a final answer to certain questions, and to place
one's trust in faith as the 'better guide'.[185] Without this trust, Bayle argues,
the dogmatists who refuse to recognise their ignorance and the sceptics
who insist on nothing but their ignorance and pursue the 'path that leads
us astray' face each other in a confrontation which is only overcome by
the insight that the 'enslavement of the understanding' through belief in a
benevolent creator of the world can point the way out of the aporias of earthly
existence. Bayle describes this as an act of self-transcendence in this passage in
which he appeals to Pascal, though it also reveals his Calvinist understanding
of religion.[186] Hence, what justifies faith is, on the one hand, such an act
of self-entrusting in an awareness that the divinity of scripture cannot be
proven mathematically or metaphysically, but can only be demonstrated
'morally'.[187] On the other hand, it is the concrete human questions which
plunge reason into confusion and thus provide a motivation for faith as an
answer that is not required by reason but is nevertheless something rationally
desirable – and the main example Bayle offers for this is the explanation of
the existence of evil.

The two articles in which Bayle chiefly addresses this problem, and which
became the focus of heated controversies that led him to offer a 'clarification',
are those devoted to the 'Manichaeans' and the 'Paulicians', hence to those
'heretics' who trace the existence of good and evil in the world to two
different conflicting sources. Bayle's central thesis in this regard is that

---

184. Remark G to the article on Uriel Acost, quoted by Popkin in his 'Introduction' to Bayle,
    Historical and Critical Dictionary, xxi.
185. *Ibid*. article 'Pyrrho', 204.
186. *Ibid*. Note C, 206; see also article 'Pascal', in particular remarks B and I.
187. 'Beaulieu', remark F.

the negative arguments of the Manichaeans (though not the counter-theory they propose) cannot be refuted by rational means that appeal to human experience; for it cannot be adequately explained how far God can be the author of the evil encountered everywhere in the world, or how, if he is not its author, the existence of evil in the order of creation is to be explained as long as one does not *believe* – beyond all experience – the story of the Fall of Man.[188]

> Human reason is too feeble for this. It is a principle of destruction and not of edification. It is only proper for raising doubts, and for turning things on all sides in order to make disputes endless; and I do not think I am mistaken if I say of natural revelation, that is to say, the light of reason, what the theologians say of the Mosaic Dispensation. They say that it was only fit for making man realize his own weakness and the necessity of a redeemer and a law of grace. It was a teacher – these are their terms – to lead us to Jesus Christ . . . Let someone tell us with a great apparatus of arguments that it is not possible that moral evil should introduce itself into the world by the work of an infinitely good and holy principle, we will answer that this however is in fact the case, and therefore this is very possible.[189]

Note that Bayle's position here is not that revelation is believed entirely without reasons; it is rather that it offers 'the best solution' to the problem posed, although the latter cannot be proved by rational and empirical means. The 'natural light of philosophy' ties the 'Gordian knot' of the need for explanation ever tighter;[190] yet an answer can be found on the basis of faith and with the aid of the principle *ab actu ad potentiam valet consequentia* (i.e. from the act to the possibility is a valid inference) – in the sense of '*the elevation of faith and the abasement of reason*' (*de l'élévation de la Foi & de l'abaissement de la Raison*).[191] This does not mean that the articles of faith are irrational but only that contents which transcend reason are believed in order to satisfy a desideratum of reason, that is, in order to provide an answer which reason itself is unable to provide. This answer will always remain contested in the realm of reason, according to Bayle, and thus the dogmatists should be as modest in their claims to absoluteness as are the philosophical sceptics who

---

188. Bayle's arguments formed a central motif for Leibniz's *Theodicy*, as the latter makes clear in particular in the Preface and in the treatise on the agreement of faith with reason. On Bayle's critique of Leibniz's idea of a 'preestablished harmony', see, for example, the article 'Rorarius'.
189. *Ibid.* article 'Manicheans', remark D, 151–2.   190. *Ibid.* article 'Paulicians', 168.
191. *Ibid.* remark E, 177 (French 860).

only succeed in posing riddles. Questions such as those concerning the reason for the existence of evil exceed human beings' metaphysical possibilities,[192] and thus reason should recognise that this marks the beginning of the sphere of faith and that acrimonious disputes concerning demonstrations of the truth are pointless; they should be met with nothing except 'silence along with the shield of faith'.[193] Questions of this kind are, to use a different vocabulary, matters of reasonable disagreement, of a rationally admissible dispute among reasonable human beings who realise that reason cannot settle this disagreement, though it is capable of clarifying it up to a certain point.[194]

In his second 'clarification', which was necessary because Bayle himself was suspected of Manichaeanism, he further clarifies this point using formulations which skilfully trace the narrow line between, on the one hand, his radical reduction of the claim to truth of the Christian religion to the domain of pure faith, which made him into a spoiler and sceptic in the eyes of those who wanted to unite philosophy and theology under the supremacy of theology, and, on the other, his restriction of the claim to authority of philosophy in the religious domain, which made him into an obdurate fideist in the eyes of those who wanted to unite both under the supremacy of philosophy. He emphasises 'that all articles of the Christian faith, maintained and opposed by the weapons of philosophy alone, do not emerge in good shape from the battle', and hence they must abandon this battlefield and look for a different fortress, namely Holy Scripture.[195] This is not an admission of weakness but is a result of the insight that '*the mysteries of the Gospels are above reason*' (*dessus de la Raison*), that 'it is impossible to solve the difficulties raised by philosophers; and, consequently, a dispute in which only the natural light will be employed will always end to the disadvantage of the theologians; and they will find themselves forced to give ground and take refuge under the protection of the supernatural light'. That is an insight, Bayle continues, into the 'limits' of reason which 'can never attain to what is above it',[196] and it is also at the same time a self-limitation of religion, which thereby abandons the scene of the battle over the absolute truth which could justify faith rationally.[197] Religion preserves only the freedom of not having to 'subject' its 'mysteries' to philosophy, but only if it regards its faith as a 'gift of God', as 'a grace of the Holy Spirit', which should not be an object of scholarly dispute except for the purpose of clarifying these mysteries.[198]

---

192. *Ibid.* remark M, 191.   193. *Ibid.* 193.   194. On this, see §33 below.
195. Bayle, *Historical and Critical Dictionary*, Second Clarification, 409.
196. All quotations *ibid.* 410–11 (French 1223).   197. *Ibid.* 414.   198. *Ibid.* 412.

The message of this way of tracing the boundary between reason and faith for toleration is evident: outside of faith itself there is no legitimation for upholding and enforcing a religious claim to truth; the truths of religion become accessible only through inner faith. As regards sects such as the Manichaeans, this means that there is no reason not to tolerate them; and also with respect to the unbelievers who fail to overcome the confusion of reason, this view implies that there is no reason for intolerance, for the natural light remains in any event a reliable guide in moral matters.[199] Although the controversies between Catholics and Protestants do not lose their point, they are relativised as regards the possibility of an absolute resolution.[200] At the same time there is no justification, conversely, for a form of intolerance of reason which would represent every empirical faith as superstitious and irrational, because faith has its own sphere in which it offers answers to metaphysical questions which cannot be discovered by rational means alone. One must choose – and in order to avoid misunderstandings it must be added: *in these questions –*

> between philosophy and the Gospel. If you do not want to believe anything but what is evident and in conformity with the common notions, choose philosophy and leave Christianity. If you are willing to believe the incomprehensible mysteries of religion, choose Christianity and leave philosophy. For to have together self-evidence and incomprehensibility is something that cannot be. The combination of these two items is hardly more impossible than the combination of the properties of a square and a circle. A choice must necessarily be made . . . [A] true Christian, well versed in the characteristics of supernatural truths and firm on the principles that are peculiar to the Gospels, will only laugh at the subtleties of the philosophers, and especially those of the Pyrrhonists. Faith will place him above the regions where the tempests of disputation reign. He will stand on a peak, from which he will hear below him the thunder of arguments and distinctions; and he will not be disturbed at all by this – a peak, which will be for him the real Olympus of the poets and the real temple of the sages, from which he will see in perfect tranquillity the weaknesses of reason and the meanderings of mortals who only follow that guide. Every Christian who allows himself to be disconcerted by the objections of the unbelievers, and to be scandalized by them, has one foot in the same grave as they do.[201]

199. *Ibid.* 411.   200. *Ibid.* 413.   201. *Ibid.* Third Clarification, 429.

It is hard to imagine a better response by an enlightened mind to the accusation of making philosophical concessions to the Manichaeans and Sceptics, and thereby of placing the foundations of religion in question. For Bayle accepts the first accusation, only to charge those who view this as a challenge for religion not only with having a falsely grounded faith which confuses the domains of reason and faith, but also with having a weak faith. He rescues the purity and possibility of faith – and the stoic calm of the believer – at the cost of relativising the claim to absolute, rationally redeemable truth; and he thereby makes clear that there is no rational ground for either side in the above-mentioned dispute not to tolerate the other side, whichever choice one happens to make. Anyone who has 'witnessed the mighty contests between reason and faith'[202] will not fall back into the dogmatic slumber which effaces the boundary between these two domains. With this definition of the relation between faith and reason, Bayle's conception of toleration is both normatively and epistemologically complete.

5. Bayle succeeded in this way in developing the above-mentioned (see §10.3) *third path in modern justifications of toleration* extending from Castellio through Bodin to Montaigne – alongside the humanist-irenic path of reducing religious difference by stressing a universally shared core religion and the Protestant path of emphasising the freedom of the individual conscience bound to God (in combination with the two-kingdoms doctrine) – into a comprehensive conception of toleration superior to the other two. It is superior to the first because it does not purchase the possibility of toleration at the price of declaring religious differences, which give rise to the most acrimonious conflicts, to be merely 'incidental matters', and in addition at the risk of according primacy to the contents of one's own religion in a supposedly higher-level, neutral core religion. This is shown not least by where the limits of toleration are drawn, namely with those who do not agree with this core religion, and this concerns not just atheists. Of course, this does not mean that this path ends here. For Leibniz's endeavours to bring about a reunion of the Christian churches on the basis of common basic truths (in the hope of an ecumenical council), in which he counted on the support of Bossuet (of all people)[203] – which were not crowned with success – show the importance of this humanist-Christian tradition, as do the Enlightenment ideas of a natural 'rational religion', which were more critical towards positive religions.

---

202. *Ibid.* 435.
203. On this, see Werling, *Die weltanschaulichen Grundlagen der Reunionsbemühungen von Leibniz im Briefwechsel mit Bossuet und Pellison.*

Bayle's conception is superior to the second, 'liberal-Protestant' path[204] – which nevertheless remains the most influential[205] – because it avoids the following *aporias of freedom of conscience*:

(a) It circumvents the problem cited by Augustine and Proast that the emphasis on the necessity of a serious faith based on inward conviction, which is the only one pleasing to God, is compatible with the exercise of mild or 'good coercion' by skilful means to break down false, and bring forth 'authentic', convictions. Hence, this argument is insufficient, as Bayle and (later) also Locke recognised.

(b) If freedom of conscience is justified by appeal to the inviolability of inward, serious convictions (before God), then the problem could arise which Locke cited in a different form against Proast, namely, how to ascertain whether a conviction really is a serious, 'truly examined' conviction of conscience – for only such convictions can be tolerated. The result could be that very narrow limits are set to toleration.

(c) Very wide limits on toleration, or none at all would follow, however, from tolerating all decisions which can be invoked as decisions of conscience (that concern the individual and God alone). Bayle's paradox of the 'conscientious persecutor' is only the most extreme example which shows that this argument does not serve either.

204. A complex amalgamation of the first and second paths, associated with the Erastian tradition from Grotius to Hobbes, can be found in Samuel Pufendorf's conception of toleration. Based on his highly influential doctrine of natural law and the social contract which combined Hobbesian and Aristotelian premises (especially in *Of the Duty of Man and Citizen According to Natural Law*; 1672), Pufendorf, on the one hand, follows Locke in restricting the purpose of the state to securing the secular order and leaves the inalienable concern with salvation to individuals themselves. In his work *Of the Nature and Qualification of Religion in Reference to Civil Society* (1687), on the other hand, he points out that it is the right of the state to ensure the uniformity of the official form of worship and a public religious creed on the basis of a 'natural religion' (largely synonymous with the Christian religion), and to erect – in accordance with *jus circa sacra* – an official state ecclesiastical regime, because respect for this religion is the moral foundation of the state. Thus, atheists and idolaters cannot be tolerated under any circumstances, and dissenting sects only insofar as this is necessary to preserve public peace. On this, see Dreitzel, 'Gewissensfreiheit und soziale Ordnung', 11–14, and especially Zurbuchen's study, *Naturrecht und natürliche Religion*, which discusses Pufendorf's argument and traces its reception in French Protestantism (Barbeyrac, Burlamaqui) – in the controversy over Bayle's provocation – up to Rousseau's conception of a *religion civile*. On the controversy over the issue of how narrow the limits of toleration are drawn in Pufendorf, see Döring, 'Samuel von Pufendorf and Toleration', and the contrasting view of Zurbuchen, 'Samuel Pufendorf's Concept of Toleration'.

205. A defence of toleration based on a pietistic conception of religious inwardness free of objective 'ossifications' of religion inspired by Sebastian Franck, though one which regards inward freedom and external conformity as compatible, can be found in Gottfried Arnold, *Unpartheyische Kirchen- und Ketzerhistorie, vom Anfang des Neuen Testaments bis auff das Jahr Christi 1688.*

(d) Moreover, as is especially apparent in Locke, the argument of the 'unfree free conscience' excludes atheists (and potentially other 'unbelievers') in a twofold sense: they neither share the key religious-normative assumptions about what constitutes the value of a conscience, nor can they appeal to such a conscience in order to claim toleration.

As we have seen, the path by which Bayle avoids these aporias is not a direct one but involves various detours. The only way out of the latter is by connecting the normative thesis involved in the non-religious principle that actions which affect the freedom of others are in need of reciprocal justification with the epistemological thesis of the finitude of reason in religious questions, which are thus matters of reasonable disagreements. It is these two components of practical and theoretical reason which ground the central insight into the *non-justifiability of religious coercion*, and hence the duty of toleration – the simple yet at the same time complex truth that, among human beings *as human beings*, coercion must always be justified in accordance with rules of reciprocity and that there are no good reasons for imposing one's religion on others. Bayle discovered the kernel of this superior justification of toleration and he pursued this approach further than any thinker before him – as well as many after him, as we shall see. Only this conception, suitably reformulated, will be able to resolve the paradoxes of toleration (see §1) and establish a justified form of toleration. For it alone has the conceptual resources to differentiate sufficiently clearly not only between knowledge and faith but also between moral norms and ethical values. Both the former and the latter distinction reside, as Bayle's theory shows, in the logic of the 'rationalisation' of the discourse of toleration: the distinction between an intersubjectively strictly binding, universal rational morality, on the one hand, and specific normative convictions concerning what makes a life, an ethos, into a good and godly life or alternatively into a bad, or even a blasphemous one, on the other. Only these epistemological and normative distinctions make it possible to conceive of a profound difference between persons who utterly reject the convictions of others and regard them as false, yet who cannot reasonably regard them as immoral or irrational – and hence can and should accept and tolerate them.

In one important respect, however, Bayle lags behind Locke and the theories of the English Revolution. Beholden to the ideas of the *politiques*, he thinks that connecting religious freedom with political self-determination represents too great a threat to the stability of the state, for he fears that it would lead in turn to the empowerment of the largest religious party in the state and the imposition of uniformity of religion. Therefore, his argument against democracy is a rather pragmatic one. There can be no doubt, however, that the idea of the reciprocal justification of coercion, as a conception of the justification of *political* power, points towards a democratic constitution of the exercise of political power, properly understood, and hence that civil, horizontal and political-vertical toleration cannot be separated in the way that Bayle thinks. Even in the eighteenth century of 'enlightened absolutism', however, conceiving of both together would still not be a matter of course, as will become apparent in the next chapter.

6

The Enlightenment – for and against toleration

§19 The gulf between social toleration and toleration by the state

1. Notwithstanding the difficulty of characterising an epoch such as the Enlightenment in general terms – one need only think of the different national contexts – the demand for toleration and the struggle against religious paternalism can be regarded as central features of this era.[1] Philosophers as diverse as Rousseau and Voltaire were in agreement on this and Kant relates his plea in support of the public use of reason as a means of promoting 'people's emergence from their self-incurred minority' to 'matters of religion' in particular, because 'that minority, being the most harmful, is also the most disgraceful of all'.[2]

However, it is noteworthy in this regard that the Enlightenment, during which the struggle for religious freedom became markedly more acute into the period of the social revolutions, brought no fundamentally new arguments for toleration. Thinkers fell back instead on the existing spectrum of justifications, though the latter were so radicalised in important respects that they acquired a new form. Three of these respects merit special mention.

First, criticism of religious intolerance was increasingly levelled not only against the Church with its social privileges which was seen as despotic (paradigmatically so in France, where membership in the Catholic Church was a precondition for enjoying full legal status as a citizen),[3] but also

1. Cassirer, *The Philosophy of the Enlightenment*, 163–4; Oelmüller, *Die unbefriedigte Aufklärung*, XIII–XIV; Möller, *Vernunft und Kritik*, 1, 5; Fitzpatrick, 'Toleration and the Enlightenment Movement'.
2. Kant, 'What Is Enlightenment?', 21 (Ak. 8: 41).
3. On the French context see Fetscher, 'Politisches Denken im Frankreich des 18. Jahrhunderts vor der Revolution'.

increasingly against positive religion as such. The revealed religions and their 'superstition' and belief in scripture, which were regarded as author-itarian, were contrasted with a 'natural' or 'rational' religion which – in a heightening of humanist irenism – was supposed to assimilate, as a 'universal religion', the rational and moral substance of the existing religions, in par-ticular of Christianity (which was generally regarded as superior to the other religions, though also as obsolete). As a result, the existing positive religions and confessions, with their additional dogmatic and ritual content, reverted in the eyes of the thinkers of the Enlightenment to the status of *adiaphora* which were the object of unnecessary strife. Seldom did these thinkers – for example, the authors of the great *Encyclopédie* – push this critique of reli-gion as far as the materialists, who criticised religion, even in this reduced form, as a reason for intolerance to be eliminated; nevertheless, it becomes apparent how far they went beyond Bayle and his conception of a separation between knowledge and faith, leading to new problems for a 'tolerant' rela-tion between reason and faith. In addition, some of the theorists of natural religion regress behind Bayle in a different respect, namely, that they can resolve Bayle's paradox only by claiming that belief in God is necessary in order to be able to act morally. This reveals certain limits of enlightenment among the philosophers of the Enlightenment themselves.

Second, it is typical for the Enlightenment – and here, too, the French authors take the lead – that, although on the one hand the idea of a religiously impartial state acquires increased prominence, on the other hand criticism is levelled primarily against the Church as an institution and its privileges and only secondarily against the inadequate political legitimation of the author-ity of a monarch, provided only that he guarantees religious freedom and abolishes censorship.[4] The thought of the *politiques* casts a long shadow in this regard. With the exception of Rousseau's thought, which raises prob-lems of its own, it was only in the revolutionary situation in North America, and finally in France, that the connection between religious and political liberty which was already apparent in the context of the Dutch Revolt and later in the English Revolution was underscored. Only then was 'enlight-ened absolutism' replaced by a political implementation of human rights – also of the right of political and not only of religious self-determination. Thus, the respect conception of toleration finally migrated from the civil into the political sphere, and the two different logics of a rationalisation of morality and of a rationalisation of power converge in a discourse of political

---

4. Thus also Kant in 'What Is Enlightenment?'

justification which is critical of authority and presupposes a 'public reason'.[5] Only in the course of this development was the autonomy of this form of political legitimation and of the political system as a whole from religious foundation defended, for example by Kant; however, the idea of a state entirely 'neutral' towards religion remained foreign to most of the Enlightenment thinkers. As the following discussion of Montesquieu and Rousseau will show, a gulf opens up especially in their case between their justification of intersubjective, horizontal toleration at the social level and their treatment of the problem of vertical toleration in the theory of the state.

Third, it is sometimes overlooked that the discourse concerning toleration in the Enlightenment is marked by an increasing awareness of the historical and cultural distinctiveness of the different nations, something which becomes especially apparent in Montesquieu. This involves, on the one hand, accepting the difference between moral conceptions as well as between religions and confessions, which allows for a form of criticism of one's own society in comparison to others and even (as in Montesquieu's *Lettres persanes* or Diderot's *Supplément au voyage de Bougainville*) from the perspective of others, leading to a relativisation of one's own conceptions. On the other hand, this is also taken as a sign of the deeper unity of all positive religions at the core of a universal religion and an inclusive moral identity. Thus, this awareness of difference could give rise to both Herder's philosophy of the plurality of cultures and Voltaire's cosmopolitanism. The former leads to a Romantic strain in the discourse of toleration which stresses individual and collective difference which is no longer understood only as religious difference.

Thus, it should be pointed out, to bring these introductory remarks on this epoch to a close, that the message of the Enlightenment concerning toleration is *ambivalent* in a twofold sense. Apropos the first point – namely, the idea of a natural religion of reason – although the underlying intention is to overcome dogmatic religious intolerance, this comes at the cost of relativising, and in a certain sense superseding, religious difference itself – that is, at the cost of a reduction of religion. At the extreme, therefore, this is more a programme of abolishing intolerance and the situation that calls for toleration than a programme of justifying toleration.

Apropos the second point, it is important to recognise that the demand for and the implementation of religious freedom based on human rights goes hand-in-hand with an unequivocal critique of toleration, specifically a

---

5. On the progressive development towards a normative, public critique of power in the eighteenth century, see the (contrasting) accounts of Koselleck, *Critique and Crisis*, especially 112–23, and Habermas, *Structural Transformation of the Public Sphere*, in particular chs. 3 and 4.

critique of the permission conception of toleration which leads Kant, as I already mentioned in the Introduction, to speak of the 'arrogant name of tolerance'[6] as something merely granted by the political ruler. This criticism of toleration, which remains influential, can be found in all contexts, from the North American to the French and the German; yet it is clear that it merely involves a *different* conception of toleration, not a rejection of the concept as such. For as long as the legitimate state is shaped by ethical and religious differences among the citizens, the latter will be required, both as the subjects of the law and as legislators, to tolerate one another by demonstrating their ability and willingness to engage in reciprocal justification in order to arrive at legitimate norms.

2. The treatment of toleration in the work of Charles-Louis de Secondât, Baron de la Brède et de Montesquieu, illustrates the complexity of contemporary arguments about toleration, especially as regards the relation between social and political toleration. Here a difference, to which I have already alluded and which is especially apparent in Bodin and Montaigne, opens up between a *broadly* conceived intersubjective-religious and a *narrowly* conceived political-vertical form of toleration. This difference finds expression in two contrasting works in which Montesquieu analyses the cultural and political situation of his time, the *Lettres persanes* (1721) and his principal work *De l'esprit des loix* (1748).

In the *Persian Letters*, Montesquieu chooses the literary form of an exchange of letters between Persians travelling through Europe and their friends and servants at home. Invoking the genre of the travelogues of conquistadores, merchants and missionaries reporting on the customs of other peoples which were popular at the time enables him to pose the question of how strange one's own customs must appear in the eyes of others. Montesquieu, who was himself a deist and a freethinker in religious matters, while nevertheless professing his Christianity,[7] represents his Muslim protagonists Usbek and Rica as adopting an 'enlightened' attitude towards their own faith in that they justify the superiority of the latter over Christianity primarily in terms of rational insights into the futility of theological hairsplitting and the primacy of a universal morality. The plea for toleration to be found in the *Letters*, which clearly exhibit the influences of Bayle's thought, plays a central role in this argument.[8]

---

6. Kant, 'What Is Enlightenment?', 21 (Ak. 8: 40).
7. See Montesquieu, *The Spirit of the Laws*, Books I, 1 and XXIV, 10.
8. On Bayle's influence on Montesquieu (and the changes it undergoes) see Shackleton, 'Bayle and Montesquieu'.

Of special importance is the criticism of the narrow-mindedness of the dominant Catholic Church in France and its support for the policy of the king, which in Montesquieu's view was unjust and ineffectual. The pope is described as an 'old idol'[9] whose 'dervishes' – by which is meant the Jesuits – continually find or invent new theological controversies in order to create new heretics to be persecuted by establishing arbitrary orthodoxies.[10] By contrast, Islam, according to Usbek, eschews violence in two senses: it does not use violence because faith can spread only by peaceful means, through persuasion, and it has no need of coercion because its truth prevails of its own accord (29). Religious intolerance is not merely a sign of weakness but is also pointless and, even worse, leads only to social turmoil (61). As Montesquieu puts it in Letter 85, which is devoted to toleration: 'It signifies nothing to say, that it is not the prince's interest to permit several religions in his kingdom'; it is even advantageous to promote religious plurality, since in this way the state can take advantage of the *disciplining* effect of toleration because all of these communities compete to be the best citizens (and to merit toleration). Therefore, a policy of toleration is also to be preferred for economic reasons (85, 121). In addition to this compilation of familiar arguments for toleration, which already prefigure Montesquieu's later theory of the state, the *Letters* also exhibit a mixture, reminiscent of Bayle, of an idea of justice and moral reciprocity independent of the positive religions with references to the limits of reason in religious controversies. Montesquieu stresses the former in several places: in the fable of the troglodytes (whose target is Hobbes), where the troglodytes successfully establish a society founded on natural justice by attending to the 'pure voice of nature' (12); and in the sketch of a natural religion consisting of a universal ethical-moral core accessible to all human beings:

> And indeed, ought not the first object of a religious man to be, to please the deity who hath established the religion he professes? But the surest way to do so is, without doubt, to obey the laws of society, and to discharge the duties of humanity; for whatever religion a man professes, the moment any religion is supposed, it must also necessarily be supposed, that God loves mankind, since he establishes a religion to render them happy: That if he loves men, we are certain of pleasing him if we love them also; this is, in exercising toward them all the duties of charity and humanity, and not breaking the laws under

9. Montesquieu, *Persian Letters*, Letter No. 24 (citations in the text refer to the number of the letter in question).
10. See Letters Nos. 24, 29, 57, 75, 78, 101, 134–5.

which they live. By this means we are much surer of pleasing God, than by observing such and such a ceremony; for ceremonies in themselves have no degree of goodness.   (46)

This quotation, which is characteristic of the *Letters* as a whole, shows how Montesquieu combines the emphasis on moral duties which also hold *prior to* religion[11] with the insight into the limits of finite human beings' cognitive abilities in religious matters. Human beings are confronted with a wide variety of religions, confessions and cults which from an *enlightened* perspective can represent nothing more than historically and culturally conditioned human products: 'It has been well said that if triangles had a god, they would give him three sides' (113). Montesquieu takes a correspondingly sceptical view of missionary attempts to propagate one religion to all human beings; it is as if the Europeans were to try to 'wash the African white' (61). Both components together – the normative and the epistemological – enable Montesquieu to apply the rule of reciprocity to the question of toleration: 'He who would have me change my religion, no doubt, desires me to do so, because he would not change his own if he was forced to do it; he yet thinks it strange, that I will not do a thing which he himself would not do, perhaps, for the empire of the world' (85).

3. Although Montesquieu's principal work on the theory of the state, *The Spirit of the Laws*, contains a series of ideas from the *Lettres*, the new perspective transforms the treatment of toleration in a way which was also noticeable in other authors, such as Bodin, if one compares the *Colloquium heptaplomeres* with the *Six livres*, or Montaigne, who developed a fundamental argument for toleration only to reject religious controversy and innovations in religion for political reasons (see above §§12 and 13). Something similar holds for Montesquieu, who, although he does not abandon his endorsement of toleration, now clearly qualifies his position regarding vertical toleration as opposed to horizontal toleration. For the overriding perspective which Montesquieu adopts in *The Spirit of the Laws* is that of the compatibility of *political freedom* and *stability*, more precisely the question of how the laws must be adapted to the requirements of justice, on the one hand, and to the specific religious-cultural and natural-climatic characteristics of a people, on the other, in order to facilitate a polity which grants liberty and follows not the principle of fear (despotism) but instead that of virtue (republic) or that of

---

11. In another passage he describes the immutable idea of justice in such a way that 'though there was no God, we ought always to love justice', and he continues: 'Though we should be free from the yoke of religion, we ought not to be so from that of equity' (83).

honour (monarchy). Here we encounter the enlightened relativisation of the peculiarities of peoples and customs (albeit without normative relativism);[12] however, in this case it is primarily associated not with a plea for intersubjective tolerance but with the *functional* question of which religion is the most politically expedient – and hence also of how useful toleration is and where its limits reside from this perspective.

Here Bayle again plays an important role, though now as a figure from whom Montesquieu distances himself. Having made clear in the first chapter of Book XXIV that in his role as a 'politician' he is only interested in the utility and not in the truth of religion, he discusses the 'paradox of Mr. Bayle's' which is that 'it is less dangerous to have no religion at all than a bad one' (XXIV, 2). In arguing thus Bayle commits a fallacy, Montesquieu argues, for in fact the opposite is the case. Even an idolatrous religion[13] has a 'restraining' influence on human beings – not only on citizens but also on princes – and deters them from transgressing the civil laws through this second instance of justice and fear (*ibid.*). Moreover, religion and the laws could complement each other in generating this effect (XXIV, 14) – provided one bears in mind that they point substantially in the same direction – in order to avoid the problem of the fear of God outweighing fear of the sovereign so that the secular laws are merely secondary: 'How shall the man be restrained by laws who believes that the greatest pain the magistrate can inflict on him will end only for his happiness to begin?' (*ibid.*). Montesquieu does not want to embrace the Hobbesian solution to this problem – namely, a minimal state religion – yet his way of posing the question commits him to the demand for a strong *unity* of religion and the form of government.

Hence, *against* Bayle, Montesquieu insists that religion is a useful foundation of the state; even 'false' religions (XXIV, 19) are superior to atheism which harbours the spirit of rebellion (XXIV, 2). In contrast to the *Persian Letters*, however, it is now the Muslim religion which is more compatible with the despotic form of government, whereas it is the Christian religion, according to Montesquieu, which is more conducive to a moderate government (XXIV, 3–6; also XIX, 18). *With* Bayle, however, he continues to appeal to an independent kernel of justice shared by all religions which provides the normative political standard for measuring their compatibility with liberty: 'In a country so unfortunate as to have a religion that God has not revealed, it is necessary for it to be agreeable to morality; because even a false religion

---

12. See Montesquieu, *The Spirit of the Laws*, Book XIX, 10 (cited in the text in the following).
13. On the distinction between idolatry and the 'religion of enlightened nations' who worship a purely spiritual being, see XXV, 2.

is the best security we can have of the probity of men' (xxiv, 8). That he nevertheless does not draw more far-reaching conclusions from this is due to the preoccupation of his theory of the state with stability and to a conservatism concerning the political importance of religion, which, however paradoxical it may appear, follows from this very emphasis on difference. For Montesquieu repeatedly emphasises that positive religions are a human creation influenced by a variety of factors, not least a country's climate (see xiv, 4 and 10). On the other hand, although this correspondence between religion, custom, history, form of government and natural situation gives rise to a plurality of religions, it is also the reason for the limitations on a society's capacity for innovation specifically in matters of religion. For such a 'national spirit' (xix, 4 and 5) cannot be easily altered, assuming that one wants to avoid turmoil; not every religion is suitable for every country (xxiv, 24–5).[14] This is why Montesquieu pleads for maximum restraint when it comes to religious innovations – *contrary to* the *Persian Letters* (no. 85), where he stressed the benefits of introducing new sects:

> As there are scarcely any but persecuting religions that have an extraordinary zeal for being established in other places (because a religion that can tolerate others seldom thinks of its own propagation), it must, therefore be a very good civil law, when the state is already satisfied with the established religion, not to suffer the establishment of another. This is then a fundamental principle of the political laws in regard to religion; that when the state is at liberty to receive or to reject a new religion it ought to be rejected; when it is received it ought to be tolerated.   (xxv, 10)

This makes clear once again how much the perspective of theory of the state, which remains completely captive to the permission conception of toleration, argues for or against toleration primarily on pragmatic grounds of avoiding internal political turmoil. Therefore, as long as the state has a choice it should not be overly tolerant of innovations – in a footnote Montesquieu makes an exception in this regard for the Christian religion – but, having come about, the state should not curb them, because religious coercion only leads to more hatred and should have no place in a state granting liberty (xix, 27; xxiv, 9). Thus, this perspective always involves a presumption in favour of the dominant religion because to challenge it is too precarious (xxv, 11), and

14. It is noteworthy that Montesquieu's diverse reflections on the climatic differences between nations contain a series of disparaging judgements concerning the peoples of the South and their character traits. See in particular Books xiv–xvii.

hence a presumption in favour of religious unity. Only where religious unity no longer exists is toleration required for reasons of internal pacification and because religious coercion is ineffectual (xxv, 12).

Montesquieu does not elaborate further on what it would mean to refuse to admit a new religion and on the point at which such a refusal would become illegitimate. The result could be a conflict with his other accounts of a liberal state in which he supports a secular administration of justice free from divine and ecclesiastical law (xxvi, 1–13) and describes the crimes of blasphemy and heresy as either of no concern to the state (xii, 4) or as difficult to judge, and in this way seeks to defend civil liberties: 'Penal laws ought to be avoided in respect to religion' (xxv, 12).

Thus, there is not only a gulf between the conceptions of toleration of the *Persian Letters* and *The Spirit of the Laws*, stemming from the different perspectives adopted in these two works; it can also be found within the political work itself. Apropos the latter, it should be noted that a tension exists in Montesquieu's concept of a liberal state and its conditions of survival between the pragmatic emphasis on the moral (and hence also the religious) unity of a particular people and the general requirements of a state that respects liberty.[15] And, apropos the former, it has once again emerged how different a philosophical perspective devoted to toleration between people of different religions on a horizontal level is from one which enquires into the stability of the state. As in other theorists of toleration, these two perspectives in political philosophy lead to different results. The toleration called for between persons or even communities no longer seems to be possible from the vertical perspective, for here – contrary to Bayle's paradox – a stronger moral and ethical unity of the citizens is advocated and it is assumed that the state is in need of a religious foundation.

4. Against this background it can be shown that in Jean-Jacques Rousseau, of all thinkers, whose idea of the political autonomy of the citizen is an important key to redefining the relationship between horizontal and vertical toleration, this gulf between an intersubjective moral perspective on tolera-tion and one informed by a theory of the state can also be found, though in a different form than in Montesquieu.

As with Hobbes, interpretations of Rousseau's political philosophy often overlook how central the problem of toleration – or, to be more precise, of overcoming intolerance – is to his work; and when it is alluded to, this is generally in connection with the chapter on *religion civile* in the *Contrat*

---

15. On this tension see also Böckenförde, 'The Rise of the State as a Process of Secularisation'.

social,[16] though this represents only a small portion of Rousseau's treatment of the issue of toleration as a whole. Combating religious fanaticism was one of Rousseau's chief concerns already in his earlier writings, and it leads him to say of himself that, like everyone else, he has his own fanaticism, the 'fanaticism of toleration'.[17] How the latter is reflected in his writings will be reconstructed in what follows, taking as central the issue of how Rousseau relates his idea of a 'natural religion', which in contrast to the encyclopaedists is less a rational religion than a religion of feeling, to the positive religions, on the one hand, and to moral and political principles, on the other.

Especially important in this regard is the connection between 'natural morality' and 'natural religion' which Rousseau already makes in the *Discourse on the Question Whether the Restoration of the Sciences and Arts Has Contributed to the Purification of Morals* (1750). Whereas there he presupposes a kind of natural virtuousness whose principles are 'engraved in all hearts', so that one need only listen to the 'voice of one's conscience' beyond all passions and social dissimulations in order to hear them,[18] in a self-defence written in 1751 he connects this with the point that the aim of his critique of the sciences and emphasis on natural virtue was by no means to criticise the Christian religion but, if anything, the 'wretched hair-splitting' of scholasticism which distracts from the 'sublime simplicity of the Gospel'.[19] This anticipates the connection between original, undogmatic and essentially moral Christianity and natural virtue which is a constant theme in the remainder of his writings, and it leads Rousseau to criticise the distortions of this doctrine in the various religious disputes which, he argues, constantly give rise to new conflicts but have no social utility: 'we have all become Doctors, and have ceased to be Christians'.[20] The Gospel alone is sufficient to lead a pious life; no additional learning or authority is needed. This reveals the Protestant aspect of Rousseau's conception of religion, whose life was marked by the religious strife of his time. When he left Calvinist Geneva as a sixteen-year-old 'he changed his religion in order to have bread',[21] as he later expresses through the character of the proselyte in *Émile*, by converting to Catholicism in a Turin hospice under the influence of Madame de Warens, a step which he

16. Thus, also in Fetscher, *Rousseaus politische Philosophie*, §14; Zurbuchen, *Naturrecht und natürliche Religion*, ch. 7. Dent, 'Rousseau and Respect for Others', 131, mistakenly asserts that the chapter on civil religion represents the most extensive explicit treatment of toleration in Rousseau's writings.
17. Rousseau, Outline of *Nouvelle Héloise* (1760), 1782.
18. Rousseau, *Discourse on the Sciences and Arts*, 28.
19. Rousseau, Observations [to Stanislas, King of Poland], 40.   20. *Ibid.* 44.
21. Rousseau, *Émile*, 260.

felt to be coerced because of his misgivings, as he states in the second book of the *Confessions*. Only in 1754 would he officially reconvert to Calvinism and regain his Genevan citizenship to which he attached great importance – only to witness how, in 1762, *Émile* was banned not only in France but also (along with the *Contrat social*) in Geneva.

The relation between religion and morality is defined in greater detail in other writings, in particular where Rousseau, in the *Discourse on the Origin and Foundations of Inequality among Men* (1755), founds the capacity for moral action not on the faculty of reason but on the natural feeling of compassion[22] – and where, in his famous Letter to Voltaire (1756), he rejects the latter's critique of religious and metaphysical optimism prompted by the earthquake in Lisbon and defends such optimism by appeal to the hope and consolation inspired by belief in a benevolent God. To the 'equilibrium of reason' the 'weight of hope' must be added.[23] Following Bayle, Rousseau defends a fideist religion which, although it does not contradict reason, is aware that it is not required by reason either; but Rousseau goes beyond Bayle in assuming that religious belief responds to an emotional need of human beings. This leads him to the idea of a natural core religion which can be associated with different positive religions and to a justification of toleration which underlines the subjective inwardness of faith. Thus, he writes to Voltaire:

> But, like you, I am indignant that each individual's faith does not enjoy the most perfect freedom, and that man dares to control the inner recesses of consciences which he cannot possibly enter; as if it depended on ourselves to believe or not in matters where demonstration has no place, and reason could ever be enslaved to authority. Are the Kings of this world then inspectors in the next? and have they the right to torment their Subjects here below, in order to force them to go to Paradise? No; all human Government is by its nature restricted to civil duties.[24]

Whereas here the emphasis on the subjectivity and steadfastness of religious sentiment and faith leads, entirely in the spirit of Locke, to a limitation on the authority of the state, Rousseau immediately adds:

> There is, I admit, a kind of profession of faith which the laws may impose; but beyond the principles of morality and of natural right, it ought to be purely negative, because there can exist Religions that

22. Rousseau, *Discourse on the Origin and Foundations of Inequality among Men*, 152. See also Rousseau, *Émile*, 222–3.
23. Rousseau, Letter to Voltaire, 243.   24. *Ibid.* 244.

attack the foundations of society, and one has to begin by
exterminating these Religions in order to ensure the peace of the State.
Among these dogmas that ought to be proscribed, intolerance is easily
the most odious; but it must be checked at its source; for the most
bloodthirsty Fanatics change their language as their fortune changes,
and when they are not the strongest, they preach nothing but patience
and gentleness . . . And if there were intolerant nonbelievers who
wanted to force the people to believe nothing, I would banish them no
less sternly than those who want to force the people to believe
Whatever they please.[25]

Here Rousseau sketches for the first time the idea of civil religion to which
he would return in the *Contrat social*, and it shows where his 'fanaticism
of tolerance', his fanatical opposition to fanaticism as it were, leads him:
not only (a) to a fideist conception of natural religion which fosters more
understanding for the existing positive religions than a rational religion such
as that of Voltaire, but also (b) to a political minimal religion which, on the
one hand, excludes intolerance and, on the other, places the state itself on a
religious foundation. Thus, against Voltaire's 'Catechism of Man' he calls for
a 'Catechism of the Citizen'. However, there is a conflict here, as can be seen
from the two quotations. For the idea of an undogmatic natural religion and
morality leads to a demand for mutual toleration and individual freedom of
conscience which seems to be placed in question by the conception of an
official civil religion. In order to clarify this conflict, let us briefly consider
how Rousseau develops these two components of his doctrine of toleration.

(a) In his letter to d'Alembert (1758), Rousseau criticises the latter for his
article on 'Geneva' in the *Encyclopaedia* on the grounds that, in addition to
recommending the establishment of a theatre which does not challenge strict
morality, d'Alembert praises the Genevan clergymen for overcoming their
intolerance by adopting an almost deistic or Socinian position. Rousseau,
who with this letter set the final seal on his break with the encyclopaedists,
confirms that the Genevan clergy were tolerant (a view which he would later
recant), but does not see any justification for describing them as deists. It
is not necessary to reduce religion in this way in order to be tolerant, he
argues, nor is it conducive to toleration to foist concepts on others which
would make them heretics in their own eyes.[26] Rather, toleration is possible
between religions when the limits of reason in questions of faith are taken
into consideration, as Rousseau explains:

25. *Ibid.* 245.   26. Rousseau, Letter to M. d'Alembert on the theatre, 13.

I think I see a principle, which, well demonstrated as it could be, would immediately wrest the arms from the hands of the intolerant and the superstitious and would calm that proselytizing fury which seems to animate the unbelievers. This is that human reason has no well-determined common measure and that it is unjust of any man to give his own as the rule to that of others . . . The intellectual world, without excepting geometry, is full of truths incomprehensible and nevertheless incontestable; because reason, which demonstrates their existence, cannot, as it were, touch them across the limits which arrest it but can only perceive them at a distance. Such is the dogma of the existence of God; such are the mysteries admitted in the Protestant communion. The mysteries which shock reason, to employ the terms of M. d'Alembert, are an entirely different matter. Their very contradiction makes them return within the limits of reason; it has every imaginable advantage for making felt that they do not exist; for, although one cannot see an absurd thing, nothing is so clear as absurdity.[27]

With this emphasis on the role of the limits of reason in including and excluding, Rousseau grounds the principle of the illegitimacy of coercion in matters of faith which, on his conception, holds for and towards every religion that itself recognises this principle. God alone is the ultimate judge of the true faith.[28] Thus, we are dealing here with a conception of toleration which does not purchase toleration at the price of reducing it to a rational religion.

Nevertheless an unmistakable tension remains between the undogmatic, primarily ethically and morally oriented, 'natural religion' and the positive religions and confessions – in this case, Rousseau's option for Calvinism – which he attempted to resolve only in his most famous text on religious toleration, the 'Profession of Faith of the Savoyard Vicar' in the fourth book of *Émile* (1762). It is in Rousseau's own estimation 'the best and most useful Writing in the century', for he presents himself merely as its 'publisher'.[29] The Vicar first explains his conception of a natural religion to the proselyte who is plagued by religious doubts and goes on to justify the reasons for adopting a positive religion. Reason, whose function is mainly a problematising and destructive one, is not sufficient, according to the Vicar, to justify the three dogmas of his faith; it is more important for each to follow his own 'inner light'[30] and to recognise that a will moves the universe, that 'matter

---

27. *Ibid.* 11–12 (fns).   28. *Ibid.* 14.
29. Rousseau, Letter to M. de Beaumont, 46–7.   30. Rousseau, *Émile*, 269.

moved according to certain laws' points to an 'intelligence' and that man is 'animated by an immaterial substance'.[31] From this springs almost naturally a religion beyond dogmas and confessions; any attempt to achieve greater certainty and determinateness fails and can only lead to irresolvable disputes.

Hence, faith, whose truth cannot be *demonstrated* though it can be practically *exhibited*, begins where rational comprehension reaches its limits. Faith finds expression primarily in moral action, for conscience is the authority through which God speaks to human beings and combines justice with worthiness to be happy. The rules of moral conduct are 'written by nature with ineffaceable characters in the depth of my heart' and 'conscience never deceives'.[32] Freed from philosophical scepticism, conscience leads human beings both to God and to morality, for '[i]f the divinity does not exist, it is only the wicked man who reasons, and the good man is nothing but a fool'.[33] Although Rousseau manages in this way to reconcile an undogmatic natural religiosity with a conception of moral principles, he does so at the cost of denying the possibility of a morality independent of religion, which seemed at least possible in the two *Discourses*; now he states that 'The forgetting of all religion leads to the forgetting of the duties of man'[34] and the Baylean virtuous atheist has receded into the distance.

But the result is the above-mentioned problem of why, if one needs nothing more than a natural religion in order to be good and pious, as the Vicar claims, religions which contain 'more' than this should be tolerated. What more can speak for them than custom or superstition, since they appear to be merely historical products? The Vicar's answer distinguishes between a universal core of all religions and their specific forms, forms of concrete worship of God concerning which it would be pointless to claim that one of them is certainly the true one. Nevertheless such forms are valid in the different societies in which they have put down historical roots, and thus living in such a context means not only *condoning* these forms but also oneself *embracing* them. The Vicar justifies his own decision in favour of the Catholic religion on the grounds that his researches into the best religion 'were and always would be unsuccessful, and that I was being swallowed up in an ocean without shores', and thus 'I retraced my steps and restricted my faith to my original notions'.[35]

Thus, Rousseau connects Montesquieu's insight into the contingency and appropriateness of particular forms of religion with the idea given

---

31. *Ibid.* 275 and 281.   32. *Ibid.* 286.   33. *Ibid.* 292.
34. *Ibid.* 263.   35. *Ibid.* 306 (translation amended).

currency by Montaigne that it is a sign of arrogance to extend scepticism concerning truth to the institutionalised religion of a country and to refuse to observe it – the point at which Montaigne's scepticism inverted into social-religious conservatism. Something similar holds for Rousseau, though he cannot disguise his partiality for Protestantism entirely when the Vicar advises the proselyte, who was originally a Calvinist, to return to his country and to the religion of his fathers, for '[i]t is very simple and very holy. I believe that of all the religions on earth it is the one which has the purest morality and which is most satisfactory to reason.'[36] In this way, the emphasis on the undogmatic character of natural religion changes under the influence of the requirement of mutual toleration of all religions which exhibit this kernel into the requirement to 'respect' the *established* religion in *each particular* country and the public worship which it prescribes:[37] 'God wants to be revered in spirit and in truth. This is the duty of all religions, all countries, all men. As to the external worship, it must be uniform for the sake of good order, that is purely a question of public policy [*une affaire de police*]; no revelation is needed for that.'[38] This quotation shows how the observation, which is meant to be critical of positive religion, that the outward organisation of religious worship does not come from God but is prescribed exclusively by the public authorities, becomes an assertion that the required freedom of conscience does *not* extend to the freedom of worship. As long as the 'internal form of worship' is guaranteed and there is no intolerance in this respect, Rousseau accepts the right of the secular powers to demand *external conformity*: 'The duty to follow and love the religion of one's country does not extend to dogmas contrary to good morals, such as that of intolerance.'[39] With the idea of such a duty Rousseau aligns himself with a long series of Erastian thinkers, not only with Montaigne who restricted the toleration necessary for those who deviate from the established religion to the *exercitium privatum*, but also with Lipsius's distinction between private *fides* and public *confessio*, with Hooker's idea of an *outward conformity* in questions of ceremonial *adiaphora*, with Spinoza's separation between freedom of thought and freedom of worship – and, of course, with Hobbes who in addition thought that a core religion which goes back to the sovereign is necessary. And this is precisely the step which Rousseau also takes – for the same reason as Hobbes, namely the eradication of intolerance.

(b) The chapter on *religion civile*, the final chapter of the *Social Contract* (1762), represents the final stage in the evolution of a conception of vertical

---

36. *Ibid.* 311.   37. *Ibid.* 310.   38. *Ibid.* 296, French 608.   39. *Ibid.* 309 n.

state toleration which is separated by a gulf from the conception of intersubjective tolerance that follows from the idea of an undogmatic natural religion (in combination with the emphasis on the limits of reason and on mutual respect). The unifying link is the connection between religion and morality; already in *Émile* Rousseau observed with reference to Bayle that, although it is true that fanaticism is worse than atheism, atheism nevertheless 'saps the true foundations of every society'.[40]

What led Rousseau to the idea of a generally valid civil religion, whose point is not to proscribe an *external* form of worship but which aims to formulate and impose the ethical-moral, *internal* content of the natural religion, so that love of God and love of the law complement rather than conflict with one another, is the Hobbesian logic of his conception of political autonomy. For Hobbes the point of entering the contract was to create a body politic with *one* will which is the only one that can give normative guidance and has the last word in questions of justice here on earth. Rousseau, by contrast, attempts to achieve the very same goal through the 'total alienation' of individuals and their rights to the community provided that all do the same thing, but in the process he locates sovereignty in the newly created entity of the community of all, this *corps moral et collectif*, of a 'moral community' which 'receives by the same act its unity, its common *self*, its life and its will'.[41] Its elixir of life is not fear as in Hobbes but the ethical willingness to obey only those laws which one gives oneself and in the process of making them to subordinate one's individual will to the common will (which Rousseau calls 'moral freedom' (*liberté morale*) in contrast to 'natural' or 'civil' freedom under natural or positive laws).[42] Although Rousseau in this way seeks to establish the rule of reciprocally justified public reason in the form of general laws, he nevertheless regards an ethical unity of the citizens as a precondition for this rule, which leads him to consider the role of religion.

At this point the tension between individual freedom of conscience vis-à-vis political authority and a civil religion reappears which we noted above in connection with his assertions in the letter to Voltaire. Rousseau follows Hobbes – 'the only one who clearly saw the evil and the remedy, who dared to propose reuniting the two heads of the eagle, and to return everything to political unity'[43] – in demanding that the separation of the two kingdoms be *rescinded* to such an extent that a fundamental conflict between God and the law cannot arise. In the same passage Rousseau is equally explicit in

40. *Ibid.* 312 n.   41. Rousseau, *The Social Contract*, I, 6 (50), French 361.
42. *Ibid.* I, 8 (53), French 364–5.   43. *Ibid.* IV, 8 (146).

asserting that in this he is contradicting Bayle and the idea that a state can exist without a religious foundation.

Rousseau classifies religions accordingly from a political point of view into three or four classes: the religion of man, the religion of the citizen, the religion of the priests and, finally, civil religion as a partial synthesis. The third of these – Rousseau has in mind the Catholic religion – is the worst because it divides sovereignty and subjects human beings to two different legislations. The first corresponds to the undogmatic, natural Christian religion confined to internal worship. Its advantage is that it contains a universal morality of humanity and is free from superstition; its disadvantage, however, is that 'it has no particular relation to the body politic', so that it not only does not support the validity of the laws of the state but alienates the 'Citizens' hearts' from the laws.[44] Its kingdom is not of this world, and hence it is not suitable for the temporal domain and encourages tyranny. The second, in turn, corresponds to a kind of theocracy in which the prince is the high priest and the gods exist only for this particular state, which turns all other peoples into infidels and enemies. Although this form of religion has the advantage for Rousseau 'that it combines divine worship and love of the laws',[45] it nevertheless leads to idolatry and superstition – not to mention external intolerance. Thus, the goal is to combine the benefits of the religion of man with those of the religion of the citizen and to eliminate their shortcomings, and this is what the *religion civile* is supposed to accomplish.

That this must be 'a purely civil profession of faith the articles of which it is up to the Sovereign to fix' – as 'sentiments of sociability' (*sentiments de sociabilité*)[46] – Rousseau explains in terms of the following definition of religious freedom:

> The right which the social pact gives the Sovereign over their subjects does not, as I have said, exceed the bounds of public utility. Subjects therefore only owe the Sovereign an account of their opinions insofar as those opinions matter to the community. Now it certainly matters to the State that each Citizen have a Religion which makes him love his duties; but the dogmas of this Religion are only of concern to the State or to its members insofar as the dogmas bear on morality, and on the duties which anyone who professes it is bound to fulfil toward others. Beyond this everyone may hold whatever opinions he pleases, without its being up to the Sovereign to know them: For since the Sovereign has no competence in the other world, whatever the subjects' fate may

44. *Ibid.* 147.   45. *Ibid.*   46. *Ibid.* 150 (French 468).

be in the life to come is none of its business, provided they are good citizens in this life.[47]

Rousseau's argument here is reminiscent of Spinoza. There is no natural law which is in principle beyond the authority of the sovereign, but this authority reaches its limits in the case of convictions that no longer concern the citizens' lives here on earth. Like Hobbes, Rousseau adds that the sovereign *may* oblige all citizens to affirm the civic creed but, because of the factual limit of his effectiveness, he *cannot* oblige them also to believe it. He can banish anyone who does not believe it, but for political, not for religious reasons – 'as unsociable, as incapable of sincerely loving the laws, justice, and, if need be of sacrificing his life to his duty'.[48] He can likewise punish someone who merely feigns belief, but acts contrary to the creed, with the death penalty.

The positive dogmas of the civil religion, which according to Rousseau can be reconciled with a range of more far-reaching religious beliefs, but represent their point of intersection, comprise the existence of an all-powerful, prescient and beneficent Deity, the life to come, the happiness of the just and 'the sanctity of the social Contract and the Laws'.[49] As the sole negative dogma Rousseau cites intolerance; it is not to be permitted under any circumstances. By intolerance Rousseau understands not only 'civic' but also 'religious intolerance' because – contrary to Diderot[50] – he regards them as inseparable. 'It is impossible to live in peace with people one believes to be damned; to love them would be to hate God who punishes them; one must absolutely bring them back [to the fold] or torment them.'[51] Therefore, whoever asserts that there is no salvation outside the Church is to be banished from the state.[52]

It is clear where his 'fanaticism of tolerance' leads him in this context, namely to the exclusion of all those from the state who (a) like the atheists reject this religion, who (b) transgress against these core principles by denying the attributes of God – 'all-powerful, all knowing, beneficent, prescient, and provident' – or the life to come, or who (c) like the Catholics recognise another sovereign or believe that there can be salvation only within the church and want to impose this view. Hence, the limits of toleration do not follow, as Rousseau assumes, a moral-political line but are located where the 'generally required', supposedly 'minimal' religion mutates into a particular, Christian religion and where it acquires binding legal force as a state religion. There can be no doubt that Rousseau's intention with this

---

47. *Ibid.* 149–50.   48. *Ibid.* 150.   49. *Ibid.* 151.   50. See below §20.2.
51. Rousseau, *The Social Contract*, I, 8 (151).   52. *Ibid.*

proposal was to put an end to intolerance; but the citizens of his state pay a high price for this – or, at any rate, those who on this basis would count as dissidents. Although, in contrast to Hobbes, he does not envisage political religious services and does not make the sovereign the supreme leader of the church, his intention is nevertheless to strengthen and secure the political-moral unity of the state and the ultimate authority of the general will with the aid of religion.

What Rousseau does not mention in the *Contrat social*, though it is found in *Émile* – namely, the binding power of a shared *external* cult – also crops up in the two writings in which he defends himself against the prohibitions of his books in France and in Geneva. In his letter to the archbishop of Paris, Beaumont (1763), he again explains his religious doctrine, which is directed against both fanaticism and the atheism of which he was accused: 'I am Christian not as a disciple of the Priests, but as a disciple of Jesus Christ. My Master quibbled little over dogma and insisted much on duties.'[53] Above dogmas, he states, stands the inward truthfulness and morality of the individual; the quality of a religion can be judged by its moral usefulness, in particular by its capacity for toleration.[54] As far as politics is concerned, the state has the right to exercise control over the faith of its citizens only insofar as this concerns morality and obedience to the laws; and Rousseau adds: 'Moreover, national forms ought to be observed; I have insisted upon that greatly.'[55] Moreover, his plea for a mutual, civil toleration based on a universal 'human and social religion' concludes with the following appeal:

> Moreover, dispute no more among yourselves over the preference due to your forms of worship. They are all good when they are prescribed by the laws and when the essential Religion is found in them. They are bad when it is not found there. The form of worship is the regulation of Religions and not their essence, and it is the Sovereign's function to administer the regulations in his country.[56]

Here Rousseau sides with the doctrine of the legislative authority of the state in 'inconsequential matters' which in spite of external conformity does not affect 'internal conviction'. But then toleration means only that 'nonconformists' are tolerated provided that they do not claim any form of public worship; as a minority tolerated in accordance with the *permission conception*, they can enjoy at most the freedom of *exercitium privatum*. And in fact Rousseau concurs with Montesquieu (and Bodin) in stating:

53. Rousseau, Letter to Beaumont, 189.   54. *Ibid.* 198–9.   55. *Ibid.* 199.   56. *Ibid.* 201.

I believe that a good man, in whatever Religion he lives in good faith, can be saved. But I do not therefore believe that foreign Religions can legitimately be introduced into a country without the permission of the Sovereign. For that is not directly disobeying God, it is disobeying the Laws, and whoever disobeys the Laws disobeys God. With regard to Religions that are established or tolerated in a country, I believe it is unjust and barbaric to destroy them there by violence, and that the Sovereign does wrong to himself in mistreating their sectaries . . . One should neither allow the establishment of a diversity of forms of worship nor proscribe those that have been established.[57]

Rousseau is ready to accept the unavoidable conclusion that the Huguenots did not originally have any right to be tolerated in France, but acquired it only when they were recognised as part of the nation in the Edict of Nantes.

In his *Letters Written from the Mountain* (1764), in which he responds to the for him particularly hurtful condemnation of his works by the Geneva Council, he expresses his incomprehension at how the republic which had served him as a model for the *Social Contract* could condemn him.[58] Here he outlines once again his conception of religion. In addition to the ceremonies, the form of the religious service, he distinguishes two parts of religion, the doctrine of the faith and morality. It is not a matter for the sovereign, according to Rousseau, to make judgements concerning the speculative articles of faith; they concern only the individual in question. But where the articles of faith affect morality, 'obedience to the natural and positive Laws, the social virtues and all the duties of man and Citizen, it is the business of Government to take cognizance of them', in order to prevent opinions harmful to society.[59] So, too, it is within the authority of the secular power to prescribe the external form of worship.[60]

At the same time, this reveals the weaknesses of this conception of toleration both at the level of the theory of the state and at the level of civil society, and in both cases it is a fatal *logic of identity* that leads to restrictions on toleration. According to this political logic, only a citizenry with a common morality and religion can constitute a *corps moral et collectif* with *one* will and *one* identity. Thus, the undogmatic natural religion mutates into a civil religion with generally valid positive and negative dogmas which declare the adherents of a range of religious and metaphysical positions to be 'bad citizens' who are not to be tolerated.

---

57. *Ibid.*   58. Rousseau, *Letters Written from the Mountain*, 233.   59. *Ibid.* 140.   60. *Ibid.* 145.

According to a second, religious logic of identity, the claim of the core 'natural' faith to be neutral towards the positive religions conflicts, in spite of the attempts at mediation of the Savoyard Vicar and the critique of a deistic rational religion, with the established religions and confessions, so that the latter sink back into the status of mere *adiaphora*. However, this means that respect for the existing religions becomes a precarious matter since they seem to express merely a form of religious conventionalism; and the result at the political level is not only the above-mentioned civil religion but also the authority of the sovereign to regulate 'external' matters and enforced conformity.

§20 The religion of reason and overcoming intolerance

1. Important commonalities and differences among the thinkers of the French Enlightenment, the *philosophes*, insofar as they bear on the issue of toleration, can be shown by comparing Rousseau with his famous adversary François-Marie Arouet, known as Voltaire. For, regardless of how sharply their views diverged – over whether feeling or reason constitutes the essence of morality, over 'natural' versus rational religion, over the contribution of the arts and sciences to social progress, over the possibility and desirability of social equality, over the relative merits of democracy and enlightened absolutism, or over patriotism and cosmopolitanism – they nevertheless agreed that the most important challenge facing the age was to combat religious fanaticism and that the effective means to achieve this was a non-dogmatic religion consisting, in essence, of the moral duties of all human beings (and of citizens). However, Voltaire, the most influential and eloquent voice of the mid-eighteenth-century European Enlightenment, exhibited the profile of the Enlightenment thinker more clearly than the ambivalent Rousseau. The rallying cry with which he signed his letters – 'écrasez l'infâme' – signified that the only way to overcome superstition and intolerance was by combating the supremacy of the positive religions, for which rational insight into the absurdity and barbarism of religious conflicts, which in Voltaire's view turned on *nothing*, is indispensable. Voltaire excelled in exposing these absurdities in his literary works and philosophical writings; whenever the representatives of religions are allowed to have their say, they exhibit the mixture of blind superstition, idiotic conceit and lust for power which, according to Voltaire, is at the root of intolerance.[61] That which Bayle had to combat with all his

---

61. See, for example, Voltaire, *Dialogues chrétiens, ou préservatif contre l'Encyclopédie*; in addition, the articles 'Dogmas', 'Superstition', 'Fanaticism' and 'Religion' in Voltaire, *A Philosophical Dictionary*.

might (though he, too, used the weapon of irony) became in Voltaire an object of caustic derision. A new, more biting tone prevails in which not only the theologians become objects of ridicule but also philosophers such as Leibniz – for instance in *Candide* (1759), in which Voltaire also responds to Rousseau's objections against the poem on the earthquake in Lisbon.

Voltaire is convinced that fanatical intolerance is an illness rooted in a perverted conception of religion and that it can be healed only by enlightenment, the purification of reason, as he states in his *Philosophical Dictionary* (1764): 'When once fanaticism has gangrened the brain of any man, the disease may be regarded as merely incurable ... There is no other remedy for this epidemical malady, than the spirit of philosophy, which, extended itself from one to another, at length civilises and softens the manners of men, and prevents the access of the disease.'[62] Voltaire is aware of the limits of this enlightenment and of the arduousness of the struggle: 'What can be said in answer to a man, who says he will rather obey God than men, and who consequently feels certain of meriting heaven by cutting your throat?'[63]

As long as the 'frenzy' of intolerance can be attributed to a contaminated religion, self-enlightened reason leads by no means to a 'crushing' of all religion and to atheism, but instead to a *pure religion*. On Voltaire's deist conception of religion, which he calls 'theism' in order to underscore its moral-practical character, this is the first among all religions; it asserts that God is the 'master of universal reason', and its first commandment is 'worship me and be just'.[64] However, this religion is not a kind of universal-moral, undogmatic core religion which is supposed to be combined with the other, positive religions, as Rousseau thinks (to some extent); rather it represents the *only rational alternative* to them. If all human beings 'hearkened to their plain reason, the earth would be covered with men such as ourselves'.[65] The dogmas of this religion are extremely simple: 'We condemn atheism, we revile barbarous superstition, we love God and the human race: these are our dogmas.'[66] From this vantage point, the established religions and confessions are mere aberrations which developed over the course of history and are often misused; the rational religion, by contrast, is 'the only sacred religion'.[67] It is the only religion which is capable of protecting itself against itself, as it were, because it implies a universal morality and a belief in God free from controversial dogmas and scriptural faith or revelations. Moreover, it cannot

62. Voltaire, 'Fanaticism', 481.   63. *Ibid.*
64. Voltaire, *Proféssion de foi des théistes*: 'maître de la raison universelle ... adore-moi, et sois juste'.
65. *Ibid.*: 's'ils écoutaient leur simple raison, la terre serait couverte de nos semblables'.
66. *Ibid.*: 'Nous condamnons l'athéisme, nous détestons la superstition barbare, nous aimons Dieu et le genre humain: voilà nos dogmes.'
67. *Ibid.*: 'la seule religion divine'.

clash with scientific knowledge because the divine plan 'which is manifested in all nature' is rational and orderly.[68] Voltaire expresses the indispensability of this religion in a rhetoric which makes abundantly clear that it is not merely a matter of a core or substitute religion, but that this religion makes a claim to *absoluteness*: 'All religions inadvertently pay homage to theism even as they persecute it. They are the putrid waters divided into channels on the muddy ground, but the spring is pure.'[69]

This stands in sharp contrast to Bayle's conception of the relation between faith and reason, notwithstanding the affinity with Bayle's critique of superstition which Voltaire defends in many places.[70] Whereas Bayle thinks that reason, even though it constitutes the framework for rational religions, speaks neither for nor against religion in general nor for any particular religion, Voltaire thinks that reason clearly supports one and only one religion of reason. His goal, therefore, is not to lead religions to embrace toleration; he wants to bring them 'to reason' in the sense that they are absorbed into the one true undogmatic religion. Only in this way, Voltaire assumes, can intolerance be eradicated: 'Therefore, our religion . . . is the only universal one, just as it is the most ancient and the only sacred religion.'[71] This programme of overcoming intolerance obviously remains beholden to the ideal of the *one*, universally valid religion.

No matter how undogmatic this theistic religion may be, it is equally clear in its rejection of the 'foolishness' of atheism as defended by the materialists, on the one hand, and in its moral injunctions whose observance is commanded and enjoined by the righteous deity, on the other. The 'pure religion' which unites all human beings entails a 'pure morality' which makes itself heard in the individual's conscience.[72] The theists' fundamental principle is: 'Morality is the same among all men, therefore it comes from God, worship is various, therefore it is the work of man.'[73] Furthermore, one of the gravest crimes which this morality condemns is that of intolerance and the imposition of religion by force. With this the idea of a tolerant religion, or rather the *religion of tolerance*, is complete, a religion which unites men

---

68. Voltaire, *Philosophical Dictionary*, 'God, Gods', vol. I, 568.
69. Voltaire, *Proféssion de foi des théistes*: 'Toute religion rend, malgré elle, hommage au théisme, quand même elle le persécute. Ce sont des eaux corrompues partagées en canaux dans des terrains fangeux, mais la source est pure.'
70. See, for example, the article 'Philosopher' in the *Philosophical Dictionary* where Voltaire speaks of the 'immortal Bayle', this 'honour of human nature' (vol. II, 308).
71. Voltaire, *Proféssion de foi des théistes*: 'Notre religion . . . est donc la seule qui soit universelle, comme elle est la plus antique et la seule divine.'
72. Voltaire, *Philosophical Dictionary*, 'Conscience', vol. I, 322.   73. *Ibid.* 'Atheist', vol. I, 166.

'rather than which divides; the religion which is not bigoted, which forms virtuous citizens and not worthless scholars; the religion which is tolerant and does not persecute; the religion which says that the only law consists in loving God and one's neighbour rather than that which makes God into a tyrant and turns neighbours into victims'.[74]

This highlights another difference from Bayle which is important for the issue of toleration, as Voltaire himself observes. In his article 'Atheism' in the *Philosophical Dictionary* he concurs with Bayle that fanaticism is a greater evil than atheism. Nevertheless, he rejects Bayle's paradox that a society of atheists could endure, citing the classical argument that there is a connection between a higher justice and just action here on earth which also informs 'Locke's fear': 'It is clear that the sanctity of oaths is necessary; and that those are more to be trusted who think a false oath will be punished, than those who think they may take a false oath with impunity. It cannot be doubted that, in an organised society, it is better even to have a bad religion than no religion at all.'[75] Hence, Voltaire not only believes that there is a constitutive relation between religion and morality; when he adopts the perspective of the theory of the state he also switches to a pragmatic, strategic level and argues that it is 'absolutely necessary' for the mass of the people and for the princes that there should be a God who rewards justice and punishes evil, even one conceived in conventional terms.[76]

As regards the justification of toleration, the first thing to note is that Voltaire's programme of enlightenment is in the first instance one of *overcoming intolerance* through a religion (and morality) of reason and only secondarily a programme of toleration. For toleration is only the second-best solution compared to achieving a unified rational religion, which would greatly reduce the occasions for conflicts that put toleration on the agenda in the first place. On this view, overcoming intolerance would also amount to an *abolition of toleration*. But since this must remain a mere idea of reason among fallible human beings, who are susceptible to errors and are slaves to habit, toleration is mandatory. When Voltaire describes it as *l'apanage de l'humanité* (the appurtenance of humanity) which is necessary and a 'law of nature'[77] on account of human fallibility, therefore, this is ambivalent. Toleration must clearly be interpreted, on the one hand, positively as a 'sign' or 'gift of true humanity', as a sense for morally required consideration but, on the other,

---

74. Voltaire, 'An Address to the Public', 130–1.
75. Voltaire, *Philosophical Dictionary*, 'Atheism', vol. I, 161–2.
76. *Ibid.* 162; see also 'God, Gods', vol. I, 569.   77. *Ibid.* 'Toleration', vol. II, 544.

as an 'inheritance' or even 'fate' of human beings who seem to have no alternative but to forgive their own 'weaknesses and errors' and those of others. From the standpoint of the 'true religion', these would indeed be primarily the errors and failings of others which one must first tolerate while working towards overcoming them. Voltaire's conception is torn between these poles. At times he emphasises (in Bayle's sense) the insurmountability of the metaphysical limitations of reason;[78] at others he stresses the need to protect the demonstrably pure source of the theistic truth from contamination.

The key text on the justification of toleration in Voltaire is the *Traité sur la tolérance, à l'occasion de la mort de Jean Calas* (1763). As so often in the history of the discourse of toleration, the text was occasioned by an actual historical occurrence. It is an appeal to an enlightened 'public' passing judgement in this case on a judicial scandal, and hence on the deluded judges.[79] In 1762 in Toulouse, Jean Calas, a Protestant, was sentenced to death on the wheel and was executed on the charge of having collaborated with his wife, his son and a friend in murdering his other son Marc-Antoine because the latter allegedly wanted to convert to Catholicism. Against all the evidence, Calas was convicted and executed in a manifestly flawed procedure, borne along by the fanaticism of the 'crowd' (5), as Voltaire writes; the rest of the family was spared and Madame Calas finally succeeded with Voltaire's assistance in having the judgement annulled and her husband rehabilitated.[80] The Enlightenment philosopher had achieved a victory with the aid of the public.

Having presented an account of the case in his *Traité*, Voltaire offers an exhaustive discussion of the reasons for toleration drawing on the spectrum of justifications developed up to that time, which he combines into an effective plea for toleration. The decisive arguments are the following:

(a) The central argument is addressed to reason itself, which must recognise that fanatical superstition is an illness in need of healing through the 'influence of reason' (25): the intolerant person regresses to the level of a barbaric animal (28, also 85), though one which does not kill for the rationally understandable reason that it is hungry but only because of a dispute over 'paragraphs' (28). To be more precise, the necessary insight

78. 'In metaphysics we scarcely reason on anything but probabilities. We are all swimming in a sea of which we have never seen the shore. Woe be to those who fight while they swim! Land who can.' *Ibid.* 'God, Gods', vol. 1, 567.
79. Voltaire, *Treatise on Tolerance*, 11 (the page numbers in the text refer to this edition).
80. On the background of the case see the editor's introduction to Voltaire, *Treatise on Tolerance*, xff. and Bien, *The Calas Affair*.

of reason has three aspects. First the insight into the metaphysical limitation of reason according to which 'it would be the height of folly to
attempt to bring all men to think alike on matters of metaphysics' (87) –
and correspondingly the recognition of the futility of an endless and
acrimonious dispute over dogmatic truth. Connected with this, second,
is the insight into the priority of the morality of reciprocity, the Golden
Rule, which Voltaire describes as a 'natural law' (28) and according to
which the coercion of conscience cannot be reciprocally justified. Third,
however, Voltaire thinks it consistent that reason should confine itself to
an undogmatic and moral religion, a conclusion which is not necessary
and is in tension, as previously noted, with the first insight. For if a religious or metaphysical unity cannot be achieved among limited rational
beings it cannot be achieved within a rational religion either.

(b) Voltaire draws on the traditional justification of freedom of conscience
when he says that whether and what somebody believes cannot be influenced by human beings; faith is produced by God and thus the true
Church will be able to prevail without human coercion. Anything else
would be a distortion of faith, tending only to produce hypocrites.

(c) Voltaire also demonstrates complete mastery of the gamut of Christian
arguments for toleration. Thus, he appeals to the Christian virtue of
patience (49), to the example of Christ's mercy, to Christianity's own
experience of persecution (38ff.); and he challenges the literal interpretation of the parable of those who were forced to enter (*compelle intrare*)
(65ff.).

(d) At the level of the theory of the state, Voltaire attempts to show in the
spirit of the *politiques* that toleration, in contrast to religious zealotry,
promotes political peace; in support he cites a variety of examples ranging
from the Netherlands to the Ottoman Empire and China.

(e) Finally, he cites economic arguments which speak against the repression and punishment of dissenters, and cites in particular the disadvantages resulting from the banishment of the Huguenots from France
(23, 95–6).

It is instructive how Voltaire defines the *limits* of toleration in the light of this
conception. In the first place, this boundary serves to exclude intolerance
itself: 'to be entitled to society's toleration, men should start by renouncing
fanaticism' (78). For Voltaire it is not religious reasons that lead to the
exclusion – for example of the Jesuits, who were banned in France at the
time – but the public good and the universal laws.

But this is not enough. For Voltaire insists in addition that a bad, super-stitious religion in a state is still better than none at all:

> Mankind has always been in need of a restraining influence, and however ridiculous it may be to sacrifice to fauns, elves and water-nymphs, it was certainly both more reasonable and more serviceable to worship these fantastic images of the deity than to give oneself over to Atheism. A committed, violent and powerful Atheist would be as pernicious a scourge as the most bloodthirsty religious bigot.   (83)

Hence, atheists must not be tolerated in a society because they challenge its foundations: 'while laws are established to place a curb upon open crimes, religion deals with private ones' (*ibid.*).

Of course, this does not mean that superstition should be tolerated as a general rule. After all, provided that a society is progressing towards enlight-enment and 'men have come to embrace a pure and holy religion, superstition becomes, not merely useless, but dangerous. We must not feed on acorns those to whom God offers bread' (*ibid.*). A religion which has become 'more pure' (84) must replace the false, superstitious religion and, inasmuch as it is historically possible, the reason for tolerating the older religion loses its relevance unless pragmatic reasons speak in favour of tolerating it. From the standpoint of enlightened reason, those who stubbornly insist, contrary to the findings of the natural sciences, that the earth does not rotate around the sun, should be regarded as beings devoid of reason, as 'animals', and if they resort to violence in support of their cause, as 'wild animals'.

With this, however, Voltaire's plea for universal toleration becomes ambivalent. It amounts to a plea for a form of toleration not only between Christians but one which for universal moral reasons also regards the Turk, the Chinaman and the Jew as 'my brother' (89) who should be tolerated, as 'children of *the same* Father' (though this does not imply a model of equal rights at the level of the theory of the state; here Voltaire remains captive to the permission conception).[81] Not only does he exclude fanat-ics for the simple reason that they defend fanatical views (even if they do not act accordingly) but he also excludes atheists and, under 'enlightened' conditions, all supporters of false, superstitious religions. These exclusions

---

81. 'I do not say that all those who profess a different religion from that of the reigning prince should share in the places and honours of those who follow the dominant religion. In England, Roman Catholics are considered as belonging to the party of the Pretender, and are therefore denied office; they even pay double tax; yet they still enjoy all other privileges of the citizen' (20).

are not just a consequence of Voltaire's acceptance of a traditional linkage between religion, morality and obedience to the law or political stability; they also follow from the fact that his programme is primarily one of abolishing intolerance by establishing a rational religion, and only secondarily one of justifying toleration. Although his rational religion would permit certain variations in teachings, it aims to abolish differences between religions, which Voltaire regarded as the chief evil leading to fierce competition, and thereby to establish *one* undogmatic religion. It not only marks the return at the heart of the Enlightenment of the fatal connection between morality and religion which Bayle combated, but also the problematic, though morally motivated, humanist idea of an undogmatic universal religion that unites all human beings and puts an end to religious strife. In this way, the thought which launched a crusade against the principle 'one king, one law, one faith' itself establishes the principle 'one reason, one morality, one religion (or one God)'; in its crusade against the 'infamy' which must be 'crushed' it continues to pay homage to the ideal of a unified religion which grounds morality – in particular a religion that is unable to shake off its Christian roots. Thus, not only are narrow limits set to the 'godless' but a boundary is also drawn to the 'false', unenlightened faith. Its error is not seen as residing primarily in a failure to appreciate the finitude of reason but in a backward adherence to a positive religion (Voltaire singles out the Jews as an example for this in many places in his work).[82] However, the fact that reason *opposes* a dogmatic claim to absoluteness which regards itself as beyond reasonable doubt and from this derives the legitimation for religious compulsion does *not* mean that it *supports* a religion of reason, as Voltaire believes. Rather, it would have to treat this religion itself as one faith among others which may have certain moral advantages but is required by neither reason nor the only rationally defensible faith. Bayle defended this 'religious agnosticism of reason', in which he is one crucial insight ahead of Voltaire's religion of reason.

2. The *Encyclopédie ou Dictionnaire raisonné des Sciences, des Arts et des Métiers* (1751–80), edited by Denis Diderot and (until 1757) by Jean le Rond d'Alembert, was the ambitious and epoch-making attempt to assemble the entire knowledge of the Enlightenment era, and thereby to advance the

82. See, for example, Voltaire, *Philosophical Dictionary*, 'Atheism', vol. 1, 166: 'It is singular that the latter [i.e. Judaism], which is the extreme of superstition, abhorred by the people, and contemned by the wise, is everywhere tolerated for money; while the former [i.e. Theism], which is the opposite of superstition, unknown to the people, and embraced by philosophers alone, is publicly exercised nowhere but in China.'

enlightenment of contemporary society and culture. Notwithstanding the differences among the (some 170) individual authors, they were united in their espousal of the ideal of toleration, based largely on a critique of religion which sought to reduce it to the rationally justifiable dimensions of a deistic conception of God. As far as the problem of the justification of toleration is concerned, however, there were important differences within this project which should be mentioned briefly. The most important authors in this regard were Diderot himself, the Huguenot Louis de Jaucourt who virtually assumed an editorial role following d'Alembert's withdrawal, and, finally, Jean-Edmé Romilly, a Genevan theologian who wrote the article 'Toleration'. I will examine more closely first (a) deism, then (b) the conception of the state informing the central articles on politics, (c) the definition of the relation between religion and morality, and finally (d) the discussion of toleration itself.

(a) Diderot developed his conception of a 'natural religion' in a number of works in the late 1740s, in particular the *Pensées philosophiques* (1746) and the treatise *De la suffisance de la religion naturelle* (1747). Diderot was convinced that superstition represents a greater evil than atheism, though the latter should also be avoided.[83] Therefore, the only route specified by reason, which should be the sole guide of faith, is that of deism: 'Only the deist can oppose the atheist. The superstitious man is not so strong an opponent.'[84] A rational faith cannot be based on revelation or miracles; if a religion claims to be true then 'its truth can be demonstrated by unanswerable arguments'.[85] Rejecting Bayle's separation of faith and reason, Diderot explains: 'When God, from whom we receive reason, demands its sacrifice it is like a prestidigitator who takes back what he has given.'[86] Reason enlightened by natural science is capable of knowing that a 'supreme intelligence' must operate in the system of nature and the laws of matter. All positive religions that go beyond the minimal 'natural religion', which also implies faith in a just God who rewards goodness, are historically contingent and finite: 'Now Judaism and Christianity had their beginning, and there is not a single religion on earth whose year of birth is not known, with the exception of natural religion. Therefore, it alone will never end, whereas all the others will pass.'[87] In comparison to the original religion all others are deviations and signs of degeneration that lead away from the initial unity. As enlightenment progresses, humanity will return to this unity of religion through reason. The testimonies of the

83. On this, see Diderot's article 'Philosopher' in the *Encyclopedia*.
84. Diderot, *Philosophic Thoughts*, vol. XIII (31).   85. *Ibid.* L (59).
86. Diderot, *Thoughts on Religion*, III.   87. Diderot, *De la suffisance de la religion naturelle*, IV.

positive religions have been 'recorded by superstitious men in parchment and marble', the testimony of natural religion 'I find written in me by the finger of God.'[88]

(b) A similar attempt to connect modern reason with enlightened religiosity can also be found in the political philosophy of the articles from the *Encyclopaedia*, which were authored especially by Diderot and Jaucourt and are profoundly influenced by the natural law theories of Locke and Pufendorf.[89] Correspondingly, both emphasise the natural – moral – equality and liberty of individuals,[90] who, as Diderot asserts in the famous article 'Political Authority', have received their liberty as a 'gift from heaven' and hence, because they belong 'entirely' to God, cannot subordinate themselves without reservation to other men. Therefore, they establish a state which guarantees their natural rights by contractual agreement and thereby become members of the sovereign 'moral being' of the community as citizens, as Diderot states in the (Rousseau-influenced) article 'Citizen'.[91] Even more than Jaucourt, who leaves room for a right of resistance,[92] Diderot is also at pains to allow for the possibility of a hereditary monarchy, given the political situation in France at the time, and rejects a right of resistance.[93]

However, the two thinkers are in agreement that freedom of conscience is an inalienable right, as is freedom of the press.[94] Since human beings are beholden in the first instance to God, and only secondarily to the sovereign, conscience remains beyond the reach of politics. Jaucourt also defends the right to be wrong in the articles 'Conscience' and 'Heretic' as long as this does not lead to immoral acts – which excludes the right of a 'conscientious persecutor', thus avoiding Bayle's problem with this case.[95]

(c) Diderot takes his lead from Bayle rather than from Locke when he defines the relationship between religion and morality, for he defends a rational conception of morality which is substantially independent of religious foundations:

> People hold different beliefs, both religious and *irreligious*, according to where on the surface of the globe they happen to go or where they live. But morality is the same everywhere. It is the universal law that God has engraved in all our hearts . . . So immorality and irreligion

88. *Ibid.* XVIII.   89. On this, see Zurbuchen, *Naturrecht und natürliche Religion*, chs. 5 and 6.
90. See in particular the articles 'Natural Rights' (Diderot) and 'Natural Equality' (Jaucourt).
91. See 'Political Authority' (Diderot); 'Citizen' (Diderot).   92. See 'Government' (Jaucourt).
93. 'Political Authority' (Diderot).
94. On the latter see 'Press' (Jaucourt).   95. 'Conscience' (Jaucourt).

should not be confused. Morality can exist without religion and religion can exist and even often does exist alongside immorality.[96]

Diderot not only attributes to all human beings the capacity for moral insight independently of their religion but also associates this with the criterion of the universal human will, thus universalising Rousseau's doctrine of the *volonté générale* and anticipating Kant. In order to determine the universal rights and duties of human beings through an 'act of understanding', he writes, the virtuous person must enquire into 'the general will of the species' and submit himself to it as if it were a universal law equally binding on everyone.[97]

(d) Combining the arguments from (b) and (c) yields reasons in favour of a maximally inclusive conception of toleration which would permit interference in the domain of religion only for moral reasons, as required by Jaucourt.[98] Anything else would contradict the natural rights of individuals and the insight that an error does not represent a crime and that respect for persons is not contingent on esteem for their thoughts or deeds.[99] In contrast to Rousseau, Diderot distinguishes between *ecclesiastical* and *state* intolerance in this connection. The former is the legitimate criticism of religions which one regards as untrue, the latter the illegitimate attempt to subject conscience to political and religious compulsion, ranging from censorship to direct violence: 'One should not persecute men of good faith or men of bad faith, but leave it to God to judge them.'[100]

There is a tension between this conception of toleration, which advocates a strong separation between state and religion and must also include atheists (though Diderot does not say so explicitly), and Romilly's article 'Toleration' (in the sixteenth volume, 1765). Although he takes his cue entirely from Bayle's *Commentaire*, to which he refers the 'curious reader' at the end, he follows tradition in setting narrow limits on the scope of toleration. He appeals to Rousseau's concept of a civil religion and the duty of the citizens to embrace this. Hence, there can be no question of tolerating atheists: 'They strip the powerful of the final restraint which could hold them in check, and the weak of their only hope; they weaken human laws by robbing them of the force which derives from the divine sanction.'[101] Apart from the atheists,

---

96. 'Irreligious' (Diderot); see also 'Superstition' (Diderot). In the article 'Atheist', by contrast, Yvon regards religion as a necessary 'restraint' for the masses.
97. 'Natural Rights' (Diderot), §9.   98. 'Conscience' (Jaucourt).
99. 'Heretic' (Jaucourt).   100. 'Intolerance' (Diderot) (translation amended).
101. 'Tolérance' (Romilly), *Encyclopédie*, vol. XVI, 394.

Romilly continues, any religion which subjects 'its members to a twofold government' and thus creates a 'state within the state' – he means the Catholic religion – cannot be tolerated. Here the traditional limits of reflection on toleration become apparent. They reveal the distance that still had to be travelled, even in the century of the Enlightenment, to a truly general and shareable justification of toleration.

3. Thus, neither deism nor the idea of civil religion seems to lead to a comprehensive justification of toleration. From this materialist atheists such as La Mettrie, d'Holbach and Helvétius concluded that genuine toleration cannot be achieved as long as religion as such, be it a traditional positive religion or a religion of 'reason', continues to exist. Although they continued to cite reason as the sole guide in questions of religion, in their eyes it spoke in principle *against* religion. The most radical approach in this regard can be found in Paul Thiry d'Holbach's *Système de la nature* (1770). In the context of his attempt to explain all phenomena of intellectual and moral life on the basis of the laws of the physical world, d'Holbach declared a range of metaphysical and all religious interpretations of the world to be aberrations that lead away from the truth concerning nature and from the essence of morality – 'delusions' which should be viewed primarily from the perspective of a critique of ideology.[102] According to d'Holbach, the concept of a God is empty and meaningless; however, in any given religion it acquires a content which, given the natural differences between human beings, can never be the same for any two persons, leading inevitably to senseless, irresolvable disputes over the supposedly 'most important things': fanaticism is not just a reverse side of religion, fanaticism is *the essence* of religion (I, 111–12, 190–1). Religions which infuse human beings with supernatural inspiration either ensure that earthly crimes are justified by appeal to divine truth or divine reward or lead to complete submission to ecclesiastical or political rule in the fear of eternal punishment: 'It is thus the doctrine of a future life that has been made fatal to the human species' (190).

This verdict also holds for the deists' or theists' conception of religion. The deist conception of a 'natural religion' of reason – 'which is anything but *natural* or founded upon reason' (II, 75) – either is completely empty and only an expression of perplexity or a lack of intellectual consistency, or (as in the case of the theists) has a content – the belief in providence and in divine justice – and hence is a no less dangerous, contradictory and superstitious

---

102. See in particular d'Holbach, *System of Nature*, vol. I, ch. 1; vol. II, chs. 1–3, 8–10. Page numbers in the text refer to the English translation.

product of optimistic fanaticism than the belief in an avenging or despotic God.

D'Holbach not only cites Bayle's paradox (cf. II, 136) that even atheists can act morally and form a society but inverts it: as long as people remain under the sway of religion a society conducive to morality cannot exist (I, 137; II, 86–108). Not only are education, positive laws and the rules of social esteem entirely sufficient to lead people to the rational insight that their natural striving for self-preservation and happiness depends on promoting the happiness of those with whom they stand in relations of dependence (I, 145–59); it is rather the case that the idea of the Deity, by leading to exclusions and disputes, is 'contrary to sound morality' (II, 96). The many religious moral conceptions, which take their cues from the most diverse gods, do not allow any uniform, stable and clear 'morality of nature' (II, 102) among human beings. Only atheism is truly compatible with morality because it is immune to fanaticism (II, 134–6); the best society possible would be a society of atheists (II, 150).

As regards toleration, it seems therefore that the only route to a tolerant society which respects the natural and irreducible differences between individuals (and their temperaments) is to overcome religion itself:

> Let us then conclude, that those divine and supernatural ideas with which we are inspired from our infancy, are the true causes of our habitual folly, of our religious quarrels, of our sacred dissensions, of our inhuman persecutions. Let us at length acknowledge, that they are the fatal ideas which have obscured morality, corrupted politics, retarded the progress of the sciences, and even annihilated happiness and peace in the heart of man. Let it then be no longer dissimulated, that all those calamities, for which man turns his eyes towards heaven, bathed in tears, are to be ascribed to those vain phantoms which his imagination has placed there; let him cease to implore them; let him seek in nature, and in his own energy, those resources, which the Gods, who are deaf to his cries, will never procure for him.   (II, 109)

Although d'Holbach had his doubts whether this radical enlightenment could reach the general mass of humanity of his time, he placed his hopes in a slow process of persuasion and of overcoming the prejudices on which religion is founded.

Hence, d'Holbach's programme draws the radical conclusion from the insight shared by many Enlightenment thinkers that religion by its very nature tends to promote intolerance and that reason alone can overcome this. He has his doubts concerning the possibility of a 'rational religion' in Voltaire's and Diderot's sense – or indeed in Bayle's sense, that is, one which recognises the limitations of reason and the idiosyncrasy of religious truth claims. D'Holbach believes that atheism alone can withstand rational examination, as well as his idea of a 'natural morality' and his physicalistic naturalism. In this way, however, he remains captive against his own will to the ideal of a *unified* religion – the 'non-religion' of nature which becomes the 'only Divinity' (II, 167), as it were – and to the idea, which Bayle rejected, that the plurality of religions *must* collapse under the gaze of reason, an idea which does not ultimately take the finitude of reason seriously enough and is metaphysically presumptuous. As a result, his programme of overcoming fanatical intolerance collapses into a kind of 'fanaticism of tolerance' that itself promotes intolerance because it cannot tolerate any religion, positive or otherwise. The dividing line between the morally good and the morally reprehensible then runs between atheism and religious faith, so that *overcoming intolerance* collapses into *overcoming toleration*. A religion of the people could be tolerated at most for pragmatic reasons – but only in order to enlighten the people step by step. In brief, the abolition of intolerance via the abolition of religion is not a programme of toleration but an attempt to establish a world in which there is no longer any occasion for religious tolerance.[103]

4. As the intellectual movement of the Enlightenment spread, it also led to – contextually varying – versions of the 'struggle' between faith and reason in other European countries.[104] The German Enlightenment, in particular, made a series of attempts to justify toleration by redefining the relation between religion and reason in a way which goes beyond atheism. The most famous and, to the present day, most influential is Gotthold Ephraim Lessing's parable of the three rings. However, in order to reconstruct his position – and the related position of Moses Mendelssohn – we must first

---

103. The inversion from a critique of intolerance into an intolerant critique of religion is typical of the Enlightenment, according to Koselleck, and involves an inherent tendency towards an 'educational dictatorship' ('Aufklärung und die Grenzen ihrer Toleranz', 265). As the above discussion of Voltaire and d'Holbach showed, there is a tendency towards such an inversion, yet not only is it far removed from a dictatorship but it is just *one* aspect in certain authors and is not characteristic of 'the Enlightenment' as such. Locke and Romilly, whom Koselleck cites, are counter-examples to this thesis. However, it is indisputable that 'reason' gives rise to exclusions of its own when it elevates itself into a religion. Although Horkheimer and Adorno do not discuss such a dialectic themselves, they allude to it when they criticise the disavowal of God as a new form of metaphysics; see *Dialectic of Enlightenment*, 20, 96–7.
104. See for example Hume's critique of religion and his deist conception in the *Dialogues concerning Natural Religion* (1779).

examine briefly the most challenging contemporary German deist theory which would draw Lessing himself into the maelstrom of the conflicts over religion of his time, that of Hermann Samuel Reimarus.

In his work *Die vornehmsten Wahrheiten der natürlichen Religion* (1754), which was profoundly influenced by Christian Wolff's *Theologia naturalis*, the Hamburg Professor for Oriental Languages Reimarus defended the conception of a religion of reason devoted to combating the spread of atheism by grounding 'natural religion and morals'.[105] He claimed that this religion represents the foundation of all possible positive religions, such as Christianity, which build upon it; and inasmuch as the latter is led onto other paths by blind obedience to scripture and authority, it effectively endangers itself. Only when reason has opened up the path to faith, according to Reimarus, does it become possible to extend the latter in the direction of revelation.[106] However, such a revealed faith then must be able to withstand the scrutiny of reason.

That it does not withstand rational scrutiny Reimarus demonstrates not in the work mentioned but in his *Apologie oder Schutzschrift der vernünftigen Verehrer Gottes*, although this work remained unpublished and only appeared (after Reimarus's death) in the extracts published by Lessing in 1774–78 under the title 'Anonymous Fragments' in his series 'On History and Literature: From the Treasures of the Ducal Library in Wolfenbüttel'. In the first fragment, 'On Toleration of the Deists', Reimarus associates his deism with the demand for toleration, in particular toleration for the deists who, although they defend the 'pure teaching of Christ', which is nothing more than a 'rational practical religion', everywhere suffer much more severe persecution than 'Jews, Turks, and heathens' and even atheists.[107] For Reimarus this is a sign that Christianity has strayed from its rational roots and now fears the confrontation with this original religion. Hence, intolerance is a sign not only of unreason but also of the weakness of the faith. True faith is instead in need of a rational foundation, in the sense not only that it must spring from one's own inner conviction but also that it must be founded on independent rational arguments. And this is possible only through free discussion and criticism of religion.[108] Reimarus goes on to argue in the five additional fragments published by Lessing that such a discussion would demonstrate that the positive religions are based entirely on the prejudices

---

105. Reimarus, *The Principal Truths* (this quotation from the 'Vorbericht' does not appear in the abridged English translation).
106. *Ibid.*   107. Reimarus, 'Von Duldung der Deisten', 314, 318.   108. *Ibid.* 325–6.

instilled by upbringing and religious authorities and that the belief in a revelation 'that all men could accept on the basis of reasons' (as the title of the second fragment puts it) is neither possible nor necessary for a rational religion. Furthermore, in a historical Bible critique Reimarus identifies a series of contradictions in the writings of the Old and New Testaments which should cast doubt on their narratives.

As the publisher of these writings, Lessing found himself in a delicate position. Himself torn between the deist critique of positive, scriptural religions and the defence of the Lutheran confession as 'rational' Christianity, he makes a plea for public toleration and discussion of the objections of Reimarus. With this position he fell between all of the philosophical-theological stools of his time, as opposed to atheism as to the 'orthodoxists', to the radical deist repudiation of all forms of revelation as to the attempts of the 'neologists' to reduce Christian teachings to rational principles: 'For what is a revelation which reveals nothing?'[109] Hence, for Lessing, toleration is a genuinely *rational matter of faith*: at a time of religious crisis, only the free and unbiased exchange of views can nourish hopes of enlightenment; hence, in a certain sense toleration externalises the internal conflict of faith. Thus, Lessing argues for accepting Reimarus's challenge, while at the same time exhorting the latter to greater tolerance, because he recognises the ambivalence of calling for tolerance while simultaneously absolutising the rational religion of the deists: 'But our deists want unconditional toleration. They want to have the freedom to dispute the Christian religion, and nevertheless to be tolerated. They want to have the liberty to mock the God of the Christians, and yet to be tolerated. However, that is asking too much.'[110]

Thus, Lessing presented his 'Counter-propositions' as an appendix to the fragments of Reimarus. Of these his most important adversary, the Hamburg orthodox Lutheran minister Goeze, would later say they were 'a medicine which was even more poisonous than the very poison to be found in the fragment'.[111] Although Lessing undertakes to relativise the positions of Reimarus, he does not regard himself as the one 'who comes at least so close to the ideal of a true defender of religion'[112] – and for whom be hopes. In this Lessing, who had been a member of a Freemasons' Lodge since 1771,

---

109. Lessing, 'Editorial Commentary on the "Fragments" of Reimarus', 66. On Lessing's criticism of these positions and his own crisis of faith see Oelmüller, *Die unbefriedigte Aufklärung*, ch. 2. Schultze likewise draws attention to the ambivalences in Lessing in *Lessings Toleranzbegriff*.
110. Lessing, 'Bemerkungen zu "Von Duldung der Deisten"', 329.
111. Goeze, 'Lessings Schwächen', II, 257.   112. Lessing, 'Editorial Commentary', 64.

remained true to his inner struggle, which he would later (in 1779) describe as follows:

> The larger part of my life has fallen – fortunately or unfortunately? – during a time in which writings in support of the truth of the Christian religion were fashionable to a certain extent . . . Not for long; and now I sought out every new work *against* religion just as eagerly and lavished on it the same patient, impartial attention which I otherwise believed myself duty-bound to show only to the writings *for* religion. And so it remained for a considerable time. I was pulled from one side to the other; neither satisfied me entirely . . . The more conclusively the one side sought to prove Christianity, the more dubious I became. The more wantonly and triumphantly the other side sought to beat it down before my eyes, the more I felt inclined to uphold it at least in my heart.[113]

In the 'Counter-propositions', Lessing objects to Reimarus – a point which Goeze would criticise especially vehemently – that the Christian faith cannot be refuted by criticising central assertions of the Bible: 'In short, the letter is not the spirit and the Bible is not religion.'[114] In attempting to conceive of positive religion as rational, Lessing also views reason as the highest authority; but, in contrast to Reimarus, Lessing allows '*a certain* subjugation of reason to the discipline of faith',[115] specifically when revelation reveals truths that reason can make its own. Then reason surrenders itself, as Lessing puts it, aware of its own finitude – so that it recuperates and accepts revelation by rational means, though it does not 'prove' it. Although the (hypothetical) path proposed by Reimarus, leading from rational truth to revealed truth, cannot succeed, the reverse path can.[116] Moreover, Lessing explains how this path beyond orthodoxy and the critique of religion should be understood in his reflections on *The Education of the Human Race*, Part 1 of which was appended to the 'Counter-propositions' (and which he presents as having been written by someone else).[117] There he proposes that revelation should be understood as the education of the human race as a whole to the autonomy of reason. The revealed truths give human beings nothing which they could not have produced through their own reason, but they give it to them sooner (§4). Even if faith in this way precedes reason, in the end reason catches up with it and becomes independent, though it can accept revelation as part of

---

113. Lessing, 'Bibliolatrie', 671–2 (emphasis in the original).
114. Lessing, 'Editorial Commentary', 63.   115. *Ibid*. 66.   116. *Ibid*.
117. Lessing, *The Education of the Human Race* (1780).

its own history. Thus, Lessing explains the absence of the doctrine of the immortality of the soul in the Old Testament in terms of the immaturity of the Israelites at that time as a 'barbarous' people; being an 'uncouth people' (§ 50), what was needed was a clear book of laws. At a later stage this was torn from its grasp by a 'better instructor' (§ 53), Jesus, in order to elevate moral action to a new, more refined level through the doctrine of eternal life: 'And so Christ became the first *reliable and practical* teacher of the immortality of the soul' (§ 58, emphasis in original). Though at first revealed, this truth – like others, such as that of the Trinity – was later assimilated by reason: the revealed truths were 'so to speak, the result of the calculation which the mathematics teacher announces in advance, in order to give his pupils some idea of the direction of their thoughts' (§ 76). In a new, third phase, the 'time of fulfilment', rational moral consciousness will emancipate itself further and do good 'because it is good, not because it brings arbitrary rewards' (§ 85).

With this attempt to reconcile Christianity and enlightenment without threatening the autonomy of reason, Lessing offers the possibility of recognising the positive, historical form of religion as part of the history of reason, albeit of a history that reason gives *itself*. Although Lessing in this way wishes to accord revelation an independent status, so that it can withstand the scrutiny of critical reason, he simultaneously denies that it has a truth content of its own. In a fragment from the period 1777–78 he duly asserts 'that a revealed religion based on human testimony cannot possibly provide unquestionable assurance in any matter'.[118] Even though revelation remains a doubtful historical fact, it can possess a truth of its own provided that reason is able to embrace it, even if scripture contains contradictions. The essential point remains that revealed truths can be regarded neither as demonstrably correct nor as demonstrably false (these being the complementary errors of the orthodoxists and the critics), but they can be deemed to be in conformity with reason. Besides scripture, religion has an 'inner truth'.[119] It is an inner truth of reason that knows its own limits, but also – and perhaps chiefly – a truth of the 'heart', as Lessing maintains against Goeze: 'I said that, even if we were not in a position to counter all the objections which reason is so intent on making to the *Bible*, *religion* would nevertheless remain unshaken and unharmed in the hearts of those Christians who have attained an inner feeling for its essential truths.'[120]

118. Lessing, 'Womit sich die geoffenbarte Religion am meisten weiß, macht sie mir gerade am verdächtigsten', 643.
119. Lessing, 'Axioms', x, 139.   120. Lessing, 'A Parabel', 115.

When the censor prohibited the continuation of the polemic with Goeze, Lessing fell back on a different literary form – his 'dramatic poem' *Nathan the Wise* (1779) – to explain how this 'inner truth' could be conceived in the field of tension formed by enlightened reason, for which the 'religion of the forefathers' is only a historical inheritance, and this very inner feeling of faith. As already in his youthful comedy *The Jews* (1749), a respectable Jew – a clear antithesis to Shakespeare's Shylock, for instance – is the central character in the play, which thus denounces the customary anti-Semitic prejudices. Moreover, the famous parable of the three rings, which is central to the doctrine of toleration in the play, does not first express the crux of this doctrine. At several points in the play Lessing stresses that, although the differences dividing Christians, Jews and Muslims are not completely insignificant externalities which could simply be discarded, nevertheless all individuals *as human beings* are united by shared needs, feelings, moral standards and belief in a divinity. Thus, Nathan addresses the Templar: 'Are we our people? What is a people? Are Jew and Christian sooner Jew and Christian than man? How good, if I have found in you one more who is content to bear the name of man!'[121] And the end of the drama, when with Nathan's assistance the protagonists discover their complicated kinship relations, reinforces the point that Lessing's humanist message is one of 'fraternity' beyond all contingent historical differences. That the latter are nevertheless important is explained by the parable of the rings, which can be traced back to the late medieval period. The direct literary model for Lessing was the third story of the first day of Boccaccio's *Decameron* (1349–52) in which the Jew Melchisedech is forced by the sultan Saladin into saying which religion is the true one and avoids the question with the help of the parable of the three rings.

Lessing outlines the framing action of the parable in the same way. In order to trap Nathan, from whom he wants to borrow money, Saladin asks him directly which of the three religions, Judaism, Christianity and Islam, is 'the true one'. 'A man like you does not remain where chance of birth has cast him: if he so remains, it's out of insight, reasons, better choice' (Act 3, Scene 5). In his predicament, Nathan has the saving idea of the 'fairytale' which he relates to Saladin. The ring which was in the possession of the 'eastern man' was precious in itself but especially because it had 'the magic power that he who wore it, trusting its strength, was loved of God and men' (Act 3, Scene 7): it is the ring of the true revelation. It came to pass that the father, who loved his three sons, Moses, Jesus and Mohammed equally,

121. Lessing, *Nathan the Wise*, Act 2, Scene 5 (translation amended).

had two additional rings made in order to be able to bequeath a ring to each son without disappointing the others. These were such exact copies that the father himself no longer knew which was the real one. This is an important point in Lessing because in this way he not only distances himself from the (equally hallowed) story of the 'three deceivers' who only possessed false rings but also states that the true ring, which continues to exist, can no longer be identified even from the standpoint of the original revelation. From this perspective the three rings are *equivalent*, like the love of the father for each of his three sons. Therefore, a *different criterion* must be found in order to prove the authenticity of the ring; appealing to revelation is not sufficient.

To Saladin's objection to this equivalence thesis, Nathan revealingly responds that the positive religions differ from each other 'in all respects except their basic grounds. Are they not grounded all in history, or writ or handed down? – But history must be accepted wholly upon good faith. – Not so?' And having presented this historical relativisation of the religions, Nathan then proceeds to legitimise belief in the religion of 'our people'. 'How can I trust my fathers less than you trust yours? Or the contrary. – Can I demand that you should give the lie to your forebears so that mine be not gainsaid?' The adoption of the faith cannot be justified from the standpoint of the truth of revelation, though it can be on the basis of trust, 'good faith' – the belief that one is the descendant of the owner of the *genuine* ring.

But how can the truth be proven? According to the judge to whom the contending parties appeal, it cannot be demonstrated through controversy or conflict. Since the ring is supposed to make the one who possesses it 'loved of God and man', a contentious religion cannot be the true one; and if all three should lapse into dispute, the conclusion must be that the true ring has been lost and that all three are mere imposters. Therefore, the judge gives the following advice: in the firm belief that he possesses the true ring, 'let each aspire to emulate his father's unbeguiled, unprejudiced affection! Let each strive to match the rest in bringing to the fore the power of the opal in his ring! Assist that power with humility, heartfelt tolerance, benefaction, and profound submission to God's will!' Hence, the solution states that the rivalry between the three should remain, only that it should be a positive rivalry over the morally best and most reasonable religion – in other words, a *rivalry over toleration*. If this combination of faith, morality and reason should be achieved, one need not fear the judgement to be pronounced 'in a thousand thousand years' concerning who possessed the true ring.

The parable of the rings is an ingenious attempt to combine the particularity of the positive religions and belief in them with the universality of a common basis in a God, the father of all three religions, and of a universal human morality. Lessing in this way chooses the path of 'competitive unity' (see §6.2 above): only the outcome of a fair and tolerant contest will reveal who possesses the truth – though not of course before a human judge, a further guarantee of toleration. A precondition for this is the recognition of a shared religious root, however, a profound kinship which turns this rivalry into a family quarrel. From this perspective, all three particular religions are after all descendants of the *first* natural religion, to which they may have added many superfluous things. And the more they do this, the more they run the risk of deviating from the original truth. Of course, this first, revealed truth is no longer directly accessible to the later generations, but only with the help of reason. Thus, that religion will be the best which is the most reasonable and morally irreproachable. The aspects of rational religion and deism come to the fore once again in Lessing, for all his understanding for the 'religion of our forefathers'. And thus we read in an unpublished outline of a preface to *Nathan*: 'Nathan's opinions against all positive religion have always been mine. But here is not the place to justify them.'[122]

With this, however, the gulf with which Lessing repeatedly struggled opens up again. For, on the one hand particular faith is supposed to remain a belief in the revealed truth, in one's own ring, while on the other, mutual toleration is supposed to be justified in the eyes of the believer himself by the postponement owing to ignorance of the real ring and by the injunction issued by the common father to behave morally. Hence, this form of self-relativisation is a function of knowledge of the historical facticity of the evolution of religion, of the *unity* in the natural religion and of belonging to a family whose members are all loved equally by the father. As a result, the particularity of the individual religions is restricted as regards its legitimacy; according to the logic of this story, it would be better if they were all to converge once again on a shared point of unity, though without forgetting the deference implied by continuity with one's historical heritage. But since all 'religions of our forefathers' ultimately point back to one and the same father, toleration becomes contingent on how this family membership understands itself. The fundamental unity of all human beings as children of a single father gives rise to toleration; and the most reasonable form of rivalry among the three would be agreement upon and reversion to the original truth.

122. Lessing, 'Preface to *Nathan the Wise*', xix.

What unites is accessible to human reason; what separates is the historical faith. And inasmuch as this unifying element depends on shared belief in the single origin, Lessing presents this belief as the reasonable one. But, contrary to Lessing's intention, this remains a particular, humanist *faith*, which reason, on a critical examination, by no means enjoins. Hence, in the final analysis Lessing's toleration also rests on belief in the common rational origin of the three major religions. Moreover, even if Lessing does not go so far in this respect as Voltaire – who in attempting to overcome the mutual rejection which leads to intolerance also tries to overcome the objection component which is constitutive for toleration – nonetheless his conception of toleration remains captive to the deist-irenic notion of the unity of the 'reasonable' religions.

5. Even aside from whether Lessing wanted to erect a memorial to his friend Moses Mendelssohn with the figure of Nathan, it seems obvious to regard Mendelssohn's conception of religion and toleration as an exemplar of a *reasonable, positive religion*, given the ideal of the sons in the parable of the rings. Mendelssohn emphasises that, in order to promote truth and toleration, reason should not seek to transcend the differences between the religions by creating a unified religion of reason; it should only *enlighten* the individual religions and permit them to engage in a rivalry over which is the most reasonable. Mendelssohn's treatment of toleration is important in various respects: first for his attempt to interpret Judaism critically as a rational religion, which led Heine to dub him the reformer of Judaism;[123] second for the clarity of his attempt to demonstrate the rational superiority of the Jewish religion over Christianity; third for his plea that these differences should be relevant neither at the human-moral level nor at the political-civic level for the question of equal rights; and fourth for his keen awareness of the ambivalence of the concept of toleration. Mere 'indulgence' of the Jews, he argues, leaves them in a condition of subordination and deference, whereas Jews are all too often required to renounce their 'unenlightened' religion in order to achieve full civil rights.[124] Both, according to Mendelssohn, violate the 'rights of mankind':[125] mere permission toleration violates the rights to legal and social equal treatment, as does the connection between emancipation and assimilation, which, as Mendelssohn insightfully observes, often lurks behind a seemingly neutral call for the 'unification of religions'. Even

123. Heine, *Religion and Philosophy in Germany: A Fragment*, 94.
124. An exhaustive account of the complex situation of the Jews in the Enlightenment era is provided by Berghahn, *Die Grenzen der Toleranz*.
125. Mendelssohn, 'Preface to Manasseh Ben Israel, *Vindiciae Judaeorum*', 80.

deism is often a mask for Christian fervour. With Mendelssohn, therefore, the discourse of toleration enters a new, self-reflexive phase which identifies the dangers of authoritarian political toleration as well as the problem of deist-irenic conceptions of unification.

As Lessing's works demonstrate, it belongs to the logic of the Enlightenment to place the question of the emancipation, and not 'only' the toleration, of the Jews on the agenda and to expose the numerous religious-cultural prejudices against them which Mendelssohn eloquently attacks[126] (which is not to imply that the Enlightenment thinkers themselves overcame all prejudices against the Jewish religion, as is shown, among others, by the example of Voltaire). For the social situation in which the Jews found themselves even under the rule of the 'enlightened' Frederick II was marked by a policy of toleration as domination, of simultaneous inclusion and exclusion, of protection and simultaneous stigmatisation. They were carefully divided into groups of so-called 'protected Jews' who could attain or purchase various forms of legal protection and narrowly defined liberties, while alongside them were other groups, such as the 'tolerated Jews', who were tolerated because of certain social functions they performed and had to pay onerous taxes. Only from 1763 onwards, after he had become a respected author, did Mendelssohn belong to the 'extraordinary' protected Jews, though his protection did not extend to his entire family.[127] The Jews lived in narrowly circumscribed ghettos and led a largely isolated social and cultural existence. Therefore, Enlightenment thinkers like Mendelssohn who had succeeded in winning universal social recognition without having to renounce their Judaism faced a twofold task: on the one hand, to overcome exclusionary, stigmatising permission toleration and achieve legal and social emancipation based on an 'enlightened' spirit of toleration, and, on the other, to transform the self-understanding of the Jewish religion in the spirit of the Enlightenment, a goal which Mendelssohn sought to promote by translating the Pentateuch into German in order to reduce the authority of the scriptural scholars. Mendelssohn believed that genuine social toleration of the Jews which was no longer oppressive should not be purchased at the price of conversion, but he did believe that it required the development of reformed Judaism.

Mendelssohn had already acquired the reputation of a 'new Socrates' through his philosophical writings when he was drawn into the religious conflicts of his time, which he had previously avoided. It was the Swiss

126. *Ibid.* 82–3.   127. See Thom, 'Einleitung', 10; Berghahn, *Grenzen der Toleranz*, ch. 2.

deacon and Christian proselyte Johann Caspar Lavater, in his perplexity as to how such an educated man as Mendelssohn could remain a Jew, who in 1759 dedicated his translation of a book by Bonnet on the proofs of Christianity to Mendelssohn and in the preface challenged him either to refute these proofs or to convert.[128] Mendelssohn felt obliged to respond publicly to this challenge, but in his response made no secret of how much he disapproved of Lavater's unfair demand and of his breach of trust in referring to private conversations. Mendelssohn also emphasised how precarious it is for a merely 'indulged' minority to allow itself to be drawn into such disputes: 'I would like to be able to refute the contemptuous opinion people have of the Jew by virtuous behavior, not by polemics.'[129]

In his reply, Mendelssohn emphasises that the Jewish religion is a tolerant and reasonable religion. The exclusiveness of the revelation to a single people prevents proselytism (like that of the Christians), according to Mendelssohn, and he appeals to a particular interpretation of Maimonides[130] to argue that the path to blessedness is not confined to the adherents of his own religion:

> He who has not been born under our law may not live according to our law. We alone hold ourselves bound to observe these laws, and this cannot give our fellow men cause for anger . . . Oh! I could scarcely think that he who leads men to virtue in this life can be damned in the next, and I need not fear that any venerable college will trouble me because of this opinion.[131]

The decisive point is that Judaism is not based on the conviction that there can be no redemption outside of the Church; the belief in the revealed truth, because of its very exclusiveness, is a tolerant faith, especially as it agrees in principle with the 'natural religion' and 'natural morality'.[132] Hence, rational deism constitutes the universal core of the particular religion, whose revealed part claims only particular validity for one people.

Mendelssohn attempts to clarify this complex construction in further writings, in the preface to a translation of the plea by Manasseh ben Israel for the readmission of the Jews under Cromwell (originally written in 1656, translated into German in 1782) and, in particular, in his central work *Jerusalem oder über religiöse Macht und Judentum* (1783). The preface was written under the influence of two auspicious political developments, the toleration

---

128. See Bohn, 'Mendelssohn und die Toleranz', 28–30.
129. Mendelssohn, 'Open Letter to Deacon Lavater of Zurich', 3.
130. On this, see §6.4 above and (critical) Katz, 'Aufklärung und Toleranz'.
131. Mendelssohn, 'Open Letter to Deacon Lavater', 4.   132. *Ibid.* 5.

policy of the Austrian emperor Joseph II (see below §22.1), which granted the Jews certain improvements in their condition, and the more radical ideas concerning civic equality for the Jews in the work of the Prussian military councillor Christian Wilhelm Dohm, *Über die bürgerliche Verbesserung der Juden* (1781). In this work Dohm combined a sweeping self-condemnation of the Christian majority culture with a plea for the emancipation of the Jews and the hope for reconciliation among the religions.[133] Although Mendelssohn had his doubts about the latter, he placed Joseph II and Dohm alongside Reimarus and Lessing as models of a way of thinking and a policy which 'takes no notice of difference of doctrines and opinions, [and] beholds in man *man* only'[134] – and, one could add, in the citizen *the citizen* only. However, the condition for social emancipation, Mendelssohn argued, was the acceptance of toleration by religion, including the Jewish religion, and not only with regard to the separation between Church and State, but also to religious-ecclesiastical life itself: 'True divine religion needs neither fingers nor arms for its use; it is all spirit and heart.'[135] Accordingly, it not only has to liberate itself from all political-legal power, but must also respect the freedom of judgement in its own sphere and tolerate dissension. Hence, the true Church, contrary to Locke, does not have any right of excommunication, whether based on its self-understanding as a 'house of rational devotion' or from the perspective of the state, because excommunications all too often entail the loss of 'civil respectability'.[136] Therefore, the state should not tolerate the internal intolerance of the churches.

In *Jerusalem*, Mendelssohn presents his conception of toleration as it concerns the relation between faith and reason, on the one hand, and the separation between church and state, on the other. As regards the latter, he argues for a strict demarcation and complete civic equality for the different religions based on arguments from natural and contractual law; the right to impose subjective convictions coercively can be transferred neither to the state nor to the Church.[137] But since the state is confined to a purely external, legal regulation of individual actions and has no access to convictions, Mendelssohn nevertheless envisages a form of cooperation between state and religion, in that the religions, inasmuch as they harbour the core of natural religion and moral teaching, instil convictions and harmonise obedience to the law with obedience to God. In this sense the state needs the churches, which constitute (at least in part) the ethical-political foundation

---

133. See Detering, 'Christian Wilhelm von Dohm und die Idee der Toleranz'.
134. Mendelssohn, 'Preface', 80.   135. *Ibid.* 104.   136. *Ibid.* 113.
137. Mendelssohn, *Jerusalem*, vol. II, 61–70.

of the state.[138] This leads Mendelssohn to the issue of Bayle's paradox. He explicitly addresses the latter and states unequivocally, both here and in his preface, that neither 'fanatics' nor atheists can be tolerated under any circumstances: 'So every civil society will act rightly in not suffering fanaticism or atheism to strike root and spread about.'[139]

In the second section of his work, Mendelssohn again confronts a Christian counter-attack, in this case the objection of August Friedrich Cranz who sees in Mendelssohn's plea for a tolerant church and a tolerant Judaism a rapprochement with Christianity, a partial conversion. Although Mendelssohn admits that many of his 'brethren in the faith' think that a strict church government is imperative, in his opinion this is at odds with the core of Judaism. Mendelssohn explains even more clearly than in his response to Lavater that the comparison between the religions tends to favour Judaism on account of the differences between the Jewish and Christian conceptions of revelation. Whereas God revealed himself to the Jews only as a lawgiver with rules of behaviour addressed to this people alone, he communicated everything which is generally counted among the contents of natural religion not through the spoken or written word but through the reason in which all human beings share. Christianity, by contrast, believes that these contents, too, and additional 'truths of salvation', were revealed, and to the Christians alone as the representatives of all human beings. Thus, Judaism is essentially universal and tolerant, since the laws revealed to it in particular concern it alone. Christianity, by contrast, is at once universal, exclusive and superstitious because it assumes that God revealed all religion to the Christians by means of supernatural revelation with the aid of miracles.[140]

Mendelssohn sums up his thesis that Judaism does not vaunt an exclusionary 'revelation of religious proposition and tenets, necessary for the salvation of man'[141] and thus is free from all 'religious fetters', in a threefold distinction. It is composed in the first place of '*immutable truths* of God, of his government and providence, without which man can neither be enlightened nor happy'.[142] These truths are not revealed through the spoken or the written word but 'the Supreme Being revealed them to all rational beings, by *events* and by *ideas*, and inscribed them in their soul, in a character legible and intelligible *at all times*, and *in all places*'.[143] These truths are therefore shared by all reasonable religions and represent the basis for toleration. Of course, Judaism is aware, according to Mendelssohn, that these involve rational

138. *Ibid.* 46–7.   139. *Ibid.* 50.   140. *Ibid.* 89–90.   141. *Ibid.* 90.
142. *Ibid.* 150.   143. *Ibid.*

truths, not revealed truths. Second, the Jewish religion contains 'historical truths' concerning the covenant between God and the people of Israel which must be taken 'on trust'. Finally, third, there are particular laws and rules of life which God revealed to the Jews, not in his capacity as 'Creator and Preserver of the universe', but as 'king and ruler of that people' – and which are addressed as rules of conduct, in the form of ceremonial laws, to the descendants of this people. With the disappearance of the Mosaic constitution, in which state and religion were one, these rules have lost their coercive character entirely, so that today Christ's principle that one should give to Caesar what is Caesar's holds for the Jews, though they should simultaneously 'be constant' to the faith of their forefathers.[144]

Mendelssohn concludes on the basis of the argument for the separation of Church and State and for the advantages of Judaism as regards toleration that there cannot be any reasons, either from the perspective of natural law or from a religious perspective, to deny the Jews legal and social equality: '[I]f civil union cannot be obtained on any other terms than that of departing from the law, which we consider still binding upon us, we are heartily sorry for what we deem necessary to declare – that we will rather renounce civil union.'[145] Yet not only is the assimilation to Christianity too high a price to pay for civic emancipation; so, too, is the reconciliation of religions to which many Enlightenment thinkers aspired. Mendelssohn clearly recognised that this attempt to overcome fanaticism by negating religious differences could neither really transcend the differences between religious perspectives nor offer a realistic prospect of reconciliation. For a dominant faith would nevertheless secretly gain a foothold which would seek to dominate the others and would in this way stifle freedom of conscience. Then, Mendelssohn warned, fanaticism

> perhaps . . . puts on the mask of meekness, to impose upon you; feigns brotherly love, and cants general toleration, all the while that it is secretly forging the fetters in which it means to put human reason . . . Brethren! if it be genuine piety you are aiming at, let us not feign consonance, when manifoldness is, evidently, the design and end of Providence . . . For your happiness' sake, and for ours, *religious union is not toleration*; it is diametrically opposite to it.[146]

With this argument Mendelssohn opposes the view that a deist religion of reason could incorporate and supersede positive religions. However, this steadfast insistence on the 'religion of our forefathers' has been passed through the

144. *Ibid*. 161–2.   145. *Ibid*. 165.   146. *Ibid*. 168–71.

filter of the critique of religion of his time and can defend the faith he advocates only – entirely in Lessing's spirit – by appeal to its rational religious core and its dogmatic self-restriction. Thus, whereas Mendelssohn distances himself from the in its own way intolerant idea of overcoming religion through Enlightenment, he nevertheless remains captive to the idea of a natural religion of reason which forms the link between the religions. This in turn has two sides: on the one hand, it entails that the Enlightenment discussion is carried into the positive religions themselves, leading to the emergence of reform movements – for example the Jewish *Haskala*;[147] on the other hand, reason is in this way so closely associated with the ('purified') religion that new exclusions follow. It leads to the exclusion of those who do not recognise this connection and hence are open to the suspicion of overthrowing the moral foundations of society – hence the complementary condemnations of fanaticism and atheism to be found not only in Mendelssohn but also in Voltaire. With this, Mendelssohn also exhibits the Enlightenment paradox that *the same* insight into the universal human rationality which justifies toleration among human beings regardless of religious differences nevertheless leads to an inadequately justified restriction of the sphere of those who count as rational human beings and can be tolerated.

In 1783 Kant wrote in a letter to Mendelssohn that *Jerusalem* had made a deep impression on him, and by the same token reveals how much he interpreted Mendelssohn's work in accordance with deist-irenic Enlightenment ideas, in spite of Mendelssohn's insistence on the truth of Judaism:

> I regard this book as the proclamation of a great reform that is slowly impending, a reform that is in store not only for your own people but for other nations as well. You have managed to unite with your religion a degree of freedom of conscience that one would hardly have thought possible and of which no other religion can boast. You have at the same time thoroughly and clearly shown it necessary that every religion have unrestricted freedom of conscience, so that finally even the Church will have to consider how to rid itself of everything that burdens and oppresses conscience, and mankind will finally be united with regard to the essential point of religion. For all religious propositions that burden our conscience are based on history, that is, on making salvation contingent on belief in the truth of those historical propositions.[148]

---

147. See Schulte, *Die jüdische Aufklärung*.
148. Kant, Letter to Moses Mendelssohn, 204 (Ak. x: 347).

§21 Toleration, respect and happiness

1. Kant did not devote any single writing to toleration, yet the problematic runs through his whole work. In view of the complexity of Kant's philosophy, this can only be discussed briefly in what follows, with reference to (1) his moral philosophy, (2) his philosophy of religion and (3) his political philosophy.

Seen in the context of a reconstruction of the logic of a 'rationalisation of morality' which is a hallmark of the discourse of toleration, Kant's moral philosophy must be deemed the culmination of that development. For it is here that the idea of an *autonomous morality* comes to full fruition, a conception of morality that liberates itself from the traditional religious foundations which were increasingly called into question in the course of the controversies over toleration, culminating in Bayle's thesis that the connection asserted between the fear of God and morality does not exist. Kant's key idea is that the capacity for moral judgement and action must be located exclusively in the faculty of practical reason and that moral action presupposes not only moral autonomy – the freedom to determine one's will in accordance with self-imposed laws – but also the autonomy of morality from heteronomous determinations of its principle and 'incentives', be they doctrines of earthly happiness or heavenly blessedness.[149] A 'pure moral philosophy' must be explained in terms of principles of practical reason and its imperatives must be justifiable *without exception* because they claim *unconditional* validity. Thus, Kant links the question of which actions are morally justifiable with a procedure which tests their universalisability in such a way that no moral person serves 'merely as a means' to someone else's end. For, as Kant explains using the example of a false promise, 'he whom I want to use for my purposes by such a promise cannot possibly agree to my way of behaving toward him, and so himself contain the end of this action'.[150]

Here it will not be possible to examine in greater detail how an interpretation of the categorical imperative as turning on a procedure of reciprocal and universal justification coheres with the Kantian idea of testing the possibility or desirability of a universal law.[151] For the problem of toleration it is important to note that Kant brings the need to justify actions that impinge on the moral interests of others in the relevant ways to bear in such a way

---

149. See Forst, *The Right to Justification*, ch. 2.
150. Kant, *Groundwork of the Metaphysics of Morals*, 38 (Ak. IV: 429–30).
151. On this, see Forst, *Contexts of Justice*, chs. IV.2 and V.2.

that a restriction on individual freedom – for example, to exercise one's religion – which is grounded in religious terms counts as unjustified because it would mean restricting the autonomy of the person in favour of a unilateral positing of the truth. Thus, not only must happiness not serve as a motive for acting morally so as not to lead to heteronomous actions, but the happiness of a (responsible adult) person must not be made the end of the action (which affects this person in the relevant way) against his or her will either. Happiness is an object of irresolvable conflicts of opinion, 'not an idea of reason but of imagination':

> But it is a misfortune that the concept of happiness is such an indeterminate concept that, although every human being wishes to attain this, he can still never say determinately and consistently with himself what he really wishes and wills. The cause of this is that all the elements that belong to the concept of happiness are without exception empirical, that is, they must be borrowed from experience, and that nevertheless for the idea of happiness there is required an absolute whole, a maximum of well-being in my present condition and every future condition. Now, it is impossible for the most insightful and at the same time most powerful but still finite being to frame for himself a determinate concept of what he really wills here.[152]

Hence, the obligation to promote the happiness of others must take its cue from *their* conception of happiness, even though this need not be accepted as binding or represent the reason for moral action: 'It is for them to decide what they count as belonging to their happiness; but it is open to me to refuse them many things that *they* think will make them happy but that I do not, as long as they have no right to demand them from me as what is theirs.'[153] Neither the imposition of my notions of happiness on them nor, conversely, of theirs on me would be reconcilable with the dignity of a moral person endowed with reason and capable of self-determination. The dignity of the person can accordingly be understood in such a way that every moral person has a basic *right to reciprocal and general justification* of all action-legitimating norms that claim reciprocal and general validity.[154] The decisive point is, contrary to a 'liberal ethical' reading, that the respect for the autonomy of the other person is *not* grounded in the fact that this enables him or her to lead a 'good life', for then a specific conception of the good life would

---

152. Kant, *Groundwork*, 28 (Ak. IV: 418).
153. Kant, *The Metaphysics of Morals*, Doctrine of Virtue, 151 (Ak. VI: 388).
154. For a detailed account see below §30 and Forst, *The Right to Justification*.

once again be guiding. Rather, it constitutes respect for the dignity of the other person as a morally self-determining reasonable being who offers and receives reasons, whom one encounters *as an equal* and to whom one owes reasons for morally relevant actions. This is the substance of the requirement of respect for maturity (*Mündigkeit*) and the right to make an independent use of one's reason – not just in 'religious matters' – which for Kant is the hallmark of an enlightened morality. Hence, in the history of morality which I have reconstructed parallel to the history of toleration (without wishing to claim that this represents *the* history of morality) it is Kant who works out in detail what has emerged within the discourse of toleration, namely that human beings, apart from all of the particular ethical, and especially religious, identities which divide them, have a common identity that binds all human beings morally simply as human beings, namely that of being a moral person. This *persona* – the dignity of a justifying being – emerges from the more comprehensive ethical-religious horizons into the foreground and calls for morally justifying reasons that hold equally for human beings who have completely different convictions concerning the true and godly life.

The focus of Kant's emphasis on the 'purity' of morality is not so much on specifying the content of what is morally obligatory as on the motives for the action itself, on the 'incentives' (*Triebfedern*) of the good will. The latter must remain free from imperatives of prudence and all considerations of the good, whether one's own or that of others, which set other values or ends in the place of acting from duty, that is from respect for the dignity of the autonomous human being. Once action is determined by particular concerns, such as special ties, religious motives, ethical goals or the prospect of personal advantages – be it a reward in the afterlife or here on earth – the unconditional respect owed to others is relativised. Hence, it is the respect for the other as a human being and an 'end in himself' that underlies the Kantian idea of acting from duty and excludes other material factors. For the latter replace respect with something else, or at least qualify the required respect – for example in the light of a religious truth concerning the spiritual welfare of the other who must be saved. The respect which persons owe each other as autonomous members of a 'Kingdom of Ends' – a kingdom in which they mutually recognise and uphold each other's freedom by acting in conformity with laws which they could have given themselves as equals among equals – is an unrestricted respect subject to no further qualifications.[155] Hence, the

---

155. See Kant, *Groundwork*, 41–2 (Ak. IV: 433–4).

essential point of the Kantian conception of morality is precisely that other persons must be respected unconditionally as moral persons *without* any need of a further reason that refers to one's own well-being or that of the others or to the will of God, and thereby imports a relativising element into moral respect. Someone who asks for a further reason of this kind fails to understand the crux of morality, according to Kant.[156]

Hence, Kant was the first to develop a rational conception of morality which makes such a clear separation between norms and principles, which achieve categorical moral validity in virtue of being strictly justifiable and universalisable, and those systems of values or doctrines of happiness which do not and hence are unsuited to defining a universally binding morality – though they are suited to providing human beings with orientation in their lives. The morally good and the happy life are two different things according to Kant.[157] Moreover, among the conceptions which pervert morality by substituting something else for unconditional respect Kant counts those derived from anthropology as well as those based on theology.[158] Regardless of whether an ethical doctrine of happiness has a religious or a materialistic or some other basis, it cannot provide the reason for what is morally required. The categorical distinction between ethical doctrines and universally valid moral norms is developed explicitly here and it is of major importance for a moral-philosophical perspective on the discourse of toleration. For not only does it resolve Bayle's paradox in such a way that from now on there can be no doubt that morality does not need a religious justification; it also leads to a new perspective on the 'paradox of moral toleration' discussed at the beginning according to which it seems that toleration is morally required to condone what is immoral. Should the distinction outlined make it possible to differentiate normatively between the objection and the acceptance components of toleration, then this paradox could be resolved. Moreover, it would also be apparent how such a form of toleration could become a universally binding *requirement* of reciprocal respect – especially among persons whose ethical convictions not only diverge but contradict one another. This would also open up the prospect of a solution to the equally problematic 'paradox of drawing the limits' (see above §1). I will return to this in the second part of the book.

2. To be sure, in his conception of an autonomous morality Kant takes a further step in the direction of a 'Copernican turn' in the relation between

---

156. On this, see Forst, *The Right to Justification*, chs. 1 and 2.
157. See Kant, *Groundwork*, 48 (Ak. IV: 442).   158. See *ibid*. 22 (Ak. IV: 410).

morality and religion. Religion no longer grounds morality but, conversely, moral consciousness arrives of itself at the justification of a 'moral religion of reason'.

The path to this conception leads through the idea of a 'supreme good' in which each of the three critiques of the *finitude of reason* culminate in different ways. For Kant believes that they repeatedly run up against the problem of this limited, finite reason, namely how are 'supreme ends' which enable reason to 'find peace' conceivable from a *practical*, if not from a speculative, point of view. In short, how can we conceive of the practical freedom of human beings proven by experience such that a 'moral world' becomes possible – as a 'practical idea which really can and should exercise influence on the sensible world, in order to make it agree as far as possible with this idea'?[159] The two questions which concern the practical interest of pure reason – namely 'What should I do?' and 'What may I hope?' – should therefore be viewed in such a way that the answer to the first is: 'Do that through which you will become worthy to be happy', so that the second question asks: 'If I behave so as not to be unworthy of happiness, how may I hope thereby to partake of it?'[160] The question of hope, according to Kant, necessarily points to happiness but, given that morality is free from empirical motives of happiness, it can be referred only to the 'worthiness to be happy' as an answer to the first question, and hence it becomes the question of how this worthiness is possible, i.e. the question of a happiness that is 'proportionate' to morality. Such a 'system of self-rewarding morality'[161] is possible, according to Kant, only on the basis of the idea of a 'highest reason' which 'commands in accordance with moral laws, as at the same time the cause of nature'.[162] Thus, the two questions concerning morality and hope which are guiding for the practical interest of reason come together in an 'ideal of the highest good', in the ideal of a perfect harmony of the morally most perfect will with the 'highest blessedness' which is only conceivable through a divine 'author and regent' of the world. According to Kant, such a perfect world presupposes the idea of God and the idea of the life to come because we must regard it as a 'future life' in which nature and reason achieve a unity. Following Leibniz, whose influence on Kant is clear at this point, he calls this a 'realm of grace'.[163]

It is equally important to recognise that, on the one hand, this argument rests on the need of human beings as finite beings who hope and strive for

---

159. Kant, *Critique of Pure Reason*, 679 (B 836/A 808); the preceding quotations can be found on 673 (B 825–6/A 797–8) and 675 (B 830/A 802).
160. *Ibid.* 679 (B 836–7/A 809–10).   161. *Ibid.* 679 (B 837/A 809).
162. *Ibid.* 680 (B 838/A 810).   163. *Ibid.* 680 (B 840/A 812).

happiness, which Kant expressly allows in this context as a practical interest of reason, and that, on the other hand, it is precisely on account of the need to avoid reintroducing the empirical striving for happiness as the telos and motive of morality that Kant introduces the idea of 'worthiness to be happy', an idea which, as he says, 'strives upwards' and leads into the realm of the speculative:

> Happiness alone is far from the complete good for our reason. Reason does not approve of it (however much inclination may wish for it) where it is not united with the worthiness to be happy, i.e., with morally good conduct. Yet morality alone, and with it, the mere worthiness to be happy, is also far from being the complete good. In order to complete the latter, he who has not conducted himself so as to be unworthy of happiness must be able to hope to partake of it.[164]

Hence, at the limit of finite reason only the idea of a transcendent being can render the unity of the ends of morality and happiness intelligible. And *pace* Kant's insistence that in so arguing he remains within the architectonic of his critique of reason, he here switches to a 'moral theology' which, although not a purely speculative one, nevertheless leads from the simultaneously practical and speculative question 'What can I hope for?' into the realm of speculation, or at any rate into the realm of faith, although Kant regards it as a pure 'rational faith': the belief in the creator of a world in which moral action, though still categorically required, will not have been in vain. 'For this reason, again, *morals* is not properly the doctrine of how we are to make ourselves happy but of how we are to become *worthy* of happiness. Only if religion is added to it does there also enter the hope of some day participating in happiness to the degree that we have been intent upon not being unworthy of it.'[165]

This is reinforced in the *Critique of Practical Reason*, from which this quotation is taken. There Kant believes that he can resolve the 'antinomy of practical reason' only through the idea of worthiness to be happy, and although he describes the supreme good as the 'whole *object* of a pure practical reason' he does not allow that it is the '*determining ground*' of moral action since that would lead to heteronomy.[166] The idea of the supreme good arises from the 'need of reason'[167] (*Bedürfnis der Vernunft*) that happiness in

---

164. *Ibid.* 681 (B 841/A 813).   165. Kant, *Critique of Practical Reason*, 108 (Ak. v: 130).
166. *Ibid.* 91–2 (Ak. v: 109).
167. As Kant also puts it in 'What Does It Mean to Orient Oneself in Thinking?', 8 (Ak. VIII: 139), and 'On the Common Saying', 282 n. (Ak. VIII: 279–80 n.).

proportion to morality 'can at least be thought as possible'[168] even if it can neither be known nor realised. This is the decisive point for Kant: whereas the morality founded on human autonomy is strictly binding for reason, the faith corresponding to the postulates of the immortality of the soul and the existence of God is not, 'for there can be no duty to assume the existence of anything'. The 'morally necessary' assumption of the existence of God is thus merely a 'subjective' need, albeit also a need of consistent reason.[169] Thus, the talk of a 'moral proof of the existence of God' in the *Critique of Judgement*, which Kant proposes as a substitute for the traditional proofs of God's existence which he has demolished, means not only that this follows from the primacy of practical reason but also that morality is primarily an autonomous obligation of reason, whereas belief in a moral creator is merely an implication of the notion of happiness which can correspond to this morality:

> This proof. . . is not meant to say that it is just as necessary to assume the existence of God as it is to acknowledge the validity of the moral law, and hence that whoever cannot convince himself of the former can judge himself to be free from the obligations of the latter. No! All that would have to be surrendered in that case would be the aim of realising the final end in the world . . . Every rational being would still have to recognise himself as forever strictly bound to the precepts of morals; for its laws are formal and command unconditionally, without regard to ends.[170]

Here is not the place to discuss the implications of this constraint for the status of the 'supreme good' or whether it fits comfortably with the architectonics of Kant's philosophy, in particular of his moral philosophy – or whether it even could do so.[171] In short, with the idea of the supreme good Kant in my view attaches too much importance to a neither illegitimate nor necessary need of finite rational beings to lend their conduct a transcendent meaning from a moral-ethical point of view, in that he acknowledges this need as an interest of practical reason, albeit one which is not on the same level as that concerning the question of knowledge or morality. In this he follows the need to transgress the boundaries of finite reason a step too far when he regards the faith corresponding to the supreme good as something

---

168. Kant, *Critique of Practical Reason*, 99 (Ak. v: 119).   169. *Ibid.* 105 (Ak. v: 125–6).
170. Kant, *Critique of the Power of Judgement*, 316 (Ak. v: 450–1).
171. On this question I am in agreement with many authors who answer it in the negative, like Rawls, *Lectures on the History of Moral Philosophy*, 313–22, who sees no reason compatible with Kant's moral constructivism for associating the 'secular ideal' of a 'Kingdom of Ends' in this way with a 'rational religion'.

postulated by reason;[172] within the limits of finite reason it could at most be *permitted*.

Decisive for the issue of religious toleration is Kant's assumption that he has thereby discovered the kernel of a purely rational, moral faith, according to which morality remains valid for its own sake, though it nevertheless presents moral duties as 'divine commands' and affirms that the harmony between nature and morals corresponds to a 'kingdom of God'.[173] In the *Critique of Practical Reason* Kant intimates to what extent this approximates most closely to Christianity while nevertheless going beyond it (and all positive religion); this position is fully worked out in the treatise on *Religion within the Boundaries of Mere Reason* (1793). Notwithstanding the differences from the tradition of rational religion, which generally founds morality on natural religion as understood by deism, with this Kant becomes part of the tradition to the extent that he sees the possibility of overcoming the differences between the positive religions, and the associated intolerance, in a 'rationalisation' of religion which would ultimately treat all religious differences as *adiaphora*.[174]

Kant's rational religion not only is based on morality but, as far as its exercise is concerned, also essentially consists in a moral outlook, namely 'the heart's disposition to observe all human duties as divine commands'.[175] It aspires to create an 'ethical community', a 'people of God', which lives solely in accordance with ethical laws and could ultimately form the one 'true church', the Kingdom of God on earth – without any splits over doctrine or forms of worship.[176] In contrast to the 'pure religious faith' which does not admit any plurality, Kant can see in the diversity of positive religions that appeal to revelation nothing but a multiplicity of 'forms of faith', of mere 'ecclesiastical faiths', which are in essence morally indifferent:

> *Different religions*: an odd expression! just as if one could also speak of different *morals*. There can indeed be historically different creeds, [to be found] not in religion but in the history of means used to promote it, which is the province of scholarship, and just as many different religious books ... but there can be only one single *religion* holding for all human beings and in all times.[177]

172. In *Religion within the Bounds of Mere Reason*, 35 (Ak. VI: 6), Kant maintains that morality leads 'inevitably' to religion.
173. Kant, *Critique of Practical Reason*, 107 (Ak. V: 128–9).
174. As Kant argues in *The Conflict of the Faculties* (1798), 266 (Ak. VII: 40).
175. Kant, *Religion within the Bounds of Mere Reason*, 98 (Ak. VI: 84).
176. *Ibid.* 109–10 (Ak. VI: 98–101).
177. Kant, 'Toward Perpetual Peace', 336 n. (Ak. VIII: 367 n.).

According to Kant, therefore, it is 'more appropriate' to say that someone is 'of this (Jewish, Mohammedan, Christian, Catholic, Lutheran) *faith*, than: He is of this or that religion'.[178] 'Religious struggles', according to Kant, never concern the true core but only the 'ecclesiastical faith'. They involve one side declaring that their inessential doctrines and practices are religious necessities and that people of other faiths are unbelievers or heretics.[179] However, for Kant this does not mean that every ecclesiastical faith is equally inessential and unimportant. Since human beings demand 'something that *the senses can hold on to*' in matters of faith, so that ecclesiastical faith is to some extent unavoidable, that faith is to be preferred whose teaching can be harmonised most readily with the 'original' or 'natural' rational religion, while according due respect to the principle of the primacy of the moral interpretation of scripture, even if this seems 'forced'.[180] Nevertheless, one must avoid elevating an ecclesiastical faith which has only 'particular' validity to the status of the true religion:

> Thus, even though (in accordance with the unavoidable limitation of human reason) a historical faith attaches itself to pure religion as its vehicle, yet, if there is consciousness that this faith is merely such and if, as the faith of a church, it carries a principle for continually coming closer to pure religious faith until finally we can dispense of that vehicle, the church in question can always be taken as the *true* one.[181]

This rational religious conception not only sets narrow limits on the claim to validity of the religions of revelation in order to put an end to all religious disputes. It also leads Kant to a position which passes judgement on these religions, thus confirming Mendelssohn's apprehension that the rational religion of the Enlightenment not only calls the positive religions into question in principle but also involves new kinds of bias, as was shown by Lessing's work on the *Education of the Human Race*. Kant is even more clear than Lessing in preferring Christianity to Judaism in this context;[182] he regards the latter not as a moral faith but as a purely political one, as 'a collection of merely statutory laws', so that Judaism 'strictly speaking . . . is not a religion at all' or a church but rather constitutes a political community.[183] Only with Christianity does the history of the moral religion begin with its emphasis on inner belief that is the essence of a purely moral disposition which does

178. Kant, *Religion*, 116 (Ak. vi: 108).   179. *Ibid.* 117 (Ak. v: 108–9).
180. *Ibid.* 118 (Ak. v: 109–10).   181. *Ibid.* 112 (Ak. v: 115).
182. On Kant's negative stance on Judaism see Brumlik, *Deutscher Geist und Judenhaß*, ch. 1, and Berghahn, *Grenzen der Toleranz*, 206–21.
183. Kant, *Religion*, 130 (Ak. vi: 125).

what is good for its own sake. Yet Christianity subsequently became prey to the intolerant sectarianism of ecclesiastical faith, according to Kant; only in 'the present' is it possible to overcome these enmities and return to the 'true religious faith' which leads to a religious unification.[184] In his work *The Conflict of the Faculties* (1798) Kant developed this conception of unity in greater detail. And although he praises Mendelssohn for rejecting the unreasonable demand to convert, he nevertheless recommends the Jews to join a dogmatically expanded as well as purified Christianity, though the latter must then disappear as an ecclesiastical faith:

> The euthanasia of Judaism is pure moral religion, freed from all the ancient statutory teachings, some of which were bound to be retained in Christianity (as a messianic faith). But this division of sects, too, must disappear in time, leading, at least in spirit, to what we call the conclusion of the great drama of religious change on earth (the restoration of all things), when there will be only one shepherd and one flock.[185]

Thus, the humanist idea of religious unity through the reduction to a minimum of essential propositions returns in the guise of moral religion. Furthermore, in this way Kant, even though he consistently stressed the primacy of rational morality which is possible for and unites all human beings over any form of revelation, continues – at the level of the philosophy of religion, though not at that of the philosophy of morality or of law (as we shall see) – the tradition of attempts to overcome intolerance between religions (or 'forms of faith') by also transcending their differences, yet without being able to shake off the prejudices of their own Christian tradition. However much Kant polemicises in the name of toleration against the religious 'counterfeit service', which the ecclesiastical faith regards as the only true service;[186] however much he attacks the 'delusion of religion', superstition, 'priestcraft', 'fetish-faith' and dogmatic intolerance in the name of the 'true *enlightenment*';[187] however much he wants to strip the Christian religion of its claim to authority in favour of the 'natural religion'; he nevertheless singles out Christianity over the other religions because at its core it is seen as

---

184. *Ibid.* 135–6 (Ak. v: 131–2).
185. Kant, *Conflict of the Faculties*, 274 (Ak. vii: 53). Concerning the expression 'euthanasia of Judaism', it should be noted that Kant also uses this phrase elsewhere for the 'easy death' of a way of thinking, for example in the *Metaphysics of Morals*, 143 (Ak. vi: 378): '[I]f *eudaemonism* (the principle of happiness) is set up as the basic principle instead of *eleutheronomy* (the principle of the freedom of internal lawgiving), the result is the *euthanasia* (easy death) of all morals.'
186. Kant, *Religion*, 152 (Ak. vi: 153).   187. *Ibid.* 173 (Ak. vi: 179).

containing a religion of unconditional morality.[188] Thus, finally, although Kant privileges moral conscience as *'the moral faculty of judgement, passing judgement upon itself'*[189] over a conscience which posits itself as absolute in obeying divine commands (thus avoiding Bayle's problem of the 'conscientious persecutor'), he nevertheless represents moral consciousness again as religious, in spite of all references to the autonomy of morality. Hence, Kant initially detached the human being as an autonomous moral person from the religious horizon of both tradition and the Enlightenment only to relocate him in the reconstituted horizon of a universalistic religion which, on critical examination, is neither universalistic nor an implication of morality and, in its striving for unity, does not do sufficient justice to the problem of toleration.

3. However, Kant would not be Kant if he did not separate these reflections in the philosophy of religion on overcoming religious intolerance strictly from the moral-philosophical question of whether some form of religious constraint could be justified, as well as from the legal-philosophical question of whether there can be a place in the law for religion in general and for religious coercion in particular. We have already seen that he gives an unambiguous negative answer to the moral-philosophical question; and it likewise holds for his concept of law that it must remain completely free from notions of and aspirations to happiness. Thus, Kant can find the existence of a plurality of forms of faith regrettable from the standpoint of the philosophy of religion while welcoming it from that of the philosophy of law:

> On the subject of sectarianism . . . we are accustomed to say that it is desirable for many kinds of religion (properly speaking, kinds of ecclesiastical faith) to exist in a state. And this is, in fact, desirable to the extent that it is a good sign – a sign, namely, that the people are allowed freedom of belief. But it is only the government that is to be commended here. In itself, such a public state of affairs in religion is not a good thing unless the principle underlying it is of such a nature as to bring with it universal agreement on the essential maxims of belief, as the concept of religion requires, and to distinguish this agreement from conflicts arising from its non-essentials.[190]

Kant contrasts law as regards its content with all ethical doctrines of happiness and as regards its form with moral imperatives, because positive law

---

188. *Ibid.* 155–60 (Ak. VI: 157–63).   189. *Ibid.* 179 (Ak. VI: 186).
190. Kant, *Conflict of the Faculties*, 274–5 (Ak. VII: 52).

refers only to external actions and not to inner motivation. The essential difference between legality and morality resides less in the content of the respective laws than in the 'incentives': positive law is external coercive law and constrains freedom of choice, whereas moral laws determine the moral will.[191] Thus, the moral prohibition on coercion of conscience as unjustified – or, more generally, on unjustified restrictions on freedom between autonomous moral persons – is generally enshrined in law in such a way that the supreme principle of law already specifies that restrictions on freedom of choice are in need of universal justification: 'Right is therefore the sum of the conditions under which the choice of one can be united with the choice of another in accordance with a universal law of freedom.'[192] The foundation of this definition of law, according to which all forms of legal coercion are in need of reciprocal justification among free and equal persons, is a basic moral human right to freedom understood in terms of natural law: '*Freedom* (independence from being constrained by another's choice), provided that it can coexist with the freedom of every other in accordance with a universal law, is the only original right belonging to every man by virtue of his humanity.'[193] This is the implication for law of the (to use my terminology) moral basic right to justification, of the universal right to respect as an 'end in oneself', as a person whose human dignity is the unconditional basis of morality. Here once more it becomes apparent that the protection of individual freedom in no way rests on a conception of the good life for which – on a certain liberal conception – legally protected and socially enabled forms of autonomy would be necessary. Kant's conception is rather that it is already the inviolability of the person, of his or her dignity, that excludes interference by others – whether this helps the non-'violated' person to achieve a good life is a completely different matter. The barrier posed by the need to justify restrictions on freedom is raised earlier, according to Kant, and it is stricter than such an alternative conception of ethical autonomy allows:

> But the concept of an external right as such proceeds entirely from the concept of *freedom* in the external relation of people to one another and has nothing at all to do with the end that all of them naturally have (their aim of happiness) and with the prescribing of means for attaining it; hence too the latter absolutely must not intrude in the laws of the former as their determining ground.[194]

191. Kant, *Metaphysics of Morals*, 21–2 (Ak. VI: 220).   192. *Ibid*. 24 (Ak. VI: 230).
193. *Ibid*. 30 (Ak. VI: 237).   194. Kant, 'Theory and Practice', 290 (Ak. VIII: 289).

Against the background of the original right of human beings and the corresponding basic definition of law, Kant proceeds to formulate different conceptions of the 'person', thereby systematising a series of attempts at differentiation undertaken over the history of the discourse on toleration.[195] For in addition to the autonomous *moral person* who acts in accordance with the categorical imperative and is owed moral respect, Kant distinguishes three 'a priori principles' in the 'civil condition', and correspondingly three further conceptions of the person, namely an ethical, a legal and a political conception. The three principles are: '1. The *freedom* of every member of the society as a human being. 2. The *equality* of every member as a *subject*. 3. The *independence* of every member of a commonwealth as a *citizen*'.[196] The first means: 'No one can coerce me to be happy in his way (as he thinks of the welfare of other human beings); instead, each may seek his happiness in the way that seems good to him.'[197] According to Kant, this excludes a 'paternalistic government' in which the subjects are treated as 'minor children'. The legal autonomy of the person is thus protected from outside interference, and law functions on the inside as a 'protective cover' for the *ethical person* to live her life in accordance with the conceptions of the good which seem right to her, whatever her reasons may be. Thus, the freedom of the ethical person is secured and with it the possibility of living an autonomous and possibly good life – through a law which is ethically agnostic and is based exclusively on the principle of reciprocal and public justification. Correspondingly, the second principle, equality, signifies that persons as *legal persons*, as 'subjects' who are subjected to the law, stand under laws which hold in the same way for everyone and place the same restrictions on everyone's freedom of choice regardless of their social status.

Finally, the third principle spells out the role of the person as a citizen, as a 'colegislator'.[198] This follows from the fact that, according to the principle of right, only 'general laws' can be laws of freedom, and they can be general only if they are in accordance with the 'united will of the people'.[199] The citizen can be politically autonomous – and here Kant takes up Rousseau's notion of autonomy – only in this role because, as a matter of principle, he obeys only laws that he has given himself, that is no other law 'than that to which

---

195. On the following fourfold differentiation of conceptions of the person and conceptions of autonomy, see Forst, *Contexts of Justice*, in particular ch. v.2 and v.3, and 'Political Liberty', *The Right to Justification*, ch. 5.

196. Kant, 'Theory and Practice', 291 (Ak. VIII: 290); see also *Metaphysics of Morals*, 91 (Ak. VI: 314).

197. Kant, 'Theory and Practice', 291 (Ak. VIII: 290).   198. *Ibid.* 294 (Ak. VIII: 294).

199. Kant, *Metaphysics of Morals*, 91 (Ak. VI: 313).

he has given his consent'[200] – 'for it is only to oneself that one can never do wrong'.[201] As an active member of the polity, as a voting citizen, the person is a *citoyen*, not just a *bourgeois* (like legal persons): He is simultaneously author and addressee of the law. Hence, the generally and reciprocally binding law can be legitimate only if it was agreed upon in procedures of general and reciprocal justification; the 'mere idea of reason', 'which, however, has its undoubted practical reality', states that 'the touchstone of any public law's conformity with right' is its ability to command general agreement. In short, just as the moral principle which makes it a duty to justify morally relevant actions and norms becomes the foundation of the original right to freedom, in the same way it here becomes the foundation of the requirement to justify coercive laws in the medium of 'public reason'.[202] All forms of coercion are in need of justification towards those who are subjected to coercion, and it depends on the nature of the norms in question whether the form of justification required is a moral or a political one.[203]

This synopsis of Kant's arguments reveals that Kantian moral philosophy as well as his philosophy of religion and his political philosophy provide arguments for religious freedom. Freedom of religion is a direct expression of respect for the dignity of the person. Thus, toleration in accordance with the *respect conception*, which is fully developed for the first time in Kant, is required primarily for *moral* reasons. But it also follows from the principle of *rational religion* that the latter should gain acceptance only by 'rational means', without the use of force. Furthermore, the *legal principle* entails that restrictions on freedom are in need of reciprocal justification and that conceptions of happiness do not provide any legitimate grounds for coercion. And, finally, the corresponding *political principle* implies that all coercive laws must spring from 'public reason', so that the latter must itself already be formulated in pluralistic terms.[204] In all of this the basic premise remains that persons have a right to justification which cannot be annulled by a 'higher truth'. In this way, Kant, if we compare his approach to that of Bayle with which it has many affinities, raised the latter's position to a new normative level. Where he seriously deviates from Bayle, however, is in his conception of what the finitude of reason means in questions of religion. Here two

---

200. *Ibid.* 91 (Ak. VI: 314).   201. Kant, 'Theory and Practice', 295 (Ak. VIII: 294–5).

202. On this, see Brandt, 'Freiheit, Gleichheit, Selbständigkeit bei Kant', 115 and Maus, *Zur Aufklärung der Demokratietheorie*, 87 and 326.

203. I will return to this in §30.

204. That this implies an argument for toleration as a means of fostering an open, deliberative system of communication is stressed by O'Neill, 'Practices of Toleration', and Bohman, 'Reflexive Toleration in a Deliberative Democracy'. On this, see below §25 and §37.

paths of the Enlightenment diverge, the Baylean path which envisages a clear (though not absolute) separation between reason and faith, and the Kantian path which aspires to an extensive abolition of religious difference under the primacy of practical reason. As regards the issue of toleration, Bayle's path is preferable, being the more consistent for a conception of finite reason, as it leads at the epistemological level to a conception of reasonable differences which nevertheless *cannot* be overcome by rational means.

Still, Kant's decisive advance over Bayle consists in his translation of the moral principle of justification into political terms, thereby transposing the respect conception from the horizontal, civil level to vertical, political toleration – which then can no longer be called 'vertical'. If reciprocal and general justification is required between moral persons in order to justify morally relevant actions, it is also required among citizens who must decide which positive laws should regulate their common social life. Then toleration is not just a *civil*, interpersonal virtue but a *political* virtue of the democratic lawgivers who respect one another as free and equal; then the laws which are justified in the medium of public reason achieve the level of toleration and freedom implied by the limits of justification. In the exchange of positions and reasons, citizens recognise what they *cannot* force each other to do with good reasons that can stand the test of reciprocity. As a result, they will pledge one another fundamental freedoms in the form of basic rights which safeguard freedom of choice, and they will recognise that *reciprocal* toleration is an important virtue of just lawgivers *and* of reasonable legal subjects who heed these laws, and that the *one-sided*, authoritarian permission conception of toleration, which Mendelssohn also criticises, is thereby overcome.

Even if this falls short of the democratic ideal, Kant – in an allusion to Frederick the Great – can view it as an advance and as a hallmark of the 'enlightened' prince if the latter regards it as his duty as 'not to prescribe anything to human beings in religious matters but leave them complete freedom' and 'even declines the arrogant name of tolerance'.[205] Hence, it is as correct to assert that the late eighteenth-century Enlightenment sought to *overcome authoritarian toleration* (in the sense of the permission conception) and to replace it with the recognition of equal liberty rights as it is false to maintain that this renders *toleration* (in the sense of the respect conception) obsolete as a *civil and political virtue*. Goethe expresses the criticism of the permission conception of toleration which was typical of the time when he asserts (as already quoted): 'Tolerance should be a temporary attitude

---

205. Kant, 'What Is Enlightenment?', 21 (Ak. VIII: 40).

only; it must lead to recognition. To tolerate means to insult.'[206] Yet it is clear that if one does not want to replace the objection component which is constitutive for toleration entirely by mutual esteem (or by indifference), one must find a non-hierarchical form of mutual toleration that is not an 'insult' but represents a specific form of 'recognition'.

A brief examination of the absolutist toleration policy under the Austrian emperor Joseph II and the attempts in the American and French revolutions to go beyond such an 'arrogant' policy of toleration will reveal how the questions of toleration and of freedom of religion were redefined in these contexts and how the revolutionary idea of a form of political and religious civic freedom which is prior to the state and underlies it took shape.

§22 From toleration to human rights – and back

1. The two most prominent examples of the toleration policy of 'enlightened absolutism' are Prussia under Frederick the Great and his successor Frederick William II and the Habsburg monarchy under Joseph II. In both realms, which were at war with each other, important steps were taken during the 1780s towards legally guaranteeing a limited form of toleration. In this regard Brandenburg-Prussia was able to build on a tradition of relaxing the *jus reformandi* extending back to the seventeenth century – an example being the Edict of Potsdam of 1685 admitting the Huguenots – and in Frederick II had a king who regarded himself as standing above the confessions, not only in a political but also in a religious sense, and who held that 'everyone should find salvation in his own fashion'– which does not mean that, in his religious policies, Frederick II did not studiously avoid excessively weakening the position of Protestantism.[207] Under Frederick William II, Woellner's 1788 edict concerning 'the Religious Constitution of the Prussian State' granted 'all three main confessions of the Christian religion' – namely, the Reformed, the Lutheran and the Roman Catholic – equal status 'in their prior condition' and called for toleration, understood as freedom from coercion of conscience, for the remaining 'sects and religious parties', 'so long as each quietly fulfils his duties as a good citizen of the state'.[208] Hence, whereas the three main confessions enjoyed privileged public recognition, the others were granted at least freedom of belief and of religious observance (within

206. Goethe, *Maxims and Reflections*, 116 (translation amended).
207. See Rudolph, 'Öffentliche Religion und Toleranz'. The quotation from Frederick II appears on 222.
208. Quoted in Hunter, 'Kant's *Religion* and Prussian Religious Policy', 6–7.

certain limits). However, this edict was accompanied by extensive official censorship designed to ensure that the Christian doctrine would not be watered down by 'unrestrained thought'.[209] By contrast, the 'General State Law for the Prussian States' ('Prussian Civil Code') of 1794, for which Carl Gottlieb Svarez was largely responsible, imposed universal toleration of all religious parties and opposed censorship, but maintained the distinction between 'the churches expressly adopted by the state' enjoying the rights of 'privileged corporations' and merely 'tolerated' churches.[210]

The toleration policy of Joseph II is more informative than its Prussian counterpart for an analysis of the ambivalences of toleration as a progressive strategy of absolutist rule. It exhibits the role played by toleration in the 'enlightened' thought of a ruler who had learned the lesson of the *politiques* and viewed toleration as a rational form of the exercise of power, as a form of *disciplining by granting freedom* – a further stage in the history of the rationalisation of power. The conflict with his mother Maria Theresa – who during her reign from 1740 to 1780 presided over an empire marked profoundly by the Counter-Reformation in which she sought to impose the principle of a single religion in a single kingdom with the classical coercive methods[211] – arose during their joint regency. It should be seen as a personal and simultaneously as a political-religious conflict between two paradigmatic understandings of political power. The dispute over toleration broke out in 1777 when thousands of Protestants who had secretly converted were prompted to identify themselves by the issuance of a false toleration decree in Moravia. The empress first sought to reconvert them by force and then to resettle them forcibly in Hungary, which led to widespread protests and violent uprisings. This led Joseph II to call upon his mother to adopt a policy of toleration:

> If one does not accept this method, not only will one save no more souls; on the contrary, one will lose far more useful and necessary bodies . . . But if, in order that their souls shall not be damned forever after death, one expels excellent workmen and good subjects during their lifetime, and thereby deprives oneself of all the profit that one

---

209. Kant also famously fell victim to this censorship, as he relates at the beginning of his treatise on the *Conflict of the Faculties*, 239–43 (Ak. VII: 5–11). In this work, we also find the distinction between sects which are merely tolerated and protected as opposed to others which are officially recognised as churches, where 'in religious matters the only thing that can interest the state is: to what doctrines it must bind teachers of religion in order to have useful citizens, good soldiers, and, in general, faithful subjects' (*ibid.* 281n. (Ak. VII: 60n.)).
210. Quoted in Rudolph, 'Öffentliche Religion und Toleranz', 236.
211. See Karniel, *Die Toleranzpolitik Kaiser Josephs II.*, ch. 1.

could derive from them, what power is one arrogating to oneself
thereby? Can one extend it so far as to pass judgment on Divine mercy,
to save men against their will, to command their consciences?[212]

Here Joseph introduces a mixture of political and economic-pragmatic and
fundamental considerations concerning the limits of political power to persuade his mother, who responded by accusing him of religious indifference
and of destroying the monarchy:

> [T]o my great grief I have to say that there would be nothing more to
> corrupt in respect of religion if you intend to insist on that general
> toleration of which you maintain that it is a principle from which you
> will never depart. I hope all the same . . . that God may protect you
> from this misfortune, the greatest which would ever have descended
> on the Monarchy. In the belief of having workers . . . you will ruin your
> State and be guilty of the destruction of so many souls.[213]

Maria Theresa refused to accept the separation between the role of the subject
and a person's affiliation to a particular religion, which Joseph defended
against his mother as the sole means of holding on to the Protestants as
subjects. This is why for her equal political treatment could count as nothing
other than religious indifference. As she put it in another letter:

> Toleration, indifference are precisely the true means of undermining
> everything, taking away every foundation; we others will then be the
> greatest losers . . . This has ruined everything. What restraints are left
> for that sort of person? . . . I am speaking only in the political sense, not
> as a Christian; nothing is so necessary and salutary as religion. Will you
> allow everyone to fashion his own religion as he pleases? No fixed cult,
> no subordination to the Church – what will then become of us?[214]

On the death of his mother in 1780, Emperor Joseph II was free to implement his policy of toleration, which he viewed as the only way to achieve civil
peace, not least because of the external threat posed by Prussia. He launched
comprehensive reforms throughout his empire which not only concerned
religion, though toleration was a central field of this reform. In October 1781
he issued his famous 'Patent of Toleration' (or, more exactly, his patents of
toleration, since the provisions for the individual parts of the empire varied

---

212. Quoted from Macartney (ed.), *The Habsburg and Hohenzollern Dynasties in the Seventeenth and
     Eighteenth Centuries*, 149–53 (translation amended).
213. *Ibid.*   214. *Ibid.*

somewhat)[215] – an exceptional document of an 'enlightened' permission conception of toleration.[216]

The text reveals that the accusation of indifference was wide of the mark. For not only did it prescribe the dominant position of the Catholic religion, which alone enjoyed the right of 'public exercise of religion'; in addition, explicitly appealing to 'true Christian tolerance', only three confessions – the Lutheran, the Reformed and the Greek Orthodox – were tolerated in their 'private exercise'. As a motive for granting this toleration, which did not involve a long-term guarantee, the patent cited the 'harmfulness of all coercion of conscience' and the 'great utility' of toleration – revealing in turn the mixture of strategic-pragmatic and Christian motives which was a hallmark of Joseph's policy. Only the 'non-Catholic subjects' who belonged to these three confessions, but no other sects – with the exception of the Jews who, in various toleration patents from 1781 onwards, were granted an improvement in their status by comparison with the suppression under Maria Theresa, though only to a very limited extent and with substantial financial impositions[217] – were permitted (contingent on certain conditions relating to numbers of members) to erect houses of prayer and schools, though the churches could not have 'any chimes, bells, or towers and no public entrance from the street'. The obligatory 'surplice fees' had to be paid to the Catholic priests as before and, in the always complicated issue of mixed marriages, children of a Catholic father had to be raised as Catholics, whereas if the mother was Catholic only the daughters had to be so raised. As regards civil rights, it is significant that these 'non-Catholics' (*Accatholici*) could acquire certain civil and political rights provided that their 'Christian and moral conduct of life' militated in favour of granting them these rights as individuals in the form of a dispensation. Hence, these individuals were legal subjects and citizens only *dispensando*, without any claim to this status by right. In addition, a 1782 decree laid down that anyone who wanted to abandon Catholicism had to submit to six weeks of religious instruction – in part at his own expense – during which Catholic clergymen attempted to prevent this apostasy.

Joseph II's Patent of Toleration can be regarded as a document of 'enlightened absolutism' in various respects. First, the emperor assumed that *coercion of conscience* was incompatible with domestic peace and that it was

---

215. On this, see Barton, 'Das Toleranzpatent von 1781'.
216. Quoted from the reprint of the facsimile, *ibid.* 199–202.
217. See Karniel, *Die Toleranzpolitik Kaiser Josephs II.*, ch. 5.

moreover unchristian,[218] but he recognised, second, that *influencing conscience* might very well succeed in buttressing the dominance of the main confession. Third, Joseph was convinced that no other measures would be capable of consolidating his role, because the repressive mechanisms on which his mother still relied had proven inadequate. Only toleration was able, through a limited and clearly circumscribed grant of liberty, to generate a disciplining effect which would turn those who were tolerated into 'good subjects'. Since they owed their liberties to the emperor who protected them from the Catholic Church and simultaneously protected the Catholic Church from them, they would prove loyal to him provided that they did not become too strong (something which likewise had to be prevented). Therefore, the connection between *freedom* and *disciplining* typical of the permission conception, as well as that between *inclusion* and *exclusion*, comes to light here; for although the 'Accatholici' acquired certain rights, this did not lead to their emancipation. Nevertheless, fourth, they enjoyed a privileged status by comparison with the non-tolerated sects, which continued to suffer complete exclusion. Thus, 'Josephinism' involved a complex web of power in which all threads converged on the emperor, although he no longer ruled by direct repressive measures but by placing controls on freedom.[219] Toleration was supposed to enable the emperor, who strove to increase his control over the population continually and even had a plan to conduct a file on every citizen,[220] to consolidate and extend this mode of exercising power.[221]

In this way, toleration remained an ambivalent concept which led to completely different and, as we shall see, conflicting developments not confined to the twofold rationalisation of power and morality. It also left room within the discourse of power and toleration for a ruler who simultaneously espoused 'enlightened' principles (in the conflict with his mother) and used them to stabilise his rule and to exercise control over his subjects. This, too, is part of the larger picture of toleration in the Enlightenment.

218. This was also why Joseph II enjoyed the support of parts of the Catholic clergy who understood toleration, on the one hand, as an expression of 'brotherly love', but also simultaneously as the best way to preserve Christian unity and if possible to lead those of different confessions back to the Catholic Church. In this spirit Bishop Johann Leopold Hay pleaded for compliance with the Patent of Toleration in a 'pastoral letter to the clergy of the diocese of Königgrätz'.

219. This facet of 'enlightened absolutism' fits with Foucault's analysis (in 'Governmentality', 96–7) of a 'patient' government which seeks to exert a form of control over the population – a particular form of *government by granting freedom*.

220. Vocelka, 'Enlightenment in the Habsburg Monarchy', 202.

221. On the foreign and domestic political opposition to this policy, which ultimately led to the retraction of many Josephinist reforms, see Karniel, *Die Toleranzpolitik Kaiser Josephs II.*, ch. 6.

2. As the analysis of the Dutch and English revolutions revealed, the notion that human beings existed in a condition of natural freedom prior to entering the state – a freedom which the state not only must not violate but which grounds the state in the first place – did not first emerge in the context of the two major revolutions of the eighteenth century, the American and the French. Yet it is there that we first encounter a declaration of these rights as *human rights* which, as enshrined in the constitution established by the citizens themselves, become positive law binding on lawmakers. In this way, the right to justification demanded by the citizens from the monarch, who is seen as illegitimate, exercises immediate effects at the political level. No longer are particular rights and liberties claimed as something to be conferred by the ruler; rather the place of the ruler is assumed by the sovereign citizens who are now themselves the ones who pledge each other certain liberties. Their fundamental freedom consists in legally and politically recognising and guaranteeing, independently of external domination, precisely those liberties which are necessary for a just social order. For the issue of toleration this means in principle that the permission conception is replaced by a political respect conception. For it is now the mutual respect among citizens of different religious persuasions that leads to the guarantee of religious freedom as a basic right, which the citizens oblige themselves to respect as legislators and as legal subjects. With the traditional permission conception in mind, therefore, one can say that the authoritarian – in Kantian terms 'arrogant' – form of toleration is overcome by the declaration and codification of human and civil rights; with regard to the respect conception, however, it is correct to say that the question of toleration shifts to the level of the relations between the citizens in their role as legislators and subjects of law and that the concept undergoes a corresponding transformation, but without being overcome.

The role played by the issue of religious freedom in the revolutionary political upheavals of the eighteenth century should not be underestimated, in two respects in particular. First, as we have already seen, for many natural law theorists the idea of 'natural' freedom had religious roots. For then the power to assert oneself against the political sovereign was founded on the idea that individuals are not at the disposition of the state because they are the *property of God*, as Locke had put it.[222] In the light of a 'revolutionary' reading of the two-kingdoms doctrine opposing Luther's interpretation, the

---

222. Locke, *Two Treatises of Government*, vol. II, §6; see my discussion of Locke above (§17.4)
    together with those of the monarchomachs (§14.1) and of the Levellers (§15.2).

state oversteps the limits laid down by God when it infringes upon the rights of individuals stemming from their God-given natural freedom, and their duty towards God to preserve themselves.

From this it follows, second, that the right to religious freedom has a special place in this argument because it is the right in which the construct of the 'unfree free conscience', which is beholden to God, and hence is politically sacrosanct, plays a central role. Hence, as many authors stress, it *cannot* be transferred to the sovereign at all, whether the latter be a king or a democratically constituted sovereign. This right duly acquires a prominent place in the declarations of human and civil rights, though as we shall see it was the focus of a major controversy in the French National Assembly.

At the same time, it is important to distinguish between the two points of view mentioned. For although it is right to emphasise the religious components of the justification of human rights, especially in the context of the American Revolution, this does not mean that the right of freedom of conscience or religion is a kind of 'original right' and a model for all of the other rights.[223] For what was demanded was not only, or chiefly, this right, but all of the rights to *life, liberty and estate* (Locke), which together followed from the idea of dependence on God as his creatures. This included the right to political self-determination which was affirmed in the Dutch Revolt and the English Revolution by appeal to the same natural right-based justification, namely as a *birthright* (in the language of the Levellers). For claiming just religious freedom as a natural right could have remained compatible with an absolutist political system, but not religious freedom as a component of a more comprehensive political freedom. And it was only the latter claim that could develop a revolutionary force.

Moreover, as the discussion of Kant and his conception of the moral origin of the (in my terminology) right to justification which ultimately has powerful effects at the political level revealed, there is no reason to infer from the tradition of religious natural law-based justifications of human rights that these rights can *only* be justified in this way, or at least cannot be justified *without* a religious component.[224] For, as we have seen, a religious justification of human rights and human dignity always involves the danger of running up against certain limits of the religious perspective in ways which

223. This is the problem with Jellinek's important analysis of the religious roots of the Declaration of the Rights of Man and of Citizens in *The Declaration of the Rights of Man and of Citizens*, 63ff.
224. On this, see the discussions in Böckenförde and Spaemann (eds.), *Menschenrechte und Menschenwürde*, especially Spaemann, 'Über den Begriff der Menschenwürde', who argues that 'atheism definitively strips the idea of human dignity of its justification' (313).

are incompatible with the meaning of these rights – especially with respect to those who do not share this religious perspective on human beings, and who thus appear to be (potentially) beyond the scope of toleration because they seem to be insufficiently morally trustworthy. This danger is the basic starting point for Bayle's argument for the separation between religion and morality. Tracing the logical implications of this idea, Kant argues for seeing the finite rational human being *without* any further transcendent ground as the basis of the unconditional duty of mutual respect and of the validity of reciprocally justified and recognised norms and rights. Moreover, this is not only possible but also necessary according to Kant. For the question concerning a further reason for human dignity, as well as the answer in terms of human beings' nature as creatures of God, *relativises* human dignity insofar as 'humanity' alone is treated as an insufficient reason for respect – as though reverence for God were necessary in order to respect human beings and God's dignity is what one should ultimately respect. To ask for a further reason for morality apart from regarding oneself and others as human moral persons is to pose one question too many from this perspective (and entails the danger mentioned). If one nonetheless insists on posing it, one must at any rate respect the primacy of morality to such an extent that any answer that goes beyond morality does not undermine the categorical validity of the duty of respect. In this way, natural law becomes a secular 'rational law'. This idea is most apparent in Kant but it also has deep roots in the tradition of natural law, if one thinks for instance of Grotius's remark (see above §14.2) that natural law would still hold even if God did not exist. Viewed in this light, the history of toleration is also the history of the increasing autonomy of morality.

3. Nowhere did the religious and revolutionary pathos of a declaration of human rights find stronger expression than in the declaration of independence proclaimed by the Second Continental Congress meeting in Philadelphia on 4 July 1776, which was in large part the work of Thomas Jefferson: 'We hold these truths to be self-evident, that all men are created equal, that they are endowed by their Creator with certain unalienable Rights, that among these are Life, Liberty and the pursuit of Happiness.' The influence of Locke's theory[225] is apparent not only in these formulations, in spite of the

225. Recent work in the history of ideas has correctly pointed out that there were a whole range of other influences on the thought of the founding fathers besides Locke, for example ideas rooted in classical republicanism; nevertheless the theory of natural law, which found paradigmatic expression in Locke, remains central. On this, see the balanced treatment in Young, *Reconsidering American Liberalism*, chs. 2–4.

fact that 'estate' is replaced by 'pursuit of happiness', but also in the conclusion: 'That to secure these rights, Governments are instituted among Men,
deriving their just powers from the consent of the governed.' This natural
law-based logic led the founding fathers to conclude that English despotism
had to be cast off and that the colonies had the right to declare themselves
'free and independent states'. In keeping with this, the Congress had called
upon the individual states to adopt constitutions of their own, which they
proceeded to do one after the other.

The first state, Virginia, had already published such a constitution in 1776,
preceded by a Bill of Rights (authored by George Mason) which became the
model not only for analogous declarations by individual states but also for
the amendments to the new constitution of the United States (1791) and,
finally, for the French declaration of human and civil rights.[226] It opens with
the declaration:

> That all men are by nature equally free and independent, and have
> certain inherent rights, of which, when they enter into a state of
> society, they cannot, by any compact, deprive or divest their posterity;
> namely, the enjoyment of life and liberty, with the means of acquiring
> and possessing property, and pursuing and obtaining happiness and
> safety.[227]

And following this line of argument concerning the rights which are inalienable in principle, it states concerning freedom of religion:

> That religion, or the duty which we owe to our Creator, and the
> manner of discharging it, can be directed only by reason and
> conviction, not by force or violence; and therefore all men are equally
> entitled to the free exercise of religion, according to the dictates of
> conscience; and that it is the mutual duty of all to practise Christian
> forbearance, love, and charity towards each other.[228]

Yet the latter clause reveals once again the precarious character of a religious justification of religious freedom. It assumes that anyone who claims

---

226. This is stressed in particular by Jellinek in *The Declaration of the Rights of Man and of Citizens*,
though he underestimates other influences on the French authors, especially that of Rousseau.
Uncontroversial, however, is the major influence of the American declarations, especially that
of Virginia; see also Sandweg, *Rationales Naturrecht als revolutionäre Praxis*, ch. 1 (especially 1.2
on the 'American party', Lafayette, Brissot, Mirabeau and Condorcet). Gauchet, by contrast,
highlights the exceptional features of the French situation in *La Révolution des droits de l'homme*.
227. Virginia Bill of Rights, Section 1, www.gunstonhall.org/georgemason/human_rights/
vdr_final.html (accessed 10 May 2010).
228. *Ibid*. Section 16.

freedom of conscience also possesses a *religious* conscience, and it requires that this freedom be used in a largely Christian way. Thus, freedom of religion in the American states was understood as freedom to practise religion, not as freedom from religion.[229]

Jefferson, however, provides an example of the fact that a religious justification of freedom of conscience based on natural law can extend freedom before God to such an extent that it remains up to the individual how and for what he or she is to be answerable before God – up to and including atheism, which the community rejects but which does not overstep the bounds of individual responsibility. Thus, in his *Notes on the State of Virginia* (1781, published in 1785), Jefferson finds fault with the fact that the constitution of Virginia does not contain any clearer determinations concerning how the right to religious freedom should be implemented, so that, for example, statutes against heresy remained valid in common law. Therefore, Jefferson had proposed an 'Act for Establishing Religious Freedom' in 1779, though it was adopted only in 1786.[230] In this he called for a radical separation between Church and State or between religious outlook and practice, on the one hand, and civil rights, on the other – as he later put it, a 'wall of separation' between religion and politics. The thesis that conscience, which is beholden to God, cannot be coerced played a central role in Jefferson's argument: 'The rights of conscience we never submitted, we could not submit. We are answerable for them to our God.'[231] It leads Jefferson to call for an unlimited freedom of conscience, not only of the religious conscience, since only certain things fall within the domain of secular law: 'But it does me no injury for my neighbour to say there are twenty gods, or no god. It neither picks my pocket nor breaks my leg.' With this, Jefferson took issue with the established opinions concerning what it meant to have a conscience, which earned him the accusation of being an atheist. Jefferson took the view that, although freedom of conscience is grounded in individual responsibility towards God, the secular power is not authorised to interfere with it even in cases of atheism.

Jefferson reinforces this argument with further, primarily epistemological considerations which anticipate the theory of John Stuart Mill. Thus, he

---

229. See Berman, 'Religious Freedom and the Challenge of the Modern State'. On the different religious regimes in the individual states, a majority of which (with the exception of Rhode Island and Providence Plantations, thanks to the influence of Roger Williams, and, with qualifications, of Maryland) envisaged a dominant religion, extending even to theocratic structures, see Jellinek, *The Declaration of the Rights of Man and of Citizens*, 59–77.
230. The text is reproduced as an appendix to Jefferson, *Notes on the State of Virginia*, 223–5.
231. *Ibid.* 159.

relies on the idea that the truth can win out only in an atmosphere of free enquiry, whereas given the fallibility of human reason no government can be permitted to presume to be the infallible judge of the truth: 'It is error alone which needs the support of government. Truth can stand by itself.'[232] Furthermore, he argues, also anticipating Mill, that a plurality of opinions and convictions is not only inevitable but also beneficial to society as a whole by enriching it and leading the individual sects to limit each other.[233] This is proven by the individual states which do not have any established religion: 'their harmony is unparalleled, and can be ascribed to nothing but their unbounded tolerance'.[234]

In the debates over the proposed new constitution, which was rejected by the (misleadingly) so-called Antifederalists on the grounds that it would lead to an excessive concentration of power in the central government, Jefferson also argued that a Bill of Rights was necessary to set limits on the power of the government. This was duly realised in 1791 with the addition of the first ten amendments, the first of which takes up the issue of disestablishment and specifies: 'Congress shall make no law respecting an establishment of religion, or prohibiting the free exercise thereof; or abridging the freedom of speech, or of the press.' This clause established a fundamental precedent in American legal practice which shapes the understanding of the limits of toleration and the exercise of freedom to the present day.[235]

4. Whereas these were the conclusions drawn from the religious plurality within and between the individual American states, the situation in France was different. In the newly founded United States, the essential task was first to fight for the independence of the individual states, on whose existing structures the new constitutions were nevertheless able to build, and then, in a second step, to consolidate the political unity among the states and to secure the independence of the new federal state against foreign threats,

---

232. *Ibid*. 160.
233. This argument can also be found in James Madison in his famous *Federalist Paper* No. 51.
234. Jefferson, *Notes on the State of Virginia*, 161. The issue of the limits of toleration and of the understanding of freedom, however, also includes the question of the relation to the slaves in particular American states such as Virginia. In this regard, Jefferson's attitude, like that of the other founding fathers, is ambivalent. On the one hand, he makes a plea for the abolition of slavery and is aware of the contradiction between this practice and his theory of natural rights: 'I tremble for my country when I reflect that God is just: that his justice cannot sleep forever' (*ibid*. 163). On the other hand, he not only recoils from the practical problems posed by this step, but also fears, in part because he is convinced of the intellectual and physical inferiority of the black 'race', the intermingling of the races following emancipation, with the result that he argues for the return of the blacks to Africa. 'When freed, [the slave] is to be removed beyond the reach of mixture' (143).
235. See the survey in Richards, *Toleration and the Constitution*.

without triggering – or permitting – further social transformations.[236] The actors of the French Revolution, by contrast, were faced with the task of mastering a more profound social and political transformation, extending from the abolition of feudal rule, through the privileges of the clergy, to the question of what role a king could continue to play in the new social order. An awareness of the need for a new foundation shaped the self-understanding of the revolutionary party, for which political reality had become a space for autonomous change.[237]

Accordingly, the *Déclaration des droits de l'homme et du citoyen* proclaimed on 26 August 1789, which was supposed to become the preamble to the newly established constitution, had to fulfil a twofold task: on the one hand, taking the American declarations of rights, especially that of Virginia, as its model, it was supposed to set forth the 'natural, unalienable, and sacred rights of man', as it is stated in the preamble, 'in order that this declaration, [be] constantly before all the members of the Social body';[238] but it was also supposed, on the other, to form an inherent part of the founding document of the sovereign nation of all citizens, whose common will now constituted the basis of all rights. Thus, the document included, on the one hand, the natural rights of individuals as *human* rights prior to the state (for example in Article 1: 'Men are born and remain free and equal in rights' or Article 2: 'The aim of all political association is the preservation of the natural and imprescriptible rights of man'); and it was made clear, on the other, that these rights can have validity only as rights of *citizens* as members of the sovereign nation which governs itself through the common will, as it is put in Article 3: 'The principle of all sovereignty resides essentially in the nation.' This twofold perspective on the person as a human being and as a citizen, or on their rights as 'natural' and 'political' rights, involves a paradox, which at the same time contains the possibility of a new understanding of the political as well as the danger that this will lead to the well-known aporia of liberty rights and popular sovereignty.[239] The possibility consists in taking the

---

236. See Dippel, *Die amerikanische Revolution*, on the fault lines within American society.
237. See Habermas, 'Natural Law and Revolution'.
238. Declaration of the Rights of Man (1798), http://avalon.law.yale.edu/18th_century/ rightsof.asp (accessed 10 May 2010).
239. Gauchet, *La Révolution des droits de l'homme*, analyses the French declaration in the light of this dilemma and attributes the failure of the revolution to a substantialist understanding of popular sovereignty – a legacy of the monarchy going back to Rousseau – to the 'conversion of the freedom of each into the authority of all' (*la démarche de conversion de la liberté de chacun en autorité de tous*) (200). Habermas, 'Popular Sovereignty as Procedure', offers a similar analysis of the problem of sovereignty as understood in the Revolution. See also Rödel, Frankenberg and Dubiel, *Die demokratische Frage*, ch. 3.

'original' human right to justification as a starting point for justifying the core content of moral individual rights which are irreducible but must also acquire concrete legal institutional form via democratic self-determination alone (in accordance with the justification criteria of reciprocity and universality).[240] This combination of moral, legal and political autonomy reveals the possibility of a conception of individual rights and democratic sovereignty as deriving 'equiprimordially' from the fundamental right to justification that grounds human rights, on the one hand, and involves the right to enact legitimate law and to confer rights in a politically autonomous way, on the other. This is the source of the twofold meaning of basic rights as both defensive rights and rights to (reciprocal-general) legislation, both of which must in turn be legally institutionalised. In this way, we arrive at a secular conception of individual rights which acquire reality only as reciprocally justified and mutually conferred and guaranteed rights, rights which must, historically speaking, be fought for in political struggles.

Such an understanding of rights and democratic sovereignty is implicit in the attempted new democratic foundation, which however is influenced by a variety of factors. This is shown by the French case which was not only shaped by a collectivist and substantialist understanding of sovereignty that led to the attempted gradual dissolution of the paradox in the unity – and increasingly the purity – of the 'body politic' of the nation on the model of a political logic of identity. Even more important were the extremely complex social conflicts of the year 1789 in which the efforts to reform society confronted the combined forces of the monarchy, the nobility and the clergy which imposed compromises, as was shown especially by the issue of religious freedom and was also reflected in the constitution adopted in 1791. With the increasing radicalisation of the Revolution, the efforts to transform this situation through violence, leading ultimately to the terror of the 'great purge', finally gained the upper hand.

Especially important for the issue of toleration is the passage of Article 10 of the Declaration of the Rights of Man and of the Citizen, which differs strikingly from the corresponding American articles: 'No one may be disturbed on account of his opinions, even religious ones, provided their manifestation does not disturb the public order established by law.' In order to understand this we need to examine briefly the social and religious context in France which continued to be shaped by the dominance of the Catholic Church,

---

240. I develop this argument in Forst, *The Right to Justification*, chs. 4 and 5 and in 'The Justification of Human Rights and the Basic Right to Justification'.

the established church in all but name. In a tolerance edict of 1787 modelled on that of his brother-in-law Joseph II, Louis XVI had sought to grant the Huguenots a certain, extremely limited, legal status, though one which was not supposed to infringe on the pre-eminence of the Catholic Church. The socially deeply rooted supremacy of Catholicism would also prove to be the stumbling block in the negotiations in the National Assembly in August 1789 over the declaration of religious freedom.

The Sixième Bureau had been commissioned to work out a draft of the article on religious freedom, and proceeded to do this under the leadership of the clergy, which, smarting from the loss of a range of economic privileges, was determined to defend the supremacy of the Catholic Church. The Bureau proposed three articles:

> Article 16. Since the law cannot punish secret crimes, it must be supplemented by religion and morality. Thus, it is essential for the good ordering of society that they should both be respected.
>
> Article 17. The preservation of religion calls for a public form of worship. Thus, it is imperative that the public form of worship be respected.
>
> Article 18. Any citizen who does not disturb this publicly recognised form of worship should not suffer any inconvenience.[241]

The deliberations over this proposal, which closely followed the traditional emphasis on the necessity of religion for morality and law-abidingness and the call for an official form of worship with simultaneous toleration of dissidents, were held on 22 and 23 August in the National Assembly and led to the most intense of all of the disputes in the Assembly over the declaration of rights.[242] At the very opening of the session, the Comte de Castellane proposed replacing the three articles by a single article: 'No one shall be molested on account of his religious opinions or hindered in the exercise of his religion.'[243] Although it was agreed in the ensuing debates over the legitimacy and necessity of a public form of worship that Articles 16 and 17 would be dealt with in the subsequent constitution, the representatives of the clergy and other conservative forces were not willing to concede a

---

241. Quoted in Bauberot, 'Liberté religieuse et la laïcité', 95.
242. See the discussions in Sandweg, *Rationales Naturrecht als revolutionäre Praxis*, 239–44, and Gauchet, *La Révolution des droits de l'homme*, 167–74. German versions of the most important positions taken in the controversy can be found in Guggisberg (ed.), *Religiöse Toleranz*, 287–96 (page numbers in the text refer to this edition).
243. Quoted from Hersch, 'The French Revolution and the Emancipation of the Jews', 552.

comprehensive freedom of religion on the grounds that it would entail too serious a danger for the stability of the state.

The Marquis de Laborde was among the most prominent advocates of a comprehensive freedom of religion, and it was he, too, who had argued (without success) against invoking the 'protection of the supreme being' in the Declaration. He argued for the neutrality of the state in religious issues: 'Neutrality is without doubt the most judicious stance. The government has no other task but to maintain the peace, and the only way not to destroy it is to respect the different forms of worship.' He also employed religious language to underscore this right to the free exercise of religion: 'Freedom of religion is a sacred good belonging to every citizen' (289). So, too, did the Comte de Mirabeau, one of the staunchest supporters of religious freedom, who clearly expressed the tension between this freedom and the permission conception of toleration:

> I do not come here to preach tolerance. In my view the utmost freedom of religion is a right so sacred that the word toleration, by which it is sought to describe it, seems itself to smack of tyranny. For the existence of an authority which has the power to tolerate is a menace to freedom of thought from the very fact that, having power to tolerate, it has also the power not to do so.[244]

Although Mirabeau in the same speech called toleration a 'sacred word' and pointed out that a policy of toleration had not led to rebellion in any state in which it had been implemented, he nevertheless made it clear that at stake in the debate in the National Assembly was nothing less than the conflict between the permission conception of toleration and the recognition of an inclusive freedom of religion, and that the recognition of this freedom called in turn for a *different* kind of toleration based on mutual respect.

In the continuation of the session on 23 August, Mirabeau again spoke out in support of Castellane's proposal and attacked the idea of a *culte dominant*:

> Here there is incessant talk of a dominant religion. Dominant! Gentlemen, I don't understand this word. Someone must first explain it to me. Does it mean a repressive religion? But you have banned this word, and those who have declared the right to liberty do not claim a right to oppress. Does it mean the religion of the prince? But the prince does not have the right to control consciences or to regulate opinions. Is it the religion of the greatest number? But religion is a

244. Quoted from Barthou, *Mirabeau*, 195–6.

matter of opinion; such and such religion is the product of such and such opinion. Now opinions are not formed through plebiscites; your thoughts are yours alone; they are independent, you cannot pledge them. In short, the opinion that is supposed to be that of the greatest number has no right to *dominate*...Only justice should dominate; nothing is dominant except the right of each: everything else is subject to it.[245]

With this Mirabeau emphasises that the question of toleration or of freedom of religion is a central question of *justice* because it impinges on the right of individuals to enjoy equal civil rights which can be restricted only on the basis of reciprocally and generally non-rejectable reasons; this was also emphasised by Castellane in the ensuing debate by appeal to the Golden Rule (292). At his repeated urging, Article 18 as proposed by the Sixième Bureau was also dropped; but from his alternative proposal only the first part – 'No one shall be molested on account of his religious opinions' – was adopted at first, and there followed a heated debate over what should be added to this clause. The advocates of 'public worship' ultimately won out with a compromise formula for Article 10 of the new Declaration which read 'provided their manifestation does not disturb the public order established by law'. Since 'public order' here could only mean the official 'public form of worship', concerning which the supporters of this formula left no doubt, this marked a victory for the representatives of the clergy, which led to Mirabeau's subsequent remark in a commentary in the *Courrier de Provence* that 'instead of nipping intolerance in the bud, the National Assembly has kept it in reserve, as it were, by incorporating it into the Declaration of the Rights of Man' (294).

In the session on August 23, it was the Protestant Rabaut de Saint-Étienne who alerted the delegates to the fact that this Article 10 contradicted Article 1 on the absolute equality of rights and would bring about not freedom but at most toleration of the old kind: 'The word intolerance is banned forever; nobody will ever use this barbaric term again. *But I do not want tolerance instead of it*. In this word inheres the notion of pity, which is degrading to human beings. I claim freedom instead of tolerance which has to be for everybody the same' (emphasis R. F.).[246] However, his plea, which invoked not only the

---

245. Mirabeau, *Œuvres de Mirabeau*, vol. I, 216–17.
246. Quoted from Araújo *et al.*, 'The Historical and Philosophical Dimensions of the Concept of Tolerance', 10 (translation amended). See also Jellinek, 'Die Erklärung der Menschen- und Bürgerrechte', 27, who writes that Article 10 does not express 'freedom of religion but only toleration' (not included in the English translation).

history of the persecution suffered by the Huguenots but also that of the Jews, fell on deaf ears; the formulation in the new article remained unaltered. Once again permission toleration had survived and it would also be perpetuated in the new 1791 constitution which incorporated the *Declaration*. To be sure, subsequently the Catholic religion did not determine the public form of worship for much longer, but was replaced by the civil religion of the 'cult of reason'.[247]

This episode from the French Revolution does not only testify to the tenacity of the social and religious forces arrayed against the equal treatment of religions and to the extreme difficulty of combating the assumption that the stability of the state required a common religion, at least as regards its external form. It also reveals the ambivalence of the concept of toleration which, because it admits of different conceptions, could serve in one context as the war cry of the revolutionaries and in another to defend the supremacy of a dominant religion. The latter is also underlined by Thomas Paine in his treatise *The Rights of Man* (1791), in which he defended the revolution (in this respect, too optimistically):

> The French constitution hath abolished or renounced *Toleration*, and *Intolerance* also, and hath established UNIVERSAL RIGHT OF CONSCIENCE. Tolerance is not the *opposite* of Intolerance, but is the *counterfeit* of it. Both are despotisms. The one assumes to itself the right of with-holding Liberty of Conscience, and the other of granting it. The one is the pope armed with fire and faggot, and the other is the pope selling or granting indulgences.[248]

5. Thus, the motto 'from toleration to human rights', which seems to fit naturally the transitional period from the 'enlightened absolutism' of Joseph II to the codifications of human and civil rights, must be placed in perspective in three quite different respects. First, the example of the French Revolution shows that the permission conception of toleration is preserved in the Declaration (if only in an attenuated form and subject to a democratic proviso). In addition, even where complete freedom of religion was recognised, a critical examination of legal practice can show how this practice once again involved privileges for certain religions or confessions. Therefore, the interpretation of this basic right reveals a repeated tendency to transform the right to equal

247. The subsequent course of French history would be marked by an interplay leading to the establishment of the Catholic religion in 1814, only for this to be again revoked in the revolution of 1830.
248. Paine, *Rights of Man*, 136–7.

liberties into a form of permission toleration which regards this right as already fulfilled when minorities are 'tolerated', though they are far from enjoying equal status.[249]

Second, even when the separation between church and state has been substantially realised, the question remains of how to deal with religious minorities who for religious reasons reject the general duties of citizens as unacceptable and claim, for instance, an exemption from the duty to bear arms, as the Quakers did before the National Assembly in February 1791.[250] Later this exception was also enshrined in certain constitutions as a right (though one whose utilisation is always strictly regulated);[251] yet such cases raise the question of whether, structurally speaking, it is still a matter of a modified permission toleration as an exception to valid rules.

Finally, third, it must be re-emphasised that replacing permission toleration with a system of equal rights signals the appearance of a form of toleration in accordance with the respect conception. Toleration is not replaced by something else, but one conception of toleration is replaced by another. The respect conception is then demanded in both the vertical and the horizontal respects – and it integrates both dimensions in a specific way. For it is now (a) the *mutual* tolerance of the citizens as lawmakers which requires that they observe the criteria of reciprocity and generality in justifying laws and not bypass them by imposing the ethical values of a majority (in basic questions of justice). By the same token (b) the citizens as legal persons, as addressees of the law, are called upon to avoid not only illegal forms of discrimination but also such forms as slip through the grid of the law in the first place. Intolerance, which is versed not only in strategies that work within and against the law, but also in ones that operate alongside the law, cannot be banished from social space by legal means alone. This requires instead a particular attitude on the part of the citizens. Toleration retains its relevance as long as a society is marked by profound and important ethical differences.

§23 Cultural pluralism and individual uniqueness

1. As already indicated, increasing emphasis was placed on the historical and cultural particularity of peoples and nations in eighteenth-century thought. This is especially true of Montesquieu, though it is most apparent in Giambattista Vico who in his *Scienza nuova* (1725) represents history as a succession

---

249. I will use a number of contemporary examples to demonstrate this in Chapter 12.
250. On this, see Guggisberg (ed.), *Religiöse Toleranz*, 296–8.
251. Bethge, 'Gewissensfreiheit', 461, speaks in this connection of an 'exemption' (*Ausnahmenrecht*).

of different ethical worlds and individual cultures that must be understood and appreciated on their own terms, even if this succession can be regarded *in toto* as the work of divine providence. This idea that cultures and peoples are irreducibly unique while nevertheless being part of the development of the human race as a whole is also characteristic of the philosophy of Johann Gottfried Herder, which introduces a new element into the discourse of toleration. The diversity of peoples – Herder does not distinguish between 'people' and 'culture' – poses a challenge for toleration so that the latter now has to respond to more than just religious difference. *Culture* itself becomes the object of toleration. Cultural pluralism leading to new forms of diversity and conflict which bring toleration into play is a seminal idea that continues to shape the discourse of toleration to the present day, as does Herder's proposed justification of toleration – namely, an ethical and religious conception of the plurality of cultural worlds – which leads to an esteem conception of toleration.

Although Herder's philosophy contains a wealth of ideas which led to a radical critique of the Enlightenment, for instance in Romanticism, the label 'anti-Enlightenment' must nevertheless be treated with caution,[252] because it does not do justice to the complexity of Herder's thought. Although he was an important early defender of a notion of cultural nationalism, he was not a conservative thinker in political matters but a critic of the absolutist system of government. Even though he criticised the cosmopolitanism of the Enlightenment and its conceptions of international law, his primary target was its concealed imperialistic implications. Even more importantly, although he emphasised the uniqueness of cultures and emphatically rejected the linear philosophy of history of the Enlightenment, this did not lead him to reject an inclusive perspective in the philosophy of history.[253] And, finally, even though he emphasised cultural particularity, he also asserted the universality of moral and religious principles. These components of his thought led to a series of tensions and contradictions which are also noticeable in his reflection on toleration.

In *Another Philosophy of History for the Education of Mankind*, written under the influence of the *Sturm und Drang* movement and published anonymously in 1774 by Herder as the court chaplain and superintendent general of the

252. Berlin discusses Vico, Herder and Hamann under this generic heading, though he differentiates between their individual approaches. See in particular Berlin, *Against the Current and Vico and Herder*, and for a critical response Proß, 'Herder und Vico'.
253. Gadamer, who denies that Herder defends a relativist form of historicism, underlines this in 'Herder und die geschichtliche Welt'.

principality of Schaumburg-Lippe, he presents himself as an aggressive critic of the idea that human history can be understood as the emergence of the kind of universal rationality defended by the Enlightenment. Against what he regarded as the deistic watering down of religion 'full of tolerant *subjugation*, *blood-sucking*, and *enlightenment* according to the high taste of your time!'[254] – in which context he repeatedly cites the enforced colonisation of other peoples and the internal political repression entailed by 'enlightened absolutism' – he stresses the 'depth' of the national character of earlier peoples. Although he reconstructs the development of peoples up to the present as a succession of stages of life, he emphasises that, contrary to the exaggerated self-opinion of the thinkers of his time, this is a history both of *progress* and of *loss*. Every earlier people, he argues, especially the Greeks and the Romans, had *its own form of perfection* which it owed to its particular natural and historical situation, and this was irretrievably lost together with the people in question. Their 'prejudices' had rather 'ennobled' them and were a sign of a sensibility or a deeper religiosity of which the present age is no longer capable.[255] Against what he regards as the tendency of the Enlightenment to level human possibilities and to impose illegitimate uniformity, Herder asserts that between historical ethical worlds 'all comparison becomes futile' since every age has its own standard: 'Every nation has its *center* of happiness *within itself*', according to a plan of the 'good mother' nature; in particular, each possesses a specific form of blessedness of its own: 'Is not the good *dispersed* throughout the earth?'[256]

The development which Herder discerns in human history is a growth in the plurality of such particular forms of perfection, and this is the path along which humankind progresses, though not towards a grand synthesis. Here Herder exhibits an ambivalent relation to the Enlightenment: on the one hand, he makes a loss calculation which contributes a variety of motifs (together with thinkers such as Rousseau) to the later critique of the 'mechanical' Enlightenment;[257] on the other hand, he not only is aware that he cannot transcend his own era, but also believes that the ethical worlds of the other epochs and peoples cannot be defended in normative terms against his own time as the *'crown of the tree'*[258] – hence, they call for a

254. Herder, *Another Philosophy of History for the Education of Mankind*, 11.
255. *Ibid.* 28, 94ff.   256. *Ibid.* 29, 30.
257. In his critique of the 'classic aesthete who views the regimentation of our age as the ultimate achievement of mankind' (*ibid.* 40), aimed at Frederick the Great and Voltaire, and in his condemnation of the shallow Enlightenment without '*heart! warmth! blood! being human! life!*' (52), Herder anticipates, for example, elements of Nietzsche's philosophy of life and social criticism.
258. *Ibid.* 68.

limited esteem, not emulation.[259] For the question of toleration this means that although Herder certainly judges these worlds critically, at the same time he also ascribes them a value which, if one adopts a synchronic perspective on the whole development, calls for toleration on account of this intrinsic value and of the integration of all parts in an all-inclusive plan of providence, of which human beings have, needless to say, only an inadequate grasp. Against this ethical-religious background, he criticises the Enlightenment, and especially Voltaire, for a false form of toleration whose deism and universalism 'spread[s] the *light . . . tolerance, ease* in *thinking for oneself*, the *gleam of virtue* in a hundred charming *guises, little human inclinations diluted* and *sweetened*' and 'at the same time what wretched *recklessness, weakness, uncertainty*, and *chill!*'[260] Moreover, he accuses it of a paternalistic attitude which imagines itself to be objectively superior to the alternative systems of values. Genuine toleration, one can infer from this, would be aware of the particularities and the differences between ethical systems and 'national characters', and hence would neither explain away these differences nor regard them as setting limits to esteem.

However, this approach also involves a series of problems. In the first place, Herder does not make his own normative perspective sufficiently clear. It remains elusive how the distinctive ethical worlds of earlier eras can be made accessible and criticised; in particular, one cannot tell whether Herder's criticism of these worlds and of his own rests on the norms and standards of his own time or whether it can draw on a universal morality and religion. Therefore, it remains open where the limits of esteem (and hence also of toleration) lie. Both the thesis of the uniqueness of distinctive cultural wholes and frequent examples of such comparisons can be found in Herder; one can also find the idea that an inclusive perspective on the whole could only be that of a god, not of a human being, though Herder himself often adopts this perspective on '*God's course across the nations*'.[261] Here major tensions within any pluralistic ethical theory come to light which emphasise the restricted and particular character of ethical perspectives while at the same time seeking to go beyond this restrictedness in making this emphasis – that is, a theory which stresses the particularity of standards while simultaneously applying overarching standards.[262] Peculiar to Herder, however, is the further

259. *Ibid.* 40.   260. *Ibid.* 94.

261. *Ibid.* 78. Thus, for instance, *Ibid.* 73: 'I do not feel [as if I were] at *the place* where the harmony of all these voices would be gathered in one ear; but what abbreviated, confused echoes I can discern from where I am standing . . . are harmonious in their own way.'

262. This kind of problem is also characteristic of Berlin's pluralism, which is clearly influenced by Herder, especially in 'The Pursuit of the Ideal', where he argues that there is a plurality of objective values and forms of life which cannot be reconciled either in the life of society or in

problem that in defending uniqueness and individuality he generally means that of a *people*, in an essentialistic sense of the term, but sometimes also that of an *individual*. He likewise stresses 'what an *inexpressible thing* the *peculiarity* of one human being is' and 'what *depth* there is to the character of even *one nation*'.[263] Evidently Herder is firmly convinced that the one determines the other, yet he plays down the conflictual character of this relation.[264]

Herder takes up these problems in the *Outlines of a Philosophy of the History of Man* (1784–91), though in this work he aspires to reconstruct human history in its entirety as detailed natural history and at the same time as 'the ways of God in nature'.[265] Thus the religious grand narrative acquires greater prominence and the progressive perspective is also more pronounced; nevertheless the emphasis on the intrinsic value of cultures and peoples continues to play the central role, now also in a synchronic perspective. The plan of nature in which God operates in everything, in Herder's words, reveals itself in its inherent telos of reaching, through the different ages and cultures, the highest level of humanity, of exalting 'godlike man'.[266] Herder accordingly stresses the shared moral and religious foundations of all human creations, from the Golden Rule to a universal human disposition to religion, which it is the supreme task of human beings to develop.[267]

However, this does not mean that Providence, the 'good mother Nature', no longer ties the development of creation organically to the formation of specific perfections of peoples and cultures, which develop their forms of life, their own forms of blessedness, in their own place and at their own historical moment.[268] These forms of life appear to the observer to have intrinsic worth, but by no means equal worth; they have a value (a) in the eyes of the members of the culture themselves, (b) in the eyes of the unprejudiced observer and (c) in the eyes of God, who alone grasps the entirety of his creation in its

that of the individual. However, it remains unclear (a) what kind of value judgement we are dealing with here, (b) where the limits of this worth (and hence, if necessary, of toleration) lie and (c) to what extent these values, which must nevertheless be comparable if we are to be able to speak in terms of worth and incompatibility, can be 'incommensurable' (9), as Berlin argues. On this, see §31.3 below.

263. Herder, *Another Philosophy of History*, 23–4. Thus, Taylor, *Sources of the Self*, ch. 21, presents Herder as a primary source of modern 'expressivism', according to which every individual must follow his inner voice (as the voice of nature or God), with as much justification as Berlin's description of him as 'the greatest inspirer of cultural nationalism' in 'The Counter-Enlightenment' (12).

264. An even-handed discussion of Herder's notion of the attachment to a culture can be found in Larmore, *The Romantic Legacy*, ch. 2.

265. Herder, *Outlines of a Philosophy of the History of Man*, ix. Thus, in a review of this work, Kant criticises this attempt as metaphysical dogmatism; see Kant, 'Review of J. G. Herder's *Ideas for the Philosophy of the History of Humanity*', 132 (Ak. VIII: 54).

266. *Ibid*. 125.   267. *Ibid*. 102, 251–6; also *ibid*. 438.   268. *Ibid*. 192, 197.

beauty.[269] In spite of his efforts to remain impartial, Herder makes a series of value judgements concerning other forms of life which are not immune to the prejudices of his culture.[270]

The central idea concerning toleration in Herder is his religious, natural philosophical and ethical idea of the 'law of creation' according to which the multiplicity of ethical-religious worlds that arise and perish leads to human progress, provided only that the different cultures do not transgress their respective boundaries, as do the Europeans in particular, whether through crusades or colonisation:

> As far as it may be, no tree is permitted to deprive another of air, so as to render it a stunted dwarf, or force it to become a crooked cripple, that it may breathe with more freedom. Each has its place allotted it, that it may ascend from its root by its own impulse, and raise its flourishing head.[271]

Peace, therefore, is the natural condition of human beings. 'Mother Nature' has seen to it that each of the cultural plants develops to full maturity in its own place, even though each does not enjoy eternal existence; Herder views this emergence and decay of peoples as God's handiwork, and thus the most important justification of toleration is that human beings should not interfere with this plan of creation without authorisation and should not impose their values on others.[272]

The diversity of languages and traditions which leads to different ways of thinking is willed by God and is in accordance with the law of divine nature: 'the general cooperation of active powers in their most determinate individuality'.[273] Thus, each people achieves its own standard and a 'fortunate telescope'[274] enables us to see how humankind thereby progresses, with Christianity in its post-Reformation form playing the central role because it breaks down the dogmatic rigidity and intolerance that reigned in the Catholic Church.[275]

269. Thus, Taylor, *Multiculturalism*, 72, is correct in regarding the hermeneutic assumption of the value of other cultures as having religious foundations in Herder; however, both from the perspective of Herder and from that of the issue of understanding itself, it is not necessary to presume the equal worth of cultures (as Taylor does) in order to evaluate another culture, since the presumption of worth is sufficient. This raises central ethical and systematic questions of hermeneutics posed by Herder, as Gadamer emphasises in his discussion of the unavoidability of prejudgements and the need to subject them to dialogical examination; see *Truth and Method*, 267–304.
270. See, for example, the remarks on the African peoples, *Outlines*, 146–52, and on the Jews, *ibid*. 296–7, 514. However, Herder rejects the division of human beings into races in favour of a division of a single human race into peoples. See *ibid*. 166.
271. *Ibid*. 210.   272. See *ibid*. 218–19.   273. *Ibid*. 384.   274. *Ibid*. 457.   275. *Ibid*. 496, 632.

However, with this theory Herder does not solve the problem of the relation between collective cultural and individual uniqueness; just as culture has its right to particularity, so, too, does the individual: 'Every man has a particular proportion, a particular harmony as it were, between all his sensitive feelings.'[276] That the happiness of the individual might not harmonise with that of his people is inconceivable on Herder's general organicistic representation of the harmony of forces.

His arguments concerning the occasion and justification of toleration are also questionable. Apropos the former, he assumes excessively unifying, essentialistic conceptions of 'culture', 'people' and 'nation' which do not adequately reflect the flexibility and mutability of cultures that he himself emphasises. Apropos the justification of toleration, it becomes apparent that the argument is ultimately founded on a global religious and metaphysical view of 'Nature's universal plan'[277] – hence on a view which, as he stressed in his earlier work, is not even accessible to human beings. As a non-religious reason for toleration, therefore, all that remains is the possibility of finding something of worth in another culture (though not something of equal worth to one's own culture, for otherwise the objection component of toleration would no longer apply). This makes the limit of toleration arbitrary, depending on whether somebody recognises such a value. Thus, as with other esteem conceptions of toleration, this shows that the price to be paid for an esteem-based toleration, however desirable it may initially appear, is extremely high, for it is purchased at the cost of setting too narrow limits on what can count as valuable and thus tolerable. But then the actual domain of what can be tolerated, which is situated between what is esteemed and what is rejected, is in danger of disappearing.

Herder's philosophy nevertheless marks an essential stage in the discourse concerning toleration, for the idea of cultural pluralism and the emphasis on subjective singularity represents a major enlargement of thinking concerning toleration, as will become apparent in what follows.

2. It was the young Wilhelm von Humboldt who took up the question of the relation between cultural and individual particularity left unanswered by Herder. In his work *The Sphere and Duties of Government*, written in 1792 but published in its entirety only in 1851, he offers a romantically inspired answer in terms of the primacy of individuality which anticipates central arguments of John Stuart Mill's Humboldt-inspired work *On Liberty* (1859) and remains influential for contemporary liberal theory. Like Herder, Humboldt opposes

276. *Ibid*. 188.   277. *Ibid*. 466.

a conception of the state, whether absolutist or otherwise, which assigns it the function of ensuring individual happiness, so that it becomes a great 'machine' ruling over 'thoughtless member(s)';[278] yet, in arguing thus, his main concern is to highlight not the organic singularity of a people and its character[279] but instead the individuality and originality of persons. For the problem of toleration this means that Humboldt's topic is not toleration *between* cultures but toleration *within* a state.

According to Humboldt, the purpose of the state consists exclusively in being 'a means towards human development (*Bildung*)',[280] a means of education towards an ideal of supreme perfection of human intellectual and emotional powers in a unique form (108). This reflects a perfectionist ethical ideal of individuality which, however, can be accomplished only when the state refrains from any involvement in this formative process – this is Humboldt's anti-perfectionist political point. He assumes a formal conception of the good – 'it is in the prosecution of some single object, and in striving to reach its accomplishment by the combined application of his moral and physical energies, that the true happiness of man, in his full vigour and development, consists' (2)[281] – and associates this with a Romantic ideal of *Bildung* and an argument for political freedom and social pluralism:

> The true end of Man . . . is the highest and most harmonious
> development of his powers to a complete and considerable whole.
> Freedom is the grand and indispensable condition which the
> possibility of such a development presupposes; but there is besides
> another essential factor, – intimately connected with freedom, it is
> true, – namely, a variety of situations. Even the most free and
> self-reliant of men is thwarted and hindered in his development by
> uniformity of position.   (11, translation amended)

Yet neither this development of individuality nor the condition of social plurality can be brought about through direct or indirect action on the part of the state,[282] nor can the necessary connection between the individual and

---

278. *Ibid.* 223.
279. In his 1791 letter on the French Revolution to F. Gentz, 'Ideen über Staatsverfassung, durch die neue französische Konstitution veranlaßt', however, he criticises in terms similar to Burke the attempt to found a state exclusively on rational principles without a prior historical foundation.
280. Humboldt, *The Sphere and Duties of Government*, 87 (cited in the following in the text).
281. For a similar formal definition of the good and the 'Aristotelian principle' in Rawls, see *A Theory of Justice*, §65.
282. That the (in Humboldt's terminology) 'variety of situations' as a plurality of values must be guaranteed by state action is one of the theses of Raz, *The Morality of Freedom*, chs. 14 and 15.

others which first enables him to realise his potentials: '[F]or, in all the stages of his existence, each individual can exhibit but one of those perfections only, which represent the possible features of human character. It is through such social union, therefore, as is based on the internal wants and capacities of its members, that each is enabled to participate in the rich collective resources of all the others' (107).[283]

However, Humboldt is interested not primarily in toleration at the horizontal level among citizens but instead in vertical toleration by the state. And here he is consistent in rejecting positive action by the state, whose exclusive task is the necessary one of guaranteeing external and internal security. In order to make possible the 'development of individuality' (37), and in order to prevent society from becoming 'an accumulated mass of living and lifeless instruments of action and enjoyment' as opposed to 'a multitude of acting and enjoying powers' (41), the state must leave the field open for the 'free play of forces' in many areas, ranging from the economy to education and social welfare – in which Humboldt anticipates central arguments of what would later be called 'libertarian' theory.

He is strictly opposed in this context to *any* meddling by the state in questions of religion and he does not accept the – as we have seen, frequently invoked – argument that the state must make religion its concern in order to raise the level of morality and customs. Humboldt follows Kant in arguing that morality and religion should be strictly separated, that the 'purity of the moral will' (81) does not require any religious foundation and that religion, which is founded on the internal feelings and character of the individual, cannot be made subservient to moral or state purposes (75–86). It is 'wholly based on ideas, sensations, and internal convictions' (85) and it cannot be elicited by external influences; only complete freedom of mind is capable of leading to an internal religious attitude.[284] Humboldt defends this position – and the more far-reaching thesis that the education of morals is not a task of the state (94) – with a consistency scarcely encountered in his predecessors.[285] However, this comes at the cost of a radical reduction of the scope of state

283. This is the key conception also cited by Rawls in his idea of social cooperation as a 'social union of social unions', for which he adopts the image of an orchestra. See Rawls, *A Theory of Justice*, §79.
284. Humboldt had already underlined this in an early essay, 'On Religion', levelled against Woellner's religious edict, in which he also argues against the rational religious reduction of religion, which in his view 'transforms religious intolerance into a much more oppressive philosophical intolerance' (54).
285. In this context it should also be noted that in 1809 Humboldt argued (in agreement with his teacher Dohm) in favour of the legal emancipation of the Jews. It was granted only in an incomplete form in an 1812 edict.

activity, and he does not consider the problem that this could lead to social inequalities and structures of power which in turn jeopardise freedom.

Humboldt's writing reveals an important source of nineteenth- and twentieth-century liberal thought, namely the Romantic idea of the inherent potentials and 'powers' of a human being which can assume a distinctive form that is capable of enriching society as a whole only under conditions of political and social freedom. To this end the state must grant freedom without taking any positive measures to promote individuals, whereas citizens among themselves must not only respect the equal freedoms and rights of others but also grant the kind of freedom that will first allow the development of the self: 'fairer and loftier and more wonderful forms of diversity and originality' (43). Tolerance is required by respect for the potential of the individual and by esteem for the figure that emerges as a result. Yet even when this esteem cannot be mustered, the requirement of respect must remain. But the problem is that in Humboldt this respect is also ultimately justified in terms of a particular ethical idea of individuality which may be contested, and thus he fails to explain how toleration can be justified in the case of those 'figures' who do *not* measure up to this ideal in the eyes of society. What if the freedom granted leads not to the 'flowering' (14) of the individual but to its withering and to indolence? Should the state 'help' in that case or even cut these plants down to size? These questions remain open and once again serve as a warning to take a critical view of justifications of freedom and toleration that appeal to ethical ideals.

3. Apart from Herder's chiefly culturalistic and Humboldt's individualist conception of toleration, another similarly romantically inspired – only in this case a religious-pluralistic – conception can be found in Friedrich Schleiermacher's speeches *On Religion* addressed to 'its cultured despisers' and published in 1799. In these speeches, the Protestant pastor at the Charité Hospital in Berlin responds to the critique of religion of the Enlightenment and its preferred surrogate 'natural religion' – 'poorly stitched together fragments of metaphysics and morals that are called rational Christianity'[286] – by highlighting the depth and singularity of subjective religious sensibility, beyond the dogmatic and intolerant scriptural faith rightly criticised by the Enlightenment. In emphasising religious individuality freed from fixed institutional forms, Schleiermacher carries on the tradition founded by Sebastian Franck (see §9.2 above). Schleiermacher stresses the 'incomprehensible moment' (14) in which 'a holy soul is stirred by the universe' and

---

286. Schleiermacher, *On Religion*, 12 (further page references in the text).

strikes 'heavenly sparks', which is paradigmatically the moment of original religious experience of the founder of a religion but, according to Schleiermacher, is an experience which lays the foundation for true faith in every individual. Hence, religion cannot be reduced to metaphysics and morality but is independent of both (just as they are from religion). It is a matter not of thought and action but of 'intuition and feeling' (22); it is 'sensibility and taste for the infinite' (23). However, because it remains an experience of a finite being, this contact between the individual and the infinite which liberates him from his fixations, this sensation of 'infinite and living nature' in its manifoldness, is different for every individual and constitutes a 'religious individuality', a specific consciousness of the infinite, and thus ultimately a personal religion: 'Everyone can easily see that no one can possess religion completely, for the human being is finite and religion is infinite' (97). Therefore, there is an infinite number of forms of religion. Against this backdrop Schleiermacher presents a pluralistic religious argument for toleration:

> This feeling must accompany everyone who really has religion. Each person must be conscious that his religion is only a part of the whole, that regarding the same objects that affect him religiously there are views just as pious and, nevertheless, completely different from his own, and that from other elements of religion intuitions and feelings flow, the sense for which he may be completely lacking. You see how immediately this lovely modesty, this friendly inviting tolerance springs from the concept of religion and how intimately tolerance nestles up to it. How wrongly, therefore, do you turn on religion with your reproaches that it is persecution and spitefulness, that it wrecks society and makes blood flow like water. (27–8)

In this argument, an esteem conception seems to spring from the soil of religion itself, a religion which, unlike the 'refined' and 'polite' (98) natural religion of reason, is not bereft of religious feeling and living intuition, and for this very reason rejects any intolerant tendency to 'fetter it to a system' (28). A problem with this conception, however, is that as a result there no longer seems to be any occasion for toleration; for clearly the objection component is no longer present when the consciousness of the finite and limited character of one's own religious perspective leads one to regard the other's perspective as 'equally pious' and equally possible.[287] But then Schleiermacher would

---

287. This is the thesis of the religious-pluralistic theory defended by John Hick in 'Religious Pluralism'. In contrast to Mensching, *Tolerance and Truth in Religion*, who describes this as 'intrinsically tolerant' (12), Schmidt-Leukel, 'Ist das Christentum notwendig intolerant?', 205–13, points out that this is no longer a matter of toleration but instead of esteem.

be closer to the Enlightenment conception than he thinks, for this would relativise the 'depth' of religious feeling considerably because it would have to regard itself as purely contingent, so that the epistemic status of religious 'intuition' would also become questionable.

This problem is also reflected in his discussion of positive religion and of the religious community, which is a non-hierarchical community of the exchange of religious intuitions and may not draw any dogmatic boundaries to other churches; in addition, in its own interest it must support a strict separation between Church and State, because it must not allow itself to be placed at the service of the state, not even through special recognition as a corporation (85). A positive religion can arise, according to Schleiermacher, only when 'through free choice' (104) an individual intuition becomes the shared 'central intuition', thus leading to a religious harmonisation. It must, in turn, provide sufficient internal scope for religious individuality and must not become fixated on doctrinal principles. However, such a form of religion can then be understood only 'through itself' (113), through shared religious feeling.

Only at this point, towards the end of the text, does Schleiermacher switch perspective and speak – now explicitly – from the Christian point of view. Thus, he argues that Judaism is 'long since a dead religion' (113), a reflection of an early, still childlike stage of human development, and for his time he acknowledges only one form of religion as systematic, namely the Christian religion, whose intuition is 'more glorious, more sublime, more worthy of adult humanity' (115). Thus, an undogmatic Christianity and its 'fundamental intuition' is elevated here to a basic structure of the religious after all, and religious toleration has mutated into a Christian toleration which now includes the 'countless' religious intuitions within itself.

Even though with this inflation of a finite religious perspective into a religion closer to the infinite which incorporates all other finite forms Schleiermacher contradicts his own premises concerning finitude and particularity, in another respect he necessarily goes beyond this self-limitation in that he doesn't envisage any relativisation of his own religious intuition. This reflects a central difficulty of a pluralistic religious conception of toleration. On the one hand, the objection component cannot disappear entirely, for then a situation of toleration would no longer exist; on the other hand, the pluralistic global perspective renders the switch to a particular, personal intuition problematic (and leads to the temptation to confound the two). Accordingly, if there is a pluralistic justification of *toleration*, then it is only in the sense that the other forms are acknowledged as having a certain value from one's own perspective, whereas the latter is regarded as being of greater value. And this conception leads back to the problems identified in Herder and Humboldt.

4. The foregoing discussion by no means exhausts the positions devoted to the problem of the relation between faith and knowledge and the relation between Church and State in connection with the central writings of the later Enlightenment, in particular after Kant.[288] One need only think of Romanticism and, in particular, of German idealism up to and including Hegel's attempt to supersede Kant's stipulations concerning the finitude of reason in the direction of a form of absolutist thought. As far as I can see, however, no new justifications for toleration were developed in these contexts.

Thus, this chapter should suffice for a differentiated response to the question of the relation of the Enlightenment to toleration. There is no such thing as 'the' Enlightenment with a specific conception of toleration. Rather, with respect both to the philosophy of religion and to political philosophy (as well as moral philosophy), a whole range of complex positions exists with extremely diverse justifications – and criticisms – of toleration. Prominent among the justifications were the attempts, whose aporias I have discussed, to replace the established positive religions with a 'civil religion' or a 'natural religion' of reason, which led in turn to different reactions which were also characteristic of the era, ranging from atheism to the return to positive religion – a reinterpreted positive religion, of course, for a straightforward 'return' was not regarded as possible. Nor was it any more possible to uphold the classical permission conception, even though it is encountered more often in the thought and practice of the Enlightenment than is generally assumed.

Hence, this survey of the eighteenth-century conflicts, on which I could throw only a limited 'light', has once again sharpened and at the same time enriched our understanding of the concept of toleration by revealing the multifaceted character of this concept. In this way, as the following discussion of the discourse of toleration during what can be called nineteenth-century modernity shows, the basic alternatives for justifying toleration had been largely worked out, so that from then on it was a matter of applying them to a rapidly changing social situation in the light of a radicalised understanding of freedom and subjecting them to critical examination.

288. Besier and Schreiner, 'Toleranz', 547–64, offers an instructive account of further controversies in the late Enlightenment period.

7

Toleration in the modern period

§24 Different experiments of living, the utility of diversity and the harm principle

1. Although the history of the discourse of toleration has shown that this contested concept appeared at various times in very traditional (for example, religious) garbs, in one particular respect it can be described as an inherently 'modern' concept, perhaps even as the modern concept *par excellence*. For inasmuch as modernity signifies reflection on the eruption of conflicts which place traditional certainties in question and lead to a fissure in the intellectual and social order which cannot be fully fused in the traditional or in new ways, toleration marks at once this 'disenchanting' fissure and the awareness of a merely incomplete 'cure'. It bears the imprint of alienation and non-reconciliation, and of heresy, which is why, in many forms of reflection on toleration, ranging from Christian humanism to the rational religion of the Enlightenment, it is also regarded as merely a transitional phenomenon towards a higher-level unity. By contrast, other theories (Bayle's being the paradigmatic example) take a sceptical view of these hopes or, like Mendelssohn's, criticise them as attempts at enforced reconciliation which deny difference. Thus, speaking anachronistically, every profound and reflexive conflict concerning toleration involves an inherently 'modern' moment, even if this reflexivity acquires a new quality in 'modernity', a reflexivity which has become aware, as Kant puts it in the preface to the (first edition of the) *Critique of Pure Reason*, that

> our age is the genuine age of criticism, to which everything must
> submit. Religion through its holiness and legislation through its
> majesty commonly seek to exempt themselves from it. But in this way
> they excite a just suspicion against themselves, and cannot lay claim to

that unfeigned respect that reason grants only to that which has been able to withstand its free and public examination.[1]

The distinguishing feature of a specifically modern form of toleration following the disenchantment concomitant on the Enlightenment and the French Revolution is, on the one hand, the consciousness induced by this rupture of living in a new age in which political and religious truths and traditions must be subjected to a new fundamental requirement of justification and that social reality can and must be transformed accordingly. The spirit of the age is one of openness to the future and to change (combined with a critical historical self-assessment)[2] and thus to possibilities of a different form of social and individual life. For the problem of toleration this means not only an increase in and radicalisation of calls for toleration but also that the traditional justifications and conceptions of toleration undergo a renewed reflexive examination.

Thus, the counterpart of this altered understanding of history and time, on the other hand, is an altered understanding of subjectivity, and especially of freedom, which has deep roots in the Romantic, aesthetic conception of the subject, as is shown by the cases of Herder and Humboldt. This leads to a heightened emphasis on uniqueness, even to the point of eccentricity (John Stuart Mill), which renders social toleration necessary. At the political level the 'principle of subjectivity' becomes, in Hegel's words, the 'principle of modern states',[3] so that in 1819 Benjamin Constant makes a fundamental distinction between the liberty of 'the ancients' and that of 'the moderns': 'We are modern men, who wish each to enjoy our own rights, each to develop our own faculties as we like best.'[4] And Constant naturally counts 'the right to choose one's own religious affiliation' among 'the most precious' rights.[5]

However, in contrasting the political liberty of the ancients with the personal liberty of the moderns, Constant is led by his critique of the understanding of sovereignty in the French Revolution to associate the idea of the political autonomy of the citizens, which first founds the state and its institutions and guides it democratically through self-given laws – and which is no less influential in modern politics – with the 'ancient' liberty. But modern

---

1. Kant, *Critique of Pure Reason*, 100–1 n. (A xi n.).
2. On this, see especially Habermas, *The Philosophical Discourse of Modernity*, ch. 1, and Koselleck, '"Space of Experience' and "Horizon of Expectation"', 362–9.
3. Hegel, *Elements of the Philosophy of Right*, §260.
4. Constant, 'The Liberty of the Ancients Compared with that of the Moderns' ('De la liberté des anciens comparée à celle des modernes'), 323.   5. *Ibid.* 311.

toleration also involves the attempt to overcome the permission conception according to which the 'modern liberties' could also be conferred by an absolutist ruler. Thus, the close connection between basic rights and popular government also becomes apparent in the modern struggles for freedom, such as that of the democrats in the National Assembly in the Paulskirche in Frankfurt in 1848. In this context a further important extension of the concept of toleration, over and above the extension to cultural particularity and individual 'experiments in living' (Mill), can be observed, namely the idea of *political toleration* between parties competing for political power, where this struggle presupposes certain rules whose definition raises major problems (see below §25).

Ultimately, all of these discussions of toleration must be viewed in the context of a comprehensive 'modernisation' and 'rationalisation' of Western societies, in Max Weber's terms: the rationalisation (and differentiation) of the state, law and the economy, as well as the differentiation of cultural spheres of value, which involves corresponding transformations of the lifeworld leading to a more extensive problematisation of traditional forms of life.[6] This is important for a range of aspects of the discourse of toleration, in particular for the twofold rationalisation of power and morality which marks its development. This rationalisation involves, first, a trend towards the increasing autonomy of morality and the state from religious grounds of legitimation; second, the questioning of political authority in the name of toleration (and the independent morality of justification); and, third, attempts to gain and consolidate power specifically by granting toleration and no longer through direct repression. This dynamic continues in the modern era, as will be shown, inter alia, by an examination of Marx and Nietzsche (§26). Finally, the major social conflict associated with the name of Marx, which developed during the nineteenth century around the transformation of the emerging capitalist economic system, would also cast its shadow on the issue of toleration.

Other aspects associated with nineteenth-century social transformations, of which a great number could be mentioned, will be discussed in the following brief analyses. The theory in which many of these aspects come together in a complex way is that of John Stuart Mill.

---

6. Weber, *Economy and Society*, especially chs. 5–9, and, drawing on Weber, Habermas, *The Theory of Communicative Action*, who reconstructs this as a process of the decoupling of and conflict between 'system' and 'lifeworld'. I follow this conception of a twofold rationalisation with regard to the problem of toleration to some extent, though in doing so I confine myself to one aspect of the rise of modernity.

2. Different threads in the discourse on toleration converge in Mill's work *On Liberty* (1859), the last of the major classical writings on toleration and freedom. In particular, it brings together the Romantic individualism and the associated theory of the limited role of the state of Humboldt, whose book appeared in an English translation in 1854, in addition to a theory of individual liberty and of the need reciprocally to justify constraints on action indebted to social contract theory and, finally – a new component – the theory of utilitarianism adopted in a revised form from Jeremy Bentham and John Stuart's father James Mill.

It was James Mill who, in an 1826 essay on 'The Principles of Toleration', explained the close relationship between unbiased thought, the open discussion of all questions of truth, and social progress in utilitarianism, which, as a progressive social movement, crusaded against the privileges of certain social strata which could no longer be rationally legitimised. In a controversy with a work of the cleric Wardlaw on the formation of opinions, Mill sides with Locke in defending the thesis of the passivity of the mind whose convictions are not based on its own choices, though he points out that individuals are certainly responsible for how they deal with the evidence presented to them. Thus, he calls for the dianoetic virtue of 'fair dealing with evidence',[7] the search for the best possible evidence and its unbiased assessment. Only in this way, according to Mill, is social progress possible by overcoming blind prejudices and a precondition for this is a comprehensive liberty of thought and discussion. Finally, the clergy is the main target of Mill's attack on the grounds that it not only neglects this virtue but even combats it.

For all its distance from the elder Mill's thought, this reformist concern with breaking down traditional structures of thought through an open discussion of all socially relevant issues would likewise feature prominently in John Stuart Mill's work on liberty. Another shared feature is that their essential target is not the intolerance of the state but that of society and of influential social institutions such as the church, a point reinforced in the younger Mill by his critique of the social and moral conformism of the Victorian era. Nevertheless he would justify his idea of liberty and its social utility in a completely different way, one which ultimately explodes the conceptual framework of utilitarianism.

As a motto for his text Mill uses a quotation from Humboldt's *Sphere and Duties of Government* in which the latter emphasises the 'absolute' importance

---

7. Mill, *The Principles of Toleration*, 14 (appeared originally in the *Westminster Review*).

of 'human development in its richest diversity'. With this Mill specifies the key perspective governing his treatment of liberty, though this becomes fully apparent only in the central third chapter. Mill defines his topic as the 'Civic, or Social Liberty', more precisely the 'limits of the power which can be legitimately exercised by society over the individual'.[8] Hence, the question of the *justifiability of restrictions on liberty* is accorded central importance from the outset. Mill emphasises that, in modern societies in which constitutions and parliaments restrict the political power of individuals, the main problem is no longer the tyranny of the government but the 'tyranny of the majority', especially in the guise of political and social tyranny. In arguing thus, he borrows a central concept from Alexis de Tocqueville's analysis of democracy in America (1835 and 1840) in which the latter had described the dangers of the social conformism lurking in a democratic society, an analysis which left a deep impression on Mill.[9] Accordingly he is primarily concerned with the horizontal dimension of toleration, namely *social toleration*. For Mill, the struggle for religious toleration was for a long time the only 'battlefield' (47) in the struggle for the rights of the individual against society, not least because questions of faith have an inherent tendency towards intolerance. Mill accords central importance to this struggle in an extended form which is not solely concerned with religious freedom:

> The object of this Essay is to assert one very simple principle, as entitled to govern absolutely the dealings of society with the individual in the way of compulsion and control, whether the means used be physical force in the form of legal penalties, or the moral coercion of public opinion. That principle is, that the sole end for which mankind are warranted, individually or collectively, in interfering with the liberty of action of any of their number, is self-protection. That the only purpose for which power can be rightfully exercised over any member of a civilised community, against his will, is to prevent harm to others. His own good, either physical or moral, is not a sufficient warrant. He cannot rightfully be compelled to do or forbear because it would be better for him to do so, because it would make him happier, because, in the opinion of others, to do so would be wise, or even right . . . Over himself, over his own body and mind, the individual is sovereign.   (48)

---

8. Mill, *On Liberty*, 41.
9. See, in particular, Tocqueville, *Democracy in America*, vol. I (1835), part 2, ch. 7; vol. II (1840), part 3. Mill reviewed both volumes immediately on their appearance.

According to this 'harm principle', as it is called, any social or political restriction on a person's room for action calls for a justification and only reasons relating to the avoidance of harm to others are acceptable, whereas reasons supposedly concerned with promoting the well-being of those whose liberty is impaired are disqualified as legitimations of force or control. They can at most provide good reasons for exhorting, advising or criticising others. Of central importance, therefore, are, on the one hand, the distinction between actions which concern oneself alone and those which harm others and, on the other hand, the distinction between suitable legal prohibition or punishment or, in the latter cases, the moral coercion of public opinion and the legitimate criticism of wrong conduct which does not harm others. With this principle Mill defends a form of political *anti-perfectionism* which infers from the history of perfectionist justifications of intolerance that such justifications should be rejected *in toto*. However, we will have to examine whether Mill succeeds in offering a convincing explanation of the above-mentioned distinctions, especially that between *self-regarding* and *other-regarding* actions.

The 'portion of a person's life and conduct' (50) that concerns him or herself alone leads, according to Mill, to corresponding demands for liberty, to wit, freedom of thought and conscience, freedom of speech and of the press, the freedom of science, freedom of association and, finally, the freedom of 'framing the plan of our life to suit our own character' (*ibid.*). For 'the only freedom which deserves the name, is that of pursuing our own good in our own way, so long as we do not attempt to deprive others of theirs, or impede their efforts to obtain it' (*ibid.*). Before arguing in detail for this, Mill addresses one of the specific forms of liberty outlined, the freedom of thought and discussion.

In the second chapter of *On Liberty*, the components of Mill's justification of toleration and liberty mentioned above are supplemented by a new epistemological component which enables him to establish a connection with the progressive utilitarianism of Bentham and James Mill. That unrestricted freedom of discussion fosters the truth is advantageous for the development of society, according to the younger Mill; yet social utility in a criterially relevant sense does not provide the decisive argument here but instead a particular value, that of truth. It is not conducive to the value of truth, according to Mill, when public freedom of discussion is restricted, whether by law or through social intolerance. Irrespective of whether an opinion is right or wrong, it always tends to promote the truth: 'If the opinion is right, they [human beings] are deprived of the opportunity of exchanging error for truth: if wrong, they lose, what is almost as great a benefit, the clearer perception and livelier impression of truth, produced by its collision with error' (53).

Here Mill takes up the topos of the truth winning out of its own accord without any need of coercion which has a long history in the discussion of toleration, extending from the advice of Gamaliel in Acts of the Apostles (5:38–9; see above §4.2) to leave the truth to God who will ensure its success, through Milton's advocacy of freedom of thought and speech on the grounds that only error is in need of help (see above §15.2), up to Lessing's rivalry between the religions. In Mill, of course, the final verdict is reserved no longer for God but for scientifically enlightened human beings who are engaged in a continuous discursive search for truth, which must therefore remain open. The two basic epistemological arguments for toleration presented by Mill are the fallibility of human knowledge and the reinforcement of truth by contradiction. According to the former, one must always allow that the suppressed truth could be true, or at least part of the truth, so that its suppression represents a presumption of infallibility (53–4). To the objection that this conception of fallibility would place excessive restrictions on the scope for taking one's own convictions to be true, Mill responds that only if one is able to uphold one's convictions in the conflict with other views is one justified in continuing to hold them (55–6). Yet Mill must also restrict this requirement, because it would subject a person's 'private judgements' to an excessive requirement of justification. Thus, Mill limits the charge of assumed infallibility to the generalisation of private judgements and the denial of freedom of judgement to others (57). This clarification is important: one is not obliged constantly to champion and defend one's convictions in public, but only when one wants to make them mandatory *for others*. Nevertheless, public discussion remains worthwhile even for private opinions because the atmosphere of free discussion fosters general and individual education and the elimination of views based exclusively on belief in authority (66).

This leads Mill to his second argument, namely, that the truth is reinforced by criticism. Even if the opinions to be tolerated are clearly untrue, tolerating them nevertheless has value, because the roots of one's own knowledge are exposed and reinforced through the confrontation with them (70). This is also true of religion: 'Both teachers and learners go to sleep at their post, as soon as there is no enemy in the field' (74). Although Mill acknowledges that it would make no sense to speak of progress without a 'narrowing of the bounds of diversity of opinion' (75), yet here again he retreats to a weaker position according to which these boundaries must be drawn through discourse, not through prohibitions. 'Fair play' (78) must be assured for the truth.

Mill thinks that he has thereby provided the decisive arguments for the mental aspect of human well-being (82) which is fostered by the aforementioned liberties. However, that he then proceeds to shift the entire weight of his argument from the value of truth to another value, that of individuality, which had featured only once briefly in the long chapter on freedom of discussion, may be bound up with the weaknesses of the epistemological argument. For however attractive the idea of the justification of toleration on the basis of the openness of a competition for the truth may be,[10] it nevertheless remains incomplete. For inasmuch as *truth* is the supreme goal of toleration, there are insufficient reasons (without further normative considerations) for tolerating *all* possible opinions, for instance those which are demonstrably false. Granted, the argument that controversies with false views are fruitful remains valid; but even that does not include all controversies, for some may be unfruitful and may lead to a hardening of opinions and stagnation rather than to progress. Besides, completely open discussion could also entail the risk that errors may survive and spread, so that from a *purely* truth-oriented perspective there is something to be said in the assessment of costs and benefits for advocating intolerance towards senseless and false opinions.[11]

Moreover, it is doubtful whether *religious* convictions can be understood on the model of scientific hypotheses which seek confirmation through a process of falsification. This reflects a mistaken conception of the nature and function of these convictions. For, although they are based on reasons, they do not expose their truth claims to a competition of evidence and arguments in such a way that one can only continue to believe those convictions – for the time being – that have not yet been refuted. As we have seen, epistemological arguments are important for an inclusive conception of toleration; yet it is doubtful whether Mill's understanding of fallibility and truth is the best candidate for such a conception.

10. Popper would defend this position in its pure form in 'Toleration and Intellectual Responsibility (Stolen from Xenophanes and from Voltaire)'.
11. Thus, Lewis's critique in 'Mill and Milquetoast'. Marcuse, for example, expressly agrees with Mill in 'Repressive Tolerance' that the '*telos* of tolerance' is truth (90), though in his view this speaks against a 'pure' form of toleration which prevents human progress by tolerating falsehood. MacIntyre, 'Toleration and the Goods of Conflict', 149–52, likewise takes issue with Mill's thesis and points in particular to assertions such as denials of the Holocaust which should not be condoned (though they should not be restricted with the aid of the state either).

Mill switches his perspective in the third chapter which deals with freedom of thought *and* action: now he follows Humboldt in asserting that it is the value of human individuality which is central for the justification of liberty and toleration (85). Individuality is the key element of the human happiness to be promoted. In order to foster it, it is useful 'that there should be different experiments of living; that free scope should be given to varieties of character, short of injury to others; and that the worth of different modes of life should be proved practically, when any one thinks fit to try them' (84). Since 'individual spontaneity' has 'intrinsic worth' (85), personal liberty is an important good. It is the necessary means for creating original and distinctive characters who can withstand the tyranny of custom and create plans of life, not in 'ape-like...imitation' (86), but autonomously and unconventionally. This leads to a wide-ranging eulogy of these individuals who make the most of their natural capabilities, of the 'strong natures' (88) who possess an inner energy and who do not follow the herd, for whom these rare individuals are mere eccentrics. They alone extend their possibilities of ennobling themselves, and thereby the human race, the 'persons of genius' (91) who raise themselves above the 'masses of merely average men' (93). Here, too, he makes a plea, on the one hand, for liberty as a source of progress, while justifying it, on the other, by appeal to an independent ethical value for which liberty is the correct means, so that progress is measured precisely by whether this value is promoted.

Yet, here a similar picture emerges as before. The value to which Mill appeals in order to justify toleration is not sufficient. For the argument as to why the 'masses' should tolerate *all* eccentrics is not convincing, even if they accept that individuality has value as something enriching, nor is it evident what reasons this value is supposed to provide for tolerating 'undeveloped' (90) forms of life in which only mediocrity and the 'tyranny of opinion' (93) predominate. Why shouldn't this tyranny be combated through social or even state action, and *ethical perfectionism*, which Mill here explicates in Humboldtian terms, not veer into *political perfectionism*? If liberty fosters the intrinsic value of individuality, and if one ascertains that there are other ways to achieve this which rescue individuals from backwardness by 'helping them to help themselves', why shouldn't one do this? Why shouldn't one – at least gently – eradicate 'worthless' forms of life which hinder the development of individuality and thereby promote autonomy and happiness, though without prescribing plans of life to individuals, assuming that they begin to develop such plans autonomously?[12] Mill would seem to have nothing to object to in such autonomy-promoting attempts to restrict liberty in order to counteract the tendency 'to raise the low and lower the high' (98).

That he nevertheless does object is a reflection of the deontological component of his work, which comes to the fore in the final two chapters. Here it becomes apparent that only a universal right to justification for every person, whose freedom must be respected *unconditionally* – hence, not only in the light of the question of whether this person conducts his life in accordance with the ideal of originality or promotes utility in some other way – can ground the requirement that restrictions on freedom must be justified in a particular way, which for Mill remains central. Only in this way can one explain the requirement that restrictions on liberty can be justified only in order to prevent harm to others, but for *no* other reason. The typical liberal assertion that it is the individual himself who is 'most interested in his own well-being' (100) is not sufficient for this purpose, for his well-being might well be increased by an external promotion of individuality in accordance with the values of originality and self-improvement, which would thereby be stimulated.

In the context of this discussion, which is of central importance for the book, Mill's ethical perfectionism and the deontological justificatory perspective are in conflict, a conflict which he must resolve in favour of the latter in order to rescue his defence of liberty. His ethical social criticism leads him to introduce a new kind of sanction over and above the public moral pressure forbidden by the harm principle in the case of deviations from ethical norms of conduct that do not cause harm to others, namely permissible and even mandatory public criticism of someone who 'pursues animal pleasures at the expense of those of feeling and intellect' (101) and thereby rightly forfeits the respect of others. Apart from the fact that this could exert just as much social pressure as explicit moral condemnation, pressure which Mill's critique of tyranny should actually lead him to reject, here he is of course forced to distinguish between two kinds of condemnation, which should be termed 'ethical' and 'moral' condemnation: the former is the *ethical* condemnation of the way of life of a person which leads to a 'loss of consideration', the latter the 'reprobation' of a *moral* transgression which

---

12. This is the conclusion drawn by Raz, *The Morality of Freedom*, 423, from his ethical-perfectionist reading of the harm principle and which Mendus, *Toleration and the Limits of Liberalism*, 57–68, regards as the central dilemma of liberalism as such.

harms others (102). The distinction between these two kinds of condemnation is a logical implication of Mill's analysis. Nevertheless, it presupposes a deontological position which (a) stresses the right to justification of each person, which must not be relativised by other values, and (b) provides the criterion for drawing the distinction between the ethical and moral domains.

(a) Each of these is only implicit in Mill. The perfectionist political leaning of his own argument in the chapter on individuality can be overcome only by the reference to a 'greater good of human freedom' (105) vis-à-vis ethical considerations, as he himself recognises; yet he thinks it sufficient to point out in this connection that any interference in 'purely personal conduct' would in all probability occur 'wrongly, and in the wrong place' (106). This does not necessarily follow, however, if one considers what he has to say about the 'undeveloped' (90); in this case the risk of not intervening, as determined by a cost-benefit analysis, could be greater than that of a wrong interference. Hence, this cannot be the 'strongest of all the arguments' (106) for unconditional respect for liberty. Instead it must be the inviolability of the person which surpasses all other values, and which therefore means that liberty must be respected as long as this does not impair the liberty of others: 'The reason for not interfering, unless for the sake of others, with a person's voluntary acts, is consideration for his liberty' (121). And the fact that this respect is a respect for the *justificatory authority* of the individual grounds the two basic principles: 'First, that the individual is not accountable to society for his actions, insofar as these concern the interests of no person but himself. . . Secondly, that for such actions as are prejudicial to the interests of others, the individual is accountable, and may be subjected either to social or to legal punishment' (114). Hence, the freedom of the individual is neither justified on the basis of some other value nor is it absolute: it is a freedom of persons as autonomous justificatory agents subject to norms that can be reciprocally and generally justified. The moral respect for this kind of autonomy is not conditional on its ethical use.

(b) This leads to the key question concerning the criteria of 'harm', in other words concerning the criteria of justification of restrictions on freedom.[13] When, according to Mill's 'very simple principle' (48), is there a good reason for establishing that 'harmful' conduct exists and for prohibiting

---

13. Here I cannot address the widely ramified discussion of this question in the literature on Mill. Horton, 'Toleration, Morality and Harm', represents the dominant tendency when he argues that the definition of the concept of harm must appeal to substantive liberal values and that for this no higher-level principle exists. The most ambitious attempt to define the concept in theoretical conceptual terms is Feinberg's four-volume work *The Moral Limits of the Criminal Law*.

it? He presents a range of formulations in this regard, such as 'private interest' as opposed to 'public interest' or the 'interest of others', *self-regarding* versus *other-regarding* actions, duties towards oneself or towards others, 'concerns' or 'being affected'. However, these definitions are not sufficient to define the limit beyond which an ethically criticisable exercise of liberty becomes morally criticisable, for almost all actions that concern oneself also concern others and thus private and public interests are constantly intertwined and often in conflict. The controversy will turn specifically on whether an action concerns oneself 'first and foremost', and hence should be exempt from interference, or whether it harms the interests of others. Yet thus the criteria of *reciprocity* and *generality* can provide guidance here. They state that a restriction on liberty is legitimate when it can be justified in a reciprocally and generally non-rejectable fashion, that is, when a participant in a conflict over justification grounds his claim without claiming privileges for himself which he denies to others, for example the privilege of himself determining the normative reference of the justifications offered, e.g. with respect to a specific, non-shared religious doctrine or to a one-sided conception of the well-being of those concerned or of society. Hence, the boundary between ethics and morality is defined not by self-enclosed spheres of value but by the threshold of reciprocity and generality. Anyone who interferes with a person's freedom of action and exercises 'power' (50), whether it be through the law or through some other form of action, must be able to present reciprocally and generally shareable reasons, since every person has a fundamental right to such reasons; and particular justifications which appeal to doctrines that are not shareable or to the supposed interest of those who are subjected to power, where the latter cannot or could not give their consent, are not good reasons. It is immaterial whether an illegitimate restriction of freedom is grounded in paternalistic terms (the case Mill chiefly has in mind) or solely in terms of an inadmissibly generalised doctrine (without paternalistic intent); what is important is only the violation of the required criteria of validity.

This stipulation occupies a central position in Mill's text. In the case of the paradigmatic example of the non-justifiability of religious constraint, he explains (entirely in the spirit of Bayle):

> No stronger case can be shown for prohibiting anything which is regarded as a personal immorality, than is made out for suppressing these practices in the eyes of those who regard them as impieties: And unless we are willing to adopt the logic of persecutors, and to say that

we may persecute others because we are right, and that they must not persecute us because they are wrong, we must beware of admitting a principle of which we should resent as a gross injustice the application to ourselves.   (108)

It is the strict rule of reciprocal justification which forbids such coercion and which likewise is (implicitly) used in other examples of prohibited paternalism and permissible restrictions on freedom.[14] The essential point is that the 'rigid rules of justice for the sake of others' (90) which stake out the limits of freedom are ones which are reciprocally and generally justifiable, i.e. they do not privilege one side of particular ethical convictions.

Hence, the famous harm principle expounded by Mill in the first chapter of the book means that all restrictions on action are in need of justification and that only those restrictions are justifiable which cannot be rejected on the basis of reciprocal and general arguments. In this way, and only in this way, one can make a coherent distinction between actions which 'concern oneself' and those which 'concern others' – namely, between those which are not in need of moral reciprocal justification and those which must be justified towards those who are affected, and then in a further step between the actions among the latter which are morally intersubjectively justifiable and those which are not. That said, Mill did not distinguish these two steps clearly enough and he did not make the criteria of justification explicit.

This argument might prompt one to speak in terms of a 'presumption in favour of liberty' in Mill such that individual liberty is the norm and every form of constraint or restriction on freedom is in need of justification.[15] This is consistent with Mill's reflections, but viewed in the light of the foregoing analysis it does not go far enough for various reasons. In a situation involving two persons whose actions are in conflict, for example, one party's exercise of freedom is opposed to that of the other and the presumption in question is of no help since both parties insist on their unrestricted liberty. Only when it is reformulated as a 'presumption of equal liberty' does a criterion of justification come into play, though this is still too vague since more factors

---

14. Compare for instance the examples of the regulation of public holidays (111–12), polygamy (113), the sale of poisons (117), and of pimping and gambling (118–19), to name just a few, which nevertheless also reveal Mill's ethical convictions.

15. Cf. Feinberg, *Harm to Others* (*The Moral Limits of the Criminal Law*, vol. 1), 9: '[M]ost writers on our subject have endorsed a kind of "presumption in favor of liberty" requiring that whenever a legislator is faced with a choice between imposing a legal duty on citizens or leaving them at liberty, other things being equal, he should leave individuals free to make their own choices. Liberty should be the norm; coercion always needs some special justifications.' See in this sense also Gaus, *Justificatory Liberalism*, 165.

than mere equality must be taken into consideration and the requirement of equality holds only when it is *justified*. The outcome would be a 'presumption of justified liberty/liberties', though this would then be nothing other than a 'presumption of reciprocally and generally justified liberty/liberties'. But this would ultimately rest on the 'presumption of reciprocal and general justificatory authority' of the individuals. Yet given that the concept 'presumption' is itself normatively vague, this would be grounded in nothing other than the 'right to reciprocal and general justification' of morally relevant actions, to which a duty to provide justification corresponds.

Thus, following the (leading and misleading) paths traced out by Mill in *On Liberty* has shown that only a deontological perspective of respect for the other as a moral person with a right to justification can justify Mill's antiperfectionism without making rigid distinctions between domains, such as, for example, between the 'private' and the 'public' domain. Toleration is justified on the basis of respect for the moral autonomy of the other to whom one owes good, reciprocally and generally non-rejectable reasons for actions that affect him or her in morally relevant ways – be it in moral situations involving individuals or in the political and legal domain.[16] If, as Mill maintains together with the other theorists of toleration, there are no good reasons for religious or ethical constraint, then he owes us an explanation of what this 'lack' involves – and this calls for a normative and epistemological conception of toleration which accords central importance to the principle of justification. Only when embedded in such a conception does Mill's 'simple principle' acquire its meaning and allow the different *experiments of living* genuine scope for development.

§25 Political toleration

Two developments – namely, the increasing legal protection of freedom of religion in the European states (though still combined with legally stipulated privileges for certain Christian confessions)[17] and the emergence of new political system alternatives – meant that, in addition to the extension of the issue of toleration from the religious to the cultural domain, a new dimension came to prominence, namely, political toleration between parties classifiable in accordance with the 'isms' which took shape at this time, ranging from the monarchist through the liberal and the democratic to the socialist parties, to

16. I discuss the differences between these contexts of justification in §30.
17. On this, see Campenhausen, 'Religionsfreiheit', 384–6; Hollerbach, 'Grundlagen des Staatskirchenrechts', 477–9.

name just a few.[18] The demand for toleration is now situated within a new field of radical conflicts.

An important document in this regard is the article 'Toleration' by one of the most important proponents of democratic liberalism in the *Vormärz* (i.e. the pre-March 1840 period in German history), Carl von Rotteck, in the *Staats-Lexikon* which he co-edited with Carl Welcker from 1834 onwards. Rotteck's chief aim in his contribution is to emphasise against the background of the history of intolerance that there can be no good reasons for restrictions on freedom of religion in the light of the 'basic concepts of law and of personal liberty in general'. After an excursus on the history of toleration and intolerance in the European states and North America, he finally turns to political toleration, which arises when disagreements occur even for reflection unclouded by religion over what constitutes the 'well-being of society as a whole' or how it can best be realised:

> The place of religious intolerance, which is increasingly in retreat before the spirit of the age, has been taken in our time by political intolerance, which has already claimed many deplorable victims, first in France under the rule of the republican government of terror, then throughout Europe, partly as a result of the aftershocks of that great movement, but partly, or even chiefly, as a result of the influence of the aristocratic and absolutist party of reaction. This form of intolerance is also more difficult to control than its religious counterpart, because it is continually nourished by selfish interests, and hence enlightenment is not sufficient to disarm it. All religious opinions and forms of religious exercise can coexist peacefully without causing one another harm, none requires the suppression of the others in order to flourish . . . Political ideas, by contrast, are by their very nature opposed to each other not only in theory but also in practice. They cannot assert or impose themselves alongside one another, but only each at the expense of or by defeating all of the others. Republicanism and autocracy, constitutionalism and absolutism, democracy and aristocracy, are mutually exclusive, or naturally strive to suppress one of the others, at least as far as possible. Thus, sincere friendship or mutual love between them is surely unthinkable. In their case the demand for toleration is confined to the mutual permitting or sufferance of all legal means as are necessary to gain or preserve validity, or also perhaps to the inclination, by way of compromise, to

---

18. On this, see Besier and Schreiner, 'Toleranz', 583–5; Koselleck, '"Space of Experience" and "Horizon of Expectation"', 373; Fetscher, *Toleranz*, 61–9.

acquire and establish for each of the competing parties through mutual
concessions a suitable external legal basis for guaranteeing whichever
of their interests are at all reconcilable with each other.[19]

The most important demand that follows from this situation of conflict,
according to Rotteck, is the demand for freedom of speech – 'the free communication of one's grounds of justification' – so that the 'judgement seat
of reason and of enlightened public opinion' alone can decide; all opinions,
provided they are not 'criminal', must be tolerated without hindrance.

Rotteck's argument is instructive for the problem of toleration in various
respects. It is important, first of all, for his views that political conflicts have
now taken the place of religious conflicts and that political conflicts are more
fundamental than the latter and offer little room for an accommodation. They
are irreconcilably opposed.[20] Moreover, it is significant that these conflicts
forbid a narrowing down of the modern situation of toleration to tolerance
of 'private' religious 'conceptions of the good' or individual and possibly
idiosyncratic plans and experiments of life. For in this case it is not objectively or intersubjectively justified legal norms or norms of justice which provide the framework for toleration of the different conceptions of the 'good';
rather these norms themselves are the focus of the conflicts, resulting in the
demand for toleration between *incompatible alternative conceptions of justice* of
a political and social kind.[21] This calls once again for foundational reflection
on the principle of toleration even if, like Rotteck, one understands it on
the model of coexistence, for he, too, envisages a common 'legal basis'. Mill
likewise makes a plea, against the background of a long parliamentary tradition and the emergence of the socialist movement, for political toleration as
'fair play':

> In politics, again, it is almost a commonplace, that a party of order or
> stability, and a party of progress or reform, are both necessary
> elements of a healthy state of political life; until the one or the other
> shall have so enlarged its mental grasp as to be a party equally of order
> and of progress, knowing and distinguishing what is fit to be preserved
> from what ought to be swept away . . . Unless opinions favourable to
> democracy and to aristocracy, to property and to equality, to
> co-operation and to competition, to luxury and to abstinence, to

19. Rotteck, 'Duldung', 548.
20. According to Rotteck, they represent 'nondivisible' conflicts, to use the terminology of
    Hirschman, 'Social Conflicts as Pillars of Market Society'.
21. In the contemporary discussion, Waldron, *Law and Disagreement*, especially chs. 7 and 11,
    emphasises this vis-à-vis Rawls.

sociality and individuality, to liberty and discipline, and all the other standing antagonisms of political life, are expressed with equal freedom, and enforced and defended with equal talent and energy, there is no chance of both elements obtaining their due; one scale is sure to go up, and the other to go down.[22]

Like Rotteck, Mill assumes that political conflict is a conflict of arguments and that the public reason of the citizens is capable of forming a generally reconcilable unity, in Mill's case even a synthesis, out of the opposing positions. And, like Rotteck, in so arguing he presupposes an agreement on the 'rules of the game'. But this poses a problem which might be called the *dilemma of political toleration*: this basic agreement is simultaneously the *presupposition* and the *object* of the political conflicts. Certain rules of political interaction as well as of the institutionalisation of these conflicts are presupposed, yet at the same time system alternatives stand opposed which are in dispute over these very rules and institutions. How could there be a framework of political fair play in which the question 'democracy or aristocracy or monarchy' still had to be decided? Doesn't such a framework already go a long way towards deciding the question?

The dilemma in question can be avoided only by taking into consideration that, although the question of political toleration marks a new scene of conflict, in a certain sense it does not represent a special case of toleration. It follows from the extension of the right to justification to the political level at which the citizens decide for themselves as equals which rights they should have and what form the basic structure of society should assume – in short, what justice means in concrete terms. And a precondition of this extension itself being accomplished in a just manner is clearly a form of *fundamental justice* which guarantees that the individual right to justification can be exercised as a political right. Thus, political (or religious) toleration can succeed at this level and can be demanded only if this fundamental justice is accepted by all concerned. Where this is not the case toleration will not be possible and to require that those who are excluded and disenfranchised should nevertheless be tolerant – for instance of an aristocratic or economic regime which perpetuates their disenfranchisement – would be, in Marcuse's terms, repressive.[23] Without a generally and reciprocally accepted fundamental

22. Mill, *On Liberty*, 78.
23. In his essay 'Repressive Tolerance' Marcuse extends his critique of a false demand for toleration, which only masks and cements relations of social and political exclusion and exploitation, to the representative democracies of his time as well. He describes the latter as 'totalitarian' (97) because all forms of dissent were neutralised in favour of the status quo, thus rendering autonomous judgement impossible.

justice of the right to justification, the demand for toleration lacks a sufficient empirical or normative basis.[24] This holds even for a coexistence conception, which likewise includes reciprocally agreed-upon rules, though it lends plausibility to talk of a stable 'legal basis' only when it is refined into the respect conception.

Hence, the problem of political toleration points to basic presuppositions of any conception of toleration that combines the vertical and horizontal perspectives and situates the principle of reciprocal justification of rights and liberties at the political level, whether it is a case of religious conflict or of conflicts in some other dimension. For even in the case of religious freedom, autonomous citizens are called upon to guarantee these liberties within the framework of justice and to justify all restrictions of these liberties. Thus, the right to justification as a political right, as a basic right of participation in all essential political decisions, is a fundamental right and the basis of fundamental political justice on which respect toleration is founded. Hence, this kind of fundamental justice calls for[25]

(a) fair social and political conditions of participation in political processes which prevent the exclusion of any group or party. Their right of participation must not be merely formally assured but must also be backed up by concrete guarantees; it must have a 'value'.[26] This presupposes

(b) the recognition by all sides of the right to justification as a real political right, as a right to have an autonomous say in determining the underlying structure of a political community, which means to decide which rights the citizens are duty bound to grant one another. Provided that basic rights have constitutional status, the necessary toleration will be legally required; however, processes of justification at the social and political level cannot be regulated by positive law to such an extent as to render the civic virtue of observing the criteria of reciprocity and generality in basic questions of justice unnecessary. Toleration then operates

---

24. The accusation of repressiveness also holds when those to whom the demand for toleration is addressed are not themselves the immediate victims of the unfreedom. This was the case in the debates between Abraham Lincoln and Stephen Douglas in which the latter called for toleration for the freedom of decision of the southern states to decide on the issue of slavery for themselves. Douglas explained this right to self-determination as follows: 'When you will recognise that principle, you will have peace, and harmony, and fraternity between all the different States of this Union. Till you do recognise that doctrine, there will be a sectional warfare, agitating and disturbing the peace of this country' (speech of 21 August 1858), in Holzer (ed.), *The Lincoln–Douglas Debates*, 84–5.

25. On the following see the more detailed discussions in Forst, *Contexts of Justice*, ch. 3, and *The Right to Justification*, chs. 8 and 12.

26. See Rawls, 'The Basic Liberties and their Priority', 37ff.

(c) at two levels of the democratic game. It comes into play, first, when it is a question of tolerating the plurality of political positions while avoiding unjustifiable exclusions. This necessitates in particular examining whether the conditions of participation and communication are such that the established standards of 'public reason' may not be closed and biased towards certain minority positions. 'Reflexive toleration' then means critically scrutinising the conditions of justification;[27] in this context a *critical theory of toleration* would have to analyse which relations of toleration, as asymmetrical relations of justification, lead to which forms of exclusion.[28] This would call for sensitivity not only to *exclusions* but also, as the historical survey has demonstrated, to *inclusions* of tolerated groups which are granted certain liberties in order to perpetuate their underprivileged and stigmatised condition.[29]

Second, and even more important, toleration is required when, in the course of justification, a group realises that their convictions are not sufficient to justify a mutually binding legal regulation, even though they hold these convictions to be true and correct. This remains the true test of tolerance, namely the insight that the good reasons which one thinks one has are not sufficient to perform a generally defensible action or, in political terms, to justify a general law, hence that *they are not good enough in this context*. Finally

(d) certain *limits* are also part of political toleration. The debate over where these limits should be drawn, over where one takes leave of the common 'legal basis', continues up to the present day. In the terminology I have proposed, it cannot be a matter of whether the right to justification as a basis for fundamental justice is negotiable, because its substance is not negotiable. Anyone who denies it is beyond the pale of political toleration. But it does concern the question of what this substance entails, for instance whether it implies a specific form of government. This was declared to be illegitimate, for example, by the 'select committee of the patriotic associations in Württemberg' in a declaration from 1848:

> Convinced that a people which is cognisant of its true interests will always discover the appropriate form of government, we regard it as presumptuous to want to stipulate this form of government once and for all. Hence we exercise and demand political toleration. We do not believe in the exclusive redemptive power of one particular form of

27. On this, see O'Neill, 'Practices of Toleration'; Bohman, 'Reflexive Toleration in a Deliberative Democracy'.
28. Forst, *Justification and Critique*.
29. Cf. Brown, 'Reflections on Tolerance in the Age of Identity'.

government, we recognise the equal rights of the political parties, we respect all convictions, we acknowledge that both the monarchist and the republican can be a good patriot, so long as he affirms in both word and deed the principle: Everything for the honour of the fatherland. Everything for the people and through the people![30]

This position is consistent in that it is an integral part of the political autonomy of the citizens to determine the form of their state for themselves, though subject to strict observance of the right to justification. This means, conversely, that the question of the possible forms of government is *not* completely open, for a system which placed this basic right in question as a formal and material right could not be legitimised, even though this right can assume a wide variety of institutional forms (though 'monarchy' is used here in a limited sense). Protecting this right, therefore, does not call for any specific institutional stipulations which would restrict the political autonomy of citizens. But what it means in concrete terms to define the limits of toleration towards the politically intolerant, where the right to justification and further basic rights of politically autonomous citizens themselves come under attack, remains to be examined (see below §38).

§26 Half measures of toleration

1. The sense that something is not right with toleration, that it does not deserve the praise lavished upon it, trails the discourse of toleration like a shadow that it cannot shake off. And rightly so. As our analyses of the diverse forms of power and rule lurking behind the permission conception of toleration have shown, Goethe's dictum that this form of toleration is an insult, and that it must lead to recognition, is justified. That said, the notion that the concept of toleration is essentially tied to this conception of hierarchical or strategic permission is no more well founded than the view that tolerance is invariably, to borrow the terminology of Heidegger, a 'deficient mode of being-with' which should be overcome in favour of genuine esteem or even solidarity. For the conflicts which call for toleration in the political domain or in interpersonal relations cannot be entirely overcome by dismantling the respective objection components. That would amount to nothing less than a transformation of the *condition humaine*. Conversely, however, the critical gaze must be sharpened for situations in which the concept of toleration tends to disguise rather than to rectify unjustifiable social trends. The critiques of Karl Marx and Friedrich Nietzsche are those which have

---

30. Quoted in Besier and Schreiner, 'Toleranz', 585.

exerted the most profound influence on the modern discourse of toleration in this regard up to the present day.

2. It is no accident that one of these critiques, namely, the Marxian, was sparked by the issue of the emancipation of the Jews. For a whole complex of long-running historical conflicts come together in this issue, ranging from religious and (increasingly) racist prejudices, from fierce intolerance to different policies of always precarious permission toleration. What could 'emancipation' mean against this background? What form of recognition could or should a minority such as the Jews aspire to: a merely legal-political form or a more sweeping social form? Which rights and liberties did it involve, and would these rights lead to genuine freedom?

In order to throw (at least partial) light on these problems, three positions on the 'Jewish question' should be distinguished which developed in the mid nineteenth century and continue to mark debates over what it means to recognise minorities to the present day. The first is the liberal position as defended, for example, by K. Steinacker in his article 'Emancipation of the Jews' in the above-mentioned *Staats-Lexikon* (1834–) of Rotteck and Welcker, the second the democratic, left-Hegelian position of Bruno Bauer (1843), which, in a third position, Marx attacked in his work 'On the Jewish Question' (1844). Each of the three approaches exhibits a different ideal of emancipation and a different dimension of the dialectic of emancipation and unfreedom which makes toleration seem like a 'half measure'. At the same time, even these progressive writings show how anti-Jewish and anti-Semitic stereotypes continued to operate surreptitiously.

In his wide-ranging article Steinacker seeks to refute the arguments offered against according the Jews complete legal and political emancipation, whether these objectives were based upon positive law, natural law, canon law, morality, religion or economics. He embeds his treatment within a historically informed survey of the situation of the Jews in different European countries, placing particular emphasis on Christian intolerance of the Jews and pointing out the ambivalence of 'grants' of permission toleration which meant that the tolerated Jewish minority all too often had – literally – to 'purchase' certain liberties and concessions and had to live in constant fear of being stripped of their rights entirely when it so pleased the ruling powers. Accordingly, the protection relation amounted to 'a condition of subordination marked by unfreedom'.[31] Permission toleration is a half measure from this perspective because it does not lead to any genuine equality among the citizens; it remains a one-sided relation between ruler and ruled.

31. Steinacker, 'Emancipation der Juden', 24.

It is not possible to present Steinacker's normative discussion in all of its facets here. His central argument involves a rational legal concept of justice according to which no citizen can be denied certain rights without good reasons. Thus, the *ius soli* constitutes a legal argument in favour of the emancipation of the Jews, according to Steinacker. Although the state needs a moral foundation for which religion is of major importance, there is nothing to suggest that the Jewish faith is disadvantageous in this respect. If one considers the many differences among the Christian confessions which are viewed as compatible with the state, there is no reason to assume that the overlapping consensus between them excludes the 'mosaic teaching', which is, after all, the 'root religion of Christianity'.[32] The religious differences, according to Steinacker, should be regarded more or less as *adiaphora*, and views that dispute this must be attributed to anti-Jewish prejudices. There is no reason to make the renunciation of Judaism the price for emancipation, as is often demanded. Moreover, the Jews had not behaved as an independent nation, and thus disloyally, in the past but, on the contrary, had shown themselves to be good citizens. Inasmuch as they exhibited symptoms of social alienation, these were a consequence of the fact that Jews had been excluded from normal social life; but this could not now be held against them. Nor was the other commonplace anti-Semitic accusation – namely, that Jews had resorted to trade and financial dealings – justified because other occupations remained closed to them. If, as was undeniable, according to Steinacker, a certain 'inclination towards self-interest, towards usury and fraud' had developed,[33] this had social causes and was not a permanent feature of the Jewish character, regardless of what the 'rabble' might think.

This argument shows how ambivalent even Steinacker's plea for unrestricted legal and political emancipation remains. Even though he makes a clear distinction between the religious and political levels and unmasks religious and other anti-Semitic biases against Jewish fitness for emancipation, he himself remains captive to certain prejudices concerning the 'tireless speculation' of the Jews, though he simultaneously acknowledges their 'admirable energy' and sees them as victims of gross injustices.[34] Hence, the Jews remain the alien and other, and also in a certain sense a suspect 'Volk' which must be integrated and which still has to *prove* that it can be integrated – Steinacker's point being his conviction that the Jews can prove this. The Jews continue to be measured against the Christian 'norm', even though Steinacker categorically rejects the view that they can be granted full

32. *Ibid.* 38–9.   33. *Ibid.* 46.   34. *Ibid.* 50–6.

citizenship only if they renounce their religion. This is his contribution to developing reflection on toleration in a consistent fashion beyond the 'half measure' of permission toleration. Yet this minority discourse, although progressive for its time, remains precisely that, namely, a discourse about a minority from the majority 'We' perspective.

This dialectical tension between advocating emancipation and testing fitness for integration (undertaken from the perspective of a dominant group) is, in turn, the 'half measure' which marks Steinacker's liberal toleration in the eyes of Bruno Bauer (in his works *The Jewish Question* and *The Capacity of Present-Day Jews and Christians to Become Free*, both published in 1843). He calls for a more radical form of political emancipation and dissuades the Jews from making their goal toleration or equal rights in a state which remains largely dominated by Christians; instead they should aim for freedom *from* religion, both on the side of the state and on that of the Jews themselves. Bauer's goal is the laicist state of the *citoyens* who have sloughed off their religious and national particularisms and no longer encounter each other as strangers. Religion can then be accorded at most a restricted space in the private sphere; the key issue is the formation of a new way of ethical life which overcomes religious divisions and the old network of privileges and concessions. In order to become part of such a state, however, the Jews must first emancipate themselves from their religion and cease to be a nation.

This argument involves different ambivalences from Steinacker's, though they have similar effects. Although the Jews should no longer be measured in accordance with the Christian norm and should no longer claim toleration, but instead genuine social and political emancipation, nevertheless they must 'have ceased to be Jewish'[35] and become citizens – a requirement rejected by Steinacker – just as the Christians for their part must become citizens. In emphasising the aspect of separation and segregation that in his view attaches to the Jews as a nation and a religion, however, Bauer perpetuates the very discourse of exclusion which he seeks to overcome, for he can envisage political emancipation only at the cost of the abandonment of the citizens' religious identity. Of course, for him this is not a high price; religion is ultimately seen as the main obstacle on the path to freedom. It must be politically 'abolished' (*aufgehoben*). Whereas this takes issue with the one-sided Christian perspective of compatibility with the state, on the other hand it replaces it with a republican perspective which sees Judaism just as much as an impediment to equal rights that needs to be overcome. The

---

35. Bauer, quoted in Marx, 'On the Jewish Question', 29.

Jewish 'Volk' remains a people which is difficult to integrate and must first be liberated from itself.

Marx regards this in turn as a '*half measure of political emancipation*':[36] Bauer's standpoint does not have the right to demand that the Jews should abolish Judaism or to demand that human beings in general should 'abolish religion' (30). However, this objection does not rest on the assumption that the state would thereby violate individual liberty rights (as Steinacker thinks), but on the assumption that the political emancipation which Bauer seeks (and which is supposed to overcome the liberal standpoint) is itself only a half measure. Bauer's error consists in 'his lack of critical sense in confusing political emancipation and universal human emancipation' (*ibid.*), in erroneously thinking that equal political rights would entail a true liberation capable of overcoming the religious consciousness which Marx, like Bauer, regards as a mark of the 'existence of a defect' (31). Just as Bauer regards a political emancipation without emancipation from religion as a half measure, so, too, Marx regards this political emancipation without genuine human emancipation, without emancipation from the bourgeois state as such, as a half measure.

Contrary to Bauer, in Marx's view political, bourgeois emancipation leads not to the suppression, but to the strengthening of religion, and that in various respects. First, the example of the United States shows that a political emancipation which displaces religion into the social domain first enables it to flourish (*ibid.*). Moreover, second, this is perfectly understandable in a society such as the Americans in which religion, given the coexistence of political freedom (and equality) and social unfreedom (and inequality), can first fully exercise its compensatory effect (34, 39). And, therefore, third, the religious splitting of the world into a free heavenly and an unfree terrestrial sphere mirrors precisely the characteristic doubling of the bourgeois state, which thus represents the consummation of the Christian state (36, 39): the splitting into the *citoyen* who imagines himself to be free, and the *bourgeois* who, in the sphere of civil society dominated by private property, 'treats other men as means, degrades himself to the role of a mere means, and becomes the plaything of alien powers' (34). Political liberty is accordingly a *false liberty* because it not only disguises, but in addition cements, the real unfreedom in society. The half measure consists in the merely imaginary emancipation of the citizens, even if political emancipation represented genuine progress in real historical terms for Marx (35).

36. Marx, 'On the Jewish Question', 30, emphasis in original (further page references in the text).

Marx's concern is thus not to emancipate the Jews from their Judaism towards the political state, but to liberate them from their Judaism and from the state towards an emancipated society:

> We do not say to the Jews, therefore, as does Bauer: you cannot be emancipated politically without emancipating yourselves completely from Judaism. We say rather: it is because you can be emancipated politically, without renouncing Judaism completely and absolutely, that *political emancipation* itself is not *human* emancipation.
>
> (40, emphasis in the original)

Here, too, Judaism is an obstacle to emancipation, though now the issue is emancipation towards a truly human condition. Human rights as *droits de l'homme* are false promises of freedom, according to Marx, because they only lead to the detachment of the egoistic, isolated and monadic private human beings; they are the rights 'of man separated from other men and from the community' (42), rights of 'limited' beings who cling to their religious identity. Hence, religious freedom is not the true liberation 'from religion' (45) towards the human condition of a communal 'species-being' (43) who becomes free only as a social being.

At this point there is no need to highlight the anti-Semitic theses which dominate the second part of Marx's text in order to reveal the ambivalence of this conception of emancipation: the theses according to which the 'profane basis of Judaism' is 'practical need, self-interest'; that 'the worldly cult of the Jew' is 'huckstering' and his 'worldly God' is 'money' (48); that the 'chimerical nationality of the Jew' is the nationality 'of the trader, and above all of the financier' (51). With these assertions Marx assimilates the spirit of the Jews to that of capitalism, so that, in emancipating itself from Judaism, 'our age would emancipate itself' (48).[37] The ambivalence resides elsewhere, namely where in Marx, too, genuine emancipation is emancipation from religion in general and from Judaism in particular, which on account of its 'limited nature' (thus Marx following Bauer, 42) represents an obstacle on the path to genuine freedom, that is to say the path of society as a whole as well as of the Jew himself who, as an 'antisocial element', remains trapped in a particular condition of 'self-estrangement' (48). This ethical-political perfectionism of the freedom of human beings towards themselves as 'species-beings' enables Marx to condemn as half measures the liberties which would constitute legal and political emancipation: a toleration of the religious identities on which these liberties would confer equal rights would amount to a perpetuation

---

37. On anti-Semitism in Marx, see Brumlik, *Deutscher Geist und Judenhaß*, ch. 6.

of social and individual unfreedom. And thus the aim must be to liberate human beings – in this case, the Jews – in the first instance from themselves to themselves.

However, this general perfectionist critique of toleration, which involves the danger of an inverted dialectic of ideal freedom and real unfreedom, is not the entire lesson to be drawn from Marx's treatise. For it represents an important, productive stage in the discourse of toleration insofar as Marx points out that even the form of legal and political emancipation which overcomes permission toleration can represent a half measure when it simultaneously conceals or entrenches social mechanisms of power, be they of an economic or, to go beyond Marx's perspective, a cultural kind.[38] If formal legal freedoms and toleration are not accompanied by social freedom, according particular rights to minorities can also have the effect of fixing them in a socially underprivileged position, because either they lack the means to make use of these rights or the rights in question do not go far enough. *Exclusion* would then turn into a form of *inclusion* which merely further solidifies cultural stigmatisation and social powerlessness. Thus, even particular rights for minorities can liberate them and at the same time subject them to stronger forms of legal and political control. This makes evident once again that the respect conception of toleration must replace the permission conception and exercise structuring effects at the political level, so that excluded and 'locked in' groups have the opportunity to lend political force to their claims, even against socially established conventions and prejudices. The critique of false liberty and toleration by half measures must itself become a political issue, and this will continue to require toleration and respect among citizens who may *not* demand of one another, as Marx's perfectionism implies, that they should renounce their ethical or religious identity for the sake of freedom as 'species-beings'. However, they may demand from one another what is implied by Marx's justice perspective, namely, that they expose the social, economic and cultural (and not just the political) mechanisms of power to which they are subject to critical discourses of justification. The toleration situation must include a critique of power, and the power to conduct this critique. We can leave it open whether this will entail an abolition of 'alienation'; at least it will seek to abolish repressive forms of toleration and to render the toleration situation reflexive. In this context it should be possible to combine Steinacker's emphasis on individual liberty, Bauer's emphasis on political self-regulation and Marx's emphasis on the necessity of social

---

38. Wendy Brown places particular emphasis on this in her reading of Marx's text in *States of Injury*, ch. 5.

self-determination into a fourth position without regressing behind the differentiations between the conceptions of the ethical person, the legal person, the citizen and the moral person achieved by Kant, and especially without imposing a prior ethical definition of what it means to live a 'human' life.

3. Toleration is criticised as a half measure in a different – namely, an existential-ethical – sense by the second great critic of morality and religion of the nineteenth century: in this case as a half measure, not from the perspective of those who are the beneficiaries of (dubious) toleration, but from the perspective of those who show tolerance. Hence, with Nietzsche's critique the discourse of toleration is pointed back towards its origins, to the Stoic conception of *tolerantia* as an attitude towards oneself, as a virtue of dignified self-control in the face of the most diverse ills and as courageous self-overcoming in being tolerant. This dimension of toleration cropped up repeatedly – for instance in Montaigne, Bayle and Kant – but it regains pride of place only with Nietzsche, provoked by his charge that the posture of tolerance is not a sign of strength at all but of weakness of intellect and character, a typical sign of modern self-lessness. The freedom and nobility which it purports to represent are merely conceit; in reality tolerance is a sign of cowardice and denial of self.

Nietzsche develops this idea in different contexts. In his reflections 'On the Uses and Disadvantages of History for Life' (1874) he contrasts the virtue of justice, which demonstrates the courage to make judgements, with tolerance, which is all that the mass of people are capable of, namely 'allowing validity to what they cannot deny happened . . . explaining away and extenuating, on the correct assumption that the inexperienced will interpret the mere absence of strong judgements and expressions of hatred concerning the past as evidence of a just disposition'.[39] In *Beyond Good and Evil* (1886), too, he sees this typically modern weakness at work where the enlightened scholar has preserved only a superficial sense for religion and makes of his indifference a virtue of tolerance that imagines itself to be superior to religion.[40]

In other writings from the 1880s, in particular the *Nachgelassene Fragmente* (*Posthumous Fragments*), he generalises this critique and situates it in the context of his analysis of the essence of moral prejudices. Thus, tolerance appears here as an expression of the 'indolent peace' of modern consciousness, as '*largeur* of the heart that "forgives" everything because it "understands" everything',[41] as a false 'recognition of the ideals of

---

39. Nietzsche, *Untimely Meditations*, 90 (translation amended).
40. Nietzsche, *Beyond Good and Evil*, 53.   41. Nietzsche, *The Antichrist*, 4.

others! Anyone who profoundly and unshakeably affirms his own ideals cannot believe in other ideals without belittling them – as ideals of inferior beings to himself... Thus, tolerance, historical sense, so-called justice are a token of mistrust – or of the lack – of an ideal of one's own.'[42] Tolerance is a typical 'virtue of the herd', 'the fear of asserting one's right, of judging', the first 'pomposity' on the list of 'depravities of the modern spirit': the 'inability of saying yes or no'.[43]

In this critique Nietzsche expresses what many regard as the characteristic feature of the concept of toleration, namely the posture of indifference, the refusal or even the cowardice to take a stance, the attitude of emptiness. However, this rests on a misunderstanding because the concept of toleration is used incorrectly when it is applied to an attitude of indifference; for without a sufficiently strong objection component (cf. §1) there is no occasion for toleration. A repudiation of one's own ideals would not be toleration. To this extent Nietzsche's objection misses the mark. Nevertheless, it is fruitful insofar as it suggests how difficult it is to strike a balance between objection, acceptance and rejection, or, to put it more precisely, how fine the line is between remaining true to one's convictions while simultaneously relativising them vis-à-vis intolerant opposition towards others, on the one hand, and resignation or indifference, on the other. For Nietzsche, however, only the latter alternatives are conceivable. Against him, it must therefore be insisted that only those who trust in their own ideals can be tolerant. For tolerance means being able to say *yes* or *no* in a differentiated manner. It involves, first, clearly grasping and affirming differences of opinions and beliefs and thus deep disagreement, while, second, nevertheless heeding reasons which speak against the unjustifiable suppression of others. This is what makes toleration an act of freedom and of inner *fortitude*:[44] freely limiting, and in part also overcoming, oneself for moral reasons (according to the respect conception, for which tolerance is a virtue), *without* abandoning one's most deeply held convictions in the process. This calls for a certain, unshakeable self-confidence and precisely the ability to distinguish good reasons in different contexts of justification and to act accordingly. The awareness of one's own autonomy as an ethical and a moral person, as a legal person and a citizen, must be correspondingly well-developed if one is to be able to strike the correct balance between objection, acceptance and rejection. An insecure sense of

42. Nietzsche, *Nachgelassene Fragmente 1880–1882*, 476–7.
43. Nietzsche, *Nachgelassene Fragmente 1885–1887*, 274–5, 432.
44. On this, see Mitscherlich, 'Toleranz'.

self, a herd virtue, would be incapable of this.[45] However, to remain tolerant where there are reasons for rejection, thus for limits to toleration, would be tolerance from cowardice, in which case Nietzsche's critique would be justified.

Properly understood, therefore, toleration presupposes something which Nietzsche criticises, namely *tolerance towards oneself*, though in a different sense than he intends. By this Nietzsche understands the posture of allowing the extremely diverse convictions one holds to coexist without any attempt to order them or to draw a 'conclusion'.[46] In this he overlooks, in turn, that only a reflexively 'ordered' self, who knows how to make negative and positive judgements, is capable of tolerance; however, it is true that in the virtue of tolerance a person encounters opposing convictions within herself which she can reconcile, if not entirely, only through tolerance. Thus, ethical objections may conflict with moral acceptance, in which case the virtue of tolerance nevertheless demands that they be brought into harmony by following the stronger reasons. But in the process an inner conflictuality remains intact. I will return to this in the more detailed discussion of the virtue of tolerance (see below §36).

However, these scant remarks should suffice to show that tolerance, especially when it is understood as an attitude in accordance with the respect conception, involves a complex relation to self which, although it differs from Nietzsche's conception, raises the question concerning a 'labour on oneself', concerning what it means to be a 'sovereign individual',[47] and for this very reason tolerant. This would then also call for a response to a final, and arguably the greatest, challenge posed by Nietzsche, namely the accusation levelled at the 'preachers of toleration' that, just like the intolerant persecutors, they absolutise a particular, arbitrary conception of reason, as a matter of taste – and bad taste at that.[48] If a generally justifiable theory of toleration is to be possible, this accusation must be wide of the target.[49] Otherwise toleration would indeed be nothing more than a half measure.

45. In other places Nietzsche certainly recognises that toleration can also flow from a posture of strength, but only in the sense of a hierarchical permission conception; see *The Gay Science*, 222, on the 'luxury' of tolerance, 'which every victorious, self-confident power permits itself'; and *Beyond Good and Evil*, 67, on the 'noble and frivolous' toleration of the Romans.
46. Nietzsche, *Twilight of the Idols*, 200.   47. See Nietzsche, *On the Genealogy of Morals*, 37.
48. Nietzsche, *Nachgelassene Fragmente 1880–1882*, 480.
49. On this, see also §1 on the 'paradox of drawing the limits'. I will return to this in Part II.

§27 Without end

1. In thus tracing the discourse of toleration back to its point of departure, where the latter is intended at the same time to provide the point of departure for the proposed theory of toleration in the second part, we conclude our historical survey for the present. Of course, this is not to imply that this marks the end of the history of toleration, quite the contrary. For the twentieth century, which has been described as the 'age of extremes',[50] was dominated by profound political-ideological conflicts which led to two world wars and ended with a multitude of struggles and wars involving complex political and religious antagonisms. The call for toleration was ubiquitous and no less urgent than in earlier times. The point is that, since my primary concern in the foregoing was not to present an exhaustive history of toleration but to reconstruct a *history of argumentation*, the discourse of toleration has reached a provisional conclusion with Marx's and Nietzsche's critique, in the sense that we now have at our disposal the full spectrum of the classical justifications (and critiques) of toleration in a differentiated form (with one exception, that of value relativism, as I discuss below). In what follows, therefore, I will offer only a very brief and sketchy historical survey of the most important developments during the twentieth century, before turning in the second part of the book to a discussion of the systematic problems which shape the contemporary philosophical and political discourse concerning toleration. More recent relevant justifications of toleration will be addressed, though it will become apparent that generally speaking they do not add anything essentially new to the classical arguments.

The developments I would like to mention concern the legal implementation of the liberties fought for over the course of the history of toleration, furthermore political toleration, cultural and ethnic toleration, religious toleration and, finally, toleration on a global scale – allowing that these dimensions overlap in a variety of ways.

2. From the perspective of positive law, the history of toleration would take the form of a history of the codification of basic liberties, not only freedom of religious exercise but also freedom of conscience, of speech and of the press. In the German context, this history extends from the German Imperial Constitution of 1849 (which did not come into force), through the basic rights in the Weimar Constitution (1919), to the Basic Law of the Federal Republic of Germany and the constitution of the German Democratic Republic (both 1949).[51] Taking this as one's standpoint, one needs

---

50. Hobsbawm, *The Age of Extremes*.   51. On this, see Herdtle and Leeb (eds.), *Toleranz*, 92–118.

to examine in what sense such constitutional systems implement the idea of toleration or neutrality, for example in constitutional court decisions.[52] For no less important than the legal stipulations is the issue of how they are interpreted in practice, and the question of the relation between legally guaranteed liberties and social tolerance or intolerance (I will come back to this in §38).[53]

A further important aspect of legal toleration is the codification of fundamental freedoms at the international level, first and foremost in the Universal Declaration of Human Rights of 1948, which in Article 2 prohibits discrimination on the basis of 'race, colour, sex, language, religion, political or other opinion, national or social origin, property, birth or other status' and in Articles 18 and 19 guarantees 'freedom of thought, conscience and religion' and freedom of opinion and expression. These freedoms are underlined once again in the declaration of the United Nations on the elimination of all forms of intolerance and discrimination on the basis of religion or belief of 1981 (Resolution 36/55); and in 1995, the official international year of toleration, UNESCO issued a declaration on toleration which explains that tolerance means 'respect, acceptance and appreciation of the rich diversity of the cultures of our world' and places particular emphasis on the fact that tolerance cannot be realised exclusively at the legal level since it is no less an individual virtue than a political practice. Therefore, aspects of education will be accorded special importance.[54]

This shows once again that the toleration situation in any given country is not just a matter of which freedoms are legally codified in which ways but of how the legal and social *practice* of toleration is configured in certain contexts.[55]

3. A special aspect of toleration in a constitutional state is political toleration, specifically the question of its limits: how tolerant should one be of the enemies of toleration?

---

52. For Germany, see Püttner, *Toleranz als Verfassungsprinzip*; Schnapp, 'Toleranzidee und Grundgesetz'; Neumann, 'Toleranz als grundlegendes Verfassungsprinzip'; Volkmann, 'Grund und Grenzen der Toleranz'; Debus, *Das Verfassungsprinzip der Toleranz unter besonderer Berücksichtigung der Rechtsprechung des Bundesverfassungsgerichts*; for a detailed treatment of the issue of neutrality, see Huster, *Die ethische Neutralität des Staates*. For the United States, see, among others, Richards, *Toleration and the Constitution*. On the relation between toleration and neutrality, see below §37.

53. The sundry discussions of toleration in Germany since the founding of the Federal Republic are documented in the review essay of Wierlacher, 'Toleranzdiskurse in Deutschland'.

54. See the wording of UNESCO, Declaration of Principles of Toleration, www.unesco.org/cpp/uk/declarations/tolerance.pdf (accessed 24 September 2010).

55. On this, see the detailed report on freedom of religion in over fifty countries by Boyle and Sheen, *Freedom of Religion and Belief*.

A striking position in this regard is the one defended by Hans Kelsen in 1932 and 1933 that it is inconsistent with the tolerant character of a democracy to defend itself against antidemocratic movements by prohibiting them.[56] He reiterates this thesis in his 1953 essay 'What Is Justice?' (though he acknowledges that democracy, like any other form of government, has the right to defend itself against violent attempts to overthrow it).[57] He sees the reason for this as residing in the fact that no form of government can claim for itself absolute truth or objective value, i.e. it is based on an epistemologically grounded value relativism. From this 'fact'[58] of ethical pluralism and subjectivism, however, he derives the thesis that it implies a 'moral principle', namely that of tolerance:

> The particular moral principle involved in a relativistic philosophy of justice is the principle of tolerance, and that means the sympathetic understanding of the religious or political beliefs of others – without accepting them, but not preventing them from being freely expressed.[59]

Democracy, according to Kelsen, is a just and preferable form of government because it guarantees freedom, 'and freedom means tolerance'.[60] And from this follows the requirement also to tolerate antidemocrats. This marks the appearance of an important new justification of toleration, namely, that of value relativism. It suffers from a manifest weakness, however: either such a relativism exists, in which case the 'value' of freedom or toleration is not immune against it and cannot represent a higher-level principle of any kind; or such a principle exists, in which case the relativism thesis is false, not to mention that it is also contradictory from an epistemological point of view because it insists on the limitations of human reason in ethical questions on the one hand, but claims to have a global perspective on ethical reality on the other.[61] Aside from this relativistic justification of toleration, Kelsen's argument concerning the limits on democracy's scope for 'defending itself' is also open to question. For even if democracy rested on the merely relative value of freedom, or even on the principle of toleration, it would have just as much right as other value systems to defend itself, in the conflict between subjective values, against the proponents of restrictions on freedom and toleration. *Pace* Kelsen, that would still not make it into an autocracy.

---

56. Kelsen, 'Verteidigung der Demokratie'; 'On the Essence and Value of Democracy'.
57. Kelsen, 'What Is Justice?', 23.   58. *Ibid.* 7.   59. *Ibid.* 22.   60. *Ibid.* 23.
61. Cf. Putnam's critique of relativism in *Reason, Truth and History*, ch. 5.

A position contrary to Kelsen's was taken at the time by Carl Schmitt. Schmitt placed no less emphasis on the subjectivity of values than Kelsen but was led by his substantialist conception of the state to reject the neutralisation of the state, its internal 'undermining'[62] and the corresponding 'passive tolerance':

> The unavoidable conclusion is that this principle must lead to a general neutrality towards every conceivable opinion and problem and to an absolute equal treatment, such that, for example, the man of religious convictions may receive no more protection than the atheist, the man of national convictions no more than the enemy and despiser of the nation. This further implies absolute freedom for every kind of propaganda, religious as well as antireligious, national as well as antinational; absolute 'deference' to 'dissenters' as such, even if they make a mockery of decency and morals, undermine the government and agitate in the service of a foreign state. This kind of 'neutral state' is the *entirely indiscriminate, relativistic* stato neutrale e agnostico, the state without content or at least one whose content is reduced to a *minimum*.[63]

According to Schmitt, this 'minimum' nevertheless leaves the liberal state a residuum of political substance, since, in contrast to the completely neutralised instrumental state, it can still at least exclude those who do not share this idea of neutrality as 'enemies'; but if this is combined with 'neutrality in the sense of equal opportunities in the formation of the political will', then the apparatus of the state must abandon itself to the free play of the forces that place it in question. By contrast, Schmitt calls for the 'total state' which, in complete conformity with the unity of Church and State of the Hobbesian Leviathan, does not recognise any prior individual liberty rights and 'does not permit any internal forces which are hostile to the state or which tend to constrain or divide it'.[64] It performs the task of

---

62. For this undermining of the state he blamed, as already noted above, the development of subjective freedom of conscience, the 'crack' in the Leviathan which attracted the attention of 'the first liberal Jew' Spinoza, just as later it was the 'restless spirit of the Jew' embodied by Mendelssohn which 'validated the distinction between inner and outer, morality and right, inner disposition and outer performance and demands from the state freedom of thought', because he recognised that such an 'undermining of state power . . . served to paralyse the alien and to emancipate his own Jewish folk'. Schmitt, *The Leviathan in the State Theory of Thomas Hobbes*, 57 and 60.
63. Schmitt, 'Übersicht über die verschiedenen Bedeutungen und Funktionen des Begriffes der innerpolitischen Neutralität des Staates', 97–8 (italics in original).
64. Schmitt, 'Weiterentwicklung des totalen Staates in Deutschland', 186.

392 Toleration in Conflict

defending the 'substantial homogeneity of a nation'[65] and ultimately the 'racial affinity among its members' (*rassische Artverbundenheit*).[66] Intolerance thereby becomes one of the chief virtues of the total and fascist state.

In the wake of the catastrophes caused by the total state in its National Socialist guise, which prided itself on its intolerance[67] and attempted to annihilate the minority which had been a primary target of persecution and suppression in European societies from time immemorial, the Jews, a third position was sought which went beyond a relativistic liberalism, whose form of toleration ultimately led in the eyes of many 'to its own abolition, namely to intolerance',[68] and beyond a substantialist-totalitarian conception of the state and nation, and which offered a justification founded on natural law of the motto: 'No tolerance of the enemies of toleration!', as Dolf Sternberger put it in 1946.[69] The newly founded political system should be normatively and legally armed against its inner erosion by the enemies of democracy; it should be a 'militant'[70] democracy. And in order to avoid positivistic relativisation and 'neutralisation', particular emphasis was placed on the *religious* foundations of this natural law[71] and on the need to replace a 'formal' with a value-bound, 'substantial' form of toleration.[72] From this is derived the possibility envisaged in the Basic Law (Art. 21 (2) GG) of the Federal Republic of Germany of banning political parties as unconstitutional, as well as the 'guarantee of perpetuity' (*Ewigkeitsgarantie*) of its basic principles in Article 79 (3). Setting aside the resulting concrete legal problems, however, this conception of toleration raises the problem that according to it the general toleration guaranteed by the state, expressed in the liberty rights, rests on a substantial basis of values which *cannot* be shared by all as long as it still contains residues of Christian natural law and pursues the goal of avoiding dangerous political-moral (and to some extent religious) 'neutralisations' and 'erosions'.[73] Especially approaches which presuppose that the state is founded on a moral 'homogeneity', though it cannot guarantee this

---

65. Schmitt, 'State Ethics and the Pluralist State', 306.
66. Schmitt, 'Wesen und Werden des faschistischen Staates', 42.
67. Cf. Besier and Schreiner, 'Toleranz', 594–5.   68. Leibholz, 'Vorwort', ix.
69. Sternberger, 'Toleranz als Leidenschaft für die Wahrheit', 166.
70. Thus, the German Federal Constitutional Court in its 1956 decision declaring the German Communist Party to be unconstitutional. On this, see Mandt, 'Grenzen politischer Toleranz in der offenen Gesellschaft'.
71. On this, see Maihofer (ed.), *Naturrecht oder Positivismus?*
72. Cf. Besier and Schreiner, 'Toleranz', 597.
73. The specific combination of religious motifs founded on natural law and ideas of Carl Schmitt represents a special problem in this connection; see Maus, *Bürgerliche Rechtstheorie und Faschismus*.

foundation with its own means,[74] lead to major conflicts over the limits of toleration, as will become apparent in Chapter 12.

4. The problem of the substantiality of a polity becomes especially apparent with regard to the extension of the discourse of toleration in the cultural dimension which can be traced back to Herder. The phenomenon of nationalism was the first to acquire prominence in this regard during the nineteenth century, since 'culture' was understood primarily in terms of 'people' or 'nation', and with it the question of how different nations can tolerate each other which dominated many of the subsequent discussions.[75] Were one to write the history of this development, this discourse would have to be reconstructed up to the present, including the important aspects of colonisation and decolonisation in which the essentialistic assumption that a people has a cultural substance played a major role, though in more recent times this assumption has been increasingly exposed to critical scrutiny.[76]

Since the 1960s this discussion has been progressively supplanted by the discussion of *multiculturalism*,[77] that is, of the coexistence of and toleration among (mainly) ethnic groups within a state (where these groups are also generally classified according to religion or confession). With this, issues of horizontal and vertical toleration arise in connection with conflicts which vary according to the history and structure of the state concerned (whether it is a classical nation-state or a country of immigration, or something in between) and with the groups involved (native groups, immigrants, former slaves, etc.).[78] In these debates the discourse of toleration becomes more intense, leading to a recapitulation of many of the justifications of toleration worked out over the course of history. In the midst of European democracies, though not there alone, a range of conflicts over the political and religious identity of societies arises which challenge their self-understanding.[79] Central to these conflicts are questions concerning the social and political integration of a political community and the rights of minorities, and accordingly the issue of the limits of toleration. I will take this up again in Chapter 12, with particular attention to the question of what is supposed to constitute the normative basis of a conception of multicultural justice.

---

74. Thus, Böckenförde's famous thesis in 'The Rise of the State as a Process of Secularisation', 44–5, 46.
75. Ignatieff emphasises the virulence of this question in 'Nationalism and Toleration'.
76. Cf. Anderson, *Imagined Communities*.
77. In this context attempts have also been made to define 'liberal nationalism'; see Tamir, *Liberal Nationalism* and Kymlicka, *Politics in the Vernacular*.
78. See, among many others, Kymlicka, *Multicultural Citizenship* and Walzer, *On Toleration*.
79. See Balke *et al.* (eds.), *Schwierige Fremdheit*; Heitmeyer and Dollase (eds.), *Die bedrängte Toleranz*.

Closely related to the problem of cultural toleration is, furthermore, the question of how tolerant a society is towards nonconformist, though not primarily ethnically and religiously defined, persons or groups,[80] for instance towards homosexuals.[81] These groups are targets of a range of deep-seated, often religiously motivated rejections, and thus provide important indicators of a society's capacity for toleration. This issue will also have to be addressed later.

Another increasingly important potential for conflict, which places major demands on toleration, should also be mentioned in this context. For not only the long-running controversy over abortion but also the questions raised by biotechnology concerning the legitimacy of so-called 'destructive' embryo research, cloning and (therapeutic or eugenic) manipulations of the genetic make-up of human beings seem to place in question the distinction between unconditionally binding moral norms, which concern action towards other persons, and ethical values, which concern the quality of one's own life and rely on particular (for example, religious) sources. The challenge resides in the fact that determining the moment from which one can undeniably speak of a 'moral person' is precisely the ethical-moral point at issue.[82] What appears to one person to be a practice which is only subject to ethical evaluation, whether positive or negative, without strict universal validity, is for another a practice which is clearly to be judged in moral terms.[83] Here we must ask whether and, if so, how this conflict can still be resolved within the framework of the respect conception of toleration.

5. Religion evidently plays an important, though not the central, role in all of the contexts mentioned. For it remains controversial whether the state can do entirely without a religious and ethical foundation shared by the majority (and thus it is apparent how effective 'Locke's fear' continues to be); and religious objections to particular groups and their practices are of cardinal importance in political conflicts. In many of these conflicts one can even observe a revival of religious identities, be they collective or individual, at the heart of 'secular' societies.[84] This seems to render the question of religious toleration more relevant than ever, even if very many of the controversies mentioned exhibit a complex mixture of sociopolitical, cultural and religious aspects.

---

80. On the controversies surrounding this question in Germany in the 1970s, see Schultz (ed.), *Toleranz*.
81. The classical controversy on this question is that between Lord Devlin (*The Enforcement of Morals*) and Hart (*Law, Liberty, and Morality*).
82. On this, see §31.4 below.   83. See the controversial discussions in Geyer (ed.), *Biopolitik*.
84. See Kallscheuer (ed.), *Das Europa der Religionen*.

If one examines the history of religious toleration, the assumption that, with the breakthrough of the principles of the French Revolution, the issue was basically decided in favour of a secular legal system is in need of qualification. For the Catholic Church, for example, made its peace with the right to religious freedom only with the declaration of the Second Vatican Council, *De libertate religiosa* (1965), in which it is acknowledged as a right which 'has its foundation in the very dignity of the human person as this dignity is known through the revealed word of God and by reason itself', and thus which is granted also to those 'who do not live up to their obligation of seeking the truth and adhering to it'.[85] Although this right remains one which is primarily justified in terms of the service it performs for religious truth,[86] the truth can now no longer claim priority over freedom in the sense that freedom would only have value as long as it conforms with the truth, and hence that the right of truth would have priority.[87]

A long and arduous path had to be followed in order to arrive at this result. Traditionally the principle of universal toleration and the right to religious freedom were categorically rejected by the Church, and if they were accepted then only 'as the acceptance of an evil and a concession to the actual circumstances',[88] primarily for strategic reasons. The encyclical *Mirari vos* of Pope Gregory XVI (1832), for instance, states that: 'This shameful font of indifferentism gives rise to that absurd and erroneous proposition which claims that liberty of conscience must be maintained for everyone. It spreads ruin in sacred and civil affairs, though some repeat over and over again with the greatest impudence that some advantage accrues to religion from it.'[89] This established a basic anti-liberal posture which Pope Pius IX reiterated in his encyclical *Quanta cura* (1864) when he described the notion that every human being has the right of religious freedom as a 'delirium' and appended a 'syllabus' comprising eighty propositions condemned by Rome, featuring, among others, the following: '15. Every man is free to embrace and profess

85. *Declaration on Religious Freedom*, www.vatican.va/archive/hist_councils/ii_vatican_council/ documents/vat-ii_decl_19651207_dignitatis-humanae_en.html (accessed 25 September 2010).
86. This also holds for the – albeit, on account of the importance of the concept of conscience and of the two-kingdoms doctrine, sharply contrasting – Protestant conception of the necessity of freedom for individual obedience by faith – that is, in my terms, the conception of the unfree free conscience. On this, see Wolf, 'Toleranz nach evangelischem Verständnis', 151.
87. For a critique of such a conception, see Böckenförde, 'Toleranz', 62–3. However, he is also of the opinion that 'freedom of religion exists as a right not in opposition to the truth but for the sake of the truth' (68).
88. Böckenförde, 'Einleitung zur Textausgabe der "Erklärung über die Religionsfreiheit"', 402.
89. Pope Gregory XVI, *Mirari vos* (On Liberalism and Religious Indifferentism), www.ewtn.com/library/encyc/g16mirar.htm (accessed 25 September 2010).

that religion which, guided by the light of reason, he shall consider true. 16. Man may, in the observance of any religion whatever, find the way of eternal salvation, and arrive at eternal salvation . . . 77. In the present day it is no longer expedient that the Catholic religion should be held as the only religion of the State, to the exclusion of all other forms of worship.'[90] This position was moderated over time, yet even in the so-called 'Tolerance Address' of Pius XII of 1953 one reads: 'First: that which does not correspond to truth or to the norm of morality objectively has no right to exist, to be spread or to be activated. Secondly: failure to impede this with civil laws and coercive measures can nevertheless be justified in the interests of a higher and more general good.'[91] Therefore, toleration may be required for the sake of a higher good, yet there is emphatically no right to toleration.

These brief remarks should be sufficient to refute the claim that the modern period marked the inexorable rise of the respect conception of toleration; the reasons for, and also those against, toleration were simply too diverse. The route leading to a conception of religion that succeeds in relativising its own truth in the light of respect for others – though not in the light of their truth – was and remains a long one.

In current critical discussions of *religious fundamentalism*[92] one should thus first keep in mind the history and the present of Christianity when other religions are criticised. Second, fundamentalism should be understood not as the unwillingness to be doctrinally tolerant, for example to relativise one's own truth, but as the inability or refusal to acknowledge the primacy of a morality of individual dignity and reciprocity as setting a limit on one's own truth in social and political matters and to allow the possibility of 'reasonable differences' in the religious domain. However, the demand for this primacy of morality is *not* relativisable where the point is not to impose a 'liberal' lifestyle or even a liberal 'world order', but to prevent possible victims of a lack of moral respect. Its protest against repressive practices is decisive. Thus, counterposing a 'premodern or antimodern' fundamentalism, a 'modern' universalism and a 'postmodern' relativism, where the latter can understand the moral objection only in terms of the self-assertion of a liberal culture

90. Pope Pius IX, *Quanta cura* (Condemning Current Errors), www.ewtn.com/library/encyc/p9quanta.htm (accessed 25 September 2010); The Syllabus of Errors Condemned by Pius IX, www.papalencyclicals.net/Pius09/p9syll.htm (accessed 25 September 2010).

91. Pope Pius XII, *Ci riesce* (Address to Italian Jurists), www.ewtn.com/library/PAPALDOC/P12CIRI.HTM (accessed 25 September 2010).

92. Cf. Marty and Appleby, *The Glory and the Power*; Bielefeldt and Heitmeyer (eds.), *Politisierte Religion*.

for which religion is at most a private game of ethical self-invention,[93] is all too easy and not especially helpful. The point is rather to recognise the reasons for absolutising religion which are all too often not primarily of a religious nature, even if religion offers a major ideological potential, and to recognise where the moral objection must be raised. In this regard, the 'modern' normative standards themselves are not beyond justification but must prove their validity in the relevant justification situation.

The history of toleration, as reconstructed above, should immunise us against assuming that toleration is an invention or possession of 'Christianity'. Although, as we have seen, a range of justifications of toleration appeal to Christian foundations, this is equally true of many no less sophisticated justifications of intolerance, so that principles for a reciprocal justification of toleration had to be sought elsewhere. The Christian history of toleration is a history of acrimonious internal struggles for and against toleration, struggles in which it was always the dissidents, the 'heretics', who demanded and argued for toleration. Non-Christians also make use of some of these religious justifications, yet they were also able to fall back on other roots of the notion of toleration, if one thinks, for example, of Maimonides or Averroes. Connecting up with this, a truly universal analysis of toleration would have to examine the potentials for toleration of all religions as to their kind and what forms of self-relativisation they make possible. Only such a study could shed light on whether, for example, the statement in the Qur'an (Sura 2/256) 'There is no compulsion in religion' could serve as the point of departure for a development towards general toleration and the ascription of a right of freedom of conscience, just as the traditional Islamic practices of toleration should be examined as to whether they contain possible inspiration for contemporary thought.[94] Given the complexity of this task, which is, of course, not confined to Islam, it could not be accomplished within the scope of the present study.

6. These few indications broach a problem which is acquiring increasing urgency in a world in which not only are states becoming more 'multicultural' and multi-religious, but the international community also increasingly sees itself as a community which must develop shared norms of action: the question of global toleration, which has been the focus of intense debates in recent decades, whether against the backdrop of a supposedly impending

---

93. Thus, Rorty in *Contingency, Irony, and Solidarity*, chs. 1–4, 9, and 'Postmodernist Bourgeois Liberalism'.
94. See Schulze, 'Toleranzkonzepte in islamischer Tradition'; Khoury, *Toleranz im Islam*.

clash of civilisations[95] or in the interest of a universally acceptable, because tolerant, international law.[96] This replicates the tolerance situation on a larger scale: which shared principles make a justified form of toleration possible, and what are its limits? Here, too, human rights are also often seen as providing such a basis, though they are themselves open to the suspicion of being intolerant and of implying a global reform of societies and 'modernisation' on the Western model, where such fears are nourished by very diverse sources. Hence, this opens up a further field of conflicts and arguments, many of which are not so new after all, if one considers the history which I have presented.

This completes the all too brief outline of the further development of the discourse of toleration, with the explicit indication that this is a discourse *without end*. It goes without saying that the theory of toleration to be developed in what follows will have to prove its worth in the light of these developments, which represent the central conflicts over toleration of our time.

95. Huntington, *The Clash of Civilisations*.
96. Rawls, *The Law of Peoples*. For a critique, see Forst, *The Right to Justification*, ch. 10.

8

Routes to toleration

§28 History and concept of toleration

1. The plurality of conceptions and justifications of toleration set forth in the previous chapters suggests a series of routes by which one can arrive at a higher-level philosophical theory of toleration.

A Hegelian route would involve the attempt to comprehend the succession of individual justifications as a cumulative dialectical learning process in which each successive theory incorporates the truth of the previous one, leading to the formation of a single comprehensive conception, the Spirit of modern toleration as it were.[1]

The antithesis of this would be a history of decline, along the lines of MacIntyre's *After Virtue* and *Whose Justice? Which Rationality?*, which postulates that an increasing dissociation from an original unity of religious faith, lived tradition and specific, recognised standards of rationality towards a relativisation and pluralisation is taking place in which, as a consequence of the 'catastrophe' of the Enlightenment, only incompatible fragments of past worlds remain floating on the surface of culture.

By contrast, a pluralistic approach, such as the one proposed by Isaiah Berlin, could point to the irreducible diversity and validity of each of these different, mutually exclusive, approaches to toleration, so that only some of them can survive in relations of tension in a confined social space, and tragic conflicts will be unavoidable.[2]

Against this, monistic approaches could question the meaningfulness of such comprehensive perspectives and defend the thesis that one of the

1. See, for example, the reconstruction of the spirit of modern identity by Taylor in *Sources of the Self*, though he reconstructs it as a history of diremption and still pending reconciliation.
2. See, for example, Berlin, 'The Pursuit of the Ideal'.

classical justifications is the true and correct one, whether it be justified by appeal to divine reality or to scepticism, in terms of a particular theory of the good or through a formal theory concerning the preconditions of the good life.

An 'ecumenical' theory indebted to Rawls's political liberalism could work towards an overlapping consensus among the proposed theories which share a subset of particular assumptions, and thus contain a 'reasonable kernel' which avoids contentious metaphysical and ethical assumptions.

In what follows I will refrain from such attempts and return to our point of departure in the original definition of the concept of toleration (§§1–3). Taking the paradoxes identified there and confirmed in a variety of ways in the course of the historical survey, I will first develop criteria for their possible resolution before going on to examine which of the available justifications of toleration can optimally satisfy these criteria.

But here the following problem arises. Even though the concept of toleration contains a range of formal criteria for justifications of toleration, these criteria remain underdetermined because the concept is itself normatively dependent (see §3). Then the question arises as to which values, truths or principles can provide the most viable normative foundation for a theory of toleration, and how the special problem with such a theory which follows from the principle of 'self-application' can be avoided, namely that the theory could itself become particular and potentially intolerant through a certain justification. Conversely, the theory needs concrete foundations, since otherwise it becomes amorphous and devoid of content. It will turn out that the only answer to this question is a recursive, reflexive one: No other values or norms except the *principle of justification itself* can provide the foundation of the higher-level, generally justified and itself tolerant theory of toleration. This meta-principle, which – as I tried to show – determines the normative grammar of the dynamic of toleration by exposing all justifications of intolerance or tolerance to a reciprocal and general duty to provide adequate reasons, as a substantive normative principle will ultimately provide the basis for toleration and thus trump the alternative approaches, all of which seek to justify particular relations of toleration. This reflexive turn towards the principle of justification as a principle which shapes the history of the discourse of toleration – in the twofold sense of a discourse of toleration in a specific social situation and as a discourse concerning different justifications of toleration – and, as a principle of practical, justifying reason, will constitute the thrust of the following remarks.

Before this can be shown, the justifications of toleration reconstructed up to this point will have to be examined against the background of the criteria provided by a dissolution of the paradoxes of toleration. In the process, the approaches which I initially reconstructed in the context of their social and philosophical histories will be gradually detached from these contexts in an attempt to reveal their systematic content, though without, I trust, running the risk of reductions and anachronisms. However, the simultaneity of argumentative *reconstruction* and *deconstruction* in which most of the 'classical' routes to toleration – whether based on Christianity, humanism, theories of sovereignty, scepticism, liberalism, rational religion or pluralism – have proved to be inadequate or to be dead ends, will become even more evident than in the foregoing chapters. Moreover, it is also part of the considerable 'revisionism' of my approach that the route leading through Castellio, and especially Bayle and (in part) Kant, which turns out to be the most far-reaching, is not among the ones which are generally favoured, although, suitably interpreted, it avoids the normative and epistemological problems of the other paths of justification. This is the decisive finding of the critical history of argumentation.

Here it should be borne in mind, however, that the concept of toleration remains a concept which refers to concrete conflicts and contexts.[3] Even if one of the routes proves to be normatively superior, therefore, this does not mean that it can be applied to all social situations; the conception and justification of mutual respect is a precept of practical reason, yet the other conceptions and justifications of toleration preserve their value in situations where it is not possible to establish a respect conception in the preferred sense. Under certain conditions, they can serve as toleration- and confidence-building routes to this goal.[4]

Another observation on the history of toleration may be in order. I have reconstructed this history as the conflictual history of a dynamic of power and morality, which already makes sufficiently clear that this is also a history of power and of morality. But, more than that, it is also a history of the state, of law, of freedom, of religion, of autonomy, of the person, of recognition, etc. In short, it represents a multifaceted history of ourselves. I can only allude to this aspect here without being able to explain it in detail. The hope is that the history which I have presented casts a useful light on these issues and that the critical reconstruction of the discourse of toleration will lead to a sufficiently complex, yet cogent, overall picture.

2. In §1, I highlighted the three essential components of the concept of toleration, namely the objection component, the acceptance component and

3. This is especially emphasised by Walzer, *On Toleration*.
4. On the relation between trust and toleration, see Dees, *Trust and Toleration*.

the rejection component. Only all three together characterise a situation of toleration: a belief or practice is rejected on certain grounds, but is accepted on other grounds up to the point at which particular reasons again speak for rejecting it. Therefore, we must distinguish between three kinds of reasons or, to be more precise, three functions reasons have within reflection toleration.

Each of these components involved specific paradoxes which haunt the concept of toleration and it is the task of a theory of toleration to resolve them. At the level of the objection component, the *paradox of the 'tolerant racist'* arose in the particular case in which toleration is understood as a virtue. According to this paradox, someone who rejects others on the basis of racist prejudices exhibits the virtue of tolerance to an even greater degree the deeper and more extensive his prejudices are, provided only that he does not act upon them. In order to avoid this paradox, a *minimally justified objection* must be required, hence one which satisfies certain rational and moral criteria, though without thereby neutralising the particular, and perhaps also idiosyncratic, character of grounds for objecting. For a variety of objections must be admissible in order not to place undue restrictions on possible constellations of toleration. However, someone who defends racist convictions cannot exercise the *virtue* of tolerance. For the point is not that he should become tolerant but that he should renounce his racism. The very objection he raises is the main problem – to which toleration is not a solution.

More important, however, are the paradoxes that affect the reasons for acceptance. Such reasons must not annul or negate the reasons for objecting, yet they must outweigh them and bring overriding points of view into play which speak in favour of toleration in spite of ongoing condemnation. As we have seen, the different justifications of toleration differ primarily in how they define these reasons. In the case where both the grounds for objecting and the grounds for accepting are characterised as 'moral', the result is the *paradox of moral toleration*, the paradox that it seems morally right or obligatory to tolerate what is morally wrong or bad. This paradox can be resolved only by making a *deontological distinction between justifications* which (a) differentiates within the predicate 'moral' between an 'ethical' objection and a 'moral' acceptance or, in particular cases in which the meaning of 'moral' is itself in dispute, between first-level and second-level 'moral' condemnation. At any rate, this presupposes (b) a morally grounded acceptance which lends the demand for toleration generally binding force, notwithstanding the controversy between mutually exclusive ethical convictions. Therefore, this resolution implies a higher-level moral conception. The discourse of toleration, in which the search for an overriding and mutually binding normative basis manifests itself, leads to such a deontological difference. Every justification of toleration can be understood as a (more or less plausible) attempt to provide such a normative basis. And as long as the latter must be reciprocally and universally acceptable, the principle of reciprocal and general justification of existing norms *itself* provides the most promising foundation, reflexively speaking.

The paradox in question has an epistemological counterpart, namely the *paradox of the relativisation of truth*, the paradox that it seems as though, in objecting to the conviction of others, the tolerant person assumes that his own conviction is true, whereas in accepting the conviction of others he simultaneously brackets his own conviction or places it in question. This paradox can be avoided only through a form of *self-relativisation without relativism*, a limited relativisation which combines continued adherence to one's own claim to truth with the primacy of toleration by providing coherent grounds for a 'moderate' self-limitation of one's own truth.

Two paradoxes arose, in turn, regarding the reasons for rejection. The first is the *paradox of self-destruction*, the paradox that unlimited toleration is in danger of annulling itself by failing to distinguish itself critically in any way from intolerance. If this paradox is avoided only by placing certain *limits on toleration*, the second and more intractable *paradox of drawing the limits* follows: demarcating what is tolerable from what is not tolerable itself involves the danger of the most extreme intolerance, for then one party claims the right to base this distinction on its own values and to declare the others to be intolerable or intolerant. But the latter then seem to be denied any possibility of making a 'legitimate' objection against such a self-immunising strategy. This paradox, which correctly identifies the dangers of one-sided definitions of toleration and corresponding exclusions, can be overcome only if a form of *reciprocally and generally justifiable rejection* can be found that does not stipulate the normative basis of toleration from the outset in particular terms and remains open to objections and contradictions, while at the same time insisting that the demand for toleration is normatively binding. With the demands for impartiality, openness and binding power, this links up with the resolution criteria cited above in relation to the paradox of moral toleration. Taken together, this results in the desirability of a higher-level conception of toleration which connects the inclusive and open character of the fixing of limits with a deontological component which can justify both acceptance and rejection in moral terms.

Thus, it transpires that all of these paradoxes place demanding requirements on the quality of the reasons for objection, acceptance and rejection,
requirements which can be fulfilled only by a theory that gives the principle
of justification itself a normative turn and as a result becomes reflexive. It
does not leave the place of justification empty, but does not occupy it in
a one-sided manner either. In this way, it opens up justification potentials
for this space which go beyond the limited possibilities of the alternative
justifications, which founder on one or another of the paradoxes and each
of which involves the danger of an *inversion of the arguments for toleration into
arguments for intolerance*. I will use the term *dialectic* to designate this tendency
in the following discussion. It will turn out that only one justification of the
respect conception of toleration is immune to this danger; on the basis of
the principle of justification, it can lend the normatively dependent concept
of toleration a form which satisfies the criteria of higher-level independence,
impartiality and binding power (see §3).

§29 Justifications of toleration – and their dialectics

1. If the concept of *tolerantia* in Stoicism stood for a particular kind of
dignified relation to oneself, in the Christian context it not only changed
in this respect into a patient ability to endure evils nourished by faith, but
also expanded as regards the relation *to others*, though the latter, of course,
is always mediated by the relation *to God*. This led, by appeal to the Gospels,
to a series of toleration justifications (TJ):

> (TJ 1) Toleration of the weaknesses of others is justified from the motive of
> compassionate *love* of one's neighbour following the example of Christ's
> indulgence. However, this love is graduated depending on whether it is a
> matter of the weaknesses of brothers and sisters in the faith to whom the
> tolerant person is bound by a deep bond of concord, or of members of
> different faiths or unbelievers who should be treated with patience. This
> humility, coupled with pious trust, proves the strength of faith. – Yet
> the limits of this argument likewise became apparent, especially in the
> discussion of Augustine. In the first place, as regards the acceptance com-
> ponent, this is not a generalisable argument for toleration because this
> kind of love is founded on faith and thus is addressed only to Christians
> who embrace this faith. But this leads to the more serious problem that
> ambivalences arise concerning the rejection component, indeed even the
> danger of an inversion into a justification of intolerance. Since love is

concerned to promote the salvation of others, its counterpart is the duty to protect them against the eternal damnation which is the result of the wrong faith. This can entail a duty of intolerance in order to cure others of the virus of error. This shows the danger, typical of perfectionistic approaches, of splitting the subject into a factual self and a 'true' self which must be realised. The lover cannot stand idly by as the loved one races towards his destruction and must therefore resort to 'liberating force' – a dialectic of Christian love.

(TJ 2) Opposed to this is the second important Christian argument from the *freedom of conscience of the believer*. This involves the normative component that one must not coerce conscience since only a faith-based or inner conviction which is not hypocritical can be pleasing to God, and the empirical component that it is not possible to coerce conscience since true convictions can be brought about only through genuine insight: *credere non potest homo nisi volens*. This kind of freedom is interpreted in different ways. It can refer only to *adiaphora* of faith but, in a more far-reaching interpretation, it can make not just a 'weak' conscience but also an 'errant' conscience, which believes in good faith that it is obedient to God, into the object of toleration. The decisive point remains, however, that the free conscience is at the same time a *bound* one, a conscience of the person of faith: conscience is the locus of the divine light in the human being which leads him to God. Only as such does it deserve respect. – Here, too, Augustine's controversy with the Donatists reveals the limitations of this justification of toleration, in particular in the form of an argument which Proast would continue to cite against Locke to demonstrate the aporias of freedom of conscience. In this controversy, Augustine does not abandon the principle of the voluntariness of faith but regards liberating human beings from false doctrines through compulsion or *terror* as a Christian duty intended to enable them to see the truth to which they were previously blind and to comprehend it. Thus, one *may* liberate conscience through force, indeed one even *must* do so, in order to save the conscience of those who are in error, and it is also *possible*, as is proven, according to Augustine, by the many cases of successful conversions which are also welcomed by those concerned. This makes it clear that the normative argument for freedom of conscience within the Christian context becomes problematic because it does not imply any unconditional respect for individual decisions of conscience but remains beholden to the truth and salvation of the individual. It follows that there can be no freedom to err and to reject God (as Thomas Aquinas also stresses against Abelard); and as long as the empirical argument of non-coercibility is supposed to be decisive, Augustine's objections concerning the possibilities of inducing 'genuine' and authentic convictions through manipulation or education carry considerable weight. The decisive issue, according to Augustine, cannot be the coercion but whether there are good grounds for a gentle and careful *compelle intrare*, especially in the light of the doctrine that there cannot be any salvation outside the Church: a dialectic of religious freedom of conscience.

(TJ 3) A third Christian argument is based on a particular reading of the two-kingdoms doctrine and emphasises the judgement seat of God. According to this argument, it is up to God alone to separate the wheat from the chaff. Finite human beings on earth cannot presume to make such a judgement. The unbelievers will not escape their punishment, but this will be a divine punishment; earthly tolerance among human beings can rest assured that God sets just limits to toleration. – Here, too, a fateful ambivalence and danger of inversion becomes apparent. For if God's justice, according to his own revelation, will be levelled against the unbelievers, and if it should prove to be possible to recognise the weeds, and perhaps even their roots, here on earth and to pull them out without endangering the wheat, then such an act cannot be displeasing to God. After all, it is not only the salvation of those who are coerced which is at stake in such conflicts but also that of other innocent souls who could be infected by the virus of unbelief and heresy. Once again, the argument for toleration becomes inverted into an argument for the duty to be intolerant.

(TJ 4) Although the two-kingdoms doctrine supports a separation between *temporal and spiritual power* and regards the latter as exclusively the power of the word and the truth, this separation does not necessarily entail that, when the church authorises the temporal power to employ force in the service of the truth, such force is illegitimate. And to the extent that the Church itself employs force, it justifies this primarily in terms of its liberating effect as regards receptiveness to the word. The transformation of religion from one which is persecuted into one which persecutes, therefore, does not presuppose a complete transformation, only a changed situation – a dialectic of the two-kingdoms doctrine.

This is not to assert that the aforementioned Christian toleration arguments necessarily become inverted into their opposite; nor does it mean that they were not the source of a whole series of further advances which sought to evade this danger. The point is only to show how qualifying the respect for people of different religious convictions in terms of the connection to divine truth not only makes these arguments for toleration limited as regards their binding force but also to show what narrow limits they could entail under certain conditions. This follows especially from the perfectionistic structure of the argument, which views toleration only as a *means* for promoting the good or the salvation of the other, where the latter is to be defined *independently* of the 'real' person of the other and promoted accordingly. Should some means besides granting freedom prove to be suited to promoting this goal, the argument for toleration would lose its force and the other person's objection would become groundless, because his 'true' self would not be speaking from him but only a deluded self. This explains why later justifications of toleration, especially those of Bayle, who more than anyone else engaged critically with Augustine, sought an *unconditional* moral form of respect for the other without a relativising religious justification. This is a crucial point: if the acceptance component is ethically or religiously particular, this will generally imply a significant relativisation of the rejection component.

2. As the conflicts within Christianity and between the different religions became more acute, new ways of dealing with the problem of religious difference developed during the late Middle Ages. Couldn't mutual toleration be made possible by a *deeper unity* underlying all differences? But which unity should this be? A variety of answers was offered to this question. Abelard asserts an *ethical-moral unity* among the different religions; yet even a reason striving for independence cannot avoid privileging its Christian variant as the most coherent. Llull, by contrast, aims for a stronger *religious-metaphysical unity*. Yet in Llull, too, this is only conceivable in Christian terms. Nicholas of Cusa calls for a Catholic *una religio in rituum varietate*, but regards toleration, restricted to ritual *adiaphora*, ultimately as a pragmatically justified necessity. Maimonides's attempt to reconcile philosophical reflection with the Jewish belief in the law leads to certain, albeit ambivalent, arguments for intra- and interreligious toleration, that is, for a certain toleration in interpretations of scripture among the few who choose and follow the path to truth, which seems to be situated beyond the positive religions. Averroes attaches even greater importance to the freedom of philosophy and the freedom to err

(though this is also restricted to just a few); toleration follows as a requirement of a philosophical discourse and from the insight that different religions
can be conducive under different conditions to the ethical stabilisation of
society based on a faith of the mass of the people. This represents the most
far-reaching conception among the theorists of religious dialogue. Different
routes to toleration can be derived from these conceptions which would
subsequently play an important role, for example, in humanism, though also
in the Enlightenment:

> (TJ 5) The route of *reductive unity*, which asserts that toleration springs
> from the consciousness of a shared core faith in the light of which disputes
> over incidental matters – i.e. *adiaphora* – must be endured. – However,
> this leads, on the one hand, to the problem of how 'neutral' the various
> definitions of this core were and, second, to the question of whether
> such reductions do not go too far in declaring essential articles of faith
> to be incidental matters, so that they become attempts to overcome
> intolerance through religious dedifferentiation instead of justifications of
> toleration.

> (TJ 6) The route of *unity through amalgamation* according to which the
> peaceful and tolerant exchange among religions will give rise to an all-
> reconciling faith. – But here, too, it remains questionable whether this
> does justice to the plurality and singularity of the different religions and
> what kind of result will be striven for in each case, i.e. with which of the
> original religions it has the greatest affinity.

> (TJ 7) The route of *competitive unity* which states that only as the result
> of peaceful and tolerant competition will the best religion prove itself
> and the truth prevail of its own accord. – This conception presupposes
> a strong self-relativisation according to which a religious conviction is
> defended on an analogy with a hypothesis in need of confirmation, a
> view which is especially difficult to reconcile with revealed religions.
> Moreover, the hope that truth will win out of its own accord is nothing
> more than a hope, and, should it be disappointed, it can become inverted
> into the attempt to help the truth to prevail (at least by excluding what
> is demonstrably false).

> (TJ 8) The route of *inclusive unity* along which a religion will be able
> to incorporate the (limited) truth of the other religions to be toler-
> ated. – Here it remains arbitrary with which religions a partial truth to be
> assimilated is correlated; the others would accordingly be excluded from

toleration, whereas the 'partially true' religions would only count as a means to an end.

(TJ 9) A variant of this route is that of *unity through refutation*, which views toleration as a means of achieving a discursive victory over the other religions. – On this justification of toleration, the latter merely a strategic means of imposing one's own truth and it is obligatory only as long as the goal of refutation seems to be achievable; if it is not, other means may be preferable.

(TJ 10) Finally, the path of *pluralist unity* states that the different religions are possible ways of interpreting the infinite divine reality. – First, it is debatable whether a rejection component is still present here and what it could involve; yet even if one's own religion is regarded as superior, it does not follow that all others are equally worthy of being tolerated or esteemed from this perspective.

Each of these routes speaks for toleration from a particular religious perspective, yet none of them satisfies the above-mentioned criteria (§28.2) with regard to the three components of objection, acceptance and rejection. Each of these justifications proves to be inadequate, especially when it comes to the corresponding limits of toleration. One's own religious perspective remains guiding concerning this question and resists any more far-reaching, higher-level normative reflection. Accordingly, it transpired in the critical discussion of the medieval religious discourses that they were discourses more of the imposition than of the discovery of truth. Structurally speaking, they were expressions of the quest for a *shared basis of discursive reason* for the purposes of mutual understanding as well as for a *universally shareable morality* and a *universalisable conception of God*. The only problem is that behind them there generally lurked an obfuscation of specific moral or metaphysical positions proper to some particular religion. The result was that the quest for a higher-level position remained unsuccessful and neither the normative acceptance component of toleration nor the limits of tolerance were generalisable, for example towards those religions which either were marginalised or did not feature in the discourse at all, not to mention towards the 'godless': a dialectic of religious understanding.

3. As regards political toleration, the discourse at that time was completely dominated by the search for reasons for a permission conception which, in the case of the two-kingdoms doctrine and of freedom of conscience, for example, stemmed from the Christian store of arguments. As

Tertullian's position concerning a *humani iuris et naturalis potestatis*, a 'human and natural right' to a *libertas religionis*, shows, this discourse already involved fundamental considerations which spoke in favour of a more wide-ranging form of toleration that amounted to more than permitting wrong for the sake of preventing worse wrong. Yet not only did the permission conception remain dominant, but, in virtue of the subordination of the *regnum* to the *sacerdotium*, it was also clearly under the sway of the dictates of the Church, so that heresy became a religious *and* a political crime. Where toleration was exercised, its chief aim was to uphold the religious-political order through a strictly controlled and disciplining grant of liberty; yet it always remained the second-best solution by comparison with religious unity.

The connection between ecclesiastical and political rule only broke down over the course of time, to the point where a thinker like Marsilius of Padua could defend what was for his time a maximally 'secular' conception of the state which inverted the classical relation of subordination and underlined the supremacy of the state also in a range of ecclesiastical affairs. Tolerance and intolerance were now determined by *political* criteria, even though the state did not liberate itself entirely from religious assumptions. This involved at the same time the suppression of the coercive power of the Church and the promotion of the power of the state; this could lead to more toleration, though not in principle, because how much liberty the state grants depends on its functional requirements. At the very moment the state emancipates itself to a certain extent from religion, it gains the power to tolerate according to its own imperatives.

(TJ 11) Structurally speaking, this does not alter the fact that the permission conception characteristically grants toleration for *pragmatic* reasons, for instance in order to prevent conflicts among and with minorities, so that peace and order prevail and the state remains stable. – The problems with such a justification of toleration are manifest, regardless of its effectiveness at particular historical junctures. Each of the three components of objection, acceptance and rejection are subject to the discretion of the rulers. This leads to a dialectic of permission toleration which can assume different forms: should the power interests require it, this toleration can change into intolerance; moreover, toleration is granted, if at all, for strategic reasons and as a means of stabilising political authority.

At the same time, to this 'rationalisation' of political power in the sense of an increase in state autonomy is added a further, normative rationalisation.

For Marsilius also stresses, albeit still within a corporative framework, the importance of the principle *quod omnes similiter tangit, ab omnibus comprobetur* (i.e. what affects everyone should be approved by everyone) with which the newly acquired toleration power of the state can be subjected to justification pressure. This initiates a new dynamic of toleration which unfolded in what followed.

At the threshold of the modern era, therefore, not only did there exist an already extremely broad spectrum of justifications of toleration, albeit still of a traditional, religious kind, but the levels on which justifications of toleration were sought also evolved: the religious level, the moral or ethical level, the epistemological level and the political level, at which toleration represents, respectively, a requirement of faith, of moral duty, of the good, of truth or of political prudence or stability.

4. The distinguishing feature of humanist reflection on toleration is its radicalisation of the reduction approach based on a new view of humans and their dignity as beings created by God for the sake of free self-development. On this view, religious differences are as legitimate as they are incidental, since all human beings are united by a core religious truth – though this is a Christian truth in the eyes of Ficino and Pico as well as of Erasmus, notwithstanding the differences between them:

(TJ 5a) This version of the route of *reductive unity*, which also includes elements of the route of unity through amalgamation, states that religious dissenters, be they Christians or adherents of different religions, should be esteemed (according to Ficino and Pico) and tolerated as part of the divine, plural creation, provided that they do not reject the tenets of the core religion. – From this also follow the limits of toleration which are located at the point where these tenets are abandoned or negated. Dissenters are tolerated only if they contribute to the Christian truth. This is the first problem with this conception.

Two further problems become apparent in Erasmus, who is less concerned with justifying toleration than with overcoming intolerance. According to Erasmus, religious differences are not estimable but instead involve disputes over trifles or *adiaphora* which obscure the deeper-lying unity in the *christiana philosophia*. In so arguing, he chooses what is for his time a very broad concept of the 'incidental' matters of faith which are unnecessary for salvation. Thus, he becomes embroiled in the dilemma of either watering down the shared core religion so much that it looks like a pallid, irenic utopia from the perspective of comprehensive religious doctrines, or of enriching it with substantive contents at the risk of failing to realise the goal of reconciliation. The humanist position of an Erasmus remains trapped in this dilemma. Moreover, it is problematic in that it also recommends toleration only as a means to the end of promoting religious unity, so that those who seem to represent an obstacle – schismatics, though also the Jews – cannot be tolerated. Hence, the three problems outlined lead to a dialectic of humanist toleration.

It nevertheless remains the merit of humanist irenism, with its critical stance towards tradition, that it seeks the *human being* beneath the manifold religious conflicts, even though it continues to conceive of him in the Christian-humanist, perfectionist terms of a philosophy of the aims of creation.

5. With the breakdown of the traditional religious-political order in the early modern period, the scope for a complex rationalisation of power, through which the latter increasingly emancipated itself from its religious prescriptions, expanded in the vertical, political dimension. This led, on the one hand, to Machiavelli's strategic use of religion for maintaining political power, though, on the other hand, it also opened up the 'space of reasons' to claims to acceptable political justifications. Thus, important further developments in the permission conception are to be found in More and Machiavelli. Thus, in More, toleration for atheists, for instance, is excluded on *political* grounds, which shows that this notion of toleration can again lead to traditional exclusions, albeit ones based on non-traditional considerations – a 'rationalised' form of the dialectic of permission toleration announces itself. It remains characteristic of the permission conception that it *can* lead to greater toleration, but only provided that this is required for strategic reasons. The 'political rationality' of the modern state remains ambivalent for toleration. The fact that intolerance is prohibited in Utopia, for example, does not automatically entail that toleration prevails there. Here a further risk of inversion characteristic of a number of subsequent justifications of toleration becomes apparent: a dialectic of the abolition of intolerance which can itself lead to intolerance.

6. Although Luther opposed the humanist conception of freedom and dignity and stressed human sinfulness, the Reformation led in an almost paradoxical way to an unprecedented intensification of religious individualisation through the doctrine of the direct responsibility of the individual before God. The critique of early modern subjectivity in the religious domain gave rise to the very thing it criticised. Crucial for the discourse of toleration

in this regard, apart from the intensification of religious subjectivity, is the Protestant interpretation of the two-kingdoms doctrine. This leads first to

(TJ 2a) a radicalised version of the argument of *Christian freedom of conscience* which asserts that the latter is a freedom from false doctrines and for the truth of the word of God. The path leading to this truth, which can only be based on one's own insight, involves overcoming oneself and subjecting oneself to the word without the mediation of religious authorities: it is at once a self-appropriation and a loss of self in God's will. Hence, respect for conscience is a matter not of respect for subjective autonomy but ultimately of respect for God, since conscience is God's handiwork; he alone is sovereign in this domain where religious constraint by human beings is illegitimate. – This renewed version of the doctrine of the freedom of the bound conscience also remains vulnerable to arguments for using 'good' and 'gentle' coercion to compel the renunciation of false doctrines, since Luther does not envisage any relativisation of doctrine either; in later writings he even argues in favour of such coercion. This line of argument also makes it possible to deny toleration to heretics who profess an 'unconscionable' form of religion.

Luther's second important argument for toleration is

(TJ 4a) a radicalised version of the *two-kingdoms doctrine*, which draws sharp boundaries between the kingdom of God or divine rule through the word and the temporal rule established by God to contain evil. The latter must be obeyed unconditionally but does not have any right over the 'soul', not even as the extended arm of the Church. – However, when the correct relation between the two kingdoms is disrupted, for example through a social-revolutionary 'carnal' interpretation of Christian freedom, which for Luther is precisely *not* secular freedom, this argument for toleration changes into a legitimation for restoring secular political subordination. This became apparent in the peasant revolts, in which religious and political definitions of heresy were brought in a close relation. Furthermore, although Luther later rejected any right of religious coercion for secular rulers, he nevertheless assigned them the duty of ensuring the institutionalisation of the Protestant national churches and granted them the right to establish a state ecclesiastical system.

7. Opposed to these aspects of a dialectic of Protestant toleration on the part of the reformers (and also, in particular, of Zwingli and Calvin) was an

individualist-spiritualist orientation in Protestantism, in Sebastian Franck for example, which calls for

(TJ 12) an extensive doctrinal toleration based on the irreducible *subjectivity of faith* and of the 'inner light', i.e. the inspiration of the Holy Spirit. All forms of positive religion are accordingly criticised as moments of religious alienation and stasis, thereby undercutting the customary definitions of heresy. All of those who earnestly seek him are pleasing to an 'impartial God', irrespective of their religion, according to Franck, and thus he can call for a 'universal' toleration which also includes non-Christians. – However, in a dialectic of subjective spiritualism, these considerations do not prevent a possible inversion of this position into intolerance of those who cling to a positive interpretation of religion or who refuse to accept a doctrinal relativisation of religion, or of those who believe that the kingdom of God on earth is possible.

8. The idea of placing the possibility of clear definitions of heresy in question through normative and epistemological relativisation of articles of faith is crucial for Sebastian Castellio's treatment of toleration. Two central arguments for this position can be found in his works.

(TJ 13) The important argument concerning a *normative difference* distinguishes between (a) a morality of behaviour towards others and of the correct conduct of life which is common and accessible to all human beings regardless of their religion, and (b) religious doctrines which go beyond this but which are unavoidably controversial among finite beings. It follows for Castellio that definitions of heresy based on the second category cannot provide good reasons for a punitive condemnation, whereas offences against the requirements of the first category can be rightfully punished. – In Castellio's thought, however, the former category is constituted by a Christian moral teaching which not only confuses moral norms with religious-ethical duties concerning how to conduct one's life (in order to achieve salvation) but also implies that 'atheists' cannot be tolerated.

Nevertheless, with this distinction he paves the way for a third justification of toleration, in addition to the dominant humanist and Protestant justifications, which will ultimately lead to Bayle and Kant and prove to be the one which escapes the dead ends into which the other justifications lead. In his normative argument, which he understands in terms of natural law, Castellio already places the main emphasis on the reciprocity of justification, which is supposed to prevent particular standpoints being inadmissibly generalised. This enables him to respond forcefully to Calvin who regarded the defence of divine truth as the supreme good even when weighed against the life of the individual: 'To kill a man is not to protect a doctrine, but it is to kill a man.'

(TJ 14) In Castellio, the counterpart of the aforementioned normative difference is an *epistemological difference* between the 'gold coin' of manifest moral-religious truths and the particular 'impressions and images' of more extensive religious convictions which, on account of the limitations of human knowledge, cannot rely on any objective attestation of the truth and thus are the object of ultimately irreconcilable differences of opinion. – Castellio integrates this epistemological difference into a Christian framework, with reference to the truths of morality and faith 'inscribed in the human soul' by God and to the difference between divine and human knowledge. Yet with this distinction he also anticipates later attempts to explain within the framework of a critique of finite reason how profound differences can arise in the religious domain and why this does not imply any moral scepticism. Hence, both of the arguments to be found *in nuce* in Castellio represent important stages in the evolution of the rationalisation of morality.

9. As regards the practice of toleration on the part of the state, the analysis of the situation in the wake of the Religious Peace of Augsburg showed how a regime of toleration based on the coexistence conception developed between the different territories in accordance with the principle *cuius regio, eius religio*. Within the principalities, this went hand-in-hand with a confessionalisation and disciplining which made toleration possible at best in the sense of a restricted permission conception informed by pragmatic considerations. Its rational power calculations geared towards an exclusionary inclusion of minorities once again reveal the Janus-faced character of toleration between power and morality.

If that already marked the end of the principle of confessional unity in the Holy Roman Empire without annulling it at the level of the principalities, the development in France led to an understanding of state sovereignty which asserts that the ruler could and should defer the goal of religious unity for the sake of preserving political unity. Although the ruler was still bound to the majority Catholic confession, he understood himself at the same time as a higher-level arbitrator of disputes and a bringer of peace. Corresponding to this position, most strikingly in the Edict of Nantes, is a revised *permission toleration*:

(TJ 11a) Although the state sovereign remains beholden to the goal of establishing religious unity among the citizens, he grants a limited form of toleration, based on various pragmatic and normative considerations – such as those to be found in L'Hôpital, for example – whose supreme maxim is the avoidance or containment of religious conflict. Bodin and the *politiques* argued in the first instance for avoiding religious conflicts, even to the point of supporting prohibitions on discussion, and only subsequently for toleration if peace was not possible by any other means. The sovereign must strive to stand above the parties to the conflict. – This conception represents a decisive step towards a differentiation between the role of the citizen (or of the legal person) and that of the ethical-religious person bound to a particular confession, and in this way represents an important stage in the history of the process of normative political rationalisation leading to a secular understanding of the state. However, this not only involves the problem that the role of the citizen remains the preserve of Christians. Even more important is that it represents a further form of the rationalised exercise of power. For, given that this permission toleration does not entail any permanent and secure rights for minorities, it can be revoked at any time and obliges the protected minorities to show greater loyalty towards the side which grants the permission. This dialectic of the permission conception – or dialectic of sovereignty – leads, in turn, to a disciplining effect through toleration, not only through the narrowly circumscribed and supervised liberties, but also through the dependence on the sovereign. As a consequence, this practice represents simultaneously an advance in freedom and an advance in the rationality of power – one additional ambivalence among many in the history of toleration.

10. Just as in the sixteenth century a concept of sovereignty emerges at the political level which derives particular conclusions from the fact of irreducible religious plurality, at the social and individual level we encounter a corresponding understanding of individual sovereignty, leading to new attempts to justify toleration especially in Bodin and Montaigne.

Bodin is a clear example of the (often encountered) difference between how toleration is thematised from the perspective of the *theory of the state* and from an *intersubjective-normative* perspective. Whereas from the former perspective he pleads for permission toleration, the latter leads him to elaborate a conception of mutual toleration which is closely affiliated with the respect conception. His colloquium on religion documents the insight into the futility of Christian-humanist irenic aspirations and into the perilousness and pointlessness of the acrimonious struggles over proving the true religion. Contrary to tradition, in the discourse on religion there are no winners and no reconciliations; instead the plurality of religious convictions turns out to be an ineluctable destiny of human reason. The latter, as discursive reason, nevertheless constitutes the link between the different positions, which can still reach at best a *concordia discors*. The central argument in this regard is

(TJ 14a) a radicalised version of the *epistemological difference*, though this time, in contrast to Castellio, it leads to a strict separation between faith and knowledge: because of the finitude of human reason, proofs and secure knowledge are impossible in the religious domain, and hence not only are ineradicable differences preprogrammed even among rational human beings; it also follows that faith consists *in assensione pura, sine demonstratione*, in a trusting consent without proof. Hence, tolerant individuals recognise that, although they think that other people's religious convictions are false, these convictions are neither irrational nor immoral because, to adapt the argument of normative difference (TJ 13), a fundamental moral agreement exists beyond divisions of faith; tolerant persons recognise that religious strife is as destructive as it is irresolvable. They preserve their religious faith in the knowledge that it is a faith, and tolerate that of others with whom they are able to reach an understanding concerning the limits of mutual understanding. – Bodin's thought also remained captive to a religious framework which led him to exclude atheists together with those who, like witches and wizards, disrupt the divinely ordained plural harmony. Yet, in spite of this very specific interpretation of that over which there are no 'reasonable disagreements', he took an important step towards clarifying the epistemological components of toleration on the model of a self-relativisation without relativism.

11. Montaigne's thought expresses the new pluralistic consciousness in an extreme form as an awareness of religious and ethical plurality and also of Plurality *within* the self. His most important argument for toleration is that of

(TJ 15) *sceptical perspectivism*: given the unlimited diversity of limited individual perspectives, not only is a diversity of convictions and values unavoidable, it is also advisable to adopt a fundamental scepticism in questions of truth. Montaigne gives this scepticism an ethical turn towards a stance of ataraxia. Although it is an attitude of tolerance towards ethical plurality, at the same time it is part of a 'Pyrrhonian' perfectionist ethics of the wise man. Moreover, this internal sovereignty is also compatible with an attitude of external conformity; scepticism and plurality should lead neither to internal nor to external strife.

When combined with a particular version of the distinction between faith and knowledge, this points to the limits of Montaigne's argument. He does not extend his scepticism to religion in the sense of a reservation of judgement; instead, he thinks that the search for clear proofs reflects a misunderstanding of religion. According to his fideism, faith should instead be regarded and accepted as a gift from God without demanding additional supporting reasons. And thus not only should one avoid the dispute over the true religion but, in addition, one should not question the established religion or incite the danger of revolt. This entails an affirmation of the religious status quo, which leads Montaigne to argue on political grounds against religious innovations, which in any case cannot lead to religious progress. In this way, scepticism concerning truth, in combination with fideism and a preference for political peace and order, becomes inverted into potential intolerance – a dialectic of scepticism also to be found in Lipsius, who associates a neo-Stoic, sceptical ethics with political-religious unitary thought (and anticipates the distinction between public *confessio* and private *fides*). The thesis of the insuperability and irreconcilability of religious disputes leads to the thesis of the political necessity of avoiding such disputes, even at the cost of religious suppression.

Yet even if scepticism were to be extended to religion itself, this could, of course, lead to another dialectic of scepticism, in the shape of intolerance of those who have a non-sceptical conception of religion. It is a mistake to assume that scepticism is necessary for an argument concerning toleration.

Therefore, Coornhert rightly opposes Lipsius's intolerant scepticism with a mixture of different, familiar considerations. New in Coornhert, however, is his interpretation of the argument concerning faith as the handiwork and gift of a merciful God, such that atheists, who apparently have not yet had the benefit of this gift, must be tolerated. This makes him the first to entertain the idea of tolerating atheists on the basis of the traditional justifications.

12. In the context of the Dutch Revolt we encounter a characteristically modern connection between the demand for toleration and a more extensive demand for political *justice* based on an early natural law-based understanding of political legitimation. The Calvinist monarchomachs called for freedom of

religion as a right while at the same time insisting on the right of resistance against a ruler who had broken the covenant (*foedus*) with God *and* the contract (*pactum*) with the people. This constitutes a new justification of toleration

(TJ 16) which appeals to an early modern (religiously grounded) under-standing of freedom of conscience and religion as a *natural individual right* which is part of a set of original rights to political freedom and political legitimation. Although this justification draws on several other argu-ments (for example concerning freedom of conscience), the affirmation of an individual natural right represents an important new element.

With this the demand for justification, which raises doubts concern-ing the reasons for existing relations of religious and political intolerance or toleration and brings them before the 'judgement seat' of the citizens, takes aim at the heart of the state and of sovereignty itself. The deci-sive point is that intolerance or inadequate toleration are understood as a form of political *injustice* for which there are no good legitimating reasons, and which is therefore part of a denial of the political self-determination of the people criticised as tyranny. Here the possibility of combining vertical and horizontal toleration within the framework of the political autonomy of a sovereign people emerges for the first time.

The ambivalence of modern natural law is apparent in authors such as Althusius and Grotius in whom the natural law legitimation of the state by the citizens continues to be associated with the Erastian affir-mation and defence of the particular religious foundations of this very right and of the state. This leads to a dialectic of natural law insofar as the latter rests on particular religious foundations which accordingly cannot be doubted. However, Grotius's remark that natural law, since it is in principle rationally accessible, would also hold even if God did not exist, points to an overcoming of this dialectic in the direction of a reason-based conception of natural law.

13. Even before Locke lent it paradigmatic form, a radicalised version of the argument from natural law appeared in the middle of the seventeenth century in the context of the English Revolution:

(TJ 16a) In the concept of 'birthright', this *early liberal, contractualist* argument *from natural law* expresses the view that individuals have God-given natural rights to religious and political liberty which they cannot alienate or transfer, not only for reasons of self-interest, to the artifi-cial state they have constructed; they cannot dispose over these rights themselves because they are merely 'lent' by God and the individuals remain beholden to him. Conscience is a divine creation and is therefore beyond the scope of political action. Hence, the normativity of the state is framed 'from below', as it were, by the liberties of the people and 'from above' by God's will, leading to the apparently paradoxical picture of a secular state being defended on religious grounds. This is shown by the writings of the Levellers and the Independents as well as by those of Williams. The connection between the basic claims to religious *and* political freedom emphasises the principle that the political, and hence also the religious-political, exercise of power and coercion is in need of justification and considers this to be a 'fundamental law'; toleration changes accordingly from being a *good* bestowed by the state to a *right* which the citizens reciprocally grant one another and for whose preservation the state is established. – The limits of this argument follow from its religious justification. Since the liberty declared by the birthright is a *Christian liberty* (Milton), there is no reason in principle to tolerate non-Christians, much less atheists. But, even more, this dialectic of the birthright idea also involves the danger of a more extensive restriction, because even tolerating non-Protestants presents difficulties. It was claimed, especially concerning the Catholics, who were vulnerable to the general suspicion of being traitors and of serving foreign rulers, not only that they were bent on abolishing freedom of conscience but that they did not even have a free religious conscience in the sense in need of protection, any more than did blasphemers or atheists. The structure of a dialectic of religious justifications becomes apparent here once again: where those to be tolerated do not share the foundation on which toleration is justified, they can be excluded by appeal to the necessary limits of toleration.

Roger Williams represents an exception in that, even though he clearly bases his argument on Christianity and, in particular, on the two-kingdoms doctrine, he makes such a sharp separation between Church and State that neither the government nor the citizens need adopt a particular religious stance. Nevertheless, this for its time 'pure' concept of the citizen remains anchored in a religious justification founded on natural law. Hence, this argument for 'universal' religious toleration by the state cannot be reciprocally shared and it must draw its universal binding force from other sources, though Williams does not specify what they could be. Only a normatively independent, reciprocally justifiable grounding of toleration could in principle avert the danger of its becoming inverted into its opposite.

14. In Milton, we encounter a further justification of toleration which marks the beginnings of a bourgeois public sphere and, although related to several other justifications, in particular that of competitive unity, possesses a new quality (TJ 7):

> (TJ 17) This justification points to the necessity of toleration for a functioning *public sphere* in which the *truth* in both politics and religion will emerge, without external assistance, and especially without force, from the exchange of opinions and positions. Only an open discourse is capable of sifting arguments and enabling citizens to gain a clear view of their interests. – However, this line of argument can lead, through a dialectic of the principle of publicity, not only to the exclusion of 'manifestly' false conceptions from the scope of toleration because they are regarded as too disruptive of the process of ascertaining the truth (to which Mill would later respond), but also to the wholesale exclusion of those who, like the 'papists' in Milton, are suspected of wanting to restrict the public discussion, and even of denying its value on religious grounds.

15. Hobbes's importance as a stage in the development of the discourse of toleration resides in the particular attention his political thought devotes to the problem of religious intolerance, for which he proposes a radical solution:

> (TJ 18) According to Hobbes's thesis of *political-religious identity*, the problem of ecclesiastical and civil intolerance must be attacked at its roots in religious plurality and in the reservation concerning the 'two kingdoms' or freedom of conscience: a lasting peace in society will be possible only when a rationally grounded unity of sovereign, citizens and religion, based on a modern understanding of natural law, is achieved, so that the sovereign is able to exploit the dual motivations of fear of earthly death and fear of eternal death which are decisive in the human domain. Only a Leviathan, as a 'mortal God', would possess the necessary political and religious authority to overcome the causes of conflict which tear states apart, though only if the individual members relinquish to him the final authority to judge temporal and spiritual matters. Paradoxically, the route to peace and to freedom, and hence also in a certain sense to toleration, leads through the unconditional renunciation of individual liberties and hence also of rights of religious freedom. According to Hobbes's identity logic, the sovereign functions as the 'public conscience', his laws hold as universal norms, he has the final say in the interpretation of Scripture, he is the ruler over the church and is 'God's Lieutenant' on earth. And,

what is most important, he decides what counts as heresy and only he can persecute it.

Hobbes assumes that, in order to secure the religious loyalty of the citizens, the sovereign reduces the binding truths of salvation to an absolute minimum, namely to belief in Jesus Christ and the precept of obedience (towards the sovereign). Whatever go beyond this are incidental matters which are subject to the regulatory authority of the sovereign, who can accordingly impose a public form of worship, though they do not provide any occasion for wide-ranging definitions of heresy. With the idea of regulatory authority over *adiaphora* in the sense of an outward conformity with the official Church, which by the same token is permissive as regards dogma, Hobbes aligns himself with a certain current in Anglicanism (Hooker, Chillingworth), but without granting the Church any independent right. Thus, this conception involves a striking variation on the doctrine concerning 'incidental matters' of faith, which once again reveals how susceptible this doctrine is to becoming inverted into its opposite (see above the dialectic of humanism or of the route of reductive unity).

Even more germane to the problem of toleration is the fact that, although Hobbes does not recognise any legal restriction on the authority of the sovereign in religious matters, he does recognise a *factual* limit, namely that of inner *fides* as opposed to public *confessio*, the refuge of private faith based on personal conviction, which Hobbes also believes cannot be brought about by coercion or laws, which apply exclusively to external behaviour. However, this does not entail any 'right' to freedom of conscience or even of worship, but only a space of freedom into which the commands of the sovereign do not intrude. According to Hobbes, the sovereign not only protects the citizens against religious hostility and coercive measures but also grants them a certain freedom of thought, especially since the official religion is reduced to a minimum core content. On the other hand, the sovereign also rules over religion and is an object of religious devotion, and thus directs not only actions but also souls. Still more, the apotheosis of the state based on the Hobbesian logic of identity means that the sovereign does not have any normative duties to justify any restrictions he sees fit to impose on the space of toleration, since religious and political dissent pose an equal potential threat to him. The price to be paid for protection against ecclesiastical and civil intolerance in Hobbes's state is complete defencelessness against possible intolerance on the part of the sovereign by renouncing all liberty rights (except for self-preservation) to him. The absolute duty of obedience is the price of peace. The danger that this conception can be inverted into its opposite resides in this attempt by the sovereign as public reason to assimilate the power of justification entirely. This amounts to a dialectic of the political-religious identity of the Leviathan who, according to Hobbes, can only have one body, one will, one head and one faith – and a further dialectic of the attempt to overcome intolerance that can itself in turn lead to intolerance. The struggle against intolerance is not automatically a struggle for toleration.

16. Like Hobbes, Spinoza's aim is to undermine the foundations of religious intolerance and, like Hobbes, he regards sovereign power as the guarantor of this goal. Yet, at the same time he stresses that the purpose of the state is to assure the citizens' freedom of thought and speech or, to be more precise, their freedom to philosophise. In support of this he cites

(TJ 19) a complex combination of metaphysical, political-theoretical and perfectionist reasons. According to his doctrine of substance, philosophical questions concerning divine truth have a much more solid foundation than positive religions, which he subjects to a radical historical critique. The substance of religion should be limited to a few dogmas in order to remove the pretext for disputes, he argues, and these dogmas should call in essence for love of one's neighbour, obedience to God and toleration. 'Heretics' are those who contradict these dogmas, not the philosophical truth seekers. At the level of theory of the state, Spinoza argues for a sovereign who is equipped with unbound authority, though, in contrast to Hobbes, the sovereign is democratic. He is not bound by any pre-political norms, he alone establishes justice on earth and he enjoys supreme temporal and spiritual authority concerning the external forms of worship and the resolution of religious disputes. Yet even this sovereign reaches a de facto limit which, according to Spinoza, is at the same time grounded in natural law: since conscience cannot be redeemed by force, it is *impossible* that anyone could have ceded the right to freedom of conscience and freedom of speech (as opposed to freedom of worship) to the sovereign. This domain remains beyond the reach of state action. That the purpose of the state is to safeguard freedom, however, presupposes the perfectionist notion that the supreme good of the mind and of free thought, human perfection, resides in approaching God through knowledge; this 'intellectual love of God' is the human telos, and the previously justified religious and state toleration finds its meaning and deepest grounding in this.

Yet Spinoza's argument is in danger of becoming inverted into its opposite at all three levels. In the first place, the religious reduction he proposes is too radical to be able to function as a mediating position; moreover, even this position can still lead to exclusions on substantial grounds, and not only of atheists (see above TJ 5 and 5a). Second, he does not do complete justice to his notion of democratic freedom, which was important for Rousseau, for instance, but follows Hobbes in installing the unitary sovereign as the supreme religious authority on earth who regulates religious worship. All that remains is a freedom of thought in which the sovereign could place restrictions on the component of freedom of speech stressed by Spinoza on the grounds that religious dissent threatens the foundations of the state. In addition, what was stated above with reference to Augustine also holds here, namely that the (empirical) thesis that conscience is impervious to force is dubious. As regards the third level, the speculative perfectionist argument which sees toleration as a means of achieving self-perfection through the 'intellectual love of God' could itself give rise to a situation in which certain obstacles along this path, such as patent errors, may, and perhaps even must, be removed. Placing toleration in the service of knowledge and truth could entail narrow limits on toleration – a further dialectic of perfectionism.

17. Locke's route to toleration, both prior to and following his famous first *Letter Concerning Toleration*, was by no means a direct one. Already discernible in the early writings, however, is the central idea of the *non-transferability* of care for the well-being of one's soul to the state, and ultimately the demand for an 'absolute and universal right of toleration'. Of central importance for Locke, too, is the notion that the natural and political liberty of individuals springs from their dependence on God. He justifies their right to property, for example, on the grounds that they are 'God's property'. This involves, generally speaking, a 'twofold' theory of property according to which human beings enjoy earthly freedom because they are subject to another, non-earthly power who has set them the task of discovering their own path to salvation and to the truth, so that they will ultimately be able to answer for it before God. This idea of ethical self-responsibility and of the 'supreme duty' to care for one's salvation is fundamental for Locke. It leads to his most important argument for toleration, which is related to the argument from birthright (thus, all things considered, although there are no new arguments for toleration in Locke, there are important reformulations of the existing arguments):

(TJ 16b) the *liberal, natural law-based contractualist* argument that the right of caring for the spiritual welfare of the citizens was not transferred to the state; this 'supreme interest' is and remains the citizens' alone, whereas the state is only entrusted with caring for 'civic interests', which are confined to external conduct. This argument integrates a large number of traditional justifications of toleration, yet two stand out which would ultimately diverge in Locke's own theory. The first is

(TJ 2b) the argument of *freedom of conscience*, which is reformulated on the basis of an empirical theory of knowledge, though it retains its religious origin. It states that the supreme care for the well-being and salvation of the individual is a matter of individual conscience which cannot be entrusted to the state. In the first place, it is a matter for God alone to guide the conscience and, second, genuine, authentic religious convictions can arise only on the basis of subjective insight and rational examination, not through external pressure or coercion; coercion can lead only to the (sin of) hypocrisy or to confusion but not to redemptive faith for which the individual can take responsibility: 'Faith is not Faith without believing.'

The other argument for the non-transferability of the 'care of souls' is

(TJ 14b) an argument from the *limits of religious knowledge*. Since nobody on earth has privileged access to divine truth and all depend equally on their reason and on God's mercy on the 'path to heaven', it would be much too great a risk to submit oneself in this matter to equally fallible authorities, and all the more so to political authorities who may have other interests. This is not to doubt the existence of religious truth but merely implies that the finitude of reason excludes a right of religious coercion, for then all churches and rulers could demand such a right for themselves on the grounds that they possess the truth. Thus, Locke connects this epistemological argument with the normative argument

(TJ 13a) from the *need for reciprocal justification of the use of coercion* and the thesis that religious justifications of coercion are not reciprocally justifiable. The religious differences remain, but they do not legitimate any general norms and duties. The result is a normative difference between universally binding norms and other convictions concerning values which are the objects of legitimate disagreements.

Locke provides a clear answer to the question of which of these justifications of the non-transferability argument is the strongest in his (first) *Letter Concerning Toleration* when he indicates that the 'principal consideration' is the non-coercibility of conscience, an answer which he would have to retract in the controversy with Proast who cited the late Augustine against Locke's argument. Although conscience cannot be immediately compelled to accept specific convictions, Proast argued, there is ample evidence that indirect force, which opens the eyes of the deluded by laying so many obstacles across their erroneous path that they are 'compelled' to abandon it, is helpful, necessary and pleasing to God; once liberated, they are receptive to the truth, which they then embrace with even greater enthusiasm and sincerity. According to this perfectionist view, the secular authority has a duty to care for the well-being of the citizens, and it violates this duty if it fails to make use of the proper means of promoting truth and salvation. It cannot enforce the true religion, but it can suppress false religion.

Although Locke succeeds in unmasking Proast's perfectionist intolerance, at the same time he has to abandon the argument of non-coercibility and fall back on the other justification which challenges the presupposition of the perfectionist argument, namely that here on earth there are sufficient reasons for assuming that one possesses the single religious truth which would authorise one in prescribing, however gently, this path to salvation to others. According to Locke's argument, it remains possible to affirm religious truth, though it likewise remains a matter of reasonable disagreement among finite beings; and given that human beings have equal rights, it follows that the reasons for religious coercion are insufficient. Although this represents a Pyrrhic victory for Locke because he has to abandon his main argument, at the same time he advances towards the epistemological-normative justification of toleration which would make its complete breakthrough with Bayle and represents the most effective refutation of intolerance.

Locke's argument from freedom of conscience leads him to set narrow limits on toleration and to regress behind certain earlier authors by rejecting toleration both for Catholics and for atheists. He rejects toleration for Catholics on the grounds that they are more beholden to other authorities, especially spiritual authorities, than to the laws of their land and refuse to practise tolerance themselves, and for atheists because they are practically devoid of conscience: according to *Locke's fear*, no state and no morality can survive without the transcendent authority of God – another form of the dialectic of religious freedom of conscience.

Locke's theory is not only a special example of the failure of one of the most important traditional justifications of toleration, which nevertheless remains influential and salient up to the present day. It also marks the point of divergence of two routes to toleration which remain extremely important into the present, namely the route of ethical liberalism according to which toleration is a necessary precondition for an autonomous, personal quest for and realisation of the individual good, and the route of the reciprocal justification of power (and, more generally, of constraints on action) between human beings who, regardless of the issue of what constitutes the good life, acknowledge a duty to grant each other a right of justification. I will return to the differences between these two routes.

18. The normative-epistemological justification of toleration at which Locke arrived in his controversy with Proast can be found in an elaborated form in the theory proposed around the same time by Pierre Bayle, which can be regarded as the culmination of the modern discourse of toleration because it establishes a new level of argumentation. Bayle is aware not only that the most influential justification of intolerance, that of the Christian perfectionism of an Augustine, must be combated at the normative and the epistemological (in addition to the religious) levels, but also that a higher-order conception of practical and theoretical reason is necessary to accomplish this and to present a *reciprocally justifiable* conception of toleration.

Central to Bayle's argument are revised versions of the aforementioned normative and epistemological components:

(TJ 13b) The normative difference between universally binding moral norms which can provide the basis of coercive law in a pluralist society and convictions concerning values which are contested by reasonable human beings can be found in a clearly articulated form in Bayle; the former, according to Bayle, are founded on the practical *raison universelle* which is *prior* to all positive religion and is shared by all human beings, even atheists. The radicality with which he opposes his famous 'paradox' that atheists are also capable of morality, and that even a stable society of atheists is possible, to 'Locke's fear' shows how dominant a role the idea of the need for an *autonomous moral* justification of toleration plays in his thought. In arguing for this he defends, on the one hand, a rational and moral universalism and, on the other, also a separation from value-based convictions – in this case, religious convictions – which are particular in nature and do not have the status of universal norms. In order to make this separation, Bayle falls back on the *principle of reciprocal justification*:

in religious controversies, those persons are in the wrong who claim a practical privilege for their 'truth' which they refuse to grant to others; this is to exercise coercion which cannot be reciprocally justified and to confuse the universal language of morality with their own language, so that a crime seems to become a virtue – 'good coercion', for example. Hence, the foundation of all morality is the Golden Rule of reciprocity and only truly 'shared principles' can count as universally binding, but not specific conflicting conceptions of the truth which are beholden to a religious perspective.

(TJ 14c) This normative difference clearly entails an epistemological difference which must clarify what kind of 'truth' is involved here and whether behind this relativisation of religious truth a scepticism or relativism may not be lurking after all. Bayle responds by developing a sophisticated theory of 'reasonable disagreement' which has lost none of its relevance: accepting the normative principle of justification and being ready to relativise one's own truth in the light of the limit of reciprocity does not presuppose that one can no longer regard one's own convictions as true. Rather, it presupposes a fundamental insight into the *finitude of reason* according to which the separation of faith and knowledge means that the domain of faith transcends reason insofar as faith, although not irrational, is suprarational (*dessus de la Raison*). Bayle's 'rational fideism' states that faith offers answers to metaphysical-religious questions that reason itself cannot provide or demand, though it cannot forbid them either. Reason can lay down minimal preconditions for such answers, but it can neither falsify nor verify them and hence it can and must tolerate them. They are situated in a domain of rational differences which can be played out within the context of reason, but which do not bend to its ultimate authority. With this theory, Bayle is treading a fine line which seeks to undercut the controversy among dogmatic theologians of different religions as well as between such dogmatists and philosophical sceptics concerning the 'true faith', since neither the one side nor the other can claim for itself the 'ultimate' stance of reason in the sense of the demonstrability of their faith (or of the demonstrability of the absurdity of faith). The different forms of religious beliefs do not become relative or subjective as a result, but they do not become intersubjectively binding either. Although people of faith regard the convictions of others as *false*, they do not regard them as grossly *unreasonable* or *immoral*. Religious disagreement continues, but it no longer develops into the fight against 'heretics'. With this the epistemological difference, which opens up the space for toleration in principle, is in place. It completes the normative difference mentioned above, for now those norms are considered binding which cannot be reciprocally and rationally rejected, by which Bayle understands the central moral precepts, whereas truths that go beyond these and are rationally rejectable (though also rationally acceptable) cannot ground any claim to coercive validity.

However, Bayle remains too captive to the traditional discourse of toleration that a series of other justifications cannot also be detected in his work, in particular

(TJ 2c) an even more radicalised version of the argument for freedom of religious conscience, which is supposed to avoid the dialectic of this argument in Locke which Bayle perceptively foresaw. Therefore, he subjectivises the conscience which must answer for itself before God to such a degree that it becomes downright sinful not to follow it or to subject it to external coercion, regardless of what it seems to enjoin. – However, this leads to the paradox of the 'conscientious persecutor' whose conscience commands him to force others to accept the truth, with the result that to require him to be tolerant would itself involve a form of intolerance. Even worse, since Bayle stresses the unconditional right to obey one's conscience, this would entail a moral right to do something immoral. Bayle ultimately escapes from this dead end only by returning to the normative-epistemological justification mentioned above.

In this way he succeeded in making the decisive breakthrough to a justification of toleration which avoids the dangers of collapsing into its opposite that beset the other justifications, though he did not himself arrive at the conception of the self-sufficiency of practical and theoretical reason which became possible in the wake of Kant. The comparison between Locke and Bayle shows in particular not only how the latter avoids the problems which forced the former to abandon the argument of the non-coercibility of conscience, but also into what difficulties Bayle's own attempt to pursue this traditional route further leads him. Thus, it is possible to uncover the aporias of the concept of freedom of conscience and to formulate an alternative justification of toleration which assigns a central role in the definition of toleration to the reflexive principle of justification itself.

19. In spite of Bayle's extensive influence on the French Enlightenment in particular, the two most important differences between his thought and that

of the philosophers of the Enlightenment are no less apparent. Regarding Bayle's paradox, many of the latter recoil at the prospect of severing the ties between religion, morality and justice entirely, whereas when it came to criticism of religion they go beyond Bayle and seek to overcome intolerance by replacing positive revealed religion with a 'natural' or 'rational' religion which is supposed to provide a new basis for toleration.

A particularly important feature of the Enlightenment is that the two perspectives on toleration – the horizontal, intersubjective perspective and the vertical perspective of the theory of the state – at first diverge sharply, for example in Montesquieu and Rousseau, though ultimately they are combined into a democratic conception of toleration in Kant and in the context of the American and the French revolutions. Montesquieu argues at the horizontal, social level for mutual tolerance founded on recognition of the moral-ethical commonalities among the positive religions which form a universal natural core religion. At the level of the theory of the state, by contrast, the notion of the plurality of religions, cultures and peoples leads to a different conclusion:

> (TJ 11b) Montesquieu's treatment of the role of religion in the state primarily in terms of functional considerations oriented to stability not only leads him to reject Bayle's paradox and to argue for the need to bring obedience to the law and obedience to God into harmony; in addition, given his conception of the limits of a society's capacity for religious and ethical innovation and transformation, it leads him to argue for a prohibition on religious innovations. It follows that toleration can be granted only within the framework of a modified *enlightened permission conception* if religious plurality already exists within the state and its suppression would provoke rebellion and injustice. Thus, this conception is indeed linked with normative points of view, but the latter continue to be shaped by a primarily statist utilitarian perspective which draws restrictive conclusions from the awareness of religious plurality, national particularity and the threat of religious strife – a dialectic of the enlightenment permission conception.

20. In Rousseau, too, a gap opens up between the social perspective on toleration and the perspective of the state. From the former perspective, Rousseau justifies toleration with

> (TJ 5b) a new version of the argument from reductive unity that mutual tolerance is facilitated and promoted by a natural religion which is prior to all positive religion. It contrasts with a 'rational religion' in that it

is derived from certain human emotions and develops an understanding for the loyalty towards the positive religion into which a person was socialised, provided that this does not give rise to a justification of intolerance. Nevertheless, there remains a tension between the natural religion and the positive religions.

In Rousseau's works in political theory, his perspective changes as dictated by his concept of sovereignty and the overriding goal of ridding the state of intolerance:

(TJ 20) If the body politic is to be able to form a common will, according to Rousseau, it requires a common ethical religious foundation, which must be laid down in a civic profession of faith, a *religion civile*. Thus, Rousseau also rejects Bayle's paradox and believes that a minimal religion is necessary in order to justify morality in general, and for political cohesion in particular. In so arguing, he follows the Hobbesian logic that successfully combating civic (and especially ecclesiastical) intolerance requires not only that sovereignty be respected on religious grounds but also that no other supreme authority should exist alongside it. In common with Spinoza, Rousseau points out that the civic profession of faith must be of a minimal and open kind and must condemn the dogma of intolerance and that the sovereign can only prescribe the external form of religious worship; his authority does not extend to the inner sanctuary of faith itself. – However, the fact that natural religion is transformed into a civil religion gives rise to the following dialectic. In seeking to establish a general basis for civil tolerant conduct, all of the religious and non-religious stances which seem to be incompatible with this, first and foremost those of the Catholics and the atheists, are excluded. Freedom of religion then ultimately shrinks to the internal freedom of conscience without freedom of worship, moreover with the obligation to observe the external form of worship and to accept the official profession of faith. Here a different dialectic of the political-religious logic of identity (cf. Hobbes (TJ 18)) becomes apparent, which likewise shows how the struggle against intolerance can become inverted into this very intolerance.

21. Voltaire's approach represents the clearest attempt to resolve dogmatic religious conflicts and the associated intolerance in the spirit of the ideas of the Enlightenment, in particular by

(TJ 5c) replacing the positive religions with a deistic *rational religion* which is understood not as a core religion uniting the positive religions but as a complete rational alternative to them, as a 'holy and unique religion'. In this way alone can the disease of fanaticism be cured, according to Voltaire. Contrary to Bayle, Voltaire believes that reason alone should be decisive when it comes to religious truth and that it privileges just one religion; thus, he retains the ideal of the one, unified religion for all human beings. Therefore, his route of reductive unity is related in part with the route

(TJ 8a) of *inclusive unity*; for he believes that this religion alone is capable of incorporating the rational elements of all of the others. They are therefore to be tolerated only as transitional stages in the emergence of an enlightened culture.

This programme is first and foremost one of overcoming intolerance and only secondarily one of toleration; its aim is to overcome religious difference itself and to translate it into a new unity from which vantage point it will become apparent how absurd the past religious disputes were. However, this programme is beset with difficulties in two respects. First, even Voltaire (as opposed to Diderot) still thinks that there is a necessary connection between rational religion, morality and the ethics of the state, so that not only atheists are excluded from state toleration but potentially also those who hinder the progress of enlightenment. This already highlights the second problem. For, even though the abolition of intolerance aims to bring about a tolerant social-religious order, in the process toleration towards the existing positive religions becomes precarious, because the latter – Voltaire singles out the Jewish religion – appear to be primarily antiquated remnants of an unenlightened era, hence to be 'false' religions. This overlooks the fact not only that the rational religion itself is just one, by no means completely neutral or higher-order, faith among others, which (like others) assumes that it is the only rational faith, but also that, by appealing to the goal of toleration and the rule of reason, which then is inflated into a religion, it runs the risk of itself legitimating new religious exclusions – a particular form of the dialectic of enlightenment.

22. From this, materialist atheists such as d'Holbach conclude that

(TJ 21) even the minimised rational religion remains captive to the logic of religious intolerance and thus that the only route to toleration consists in overcoming religion entirely, in *atheism*. They argue that fanaticism is not an aberration but the essence of religion; moreover, it is a serious error to connect morality with the fear of God; on the contrary, fear of God is more likely to undermine morality. – However, this would mean the end of toleration in a twofold sense: an end to the occasion for religious toleration because religious plurality would no longer exist in any meaningful sense, and an end of toleration for existing religions, all of which would stand accused of fanaticism and intolerance. Again we encounter the problem of the search for a single religion of reason, only this time with a negative outcome. In a dialectic of atheism, its battle against intolerance can itself lead to intolerance.

23. The status of the positive revealed religions vis-à-vis the deistic rational religion is the topic of Lessing's justification of toleration, which seeks to reconcile both poles. Toleration is grounded primarily

(TJ 7a) via the path of *competitive unity*, such that toleration signifies the space of freedom laid down by God and by reason within which the revealed truths are supposed to demonstrate their reasonableness. Based on an original unity in God and a shared reason and morality, one can no longer inquire into the 'true' revelation. Instead the best and the true religion should be able to prove its truth by the fact that it remains true to the spirit of the shared origin and the spirit of toleration without betraying itself or the 'religion of the forefathers'. This conception of toleration and religious plurality thereby acquires a pronounced humanist-irenic character, which suggests that the enlightened religions are converging not just on a moral, but also on a theological consensus. – At the same time, the tension between the positive revealed religions and their relativisation through the rational insight that the genuine ring is no longer identifiable remains unresolved; as a result, the strong emphasis on the joint origin lends religious particularities the appearance of conventions which are the object of meaningless disputes. The genuine, secure faith is then reduced to what unites, a humanist faith in humanity as it were; and the participants in the competition between religions can understand their particular beliefs which go beyond this only as hypotheses which may prove fruitful in the moral rather than in the theological domain. All told, this amounts to a radical self-relativisation of the religious perspectives: in a dialectic of the competition between religions, those who are supposed to stage this competition become uncertain whether it will ever be able to demonstrate the truth which is the principal concern of their faith.

Mendelssohn takes up the idea of the competition between religions and tries to show that there is much to be said for Judaism as a reasonable and tolerant religion by comparison with Christianity. However, he is sceptical concerning Lessing's overriding rational religious deism; both against such a reduction of religion and against the idea of a reconciliation of religions he objects that these are all too often merely disguised Christian attempts at appropriation. Nevertheless, his conception also involves the problem identified in Lessing, albeit in a different form; for in Mendelssohn the rational, enlightened and tolerant faith is likewise accorded priority over the (merely particular) revealed faith. At the same time Mendelssohn criticises a confusion of the religious and political levels which implies that the emancipation of the Jews, which he demands in contrast to mere toleration in accordance with the permission conception, has to be purchased at the price of religious assimilation.

24. In the history of the rationalisation of morality, which is a distinguishing feature of the discourse of toleration, Kant's moral philosophy represents the culminating point insofar as he develops

> (TJ 13c) an *autonomous* conception of morality which captures the normative difference of toleration as a *deontological difference*. Morality presupposes a faculty of practical reason which is independent and not founded on any other values or convictions, for example religious ones; it is free from heteronomous definitions of happiness here on earth or in the afterlife. It calls for unconditional respect for human beings as moral persons which does not involve any further ethical justification, qualification or relativisation. Accordingly, here the development of the idea of the normative priority of 'pure' humanity, as formulated for example in Castellio and Bayle, over other aspects of human identity is followed through to its logical conclusion; the human being as a 'moral person' in his own right takes his place alongside the 'ethical-religious person'.

The deontological difference follows from the insight that only those norms can claim moral validity which can be justified reciprocally and generally among autonomous persons, so that restrictions on action which absolutise a one-sided positing of the truth are illegitimate, even if they are justified with reference to the good of the person subject to the restrictions. Notions of happiness are the object of reasonable disagreements, according to Kant, so that categorically valid moral norms capable of justifying restrictions on action will not contain such particular ethical notions. Hence, the normative difference will always have to be the result of a process of reflexive universalisation and cannot fall back on a reservoir of fixed values.

The objection against paternalistic justifications of intolerance is not grounded in the 'good' of ethical autonomy which would be necessary for a 'good life' but follows from the *dignity* of every autonomous moral person who has a right to demand that all moral actions that affect him or her should be justifiable on the basis of reciprocally shareable reasons. Religious coercion, therefore, cannot be justified in reciprocal terms. In contrast to perfectionist thought, for which toleration counts as a means to the end of achieving the good life, with the danger that other means could prove to be more conducive to this end, here the justification requirement implies that other people must be respected as 'ends in themselves', which simply means that the duty of justification must be strictly observed.

Even though Kant's moral philosophy thus provides the desiderata of an autonomous morality and of the deontological difference which, as remains to be shown, are necessary for resolving the paradoxes of toleration within the framework of the respect conception, nevertheless a particular aspect of this approach leads him to return to the conception of a rational religion, with its attendant problems. Although, in contrast to Enlightenment thinkers like Voltaire, he no longer thinks that morality is grounded in religion but, conversely, that religion is grounded in morality, the idea of a 'supreme good', which follows from the 'need of reason' to conceive of a happiness in proportion to morality, leads him to embrace a moral rational religion which he regards as the only rational form of religion and as capable of rationally resolving the disputes between the positive 'forms of faith'. This is supposed to undercut dogmatic intolerance, though it does so at the cost of a 'rationally grounded' hierarchisation of the positive religions which favours Christianity, even though the latter, as a form of ecclesiastical faith, can also serve only as a 'vehicle' leading to the uniquely true, extremely reduced religion. With this, Kant draws a different conclusion from the finitude of reason from Bayle who, by contrast, is more consistent in stressing the difference between faith and reason and thus offers a more appropriate basis for toleration from an epistemological point of view (see above TJ 14c).

In his philosophy of law and politics, Kant conceives of law parallel to morality as a system of norms which are free from particular doctrines of happiness. They spring from procedures of public, democratic justification, which call for the virtue of tolerance on the part of the legislators who must recognise where the limits of good, publicly defensible reasons lie. In this way, the right to justification migrates into the political-legal domain and excludes religious coercion as illegitimate. This gives rise to the possibility of extending the respect conception from the horizontal to the vertical dimension and of superseding the one-sided, authoritarian toleration of the permission conception, which Kant describes as 'arrogant'. Tolerance becomes an essential virtue of democracy.

Kant's philosophy as a whole involves a differentiation between *four different normative conceptions of the person* which emerged in the development of the discourse of toleration. In addition to the autonomous *moral person* who must be respected unconditionally in his dignity as a justifying being, there is the *ethical person* who has specific conceptions of the good and of value which can, for example, be justified in religious terms; to these two roles are added the roles of the *citizen* and of the *legal person* as authors or addressees of the law, which has to be discovered and decreed in procedures of public legitimation.[5] Just as the moral person has a right of justification concerning one-sided impositions of values, so, too, the legal person has a claim to equal rights and to participate in legislating discourses as a citizen in order to bring his own perspective to bear in these discourses.

25. The normative power of the logic of justification connecting the horizontal with the vertical axis unfolds in the two major revolutions of the eighteenth century. This shows how the twofold rationalisation of power and morality, which is the distinguishing feature of the history of the discourse of toleration, leads to a crisis in the direct conflict between a permission toleration in accordance with 'enlightened absolutism' and a political respect conception; thus, the revolutionaries called for equal freedom of religion as part of a more comprehensive political freedom and resisted an authoritarian, 'despotic' and 'degrading' understanding of toleration. At the same time, however, tolerance was supposed to be one of the central virtues of the emancipated citizens as lawmakers and as subjects of the law who had learned not to translate religious differences into legal-political discrimination. Hence, toleration is justified, especially in the human rights declarations,

> (TJ 22) on the basis of the mutual *respect* between morally and politically *autonomous citizens* who accord one another the rights which they can justify reciprocally and universally as free and equal persons. In this way, the right to justification finds application at the political level in such a way that a moral and political claim to a series of rights calling for legal and political institutionalisation, both as defensive rights and as rights of participation, can be justified.[6] Rights and liberties are no longer granted 'from above' but instead are legitimised and secured among equals, resulting in a close interrelation between rights to religious freedom and political participation rights.

5. On the four conceptions of the person, see Forst, *Contexts of Justice*, ch. 5.
6. See Forst, 'The Justification of Human Rights and the Basic Right to Justification', in *Ethics* 120, July 2010, 711–40.

Nevertheless, the understanding of liberty and of law continued to be shaped profoundly by religious conceptions, especially in the United States, whereas in France an autonomous political justification of basic rights took shape. In France, however, not only did the relation between individual liberties and the principle of popular sovereignty remain obscure but also a residual form of religious permission toleration could initially prevail. The opposition which this provoked in the National Assembly revealed the internal relation between the democratic respect conception of toleration and the principle of political *justice* according to which the basic structure of a society must rest on reciprocally and generally justifiable norms.

26. A further aspect of the debate on toleration in the Enlightenment is that the heightened awareness of the cultural and ethical differences between peoples led to the formation of theories which are critical of attempts to privilege a universal religion of reason. In Herder we encounter for the first time a shift within reflection on toleration away from religious differences and towards ethical-cultural differences between groups and likewise a

(TJ 23) *cultural-pluralistic justification of toleration*. According to this argument, human history should be understood in terms of a divine providential plan as a succession of culturally unique and incompatible forms of human perfection – ethical worlds, as it were – each of which contains its own measure, so that they cannot be assimilated into a universal synthesis: the good is scattered across the earth. An esteem toleration is justified by the idea that these forms can be valued for their uniqueness and their ethical character, even if they are rejected on account of other features or of their one-sidedness. – This conception not only suffers from an essentialist conception of culture and peoples, however, but it is unable to resolve the tension between the emphasis on the limits of ethical perspectives and the comprehensive perspective (on the plan of creation) that this ethical-pluralistic theory must itself be able to adopt. In addition, its organicistic vocabulary masks the potential contradiction between collective and individual claims to singularity. And, finally, there is the danger that the argument could become inverted into its opposite when a form of life is not held to be worthy of esteem in any of its features but is seen as a deviation from the beauty of creation; the fact that the ethical standards of esteem and tolerance remain open entails the danger of arbitrary demarcations. This dialectic of cultural-ethical pluralism is characteristic of esteem conceptions in general: the closer the connection drawn between the persons or cultures who tolerate and esteem each other, the narrower may be the resulting limits of toleration because they are marked by what one is able to value. However, toleration should include more than what one can judge to be ethically valuable from one's own – or a putatively divine – perspective.

27. A Romantically inspired, pluralistic conception of religious toleration can be found in Schleiermacher:

(TJ 10a) a variant of the *religious-pluralistic* argument, in this case with an emphasis on the uniqueness of subjective religious experience (related to TJ 12), which, according to this conception, takes a different direction in the case of each finite being from the moment of 'contact' with the infinite onwards. Thus, individuals are not only able to explain the differences between religious views but they can also adopt an attitude of tolerant esteem towards the paths pursued by others. – This leads in turn to the dilemma of too strong versus too weak self-relativisation: too strong insofar as the awareness of the finitude of one's own perspective requires one to regard the perspective of the others as 'equally pious' or as equally true, so that it becomes unclear whether a situation of toleration still pertains; the self-relativisation would be too weak, on the other hand, assuming that one understands one's own perspective in such a way that it reflexively incorporates those of the others. This dilemma is characteristic of a pluralistic conception of religion, whose notion of esteem toleration also faces the problem that, from this perspective, what can be esteemed is also identified with what can be tolerated, which can lead to excessively narrow limits being placed on toleration.

28. In his liberal-Romantic theory, Humboldt, in contrast to Herder, emphasises the primacy of individual over collective singularity. This leads to an

(TJ 24) *ethical-liberal justification of toleration* founded on a conception of human self-perfection. Tolerance among the citizens, and especially toleration by the state, is justified in terms of the need for a space of freedom to enable individuals to develop their individual potentials by their own efforts, albeit in harmony with the efforts of others, while pursuing their respective paths to perfection. Individual originality is the goal and the purpose of the state; political freedom and toleration are the means to its realisation. Hence, toleration is ultimately founded on esteem for the potentials for originality residing in individuals and what they produce in a society of 'fairer and loftier and more wonderful forms [of diversity and originality]'. – However much Humboldt is at pains to distinguish his conception of ethical perfectionism from political perfectionism, the fact that toleration is regarded primarily as a means to achieving the ethical goal of the development of originality involves in a variety of ways the danger of an inversion into its opposite. This danger arises, first, where the liberty granted leads to the development of 'forms' which fall far short of the ideal of singularity or which even lack the drive towards self-perfection, so that their freedom appears 'worthless'. It arises, second, where forms develop which do not challenge the rights of others but nevertheless jeopardise their 'flourishing', for example by offering bad examples. And this danger arises, third, where it proves to be possible to create ethical forms of originality other than by granting liberty, i.e. not through direct force but through positive incentives or educational measures. In all of these cases, ethical perfectionism could turn into a form of political perfectionism which imposes narrow limits on toleration.

29. Mill's conception of social toleration involves a variety of justifications of toleration,

(TJ 24a) one of which is closely related to Humboldt's *ethical-liberal perfectionism*. Toleration is supposed to create a space of freedom for social experiments which promotes the development of unconventional plans of life which, taken together, are conducive to social progress. The value of individuality, the production of 'strong natures', is of central importance in this respect. Mill seeks to avoid the problems of the inversion of ethical perfectionism into a form of political perfectionism identified above in that he regards the *autonomous* conduct of life as a precondition for the development and realisation of a conception of the good, and correspondingly calls for respect for this autonomy insofar as doing so does not involve harm to others. – However, because this connection between political liberty or social toleration, personal autonomy and the development of individuality, is primarily grounded ethically in terms of the ideal of originality, the argument for toleration remains conditioned and relativised by this circumstance. Toleration and respect for autonomy are 'good' only when they lead to something good, that is, when they are employed in the ethical sense specified. If they are not, perfectionist political interventions not only may be justifiable but may even be required.[7] One would only need to ensure

7. Raz draws such conclusions in *The Morality of Freedom*, chs. 14 and 15, and 'Autonomy, Toleration and the Harm Principle'.

that they achieve their goal with the least possible impairments of individuality, beginning, for example, with the prevention or suppression of worthless forms of social life or those which impede autonomy and originality.

Even more important is the problem that the thesis about the connection between political liberty, personal autonomy and the good life, which developed against the background of the traditional justification of freedom of conscience as a precondition of an authentic and inner faith, remains captive to a specific, albeit higher-level, liberal conception of the good, namely the assumption that only an 'autonomously chosen' life plan can lead to a good life. However, this remains a quite particular conception. For, however reasonable it may be, one can also reasonably argue that a life which is *not* autonomously chosen in this sense can constitute a good life, for instance, one which is devoted to fulfilling duties towards others which are not chosen and are not critically examined or one which is grounded in traditional religious terms. The politically *free*, the ethically *autonomous* and the *good* life may be three different things. Thus, even when the quest for the good is not confined to specific 'valuable options' but is left open, a form of perfectionism may become established which implies that the promotion of the necessary good of autonomy is regarded as an obligation of the state. The result would be intolerance towards those forms of life which would not be deemed conducive to autonomy, even though they would not thereby cross the line to morality (for instance a religious minority which does not coerce its members into adopting a particular form of life but which has a strong sense of duty to God to observe a concrete plan of life). Moreover, one could infer that only 'genuinely' autonomously grounded plans of life and corresponding forms of life deserve to be tolerated (however one wished to confirm this). That would potentially lead to very narrow limits on toleration, whereas tolerating (without further criteria) all the options which are chosen by individuals 'independently' would lead to very wide limits. And a final point: an ethical justification of toleration along these lines not only would fail to fulfil the criterion of the reciprocal justification of the limits of toleration; it would not satisfy the criterion of the reciprocal moral requirement of toleration either, because it adheres to a particular 'liberal', and hence non-generalisable, justification.

In order to ground the requirement that any restriction on freedom of action is in need of reciprocal justification, as his harm principle implies, Mill duly avoids this kind of ethical relativisation and (implicitly) falls back on a

(TJ 13d) *deontological justification* which presupposes a duty of unconditional respect for the right to freedom of individuals. This is founded (a) on the overriding right to justification and must (b) employ the criteria of reciprocity and universality to distinguish between actions which concern a person himself and those that are in need of reciprocal justification, and are potentially reciprocally rejectable because they could cause 'harm' to others. Only these criteria can ground such a distinction, for any other specification of what is in the 'private' or in the 'public' interest could prove to be one-sided. In this way, standards for a moral, in contrast to an ethical, condemnation of a practice can be found which lead to judgements concerning the limits of toleration that can be justified in general terms and exclude religious coercion, for example.

This approach can also offset the disadvantages of another argument for toleration (regarding freedom of opinion and speech) to be found in Mill. It is

(TJ 17a) a variant of the justification of toleration based on its functionality for a deliberating *public sphere* which, through the discursive exchange of opinions, however false they may be, leads to a collective process of searching for the truth which makes productive use of individual fallibility. In Mill's specific version of this argument, which also incorporates motifs from the route of competitive unity (TJ 7), it is once again a value which determines the utilitarian calculation – namely, that of truth – and entails the paradox that it should be permissible to speak any falsehood in order to strengthen the truth. – This justification reaches its limits, however, where the advance of knowledge itself speaks against always permitting certain discussions, because they lead either to stagnation or to the danger of the dissemination of errors; even if it were correct that the truth will always prevail of its own accord, nothing would speak against lending it a helping hand if truth is what counts. Certain false assertions will be conducive to the search for the truth, but presumably not all.

30. If the discourse of toleration expanded at the end of the eighteenth century from the concentration on religious conflicts to include toleration between nations and cultures, in the nineteenth century it expanded to include the issue of political toleration in the light of the antagonisms between comprehensive alternative social systems. This affects the distinction between ethical values, which refer to the good life of individuals, and

moral norms, which concern just social relations and provide the frame-work for toleration of the former, insofar as these norms *themselves* now seem to be the object of controversy. To ensure that this framework remains within the bounds of mutual toleration, however, higher-level norms are required which correspond to a shareable fundamental standard of justice. The dispute over justice itself presupposes certain rules of justice, in the first place safeguards that guarantee the right to justification at the political level. Toleration is then grounded

> (TJ 22a) in the reciprocal *respect* for this basic right in the sense of *minimal or fundamental justice* which is necessary in order to be able to conduct further justice discourses, discourses from which nobody is excluded through a formal or material disadvantage regarding the required basic rights. Hence, this form of political toleration is required in order to justify and interpret the rights of citizens, including the right to religious freedom; in this respect, it is a matter not of a particular case of toleration but of the political-legal institutionalisation of the respect conception in general.

Toleration is required here in two places. It is involved, first, where it is a question of securing just access to political processes and public discussions without illegitimately excluding opinions, even if one holds them to be wrong. Thus, the respective relations of toleration and justification must be scrutinised as to the existence of potentially hidden mechanisms of exclusion (and, in a reflexive move, this scrutiny must be lent institutional form). Furthermore, toleration is required where one of the parties to political discourses of justification recognises that its reasons are not sufficient to overcome the threshold of reciprocity and generality and ground generally binding norms, even though they continue to regard their reasons as well founded from within their ethical perspective.

The problem of where to draw the limits of political toleration and whether, for example, a particular form of state should be stipulated has led to a multiplicity of complex discussions. According to the justification mentioned, the fundamental limit lies where others are denied their right to justification, or are denied justified basic rights and their exercise; this exercise, however, is compatible with a variety of institutional arrangements. In this connection, one can find an alternative

> (TJ 25) *relativistic* justification of toleration in Kelsen which states that democracy cannot forbid antidemocratic movements because it itself

rests on particular values which lack an overriding status. According to Kelsen, however, value relativism implies toleration as a 'moral principle' that calls for recognising the diversity of values. – But here the status of toleration as (a) one value among others or as (b) a higher-level principle remains unclear. Both cannot hold simultaneously. If the former were true, then intolerance (in the name of certain values) would be no less justified than toleration (in the name of liberty, for instance); and if the latter were true, there would be no relativism.

31. The discussion of Marx's critique of toleration in the context of the problem of the emancipation of the Jews made clear not only how certain forms of toleration can be criticised in the light of different conceptions of emancipation as 'half measures', but also what snares are lying in wait for such a critique itself when it works with a conception of 'true' freedom which makes toleration of religious identities, for example, appear regressive. However correct it may be (against the background of the principle of justification) to describe a merely formal legal 'liberal' emancipation, which is politically ineffective and lacks material guarantees while leaving the standards of a religious majority culture intact, as a half measure, and however correct it may be to criticise a 'republican' political emancipation when it persists in obscuring sociocultural and economic mechanisms of power, it is equally unjustified to require individuals to renounce their religion as the price for 'genuine' emancipation. The critique of false, 'repressive' or 'productive', forms of toleration which perpetuate relations of power and government must not presuppose a perfectionist ideal of liberty which in turn leads to a narrowing of the space for toleration (on this, see §37 below).

32. From Nietzsche's critique of toleration as the 'inability of saying yes or no' we can learn not only the negative lesson of how widespread the confusion between toleration and indifference is, but also the positive lesson (in an inversion of Nietzsche, as it were) of how important is the first, 'original' meaning of *tolerantia* as an attitude towards oneself, as a virtue of dignified self-mastery and sovereignty, and how difficult it is to strike the correct balance between objection, acceptance and rejection. The virtue of tolerance presupposes a complex *ability to say yes or no in a differentiated manner*, the ability to harmonise ethical objection with moral acceptance on the basis of autonomous reflection and to endure an internal antagonism. In a certain way, this also implies the ability to be tolerant towards oneself.

33. Perhaps the most important challenge posed by Nietzsche's thought, however, is to be sought at a different, more fundamental level:

> These preachers of tolerance! They always make an exception of a couple of dogmas ('fundamental truths')! They differ from the persecutors only in their opinion of what is necessary for salvation. Adhering to reason would be all well and good if there were *one* reason! But the tolerant person must make himself dependent on *his own* reason, its weakness! Moreover: ultimately it *isn't* even this which listens to the proofs and refutations and decides. It is instead the inclinations and aversions of *taste*. The persecutors were certainly no less *logical* than the freethinkers.[8]

If this criticism – a variation on the 'paradox of drawing the limits' which, in view of the numerous dialectics of toleration discussed, has a certain cogency – were invariably true, there would be no toleration in the strict sense. There would only be different forms of intolerance which owe their existence to human tastes, of which some are at least honest in their urge to exclude and dominate, whereas others disguise their claim to power rhetorically as impartiality because they are too weak to acknowledge themselves and their aversions.

If we are not to close the book of toleration at this point, however, if it is to be at all possible to make a conceptual distinction between the intolerance of a religious persecutor and the attitude of the person who opposes such persecution and to defend the latter with good reasons, if the talk of a 'critique of power' and the many struggles for toleration and justice are to have any normative meaning, it must be possible to identify a justification of toleration which is not reciprocally rejectable in that Nietzschean way and which does not succumb to any of the aforementioned dialectics: a justification which, to echo Nietzsche's criticism, does not absolutise any contentious 'promise of salvation'. And, if we apply the discourse of toleration recursively to itself, this justification can only be the one which rests on nothing other than the *principle of justification itself*. In order to prevent the threat of a particular (i.e. reciprocally rejectable) justification of toleration becoming inverted into its opposite at the point where it meets with opposition and reaches the limits of its grounds, recourse to a higher-level reflection on the justifiability of how boundaries are drawn is necessary. And this reflection must liberate itself, in turn, from such partial justifications by making the principle of reciprocal-general justification, which was always implicit as a higher-level principle *both* in historically concrete, social conflicts over toleration *and* at the philosophical level in the discourse of justifications of toleration, the

---

8. Nietzsche, *Nachgelassene Fragmente: 1880–1882*, 480 (emphasis in original).

basis (a) of the demand for toleration and (b) of the drawing of boundaries. This justification alone – a *combination of TJ 13 c/d and 14 c (interpreted in political terms as TJ 22a)* – can banish the dangers of inversion analysed.

Thus, one justification has emerged from our survey of the many justifications of toleration, as the result of a *dialectic of dialectics* as it were, but a justification which, not to put it in overly Hegelian terms, must not lead us to overlook the fact that the alternative justifications persist and continue to clash in social conflicts: the 'Spirit' of toleration remains *in conflict* from this vantage point, too. The critical historical perspective teaches us which of the justifications of toleration is superior to the others. Nevertheless, this is not a historical truth in the sense that 'history gives rise to' this form of respect; even as historical, it remains primarily a truth of practical reason. It must be recognised, in addition, that other justifications remain as valid as the permission and coexistence conceptions in cases where the social situation seems to preclude any more extensive toleration.

In comparison to the argument which accords central importance to the principle of justification, however, the other routes to toleration seem too short; they end at limits which are unjustified from the perspective of the former, where by 'limits' are meant structural ones, not primarily restrictions rooted in special historical contexts. They concern, on the one hand, the shareability or rejectability of reasons for toleration, but especially the drawing of limits. Hence, the theory which, on the contrary, regards the principle of justification in a deontological sense as binding and applies it in a reflexive and critical manner in defining the limits of toleration follows from the analysis of the discourse of toleration and claims to be able to resolve the aforementioned paradoxes differently from the competing justifications (see above §28.2): not questioning fundamental respect for others counts as a criterion for a minimally justifiable objection (see the 'paradox of the tolerant racist'). The 'paradox of moral tolerance' is resolved in accordance with the deontological distinction between justifications. This means that the moral right to justification is strictly binding (and grounds acceptance) and that only those norms can claim general validity which overcome the threshold of reciprocity and generality, while the ethical values that cannot do so without violating moral norms remain defensible and tolerable. Alongside this normative component of toleration, the epistemological component, which emphasises the finitude of reason, explains how a self-relativisation without relativism is possible. And, finally, the 'paradox of drawing the limits' is resolved in such a way that every rejection of a belief or practice must be reciprocally justifiable in order to avoid arbitrariness and partiality as far as possible. Therefore, this resolution must be backed up with a theory of political justification.

Emphasising the connection between the *principle* and the *practice* of justification is an important implication of the analysis of the conflictuality of the history of toleration 'between power and morality'. Not only the manifold forms of intolerance, but also forms of false or abridged toleration, should meet with objection; the historical dynamic prompted by the situated demand for justifying reasons does not cease to operate. This calls, on the one hand, for the increasing institutionalisation of procedures of discursive justification (and, in methodological terms, a critical and discursive theory of democracy as part of a theory of toleration); however, on the other hand, the dialectic of toleration is not brought to a standstill by progressive guarantees of certain rights and liberties. This emphasises once again the extent to which the principle of justification is inherent in the discourse of toleration not only in the *philosophical* sense but also in the *historical* sense as the foundation of a 'normative logic' of concrete social struggles, of a logic of emancipation and of demands for justification between free and equal persons.

PART II

A theory of toleration

Against the background of the reconstruction of the history of toleration presented in the first part of the study, the task of a systematic theory of toleration is to present the individual components of the most promising route to toleration singled out by the reconstruction: first, the normative justification of toleration and, second, its epistemological implications. This will also mean answering the question of how far the proposed theory can itself claim to be tolerant given the conflicts between the extremely diverse justifications of toleration. It must also be shown, third, what it means to regard tolerance as a personal virtue. Finally, this theory must prove its worth in concrete conflicts involving the – contested – demand for toleration. I will address this issue in the closing chapter on the 'tolerant society'.

9

The justification of toleration

§30 A reflexive justification of toleration

1. To begin with, let us recall the different meanings of the title 'toleration in conflict' outlined in the introduction. Toleration is called for in conflicts that cannot be resolved but can only be 'defused' by adopting a tolerant attitude. The demand for toleration implies advocating as impartial a resolution of the conflict as possible, but the demand is not situated outside the dispute. Furthermore, the concept of toleration is itself contested with regard both to how it is understood and to what value is attached to it as well as regarding differences among justifications of toleration. In short, toleration is a focus of both social and philosophical conflicts.

A closer analysis of the social conflicts in which the demand for toleration arises reveals that what is at stake is always the legitimacy of practical liberties or of restrictions on the realm of freedom of action. As the examination of the historical controversies has repeatedly demonstrated, the kernel of the demand for toleration consists in critically scrutinising existing 'relations of freedom' or 'relations of toleration' and offering reasons for which liberties or restrictions on action are justifiable and which are not. Thus, the call for toleration, especially in the political context, is associated from the outset with the language of *justice*, with criticism of intolerance and false toleration which are regarded as unjust and unjustifiable. The dynamic of the problematisation of existing social and political relations triggered by an increasing radicalisation of the demands for reasons led to a continual surpassing of existing levels of toleration and called for new justifications of toleration.

Thus, turning to the philosophical dimension of the discourse concerning 'toleration in conflict', the justifications of toleration in question are nothing other than specific arguments for particular relations of toleration: they target illegitimate restrictions, though they themselves in turn place limits on toleration. Inherent in all of these justifications, as we have seen, is the claim to provide higher-level reasons for toleration and its limits which are above the conflict, a claim which often proved to be untenable. The justifications offered not only stemmed from the conflicts of their time but remained part of those controversies and a target of criticism, including emancipatory criticism. Thus, here too the demand for supporting reasons led beyond particular justifications to more inclusive and reflexive conceptions of toleration.

This perspective on the sociopolitical and philosophical conflicts over the justification of toleration shows that it is against the principle of reciprocal justification itself that relations of toleration must be measured. This principle reflects the moral logic and dynamic of the discourses of toleration and, as Bayle's approach in particular shows, when this principle is interpreted reflexively it can provide the basis for a conception and justification of toleration which does equal justice to the historical development and to the systematic comparative treatment of the advantages and disadvantages of the justifications developed in the course of this history. If conflicts over toleration, at both the social and the philosophical level, are invariably conflicts over the justification of particular relations of toleration, then that theory will prove to be superior which rests on the principle of justification *itself* and not on any other (always contentious) values or truths. It alone can provide a higher-level justification in the sense that it is connected with the structural core of the demand for toleration, namely the issue of justifying reasons for particular freedoms of action or restrictions on action. Accordingly, if the norms which are supposed to legitimise such spaces of freedom and their limits are to claim validity for all of those affected, and if it is to be possible for the latter to demand these norms of each other, they must also be generally and reciprocally justifiable; a good justification which is worthy of recognition in particular social contexts must then be able to withstand scrutiny in terms of the criteria of generality and reciprocity. Thus, recursive reflection on the structure of justification of the question of toleration and its criteria entails that the superior justification of toleration must be based on the principle of reciprocal and general justification. In other words, it must be based on the very principle which puts all existing social and philosophical justifications of toleration to the test. The actors involved in toleration conflicts (implicitly) appeal to this principle and the task of the resulting systematic theory of toleration is to make it into the *explicit* basis of the justification of toleration. The principle of justification is the trump which enables this theory to outbid the other justifications.

Therefore, the claim which I am making involves the following elements:

(a) The principle of justification follows from recursive reflection on the requirement to provide a general *moral* justification of practical liberties and restrictions on freedom of action and the requirement to provide a particular *political-moral* justification of the exercise of political power and the coercive rule of law (more on this in the following section).

(b) In this way, it is possible to reconstruct the foundation of toleration which is *immanent* in the social and theoretical conflicts over toleration. This foundation is contingent not on any external norms or values but instead on a moral understanding of the principle of justification itself whose counterpart is an unconditional duty or a fundamental right to justification to which all human beings as human beings – that is, as justifying, finite rational beings – have a claim independently of their particular characteristics, convictions and identities (more on this also below). As a principle of practical reason, it provides the autonomous basis for an interpretation and justification of toleration which invests this normatively dependent concept with a substantial, overriding and binding content.

(c) In this way, one can provide a plausible resolution of the paradoxes of toleration. An emphatic ethical objection to certain practices or convictions by a person is counterbalanced by moral considerations which make it clear to her why these practices or convictions are nevertheless not immoral, and hence not only *can* but also *must* be tolerated. This difference between normative viewpoints will have to receive a deontological explanation in terms of the right to justification. It also entails that defining the limits of toleration can rely on no criteria other than those of reciprocity and generality. Every rejection must be justified in terms of these criteria, which should preclude the limits being drawn arbitrarily. This conception avoids the dangers of becoming inverted into its opposite to which the other justifications are inherently susceptible at this point in particular.

(d) The principle of justification is located at the intersection of the twofold rationalisation of power and morality which is a diachronic feature of the discourse of toleration, that is, at the intersection of the formation of an autonomously justified state which develops its own 'rationality' of the exercise and legitimation of power in which toleration features, on the one hand, as a strategy of power but also, on the other, as an emancipatory claim. The latter is connected with the development of an independent morality of justification which, in the political context, calls for publicly shareable, and in this sense rational, grounds for the exercise of political power, whereas, in the moral domain, a conception of binding norms which is independent of particular justifications arises. In political terms, the principle of justification combines the vertical and the horizontal perspectives on toleration into a democratic conception of toleration.

(e) Finally, only this justification can constitute the kernel of a 'tolerant' theory of toleration. This is not only because it avoids as far as possible placing too narrow limits on toleration in practice, but especially because the recursively grounded principle of justification is independent of and compatible with the alternative justifications of toleration, provided that they do not overstep the toleration threshold implied by this principle.

Nevertheless, this at first seems to imply not much more than that freedoms of action or restrictions on action and, in particular, any exercise of coercion, especially legal coercion, are in need of justification. Thus, it must be asked how this principle is itself grounded and what exactly it means in the context of toleration: which reasons for restrictions and for coercion does it exclude?

2. First, I would like to make some remarks on the recursive grounding of the principle of justification. This involves reconstructing the specific *validity claim*, which is raised in moral and political contexts in which toleration is at stake, that for certain reasons certain actions may justifiably be restricted or that certain actions should not be restricted (at least not for the reasons specified). In a moral context, and this is fundamental by comparison with the political, in which at least two persons find themselves in a situation of justification because the actions of the one place restrictions in a relevant sense on the other's practical possibilities,[1] each of the actors claims that his course of action can be justified based on norms that are *reciprocally and generally justifiable and obligatory* (i.e. that the action in question is either required or permitted by such norms): according to the underlying moral validity claim, nobody can justify a breach of such norms, unless he can point to higher-level moral reasons.[2] The criteria of validity of reciprocity and

---

1. This principle also holds in general for moral condemnations of violations of perfect duties (see §35.1). There, too, it is claimed that such a judgement cannot be rejected in a reciprocal and general manner.

2. One need only think of the prohibitions on lies and stealing and the possible exceptions to these. Morality is a reflexive system of norms, not a rigid one.

generality are inscribed in moral norms. Structurally speaking, they imply that every practically rational person can grasp them and must obey them and can also require this of every other person, where the persons in question need not share a specific ethical or political context. Moral norms express a *categorical* form of binding validity.[3] Therefore, since the universal principle of justification (which is generally valid in practical contexts) asserts that normative statements must be justified precisely as their claim to validity implies, it follows in the moral context that the criteria of reciprocity and generality are necessary for redeeming validity. The recursive analysis arrives at context-specific criteria of justification by proceeding backwards from conditions of validity to the conditions of justification.

Hence, in the moral domain, persons have a duty to ensure that they can account for their actions in terms of normative reasons which *cannot be reciprocally and generally rejected*.[4] Here the universalisation of a maxim of action is not required, as in Kant's reflexive procedure in which the agent asks himself whether his action can be universally willed without contradiction, or whether he can will that any person should make the same decision as he does in the given situation. Justification is understood instead as a *discursive* process whose immediate addressees are those who are morally affected. In contrast to a pure consensus theory of moral justification, however, the criteria of reciprocity and generality permit substantive judgements concerning the justifiability of normative claims even in cases of (expectable) *disagreements*, a feature which is especially important in the context of the problem of toleration. For, insofar as some claims can be backed up by reciprocal and

3. Here I follow Habermas, 'Discourse Ethics' and 'Rightness versus Truth'. However, the programme of a 'recursive' reconstruction of criteria of justification with reference to specific criteria of validity tries to do without a general theory of argumentation and instead assumes a series of specific contexts of justification and validity claims that cannot be analysed in terms of the tripartite division into 'truth', 'rightness' and 'truthfulness' suggested by Habermas (see below §33.3). By a 'recursive' justification of rational principles, O'Neill, *Constructions of Reason*, chs. 1 and 2, understands in general terms their connection back to an open debate among free and equal persons. By contrast, I understand it in methodological terms as reflection on which form of redemption of validity is required by a particular kind of norm or value. For a detailed treatment, see Forst, *The Right to Justification*, ch. 1.

4. Here I adopt the negative formulation '*which no one could reasonably reject*' proposed by Scanlon, 'Contractualism and Utilitarianism', 110, for the validity of moral norms. There are numerous norms which one can reasonably *accept*, on altruistic grounds, for example, but which one can just as well *reject* because they are not morally binding. See also Scanlon, *What We Owe to Each Other*, ch. 5. In contrast to Scanlon, however, I interpret the meaning of 'what one could reasonably reject' in terms of the criteria of reciprocity and generality which permit a higher degree of determinacy. This also implies that here I am referring only to the domain of what is morally required strictly speaking and not to the moral good in general which includes, for example, imperfect duties and supererogatory actions (see below §35.1).

general reasons, though they are opposed by reasons which do not satisfy these criteria, one can conclude (at least provisionally) that the claims in question are justified even if a consensus is not possible. Moral reasons need not be universally *shared* but they must be universally *shareable*,[5] something which it must be possible to establish in terms of the two criteria.

Whereas in the moral context persons must be able to answer for their actions to others who are affected by them in terms of reasons which cannot be reciprocally and universally rejected (so that the community of justification potentially includes all moral persons), in the political context, where the justification of the exercise of power by law is at stake (and the community of justification is a limited, political one), this holds *only* for questions which concern the fundamental aspects of justice, i.e. those which impinge on the morally relevant status of citizens as free and equal.[6] Here a justification in accordance with the strict criteria of reciprocity and generality is called for, whereas in other issues in which no central moral questions are involved it may be majority decisions based on a consensus concerning specific procedures which lead to a legitimate justification. When which criteria hold is, of course, often decidable only in conflicts in which the strict criterion must be met. There are a series of further important differences between moral and political legislation; yet common to both is the obligation to provide reciprocal and general justifications in basic questions of *justice*.

3. What do the criteria of reciprocity and generality imply as regards the issue of toleration? In a normative conflict situated in the moral or in the basic political context, *reciprocity* means that nobody can make certain claims (to the validity of norms, to rights or resources) which he denies to others (*reciprocity of contents*), and that one may not simply assume that others share one's perspective, one's values, convictions, interests or needs (*reciprocity of reasons*) by claiming to speak in their 'real' interests (and arguing accordingly that, 'reciprocally' speaking, one would be glad to be treated or coerced as they are).[7] In addition, no party may appeal to the authority of 'higher truths' that cannot expect to meet with general approval.[8] The criterion of reciprocity calls for reasons which can be shared based on autonomous

---

5. Cf. Korsgaard, 'The Reasons We Can Share'.

6. On this, see Forst, *Contexts of Justice*, 84–5 and 'The Rule of Reasons'.

7. Such an attitude is exhibited in an extreme form by Hare's 'fanatic' who is willing to abide by his ideals even if he should turn out to be one of those who (in Hare's example) are sacrificed not for the salvation of their souls but because of their alleged inferiority. Hare, *Freedom and Reason*, ch. 9.

8. As Nagel argues in 'Moral Conflict and Political Legitimacy'. See also Nagel, *Equality and Partiality*, 159: '[I]f you force someone to serve an end that he cannot be given adequate reasons to share, you are treating him as a mere means – even if the end is his own good, as you see it but he doesn't.'

and unimpeded judgements. In this context, *generality* means that a normative solution must take the claims of every single person into consideration and cannot be brokered by two socially dominant parties, for example two religious confessions. Accordingly, each person has a moral veto right of reciprocal and general objections.

As a result, one must subordinate one's view of what is true to the normative priority of the other, to his right to justification, in the case of a regulation that claims to be generally and reciprocally binding; were the criteria of reciprocity and generality to be flouted in such a case, one's claims to truth would collapse into unvarnished claims to power and domination. This shows the extent to which intolerance constitutes a particular form of injustice, and toleration a basic requirement of (morally grounded) justice.

The norms which can claim binding validity (and can become the basis of valid law in the political context) and the values which cannot are separated by a *threshold of reciprocity and generality*, which has to be defined discursively in each particular situation. Between moral norms and ethical values (a distinction to which I will return in §31) there is no predetermined gulf which would distinguish between 'public' and 'private' validity, for instance. The crucial point is rather that, in contexts of justification in which universal obligations are at stake, toleration requires that one refrain from imposing one's own ethical convictions without appropriate justification precisely when one continues to believe that these convictions are true and right. Even if these evaluative convictions do not overcome the threshold of reciprocity and generality with the required reasons, it by no means follows that they can no longer be regarded as true or right and that they are ethically devalued, but only that they do not provide a sufficient reason, at least in this situation, for a general normative regulation. *This* is the crucial insight of toleration. A tolerant person will continue to live in accordance with his or her convictions and if necessary canvass for them, but he or she will not impose them on others who can reject these convictions on reciprocal and general grounds. Such a person is willing and able to relativise his or her beliefs in the light of moral requirements because he or she recognises the difference between different contexts of justification.

Hence, the limits of toleration are reached when others are denied their basic right to justification in general or, alternatively, this right is flouted in particular cases (corresponding to two distinct forms of intolerance). Neither of these things can be tolerated.[9]

9. I will return to such cases in §38.

4. The argument for the priority of the moral basic right to justification, and for the view that practically rational persons accept a duty to act in accordance with the principle of justification in moral (or political) contexts, implies that, on the one hand, the principle of justification is a principle of *reason* which stipulates that specific assertions must be justified with specific reasons according to specific kinds of validity, but that, on the other hand, it is also a principle of *practical* reason. The *rational* insight into the validity of this principle is itself a *normative* insight, namely, that, as a human being, as a justifying rational being who can offer reasons and is reliant on justifications, one 'owes' it to other human beings to act in accordance with this principle. In the moral context, this does not require any additional faculty of moral sense or even of ethical decision,[10] only the insight of practical reason that this is a valid principle (of reason) which no one has good, morally justifiable reasons not to obey.[11] This basic moral insight is a feature of persons who regard themselves and others as always already situated within a shared context of responsibility, a context which they feel themselves, as autonomous moral persons capable of acting responsibly, obliged to uphold – obliged, essentially, by *others* and not, for example, by abstract 'reason'.[12] To recognise oneself and others as finite, equally vulnerable, justifying beings means ascribing to oneself and others a *right to justification* and a corresponding duty, in the form of an *unconditional* duty in no need of further justification. Moreover, even to pose the question concerning additional reasons for respecting others as 'ends in themselves', as beings with a right to justification, whether they be reasons which justify this in terms of God's commandments, in terms of self-interest or in terms of particular conceptions of the good, would be to pose one question 'too many' from the perspective of practical reason, and

10. But see Habermas, 'Rightness versus Truth', 273, and especially *The Future of Human Nature*, 73.
11. For a variety of reasons, this differs from a transcendental programme of 'ultimate grounding', such as that in Apel, 'Faktische Anerkennung oder einsehbar notwendige Anerkennung?' In the first place, the connection between the principle of reason and moral duty holds *only* in the context of morality, not for all forms of rational, argumentative discourse. Besides, the insight into the validity of the principle of justification as a principle of practical reason remains an authentically *moral* insight (which cannot point to any 'ultimate' reasons in Apel's sense). In neither case are obligations of rationality and moral obligations short-circuited (as in Wellmer's critique of transcendental pragmatics in 'Ethics and Dialogue', 185). Instead, it is pointed out that it is *the same* faculty of practical reason which (in the moral context) recognises that the principle of justification is normatively valid and that no further reasons are required in order to obey it. The practical insight into this validity fills the gap opened up in Habermas's version of discourse ethics by the separation between 'a "must" in the sense of weak transcendental necessitation' through 'unavoidable' presuppositions of argumentation and the 'prescriptive "must" of a rule of action'; see Habermas, 'Remarks on Discourse Ethics', 81. I discuss this in Forst, *The Right to Justification*, ch. 3.
12. For a more detailed discussion of the following, see Forst, *The Right to Justification*, ch. 2.

thereby to miss the point of morality, which is that respect for others does not call for any additional reasons. Their 'humanity' alone must suffice. This represents an insight into the 'ground' of morality from an *original responsibility* towards others, and simultaneously an insight into the limits of moral grounding, since any further justification of the moral 'ought' from external sources, whether transcendent or empirical, threatens to relativise morality. In this resides the truth of Kant's moral philosophy, which emphasises not only the autonomy of the morally responsible subject but also the *autonomy of morality* vis-à-vis other sources of value. At the same time, this kind of autonomy is one of the main lessons of the discourse of toleration, which has shown how problematic further qualifications of 'humanity' are when it comes to moral respect. The concept 'human being' must itself acquire a certain independent normative meaning.

In the moral context, therefore, one must distinguish between a first-order practical insight into reciprocally and universally justified norms and a second-order practical insight not just into the 'how' but also into the *'that'* of justification. The unconditional duty of justification must be assumed to be based on a claim of the other that cannot be negated, to be something whose fulfilment one owes to others without any need for prior agreements. The 'dignity' of the other and of oneself as a free, and nevertheless finite, justifying being must be respected in a way that accords the shared moral identity priority over all differences separating individuals, so that a willingness exists to heed the limits of reciprocity and generality, in spite of all of these differences. The principle of justification would remain in limbo, as it were, if the recursive insight into this principle were not associated with such a second-order insight. The latter first leads to a moral self-understanding and to the readiness to accord priority to moral reasons in the moral context. It lends the principle of justification a *practical* meaning.

The form of mutual respect underlying the respect conception of toleration must be morally justified in this sense, namely, in the dignity of the other as a justifying being, not in the concern for his particular well-being (much less one's own well-being). Only thus can this respect be demanded from everyone, independently of particular ethical convictions, and, second, only in this way can a clear separation be made between the domains of (a) what is one's own, (b) what can be tolerated and (c) what cannot be tolerated, a separation which avoids questionable ethical determinations. This ensures that the sphere of what can be tolerated is not ethically grounded and restricted in the wrong way. Finally, this also banishes the danger of perfectionism which sees toleration merely as a means to other ends that has served its purpose when other, more suitable means exist to promote the good, even the good of autonomy.

In this way, the rational content of a plurality of extremely diverse and mutually contradictory demands for respect are included without embracing their problematic aspects. Certain theories call for respect for personal autonomy of choice arguing that one should respect that people have chosen, and ought to be able to choose, their conceptions of the good (the liberal version),[13] whereas other theories justify respect on the grounds that individuals have *not* chosen their own conceptions (nor are they freely 'choosable' or 'changeable') and their identities would be destroyed if one did not show them respect and regard them as merely 'unencumbered' subjects of choice (the communitarian version).[14] This dichotomy between respect for a person's freedom of choice and respect for his or her specific, constitutive identity is connected with a series of further conceptions (of the person, of the nature of convictions, etc.) which refer back to the history of the discussion of freedom of conscience, both of which involve the dangers already identified above (§29, sections 18 and 29). Whereas the liberal approach tends to respect only 'autonomously' chosen conceptions of the good and can make the active promotion of personal autonomy its (paternalistic) task, the communitarian approach tends to recognise only 'deep' identity-constitutive conceptions of the good and to neglect the importance of personal autonomy. If, on the contrary, respect towards persons is justified in terms of their dignity as persons endowed with a right to justification, the (reasonable) dispute between such particular conceptions of the person and of respect is avoided while preserving the normative content of respect for the autonomy or the identity of the person, since *both* the reference to freedom of choice *and* the reference to the existing identity, properly understood, can constitute good reasons for particular rights.

It remains to observe that the assumption, frequently encountered in the context of the justification of toleration, that toleration presupposes a 'pluralism of values', needs to be qualified. Toleration, on the one hand, presupposes a pluralism of ethical values but, on the other, excludes pluralism as regards morality or the basic principle of morality, since the demand for toleration should rest on a shareable foundation and involve more than a

---

13. See, for example, Kymlicka, *Multicultural Citizenship*, ch. 5; Dworkin, 'Foundations of Liberal Equality', 83–6.
14. See, for example, Sandel, 'Religious Liberty', and 'Moral Argument and Liberal Toleration'; Mendus, *Toleration and the Limits of Liberalism*, 150–1.

strategic modus vivendi.[15] But how should we understand in detail this distinction between a plurality of ethical values and a single moral principle? What is the nature of these values?

§31 Ethical pluralisms

1. The discourse of toleration reveals the necessity of a structural distinction between (a) categorically valid norms which support the call for toleration and make it into a moral requirement and (b) the evaluative commitments in conflict to which individuals or groups hold fast, even though their claim to be binding is relativised by the insight into toleration to such an extent that those involved recognise in what respects their evaluative commitments cannot count as generally or reciprocally valid or non-rejectable. This normative difference is captured by the distinction between moral norms and ethical values proposed by Habermas, because it preserves the binding character of 'morality' and the reference to the particular 'ethos' of convictions concerning the 'good life'. In this sense, the distinction has also become standard terminology.[16] Yet even if one rejects this terminology and prefers to speak in terms of 'moral values', for example, or to use the concept 'ethics' in the narrow sense of 'moral philosophy', this in no way alters the necessity of such a structural differentiation between, if you will, first- and second-order values or norms.

The central issue for justifying toleration is that the moral perspective attaches primary importance to the right to justification and that the question of which norms can claim reciprocal and general validity must be decided based on these criteria *alone*. The values which remain below this threshold continue to be ethically tenable: the fact that, in the context of general justification, particular ethical convictions meet with objections which explain why these convictions can be reciprocally rejected does not show that individuals cannot meaningfully follow them in their personal or social lives; it is only that such convictions cannot provide the basis for general and reciprocal restrictions on action or for the exercise of political force among persons

15. For example, Gray, *Two Faces of Liberalism*, argues for a form of toleration on the model of a modus vivendi of peaceful coexistence based on a theory of incommensurable values. Yet he does not want to relinquish a normative argument for such a coexistence and a kernel of human rights (as minimal standards of political legitimacy) either.

16. In addition to Habermas, 'On the Pragmatic, the Ethical, and the Moral Employments of Practical Reason', it is also to be found in Williams, *Ethics and the Limits of Philosophy*, 6–7, Dworkin, 'Foundations of Liberal Equality', 9, Margalit, *The Ethics of Memory* and Strawson, 'Social Morality and Individual Ideal'. See also the detailed discussion in Wingert, *Gemeinsinn und Moral*, part 1.

who are in *reasonable disagreement*[17] about them. The fact that other people's objections are reasonable does not entail that one's own convictions are false or unreasonable, only that the claim to universal validity of these convictions is thwarted by the plurality of ethical perspectives. Tolerant persons need not regard these other perspectives as equivalent in truth to their own or as true in part; they need not esteem them as ethically good or even regard the existence of a plurality of such perspectives as a good thing; they need only recognise that these perspectives are reasonable and not immoral.

Distinguishing between moral norms and ethical values in terms of the threshold of reciprocity and generality can give rise to a variety of misunderstandings.[18] First of all, this does not imply that ethical values are a kind of 'by-product' of moral discourses. They form an independent and complex normative domain that is not only more extensive than that of morality in the strict sense, which refers only to what is intersubjectively binding regardless of ethical contexts, but is also regarded for the most part as 'more profound'. Here we encounter the evaluative convictions in terms of which persons orient their lives and assess whether they merit being described as 'good'.

Associated with this is a further source of misunderstanding. The fact that ethical values provide answers to the question concerning the good life does not mean that they are purely 'private' or 'subjective'. In fact, they can unite societies and transcend cultures – one need only think of religious convictions – and they by no means only provide answers to 'existential' questions. Often they constitute entire 'worldviews' that not only concern individual and social life but also include 'supreme' values which have a bearing on the social order as a whole and on 'ultimate questions'. A case in point are debates over the beginning and the end of life (a topic to which I will return). Although the subjective dimension in which a person seeks assurance concerning the value and success of his life in dialogue with 'significant others' is central, it is by no means the only ethical dimension, for ethical reflection is always bound up with shared and often with 'ultimate' values. The decisive moral issue is only that, in all of these dimensions, when an issue of moral responsibility is at stake for which the common store of ethical convictions, however 'deeply' anchored or founded on 'higher truths' they may be, does *not* suffice to provide an answer, respect for others and

17. On this concept, see especially Rawls, *Political Liberalism*, 54–8, und Larmore, 'Pluralism and Reasonable Disagreement'. I discuss the important epistemological aspects of this concept in §33.

18. For a more detailed discussion, see Forst, *The Right to Justification*, ch. 3.

observance of the threshold of reciprocity and generality have normative priority. When ethical convictions concerning values are so inclusive as to constitute worldviews, they can bathe reality as a whole in a normative light; yet respect for others must shine through this by its own power. However, this is not an ethical requirement. For, although being moral may appear to some to be part of being ethically good, this is not necessarily so; the moral life and the good life may be two different things. The 'ethical' domain represents a complex, independent context of the justification of subjective and intersubjective normative answers, also by appeal to objective truths, a context which no more necessarily includes the moral domain than the converse. Given this differentiation within the normative sphere, the 'autonomy' of persons means in the first place that they are able to judge which kinds of reasons they must heed or offer for which kinds of actions and in which context of justification.

The reference to the intersubjective dimension of the ethical is supposed to make clear that the distinction between moral norms and ethical values does not in any sense imply a 'privatisation' of the ethical, as though ethical questions were a 'private matter' and ethical values could not play any role in the public, or at any rate the political, domain. None of this is the case. Ethical questions are generally answered in intersubjective terms, even when they concern vital personal issues which individuals mostly answer jointly with others, even though they bear sole responsibility for them. Moreover, the proposed normative distinction has nothing to do with the sociological distinction between the private and the public domains. Ethical values are part of public discussion and of political discourse. The fact that, in a particular context of justification, they are measured against certain criteria in order, for example, to justify coercive norms and may fail to pass this test does not mean that they must be excluded from political discussions, as would be implied by positions which draw on Bodin, Montaigne and Hobbes, who feared that public religious debates would lead to political strife and turmoil.[19]

Finally, the reference to the 'objective' dimension of ethical valuations makes clear what is in any case suggested by religious convictions,[20] namely, that such valuations are not purely subjective but make a claim to general validity and that corresponding judgements have a cognitive content. The latter can vary, however, because ethical valuations do not generally claim

19. Compare also Holmes's restrictive conception in 'Gag Rules or the Politics of Omission'.
20. Compare the critiques of discourse ethics in Bernstein, 'The Retrieval of the Democratic Ethos', 301, and Joas, *The Genesis of Values*, 182–3.

general validity nor do they invariably confine their claim to validity to specific subjects, groups or cultures;[21] religious value statements, for example,
may, though they need not, imply a cross-cultural validity. Ethical validity claims can assume a variety of forms and some in fact aim at universal
truth; but this in no way changes the fact that ethical values do not possess
any reciprocally and generally non-rejectable categorical force, but instead
rely on 'moving' people in their self-understanding in order to redeem their
claims to validity (whether particular or universal).[22] Therefore, a theory
which separates ethics from morality should not ascribe cognitive content
only to values that have passed through the 'filter' of morality;[23] but it
regards the ability to go beyond the threshold of reciprocity and universality
as a distinguishing feature of moral norms which does not hold for ethical
values.

2. Hence, the idea of an 'ethical pluralism' must be differentiated in
several respects. In the first place, it may refer to a plurality of substantive
conceptions of the good that specify the *content* of what constitutes a good life
and how it should be evaluated. The comprehensiveness of such a conception
is important in this respect, that is, whether it concerns just one aspect of
the good life or life as a whole and, furthermore, to what extent it relates the
quality of the good life to how the social environment is constituted (and
assumes, for example, that a good life is only possible in a just society or in
one which is organised along religious lines).

Second, it may be a question of a plurality of higher-order conceptions
of the good, that is, conceptions which determine the *form* of the good life
and are compatible with a plurality of substantive conceptions of the good:
whether the good life must be a self-determined, critical-reflective life or
instead one which is situated within a firmly established and coherent tradition; or whether it can be measured only by the standard of objective values
or is primarily oriented to subjective criteria.[24] Reasonable disagreement

---

21. *Pace* Habermas, 'Norms and Value'.
22. Compare the conception of practical reason in Taylor, *Sources of the Self*, 71ff.
23. *Pace* Korsgaard, *The Sources of Normativity*.
24. For an extensive and sophisticated treatment of what it means to speak of a good or a happy or
    successful life, see Seel, *Versuch über die Form des Glücks*. However, the 'formal concept of the
    good life' developed there, on the one hand, draws too close a connection between the 'good'
    and the 'self-determined' life from an ethical perspective. On the other hand, from the
    perspective of moral theory the good cannot constitute the 'point' of morality, because the
    good, contrary to Seel, comes into play in moral contexts only by dint of the prior and
    independent criteria of reciprocity and generality. The suggestion (in response to an earlier
    criticism from my side) that morality is concerned with 'protecting the form . . . of a good life'
    (*ibid.* 233, n. 168) does not change things, because which form this is and how it should be

is also possible at this level. When it comes, for example, to the necessity of ethical autonomy – understood as the faculty of free choice and critical revision of a conception of the good – for a good life, it is questionable whether someone who, for instance, in younger years feels a vocation to perform God's work by caring for the poor and the sick, and from that point onwards regards doing anything else as *inconceivable*, does not live a 'good' or 'successful' life because his autonomy (in the sense specified) is patently severely restricted by the fact that he regards the very idea that he 'chose' this path freely, or that he could choose a different one, as a betrayal of himself and of God and refuses to entertain it.[25] Thus, here it is also the case that the normative requirement that a person's *ethical* autonomy should not be restricted by others must be reciprocally grounded on the basis of the principle of justification and of respect for a person's *moral* autonomy as a being who should not be subjected to norms that cannot properly be justified to him or her; appealing to the necessity of this autonomy for the good life is insufficient. The good life and the autonomous life may be two different things. A person's external freedom, which affords him the freedom for ethical self-development, is *not* justified by an ethical ideal of the life of self-development or self-determination, not even by a higher-order ideal of this kind.[26]

Finally, there is a third level of ethical pluralism, namely, different conceptions of the *sources* of the good. Are the sources assumed to be 'real', thus a metaphysical reality of values in the world understood in divine or other terms? Alternatively, are the values explained in constructivist or culturally specific terms, or even in historicist or deconstructivist terms? Whole 'worldviews' or 'images of the world'[27] can be differentiated according to how people understand their place in a normative 'cosmos' and whether the latter is a purely naturalistic one in which values only admit explanation in evolutionary terms, for instance, or is instead one with objective values, one with only historical values, one with merely imaginary values, etc. A 'tolerant' theory of toleration, as remains to be shown, must also be able

protected will first have to be established in a reciprocal and general manner in a discourse among individuals who may have very different opinions on this question.

25. Frankfurt, 'On the Necessity of Ideals', 111, describes such conditions as 'volitional necessities'. He regards them in addition as conditions for ethical autonomy, which shows how controversial this concept is as well. On this, see §36.1 below.

26. I will return to this point in §37.

27. With reference to Kant, for example, see Henrich, *Aesthetic Judgment and the Moral Image of the World*. For an ontological version, Heidegger, 'The Age of the Word Picture'. Taylor, *Sources of the Self*, 91–107, speaks in this context of 'constitutive goods'.

to deal with such a highest-order pluralism, that is, it cannot put forward a single worldview at this level. The thesis that there is a pluralism of objective, mutually incompatible and incommensurable ethical values stemming from different cultures or sources which can force a person or a society into rationally irresolvable, tragic ethical conflicts, as Berlin argues,[28] is just *one* of these possible ways of seeing the world of the normative: one pluralist theory among a plurality of such theories.[29] The same also holds for a theory which sees the plurality of ethical values and forms of life as itself a *value* on which it bases the demand for toleration; this is also a highly specific ethical conception.[30]

The forms of ethical pluralism on the three levels outlined, by contrast, should be regarded not as ethical or metaphysical themselves but as an unavoidable consequence of human difference and of the diversity of individual perspectives on the world. This conclusion is not the result of adopting a comprehensive perspective of infinity, but is based on an insight into the finitude of human reason which must acknowledge that it is unable to reach a non-rationally rejectable answer to the question of what ultimately makes a life a good one and could in this sense 'justify' it. What reason can accomplish in the moral context, namely, arriving at a justification of norms in accordance with their claim to validity which is 'tenable' (though not 'ultimate') among finite rational beings, is not possible in the ethical domain. The validity claim that a particular ethical path leads to the good or to salvation, assuming that one wanted to redeem it reciprocally and generally, would presuppose not only a non-rejectable description of this goal but also the possibility of confirming that it had been reached. But this does not seem to be attainable for finite human beings.

In another sense, however, the distinction between different contexts of justification leads to a 'pluralistic' conception of the normative. Not only is the ethical domain differentiated in a variety of ways with respect to different obligations (such as towards family or friends) and values (ranging from special goals to guiding orientations), it is also just one domain alongside others, such as the moral domain or the domain of political obligations.[31] The 'space of normative reasons' is extensive and complex and the essential task of practical reason is to systematise it, a task which must reckon with deep-seated conflicts, for instance between ethical ties and moral duties.

---

28. See Berlin, 'The Pursuit of the Ideal'.
29. See Larmore, 'Pluralism and Reasonable Disagreement', 153–63.
30. Thus, Raz, *The Morality of Freedom*, 395–9, though in connection with the value of autonomy.
31. See Nagel, 'The Fragmentation of Value', who makes further differentiations; also my conception in Forst, *Contexts of Justice*, ch. 5.

3. Two objections should be mentioned which criticise the proposed differentiation between ethical values and moral norms for inadmissibly defusing the conflicts that lead to the call for toleration, that is, conflicts *over morality itself*: first in the sense that profound social differences exist (a) over what should count as morally right or politically just and, second, (b) regarding the innermost kernel of morality, namely, the question of when a moral person begins or ceases to exist.

(a) Without a doubt, disagreements inevitably arise at the moral level over the detailed application of the criteria of reciprocity and generality and over which solution has the best possible moral justification; and it is equally clear that profound differences will arise at the political level over which substantial norms of justice can be justified on the basis of these criteria.[32] However, these objections cannot challenge the validity of these recursively reconstructed criteria but instead support their optimally inclusive and prudent application. As regards the validity of the criteria in question, disagreements over which claims are reciprocally rejectable and which are not cannot be avoided entirely; the key point is that in the process the two criteria should not be placed in question and that those involved should be aware of their own fallibility in these questions. Then, in cases in which the criteria of justification are not clearly violated, being tolerant means living with such differences and seeking the best possible solution, where the latter is subject to further revision. This reciprocal toleration is required precisely because human beings are not machines for applying morality.

As regards the optimal application of the criteria, we should recall the dilemma of political toleration (see above §25) whose avoidance requires that political discourses concerning fundamental questions of justice always presuppose a *minimal* conception of justice which ensures that citizens have an effective right to justification. Discussions concerning justice can be conducted legitimately only within this framework, which must itself acquire institutional form. In these discussions, those who are potentially worst off have a qualified veto right based on their right to justification which comes into effect when their status as equally entitled citizens within a social basic structure is challenged.[33] The kernel of justice, the right to justification, calls for a constructive realisation leading to a social basic structure that maximises justice, while at the same time placing restrictions on the framework

---

32. See Waldron's critique of Rawls in *Law and Disagreement*, especially chs. 7 and 11; also, Hampshire, *Justice is Conflict*.

33. This boils down to a procedural version of the Rawlsian difference principle, to which Rawls alludes in *A Theory of Justice*, 131, when he grants those who are worst off a 'veto' according to which 'those who have gained more must do so on terms that are justifiable to those who have gained the least'. Cf. Forst, *The Right to Justification*, parts 2 and 3.

of possible social differences. In this context toleration means ensuring that procedures of 'public justification' remain as open as possible and avoiding exclusions. Moreover, in cases in which one's own view and claims are rejected on legitimate grounds, it means accepting this and abiding by the democratic rules.

(b) Whereas the objections outlined do not challenge the primacy of the principle of justification and its meaningfulness as such, the distinction between reciprocally and universally valid norms and ethical values seems to reach its limit where the ethical background assumptions determine the core of morality itself, the definition of the moral person, and draw it into the conflict. These kinds of problems seem to arise in discussions of abortion, the treatment of embryos and assisted suicide.[34] In this context, how is it possible to make an 'impartial' moral assertion and what does it mean to call for unconditional moral respect?

First, it should be noted that the criteria of justification also remain valid in such debates because the latter concern norms which are supposed to be reciprocally and generally binding and which, as legal norms, are also supposed to legitimise the exercise of coercion by the state. This excludes justifications of norms which are clearly reciprocally rejectable, for example that embryos or foetuses are created by God and hence must be regarded as moral persons. However, it would be too simple to assert that one side – for example, those who argue for ascribing moral personality from a very early stage in life onwards – necessarily relies on untenable religious arguments. The criterion of reciprocity excludes certain justifications, yet it permits a reasonable conflict over these questions.[35] As a consequence, *neither* of the two sides to such a dispute can justifiably claim that their conception should be made the basis of generally binding coercive norms. It is *precisely* here that toleration comes into play: based on the insight that, concerning the central issue in dispute, there are insufficient grounds for exercising legal force as long as the status of the embryo, for example, remains a matter of reasonable disagreement, and hence that *other* fundamental considerations (liberty rights, claims to psychological welfare, promoting health, long-term consequences,[36] etc.) must prevail. Thus, a conciliatory resolution must be sought

34. As in Huster, 'Bioethik im säkularen Staat', though he goes on to apply the principle of justification as a principle of 'political morality' that excludes particular justifications.
35. Gutmann and Thompson, *Democracy and Disagreement*, 74, speak in this case of a 'deliberative disagreement'.
36. Habermas, *The Future of Human Nature*, presents such an argument to the effect that certain practices of 'positive eugenics' entail the possibility of an 'auto-transformation of the species' (21) which involves the risk that the self-understanding of persons could be transformed to

based on mutual toleration. The impression that this seems to demand 'more' from those who call for more extensive restrictions on the autonomy of the individual is due not to the unfairness of the required self-restriction[37] but to the nature of their demands. On the other hand, those who argue for the primacy of individual freedom of choice in such matters must also acknowledge that the central moral issue remains *controversial* and that the notion of the 'inviolability' of pre-personal human life is morally relevant (though not strictly speaking incontrovertible), which calls for corresponding normative regulations that take this into account.[38] In thus agreeing to disagree, the principle of justification retains its guiding normative role. In fact, in this case toleration is a result not of a separation between ethics and morality but of the awareness that this separation can *itself* reach its limits in discourses among finite beings. The key issue, however, remains the ability to relativise one's own position, which, even when one believes that one is defending a *moral* truth, prioritises the moral obligation to offer adequate justifications to others who can reciprocally reject this truth. Toleration is also required, indeed especially so, where moral discourses do not lead to any agreement and the application of moral criteria is controversial. Not every morally relevant and rationally tenable viewpoint is reciprocally non-rejectable and

such an extent that they could no longer understand themselves as ethically autonomous authors of their own biographies or respect each other as morally equal persons (29, 40–1, 49, 56). *Insofar as* this were the case, however, the decision concerning the approval and use of such practices would be not a (species-)ethical issue, as Habermas assumes (71–4), but a question of moral conduct and responsibility towards those whose capacity for moral autonomy and whose chances of being respected as autonomous persons would be impaired as a result.

37. As Sandel, 'Judgemental Toleration', argues in his critique of liberal theories which, in his view, profess a 'neutrality of justification' while advocating solutions to controversial issues such as abortion which favour one particular answer (concerning the beginning of moral personality). Sandel suggests instead that not only citizens but also the state should take a clear, substantive position on such issues and that only from that vantage point can one ask whether deviations from this position can be tolerated (which Sandel doubts in the case of abortion; see 'Tolerating the Tolerant'). However, in so arguing, Sandel overlooks various important aspects of the problem. First, the conception of toleration which he challenges is not morally empty but has a substantive moral grounding in the principle of justification and respect. Second, toleration does in fact presuppose a clear ethical position; however, in accordance with the principle of justification, it requires that, in basic questions of justice, nobody should be forced to obey norms which rest on reciprocally rejectable reasons, for instance reasons which are clearly of a particular religious kind, which Sandel expressly wants to allow as a basis for decision in such questions. But this would violate the basic respect for others which citizens of a just society owe one another. Respecting others when legitimating fundamental legal decisions, by contrast, does not imply banishing religious positions, for example, from the public arena or political discourses altogether, as Sandel also assumes. The consequence of Sandel's position, therefore, would be a rehabilitation of the permission conception that a 'moral-ethical majority' can lay down the law in principle and then itself decide which differences from it are tolerable.

38. Thus, Habermas, *The Future of Human Nature*, 29–37; Dworkin, *Life's Dominion*, ch. 3.

strictly binding; or, to put it in terms of the concepts of the components of toleration: even a moral objection may not suffice for a moral rejection.

Should this insight of toleration in accordance with the respect conception prove to be too demanding in certain conflicts because the moral costs for those concerned are seen as too high, the discourse of toleration offers an alternative conception based on less demanding premises. The coexistence conception, which is informed primarily by pragmatic motives on the model of a modus vivendi between parties who recognise that the conflict involves too many risks and has too little prospect of success, could then undergo a renaissance. Although this situation remains unstable because it presupposes a relatively equal division of social power, it also allows that this could lead to an increase in trust that makes more extensive toleration possible. Which path prevails depends on the nature of the conflict and on the existing social constellation.

§32 Justice and toleration

1. No other work in recent political philosophy has accorded the connection between justice and toleration greater prominence than John Rawls's *Political Liberalism*, a work which has earned a special place in the further development of the modern discourse of toleration. Rawls not only sets toleration apart as a special virtue of justice, as he already did in *A Theory of Justice*,[39] but, in a revision of his original approach, he now also privileges it as a virtue of the justification of the principles of justice themselves, as a virtue of political philosophy as it were.[40] The problem of justification takes on a new form, according to Rawls, once the theory becomes aware that modern democratic societies are marked by a 'pluralism of incompatible yet reasonable comprehensive doctrines' (xvi) of a religious, philosophical or moral kind. This calls for the reconstruction of a concept of 'reason', i.e. of reasonable justification, reasonable persons, etc., which is as neutral as possible with regard to this dispute between 'comprehensive doctrines', as a basis for a 'freestanding' (xxx) and 'autonomous' (98f.), 'political' conception of justice which pursues a 'method of avoidance' in moral and metaphysical controversies. In

---

39. See §§34 and 35. On the relation between toleration and justice see also Höffe, 'Toleranz', and Ricoeur, 'The Erosion of Tolerance and the Resistance of the Intolerable'.

40. Rawls attaches central importance to the connection between justice and toleration in *Political Liberalism*, 4: 'Combining both questions [of justice and of toleration] we have: How is it possible for there to exist over time a just and stable society of free and equal citizens, who remain profoundly divided by reasonable religious, philosophical, and moral doctrines?' (See also 47; page references in the text are to this book.)

this way, the 'political' conception, which is based exclusively on a *political* understanding of practical reason, can be conceived independently of these doctrines while at the same time being recognised from their perspectives in an overlapping consensus among them. Political liberalism thus applies 'the principle of toleration to philosophy itself' (10). The justification of the principles of justice claims only that they are 'reasonable', whereas the claim to 'truth' is made for ethical positions which follow from 'comprehensive doctrines' (xix–xx).

Without being able to offer an exhaustive discussion of the complex justification proposed by Rawls, not to mention the details of his conception,[41] I will address the central problem of his attempt to develop a tolerant theory which threatens to undermine his undertaking. It concerns the *moral* quality of the 'political' justification of the principles which constitute the basis of toleration and the limits of what can be tolerated. Here Rawls's approach is marked by an ambiguity from the outset. This leads him to stress, on the one hand, that the political conception of justice 'is, of course, a moral conception' (11) but, on the other hand, that it is independent of 'moral comprehensive doctrines', be they liberal doctrines concerning the value of the ethically autonomous life or Kant's conception of moral autonomy. Hence, Rawls uses the term 'morality', on the one hand, to refer to his own conception and, on the other, with reference to comprehensive ethical convictions (in the three respects outlined above of contents, forms and sources of the good) which the political conception must avoid. This leads to a *paradox of political liberalism*: Rawls must raise an independent, autonomous moral claim to validity for the principles of justice which are supposed to form the basis of the demand for toleration, a claim which the theory simultaneously seems to preclude in virtue of the 'method of avoidance' of comprehensive moral concepts. This leads to problems and uncertainties, for instance when Rawls speaks of the '(moral) political values' (xlii) of the conception of justice in contrast to comprehensive moral values, of a 'freestanding political conception having its own intrinsic (moral) political ideal' (xlv) or of basic constitutional principles as 'political (moral) principles'.[42] This paradox can be resolved only by removing the embarrassment expressed in placing 'moral' in brackets. It must become clear to what extent it is a specific conception of *moral practical reason independent of ethical doctrines* that leads in the *political domain* to the justification of principles of justice, where the latter are valid

41. On this, see in particular Forst, *Contexts of Justice*, ch. IV.2 and *The Right to Justification*, ch. 4, with a shortened version in Forst, 'The Justification of Justice'.
42. Rawls, 'The Idea of Public Reason Revisited', 781.

for the political basic structure and acquire positive legal validity through the process of founding a constitution and making law, though they are in essence *moral* principles endowed with an autonomous moral validity. To accomplish this, however, Rawls would have to attach greater importance to these (implicit) moral components and, in particular, to modify his theory of an overlapping consensus. Let me explain this briefly.

That political liberalism has its 'philosophical background . . . in practical reason' (xiv) in the Kantian sense already becomes apparent where Rawls outlines the conception of the person which is one of the essential 'ideas of practical reason' on which the conception of justice rests. However much Rawls stresses that this is a 'political' conception of the person which merely designates the properties of democratic citizens, it is unmistakable that both aspects of their faculty of reason are moral capabilities which acquire special importance in the political context: first, the capability to justify norms of justice discursively in such a way that they can expect to meet with general approval (49) and, second, the recognition of the 'burdens of judgment'. The latter explain why reasonable differences in opinion over normative issues are unavoidable and why a pluralism of 'comprehensive doctrines' is an implication of finite reason itself (60).[43] Taken together, both aspects of the reasonable lead to the insight that the justification of general principles of justice cannot rely on reasons stemming from such doctrines; it follows that toleration is a basic requirement of justice:

> Since many doctrines are seen to be reasonable, those who insist, when fundamental political questions are at stake, on what they take as true but others do not, seem to others simply to insist on their own beliefs when they have the political power to do so. Of course, those who do insist on their beliefs also insist that their beliefs alone are true: they impose their beliefs because, they say, their beliefs are true and not because they are their beliefs. But this is a claim that all equally could make; it is also a claim that cannot be made good by anyone to citizens generally. So, when we make such claims others, who are themselves reasonable, must count us unreasonable. (61)

In explaining this – in the light of my reconstruction of Bayle, 'neo-Baylean' – approach (in the preface to the 1996 paperback edition), Rawls stresses that restricting their convictions concerning truth in accordance with the principle of justification is a *moral* achievement of individuals in the context of general justification. 'Reasonable' citizens must justify the exercise of

---

43. I will discuss this aspect in greater detail in the following chapter.

political power in accordance with what Rawls calls the 'criterion of reciprocity' in terms of reasons that can be recognised by others as free and equal persons, without domination or manipulation (xlii–xliv), which for Rawls means that 'the citizen is, of course, a moral agent' (xliii), 'for a political conception is . . . a moral conception. But the kinds of rights and duties, and of the values considered are more limited' by comparison with those which follow from a 'comprehensive doctrine'. Here it becomes apparent that the 'political' conception is based not on 'political' but on moral principles which are restricted as regards not their normative character but only their context of application. Rawls rightly points out that, in contrast to a 'comprehensive', ethical liberalism, an ethical ideal of autonomy of the self-chosen life does not have pride of place here (xlii–xliii). However, because he does not distinguish explicitly between 'ethical' and 'moral' autonomy, he does not make sufficiently clear that he is relying on a notion of *moral autonomy* (as the kernel of political autonomy) which, although it is not an ethical ideal, ascribes to citizens the capacity for moral self-limitation on which respect toleration is based: 'In order to fulfil their political role, citizens are viewed as having the intellectual and moral powers appropriate to that role, such as a capacity for a sense of political justice' (xliv).

This is also shown by the constructivist justification of the conception of justice. In contrast to a Kantian 'moral constructivism' which understands itself as an alternative to moral realist theories of normativity (such as 'rational intuitionism') and views autonomous self-legislation as the source of all normativity,[44] Rawls seeks a 'political' constructivism which remains agnostic in this metaphysical dispute. Nevertheless, following Kant, it is supposed to be characterised by 'doctrinal autonomy' (98) in that it does not rely on any other values or truths apart from the principles and ideas of practical reason which can be reconstructed in the light of the task of developing a conception of justice for a pluralistic society.

> [C]ertainly political constructivism accepts his view that the principles
> of practical reason originate . . . in our moral consciousness as informed
> by practical reason. They derive from nowhere else. Kant is the
> historical source of the idea that reason, both theoretical and practical,
> is self-originating and self-authenticating.   (100)

Hence, here too it follows that the domain of the political, as far as it is a matter of fundamental principles of justice, is not a separate normative sphere

---

44. As argued by Korsgaard, *The Sources of Normativity*.

but a particular context of application of principles and procedures of moral justification. And even if constructivism remains metaphysically agnostic, it affirms the autonomy of reason and builds upon the autonomous faculty of reasonable persons to generate and grasp the justification of the principles of justice based on their own practical reason. In short, an autonomous constructive justification of justice presupposes individuals endowed with such an autonomous practical reason.

This is the very point that inspires doubts about Rawls's idea of an over-lapping consensus, however. For, insofar as the political conception, in his view, merits the predicate 'truth' only from the perspective of the individual 'reasonable' comprehensive doctrines (126), it would have to *borrow* its moral validity from each of the comprehensive doctrines in an 'overlapping consensus'. The political conception of justice is not merely a modus vivendi, for then it would be 'political in the wrong way' (142), but a 'moral conception' (147), which is 'affirmed on moral grounds', though in Rawls's view based *not* on *shared* but on *different* reasons:

> All those who affirm the political conception start from within their own comprehensive view and draw upon the religious, philosophical, and moral grounds it provides. The fact that people affirm the same political conception on those grounds does not make their affirming it any less religious, philosophical, or moral, as the case may be, since the grounds sincerely held determine the nature of their affirmation.
>
> (147–8)

Elsewhere he states that the overlapping consensus does not represent a compromise between the comprehensive doctrines but 'rests on the totality of reasons specified within the comprehensive doctrine affirmed by each citizen' (171). Therefore, according to Rawls, the consensus which serves as a guarantor of the stability of a just (and tolerant) society is a consensus on the principles of justice but not on the reasons that support them. Therefore, the overlap between the comprehensive doctrines is not such that they share a subset of autonomous moral reasons which provide the justification of justice, but such that they remain situated at different levels and only overlap in the point of justice, like leaves threaded on a string without touching each other. This construction does its utmost to accommodate the comprehensive doctrines and their respective claims to truth, since justice does not make a claim to moral truth itself. Yet, in the context of Rawls's own constructivism, it is in danger of being tolerant *in the wrong way*. For at the very point at which the truth claims of comprehensive doctrines clash and justice is supposed to come into play, the latter must develop its *own* autonomous categorical force which makes reasonable persons accord justice *priority* vis-à-vis the various claims to impose comprehensive truths. This, after all, is the point of granting justice priority over comprehensive doctrines, a point which Rawls repeatedly stresses and which corresponds to the two aspects of the reasonable (see above). If the citizens are to avoid violating the principle of justification by absolutising their comprehensive truth and are instead to appeal only to a 'part' of their truth (61)[45] – namely, that part which is included in the *overlapping consensus* – they must have an autonomous moral insight into the 'intrinsically moral duty'[46] of fair justification (in the exercise of 'public reason'). This conception would be tolerant in the wrong way if it failed to identify the reasons for just(ified) tolerance as independent, normatively overriding, *shared* reasons which are strong enough to motivate the required relativisation of one's own truths in normative conflicts involving a reasonable disagreement. The 'freestanding' conception of justice presupposes an autonomous moral sense for and insight into justice.

For the idea of an 'overlapping consensus', this implies that, although the citizens must be able to integrate the perspective of justice into their comprehensive perspective as a 'module' (145), in so doing they must understand themselves as autonomous persons who are duty bound to their fellow citizens to seek certain kinds of reasons in certain kinds of conflicts in order to legitimise general norms reciprocally – and correspondingly to try to reformulate their comprehensive claims to truth or to subordinate them at this point. This is what it means to be tolerant out of motives of justice. Rawls himself distinguishes between two 'ideas of toleration': one justified in purely political terms and a 'comprehensive' idea, for example one justified in religious terms.[47] In this it is clear that the former is supposed to define the limits of toleration to prevent these limits from being drawn too narrowly or particularly; yet it is also clear that for this it is not sufficient, as Rawls conjectures, to leave the reasons for adopting a tolerant stance up to the comprehensive doctrines. For at the very point where their tolerance ends the 'politically' grounded tolerance must provide a corrective, and hence it requires reasons of its own. This is why the relation between the political reasons regarded as more 'superficial' and the 'deeper' ethical reasons needs to be redefined: the 'political' reasons must be strong and 'deep' moral

45. Here Rawls relies on Cohen, 'Moral Pluralism and Political Consensus', 283.
46. Rawls, 'The Idea of Public Reason Revisited', 769.   47. *Ibid.* 783 and 804.

reasons which specify what one owes to others when ethical doctrines clash.[48] If the duty to be tolerant is not itself regarded as an independent moral duty of justice towards others with whom one shares a political context of justification, it cannot have the normative force that Rawls ascribes to it. The 'political' conception of justice must have a moral basis in the principle of justification and the duty to provide justifications, where this is interpreted contextually as a duty of justice and toleration.[49] The 'hope'[50] that the citizens will accord justice priority in certain situations of conflict is a moral hope for favourable social conditions. However, the supporting argument is not addressed primarily to the different comprehensive doctrines with the claim that they should exercise toleration in the light of their own interests and their own conceptions of value; instead, the argument is that people *owe* this to each other. Intolerance is not primarily a violation of one's own ethical doctrine but a moral failing, as Bayle, in particular, makes clear.[51]

2. From the point of view of moral theory, doesn't this amount to a return to a 'comprehensive doctrine', i.e. to a specific doctrine (a) of autonomy and (b) of the sources of morality, to a moral 'worldview'?[52]

(a) Many critics who support an ethical form of liberalism, whether informed by a perfectionist or an anti-perfectionist outlook, have argued that Rawls cannot avoid privileging a particular conception of autonomy in the sense of an ethical ideal. A representative example is Kymlicka's objection that Rawls cannot uphold his argument for the primacy of liberty rights

---

48. Scanlon, 'The Difficulty of Tolerance', 231, argues along these lines concerning the primacy of the obligation of tolerance in deep-seated conflicts: 'What tolerance expresses is a recognition of common membership that is deeper than these conflicts, a recognition of others as just as entitled as we are to contribute to the definition of our society.'

49. Thus, I agree with Larmore, 'The Moral Basis of Political Liberalism', that a principle of equal respect of persons must underlie political liberalism and that Rawls does not make this sufficiently explicit. However, Larmore views this principle – in association with a 'norm of rational dialogue' (see Larmore, 'Political Liberalism', 347–52) – as playing a guiding role only in the context of the justification of political-legal coercion; moreover, he understands it as an independent moral principle and not as a principle of practical reason. In my view, by contrast, the principle of recognising others as 'ends in themselves' and of reciprocally and generally justifying actions that restrict their scope for action in morally relevant ways is a principle whose validity is not confined to coercive norms but extends to all cases where it is a matter of justifying actions that impinge on the interests and legitimate claims of others.

50. See Rawls, 'Reply to Habermas', 145.

51. In this I take the opposite standpoint to Schneewind, 'Bayle, Locke, and the Concept of Toleration', who criticises Bayle for arguing for an autonomous morality which leads to a revision of 'comprehensive' doctrines, whereas Rawls's model does without such a moral revision because the reasons for toleration remain on the side of the comprehensive doctrines. Nevertheless, even Schneewind cannot avoid stressing the normatively overriding, independent character of the 'public political commitment' to justice – with which he is back with Bayle.

52. Compare in this sense Rawls's critique of Habermas, in 'Reply to Habermas', 147.

without recognising the value of individual autonomy as grounded in the 'highest-order interest' (Rawls) in having the ability and the opportunity to choose rationally and, if necessary, to change one's own good.[53] Anyone who does not value this good of autonomy as a condition of the good life, according to Kymlicka, will not be just and tolerant in Rawls's sense; autonomy cannot be viewed exclusively in political terms without at the same time regarding it as an ethical value:

> The problem is to explain why anyone would accept the ideal of autonomy in political contexts without also accepting it more generally. If the members of a religious community see their religious ends as constitutive, so that they have no ability to stand back and assess these ends, why would they accept a political conception of the person which assumes that they do have that ability (and indeed a highest-order interest in exercising that ability)?[54]

However, Kymlicka's identification of ethical with political arguments for respecting individual autonomy overlooks the possibility that someone who is convinced that such subjectively autonomous 'choice' of a plan of life is not a necessary condition of the good life, because it lacks the 'constitutive' dimension which first lends every decision a certain direction and grounds it, can nevertheless show respect for the individual autonomy of *others*, and not on ethical but on *moral* grounds. This is because he views others as persons endowed with a right to justification and acknowledges that his own ethical conviction is not sufficient to prescribe it in a generally binding way to others, much less to impose it on them. This does not mean that he cannot continue to live his life according to this conviction or that he cannot condemn others for living differently, but only that he must respect their dignity as morally autonomous beings even though he regards their ethical notions of autonomy or the choices they made as false or mistaken. Therefore, Kymlicka's puzzle does not exist; what is puzzling is instead the assumption that only those who take a 'liberal-autonomous' stance on life could be tolerant. Members of closely knit, traditional religious communities, for example, do not have to change their ethical attitudes to life in fundamental ways in order to exercise tolerance. If they are required not to deny their young members certain freedoms and educational opportunities (the example that Kymlicka has in

53. See Rawls, 'Kantian Constructivism in Moral Theory', 312.
54. Kymlicka, 'Two Models of Pluralism and Tolerance', 91. For a more extensive discussion of Kymlicka's view, see my 'Foundations of a Theory of Multicultural Justice' and his reply in 'Do We Need a Liberal Theory of Minority Rights?'

mind)[55] this need *not* be based on the conviction that an increase in autonomy is a condition for seeking and finding the good life. The underlying reason may instead be the generally and reciprocally required respect for others as morally autonomous beings who have a right not to be forced to adopt a particular form of life which is imposed on them one-sidedly by their elders and sets severe restrictions on their opportunities for enjoying *equal* rights and opportunities within the broader society. The ground for this, therefore, is being free from domination, i.e. the exercise of illegitimate power in the 'private' or social domain, not a particular conception of the good life. For one cannot know whether the life of any given person will become 'better' as a result of such freedom; but one can judge to what extent someone presumes to have the right to determine the life of others in a reciprocally non-justifiable way. And doing something to prevent this does *not* mean simply absolutising one form of life at the expense of another.

Thus, the criticism of Rawls that he does not sufficiently clarify the moral foundations of his theory and that they must reside in a particular conception of moral autonomy that first grounds its primacy over 'comprehensive doctrines' in the context of political justice leads not to a 'comprehensive liberalism' but to an explanation of why the latter represents the wrong path. For the very emphasis that ethical liberalism places on the value of personal autonomy for the good life overlooks the moral autonomy of persons, which entails that people are indeed under a duty and capable of tolerating other forms of life on moral grounds, even if they regard these forms of life as wrong from an ethical point of view. Ethical liberalism underestimates the capability for differentiation and self-limitation that constitutes the virtue of tolerance. It can only stigmatise the form of self-reflection which implies that citizens cannot transfer their ethical convictions into the space of fundamental political questions as a form of 'schizophrenia'.[56]

(b) The kind of moral autonomy presupposed in no way implies a *comprehensive doctrine* with respect to either the content, the form or the source of the good life. It is characteristic of practically rational persons who know which reasons are required in which context of justification. This form of reason does not constitute a particular 'worldview', nor does it presuppose such a view. It is agnostic as regards the three above-mentioned forms of ethical pluralism; it is compatible with a variety of theories concerning the source of the normative, not just of ethical but *also* of moral normativity. In particular, it does not rest on any metaphysical position on whether we 'make'

---

55. I will return to this in §37.   56. Thus, Mulhall and Swift, *Liberals and Communitarians*, 220.

or merely 'apprehend' or 'see' non-rejectable reasons, that is on whether they are regarded as objectively valid because they can be shared reciprocally and generally or whether they can be shared because they are objective in nature.[57] That human beings must be regarded as moral 'legislators' does not mean that they themselves create the space of the normative in a comprehensive sense. As finite rational beings they do not have any other way to reach an agreement on good moral reasons besides through procedures of reciprocal and general justification. But this does not impinge upon the metaphysical status of reasons or of norms or principles. In this sense, the proposed conception avoids what Rawls calls 'constitutive autonomy' – the idea that 'the order of moral and political values must be made, or itself constituted, by the principles and conceptions of practical reason' (99) – in a *metaphysical*, though not a *practical* sense (to introduce a new distinction). The fact that we ascribe objective content to reasons that we take to be shareable and valid, as well as to the rational principles that we reconstruct (rather than construct) through an analysis of reason and to which we in a certain sense 'submit' ourselves,[58] allows the conclusion that they are really existing 'objects' that should be regarded as metaphysical entities in a Platonic sense, though it does not make this conclusion unavoidable.[59] A cognitivist conception of morality is not necessarily a metaphysically realist one. So, too, the insight that we justify moral norms discursively, and that only in this way can we construe them in practical terms without being able to know of the prior existence of 'universal interests' (or having to presuppose such),[60] does not necessitate the conclusion that this amounts to '*producing a world of norms*'.[61] Finite rational beings are capable of reconstructing the principles of the practice of rationally justifying norms in recursive and pragmatic terms and of distinguishing between reasons which are reciprocally and generally valid and those which can be rejected (or acknowledging conflicts over such differentiation); yet they may have different 'worldviews' when it comes to the metaphysical constitution of the 'moral world'. This remains – in Bayle's sense – a speculative question and an object of reasonable disagreement. In this sense, the conception of moral justification and moral

57. Compare the contrary positions of Korsgaard, *The Sources of Normativity*, and Larmore, 'Moral Knowledge' and 'Denken und Handeln'.
58. Larmore, 'Der Zwang des besseren Arguments', 124.
59. Thus, Larmore, 'Moral Knowledge', 116. For my view of practical reason, see Forst, *The Right to Justification*, chs. 1 and 2.
60. This, however, is the thesis defended by Lafont, 'Realismus und Konstruktivismus in der kantianischen Moralphilosophie'.
61. Thus, Habermas in 'Rightness versus Truth', 268 (emphasis in original).

autonomy can 'fit into' comprehensive ethical *and* moral doctrines. It is per se agnostic and consequently neither metaphysical nor anti-metaphysical. The constructivism involved here, which must be differentiated according to context into a moral and a political constructivism,[62] is a *practical*, not a metaphysical constructivism.

However, the adaptability of the conception of moral justification is not unlimited. For it is only compatible with the comprehensive explanations of normativity which do not place in question or qualify the unconditional validity of the right to justification. That human beings are moral persons who possess such a right is an insight of practical reason which qualifies the 'reasonableness' of the different worldviews according to whether they include this recursive insight into the principle and validity of the principle of justification. To speak both with and against Kant's idea of the 'supreme good', it is possible, though not necessary, to understand the fulfilment of moral duties in such a way that a person thereby becomes 'worthy of happiness' or deserving of reward. The point is that respect for others must not be made contingent on such notions of happiness or the good. This duty, which must be fulfilled 'gratuitously' as it were, can be invested with a transcendent ethical meaning; but in the context of toleration, in particular, the point is not to connect the duty of justification with a motivation which could relativise its exercise.

But – to entertain one final objection[63] – doesn't the obligation to understand (*erkennen*) and recognise (*anerkennen*) a human being as a 'moral person' (in accordance with the principle of justification) mean presupposing a 'moral reality', an unconditional metaphysical ground of morality which we do not create? In fact, in the practical insight into an 'original' moral responsibility (see above §30.4), a moral authority must be 'seen' in the other human being, as expressed in the notion of the 'inviolability' and 'dignity' of the person. Yet this insight also remains an insight of *finite* reason, namely the insight that human beings, as finite beings, are beings who require and are able to offer reasons and that, according to the principle of justification guiding their practice, there cannot be any good, mutually responsible reason for such beings deliberately to evade the claim to validity of morality, which implies

---

62. To be more precise, in a moral constructivism, universally and reciprocally valid norms are constructed, in a moral-political constructivism, the norms which provide the basis of a just basic structure (in particular human rights), and in a political constructivism (building on this and in relation to specific contexts), the basic structure of a society and particular legal arrangements. On this, see Forst, *The Right to Justification*, chs. 4 and 9.

63. This objection was raised by Charles Larmore. On this, see also his article 'The Autonomy of Morality'.

the criteria of reciprocity and universality. The autonomy of morality then means recognising in moral autonomy that one neither has nor can have any other reason for respecting the worth of a human being as an 'end in himself' than that of shared human vulnerability and of the resulting mutual responsibility, which one thereby accepts. Among human beings who cannot adopt a perspective of 'ultimate' reasons, this is in essence a *moral*, not a metaphysical, insight, namely an act of *understanding* one's own responsibility which is at the same time an act of *recognising* the other and his nature as a rational and finite being.

Both problems addressed in this section, the problem of the ability of persons to set limits on their ethical claims to truth and the problem of the agnostic character of the conception of morality, point to the task of defining in greater detail the notion of the 'finitude of reason' in the context of toleration. I will attempt this in the following chapter.

10

The finitude of reason

§33 Relativisation without relativism and scepticism

1. The foregoing reflections on the grounding of toleration on the principle of justification have confirmed what emerged from the reconstruction of the historical discourse of toleration, namely that two components of toleration – of the insight into the non-justifiability of ethical coercion (or of ethically justified, morally relevant restrictions on action) – must be distinguished, a *normative* and an *epistemological* component. For the paradox of moral toleration, which asks how one can be morally required to tolerate what is morally wrong and which was resolved through the deontological difference with the aid of the principle of reciprocal-general justification, has an epistemological counterpart in the paradox of the relativisation of truth, which asks how it can be possible in exercising tolerance to hold one's own conviction (on which basis one objects to others) to be true while nevertheless at the same time restricting or bracketing it by refraining from imposing it. Hence, the answer offered to the first paradox – namely, that tolerant persons are able to grasp moral reasons for tolerating convictions or practices that they object to on ethical grounds and to evaluate ethical conflicts as matters of reasonable disagreement – already implies a certain capacity for self-relativisation which must be explained in epistemological terms: how is it possible to accept the threshold of reciprocity and generality in such a way that one can continue to hold one's own ethical commitments to be 'true' in ethical contexts even though they fall below this threshold in the case of public justification? How is it to be explained that one must as it were 'forgo' 'higher truths' in a particular context as required by the 'reciprocity of reasons' (see §30.3 above), while nevertheless continuing to adhere to them in a different sense? What is meant here by 'reason' as

opposed to 'truth' and in what specific relation does reason stand to religious faith?

From these reflections it follows that it is a mistake to separate the normative from the epistemological component of toleration and to treat them as two distinct justifications of toleration or to regard the normative component as sufficient. Although it is the primary component, as we shall see, like any reflexive moral attitude it has important aspects that must be analysed in epistemological terms. More fundamentally, *every* conception and justification of toleration must be able to provide an answer to the question of how a person who is convinced of an ethical or a religious doctrine relates to the existence of a plurality of such doctrines from his or her perspective. As we have seen, the spectrum extends from sceptical, through relativist, fallibilist and pluralist, to monist approaches, all of which constitute problematic routes to toleration.

The fundamental reason for regarding Pierre Bayle as the greatest thinker of toleration is that his elaboration of the two components of toleration not only was seminal for his own time but remains so for ours as it avoids the problems of such routes to toleration (see above §18 and §29). Building on his predecessors Castellio, Bodin and Montaigne, Bayle recognised that the (structurally speaking) Augustinian, perfectionist justifications of intolerance, which govern the 'convertist' interpretation of the *compelle intrare* parable, must be rejected at two levels. A moral argument must be presented for why this interpretation of scripture transforms a crime into a virtue, so that corresponding actions can be seen for what they are, namely pure violence for which there are no good, reciprocally non-rejectable reasons. This presupposes a conception of morality that is accessible to and binding on all rational persons based on their 'natural' reason, a morality that accords primacy to the principle of reciprocal justification. Furthermore, in order to accord priority to what I have called the criterion of the 'reciprocity of reasons' – that is, in order to be able to explain why the reference to an absolute truth which is also supposed to be able to justify 'good coercion' in reciprocal terms (implying that one should always be glad to be led onto the path of goodness and truth) is illegitimate – an epistemic relativisation is necessary, as Bayle recognised, which draws the boundary between ethical or religious and moral truth. The perfectionist legitimation of intolerance fails because it is based on a false interpretation of the criterion of reciprocity and involves an inadmissible absolutisation of a truth that is merely particular in the context of general justification – inadmissible in both *moral and epistemic* terms.

Whereas Kant developed the normative component of a morality of reciprocal justification further in decisive ways, the difference between faith and knowledge as conceptualised by Bayle remains fundamental for a plausible understanding of the possibility of reasonable disagreements in the domain of religion in the narrower sense and that of the ethical question of the good in the wider sense. It is a fundamental insight into the *finitude of reason* that leads Bayle to his conception in opposition to a radical religious scepticism that calls for religious 'proofs' and to a dogmatic conception of religion which imagines that it has such proofs, and also to a radical fideism which views the leap into religion as irrational. On Bayle's conception, the religious domain begins where reason encounters a limit but does not end completely, for reason remains a criterion for rejecting incoherent forms of 'superstition' and continues to permit rational religious discussions of questions which it itself poses (for example, concerning the existence of evil) or at least allows for without being able to provide unambiguous, rationally non-rejectable answers (see especially §18.5 above). The faith which provides answers to 'ultimate' questions concerning how the world is constituted and how one should live – answers which reason *can neither falsify nor verify* – can only provide supporting grounds for these answers which reason neither demands nor forbids but permits, provided that faith *knows that it is a faith*. From the perspective of reason, its evidence is only 'relative' to a particular ethical or religious worldview; it is *suprarational (dessus de la raison*, as Bayle put it) but not *irrational* (for then it would be superstition). Hence, reason is aware that rationally irresolvable religious and ethical controversies are unavoidable; reasonable faith, by contrast, is certain that this is not an objection against its conviction concerning the truth. Hence, recognising the finitude of reason means, on the one hand, recognising that reason cannot have the final, universally and objectively binding say in ethical-religious questions and that, conversely, religion reaches its limits when it comes to objective knowledge and general moral and political obligations. For, although faith can affirm its own truth in every context, it must observe the criteria of reason which hold for theoretical or moral contexts.

The difference between faith and knowledge, religion and philosophy, still exhibits certain traces of fideism in Bayle, albeit a 'rational fideism' that restricts the 'subjugation of reason' in faith within the confines of what reason permits and does not view it as an irrational act. In this way, it attempts, on the one hand, to create a space for religion within the universe of a reason aware of its own limits and, on the other, to assign reason an independent place which is superior to faith in certain contexts. Finite reason cannot provide unambiguous or final answers to the questions it poses concerning the existence of good and evil, the proper conduct of life or the essence of God – and insofar as it recognises this, it can regard a religious position as rationally tenable while at the same time as open to rational criticism and rejection. A fideist stance is not preprogrammed from the perspective of the person of faith, however. For it is still possible to regard one's own route to faith as the most reasonable provided that one is ready not to elevate it above all others as the only one which can be objectively demonstrated by rational means, so that objections against it would have to be regarded as per se irrational. 'Reasonable' persons need not profess a particular faith, or have any faith at all, though they may have one. Moreover, they must recognise that there is a plurality of 'reasonable' religious and non-religious ethical perspectives that inevitably lead to conflicts which are rationally resolvable only within limits and which as a result call for toleration founded on universally justified norms. One can be strongly convinced of a particular ethical or religious truth while recognising that other convictions may likewise be reasonable without being true. Within the frame of theoretical and practical reason, the convictions in question must be tolerated, though given the possible particular demands of ethical truth one need not esteem them or view them even as 'true in part'.

2. A theory of toleration must be capable of explaining this stance if it is to avoid the danger of championing a particular, rejectable doctrine. For there are several possible answers to the question of how reason can require that a person should relativise her most profoundly held convictions and exercise tolerance, for example a sceptical, a relativistic and an 'ethical liberal' answer. The first answer derives the necessity of withholding judgement, and thus of being tolerant, from the epistemic uncertainty concerning ethical truth; the second answer assumes the equal worth of ethical evaluative convictions; and, for the third, toleration itself is grounded on specific ethical values, such as autonomy or pluralism, which are regarded as necessary for a good life. As has already been shown, whereas these routes lead to toleration (though, in the case of scepticism and relativism, not without further normative assumptions), they do so only on the basis of highly specific, non-generalisable premises and they potentially stop too soon, namely, where others who do not share these premises seem not to be tolerable. As a result, a historically informed theory of toleration that wants to do justice to the demand for tolerance as a normative demand must rest on different foundations; in particular, it must try to explain that and how someone who is not a sceptic, a relativist or an ethical liberal, but a staunch advocate of an

'exclusivist' religion which upholds its exclusive claim to truth, can also muster a stance of tolerance.[1] It must be asked which form of self-relativisation is required and how this is possible for such a person. Can she avoid the consequences of scepticism, of relativism or of embracing a form of ethical liberalism?

Recent philosophical discussion has thrown up a series of proposals concerning how this problem should be understood or how it could be resolved within the framework of a theory of 'public justification'. Thomas Nagel attempts to explain the 'higher-order impartiality' which is required for norms in need of general justification in terms of a primarily epistemological distinction between the 'private' and 'public' domains.[2] This would make it possible to distinguish the values to which one may appeal in the personal conduct of one's life from those which can justify the exercise of political power, on the grounds that the latter correspond to a 'higher standard of objectivity'. Each person claims that her commitments (religious commitments, for example) should be regarded as true and correct in the personal as well as in the political domain; yet in the context of political justification she must be able to substantiate this in such a way that she adopts a 'universal' and impersonal standpoint 'independent of who we are' towards her own convictions.[3] According to Nagel, viewing one's own convictions from this detached perspective as though they were those of a random person enables one to judge whether they are in fact supported by generally shareable evidence and whether those who do not agree with them commit an objective error. If this cannot be shown, then, although one can continue to take one's commitments to be true in the personal domain, one can no longer appeal to their truth in the political domain because of the lack of objective reasons – they lack the epistemic quality that would be necessary for this. Consequently, from the objective perspective, they are nothing but 'someone's beliefs, rather than . . . truths'.[4]

However, this radical form of self-detachment and self-relativisation involves too extreme a separation of the ethical from the political-moral perspective, so that one can no longer explain how someone who has adopted such a detached perspective on her own convictions (assuming that this is even possible) can still regard them as ethically true and good if they have failed the test of public justification. Nagel connects the epistemic confirmation of convictions in the ethical context too closely with their confirmation

---

1. For an explanation of 'exclusivism' see Schmidt-Leukel, 'Zur Klassifikation religionstheologischer Modelle'.
2. Nagel, 'Moral Conflict and Political Legitimacy', 216 and 230.   3. *Ibid.* 229.   4. *Ibid.* 230.

in contexts of general justification. He seems to think that the reasons which support an ethical conviction must be *the same* reasons that also speak for it in the political domain – and if they do not do so in the latter domain, then they also become questionable in the former. The logical conclusion, which Nagel expressly wants to avoid, is an ethical scepticism combined with reasonable disagreement.[5]

This approach rests on a mistaken understanding of the difference between the contexts of justification. The threshold of reciprocity and generality separating them implies that *different* questions must be answered in accordance with *different* criteria in the two contexts. That a conviction is supported by good reasons in the one context, therefore, does not mean that it is likewise supported in the other. There is a continuity of justification between the two contexts, because one's political or moral arguments are connected to one's ethical convictions; but one must be willing to recognise the respective criteria of validity. It then becomes possible to recognise that one's evaluative convictions were reciprocally and generally rejectable insofar as the context involved reciprocally and generally binding norms; but it by no means follows that one's convictions lose their value in the ethical context as a result. For, in order to understand the necessity of relativising them in the general context, instead of viewing them 'from the outside' as the convictions of 'someone or other' one would have to try to formulate (or 'reformulate') them as reasons *for a general rule* that are not reciprocally rejectable; therefore the question of the *ethical* quality of these convictions need not arise. In this way, the tolerant stance which accepts the impossibility of enforcing convictions in a generally binding manner, while nevertheless maintaining their truth, becomes possible. It would be unreasonable, by contrast, to conclude from the fact that an ethical conviction encountered objections in a 'reasonable ethical conflict' that it was a 'mere opinion' and was no longer tenable.

Joseph Raz also criticises Nagel for making too sharp an epistemological separation between personal convictions and political norms. Raz concludes that it is not possible to distinguish between ethical values and norms which are justified in universal, 'neutral' terms because that would imply a discontinuity between personal and political convictions.[6] In my opinion, this objection does not hold against the notion of different contexts of justification, which implies not a divided self (in the sense criticised by Raz) but a self

5. Nagel, *Equality and Partiality*, 162–8, referring to these problems, duly retracts the argument and opts instead for a normative, Kantian position.
6. Raz, 'Facing Diversity', especially 43–6.

who is aware of the differences between these contexts and knows when and to whom it owes certain reasons. This has nothing to do with epistemic or normative (ethical or moral) 'abstinence'. Instead, it is a question of insight into the possibility of reasonable ethical conflicts and the duty to engage in reciprocal-general argumentation.

Brian Barry, by contrast, welcomes the (inadvertent) sceptical implications of Nagel's approach. According to Barry, a conception of 'justice as impartiality' based on the principle of general justification must presuppose a form of ethical scepticism: the self-relativisation called for by this principle implies renunciation of ethical claims to truth (and a reservation of judgement). From the principle that justice calls for a normative agreement with others on grounds that no one can reasonably reject, he concludes that no conception of the good can provide a foundation for such an agreement.[7] However, he tries to explain this not in terms of the primacy of particular criteria of justification but in epistemological terms with the argument from scepticism:

> How, then, are we to establish that there is no conception of the good that nobody could reasonably reject? The answer that I wish to defend is that no conception of the good can justifiably be held with a degree of certainty that warrants its imposition on those who reject it. I shall dub this the argument from scepticism.[8]

Apart from the fact that his argument that the frequency of ethical conflicts is proof of scepticism is flawed because it can also be interpreted as proving the opposite – namely, the undiminished strength of ethical convictions – Barry's conception of ethical truth leads to a view of intolerance as its natural consequence. The readiness to impose this truth against all other ethical doctrines is taken to indicate the seriousness of the conviction concerning truth, so that the only way to overcome intolerance is to overcome ethical claims to truth. Central to this argument is Barry's doubt about 'whether certainty from the inside about some view can coherently be combined with the line that it is reasonable for others to reject that same view'.[9] Even more so than Nagel, therefore, Barry links the conviction concerning the truth of an ethical conception of the good too closely with its general shareability and non-rejectability in the domain of political morality, so that the persons in question either will attempt to ensure this shareability by illegitimate means or will have to bracket their convictions and refrain from judgement

7. Barry, *Justice as Impartiality*, 168.   8. *Ibid.* 169.
9. *Ibid.* 179. Consistently with this, Barry restricts the sceptical demand to conceptions of the good and does not extend it to the principle of justification and its normative validity; see *ibid.* 172.

about them. Yet the 'uncertainty' that arises when a conviction proves to be rejectable in the context of general political-moral justification is completely different from the uncertainty occasioned by ethical counter-arguments that lead a person to doubt her convictions. The latter can certainly be a consequence of the former, but this is by no means necessarily so. The fact that a conception of the good can be rejected as *not morally-politically binding* is far from implying for those who are convinced of its truth that it loses its ethical value as a result or that those who have rejected it in this sense are necessarily *unreasonable*. The limit barring an inadmissible generalisation of ethical convictions is not one called for by scepticism but one implied by a reasonable differentiation among contexts and the willingness to conduct oneself accordingly. With respect to religion, for example, Barry's view leaves no room for a reasonable distinction between reason and faith. From a Baylean perspective, it is puzzling why reasonable rejection of general religious norms in a pluralistic society should leave no room for holding fast to such faith in the sense of 'certainty from the inside'.

Against Raz's inference that we must abandon the idea of independently justifying reciprocal-general norms as opposed to ethical values, and against Barry's conclusion that the primacy of the principle of justification can be upheld only at the cost of overcoming strong ethical evaluative convictions, Rawls takes the view that the (above-mentioned) 'burdens of judgement' enable us to explain from the perspective of a person how she can regard certain convictions as reasonable, even though she takes them to be false, without doubting the truth of her own convictions. This second aspect of the reasonable, in addition to the normative aspect of the willingness and ability to justify and observe fair principles of cooperation, is supposed to explain why certain normative conflicts involve a reasonable disagreement, the point being that they are conflicts in which reasonable persons cannot reach an agreement and hence must be tolerant. 'Reasonable' persons possess the most important capacities of practical and theoretical reason, according to Rawls; they are willing and able to offer, ponder and judge practical and theoretical reasons in the relevant contexts of justification. Nevertheless, six burdens can hamper or prevent a consensual judgement. Rawls calls them 'burdens of judgement'; in consideration of the fact that they refer to the imperfections of theoretical and practical reason, however, his earlier terminology of 'burdens of reason'[10] is preferable. These are:[11]

10. As Rawls argues in 'The Domain of the Political and Overlapping Consensus'.
11. See Rawls, *Political Liberalism*, 56–7.

(a) It may be difficult to weigh the empirical evidence in a particular case.
(b) Even people who agree on the important aspects of a case can attach greater or lesser weight to them.
(c) All concepts, not just moral and political ones, are indeterminate and in need of interpretation in difficult cases, which can lead to divergent judgements.
(d) How people judge evidence and assess moral and political values is conditioned as a rule by their specific, biographical experiences, which inevitably differ from person to person.
(e) Different moral considerations may be relevant in a given case and differences may arise over how priorities should be set.
(f) In a society, which represents only a limited domain of the realisation of values, ethical-political decisions are unavoidable and it may not be possible to resolve them in a single way in which all can share.

Clearly, these explanations are not all situated at the same level. Thus, one might question whether the last point should not be regarded as a particular occasion for conflicts rather than as a deeper reason for them. Moreover, the fourth point is without doubt the most important: the variations among personal experiences and corresponding background convictions – Charles Larmore speaks in terms of 'conflicting backgrounds of belief'[12] – is the essential reason for the formation or persistence of 'comprehensive doctrines' leading to conflicts over particular issues which, although open to rational discussion, may not be unambiguously resolvable by rational means. Reasonable persons, and 'reasonable comprehensive doctrines', acknowledge this and recognise that they, like others, are subject to these burdens, and as a result are prepared to show tolerance:

> We recognise that our own doctrine has, and can have, for people generally, no special claims on them beyond their own view of its merits. Others who affirm doctrines different from ours are, we grant, reasonable also, and certainly not unreasonable. Since there are many reasonable doctrines, the idea of the reasonable does not require us, or others, to believe any specific reasonable doctrine, though we may do so. When we take the step beyond recognizing the reasonableness of a doctrine and affirm our belief in it, we are not being unreasonable.[13]

The readiness to be tolerant follows, in conjunction with the normative insight into the duty to provide justifications, from this insight into the

12. Larmore, 'Pluralism and Reasonable Disagreement', 173.   13. Rawls, *Political Liberalism*, 60.

space of the reasonable, which does not coincide with the space of ethical truth, so that from a given person's perspective there may be many reasonable comprehensive doctrines but only one true comprehensive doctrine.

This calls for three remarks. First, this insight must be seen as a fundamental recognition of the finitude of (theoretical and practical) reason and not primarily (as Rawls tends to see it) as a pragmatic-realist insight into the 'fact' of the 'practical' impossibility of agreement in ethical judgements as a 'normal result of the exercise of human reason within the framework of the free institutions of a constitutional democratic regime'.[14] For, in order to be able to describe this 'practical impossibility' as 'reasonable' in the first place, and to ascribe it to the limits of the faculty of reason, it must be a characteristic feature of reason itself; and, with a view to the discourse of toleration, one can regard the plurality of incompatible 'comprehensive doctrines' rather as the reason for than as a result of 'free institutions'. Hence, the distinguishing feature of reasonable persons is a recursive insight into the finitude of their own faculty of reason.

Still more important is, second, the question of why Rawls thinks that the idea of the burdens of reason does not imply scepticism or relativism. For, on a certain interpretation of the burdens, it appears as though, because reasonable persons see themselves and others as subject to these burdens, they must regard the convictions of others to be just as true as their own, or at least to be possibly true; all are subject to the same restrictions and are equally uncertain when it comes to their ethical cognitive abilities, in precisely the sense of uncertainty intended by Barry, excluding a claim to validity according to which all reasonable persons would have to accept that a particular doctrine is true.[15] However, this reading misses Rawls's point. For being aware of the limits of reason on account of the burdens means neither that one can no longer take one's own convictions to be true nor that one can no longer claim that one's doctrine has the best justification and that this should be apparent to all those with 'a clear vision and an open heart'. All that one must recognise is that those who nevertheless do not accept this doctrine are not necessarily unreasonable or immoral. Here, however, Rawls's idea must be supplemented with a clearer emphasis on the difference between contexts of justification. There is a host of convictions in the ethical domain which can be correctly taken to be true although they cannot furnish proofs in the context of theoretical justification and they are not

14. *Ibid.* 63 and xvi.
15. As on the interpretation of Wenar, '*Political Liberalism*: An Internal Critique', 44.

reciprocally non-rejectable in the context of reciprocal-general justification. Neither the theoretical nor the normative rejection automatically means that the convictions in question (bearing on particular features of the good life, for example) are false or immoral; for if they are rejected as theoretically contestable and as not morally binding, this only implies that the reasons that support them in these contexts were not, or not yet, sufficient. Their rejection does not imply that they can no longer be ethical truths which the relevant persons regard as *the* truth. In such cases, reasonable persons need not assume – and here the specificity of *religious* or *metaphysical-ethical* convictions comes into play to which I will return later – that they could be just *as much in error* as others; they only need to recognise that one cannot show by exclusively rational means that the others are clearly and demonstrably wrong or that they are committing a moral wrong. Religious intolerance, for example, begins when these limits of theoretical and practical reason are transgressed without good reasons, that is, when one regards one's own faith as the only legitimate, demonstrable and non-rationally rejectable one and from this infers the right to make it generally binding. The domain of ethical truths is broader – and perhaps 'deeper' – than the domain of what is rationally non-rejectable in the strict sense.

This shows once again how demanding is the form of autonomy that Rawls must presuppose and that it cannot be explained in purely 'political' or pragmatic terms but must be explained in terms of a fundamental faculty of reason. The reasons which can be valid in the context of reciprocal-general justification may to some extent originally stem from 'comprehensive' ethical perspectives. However, in that general context they become independent reasons which those concerned invoke, take responsibility for and grasp autonomously; then they have sufficient moral force in possible cases of conflict either to correct one's own ethical convictions or to limit their binding validity for others. This primacy of the reasonable cannot be explained in terms of the construction that citizens, in public discourses of justification, remain entirely within their own comprehensive doctrine and detach only the 'part of the truth' that corresponds to 'political values'.[16]

This already indicates, third, that here practical reason enjoys primacy over theoretical reason or, alternatively, that the normative component of toleration enjoys primacy over the epistemic component.[17] For the

16. Thus, Rawls, *Political Liberalism*, 127–8, drawing on Cohen, 'Moral Pluralism and Political Consensus', 283.
17. Thus, also Rawls, *Political Liberalism*, 62, who says 'that here being reasonable is not an epistemological idea (though it has epistemological elements)'. See also Gaus, *Justificatory Liberalism*, 129.

fundamental motive for self-restraint in the discourse of justification is the moral one: one 'owes' others certain kinds of reasons. However, the epistemic element belongs inseparably to this: one must be able to grasp such reasons and to incorporate them into one's comprehensive 'store of reasons'. The requisite faculty of 'reciprocity of reasons', in particular, presupposes both components.

In the insight into the possibility of *reasonable ethical disagreement*, convictions that may represent the essential ethical truth of a perspective on life are regarded as simultaneously reasonably disputable and reasonably defensible. However, it does not follow that such ethical truths are mere *adiaphora* or that they must be respected as 'individual decisions of conscience' (to allude briefly to alternative justifications of toleration). Respect for them is governed by the principle of justification and the threshold of reciprocity and generality vouches for their tolerability.

3. This conception of the finitude of reason also comes close to Bayle's view in the primacy it accords practical reason. Nevertheless, it is advisable in the light of Bayle's approach to examine more closely the definition of the relation between faith and knowledge and the specific nature of religious or metaphysical-ethical convictions and conceptions of the good. For the claim that ethical convictions concerning the good and correct life are reasonable, but are also *beyond* reason, means in general in the first place only that value judgements are formed against the background of specific systems of convictions of individual persons who recognise that reason alone may not be sufficient to overcome the resulting differences and conflicts. But those concerned do not see this as a reason for revising their system of convictions because it seems to them the best one from their perspective – and they have no other; thus upholding it is not merely a conventionalist or irrational act of faith but rests on good reasons.[18] In a certain sense, however, convictions grounded in this way remain subject to the still valid presupposition of a *shared* reason within a discursive framework in which the participants acknowledge in principle that their convictions could be falsified, even though not every possible reasonable objection need be understood as a falsification or as a relevant objection – as is especially true of ethical discourses.

But when *religiously* – or otherwise *metaphysically* – grounded ethical convictions or systems of convictions meet in discourse, the falsification

18. As Larmore argues in 'Pluralism and Reasonable Disagreement', 173: '[W]here we have no positive grounds for doubt, we should regard our view as true, however much it may be the object of reasonable disagreement.' See also Rescher, *Pluralism*, 119–20: 'There is no good reason why a recognition that others, circumstanced as they are, are rationally entitled *in their circumstances* to hold a position at variance with ours should be construed to mean that we, *circumstanced as we are*, need feel any rational obligation to abandon our position.'

consciousness changes. It may be possible that – still assuming a shared reason – the ethical discourse gives rise to reasons which provide occasion for questioning one's convictions or even the underlying system; but one should not expect this as a general rule in the case of a person of faith, for example. As already indicated (with reference to the justifications of toleration of Mill and Popper; see §24.2), religious convictions need not be assumed to be immune to rational revision; yet neither must they be assumed to be theories about the world which are seen as objects of a confirming or falsifying rational discourse, similar to discourse about empirical statements or even scientific hypotheses. The faith which knows that it is a faith is aware that possibilities of verification and falsification are limited in principle by the fact that the system of convictions is founded from the outset on a 'world disclosure',[19] a specific interpretation of the world conditioned by concrete experiences which first *constitutes* and colours as it were the relevant ethical 'view' of the world. This worldview is understood to be well founded, to be a meaningful view of the world, yet in such a way that it involves an inherent transcendent moment that warrants speaking in terms of a *faith*. Regardless of how this is understood and how the relation between knowledge and faith is defined in detail from the perspective of religion – and a theory of toleration must take an agnostic position on such a plurality of understandings of religion[20] – such a moment is at any rate indispensable for faith. For it is a distinguishing feature of the 'reasonable faith', which can derive a certain degree of religious certainty from this, that it is aware of the limits of reason when it comes to falsifying religious convictions, ultimately because it believes that there is an unbridgeable difference between a *divine* and the *human* perspective, which implies that human faith cannot have perfect knowledge of a divine reality. This does not mean that ethical, moral or theoretical discourses cannot give rise to religious uncertainties, but it does mean that external doubts concerning fundamental religious convictions do not necessarily give rise to such uncertainties. Faith cannot provide 'ultimate' proofs but it does *trust in* 'ultimate' reasons, even though these are fully accessible only to the faithful. Therefore, the limits of falsification are *simultaneously* also the limits of verification and of an absolutisation of faith that negates the internal logic of the contexts of justification. Hence, 'reasonable' religious consciousness reflects

19. On the discussion of this concept, albeit not with explicit reference to religion, see Lafont, 'World Disclosure and Reference', Seel, 'On Rightness and Truth' and Kompridis, 'On World Disclosure'.

20. On this, see the discussions in Plantinga and Wolterstorff (eds.), *Faith and Rationality*; Jäger (ed.), *Analytische Religionsphilosophie*; Geivett and Sweetman (eds.), *Contemporary Perspectives on Religious Epistemology*.

a different conception of finitude and fallibility than do other convictions relating to the world. Whereas the consciousness of the finitude of reason leads one person to religion, it turns another person against religion.

It follows that ethical discourses of a religious or a metaphysical kind involve a particular claim to truth whose redemption among human beings presupposes an insight of faith, and whose 'ultimate' redemption, or 'ultimate' rejection, would presuppose a truly 'ideal' communication community of the divine perspective. The finitude of reason and the 'situatedness' of human beings do not permit such a perspective.

Reflection on the particular nature of a religious-metaphysical ethical validity claim according to which certain conceptions of the good are true because they correspond to a transcendent reality raises the larger question of the nature of ethical validity claims. This question reveals a desideratum of the theory of discourse, because these validity claims do not conform to the distinction Habermas suggests between claims to truth in terms of objective truth, moral rightness or subjective truthfulness (where the latter refers to subjective experiences).[21] It is important to recognise in the first place that a whole series of *different* ethical validity claims exists depending on who is supposed to regard which values as good on what grounds. Is it a matter of subjective plans of life as a whole, only of particular aspects of such plans or of social questions of the good life as such? Are these assertions supposed to hold for certain individuals or for all human beings? And is the claim that they are grounded in a 'higher truth' or that they are contingent on experience or are shaped by particular cultural factors? I can only allude to these issues here without being able to discuss them in detail.

It is important in this context that, although understanding an ethical truth claim, even one justified in religious terms, presupposes an insight into a person's reasons for her convictions, it does not at all presuppose that these reasons are shared, that an agreement exists. A second person can regard the reasons a person has from her perspective for taking certain convictions to be true as reasonable, both in the theoretical and in the practical sense, without having to accept that these reasons are true. One can *reach an understanding* about such reasons *without sharing them*.[22] Understanding an ethical validity

---

21. See the analysis of validity claims in Habermas, *Theory of Communicative Action*, vol. 1, 77–81.
22. This is a special case of the distinction between 'agreement' and 'understanding', though Habermas analyses this in relation to pronouncements and declarations of intention in 'Some Further Clarifications of the Concept of Communicative Rationality', 320–5. In his article 'Intolerance and Discrimination', by contrast, he discusses the distinctive features of religious claims to validity which would have to be taken into account in a general systematic treatment of ethical validity claims.

claim is independent of whether one shares it. In a certain sense, not reaching an agreement is even the normal case. Knowing that someone is making such a claim to validity already means knowing that it involves very specific premises about which reasonable differences may arise. If such a conflict does in fact arise, understanding the other person's reasons is not only possible but also *necessary*, for otherwise a reasonable conflict, and hence toleration (combined with justified objection), would not be possible. Reasonable and tolerant persons recognise that others have 'their' reasons for their ethical convictions, reasons which the reasonable and tolerant persons take to be false and concerning whose falsity they might want to convince others whom they assume to be reasonable; nevertheless, they recognise that in order to achieve this they can only employ rational means that may ultimately reach their limits. Therefore, a person can regard another person's ethical convictions as false and yet as justified from the latter's perspective[23] – and feel duty bound to convince the other person of the truth by trying to change the latter's perspective by rational means on the grounds that it is too restricted.

A feature of ethical convictions, therefore, is that they may, but do not necessarily, raise a claim to universal validity. Thus, according to the general principle that validity claims should be justified in accordance with internal criteria, there may be no obligation to justify them in general terms; yet even if they make a claim to universal validity, redeeming this claim remains contingent on a specifically *ethical* insight which cannot be strictly demanded of reasonable persons. It is always open to the latter reciprocally to reject such claims, just as they can continue to believe such truths even when they have turned out to be reciprocally and generally rejectable. The threshold of reciprocity and generality protects ethical persons *in* their convictions while simultaneously protecting them *against* such convictions of others.

4. The above-mentioned primacy of practical reason, according to which the duty to justify reciprocal–general validity claims, even though it has an important epistemological component, is grounded primarily in moral rather than in epistemological terms, has a further important meaning. For it has been repeatedly emphasised that 'reasonable' persons are reasonable both in the moral and in the theoretical sense, and as such are participants in 'reasonable' conflicts which call for toleration, because the limits of reason are recognised. However, this does not explain what constitute

---

23. On this, see in particular Gaus's analysis of 'personal' justification in *Justificatory Liberalism*, 45–73 and 117–18; following Piaget, he calls this a 'de-centring' insight.

unreasonable disagreements and whether toleration is also required or appropriate in such cases. Here, in turn, one must distinguish between a moral and an epistemological perspective. From the moral perspective, being unreasonable in the practical sense means not observing the principle of justification. This can take a variety of forms, for example that the criteria of reciprocity and generality are violated regarding a single issue or, more seriously, that others are denied their right to justification in principle. Both are cases of intolerance which should not be condoned, though this does not answer the context-specific question as to the appropriate response.[24]

From the theoretical perspective, transgressing the boundaries of reason means that a person violates particular logical rules governing argument or how words are used, or that she questions contents of knowledge that cannot be meaningfully doubted. All of these rules and contents may in turn be controversial in particular cases, yet it must be possible to draw such boundaries in accordance with the presupposition of a shared discursive reason. A particularly important case in the context of toleration is that in which a person or group challenges the established and justifiable boundaries separating knowledge and faith – for example, the 'creationists' who regard Darwinian evolutionary theory as *false* by comparison with the story of creation. Whether such irrational convictions should be tolerated must be decided on *normative* grounds – and here again the primacy of morality becomes evident – depending on the social situation. That a person or a group believes this is not a sufficient reason for not tolerating such convictions in the public arena, even when it is not a case of a 'reasonable dispute'. When such groups claim the right to influence school curricula, however, and to teach both doctrines as equally valid, or even to teach the biblical doctrine as the only true one, they make a normatively relevant demand which is patently reciprocally rejectable. For no social group can claim the right to declare their ethical convictions against all evidence to be the truth which all schools are obliged to teach. Were a group accorded this right, all other groups could likewise claim such a right in violation of the standards of reason which, although finite, is nevertheless capable of making determinations. Such claims must ultimately be rejected by appeal to the legitimate interests of the schoolchildren in receiving the best possible education.[25] This demonstrates once again that the normative justification of toleration is the decisive one not only as regards the acceptance component but also as

24. I will return to such cases in Chapter 12.
25. I will also present a more detailed discussion of this in Chapter 12.

regards the rejection component in terms of which the limits of toleration are drawn, though theoretical considerations play an important role in this regard.

§34 The tolerance of the theory

1. The talk of a 'discourse' of toleration, to pick up the idea of a reflexive justification of toleration (see above §30.1), not only means that toleration is required in concrete social conflicts of an ethical, moral or political kind, but also has a meaning specifically related to the theory of justification. The reconstruction of the toleration debates in the first part showed that philosophical analysis yields a plurality of comprehensive justifications of toleration which were subjected to critical scrutiny with reference to the principle of justification (in the light of the criteria implied by a resolution of the paradoxes). The claim that the proposed normative-epistemological justification of toleration is superior to the others had to be redeemed by reflexively showing that, in contrast to the other justifications, it rests on rationally non-rejectable foundations, in particular on the principle of reciprocal–general non-rejectability itself as a principle of practical reason (combined with an epistemological component). However, such a higher-order theory of toleration has to be able to show not only that it does not rest on any particular ethical doctrine – as regards the contents, forms and sources of the good (see above §31.2) – but also to what extent it is compatible with these evaluative conceptions and worldviews, insofar as they can be reasonably defended on ethical grounds, and thus to what extent the theory is tolerant towards the latter.

This coheres in a certain sense with Rawls's idea of a 'political' conception of justice and toleration. As we have seen, however, his theory is tolerant in the wrong way in that it does not sufficiently emphasise the morally autonomous character of the justification of 'political' principles based on practical reason and wants to leave the binding force of these principles in an overlapping consensus to the 'comprehensive doctrines' (see above §32.1). In contrast to Rawls, the demand that the theory should be autonomous is not a 'political' demand but a fundamental implication of the autonomy of practical reason; such a theory, moreover, does not relinquish a moral (as opposed to an ethical) claim to truth in relation to basic norms. But since practical reason is at the same time a finite reason that is aware of its limits in the ethical and the metaphysical domains, it must be compatible with a plurality of 'reasonable' ethical doctrines of toleration insofar as the latter do not fall short of, but instead go beyond, the normative-epistemological justification of toleration. A specific doctrine may *integrate* this justification into a comprehensive worldview, yet it must not *relativise* it in the process. Otherwise the demand for toleration will no longer be reciprocally and generally binding and it would be in danger of drawing its limits too narrowly (or too broadly), as was shown by the analysis of the dialectical potentials of the alternative justifications (in §29). More inclusive philosophical doctrines of toleration can supplement the proposed justification, but cannot replace it. It remains the criterion for a non-reciprocally rejectable conception of toleration; the other justifications, by contrast, are reciprocally rejectable, though they are also acceptable, and therefore they have their own, limited legitimacy. The higher-level theory of toleration remains the primary one – an additional meaning of the primacy of practical reason.

Hence, the theory of toleration is itself tolerant in that it 'supersedes' – that is, simultaneously incorporates and normatively frames – the reasonable controversy between alternative justifications of toleration at the theoretical level. The alternative justifications preserve a certain legitimacy since they evolved out of the comprehensive ethical perspectives of persons – think, for example, of religious justifications of toleration. Yet, in conflict situations when their particular view of toleration runs up against its limits, these persons must be sufficiently *autonomous* to subject this view to further moral examination and to measure it against the other's claims in accordance with the criteria of reciprocity and generality. The principle of justification is the basis that connects moral persons, also and especially where their ethical commonalities end (and also where the detailed application of moral principles is controversial). As stated, the self-understanding of a person who is autonomous in this sense does not itself imply a particular 'comprehensive' doctrine and as a result can be associated with such doctrines. Yet, given the diversity among these worldviews, they can generally only lend the awareness of 'owing' others as human beings specific reasons different colourations, but cannot suppress it or declare it to be their exclusive property. Thus, insofar as moral consciousness is connected, for example, with a religious consciousness, this must not lead to a relativisation of moral respect, as when atheists are denied any moral sensibility. The self-understanding of persons remains complex and marked by tensions between ethical-religious values and moral duties, which can also lead to internal conflicts within a person's consciousness (a point to which I will return in the discussion of the virtue of tolerance).

Two senses in which a theory of toleration can be said to be 'tolerant' must be distinguished. First, 'tolerant' can refer to the relation between particular, reasonably affirmable, though also rejectable, justifications of toleration that respect each other based on the shared principle of justification and can tolerate the other's convictions even though they take them to be false. Someone who endorses freedom of conscience on religious grounds, for example, can tolerate someone who defends a humanist irenism even though he thinks that the hoped-for religious agreement and reconciliation is entirely unfounded. The decisive point, however, is that both sides are willing to reassess these particular viewpoints in terms of the principle of justification.

The second meaning of a 'tolerant' theory of toleration refers to the relation between the higher-level theory and theories grounded in particular terms. This is not a case of strict, reciprocal toleration because the higher-level theory tolerates the others as imperfect though reasonable, whereas the particular theories must acknowledge the priority of the former based on autonomous insight, namely insight into the priority of practical, finite reason. The latter implies the unity of morality, even though this unity cannot be realised in a perfect form among finite beings, and it implies the plurality of ethical conceptions, since the latter answer questions to which reason alone cannot provide exhaustive answers.

2. It will not be possible in the present context to provide an exhaustive account of the plurality of normative-epistemic positions and comprehensive justifications of toleration which are compatible with the proposed theory. Hence, a couple of examples will have to suffice.

(a) Person A is a *sceptic* when it comes to the existence of ethical truths; from the plurality of conceptions of the good that can be reasonably defended as well as rejected, she draws the sceptical conclusion that it is better to refrain from judging which of them are true or right. In her view, only biographical reasons can speak in favour of following a particular ethical plan of life. This of itself does not imply any argument in support of toleration, however. For, as the example of Montaigne shows, this can also support the conclusion that ethical plurality, especially when the individual doctrines are invested with objectivistic connotations, leads to controversy and strife, so that it is dangerous to permit religious innovations or excessively strong religious convictions. And that the sceptic doubts whether there are objective reasons for particular conceptions of the good does not imply that he or she could not have other reasons for attempting to dissuade people from holding certain ethical conceptions by intolerant means. The sceptical perspective could also be bound up with a series of reflections on toleration, however – for example, concerning the need for freedom to experiment with different life plans, a freedom that it is subjectively advantageous for individuals to grant one another, or that toleration is the best guarantor of social peace. Perhaps this person is also convinced that wanting to impose an ethical doctrine on others is in any case pointless, or that a society is richer in the aesthetic sense when a plurality of forms of life exists. To be sure, the decisive point for an autonomous stance of tolerance is that, in cases of conflicts over toleration, the person is willing to respect the threshold of reciprocity and generality. The tolerant sceptic cannot take a sceptical position on this principle itself; she can have her doubts about the validity of practical reason when it comes to the possibility of justified ethical judgements, but not about the possibility of moral justification.

(b) Person B defends a form of *cultural relativism* according to which each culture gives rise to its own particular evaluative convictions whose worth becomes accessible only from an internal perspective. They are incommensurable in the sense that there is no higher-order standpoint from which their value can be measured. The members of a culture can judge the values of others, but they can do so only from their own perspective, even when there are opportunities to enlarge their own horizon through dialogue. This possibility of enlarging one's perspective and learning can be viewed as a reason for toleration; but it is also possible that relativism can lead to indifference towards others and to a retreat to one's own values, even to the point of dissociation. Here, too, in order to arrive at an autonomous attitude of toleration one need not abandon ethical relativism, but one must accept the threshold of reciprocity and generality. Accordingly, the tolerant individual cannot have a relativistic mindset when it comes to morality.

(c) Person C is convinced of the truth of *value pluralism*. She believes either that a pluralistic universe of objective, incompatible values exists, all of which can be traced back to one source (for example, one understood in theistic terms), or that a pluralism of values and of 'ethical worlds' stemming from very different sources exists. These values are caught up in a struggle for the allegiance of human beings and always confront those who recognise their validity with the tragic decision of having to choose between them, since they cannot be realised simultaneously in an individual life or in a society. Toleration responds to this objective reality of values and conflict and respects the decisions of individual persons or collectivities. Toleration must then represent a particular 'value', however, or, better, a higher-order principle, for radical pluralism does not necessarily entail the preference for toleration. Here, too, the moral universe must accord the right or duty of justification a special status if it is to arrive at a principled toleration; this specifically human duty cannot be relativised by other values. This does not exclude the possibility of tragic conflicts between an ethical and a moral standpoint, but instead explains it.

(d) Person D is an ethical *pragmatist*. She seeks the best values to orient her life and thus is open for ethical alternatives. She has certain convictions but assumes in a fallibilistic way that other convictions could be superior or could contain an element of the truth that one can adopt. She conceives of the ethical life as a learning process. Therefore, tolerance is enjoined in order to ensure the greatest possible choice among ethical options; this person believes that even false ethical paths have something to teach. The truth concerning the best life is something which must be investigated both individually and collectively. This stance, too, is compatible with the autonomous justification of toleration; but only this justification prevents pragmatist toleration from ending where, for example, it is no longer possible to argue that one can learn something from specific ethical options.

(e) Person E, finally, is a *monist concerning values*. She believes firmly in the truth of a particular ethical teaching and is convinced that a pluralistic universe or an as yet undiscovered truth concerning the good does not exist. To be sure, she also recognises that special conditions must be fulfilled in order to see the truth, which is a 'gift' conferred by the mercy of God, for example. Thus, this person may traditionally assume that the truth can be propagated only through free speech and not through coercion and that a person must be open and free for the truth in order to see it. That this openness itself may not be prompted in turn by gentle pressure or by shielding persons from false doctrines may be justified in religious terms, for instance by the claim that human beings should not perform God's work; yet such justifications run the risk of becoming inverted, for propagating the truth and preparing its path without resorting to direct coercion are likewise duties that can lead to intolerance without a further moral insight into the need to reciprocally justify freedom-constraining actions. It is not enough, therefore, to recognise the epistemic autonomy of a person in the sense of freedom of conscience (as freedom for the truth) if the primacy of religious truth is not contextually trumped by the primacy of morality and the insight into the finitude of reason in religious-ethical questions. This in no sense entails scepticism concerning one's truth-convictions or any form of ethical relativisation. The truth remains the truth; one only has to recognise that particular kinds of reasons are called for in particular contexts of justification. What is trumped is not the perspective of truth but an inadequate appreciation of contextual differences. In the ethical context, this person need not entertain any doubt concerning the truth for herself or anyone else, yet she will not violate the threshold of reciprocity and generality on this account.

This brief and highly schematic discussion indicates that each one of these normative-epistemic positions can lead to toleration, though by routes which exclude those of the others and which are not generalisable or generally demandable. And it also shows that, without the corrective of an autonomous moral consciousness of justification, the limits implied by these particular justifications of toleration are potentially too narrow. This in turn means that the toleration on the part of the autonomous justification itself cannot be boundless (as no form of toleration can be), for it is not compatible with all forms of scepticism, relativism, pluralism or monism. However, it draws the limits of toleration – and this is the decisive point – not on the basis of a competing ethical-metaphysical teaching either, but on the basis of the principle of justification which is 'unavoidable' for reasonable and responsible persons. This is the essential meaning of an autonomous justification of toleration for autonomous persons.

11

The virtue of tolerance

§35 Autonomy in conflict

1. Reflection on the need for an autonomous grounding of toleration with the aid of the principle of justification points to the fact that toleration as an attitude – or, more precisely, a *virtue* – presupposes a particular form of personal autonomy. With this the theory presented here returns to one of the basic themes of the discourse of toleration from the Stoics to Nietzsche, namely, that tolerance is a complex personal virtue which implies a particular attitude towards oneself and others. How should this be understood in detail?

First, I would like to offer a couple of general remarks on the concept of virtue which plays an increasingly important role in contemporary moral philosophy, though also in political philosophy.[1] Many discussions of the concept continue to be conducted within the terms of the conflict between an Aristotelian and a Kantian conception of virtue. According to the former, virtue is understood as the 'excellence' (*areté*) of a person who, in striving for self-perfection – achieving the highest good of *eudaimonia* – is willing and able to do the good for its own sake in a good way. Her striving for perfection includes practising and improving the various ways of being good, in other words the relevant ethical and dianoetic virtues. According to this conception, virtuous goodness, which is a distinguishing mark of a character as a whole and is defined by the adequate practical insight as the mean between two extremes, cannot be reduced to general principles or to the willingness to act in accordance with them. Kant, by contrast, rejects the justification of virtue in terms of the striving for the highest good and the

---

1. See Crisp and Slote (eds.), *Virtue Ethics*; Macedo, *Liberal Virtues*; Höffe, *Democracy in an Age of Globalisation*, ch. 7.

doctrine of the correct mean on the grounds that virtuous action can be understood only as free and responsible action in accordance with maxims aiming to fulfil moral duty, that is, to respect the human being as an end in herself in each of the required actions. According to Kant, this gives rise to a series of duties of virtue towards oneself and others.

Without being able to discuss this controversy in detail, much less to offer a comprehensive solution, it should be noted in explicating the virtue of tolerance, which is likewise interpreted within this field of tension, what the proposed distinction between different practical contexts of justification means in this connection.[2] If virtue is defined in general terms as the *ability and willingness to guide one's action in the respective normative contexts by the relevant appropriate and good reasons*, then one can distinguish between different forms of virtue according to context. *Ethical* virtues, for example, would be those in which a particular 'excellence' is required in order to pursue or realise ethical values, be they objective values which make an action 'good' or communal values whose goal is to maintain special ties to others. Doing the good in the best possible way then presupposes being able to recognise and promote this good and developing an 'expertise' in this respect – in precisely the sense of Aristotle's definitions. The standards of judgement remain ethical ones, whether they are understood in objective or in culturally relative terms, which means that the normative force of these virtues remains contingent on accepting the good that is supposed to be realised through them, a good that contributes to the goodness of a life, not just of action. Hence, such virtues can be demanded only within 'thick' ethical contexts and they are not morally binding in the strict sense.

Political virtues, by contrast, have an intermediate status between ethically and morally demandable virtues. Some of them spring from the particular political context of a specific community and its expectations of 'good citizens' (as regards civic involvement, for example), but some are of a political-moral nature, that is, they are generally required in a political context. Among the latter are the virtues of the readiness to accept discursive

---

2. For a Kantian interpretation, albeit one which argues that this involves a metaphysical 'comprehensive doctrine' which is incompatible with political liberalism, see Hampsher-Monk, 'Toleration, the Moral Will and the Justification of Liberalism'; by contrast, Newey, *Virtue, Reason and Toleration*, ch. 3, defends an Aristotelian position that tries to avoid reducing the virtue of tolerance to particular principles or motives and understands it instead as a basic character trait. However, on Newey's definition of the relation between objection and acceptance, both of which he conceives of in 'moral' terms, this can be understood only as a supererogatory virtue. But in this way he not only relinquishes the deontological character of the tolerance requirement but also fails to clarify the criteria governing what is tolerable.

responsibility in normative conflicts and the virtue of tolerance. They are demanded in the name of justice.

Moral virtues, finally, are virtues which correspond either to perfect or to imperfect duties. The former are virtues which persons must exercise towards concrete others in a reciprocally and generally binding way (in fulfilling duties of justice, for example), whereas the latter are virtues which no one can reject in general even though they do not imply any distinct practical duties or rights (and which can be traced back to duties of charity, for example).[3] Both kinds of virtues are grounded in respect for others as 'ends in themselves', as beings endowed with a right to justification, but they arise in different intersubjective situations. In general, Kant defines moral respect as 'limiting our self-esteem by the dignity of humanity in another person'.[4] For this fundamental form of respect, the following holds: 'Every human being has a legitimate claim to respect from his fellow human beings and is *in turn* bound to respect every other.'[5] What is required, as Kant explains, is not esteem but respect for the other – without any further condition.

This brief outline of the distinction between different categories of virtues illustrates the complexity of the virtue of tolerance. For, on the one hand, it can crop up at each of these levels. In the ethical context, there are a range of situations in which tolerance is required for particular reasons, for example, the tolerance of parents towards their children, or tolerance between friends or between members of a particular religious community. In this context, it is founded on shared conceptions of the good and is measured by the specific character of the relation in question. In the political context, by contrast, insofar as it is an ethically pluralist one, tolerance already acquires a moral meaning. For here, the citizens have a duty to justify the norms which are supposed to be binding on all in reciprocally and generally acceptable terms and in this regard to exercise tolerance in the procedure of justification and, even more important, when they realise that there is an insuperable disagreement.[6] The fact that this represents a particular context of the application of the general moral requirement of

---

3. Of course, these brief remarks are not sufficient to address the complicated problem of the Kantian distinction between these duties; for an instructive analysis of this relation, see O'Neill, *Towards Justice and Virtue*, ch. v.
4. Kant, *The Metaphysics of Morals*, Doctrine of Virtue, 199 (Ak. vi: 449).   5. *Ibid.* 209 (462).
6. See Höffe, 'Toleranz', 76, on tolerance as a 'deliberative' and a 'dispositive' competence which designate the abilities to distance oneself from one's own convictions and to subject them to reflexive examination.

respect in no way alters its moral character. In the moral context in general, finally, in which ethical conflicts arise between persons that they must defuse even though they cannot resolve them, the capacity for tolerance must be exhibited based on respect for the right to justification, even if it is not a case of a dispute over questions of political legislation. For not only are political-legal practical constraints in need of justification but also intersubjective constraints on action in general; the latter even constitute the normal case in moral interactions. Here tolerance presupposes something which Kant calls 'self-constraint' based on moral reasons, an 'act of freedom' which places the duty of respect – more precisely, the duty to offer justifications – above the pursuit of one's own ends and thus presupposes 'inner freedom' and 'moral strength'.[7] Here the specifically moral demand on the autonomous capacity for tolerance becomes apparent. For someone who is virtuous in this sense must place restrictions on her ethical valuations in free 'self-legislation' in such a way that she complies with the primacy of the principle of justification in contexts of reciprocal–general justification. Both one's own ethical striving and attempts to generalise ethical truths must yield in the face of this requirement. In this sense, tolerance is a moral virtue of justice.

On the other hand, the theory of the difference between contexts of justification calls for not only a context-specific situating of tolerance within them but also the recognition that the virtue of tolerance itself implies a complex, higher-level virtue, namely, the *virtue of the awareness of difference* with regard to these contexts. This means that a person is able to judge which normative questions belong to which context (as determined by their validity claim) and the criteria in terms of which they should be answered. Tolerant persons are in this sense 'context virtuosi'. They have to be able not only to differentiate between different contexts of justification but also to accord priority to moral imperatives in cases of ethical disagreement. It follows that even though the higher-level virtue of contextual differentiation, which is an 'intellectual virtue' of all rational persons, is not identical with tolerance, it does have special significance for tolerance. For tolerance is the virtue which must respond to a specific *contextual conflict* and muster the 'inner' power to order different contextual claims.

Therefore, toleration is not the 'inability of saying yes or no', as Nietzsche (representative of many others) alleged (see above §26.3), but the *ability to*

---

7. Kant, *The Metaphysics of Morals*, Doctrine of Virtue, 145–6, 146, 156, 164 (Ak. VI: 380, 381, 394, 405).

say yes and no in a differentiated manner, and in particular to say an ethical no and a moral yes. Hence, it is a complex virtue and is 'hard work' (to quote Aristotle).[8] It must observe the practically reasonable, responsible 'mean' between objecting and accepting and resist the impulse to turn ethical reasons for objecting into moral reasons for rejecting (or, in the case of a dispute within morality, to make reasonably rejectable reasons for objecting into strict reasons for rejecting). Tolerant persons have to have the dianoetic skill – the 'excellence' – of an 'art of separation',[9] of separating ethical from moral truth (or, with respect to religion, faith from knowledge), which, in the case of ethical or political conflicts, must go hand-in-hand with a morally required self-relativisation, a certain self-overcoming. This presupposes a complex relation to self, as will be discussed in what follows.

2. A comparison with the Aristotelian conception of virtue proposed by John McDowell may be helpful at this point to clarify the distinctive features of the notion of virtue relevant for toleration. McDowell sees a fundamental difference between an explanation of virtue 'from the outside in', that is, from the vantage point of certain predefined principles, and an explanation 'from the inside out' in the Aristotelian sense.[10] Only the Aristotelian perspective, McDowell argues, can reveal the specificity of virtue, namely, that it constitutes a particular form of knowledge or cognition and presupposes a 'perceptual capacity'.[11] Virtue is a form of responsiveness to particular situations in which the virtuous person recognises not only the relevant facts but also the relevant normative reasons that speak for a particular action – and acts accordingly. Virtue is 'an ability to recognize requirements that situations impose on one's behaviour'.[12] People learn within a particular normative way of life to 'see' what must be done in which situation; a virtuous person will integrate this knowledge into her conception of the good life, so that her perspective on situations of action is always also a perspective on herself. This ability cannot be reduced to external principles: 'Occasion by occasion, one knows what to do, if one does, not by applying universal principles but by being a certain kind of person: one who sees situations in a certain distinctive way.'[13]

The conception of virtue that I propose, which is based on a distinction between different contexts of justification, throws a different light on the practical perceptual capacity of virtuous persons. In view of the complex

---

8. Aristotle, *Nicomachean Ethics*, II.9, 1109 a24.
9. I borrow this concept from Walzer, 'Liberalism and the Art of Separation', although he uses it in a different context, namely that of social theory.
10. McDowell, 'Virtue and Reason', 50.   11. *Ibid.* 51.   12. *Ibid.* 53.   13. *Ibid.* 73.

problems and conflicts posed by tolerance situations, the primary 'knowledge' required is of a reflexive nature: it is not an immediate knowledge of what is to be done but, in the first instance, knowledge of the criteria of validity or justification relevant for the various claims that clash in such situations. These are the first 'requirements' that must be observed in a situation of conflict. For this, a purely perceptual faculty is not enough, however. What is required is a reflexive awareness of the competition between different practical standpoints – of objection, of acceptance and of rejection – which calls for the ability to impose an order on the contexts of justification. The virtuous person must 'know' which reasons are 'owed' to whom if she is to be able, in a second step, to provide a substantive answer to the question of the best reasons for action. Although the perception of the situation and its relevant features plays an important role in this respect, in many conflict situations it is not immediately apparent, but only through discursive reflection and examination, what can be done in a responsible way. *What* should be seen in each case is itself a matter for critical reflection. McDowell is correct to point out that complex practical answers cannot be discovered through a 'mechanical' application of principles.[14] But it is equally correct to assume not just a sense of responsibility and a capacity for reflection in general but also the ability, especially in the case of moral problems, to ask from a detached perspective what norms could provide an intersubjective justification of a mode of action. The difference between a perspective 'from the inside' and one 'from the outside' with respect to virtue is an artificial one; there are no completely 'external' norms of action, yet it is necessary to subject what appears 'from the inside' to critical scrutiny.[15] Only in this way can a person involved in a particular conflict recognise, at a first-order level, which reasons should be defended, and this presupposes knowledge, at a second-order level, of which context of justification is involved and which reasons can even count as good ones. The ability to 'see' reasons presupposes this first- and second-order faculty of reflection. Otherwise, a tolerant person would not be able to distinguish between and weigh the different categories of ethical and moral reasons.

Pace McDowell's fear, this does not require a standpoint 'external' to particular contexts of justification, but instead the practical ability to reflect and judge autonomously within and between such contexts. Finally, the

14. *Ibid*, 58.
15. Axel Honneth stresses the necessity of recourse to reflexive arguments and principles in cases of conflicts between values in his critique of McDowell; see Honneth, 'Between Hermeneutics and Hegelianism'.

selectivity as regards the relevant normative standpoints in a situation cannot be defined by a particular ethical conception of life of the individual, as McDowell proposes,[16] for whether this conception conflicts with moral imperatives, for example, and how one should then decide, can be judged only through autonomous reflection on justification. Practical reason remains an independent faculty of 'seeing' reasons by subjecting them to critical discursive examination.[17]

In more recent writings, McDowell tries to connect such critical reflexivity, in particular with regard to moral imperatives, with his conception of normative realism.[18] Reason is conceived as an autonomous faculty which is capable of distancing itself from 'first nature' and its desires and needs and to judge them in moral terms: 'Reason enables a deliberating agent to step back from *anything* that might be a candidate to ground its putative requirements.'[19] Against naturalistic reductions of the normative, McDowell nevertheless regards this capacity of the *logos* – a form of practical reason understood in 'Kantian'[20] terms – as part of nature, though of the specifically human 'second nature'. The latter is the result of a shaping of practical reason by processes of training or education that gives rise to the ability to take a critical and reflexive distance from 'natural motivational impulses' and enter the 'space of reasons'. This enables a virtuous person 'to open his eyes to reasons for acting'; she acquires an eye for good reasons.[21] McDowell emphasises at this point that the existing limits of the space of reasons must themselves be subjected to reflexive critical examination, though not from a radically external perspective, but in the manner of Neurath's boat, such that particular components of the space can be examined, and if need be replaced, while others remain in place.

However, because McDowell continues to conceive of the recognition of reasons in perceptual terms, the criteria for a reflexive *justification* of good reasons remain underdetermined. He continues to assimilate 'justification' to an 'ability to see' that leaves open the question of how the 'seer' can judge in a moral situation, for example, whether she can answer to others

---

16. McDowell, 'Virtue and Reason', 68: 'Acting in the light of a conception of how to live requires selecting and acting on the right concern.'
17. On the primacy of reason as the faculty of justification see Scanlon, *What We Owe to Each Other*, ch. I, and Forst, *The Right to Justification*, ch. 1.
18. See especially McDowell, 'Might There Be External Reasons?' and 'Two Sorts of Naturalism'.
19. 'Two Sorts of Naturalism', 173 (emphasis in original).
20. 'So we can bring practical reason back into nature; but what we bring back into nature is practical reason still conceived in a somewhat Kantian fashion, as something that does not need certification from outside itself': *ibid.* 184.
21. *Ibid.* 189.

for her way of seeing things.[22] For the decisive point for the morally judging person who was 'brought up in the right way' would be that she places only as much trust in her faculty of seeing as she takes to be reciprocally and generally defensible. Moreover, this 'moral seeing' must already orient itself to these criteria. Setting aside the metaphysical problem of an ethical or moral realism for the moment (see above §32.2), from a practical perspective such an approval of the explanation of reasons cannot do without the decisive criteria of justification. Overcoming the 'myth of the given' also in moral philosophy in favour of the autonomy of the faculty of justifying reason of beings who *jointly* inhabit a 'space of reasons' should not mislead us into erecting a new myth of 'given' reasons in the second nature.[23]

Nevertheless, McDowell's idea of a 'second' nature of reason has special importance for the issue of toleration in two respects. First, although the virtue of tolerance indeed presupposes the ability to distance oneself from 'natural' motivational impulses and to arrive at a rational self-relativisation, this (to go beyond McDowell's conception) is more a matter of these 'natural' impulses themselves already being of an *ethical-practical* kind. The attitude of tolerance presupposes the possibility of a certain detachment, though not of disengagement, from the ethical impulse to object, an impulse which tends of itself to reject an ethically condemned practice or conviction and not to tolerate it. In order to arrive at acceptance in spite of the objection, the virtuous ability to 'liberate' oneself reflexively from ethical convictions to such an extent that, although one upholds them, one suspends them for (higher-order) moral reasons and exercises tolerance must prevail *within* the second nature of reason.

Second, McDowell's conception of practical training and development (*Bildung*) rightly emphasises that the virtue of tolerance, in the sense of a schooling of the faculty of practical reason and the ability to deal with reasons, is something that must be learnt. A tolerant person must be able to differentiate and order different practical contexts, that is, to know when which reasons are required. Moreover, she must be able to set limits on

---

22. See, for example, 'Might There Be External Reasons', 101: '[I]f the upbringing has gone as it should, we shall want to say that the way of seeing things . . . involves considering them aright, that is, having a correct conception of their actual layout. Here talking of having been properly brought up and talking of considering things aright are two ways of giving expression to the same assessment: one that would be up for justification by ethical argument.'
23. On the critique of the *myth of the given* (W. Sellars) and the thesis that the 'space of reasons' is the 'space of reason' which needs *justifications* and not *exculpations*, see McDowell, *Mind and World*, 5 and 8. However, there too the relation between experiences with conceptual content and judgements remains insufficiently determinate; see, for example, 62, 125.

her ethical objections in cases involving 'reasonable differences' so that she relativises them with regard to their reciprocally and generally, though not their ethically, binding character. This ability presupposes experience of conflicts and of how to deal with them correctly, a multifaceted learning process that also involves a certain complex relation to self, as we shall see. This explains why, although every reasonable person is expected to exhibit this capacity, it nevertheless also has its own individual genesis in a personal formation process.

3. In a context marked by profound normative conflicts the virtue of tolerance has, to summarise the foregoing, a moral and a closely related epistemological, dianoetic component. From the moral perspective, the unconditional respect for the other as a person who has a right to justification and to whom one owes corresponding reasons in contexts of reciprocal and general validity has pride of place. The tolerant person accepts the threshold of reciprocity and generality and recognises that a well-grounded ethical objection is not yet a sufficient reason for a moral rejection. This central insight of practical reason is supplemented by the insight into the finitude of (theoretical and practical) reason exhibited by the reasonable person. This is why reasonable differences over the good or true life or about the constitution of normative reality are possible in ethical questions and why this, in virtue of the differences between contexts of justification, is an objection neither against an ethical truth nor against the possibility of moral justification. For even though the finitude of reason leads to irresolvable ethical conflicts, reason is nevertheless capable of justifying norms – without recourse to 'ultimate' reasons – in contexts of reciprocal and general validity, norms which are independent of the conflicting conceptions of the good. Tolerance, therefore, implies respect for the *moral and the epistemic autonomy* of others, without this respect being in need of an ethical justification of its own or this implying an ethical relativisation of one's own convictions; what it implies, however, is the reasonable self-relativisation of comprehensive ethical claims to truth in the validity contexts of reciprocity and generality. The moral and the epistemological elements explain why tolerance is a *virtue of justice* and a *demand of reason*.

Here the autonomy of the person exercising tolerance should be seen as being 'in conflict' in a twofold sense. It is involved, on the one hand, in the conflict between one's own ethical convictions and those of others and, on the other, in the conflict *with oneself*, for the ethical objection against the others involves the tendency to make this negative evaluation the basis of action or general norms as well. The virtue of tolerance presupposes that this impulse is thwarted by moral insight. As we have seen, this involves a certain ability to limit and overcome oneself. And thus the question of how such a 'reasonable' posture is possible once again arises. What notion of the 'self' does it presuppose? Is it even possible to put this ideal of virtue into practice in one's life?

§36 The tolerant person

1. In order to offer a more detailed analysis of the relation to self of the tolerant person, three objections to the conception of virtue presented above should be considered. These are the objections (a) that the self presupposed is basically a self-less self, one which denies itself, (b) that it is a purely intelligible, and in this sense a characterless, self and (c) that it is a split self. None of these objections is valid, yet they point to important facets of the virtue of tolerance.

(a) Nietzsche's suspicion that tolerance is a sign of modern self-lessness, indifference and 'depravity' implies that the self-overcoming required by tolerance is a form of self-denial: only someone who is not sure of himself arrives at a stance of tolerance from inner weakness (see above §26.3). Yet, as already observed, precisely the contrary is true. Both a clear-cut ethical objection to a conviction or practice as well as its moral acceptance and the associated self-limitation call for a *strong self* which, in Kant's words characterising moral virtue, musters up the 'inner freedom' to perform this 'act of freedom' – as 'free self-constraint'[24] – and this not only once, or in single actions, but in general as a distinguishing mark of a tolerant character (for, as Aristotle says, one swallow does not make a spring).[25] The self presupposed in this context, however, is aware – and herein lies a difference from Kant's moral philosophy – of the independent validity of ethical values and obligations, which may also be situated outside the moral domain; but as a moral self it has the ability to set limits to its own ethical valuations when it is not possible to act in accordance with them in a reciprocally–generally responsible manner. Hence, both aspects of the self, the ethical and the moral, have to be educated if one is to be able to identify and evaluate such a conflict *with others* and *within oneself*.

However, such an ability to say yes or no in a differentiated manner can – as Alexander Mitscherlich puts it following Kant, though from the

24. Kant, *The Metaphysics of Morals*, Doctrine of Virtue, 165–6, 146, 148 *et passim* (Ak. VI: 407, 381, 383 *et passim*).
25. Aristotle, *Nicomachean Ethics*, 1.6, 1098 a19.

perspective of psychoanalysis – be a 'liberating experience', namely, the experience of overcoming negative ethical impulses (though these are already reflexive): 'an exhilarating experience of being free from the compulsion of intolerance'.[26] Yet it need not be experienced in this emphatic sense as a liberation from the 'vicissitudes of one's own instincts'; for although the act of tolerance presupposes an inner autonomy and a higher-level reflexivity, an 'ego-strength',[27] it is also aware of the costs of this self-limitation, which are high, especially for people with a comprehensive ethical-religious world-view. Meeting one's moral responsibility is one thing, ethically embracing it another. Tolerance may be perceived simultaneously as a reinforcement of the self and as an affront against the self. Hence, to speak once again in Aristotelian terms, tolerance maintains the just mean between excessive self-doubt and excessive self-confidence in one's ethical truth, that is, between an excess and a deficiency of self-relativisation. This calls for a kind of higher-level *sovereignty* which regards the required self-limitation as an expression of one's strength, yet also as a duty to restrict one's ethical truth in contexts of universal justification. For the tolerant person stands by her objection, in spite of the acceptance component.

(b) Hence, tolerant persons should not be seen as purely 'intelligible' reflexive beings devoid of practical character and ethical identity. They are shaped by particular ties to others and 'ground projects' which, in Bernard Williams's words, first lend life meaning: they explain 'why we go on at all'.[28] Tolerant individuals always see themselves as being situated in different contexts – but precisely in *different* contexts. Hence, their view of themselves as responsible and practically rational beings who know to whom they owe which reasons is part of their personal identity. Only a sufficiently complex explanation of identity can reveal how profound conflicts with others and conflicts within a person can be in this context, conflicts in which different 'determinations' of individual self-determination can come into conflict. Within the identity of a person who finds herself caught in a conflict between different duties and obligations, how she should decide cannot be settled by a mathematical formula. Of course, the *tolerant* person will be able to establish a responsible order among her responsibilities and to make certain 'sacrifices' for this, though not at the cost of renouncing her identity. The distinguishing feature of her 'nature', her character, is that she is aware of the different levels of her identity – of *identification* with concrete others in ethical contexts and

26. Mitscherlich, 'Toleranz', 429.   27. *Ibid.* 437.
28. Williams, 'Persons, Character and Morality', 10.

of identification with all human beings at the moral level – and tries to find a path that corresponds to these identifications. Being 'autonomous' here does not mean, to reiterate the difference from Kant, that only moral duties can be recognised as genuine duties or that one has 'chosen' or 'created' all of one's evaluative convictions and ethical ties. Instead autonomy means being aware of the different components of one's identity and of the different corresponding responsibilities (chosen or not chosen) and being able to take responsibility for oneself *overall*.

(c) Hence, the tolerant self is not a split self either, that is, a self who is torn between ethical and moral valuations and, when the latter are accorded priority, alienates part of itself. It is instead a complex self whose identity is constituted in the *tension* between different normative poles. The identity is a product of the person's ability to integrate these different poles, that is, to recognise these tensions and to conduct herself towards them in a reflective manner. Here the picture of two poles must be modified so that more than two aspects of the determination of identity become apparent. For different ties already exist within the ethical domain (for example, to family, friends and worthwhile projects) and legal obligations and political responsibilities must be taken into account in addition to moral duty. Within this normative framework a personal identity evolves which always remains tension-laden while, as an autonomous identity, remaining aware of the different contexts of justification in which it is situated. It follows that tolerance is a character trait of persons who exhibit this awareness to a special degree. Their 'integrity' flows from an accountability which does not reduce the complexity of the normative sphere and in the process exhibits a certain steadfastness.

This also shows why the tolerant person must exhibit a certain degree of tolerance not only towards others but also *towards herself*. She must do so not only in the sense of having to tolerate the conflicting inclinations and desires within herself by acknowledging them as her own and trying to shape them.[29] She must also do so in the further sense of recognising the extent to which conflicts between different standpoints can arise within her reflected 'store' of norms which do not admit of any clear resolution, or at best one which entails certain costs. Refraining from translating ethical objection into

---

29. Wollheim uses the concept of tolerance of oneself in this sense in *The Thread of Life*, 184. Mitscherlich, 'Toleranz', 440, also stresses the need for recognition and for shaping inclinations in the context of education in a tolerant attitude. Kristeva, *Strangers to Ourselves*, draws an instructive, albeit overstated, parallel between the experience of one's own difference and 'strangeness' and that of the stranger.

a strict rejection then means with regard to one's own ethical convictions that they must acknowledge the primacy of moral responsibility, whereas, in the case of moral consciousness, it means recognising the legitimacy of the ethical standpoint. The decisive point is that even such a 'decentred'[30] person exercises tolerance out of a clear conviction, even when she is aware of a continuing conflict within herself. By 'meeting' her responsibility towards others she establishes a certain internal order within the plurality of her convictions. The 'sway' she holds over herself in exercising tolerance, therefore, is a form of freedom which opposes specific ethical impulses, though without suppressing them but instead sorting them out and, if necessary, curbing them; the person does not let herself be determined by her ethical objections, though she sees these valuations as a determining part of herself. She recognises the irreducible difference between different normative standpoints, which she is nevertheless able to integrate – though, as stated, not without tension.

Hence, a tolerant person has a single practical identity, though a complex and differentiated one, whose integrity is a product of coherent behaviour in different contexts of justification in which she can answer for herself – and knows which reasons are appropriate in which context. Tolerance presupposes such knowledge of the complexity of the normative world as a world *between* individuals and (in different degrees) also *within* the individual. Once again, tolerance proves to be a virtue of practical reason.

2. In order to develop the thematisation of a 'tolerant personality' further at this point it would be necessary to supplement the philosophical perspective through perspectives of individual and social psychology. Such an extension of the study – one need only think, for example, of the theoretical foundational questions and the details of empirical research methods one would have to discuss – I will not even attempt here. However, it is worth mentioning some topoi from studies of the tolerant or the 'authoritarian' personality, such as the work conducted in the wake of the influential study by the Frankfurt Institute of Social Research (in collaboration with a group of American social psychologists) entitled *The Authoritarian Personality* (1950).[31] Although such studies subsume the most diverse kinds of objections under the concept of 'prejudice' – and correspondingly identify 'tolerance'

30. In this connection, see Honneth, 'Decentred Autonomy', on the relationship between the 'creative articulation of needs' (271), the reflexive representation of one's own life history and the context-sensitive application of moral principles (albeit not in relation to the problem of toleration).
31. On the continuing influence of the study (in spite of all criticism), see Young-Bruehl, *The Anatomy of Prejudices*, and Stenner, 'The Authoritarian Dynamic'.

(over-hastily) with the absence of prejudices or (wrongly) with the absence of objections in general[32] they nevertheless provide important pointers for analysing the complex connections between the relation to self and the relation to others and for analysing the social conditions of the capacity for tolerance. As regards the former, many of these studies point, following Freud,[33] to the connection between ego-weakness (as conditioned by socialisation) and an excessive identification with a group involving a corresponding intolerant demarcation from and an aggressive aversion to other groups, whose very 'difference' is perceived as a threat to one's own identity.[34] Contrary to what Nietzsche believed, intolerance (and not tolerance) thus appears to be a 'herd virtue', a token of the weakness and not of the strength of the ego, as the inability to endure 'ambiguity'[35] in oneself and in society because one's own identity is labile. External differences are no more endured than is internal difference and the person takes refuge in simplistic differentiations and negative attitudes towards the 'other'. It follows that internal and external (in-)tolerance go hand-in-hand. Thus, only a person whose negative and positive valuations are stable seems to be capable of exercising tolerance, and not only of withstanding conflicts but of dealing with them in productive ways (without thereby placing herself in question).

However, the corresponding self-confidence requires not only an inner freedom from fear that must be acquired through socialisation – this is generally the starting point for large-scale studies of socialisation – but also freedom from external threats; in other words, it calls for a certain social trust.[36] As regards the second point mentioned above, this once again reveals a specific connection between toleration and justice; for where this trust is shaken by perceptions of injustices and threats, whether imaginary or real, the potential for intolerance increases.

These scant remarks must suffice to indicate, on the one hand, that this represents a fruitful field of investigation but that, on the other, it involves dangers of imprecise concepts and of over-generalised causal explanations.

32. Compare, for instance, the informative study from the 1960s by Martin, *The Tolerant Personality*, 21: 'Absolute tolerance is a completely neutral attitude towards a group, without any group judgment, favorable or unfavorable. As tolerance increases prejudice decreases, and vice versa, so that absolute tolerance can be expressed as the point on a scale which indicates neither positive nor negative prejudice.'
33. See especially the classic study *Group Psychology and the Analysis of the Ego* (1921).
34. See Adorno, *The Authoritarian Personality*, 234 (in collaboration with R. Sanford, E. Frenkel-Brunswick and D. Levinson).
35. See Frenkel-Brunswick, 'Intolerance of Ambiguity as an Emotional and Perceptual Variable'.
36. On this, see especially Mitscherlich, 'Wie ich mir' and 'Toleranz'; in addition Stenner, 'The Authoritarian Dynamic'.

The latter can lead not only to the pathologisation of intolerant attitudes in general, and to setting the tolerant personality apart as the only strong one,[37] but also to the tendency to make too strong inferences back to factors relating to the family, social conditions, the role of religion, etc. Viewed from the perspectives of individual and social psychology, the paths leading to intolerance are as diverse as those leading to tolerance.

To be sure, the danger of inadmissibly generalising certain 'character types of tolerance' also exists at the philosophical level. There one can find, for example, a range of specifically ethical interpretations of what is meant by the insight into the finitude of reason. Thus, the tolerant person could be seen as an *ironist* in Richard Rorty's sense, that is, as someone who is aware of the lack of incontrovertible reasons for 'final vocabularies' and as a result adopts a stance of tolerance. However, although the tolerant person may adopt an ironic stance towards the conflict between comprehensive ethical doctrines, this is by no means necessarily so; it is an open question which conclusions should be drawn from the insight into the possibility of 'reasonable differences' in the ethical domain. More than that, Rorty's ironist is not a good candidate in this respect because she does not seem to have sufficient reason for objecting to the convictions of others, which she acknowledges are of equal value and equally contingent,[38] and for preferring her own – unless she were to reject all non-ironical, comprehensive metaphysical doctrines once again on metaphysical grounds and thereby abandon her irony (thus defined).[39]

Opposed to this are conceptions which, drawing on Isaiah Berlin's pluralism thesis, would describe a tolerant attitude as a *tragic* one, at least as regards ethical-political consciousness.[40] The tolerant person is undoubtedly aware of the irreducibly conflictual character of the normative world and that the finitude of practical reason means that errors are unavoidable; however, the fact that this can also lead to 'tragic' conflicts (both in personal and in political life) does not mean that a tolerant consciousness is *necessarily* a tragic consciousness. A person can also interpret this in the pragmatist spirit of

37. The fact that tolerance presupposes a self which is stable in a certain sense does not mean that every stable self will be tolerant – or that all those who find themselves in a precarious situation as regards their identity will tend to be intolerant.

38. Rorty, 'Private Irony and Liberal Hope', 73–4. This is why this conception lacks any basis for an objection component.

39. That the ironic posture is itself a metaphysical one becomes apparent, for instance, when Rorty (*ibid.* 74) asserts: 'The ironist . . . is a nominalist and a historicist. She thinks nothing has an intrinsic nature, a real essence.'

40. Thus, for example, Moon, *Constructing Community, passim*; and van den Brink, *The Tragedy of Liberalism*, especially ch. 2.

the striving for improvement and take an optimistic view of the gains of a successful political form of life, just as she can believe in a religious spirit that all of these losses will acquire a meaning in a higher justice.

Finally, to repeat, one must resist the temptation to conceive of the tolerant mindset as a *sceptical* one which withholds judgement when it comes to 'ultimate' truths.[41] In order to undertake the self-relativisation required by self-conscious reason, one need not renounce the claim to 'absolute' ethical truths; what is required is instead an insight into the difference between contexts of justification, each of which calls for specific reasons. Fundamental determinations of reason and its limits should not be reified into a specific, ethical-philosophical stance.

41. Thus, in addition to Barry, *Justice as Impartiality* (see above §32.2), also Schleichert, *Wie man mit Fundamentalisten diskutiert, ohne den Verstand zu verlieren*, especially ch. 9.

12

The tolerant society

§37 Political integration and ethical-cultural difference: towards a critical theory of toleration

1. Both the reconstruction of the history of toleration and the foregoing systematic discussion should have sufficiently demonstrated the contemporary relevance of this concept. Thus, in what follows, there will be no need to revive it for present-day conditions; the aim will instead be to clarify the extent to which the history of the concept lives on in a variety of ways in the present through a discussion of a number of central toleration conflicts. Here virtually all of the complex and mutually antagonistic conceptions and justifications of toleration reappear, first and foremost the conflict between the permission and the respect conception. Hence, toleration remains caught up in the tension between power and morality; it functions as much as an instrument of power and domination as it does as an emancipatory claim. Neither the authoritarian conception of toleration nor what I have called 'Locke's fear' – the fear that too much toleration could destroy the normative foundations of society – should be assumed to have been overcome in contemporary societies.

In these contexts, finally, it will have to become evident whether the justification of the respect conception which I have proposed can serve to analyse and explain such conflicts and whether it has the normative resources to show what toleration means in these conflicts, in particular whether the criteria of reciprocity and generality suffice to define the limits of toleration and whether they actually enable us to avoid particular and rejectable evaluations.

With this, the theory of toleration founded on the principle of justification becomes entirely situated within the political context and is understood within the framework of a theory of *public political justification*, that is, a theory of democratic self-legislation. Here the *citizens* as members of an ethically pluralistic political community owe one another certain reasons for reciprocally and generally valid norms, where it is important whether what is at stake are morally relevant, fundamental questions of justice or decisions that can be legitimately taken on the basis of majoritarian procedures, for instance. Therefore, the decisive perspective from which the issue of toleration should be dealt with is that of the citizens as *legislators* who, as legal persons, are simultaneously the *subjects* of these laws. They are authors and addressees of the norms to be justified.

This shows that talk of a 'tolerant society' is ambiguous. For this can mean (a) the tolerance of the citizens as individuals, (b) the space of toleration resulting from social norms and understandings concerning what is tolerable in social interactions, where the norms and understandings in question are not subject to legal regulation, (c) the 'tolerance' of the legal norms themselves, i.e. the level of freedom they bestow, (d) the tolerance of the political system and its institutions, i.e. its openness to the diverse voices of citizens and communities, and (e) the 'tolerance of the state', arguably the most problematic usage. For, however common it may be in legal discourse,[1] it nevertheless conveys the authoritarian or majoritarian meaning of toleration as captured by the permission conception. The exercise of toleration on the part of 'the state' presupposes a dismissive judgement concerning the practices and convictions of certain individuals or groups who as a result are seen from the outset as 'politically different'; even if they are tolerated, on whatever grounds, they are not counted among the 'normal' citizens or they do not conform to the official norms, but are merely 'tolerated' citizens. Hence, the state functions as the supreme authority and simultaneously as an actor who, when it comes to a conflict of toleration, abandons its higher-level, neutral status by adopting the position of one side and merely tolerating the other side. In this way, however, it not only sacrifices its neutrality but also in a certain sense is intolerant because it takes sides and lays down particular norms that privilege one side.[2] In order to avoid such a hierarchical and contradictory understanding of the 'toleration state' (to which

---

1. See, for example, Debus, *Das Verfassungsprinzip der Toleranz unter besonderer Berücksichtigung der Rechtsprechung des Bundesverfassungsgerichts* (see also above §27.2, n. 52).
2. Newey, *Virtue, Reason and Toleration*, 138, discusses this in terms of the 'paradox of political tolerance'. However, he does not consider as an alternative to this a democratic conception of toleration in accordance with a principle of justification but remains captive to a Hobbesian understanding of the state which allows toleration, if at all, only in accordance with the permission model.

I will return in §38 in a discussion of some examples), it seems more sensible to understand the 'imperative of toleration' as being addressed exclusively *to the citizens*, whereas an 'imperative of neutrality' should be addressed to *the state*.[3] Finally, this neutrality should be understood not in such a way that the state in all of its decisions should strive for 'neutrality of effects' on all possibly affected individuals and groups, which would be impossible, but such that a 'neutrality of justification' is required in the sense that only reciprocally and generally acceptable reasons, and not controversial ethical valuations, can be the foundation of general norms.[4]

Still, notwithstanding the validity of this principle for political-legal decisions, this understanding of toleration and neutrality should not disguise the fact that, in a democracy, *the citizens* themselves and not *the state* are the agents of 'neutral' – or better, reciprocal-general – justification, so that the principle of reciprocal-general justification presupposes the civic virtue of tolerance especially in procedures of public justification. If, instead of speaking of a 'tolerant' state, therefore, we correctly speak instead of a state which is 'neutral regarding justification', there is a danger that the criticised, hierarchical conception of official toleration will be stipulated as the only possible one. More importantly, there is also the danger that the central insight that the neutrality of justification called for refers to the reasons which find their way into justified norms *through the citizens* will be ignored, because civic tolerance is then reduced entirely to 'compliance with valid law'.[5] To avoid this, such a conception of justification requires a theory of *democracy*. Civic tolerance plays an important role where the citizens must be ready to justify their claims in reciprocal and general terms and especially when they must recognise what the threshold of reciprocity and generality demands – for example, relativising one's own ethical claims to truth insofar as they can be reasonably rejected. Tolerance is in this sense an indispensable democratic virtue and is essential for the success of impartial justification. Therefore, if we reject the hierarchical – for example, the 'Christian' – 'toleration state', the concept of toleration should neither be annexed to the permission conception nor be reduced to compliance with the law but must feature centrally in a theory of political justification as a capacity of the citizens. This, as we have seen, constitutes the 'revolutionary' legacy of the discourse of toleration (see §22 above), that is, the extension of the respect conception to

3. Thus, Denninger, 'Der Einzelne und das allgemeine Gesetz', 428.
4. On this, see my discussion of the ethical neutrality of law in Forst, *Contexts of Justice*, ch. 2 For an in-depth exploration in the context of German constitutional law, see Huster, *Die ethische Neutralität des Staates*.
5. Thus, Huster, *Die ethische Neutralität des Staates*, 234, in his discussion of toleration and neutrality.

the political level and the replacement of toleration 'from above' by reciprocal toleration.

Hence, speaking in terms of a 'tolerant state' involves considerable risks of conveying a particular conception of toleration. In a democracy, when it does not have the meaning of the scope for freedom left open by legal norms, this term can only refer to toleration on the part of the citizens. However, it may be legitimate to speak in terms of the 'tolerance of the state' (if only figuratively) in the special case where a group among the citizens challenges the norms essential for maintaining a political system of justification – and it remains to be examined whether the permission conception does not as a result recur at the heart of the respect conception.

Therefore, in what follows I will discuss the tolerance of the citizens and will likewise eschew the concept of neutrality on account of its ambiguity in favour of the terminology of political or reciprocal-general justification.[6] For, however legitimate it may be to speak of a 'neutrality of justification', in the sense that the reasons that legitimate generally binding norms have an impartial character and that procedures of justification should accordingly guarantee the required impartiality, it is nevertheless problematic to speak in terms of 'neutral' reasons because their quality is measured not by their (equal) distance from the conflicting positions, but only in terms of the criteria of reciprocity and generality. Moreover, only *disputed* ethical conceptions are excluded as a ground of legitimation of general norms, not a priori all possible ethical values.

Speaking in terms of a 'neutral' justification of the principle of neutrality also permits the false assumption that it does not involve a substantial moral justification – even if the latter is a higher-level justification based on practical reason. The *ethical* impartiality of justification is itself justified in *moral* terms. Finally, one can easily be misled into concluding

(a) that a conception of reciprocal-general justification calls for a 'neutralisation' of political discourses in the sense of a 'purging' of controversial ethical or religious positions, which in view of the need for discursive confrontation between such positions is unfounded,

(b) that what is meant is the (above-mentioned) 'neutrality of effects' which requires that all legal norms should have the same effects on all affected group (or even individual) interests, or

(c) that 'the state' in the Hobbesian sense is a neutral third party in the conflict among the citizens,

(d) that maintaining social relations unchanged is the preferred option.

6. Compare the seven meanings of neutrality in Forst, *Contexts of Justice*, 45–8.

Furthermore, the expression 'ethical' impartiality should not lead us to overlook the fact that toleration is not only an ethical but also a political and a moral affair, that is, that toleration is called for with regard not only to different conceptions of the good but also to alternative conceptions of justice and different interpretations of moral norms. Nevertheless, toleration with regard to ethical values and 'comprehensive doctrines', which often underlie profound political and moral disputes, remains fundamental. The hallmark of a pluralistic society in which tolerance is a necessary virtue is its ethical pluralism or, more precisely, the forms of ethical pluralism outlined above (§31.2). Therefore, in what follows, the society in relation to which the ethical implications of toleration will be discussed will be described as an *ethically pluralistic society*. Moreover, since ethical conceptions of value are bound up with ethical practices, i.e. with forms of life which have a (more or less thick) cultural character, one can speak of an *ethically and culturally* pluralistic society.

Whether this is also a multicultural society depends on what is meant by 'multicultural'. 'Multiculturalism' in the narrower sense stands for the existence of a plurality of 'cultures' which, although part of a society, represent more than just 'lifestyles'; rather they are communities which set themselves apart from others through their definitions of members and non-members, hence through their identity, and define themselves through a shared history, shared conceptions of value, and shared language and descent. Whether relatively firmly established cultures, such as those of indigenous peoples, or already pluralised immigrant cultures are meant, however, the decisive issue remains that it is a matter of ethical communities, that is, of communities marked by deep agreements at the three levels of the ethical: the contents, the forms and the sources of the good life. Correspondingly, such cultures are often also distinguished by a specifically religious component. Finally, the primarily ethical rather than ethnic definition of culture which I favour in this context also allows for a broader concept of 'multiculturalism' according to which groups that are not defined in ethnic or national terms are also counted among such 'cultures' insofar as they exhibit a high level of ethical particularity and identification – for example, religious communities or groups which define themselves through sexual orientation or other attributes and interests.[7] Hence, a primarily ethical definition of the pluralism which leads to toleration conflicts includes the cultural components in the narrower sense; nevertheless, it also includes other ethical components which mark equally important differences among forms of life.

7. For a narrower concept of multiculturalism, see Kymlicka, *Multicultural Citizenship*, ch. 2, and for a broader one, Kymlicka, *Finding Our Way*, ch. 6.

2. The society that provides the context for the toleration conflicts to be discussed should therefore be regarded as a *political community of ethical communities*. This raises the question, which is central to many debates over multiculturalism, of how such a society can be integrated as a whole, given that it seems to fall apart into a multitude of ethical 'cultures'. In answering this question, it must first be emphasised that this question primarily concerns the *normative* integration of such a community of communities. For, with the exception of the relation between a society and an institutionally clearly demarcated group with its own territory (for example, a reservation of indigenous people), it becomes apparent, from the perspective of an inclusive *social* integration, how dense are the interconnections between the members of the different ethical communities in the economic and political domains, though also at the level of culture in general. This is also important for normative reasons, for in all of these areas particular normative agreements are already necessary for the 'functioning' of normal social practices.[8] Hence, sociologically speaking it is not realistic to assume a multiplicity of normative 'islands' swimming in a sea of superficial connections.

Nevertheless, for the normative integration of the society as a whole as a *political community*, there is the problem of how conflicts over fundamental questions of social coexistence between the different ethical communities are to be resolved. Hence, an ethically pluralistic political community faces the problem of 'substanceless substance':[9] on the one hand, in its own normative identity it must be sufficiently 'substanceless' in order to avoid inadmissibly curtailing ethical plurality but, on the other, it must itself possess so much 'substance' that all of its members regard themselves, not only as ethical persons, but also as citizens who are responsible to and for one another, and thus as parts of a political *community of responsibility*. Besides all of their particular ethical languages, they must be willing and able to speak a common language and thus must share a common political culture in which the justificatory procedures intended to lead to the setting of legitimate norms are embedded. Toleration alone cannot produce this connection;[10] it rests instead on a fundamental consensus concerning justice which, on the one hand, is *procedural* because it essentially contains the principle of justification but, on the other, also has a *substantial* character. This is so not only because the principle of justification itself has a substantial moral character but because the political context as a context of justification is a historically evolved context shared by the citizens and is marked by many conflicts and

8. For a comprehensive treatment, see Peters, *Die Integration moderner Gesellschaften*.
9. On this, see Forst, *Contexts of Justice*, ch. 3.
10. This is nevertheless the view defended in Kukathas, 'Cultural Toleration'.

institutional achievements. And even if they regard these institutions as in need of improvements over which they disagree, they must presuppose the shared consciousness of these contexts, even though they interpret them in different ways. In all of these conflicts, therefore, a basic consensus, not only over the validity of the principle of justification, but also over the shared responsibility for this specific political community, is necessary.

In the light of the differentiation between four conceptions of the person worked out above (see especially §21.3 and §29.24), this means that persons understand themselves not only as *ethical persons* but also as *moral persons* and simultaneously as authors and addressees of the law of their political community, i.e. as citizens and legal persons. In all of these respects they exercise a specific form of responsibility. In the political context, this means that, as fellow citizens, they are aware that in ethical conflicts they are obliged to engage in a particular form of justification and, if necessary, to exercise a certain form of tolerance. *This* normative integration is indispensable for a political community united by the 'project' of constructing a just basic structure; integration does not arise *through* the numerous ethical conflicts, but it does occur *along with* such conflicts. More or less sharply divided in their ethical convictions, the citizens are united by an awareness of being part of a particular, historically situated community of responsibility in which they owe each other certain kinds of reasons. The self-image and structures of such a community, whether it be a classical nation-state or an immigrant society,[11] will inevitably be 'ethically impregnated'[12] by the majority culture or by dominant groups; yet, if it is to be regarded as just in the eyes of its citizens, it must be capable of exposing this impregnation to the test of reciprocal and general justification. The problem is not the existence of a particular form of 'ethical life', for this is unavoidable; what is problematic is the refusal to subject this ethical life to examination with regard to its justice. Every political community contains some prior substance, yet this must essentially include the disposition to justice.[13] The citizens of an ethically pluralistic society are always united by more than 'mere' procedures of justice. They are united by shared principles and a shared history (also of conflicts); yet whatever divides them is worked out within procedures of justice. However, it must be borne in mind that the ethical or political lines of conflict between

---

11. For these distinctions see Walzer, *On Toleration*, ch. 2.
12. Thus, Habermas, 'Struggles for Recognition in the Democratic Constitutional State', 122–8.
13. This model of integration thereby escapes the criticism of 'civic assimilationism' raised by Parekh, *Rethinking Multiculturalism*, 199–206, without (like Parekh) having recourse to a strong concept of 'national identity' in the consciousness of mutual esteem (230–8).

groups can vary from case to case and involve shifting coalitions. Ethically speaking, the conflict situation within a society is rarely a purely antagonistic matter, especially as the ethical pluralism of a society is often reflected within a person who may belong to different ethical communities.

3. The issue of the 'recognition of difference' opens up a panorama of conflicts which mark the debates over the attributes of a 'multicultural society'. In the first place, it must be asked to what extent the principle of reciprocal and general justification can legitimate particular forms of recognition for ethical communities at all, since the criteria of reciprocity and generality seem to call for norms that should not be indexed in any way to a specific group. Don't these criteria exclude any particular regard for ethical particularity? This is correct in an important sense, namely that no reasons can enter into the legitimation of norms that discriminate against or privilege a particular group on ethical grounds. To that extent the law is 'colour-blind'[14] and constitutes a *protective cover* for ethical identities precisely because it excludes the domination of specific ethical viewpoints. However, when generally valid law constitutes not a fair protection for particular ethical communities but instead an inadmissible burden because it places them at a disadvantage towards others, the law degenerates into an ethical straitjacket and must be altered – likewise with the aid of the criteria of reciprocity and generality, because in such a case a community must be able to show to what extent applicable law flouts their *justified* concerns *by comparison with the other communities*. Then it must be apparent that strict *equal treatment* has to be altered in favour of a qualified treatment *as equals*.[15] In that case, a specific recognition of ethical difference within the law is not an ethical but a *moral-political* requirement in the sense of justice. The issue remains one of avoiding injustices, which in this case means avoiding disadvantages for particular individuals or groups which cannot be justified in reciprocal terms.

Very different demands for recognition are made on this basis:[16]

(a) Members of groups who suffer discrimination, to an extent in the legal but even more so in the social domain, in ways that are concealed rather

14. Thus, Justice Harlan in his 1896 'Dissent' to the famous *Plessy* v. *Ferguson* decision which established the principle 'separate but equal' regarding the relation between whites and blacks in the United States.

15. On this distinction, see Dworkin, *Taking Rights Seriously*, ch. 12.

16. This list includes a series of differentiations to be found in a wide range of sources. Cf. Kymlicka, *Multicultural Citizenship*, 27–33; Taylor, 'The Politics of Recognition'; Habermas, 'Struggles for Recognition in the Democratic Constitutional State', 116–22; Peters, 'Understanding Multiculturalism', 28–37; Honneth, 'Redistribution as Recognition', III.1, 161ff.

than revealed by 'neutral' law, can demand legal regulations which prevent this and actively transform social inequalities on account of manifest or concealed discrimination – for example, in the form of quota systems.

(b) Members of historically disadvantaged groups who continue to suffer under the structural effects of discrimination even after this has been legally abolished can likewise claim legal means which help them to escape a socially underprivileged position.

(c) Members of particular groups who previously counted as merely 'tolerated' minorities without special status can, in cases in which a legal community confers a special legal status on certain religious communities, for instance, also demand this for themselves.

(d) Members of cultural-ethical communities can call for special means to promote their culture by appealing to the means publicly made available to other communities, even if there is no established right to such means.

(e) Members of cultural communities can point out that applicable law prevents them from enjoying general rights (for example, the free exercise of religion) or a form of equal respect because their cultural practices are incompatible with the conventional assumptions on which the law was based up to that point. Members of certain religious communities, in particular, have demanded exceptions from laws governing trading hours, from the duty to wear a helmet or uniform and from the duty to attend particular forms of instruction at school or to attend school at all. Sometimes such cases reach the point where not only exceptions from valid legal norms are demanded but fundamental revisions of these norms.

(f) Certain groups who are particularly affected by political decisions or are in danger of being ignored claim special rights of political representation, extending even to qualified veto rights.

(g) Groups with a high degree of cultural cohesion, also geographically, can claim rights to cultural-political autonomy within a federal system by citing the disadvantage they suffer within the larger society and possibly a special history of discrimination. In certain cases – indigenous cultures, for example – this autonomy can be very extensive.

(h) Finally, groups that regard themselves as nations and enjoy a large degree of institutional independence can demand their independence, though only on the grounds that this is strongly desired by their members, that it would not give rise to any new injustices and, most importantly, that it is required by justice in order to overcome an existing condition of heteronomy and domination.

This list of claims to recognition (which could be extended and differentiated further) shows, first, that different understandings of the 'recognition of difference' are involved. In some cases this recognition is explicitly intended to ensure that difference henceforth plays no role in the law or in society, in others the intention is that it should not only be positively recognised but should also be preserved or promoted.[17] Second, all of these claims are in essence raised in the name of justice and of material equality, even if the relevant viewpoints are very specific. Third, in virtually all of these cases the struggle for legal or political recognition is also a struggle for an ethical-cultural revaluation of particular social convictions or practices. Yet, as a general rule, controversy at this level also serves to place in question particular standards of justice and its primary goal is not to demand particular cultural esteem.[18]

Without being able to present the theory of multicultural justice that would be necessary here to address these questions in detail, I would like to point out in general terms the need to distinguish between the *definition of a group* (whether in ethnic term or in terms of other criteria) and the *justification of its claims* (for example, to certain rights). These two things are largely independent. For, although justification must be viewed in relational terms with reference to particular groups, the key point is nevertheless that considerations of justice should be decisive and not other considerations, such as the objective value of a community or its social value (as socially enriching) or its subjective value for a person. The latter, in particular, may indeed play a role when one group calls for equal treatment relative to another so that it has equal chances to develop and exercise its own identity; nonetheless, the decisive issue is not how 'deep' this identity is but instead the comparison with other groups and whether the specific claim can be justified in reciprocal and general terms.[19] It is also immaterial in this context whether the identity of a group is regarded as 'evolved', 'chosen' or 'constructed'; for, aside from the fact that all of these can hold simultaneously in a certain sense because no identity is simply 'given' and none is entirely 'made', this is largely irrelevant for the normative issue of whether a group's claims are justified. No clear normative conclusions can be drawn from 'ontological' views concerning 'constructed' versus 'constitutive' identities.[20] This is all

17. On this, see Nickel, *Gleichheit und Differenz in der vielfältigen Republik*.
18. On this, see the controversy between Nancy Fraser and Axel Honneth in *Redistribution or Recognition?* See also Forst, 'First Things First'.
19. See also Pogge, 'Group Rights and Ethnicity'.
20. On this, see the discussion of constructivism (and its limits) in Benhabib, *The Claims of Culture*, ch. 1.

the more so in virtue of the fact that one must anticipate a plurality of possible forms of identities (ranging from 'chosen'[21] to 'hereditary'[22]) and a plurality of interpretations of one and the same group identity.

Furthermore, we must distinguish between the *basis of normative claims* to particular rights and *how these rights are exercised*. This concerns the much-discussed issue of 'collective rights'.[23] The basis of all of the normative claims relevant here is the *individual* right to justification which, in particular contexts, may support specific legal forms of recognition of ethical identity provided that the latter can be justified on the basis of reciprocal and general reasons (in one of the above-mentioned categories). The exercise of these rights, by contrast, can take an *individual* form, for example when persons as members of particular groups have the right to drive motorcycles without a crash helmet or to be exempt from schooling. This is a case of an 'individual group right'. However, it may also be the case that particular rights which individuals are accorded as members of a *collectivity*, for example, certain autonomy rights or rights of representation, can be exercised *collectively*. This does not yet exhaust the range of variation of 'group-specific' or 'group-differentiated' rights;[24] yet it should be apparent that an individualistic foundation is indeed compatible with a collective exercise of such rights.

This is important not only for a general conception of multicultural justice but also for the issue of 'multicultural toleration'. For especially cases (e) and (g), that is, claims to special legal regulations and cultural autonomy, give rise to a multiplicity of ethical-political conflicts. These illustrate the fact that a conception of justice is required not only in order to *grant* group-specific rights but also in order to *limit* them – a conception of justice, however, which does *not* draw these limits based on a particular ethical doctrine but in such a way that they cannot be reciprocally and generally rejected. And here the conception of justice founded on the right to justification again proves to be the appropriate one because it serves to legitimate specific rights for particular groups, while at the same time highlighting the rights of potentially affected individuals or minorities *within* such groups. For it already holds on recursive grounds that a group which demands specific rights by

21. See, for example, Waters, *Ethnic Options*.   22. Especially Sandel, 'Religious Liberty'.

23. For sceptical positions on collective rights, see Kukathas, 'Are There Any Cultural Rights?', Tamir, 'Against Collective Rights' and Hartney, 'Some Confusions Concerning Collective Rights'; for positive positions, see Bauböck, 'Liberal Justifications for Ethnic Group Rights', Parekh, *Rethinking Multiculturalism*, 213–19 and Frank, *Probleme einer interkulturellen Gerechtigkeitstheorie*, ch. 3.

24. In the terminology of Kymlicka, *Multicultural Citizenship*, ch. 3.

appeal to this basic right cannot withhold this very same right from any of its members (or from anyone else for that matter). Their group-specific rights come to an end at the point where individuals within the group claim the right to curtail the autonomy of their members in inadmissible ways, though this argument does not rely on the ethical autonomy of the individuals as a value or a condition of the 'good life' but appeals to their right to justification, and thus to their moral autonomy. This represents a pivotal difference, for even an ethical-liberal argument is in danger of making particular demarcations, so that one 'comprehensive doctrine' is merely opposed to another.

4. This is shown by a brief discussion of the most important theory in this area, that of Will Kymlicka. His central argument combines an ethical-liberal understanding of autonomy with an emphasis on the importance of a culture for promoting this autonomy. From a liberal perspective, there are two essential preconditions for a good life: 'The first is that we lead our life from the inside, in accordance with our beliefs about what gives value to life ... The second precondition is that we be free to question those beliefs, to examine them in light of whatever information, examples, and arguments our culture can provide.'[25] The context of this autonomy, according to Kymlicka, is provided by a person's *societal culture*, which provides the *context of choice* within which significant ethical options become accessible. From a liberal perspective, therefore, membership in one's own 'societal culture' – for which institutionally structured and established 'national cultures' provide the model (76, 80) – is a major good worthy of protection. Kymlicka differentiates two groups: first, national minorities who possess a virtually complete societal culture of their own so that they can claim extensive autonomy rights, and, second, ethnic immigrants who, while still identifying (in part) with the societal culture they have left, also regard themselves as members of the new, comprehensive societal culture and can only claim 'polyethnic' rights which enable them to accommodate themselves to the surrounding culture without having to abandon their identity.

Kymlicka's approach poses a range of problems concerning, for example, the strong emphasis on rights to a 'national' culture of one's own, the sharp dichotomy between national minorities and ethnic immigrant groups[26] and

---

25. Kymlicka, *Multicultural Citizenship*, 81 (the following page references are to this book).
26. Compare the critiques of Carens, 'Liberalism and Culture' and Young, 'A Multicultural Continuum.

the vague connection between culture as a context of autonomy or choice and the question of identity; for only the emphasis on culture as a 'context of identity' could explain why one's *own* culture must represent the context of choice.[27]

However, the most important problem for the issue of toleration, which Kymlicka discusses at length, is the particularity and non-generalisability of the ethical-liberal foundations of his theory. This becomes apparent where Kymlicka rightly emphasises, with reference to group-specific rights, that they have the meaning of *external protections*, not of *internal restrictions* (35–44), that is, that although the integrity of groups (the model being national minorities, especially indigenous peoples) must be protected against external influences, they nevertheless do not have the right to restrict the autonomy of their members, for instance by establishing a theocratic system within their ethical-cultural community (37).

The decisive issue, normatively speaking, is how Kymlicka draws the limits of liberal toleration. For, insofar as the argument for cultural rights as well as for their limits rests on the above-mentioned liberal conception of the preconditions of the good life, it is clear that many cultures would quickly run up against these limits because they do not share such a conception of the good. As already noted (see §31.2 above), one can reasonably disagree over whether only a life which is 'autonomously chosen' can be a good life. Thus, Kymlicka's theory faces the problem not only that his justification of the limits of toleration cannot be generalised, but also that these limits would be very narrow, for a whole range of ethical communities would have to be examined to determine whether they appropriately communicate this conception of autonomy to their members. The result could be a perfectionist liberal system of promoting autonomy which would leave scarcely any independent cultural rights intact.

Since autonomy and toleration are 'two sides of the same coin' (158) for Kymlicka, he does in fact think that the limits of toleration are reached *in principle* where the liberal conception of autonomy is not realised in a cultural community. Given his view that only those persons who embrace the liberal conception of ethical autonomy can themselves be tolerant, 'illiberal' groups cannot show tolerance in principle and thus cannot demand toleration either. However, in Kymlicka's view this does not mean that the liberal state could always legitimately impose its conceptions of autonomy on illiberal groups;

27. On this criticism, see Forst, 'Foundations of a Theory of Multicultural Justice' and the answer of Kymlicka, 'Do We Need a Liberal Theory of Minority Rights?', 87 n. 6, who modifies his approach accordingly and places greater emphasis on the identity component.

on the contrary, a form of *permission toleration* is called for towards them, whose point consists in working towards the 'liberalisation' of the groups in question (168).[28]

The most serious defect of this argument is its ambiguous use of the term 'liberal' (or 'illiberal'). From an ethical perspective, a community already appears to be 'illiberal' if its members have a conception of life which does not include the idea of an autonomous 'choice' of options about how to live that is permanently open to revision. In this way, they fail to satisfy one of the essential preconditions of the good life and it would in principle be the task of the perfectionist liberal state to lead them to the good. However, Kymlicka does not emphasise this perfectionist argument (although it is a logical implication of his theory), but points out, in what is intended to be a moral sense, that people with such an attitude to life will also be incapable of themselves showing tolerance towards other conceptions of life. This inference is not valid, however, as was shown above (§32.2). For someone could accept such a non-liberal view of life for himself and also believe that it is the only correct one, all things considered, while nevertheless accepting on *moral* grounds the threshold of reciprocity and generality which enables him to exercise tolerance – both within his ethical community and within the overall society. One need not be an 'ethical liberal' in order to be able to show tolerance. More importantly, when it comes to conflicts, the ethical liberal seems to be in the unenviable position of merely opposing one comprehensive ethical doctrine to another.[29]

Therefore, the stipulation that ethical communities should not impose any inadmissible 'internal restrictions', and should in this sense be 'liberal', must be grounded in a different way, in terms not of a particular liberal

28. A similar line of argument can be found in Raz, 'Multiculturalism'. According to Raz, liberalism calls for respect for cultural communities because such communities offer their members meaningful options which they can use autonomously to shape their lives (177). A certain form of respect toleration, and even of (limited) mutual appreciation, is required between these autonomy-fostering groups (181). However, when communities do not contain any 'true values' (183), that is, when they are not only oppressive (184) but also 'inferior without being oppressive' (185), a different, no longer principled but pragmatic, permission toleration is called for which aims at transformation. See also Raz, *The Morality of Freedom*, 423–4, on the right to assimilate communities which are 'inferior' in liberal eyes and the toleration that becomes necessary when the associated costs are too high. Not unlike Kymlicka, this involves the problem that the demand that the right to justification be respected is not distinguished sufficiently clearly from the further issue of imposing a liberal 'form of life'. The ethical-liberal approaches of Fitzmaurice, 'Autonomy as a Good' and Oberdiek, *Tolerance* are beset with similar problems.

29. See also the criticisms of Kukathas, 'Are There Any Cultural Rights?' and Parekh, 'Dilemmas of a Multicultural Theory of Citizenship'. However, I do not share their alternative proposals.

ethical conception of life but of the right to justification, which also provides the normative basis for group-specific rights and can never be overruled by collective rights. Then placing 'liberal' limits on toleration does not mean imposing a specific way of life but instead means calling for a basic form of moral respect which is absolutely binding and is itself claimed by the groups who demand special rights. Reflexively speaking, the basis on which respect for a group is called for must also hold within such a group. Insofar as practices exist within a group which, for example, expose underage children to extremely painful procedures,[30] deny them medical treatment, marry them off without their consent, or structure their education in such a way that they have a markedly worse starting position by comparison with other citizens in a society, the limits of toleration are reached – *not*, to reiterate, because this would violate necessary preconditions of the *good life* but because this violates the *dignity* of morally autonomous beings who have a right to justification. And given this right, mutilations, endangerments of health, gross restrictions on liberty and being consigned to an inferior social position cannot be justified. The goal of preserving a special culture can never overrule basic claims and rights of this kind.[31] The problem, therefore, is not *advocating* or *practising* a non-liberal way of life but *imposing* such a way of life – though also, conversely, imposing a liberal way of life.[32]

Therefore, my thesis is that, in order to be able to make decisions in matters of toleration, one must be able to distinguish between an ethical and a moral condemnation of a cultural practice or community. One can regard certain conceptions of life as one-sided or wrong from a 'liberal'

30. Thus, the distinction between moral and ethical valuations that I propose would lead not to practices of clitoredectomy, for example, being tolerated as an 'ethical practice', as Benhabib, 'On Reconciliation and Respect, Justice and the Good Life', 106–7, fears, but to the possibility of rejecting this practice on unambiguous moral grounds.

31. In response to my analogous criticism in 'Foundations of a Theory of Multicultural Justice', Kymlicka, 'Do We Need a Theory of Minority Rights?', 84–5, argues that the conception of moral autonomy is no less rejectable than his conception of personal autonomy. However, in arguing thus, he does not make clear whether he thinks that the principle of reciprocal-general justification is rejectable on reasonable grounds or that it is often rejected as an empirical matter. To demonstrate the former claim it is not enough to object that this conception of morality does not adequately thematise certain moral domains (duties towards animals, for example, though also towards children). For, aside from the fact that obligations towards children as addressees of justification are included (and those towards animals can be included), the issue up for debate here is whether this principle can be reasonably rejected in the context of multicultural justice, not in general as a principle of morality. And there it is unclear what a 'paternalistic' counter-argument of a group would look like which rejects the right to justification while at the same time demanding political-legal respect and claiming that its community is one supported by its members. On this, see Forst, 'The Basic Right to Justification'.

32. I will return to what this means in the context of education in §38.

ethical perspective, but this does not provide a sufficient moral argument for rejecting them. The latter must rest on foundations which are not reciprocally and generally rejectable, for only then can the predicate 'illiberal' have a moral sense. A range of liberal theories make the mistake of not recognising this difference[33] – a difference that calls for a deontological explanation. Without doubt, appealing for respect for the right to justification and to individual moral autonomy entails 'costs' for ethical communities that reject this; but the decisive point here is to base one's argument not on a controversial conception of the 'good' – for the autonomous life is not necessarily the same thing as the good life – but on moral principles. The central issue in this regard is not *freedom for the good* but *freedom from external domination*, and in particular, on the one hand, from external domination of the *group by others* and, on the other – as the other side of the coin – from domination *within a group*. Thus, as in Kymlicka, the reason for group-specific rights also becomes the reason for setting limits to them, but in a completely different, non-ethically particular, way. Justice, not the good, defines the limits. An ethical-cultural community cannot demand legal respect if it does not simultaneously respect the basic rights of its members. But as a general lesson of the discourse of toleration, one should be aware of what one is appealing to when one criticises such practices, namely, universal rights or a particular form of life.

5. From a perspective inspired by Herder's cultural pluralism, however, neither ethical-liberal nor moral-political justifications of multicultural justice are sufficient for recognising the *inherent value* of cultural communities because these justifications regard this value only as a contribution to the development and promotion of individual autonomy or identity. This has led Charles Taylor to defend the thesis that, in contrast to a 'politics of universal dignity', only a 'politics of difference' is capable of recognising 'the unique identity of this individual or group'.[34] In contrast to a homogenising, 'difference-blind' politics of strict equal treatment, it permits political measures designed 'to maintain and cherish distinctness, not just now but forever'; in this way, the specific identity of a group should 'never be lost' (40).

Taylor explicates the political-normative distinction he is driving at in terms of the special status of the Canadian province of Québec which, in

---

33. This also holds for critics of multiculturalism like Moller Okin, *Is Multiculturalism Bad for Women*, 24, who, in her justified condemnation of immoral practices, especially towards women and girls, defends the 'fundamentals of liberalism' against explicitly non-liberal cultures. Gutmann, 'The Challenge of Multiculturalism in Political Ethics', by contrast, implies a – in structural terms, deontological – differentiation in the normative domain.

34. Taylor, 'The Politics of Recognition', 38 (subsequent page references in the text).

order to safeguard its collective Franco-Canadian identity, has passed laws which place certain restrictions on the basic rights of its citizens. Thus, one of these laws forbids francophones and immigrants from sending their children to English-language schools (52). According to Taylor, only through these kinds of restrictions can the good of the survival of a culture be secured, contrary to a strict neutralist liberalism – though he also thinks that this should not go so far as to annul fundamental rights to which all Canadians are entitled according to the Canadian Charter of Rights (59).

However, the difficulties of this position can be seen from a tension in its argument for a politics which respects 'difference' and diversity. On the one hand, it appeals to the fact that the larger Canadian society accords a province the status of a distinct society but, on the other, this status means that a 'politics of the good' is advocated *within* this province which subordinates differences among its citizens – in particular, in the case of immigrants – to this political-ethical goal and can show respect for their difference only through the allegedly 'difference-blind' fundamental rights of the Charter. The identity of non-francophone citizens of Québec is specified as a minority identity and their rights as Canadian citizens to send their children to an anglophone school are restricted. Hence, the reverse side of this 'politics of difference' is a politics of imposing a majority identity, and this by a community which, within Canada, itself confronts a majority with a different cultural identity. This entails – also taking into account the historical background – an entitlement to a special cultural status. Yet this status neither requires an appeal to the 'eternal value' of this culture,[35] which is open to the suspicion of essentialism,[36] nor is it compatible with an impairment of the fundamental rights of citizens who are not just citizens of this specific province but also of the Canadian political community *as a whole*.

Contrary to what Taylor believes, a sufficiently differentiated 'politics of equal dignity' does not require any perspective on the good which transcends the rights and interests of present-day citizens in order to recognise ethical-cultural differences. In a specific, historical-political situation, it is sufficient to assess the constellation of the respective groups and their claims in accordance with the principle of justification and to examine where supposedly 'neutral' or general legal regulations openly or covertly put one group at a disadvantage vis-à-vis others. As explained, this can lead to the justification of special rights, though they must always be examined to ensure that they do

35. Habermas, 'Struggles for Recognition in the Democratic Constitutional State', 130, criticises this as 'preservation of species by administrative means'.
36. See Benhabib, *Kulturelle Vielfalt und demokratische Gleichheit*, 39–46.

not give rise to new, unjustifiable privileges. As long as a legally recognised ethical-cultural community equipped with specific rights remains within the general federation, it does not constitute a political community in its own right but must protect the standards of civic equality with a view to the society as a whole.

Therefore, the respect conception of toleration does not imply a model of 'formal equality' (see above §2.3) which proceeds from a strict separation between the private and the public and seeks to 'privatise' ethical differences and exclude them entirely from the public domain and from valid law.[37] Based on the principle of justification, its counterpart is a model of 'qualitative equality' according to which the citizens recognise one another as persons endowed with equal rights in the legal and political sense, who nevertheless are ethically different; moreover, they recognise that ethical differences can give rise to particular legal forms of recognition – provided that this can be justified in reciprocal and general terms with reference to equal chances to form or to preserve ethical-cultural identities. No specific form of identity is prescribed in this way. The notion that observing religious obligations, such as wearing a head covering or praying at specified times, should be regarded as a mere individual 'preference' that belongs 'in the private domain' and provides no reasons for showing special deference in the public domain should be avoided no less than the converse assumption that only those practices should be respected that are justifiable, for example by appeal to the objective value of religion recognised by a majority of the citizens.[38] The arguments for respecting specific individual liberty rights as well as for group-specific rights rely neither on a liberal nor on a traditionalist conception of identity; here, too, the theory of toleration remains agnostic. The key issue in justifying such rights, just as in placing limits on them, is that the claims of the individual groups who are in conflict with the convictions of the majority should be treated just as fairly and impartially[39] as those of individuals within such groups.[40] The right to justification, in the sense of a call for *freedom from inadmissible restrictions of autonomy and thus as freedom*

---

37. See the critique of liberal toleration in McClure, 'Difference, Diversity, and the Limits of Toleration' and Galeotti, 'Citizenship and Equality'.

38. Sandel, 'Religious Liberty', rightly criticises the former assumption, from which he incorrectly draws the latter conclusion. The right to the free exercise of religion protects a person's religious identity on the basis of a generally required respect for the ethical identity of person, not of special esteem for religion.

39. Compare the emphasis placed on 'evenhandedness' by Carens, *Culture, Citizenship, and Community*, ch. 6. See also Tully, *Strange Multiplicity*, who emphasises the necessity of intercultural dialogue.

40. See Benhabib, *Kulturelle Vielfalt und demokratische Gleichheit*, ch. 2.

from domination, holds in each case: on the side of the political community in general, on the side of particular groups within this political community and on the side of the members of such groups, who do not lose their status as free and equal citizens who enjoy constitutional protections.

In view of these problems, calling for *more than toleration* in the context of multicultural conflicts over recognition is understandable, given certain conceptions of toleration, but it is nevertheless wrong[41] – specifically, calling for a 'thick' or 'positive' form of respect for ethical-cultural identities that goes beyond merely 'putting up with', both in the legal dimension and the dimension of cultural values. It is understandable because the respect called for clearly goes beyond what is implied by a permission conception or a liberal form of toleration based on a strict opposition between 'private' and 'public'; yet it is nevertheless false because what is called for is not more than toleration but the *correct form of toleration*, i.e. a toleration justified in terms of a concept of justice properly understood. If tolerance is a basic virtue of justice, then it has its foundation and limits in the latter – in which case an attitude that does not sufficiently recognise ethical-cultural groups is as unjust as it is insufficiently tolerant. But this holds only as long as the resolve to treat such a group justly continues to be allied with an objection to their convictions and practices; should this component fall away because one has come to value this group, then it is no longer a question of toleration, though it remains one of justice.[42] Hence, the virtue of justice is more inclusive and fundamental than that of tolerance. However, calling for 'more than toleration' can also mean requiring that citizens should abandon their objections, and this may be well-founded (in the case of racist prejudices, for example; see above §1.2). Yet, in many cases which do not involve simple prejudices, this can amount to nothing more than an ethical-political ideal. Thus, it remains important to point out that, in cases of persistent mutual objections, toleration and justice are intimately interconnected, in which case not 'more than toleration', but the correct form of toleration in the guise of respect is required, and this does not imply mutual esteem. When it comes to toleration, legal recognition must be differentiated from ethical-cultural esteem.

6. This discussion points once again to the need to transpose the principle of justification, and the associated demand for toleration, into the political

---

41. See, for example, Minow, 'Putting Up and Putting Down' and Deveaux, *Cultural Pluralism and Dilemmas of Justice*, ch. 2. By contrast, for a more differentiated account (albeit also one with a perfectionist component), see McClain, 'Toleration, Autonomy, and Governmental Promotion of Good Lives'.

42. The argument of Galeotti, 'Citizenship and Equality', in support of public 'acceptance' or 'recognition' of cultural difference remains ambiguous regarding this point.

context. Only institutions of *democratic discursive justification* are able to bring to light the plurality of different perspectives within a political community and to give voice to minorities, minorities within the society as a whole and minorities within these minorities. This is in the first instance a demand of justice. Yet here, too, the tolerance of the citizens as lawmakers and as addressees of the law fulfils an important function. For, in institution-alised and non-institutionalised procedures and discourse arenas, positions of groups clash which not only may be diametrically opposed but may also speak different 'ethical languages'. Although the latter are not untranslatable, they give rise to translation problems, especially as – not to be excessively idealistic – these positions are bound up with political interests. Still more, not only is such an ethical-political plurality encountered in public discus-sions, but there is in addition the problem that certain positions are *not* represented because they are formulated in a language which is not heard or is even suppressed – possibly both by the established standards of 'pub-lic reason' and by those who purport to speak 'for this group'. I can only allude to this complex problem area here in general terms without being able to explain and outline in detail what the resulting critical theory of democracy would have to look like.[43] The central issue is the need for a democratic public sphere and specific democratic procedures in which the conflicts over and struggles for toleration – or, in more general terms, for formal and material justice – can be conducted, so that one could speak of a 'reflexive' democracy which seeks to institutionalise the controversies over a better democratic elaboration of the social basic structure itself.[44] Such *public processes of justification* turn on the fact that the criteria of justification of reciprocity and generality are brought to bear through corresponding institutional and deliberative as well as contestational arrangements. This raises the question, on the one hand, concerning institutional details such as chances to participate, perhaps specific forms of group representation or even certain veto rights, but it also calls to mind, on the other hand, the limits of such institutional designs, which necessarily presuppose a certain readiness to justify and fairness on the part of the citizens. The lack of such willingness cannot be offset entirely by institutions.

43. For a more detailed discussion, see Forst, *Contexts of Justice*, ch. 3.3, and 'The Rule of Reasons'. See also the important approaches, especially in feminist theory of democracy, of Young, *Justice and the Politics of Difference*; Fraser, 'Rethinking the Public Sphere'; Benhabib, *Kulturelle Vielfalt und demokratische Gleichheit*; Williams, *Voice, Trust and Memory*; Deveaux, *Cultural Pluralism and Dilemmas of Justice*, chs. 5 and 6.
44. On this, see Habermas, *Between Facts and Norms*, chs. 7 and 8, and Schmalz-Bruns, *Reflexive Demokratie*.

Indispensable for such a political form of public justification, in which struggles are conducted not only over the legitimate forms of cooperation within culturally pluralistic societies but also over the justice of the shared social basic structure as such – and in which the latter is politically 'constructed' – is a *fundamental conception of justice* (see §25).[45] It involves in the first place the guarantee of fair political and social conditions of participation in political processes from which no group of citizens may be excluded. In concrete terms, this implies granting citizenship rights to permanent residents in a political community independently of ethnic criteria; and in cases where there are large, integrated ethical-cultural communities who speak different languages, this may call for corresponding regulations governing official multilingualism – as a measure of integration, not of exclusion. For the pivotal issue remains participation in inclusive discourses of reciprocal justification. Therefore, the right to justification must be guaranteed both formally and materially, and hence also all of the basic rights, not just the political ones, justifiable on this basis. Thus, broad inclusion must be guaranteed which enables groups to generate the communicative power they need in order to vindicate their claims. If this is impossible for structural reasons, the requirement that minorities should accept existing social relations becomes repressive.

Toleration is important in the context of fundamental justice at three points:

First, it is important where the citizens must be willing to justify their claims and politically relevant positions in public political terms and, in the process, should exhibit responsiveness in particular to the positions that conflict with their own. They do not have to accept the latter or view them as correct; however, if they want to prevail over these positions when it comes to basic matters of justice, they must be able to offer reciprocally and generally non-rejectable reasons.[46] Precisely with regard to such questions, basking in the support of the majority of the citizens and simply outvoting the minorities is *not* sufficient. This brings the *second* reason for the importance of discursive democratic toleration into play: recognising this – that is, recognising that the threshold of reciprocity and generality forbids one, in fundamental questions, from arranging the shared basic structure

---

45. See Forst, *The Right to Justification*, Pt 2.
46. As already noted, the criteria of justification hold in the strict sense only for basic questions of justice; in other questions, majority decisions arrived at through legitimate procedures are legitimate.

in accordance with one's own, reciprocally and generally rejectable ethical evaluative conceptions even when one happens to be in the majority – is the most important and exacting meaning of the virtue of tolerance in this context. Political institutions which seek to prevent violations of basic rights, through a constitutional jurisdiction for example, can contribute to achieving this goal. Yet, this is to a crucial extent a requirement of virtue addressed to the citizens, and in the first instance to the relevant majority (though in a different sense also to minorities who are equally obliged to provide reciprocal and general justifications). This virtue has a 'price' and presupposes a robust sense of democratic justice. This goes to the heart of the problem of toleration, as will be shown in the discussion of various examples below; for here the citizens must construct the correct relation between reasons for objecting, for accepting and for rejecting.

It must be emphasised that the foregoing holds not only where incompatible ethical positions clash but also where different conceptions of justice come into conflict. However, in such conflicts it is possible, building on the basic right of justification, to arrive at more substantial arguments for justice which ground a series of rights as not reciprocally rejectable and which legitimate a high level of social equality, because the principle of justification accords those members of society who are worst off materially a right of appeal and, regarding certain issues, even of veto.[47] Finally, these stipulations also hold where no non-reasonably rejectable answer can be found to an immediately morally relevant question and a solution must be sought on a different basis without negating the positions of the parties to the conflict. As the debates over abortion and embryo research demonstrate, this in turn places high demands on toleration.

The *third* place where toleration acquires importance from the perspective of the theory of democracy is the (above-mentioned) reflexive demand on the members of a political community to expose the *terms* of the public language which have become established, and their institutions, to critical examination as to whether they are really inclusive or instead exclude certain voices, interests or positions.[48] Here a democratic critique of language and reason is necessary which scrutinises existing 'public reason' with regard to its particularity. In this connection, no reasons should be excluded from political discourse, be they religious or otherwise. The criteria of reciprocity

47. On this, see §31.4 above and *The Right to Justification*, ch. 8.
48. This point is stressed by O'Neill, 'Practices of Toleration', and Bohman, 'Reflexive Toleration in a Deliberative Democracy'.

and generality should not be reified into criteria of exclusion from discourse. They do not require reasons to be characterised a priori as 'secular', though they do call for a *translation* of particular languages into a language which satisfies these criteria (in basic questions of justice).[49] As a consequence, we must distinguish between (a) reasons which should be admitted into public discourses and which may be extremely diverse (also religious ones, for example), for otherwise no meaningful and inclusive discourse and no reflection on objection, acceptance or rejection would be possible, and (b) reasons which are 'good enough' to justify reciprocally and generally binding norms. And nothing need be asserted concerning their nature except that they should not be reciprocally and generally rejectable.

That not only the *exclusions* inherent in political procedures should be exposed to critical scrutiny but also the *inclusions* that can shape a society, including a multicultural one, also belongs to the reflexive component of democratic toleration. For, as the discourse of toleration between power and morality in the first part demonstrated, legitimate criticism in the name of toleration was levelled not only against the various forms of intolerance, but also against forms of 'false' toleration, specifically against a politically 'rationalised' form of toleration which relieved minorities of social pressure through an always limited and precisely calculated, carefully monitored bestowal of liberty while simultaneously disciplining them or, in Foucault's terms, *governing* them. These groups were simultaneously integrated into the political community and partially excluded from it, i.e., they were trapped and stigmatised in a dependent, inferior position. This went hand-in-hand with certain social determinations of identity which were also partially internalised (when this exercise of power was very extensive), although such identities were always marked by a tension between different representations. W. E. B. du Bois (1903) expresses this point when he speaks of 'this double consciousness, this sense of always looking at one's self through the eyes of others, of measuring one's soul by the tape of a world that looks on in amused contempt and pity'.[50] Such a perspective could also hold for groups

49. On the frequently expressed (and to an extent warranted) criticism that certain liberal conceptions of political discourse, in particular that of Rawls, involve a general exclusion of religious positions, I would refer the reader to my discussion of this issue in Forst, *Contexts of Justice*, 94–100 and 121–37. There I also develop a notion of required public 'translation'. The call for purely 'secular' reasons can be found in Audi, *Religious Commitment and Secular Reason*, ch. 4; see also Schmidt, 'Glaubensüberzeugungen und säkulare Gründe'. On the more recent discussion, see also Weithman (ed.), *Religion and Contemporary Liberalism*. Jürgen Habermas has more recently addressed the problem of translation in the relation between religious and secular citizens in *Between Naturalism and Religion*.
50. Du Bois, *The Souls of Black Folk*, 45; on this, see also Sartre's reflections in *Anti-Semite and Jew*.

which are not victims, or are no longer victims, of direct repressions but are 'tolerated' – tolerated, that is, as deviating from the norm but nevertheless as 'tolerable' (as the example of the Jews frequently demonstrated). The primary problem here is not the complete adoption of such a stigmatised identity, since this extreme surrender of one's identity is improbable, but the danger that others henceforth regard those affected only in the light of this stereotype and that this determines the standards in terms of which they are treated.[51] Therefore, the task is to struggle against such stereotypes and for their 'revaluation',[52] to oppose reified imputations of identity and the corresponding disciplining effects.

Wendy Brown, in particular, has pointed out that such processes of the disciplining fixation of identity are also present in contemporary multicultural societies. According to her, the discourse of toleration is inevitably bound up with a differentiation between a 'normal' or 'unmarked'[53] identity and other, 'non-normal' ones, which are supposed to be tolerated and thereby acquire a marginalised status – even more, they are ascribed an identity that is supposed to be explicable in terms of a single root (sexual orientation or ethnic membership, for example) and to define the whole person. Therefore, these identity groups are conceived as mutually exclusive, as deviant and as determining persons in their essence. According to Brown, this represents a form of 'bio-power' (Foucault), a form of the disciplinary exercise of power by stipulating identity which deflects attention away from the real sources of social inequality and renders 'collective deliberation' impossible through artificially induced group antagonisms.[54]

Although this criticism argues for an overly strong conception of the external production of identity, 'deconstructs' existing self-identifications (for example, of ethnic groups) too sweepingly and ascribes the call for group-specific rights too globally to motives of resentment in Nietzsche's sense,[55] it points to a series of very important insights. In the first place, it refers to the fact that toleration is always linked in multifarious ways with the issue of *power*, not only with forms of power that operate in intolerant ways, but also with forms of power that exercise disciplining toleration. The critique is directed against phenomena of rationalisation both of power and of government, and it calls for the practice of 'desubjugation', which

---

51. On this, see the analysis in Laden, *Reasonably Radical*, 144–51.
52. Fraser, 'From Redistribution to Recognition?', 27–31, speaks of the need for 'deconstructive transformation'.
53. See Brown, 'Reflections on Tolerance in the Age of Identity', 110–11. See also her book *Regulating Aversion*.
54. *Ibid.* 115.   55. Brown, *States of Injury*, 66–76.

Foucault characterises in terms of the resolve 'not to want to be governed', of the demand for justifying reasons.[56] The point of these kinds of critique is to call for liberties which are not bound up with a dominant and stigmatising setting of norms in accordance with the permission conception, which is the primary focus of Brown's criticism, but which permit a plurality of ethical modes of valuation and presuppose a shared, deliberative justification of norms. The higher-level norm of non-domination, which finds expression in the right to justification of morally autonomous beings, is levelled not only against legal and social forms of unfreedom but also against one-sided stipulations of identity and sociocultural devaluations. The point is to prevent such devaluations from becoming the foundation of positive law and of social institutions; the more far-reaching call for a deconstruction of ethical objection judgements (as opposed to the call for a critique of prejudices) is not warranted. The stigmatisation of identities from a dominant perspective must be combated, but not the existence of identities which differentiate themselves from one another. Such critical struggles remain struggles for and against toleration: for a reciprocally justified toleration and against a permission toleration. Absolutely essential in this regard is that conflicts over toleration and recognition are not only conflicts over the recognition of particular identities (in the legal-political or the social sense) but also conflicts over codifications of identity – thus against false, disciplining fixations of identity and forms of reifying recognition.[57]

Furthermore, Brown's critique points to the fact that conflicts over legal and cultural recognition often have a material, economic component and that there is a danger of this component receding into the background.[58] Here, too, a form of critique and of public discussion is called for which differentiates between the different dimensions of exclusion and inclusion.

These reflections on the complex relation between power and morality in their modern, rationalised form lead to the call for a *critical theory of existing relations of toleration*, in the sense of the real social relations of justification and of existing identity relations. A *critique of relations of justification* presupposes an analysis of the distribution of justificatory power among the relevant groups, an analysis of the language of 'public reason', possible exclusions,

---

56. Thus, also Foucault, 'What Is Critique?', 45–7.
57. However, group-specific rights are always confronted with the 'dilemma of difference' according to which particular rights accorded to groups for the purposes of equalising their material status entrench established differences and identities. See Minow, *Making all the Difference*.
58. On this, see the emphatic position of Barry, *Culture and Equality*, especially chs. 7 and 8. The legal, cultural and socio-economic dimensions of recognition are discussed in depth in Fraser and Honneth, *Redistribution or Recognition?*

etc. And a critique of the dimension of identity calls for an analysis of the corresponding assumptions concerning identity, their roots and their disciplining and stigmatising functions. In this way, false, ideological relations of toleration can be criticised and transformed in the direction of a reciprocally justifiable form of toleration among citizens endowed with equal rights. This does not exclude a transformation towards a condition 'beyond toleration', though this would seem to represent a utopia which itself in turn potentially involves a repressive negation of difference. The point of the toleration to be striven for is to transform a problematic form of toleration towards persons or groups into a fundamental respect for these persons or groups, while simultaneously demonstrating toleration of their convictions or practices, not necessarily to foster mutual esteem.

In pursuing this goal, the aim of a critical theory of toleration is to uncover the *repressive toleration* inherent in the call on minorities to tolerate unjust social conditions and the *disciplining toleration* which consists in 'productive' rather than 'repressive' exclusionary inclusions.[59] Such a critical theory accords equal importance to the concept of justice and to the concept of power in its reflections. The critique of repressive or disciplining toleration does not presuppose any absolute normative point of reference located beyond a 'false' – either 'manipulated and indoctrinated' (Marcuse)[60] or slavish, reactive (Brown)[61] – consciousness. Instead it connects up with the multifarious demands for justification raised in social conflicts and with the awareness of having a right to such a 'desubjugation' (Foucault),[62] namely, the right to critique and to justification.

The following will present a number of analyses of toleration conflicts designed to show what this means in concrete terms and to what extent such a perspective follows from the historical and systematic reflections of my study.

§38 Toleration conflicts

1. The following analyses select a couple of paradigmatic examples from among the multiplicity of conflicts over issues of toleration encountered in many different countries. 'Toleration conflict' in this context refers not

---

59. See Foucault's critique of the 'repression hypothesis' in *The History of Sexuality*, vol. I: *An Introduction*.
60. Marcuse, 'Repressive Tolerance', 90.   61. Brown, *States of Injury*, 70–4.
62. As a critique of disciplining toleration, this presupposes a critique of oneself as a subject of power, though also the freedom (and the power) to accomplish this. On this dimension of critique and such a conception of freedom, see Foucault, 'What Is Critique?' and 'What Is Enlightenment?'.

only to conflicts in which one party demands toleration, and corresponding legal reforms, from the others but also to *conflicts over toleration*, that
is, conflicts in which different conceptions of toleration clash and lead to
sharply contrasting practical consequences. In the first place, these are the
permission conception as opposed to the respect conception, thus a primarily hierarchical and vertical conception of toleration as opposed to an
intersubjective, horizontal one – where the permission conception appears
no longer in its classical, absolutist form but in a democratic variant. Thus,
here conflicts come to the fore within the rich and complex understanding
of toleration reconstructed in the first part of the book and they exhibit
the ongoing relevance of the conceptions and justifications of toleration
which have developed over the course of history. The history of toleration,
therefore, leads to a present marked by toleration in conflict.

In this context, it will not only become apparent that what facilitates a
normative critique and the privileging of a specific conception of toleration
here is not the concept of toleration as such but a corresponding understanding of justice and justification. It should also become clear in what
way the criteria of reciprocity and generality make possible *substantial* judgements concerning which of the positions in a toleration conflict is the more
justifiable.

Finally, these analyses are also intended to show which forms of repressive
and disciplining toleration are encountered in the present. Hence, toleration,
as is characteristic of its history, remains situated within a contemporary field
of tension of power and morality.

2. The first example is the so-called 'crucifix ruling' of the German Federal
Constitutional Court of May 1995, one of the most controversial decisions
of the Court, which has prompted impassioned protests extending even to
threats of civil obedience.[63] First, a brief account of the case.

In the Federal Republic of Germany, the regulation of issues concerning school education falls within the jurisdiction of the federal states, each
of which has issued corresponding school regulations. Bavaria's 'Elementary Schools Act' (of 1983) contained the following paragraph (§13(1)): 'The

---

63. The commonly used expression 'crucifix ruling' (*Kruzifix-Urteil*) is incorrect because the case
    concerned not only crucifixes but also crosses in classrooms and, in addition, it was not a ruling
    but a decision. On the diverse reactions, see the documentation and discussions in Pappert
    (ed.), *Den Nerv getroffen*; Streithofen (ed.), *Das Kruzifixurteil*; Hollerbach *et al.* (ed.), *Das Kreuz im
    Widerspruch*. The political-legal aspects are analysed in Brugger and Huster (eds.), *Der Streit um
    das Kreuz in der Schule*; Denninger, 'Der Einzelne und das allgemeine Gesetz'; Frankenberg, *Die
    Verfassung der Republik*, ch. 7; and, for a very detailed account, Huster, *Die ethische Neutralität des
    Staates*, ch. 3.

school shall support those having parental power in the religious upbringing of children. School prayer, school services and school worship are possibilities for such support. In every classroom a cross shall be affixed. Teachers and pupils have a duty to respect the religious feelings of all.' Accordingly, a cross or, more often, a crucifix was hung in every classroom; in the case in question, it was (initially) placed directly beside the blackboard and it had a total height of 80 cm with a 60 cm figure of Christ.

When the first of their three daughters was enrolled in school in 1986, a couple who were rearing their children according to the anthroposophical teaching of Rudolf Steiner objected to the crucifix in the classroom. According to the couple, it violated their constitutional right to freedom of conscience and religion (in accordance with Article 4(1) of the German Basic Law) and the principle of state neutrality in religious matters (as underlined by the Federal Constitutional Court in other decisions). Not only were their children as a result unavoidably exposed to the influences of the Christian faith not shared by their parents, but being confronted on a daily basis with the 'suffering male body' was inflicting 'psychological damage' on the children.

Since a mutually satisfying compromise could not be reached between the parents and the school authorities, an action was brought first before the Administrative Court in Regensburg and finally before the Bavarian Higher Administrative Court. Both courts rejected the claim that the crucifix ordinance represented a violation of the basic right to freedom of conscience and religion and of the principle of state neutrality in religious matters. The reasons cited were the following:

The Basic Law grants jurisdiction over the school system to the states and within the framework of the Basic Law they have the right and a certain level of discretion to influence the religious and ethical character of the public schools. Article 131(2) of the Bavarian Constitution (of 1946) states, for example, that: 'The paramount educational goals are reverence for God, respect for religious persuasion and the dignity of man, self-control, the recognition of and readiness to undertake responsibility, helpfulness, receptiveness to everything which is true, good and beautiful, as well as a sense of responsibility for the natural world and the environment.' (The latter clause was added in 1984.) And Article 135 (as amended in a 1968 referendum to abolish denominational schools) states: 'State elementary schools shall be open to all children of school age. In them children shall be taught and educated according to the principles of the Christian creed.' Therefore, since the task of the school is not only to impart knowledge and cognitive skills, but also to educate 'heart and character' and to transmit certain values, it is not required to be fully neutral in religious matters.[64] It must not be missionary, according to the Bavarian court, and it must respect all religious convictions as well as those of non-religious persons; it cannot force anyone to participate in specific religious practices or to adopt specific beliefs. This is required by the 'precept of toleration' (which in this context is understood as a precept addressed to the state).[65] However, Christian values, understood as general 'cultural and educational values', may constitute part of ethical education. Following this argument, the courts concluded that placing the cross or crucifix on the wall is constitutional; there was no impermissible discrimination against adherents of different faiths or 'promotion of a particular Christian confession'.[66]

To this corresponded a further argument according to which the cross is not exclusively a symbol for a particular faith or denomination but represents the 'Christian-Occidental' tradition and culture which is a *common* ethical and political heritage:

> Representations of the cross in the form in question here are not an expression of the profession of a denominationally bound faith, any more than is ecumenical school prayer. They are an essential part of the general Christian-Occidental tradition and a common heritage of the Christian-Occidental culture. To require that a non-Christian or someone with different ethical beliefs of whatever kind should tolerate these representations, even assuming he or she rejects them, under the aspect of the obligation to respect the beliefs of others, does not represent an imposition, given that the precept of tolerance is also binding for him or her.[67]

Finally, the administrative courts presented an important argument concerning religious liberty according to which this constitutional right has two sides or two modes of exercise, one negative and one positive. The negative right consists in a freedom from religion, i.e., in not being forced to adopt a certain faith, whether by the state or by others. In this sense, however, it also has a positive side; for this liberty opens up a space of freedom to live according to one's own convictions, whether religious or otherwise. However, this is not quite the positive side which the courts had in mind. According to them, 'positive freedom of religion' means having the right to

---

64. Verdict of the Higher Administrative Court, Munich, 3 June 1991 (7 CE 91.1014), in *Neue Zeitschrift für Verwaltungsrecht* 1991, 1099–1101, here at 1100.
65. *Ibid.*   66. *Ibid.* 1101.   67. *Ibid.*

express one's convictions publicly – for instance, through certain symbols – and also being permitted to practise one's faith. This distinction led the courts to interpret the crucifix case as a conflict between the *negative* rights of a minority to be free from religion and not to be confronted with religious symbols, on the one hand, and the *positive* right of a majority to profess its religious beliefs in public and to express them with certain symbols, such as the cross or the crucifix, on the other. Thus, the Higher Administrative Court concluded: 'Seeking the requisite balance with due regard to the precept of tolerance, therefore, the claim of the plaintiffs founded on their basic right to negative religious liberty must yield to the state's right of school organisation which here is in harmony with the positive freedom of religion of the other pupils and parents.'[68] This view received emphatic support from the position taken by the Institute for Law on Church–State Relations of the Dioceses of Germany in the submission of the German Bishops' Conference to the proceedings before the Federal Constitutional Court. It stated that, although minorities have a claim to respect and toleration, they cannot claim that their negative religious freedom should be accorded 'absolute primacy' so that 'no room would be left over for the exercise of positive religious freedom' by the majority. The Bavarian state government also pointed out that the right to 'impose' one's own philosophy of life reached its limits in the positive religious freedom of third parties and 'the concomitant precept of tolerance'.[69]

It is remarkable how clearly the permission conception of toleration is articulated in these arguments. For, although the 'precept of tolerance' holds for the state, for the majority and for minorities, it means something different in each case. On the side of the state, which is substantially identified with the will of the majority, it means that minorities are not forced to adopt certain religious beliefs or practices and that no form of indoctrination or proselytisation takes place; toleration on the part of the minorities, by contrast, means that they have to recognise the right of the majority to display their religious symbols in public, and even to display them in public schools *by legal decree*. In the opinion of the courts, corresponding to the positive right of religion is the right of the state to uphold the culturally Christian character of schools within the framework of the constitution.

68. *Ibid.*
69. Both opinions are quoted from the account in the decision of the Federal Constitutional Court, 16 May 1995 (1 BvR 1087/91), in *Europäische Grundrechte-Zeitschrift* 22, 1995, 359–69. English translation: www.utexas.edu/law/academics/centers/transnational/work_new/german/case.php?id=615 (accessed March 2011).

The minority is 'tolerated' as a different group that deviates from the norm, whereas it must 'accept' the primacy of the majority in the legal and cultural domain. The minority is thereby cast in a negative light in several respects: as a group, which

> first, contests the generally accepted basic ethical values of the society or its symbols,

> second, is fixated on an 'extremely exaggerated subjectivism'[70] and seeks to suppress the positive religious freedom of the majority by absolutising its purely negative claims, and thus

> shows itself to be completely intolerant towards the religious feelings of the majority, and to be fundamentally hostile to religion. The minority is not only stigmatised as 'abnormal';[71] it is also accused of challenging the foundations of the state and of seeking to impose its own anti-religious and idiosyncratic intolerance under the guise of toleration. Thus, given that the precept of toleration also holds for them, it is 'not unreasonable that the plaintiffs cannot succeed in imposing their philosophy of life'.[72]

Typically for a permission conception of toleration, the toleration which the majority must exhibit in order to 'grant' minorities certain liberties is not only clearly distinguished from the toleration which the minorities must muster in the face of this hegemony. The foundation of the state itself is also connected back to the religious-ethical convictions of the majority, albeit, it is claimed, in an interdenominational sense. Accordingly, this toleration is far removed from a form of equal legal respect in basic institutional questions, such as those of the establishment of an educational system; its only requirement is freedom from religious coercion, specifically a negative freedom for minorities and a positive freedom for the majority. This fails to satisfy the criteria of reciprocity and generality in several respects, not to mention the fact that this construction is manifestly contradictory, for the cross or crucifix is interpreted in one place as a mere symbol of universal cultural values (such as toleration) but in another as an expression of a particular creed.

The case finally reached the Federal Constitutional Court which overturned the decisions of the Bavarian administrative courts and found that

70. Thus, the High Administrative Court, Munich, 1101.
71. So also Denninger, 'Der Einzelne und das allgemeine Gesetz', 429, in his critique of this conception of toleration which relegates the minority 'to the grey, peripheral area of legal inferiority'.
72. Higher Administrative Court, Munich, 1101.

affixing crosses or crucifixes in the classrooms of public compulsory schools by state decree is unconstitutional. The court conceded that there is no general negative right not to be confronted with religious symbols in public; however, it found that there is an essential difference between an expression of a belief having a public character and its being prescribed as legally binding. The right to religious freedom does not involve any entitlement to express a religious conviction 'with state support'. 'On the contrary, the freedom of religion of Art. 4(1) Basic Law implies the principle of state neutrality towards the various religions and confessions.'[73] Thus, a state cannot oblige pupils to learn 'under the cross'.

Furthermore, the court recognised the contradiction in the interpretation of the precept of toleration by the administrative courts mentioned above, because the latter require non-Christians to recognise the cross in the classroom (a) as an expression of the positive religious freedom of the Christian majority within the population and (b) as an expression of general 'Christian-Occidental values', and thus precisely not in the sense of (a). The Federal Constitutional Court did not even find a reasonable disagreement among these interpretations but concluded that the cross is the symbol of Christian belief, indeed 'its symbol of faith as such' and, even more, a symbol of the 'missionary dissemination' of Christianity.[74] Hence, neither can it be regarded as a purely ethical-political symbol nor can the claim that representations of the cross have a substantial influence on schoolchildren be dismissed. It has a clear 'appellant character', according to the court.

In so arguing, the Federal Constitutional Court did not deny that the state which is obliged to be neutral 'cannot divest itself of the culturally conveyed, historically rooted values, convictions and attitudes on which the cohesion of society is based and the carrying out of its own tasks also depends. The Christian faith and the Christian churches have in this connection, however one may today wish to assess their heritage, been of overwhelmingly decisive force.'[75] Christian values are in this sense part of the political culture, according to the court, and the state legislators may take 'Christian references' into consideration in organising the public schools (for example, when it comes to voluntary school prayer or religious instruction as a subject). When crosses are affixed in the classroom, however, the religious-ethical even-handedness required by the Basic Law (in spite of its appeal to God) in the organisation of schools is no longer assured. According to this reasoning, Christianity may be regarded as a cultural factor but not as a privileged religion in the schools.

---

73. Thus, the Federal Constitutional Court, 363.   74. *Ibid.* 364.   75. *Ibid.* 367.

Finally, the Constitutional Court takes issue with the lower courts' interpretation of the relation between negative and positive religious freedom. All citizens are entitled to a positive religious freedom, not just the majority, and this conflict cannot be resolved in accordance with the majority principle 'while taking account of the precept of tolerance'.

Although the meaning of the 'precept of tolerance' is not sufficiently clarified in this context, this underscores, in virtue of the court's emphasis on neutrality in matters of principle, the extent to which the criterion of *reciprocity* must be heeded in such questions and accordingly how the claims of minorities to equal rights or against certain privileges of a particular group, be it the majority, are justified (see §30.3 above on reciprocity of contents). According to this view, the minorities are not merely to be 'tolerated' in a minimal legal sense but must be recognised as citizens endowed with equal rights to whom one owes reciprocally and generally non-rejectable reasons in basic questions of justice. It follows that such reasons must appeal to principles, such as the right to religious freedom, or to universal, politically and normatively essential values, and the supporters of the crucifix or cross attempt to do this, too. In this case, however, they were not successful. The form of toleration corresponding to the permission conception which emerges from the judgments of the lower courts is instead *repressive* in that it calls on the minority to accept its legally unequal status and to tolerate the privilege of the majority. Moreover, this conception of toleration is also a *disciplining* conception in virtue of the fact that the identity of those who raise objections and demand reasons is presented as purely negative, deviant, hostile to religion and idiosyncratic. Finally, the fact that this minority itself is represented as intolerant shows once again how controversial the concept is, and how urgently needed is a normative analysis capable of rebutting this accusation.

The decision of the Federal Constitutional Court was passed by a vote of five to three. The dissenting opinions reiterated that the right to negative religious freedom is not some 'superior fundamental right' and that it is not a 'right to prevent religion'. The minority is urged to show tolerance; the precept of tolerance 'obliges' them 'to put up with the presence of crosses'.[76]

That the decision was extremely hostile to religion and, in addition, that it challenged the foundations of the German political community was a widely shared conviction, as was the view that it was a 'judgment of intolerance'.[77]

76. *Ibid.* 368.
77. See the reactions collected in the publications on this case (cited in n. 63 above).

The cross, by contrast, is a 'sign of tolerance', so it was claimed. The refusal to implement the decision was proclaimed by various sides and parallels were even drawn between the decision and the (unsuccessful) attempt by the National Socialists (in 1941) to banish crosses from the classrooms. At the risk of a renewed confrontation, the Bavarian government issued a decree that continues to provide for placing a cross or crucifix in the classroom but contains provisions for how objections should be dealt with when they arise. Disputes have already arisen over what could constitute 'serious and intelligible reasons' for an objection, and especially over whether atheistic convictions constitute such reasons.[78] Not only do the conflicts over equal rights persist, but so, too, do those over the exact meaning of toleration: permission or respect?

3. Conflicts such as these not only show how vital the permission conception of toleration and how controversial the general concept remain. The emphasis on the Christian character of the political community also reveals a contemporary variant of *Locke's fear* (which, to reiterate, is to be found not only in Locke but throughout the entire discourse of toleration, though it plays a special role in Locke): the fear that an excessive, 'neutralising' challenge to the ethical-religious values of the majority of the citizens could undermine the foundations of the state, especially if those making the challenge are 'unbelievers'. The concern is that no form of secular morality or positive law could provide the same kind of assurance of respect for the law as the fear of God provides (contrary to Bayle's conjecture in his famous paradox, which represents the antithesis to 'Locke's fear'). However, this argument is not generally presented in this form in a modern social context. Instead it is reformulated as the claim that the essence of democracy is misunderstood when it is assumed to be founded exclusively on abstract principles of justice; on the contrary, a democratic state is seen as the product of highly specific historical developments and as being constructed on the basis of particular values which may have a pronounced religious character. Although, with increasing social plurality, these values must be augmented and cannot be made the immediate foundation of the legitimacy of the state, nevertheless their 'substance' must not be destroyed. Liberal states, in particular – especially those which lack a rich democratic tradition – require 'inner regulatory forces of liberty' which secure their 'homogeneity', a concrete form of ethical life, in the words of Ernst-Wolfgang Böckenförde who puts the problem as

---

78. The Bavarian Higher Administrative Court expressed doubts about this and was corrected by the Federal Administrative Court (6 c 18.98) in an April 1999 decision. In essence, however, the Bavarian regulation was approved in the process.

follows: 'the liberal, secularized state is nourished by presuppositions that it cannot itself guarantee'.[79] And he goes on to ask 'whether the secularized, temporal state must not also, in the final analysis, live by the inner impulses and bonding forces imparted by the religious faith of its citizens'.

This idea has two aspects. On the one hand, it means that the state would lose its liberal character if it actively undertook to create these presuppositions, and religion would as a result be functionalised.[80] On the other hand, according to Böckenförde, the best possible promotion of these values (and of the corresponding religious communities) is an important task of the state in preserving its normative substance, its 'relative homogeneity'.[81] On this second reading, a policy of neutrality such as the one expressed in the crucifix decision of the Constitutional Court is in danger of undermining this substance because the latter can be preserved only if the reproduction of the dominant cultural form of life and its values is not disrupted.[82] For that would involve the danger of a *dialectic of toleration* in the sense that insistence on a form of civic toleration founded on the principle of justification (and corresponding legal regulations) could degenerate into ethical-political disorientation, into a loss of values and ultimately into intolerance, because the foundations of the liberal state would no longer be accepted and the political community would dissolve into islands of values alienated from (or even in conflict with) each other. Principled toleration would in this way destroy its own cultural foundations.

This leads back, as can be seen from many places in the discourse of toleration, not only to 'Locke's fear' but also to the relation between ethics, law, politics and morality in its many facets, and ultimately to the process of the autonomisation and 'rationalisation' of politics and morality vis-à-vis ethical-religious values. Against this backdrop, it becomes apparent that replacing principled respect toleration with permission toleration legitimated by the aforementioned argument entails the danger of a *second dialectic of toleration*. For the appeal to the need to preserve the ethical-cultural and religious foundations of a democratic state could lead to the justification of a series

---

79. Böckenförde, 'The Rise of the State as a Process of Secularisation', 46; the following quotation is on 44f.
80. Thus, Böckenförde, 'Religion im säkularen Staat'.
81. Thus, Böckenförde, 'Die Zukunft politischer Autonomie', 111.
82. This is not to imply that this is Böckenförde's position with regard to the crucifix; see, for example, '"Kopftuchstreit" auf dem richtigen Weg?', 726, on the difference between the crucifix case and the (still to be discussed) headscarf case. However, this is a possible implication of the application of his thought, as Würtenberger, 'Zu den Voraussetzungen des freiheitlichen, säkularen Staates', shows with reference to Böckenförde.

of regulations that discriminate against minorities in the name of toleration. The protection of toleration thus understood would lead to intolerance. This would enable a series of ethical objection judgements (and prejudices) to find their way into the definition of what is tolerable, as classically occurred in the case of the 'godless', for example. In other words, the failure to distinguish between the ethical standards of evaluation of a majority and generally share-able norms is advocated on the basis of higher-level considerations, which, however, in the process clearly take sides. But this would be to draw the wrong lesson from the discourse of toleration and the 'secularisation' of the *democratic* state.

4. The question of what the integration of a democratic society requires and where the limits of toleration lie is a constant source of conflicts. One place where these conflicts are especially prone to break out is in the education system, for there the question of the indispensable ethical-political values which should be lived out and passed on has, as it were, programmatic significance.

This is also shown by the so-called 'headscarf cases'. The first to be discussed here, a German case which exhibits important parallels to the controversy over the crucifix, is that of a Muslim trainee teacher who insisted on religious grounds on covering her hair with a headscarf during classroom instruction. Although she was admitted to teacher training, after taking her examination she was refused admission to the teaching service. In justification, it was cited that she lacked the personal presuppositions for a teaching position because, in virtue of her insistence on wearing the headscarf, she violated the official duty of neutrality which requires teachers to forgo religious symbols with which the pupils could not avoid contact and which potentially exercise a powerful influence on them. In addition, it was argued that wearing the headscarf should be regarded not only as a religious but also as a political symbol, and that in this context it conveys the meaning of 'cultural demarcation' and of the suppression of women within Islam and does not serve the goal of social integration and toleration. Someone who wants and is obliged to educate others in toleration must also provide a living example of it – which is incompatible with wearing this symbol.[83]

The trainee teacher proceeded to bring a court case. She argued that toleration enjoined respect for her Muslim identity, and the latter required her to wear the headscarf, though, in so arguing, she did not dispute that

83. See the arguments of the educational authorities cited in the judgment of the Higher Administrative Court of Baden-Württemberg (in Mannheim), 26 June 2001 (VGH 4 s 1439/00); in *Neue Juristische Wochenschrift*, 2001, 2899–2905.

there are alternative approaches to an Islamic identity which do not imply this duty. For her, however, this was a religious duty and an expression of identity and not at all a matter of political conviction. Thus refusing her a teaching position violated her basic right to religious freedom, especially as it placed her at a disadvantage by comparison with colleagues who were permitted to wear a cross or a Jewish kippah. As regards the pupils, she saw no danger of a violation of the duty of neutrality, provided that this was not interpreted in a strictly laicist fashion which forbids the wearing of any religious symbols whatsoever. Moreover, no conflicts had arisen during her training period.

The Higher Administrative Court of Baden-Württemberg concluded in its judgment, which was upheld by the Federal Administrative Court,[84] that the refusal of a teaching position did in fact violate the constitutional right to religious freedom of the candidate, but that it was nevertheless legitimate because it was outweighed in a balancing of conflicting legal interests by other 'legally protected goods', such as the constitutionally grounded principle of neutrality and the basic rights of negative and positive freedom of religion of the parents and pupils. Thus, wearing a headscarf violated the duty of neutrality of teachers in the public service because such a form of symbolism did not allow the schoolchildren any room for evasion. In so arguing, the court applied elements of the crucifix ruling to this case, even though it concerned not an officially affixed symbol but one worn by a person. Nevertheless, it argued that here, as in the crucifix case, the protection of the religious freedom of the schoolchildren potentially exposed to an excessively strong influence (or the protection of the freedom of religion of their parents) had priority, even though no intent to indoctrinate or to question the equality of men and women, for example, could be ascribed to the applicant. 'Even the sight' of the headscarf sufficed to induce effects incompatible with the duty of neutrality.[85] Anticipating protests by parents, the court argued that this entailed the danger of serious adverse effects on the 'the schools' ability to function'.[86]

This conflict shows how the neutrality principle and the idea of toleration are applied in this judgment in order to place limits on toleration. Contrary to the requirement, in principle accepted by all concerned, that one must carefully examine the individual case when it comes to such problems, a religious symbol is assessed in general as a symbol of intolerance independently

84. As outlined in the judgment of the Federal Administrative Court, 4 July 2002 (BverwG 2 c 21.01).
85. Higher Administrative Court, Mannheim, 2903.   86. *Ibid.* 2900.

of the person involved and her views. Once again, two toleration claims clash: on the one hand, the demand by the members of a minority, not that their identity should be valued in an ethical sense, but that they should be respected as equals and that their *equal* rights should not be restricted; and, on the other, the call on them to be tolerant and to recognise that their expression of their identity represents a violation of religious basic rights and of functional requirements of institutions.

There can be no doubt in this connection that teachers in public schools must be held to exacting standards when it comes to religious restraint and hence that a certain duty of neutrality exists. Yet, in each individual case it must be demonstrable whether this duty has been violated, and in none of the judgments is the candidate ascribed a motive or behaviour of this kind; a blanket condemnation of a symbol, by contrast, would be legitimate only if there could be no doubt that it would exercise an unjustifiable influence or if it stood for a grossly immoral conviction or practice. But neither was the case, for an influence on schoolchildren that exceeded certain limits was not demonstrated but merely assumed in a general way. Although a moral component is present in the guise of the reference to the fact that the headscarf can be a symbol of the suppression of girls and women, the emphasis here is on 'can be'; for, according to the testimony of many Muslim women, it cannot be generally assumed that women who wear a headscarf on religious grounds have been forced to do so or that they thereby inadvertently legitimate coercion against others. Neither is it appropriate to point out that wearing it is not a 'genuine' unavoidable, religious duty because other ways of professing their Islamic faith are open to women, since this does not do justice to what it means to feel a religious duty. It is not the task of courts or of school authorities to decide what constitutes an authentic religious duty and what does not.

Finally, the difference between the crucifix case and this one must also be emphasised. For in one case the issue was whether a community which represents one part of the citizenry has the right to the mandatory display of their particular religious symbols in public institutions by law, whereas in the other it was a question of the limits of the exercise of the right to religious freedom of a person who performs an official task. The central issue in both cases is respect for ethical-religious difference, and the comparison between the symbolic value of the crucifix on the walls of Bavarian classrooms and the headscarf of a Muslim teacher does not support the conclusion that here we are dealing with two analogous violations of state neutrality or of civic toleration; viewed critically, it is instead a matter of two forms of the disrespect of the particular identities of minorities which contradict what is customary.

Based on such considerations, the Administrative Court in Lüneburg concluded in a similar case that the constitutional right to religious freedom of a teacher was violated when, based on sweeping negative evaluations, but without concrete evidence and without regard to her person, she was refused a position on the grounds that she disturbed the 'school peace'. The precept of toleration holds for all concerned, the court argued, including parents and pupils, 'so that they cannot, contrary to the principle of toleration, demand certain basic positions – for instance, Christian or . . . non-denominational positions – for their children and the pedagogical work in the school'.[87] On the contrary, it is beneficial for the school if the pluralism in society is reflected within it in mutual toleration. Böckenförde agrees with this in his positive discussion of the judgment:

> A pluralistic society as such is vital and viable not when the different convictions and attitudes of the people are levelled down and excluded as far as possible, but when people have such convictions and attitudes, cherish them but also champion them and on this basis encounter others with respect.[88]

He argues against a blanket presumption of 'fundamentalism' and regards the disadvantages suffered by certain – in this case, Islamic – religious convictions and their 'unusual' dress codes as a matter of discrimination.[89]

5. Without doubt, the fact that such conflicts involve a moral condemnation of the treatment of girls and women in Muslim communities represents a special problem. This became especially apparent in the French *affaire du foulard*, which concerned not the wearing of a headscarf by a Muslim teacher but the wearing of the traditional head covering by Muslim girls, who were

---

87. Judgement of the Administrative Court, Lüneburg, 16 November 2000 (1 A 98/00), in *Neue Juristische Wochenschrift*, 2000, 767–71, here 768 (the judgment was nullified in 2002 by the Higher Administrative Court, Lüneburg). On 24 September 2003, the Federal Constitutional Court (2 BvR 1436/02: English translation: www.bverfg.de/entscheidungen/ rs20030924_2bvr143602en.html (accessed 19 September 2011)) upheld the constitutional appeal of the trainee teacher in Baden-Württemberg. In its judgment, it cites a range of the above-mentioned reasons; nevertheless, it ascribes the state legislators (though not public authorities or courts) a wide authority to stipulate a variety of admissible religious references in schools (which were lacking in this case). After this ambivalent ruling, a number of new state laws were enacted regulating religious dress codes, and further legal conflicts ensued.
88. Böckenförde, '"Kopftuchstreit" auf dem richtigen Weg?', 727.   89. *Ibid.* 727, 726.

forbidden to do so by the school administration. Without being able to go into the affair in detail here, it is significant how republican arguments, which insist on a laicist separation between *bourgeois* and *citoyen*, and feminist arguments, which criticise the subjugation of girls in Islamic communities, combined to support the prohibition. As regards the former, it must be emphasised that this sharp separation between private-ethical and public-political identity in cases like this, in which certain 'conspicuous symbols' belong to an identity, is too strict and leads to unfair treatment of nonconforming minorities, whose concerns, moreover, are dismissed as 'insignificant' and 'belonging in the private domain'[90] – a problematic legacy of the *adiaphora* doctrine. The second point, however, is fundamental. For, according to the principle of justification, practices of an ethical-cultural community which infringe upon people's basic rights cannot be justified – and they cannot be tolerated either. Here, if necessary, the citizenry as a whole must speak out in support of a *minority within the minority* which is subordinate – in this case, under-age girls – wherever such practices exist. This is difficult to achieve in practice because it calls for extensive controlling and interventionary mechanisms which may entail a range of undesirable paternalistic side-effects. However, the proposal to draw such limits of toleration first in the *symbolic* domain by placing the wearing of the hijab under general suspicion not only misses the problem of *real* suppression. It incorrectly infers from the fact that some girls *might* be forced to wear a head covering that the latter *is* a symbol of an oppressive practice as such – just as, from the fact that some children are forced to attend a denominational school, one cannot draw the general conclusion that such schools are part of a coercive practice. In this way, an ambiguous symbol is lent a negative moral interpretation which is in danger of disrespecting ethical-religious identities. This represents a further, very familiar dialectic of toleration: the attempt to combat intolerance itself becomes a form of intolerance.

Cases like this reveal how difficult it is, especially in educational matters, to trace the boundary between showing consideration for the particular identity of minorities and showing consideration for the precarious social position of minorities within such minorities. For the basic rights of the latter, as explained in §37, are not placed in question by group-specific rights: the community affected also has a duty of justification towards them. Therefore, religious duties must be respected, but not the exercise of religious

90. See the exhaustive analysis in Galeotti, 'Citizenship and Equality'.

force or the withholding of rights and opportunities to which the citizens of a political community are entitled in principle.[91]

6. Questions concerning compulsory school attendance and education also lead to hotly debated toleration conflicts in other countries, in particular in the United States, where a large number of extremely diverse cultural groups exist in a highly pluralistic education system. I would like to mention two (almost classic) examples of such conflicts which are instructive.

The first concerns the famous case *State of Wisconsin* v. *Jonas Yoder et al.* in which the American Supreme Court decided in 1972 that parents belonging to the Amish religious community are entitled, based on their right to the free exercise of religion, to withdraw their children from the public schools after the eighth grade. The Amish are a community whose roots extend back to the sixteenth-century Anabaptist movement, which, as we have seen, suffered extreme persecution; they represent a sub-community which broke away from the Swiss Anabaptists in the seventeenth century, and during the eighteenth and nineteenth centuries emigrated to the United States, where Amish people reside in different states, though primarily in Pennsylvania. Their lifestyle is shaped by an 'Old Order' which forbids the use of modern technology and prescribes an agrarian form of life governed by strict religious regulations. The gender roles are organised on a traditional, patriarchal model and transgressions against the regulations governing day-to-day life, such as using rubber wheels, wearing jewellery or other violations of the uniform dress code, are punished with sanctions extending to social excommunication in a kind of theocratic regime. The Amish recognise the state and pay taxes; the state, in turn, has exempted the Amish from a series of civic obligations (for instance, in the social security system) and granted them certain rights to maintain their form of life on their lands.

The partial exemption from the duty of school attendance was justified by the Amish not only on the grounds that the basic knowledge acquired until the eighth grade was sufficient for integrating the young people into their form of life, but also on the grounds that exposure to worldly influences and temptations, which is regarded as typical for the corresponding higher grades, is deleterious for the reproduction of this community. The abridged

91. Thus, the Federal Administrative Court concluded that the educational responsibilities of the state must take a back seat to the basic right to religious freedom when participating in coeducational physical education would plunge a Muslim girl into a religious and moral conflict. This was expressly presented as an exception in the sense of a qualitative reinforcement of protection of fundamental rights and of respect for religious identity, not as a partial annulment of this protection. Federal Administrative Court, judgment of 25 August 1993 (6 c 8/91), in *Neue Zeitschrift für Verwaltungsrecht* 1994, 578–81.

education, they argued, was sufficient to be able to read the Bible and to be 'good farmers and citizens' (or housewives); moreover, the spiritual welfare of the children would otherwise be jeopardised because they would become estranged from their community in which alone they could flourish.[92] On the other hand, nobody is compelled to be baptised (at eighteen) against his or her will and to remain a member of the community.

The Supreme Court under Chief Justice Burger accepted this line of argument. It stressed that the specificity of the case resulted from the unique situation of the Amish as a religious community with a long-standing tradition which had succeeded in maintaining itself and its form of life over time without incurring violations of the law. Therefore, the legitimacy of this particular religious community and its form of life is beyond doubt, according to Burger; it must be tolerated because it does not interfere with any rights of others: 'A way of life that is odd or even erratic but interferes with no rights or interests of others is not to be condemned because it is different.'[93]

Furthermore, the court held that it must in fact be assumed that the worldly influences of the school on children of a corresponding age pose a 'very real threat' to the religious way of life of the Amish, since values and attitudes are favoured in school which are incompatible with the traditional conceptions of life.[94]

Finally, the court addressed the argument that a general education is necessary not only in order to educate good citizens but also to train independent persons who are capable of being successful in society. The decisive point here is how the two communities concerned, the ethical-cultural community of the Amish and the larger society, are related to each other. According to Burger, both integration objectives should be pursued, but in such a way that the primary integration for Amish children is integration into the 'separated agrarian community that is the keystone of the Amish faith'.[95] This is why the restriction on schooling is justified and is mandated by the right of religious freedom. The integration into the surrounding society is assured not only by the fact that the Amish community is incorporated into the society in a relatively conflict-free way; there is, in addition, a real possibility of some members leaving this community. The question of whether their abridged education leaves these individuals with insufficient opportunities must be

92. *Wisconsin* v. *Yoder* (406 US 205; 1972), 209–13.   93. *Ibid.* 224.
94. *Ibid.* 218. The following examples were cited: competitive spirit, intellectual and scientific pursuits, orientation to worldly success, but also 'social life with other students' (211).
95. *Ibid.* 222.

answered in the negative: 'There is no specific evidence . . . that upon leaving the Amish community Amish children, with their practical agricultural training and habits of industry and self-reliance, would become burdens on society because of educational shortcomings.'[96] The Amish 'virtues' would also find 'ready markets' in the larger society.

But this reveals the problem with the ruling. However justified it is in emphasising that respect for equal opportunities to reproduce forms of life may in certain cases ground legal exemptions and special arrangements, and however important the reference to the high degree of closure of the Amish community is, the clear priority accorded 'small' integration over 'large' integration, in which the chances of such persons becoming full citizens in the larger society is at stake, is no less problematic. The guiding idea here is *not* the liberal one that the good life presupposes a choice between equally feasible options or that it is possible only within a 'liberal' culture, *nor* is it the republican idea that shared political duties have priority. The guiding idea is instead that group-specific rights for communities like the Amish must not give rise to a situation in which their members, because they have pursued fundamentally different educational paths, have far fewer opportunities in cases in which they want to or are forced to leave this community (where the latter scenario is not unrealistic in the light of the strict excommunication rules). The normative point of reference is not the good life, free choice or the quality of the *citoyen*; the point is instead *equality of opportunity*, restrictions on which are especially in need of justification. The decisive issue is not, as Justice Burger assumed, whether the members of the Amish community with their capabilities could find some place in the larger society without becoming a burden on it, but whether they would be condemned to a small number of subordinate places in that society. From this perspective, the question of whether a complete school education is necessary to ensure equality of opportunity is important and must be answered in the affirmative, otherwise there is the danger that a legitimate recognition of a 'partial' citizenship[97] can turn into a confinement within this partialness even when the individuals in question leave the community. Then those who were excluded from this primary community would suffer a second exclusion, now from the larger community into which they would only be partially assimilated.

96. *Ibid.* 224.
97. On this concept, see Spinner, *The Boundaries of Citizenship*, 88–108; see also Macedo, 'Liberal Civic Education and Religious Fundamentalism', 489, and the critique of Barry, *Culture and Equality*, 243.

Here, however, we encounter a dilemma which cannot be easily resolved in one direction or the other. For the danger of a twofold exclusion should not lead us to the opposite conclusion that such communities – indigenous communities are another example – should be forced to bring the education of their children completely into line with the social mainstream. For that would also give rise to tendencies towards exclusion and colonisation. What is important is that the balance between the two competing modes of integration should be maintained and extremes avoided. Based on the right to justification one can call for respect for such distinctive identities, but not for the confinement of under-age members within such structures because members of these groups are also citizens endowed with equal rights.

Instructive in this context is the parallel to another, no less striking case, namely *Mozert* v. *Hawkins County Board of Education* (1987). In this case, it was not a historically and geographically situated and integrated community which was clearly separated from the surrounding society, like the Amish, but a group of 'born-again Christians' in Tennessee who called for certain exceptions for their children from the general school curriculum on the basis of their right to religious freedom. The case is especially important for the problem of toleration because it was toleration in particular, understood as a 'value' to be accepted in a particular form, which was rejected by the parents in the name of toleration. Once again it was a case of an opposition between two mutually exclusive notions of toleration, though one driven to an extreme by the question of what it means to teach or to learn 'toleration' in school.

The parents demanded that their children, who belonged to different age groups, should no longer be instructed using a series of schoolbooks whose contents offended their religious convictions. According to the plaintiff Vicki Frost, who stressed that the Bible was the 'the totality of my beliefs',[98] some of the stories to be found in the books presented the, in her opinion, false theory of evolution, albeit as a theory, but nevertheless as a superior theory to the story of creation. In addition, the 'occult practice' that the exercise of the faculty of imagination can and may go beyond the limitation of biblical authority was taught. In certain stories – 'Pat reads to Jim. Jim cooks. The big book helps Jim. Jim has fun' – the natural relation between the sexes was placed in question and feminist positions were defended (as also argued by the plaintiff Bob Mozert). The schoolchildren were also taught to make independent moral judgements without reference to the Bible; furthermore,

---

98. *Mozert* v. *Hawkins County Board of Education*, 827 F.2 d 1058 (6th Cir. 1987), 1061.

pacifist ideas which the parents rejected were expressed. The most important arguments referred to the issue of religious toleration itself, however; for the plaintiffs argued that their children were made acquainted with a variety of religions and philosophical theories without it being explicitly stated that only the biblical teaching is true:

> Both witnesses testified under cross-examination that the plaintiff parents objected to passages that expose their children to other forms of religion and to the feelings, attitudes and values of other students that contradict the plaintiffs' religious views without a statement that the other views are incorrect and that the plaintiffs' views are the correct ones.[99]

Moreover, through the directive to adopt other perspectives and the presentation of many religions, a false form of toleration was taught, namely, according to Vicki Frost, 'a religious tolerance that all religions are merely different roads to God . . . We cannot be tolerant in that we accept other religious views on an equal basis with ours.'[100] Therefore, the preferred form of toleration in the schoolbooks was, she argued, *intolerant* towards her beliefs. As an example, a passage from *The Diary of Anne Frank* was cited in which Anne reflects on whether an unorthodox faith might be better than no faith at all; but also the depiction of a Catholic Indian community in New Mexico was criticised as promoting Catholicism.[101]

Judge Lively of the United States Court of Appeals rejected this suit on the basis of two arguments. He argued, on the one hand, that one must distinguish in principle between familiarising pupils with values and religions in school and promoting such values and religions; and it had not been shown that the school was guilty of the latter. On the other hand, however, the judge recognised the *valid* kernel of Vicki Frost's toleration objection. For it would in fact be illegitimate if a conception of toleration were taught in the school which was fundamentally relativistic or pluralistic and represented all religions as equally true (or false). But this was not the case, he argued, for the Supreme Court had correctly required that the public schools should convey fundamental democratic values such as those of toleration; however:

> The 'tolerance of divergent . . . religious views' referred to by the Supreme Court is a civil tolerance, not a religious one. It does not require a person to accept any other religion as the equal of the one to

99. *Ibid.* 1062.   100. *Ibid.* 1069.
101. On this, see Gutmann and Thompson, *Democracy and Disagreement*, 63f.

which that person adheres. It merely requires a recognition that in a pluralistic society we must 'live and let live'. If the Hawkins County schools had required the plaintiff students either to believe or say they believe that 'all religions are merely different roads to God', this would be a different case.[102]

But since this was not the case, the judge concluded, the objection of the plaintiffs was unfounded and their further claims that their ethical-religious beliefs had priority over education in the use of one's critical faculties were to be rejected, because this education did not involve the assumption that the Bible cannot provide a legitimate basis for personal judgements. The constitutional right of religious freedom in turn does not imply that one may make one's own convictions concerning the truth the basis of the curriculum.

This conflict involved a complex use of the concept of toleration. On the one hand, the parents rightly criticised a problematic conception of toleration, but in doing so they themselves replaced it with an understanding of education and of the confrontation with other positions which can be characterised as *fundamentalist* because it involves the refusal to relativise one's own claims to religious truth either in the moral or in the epistemic sense as required by the use of practical and theoretical reason. Such a position represents a violation of the criteria of reciprocity and generality for the following reasons:

First, it draws an untenable connection between the familiarisation with certain convictions and practices and promoting them, the implication of which would be to render school instruction virtually impossible.

Second, if every ethical-religious minority had the right to demand exemptions from the obligation to attend school in the case of topics which they viewed as controversial, the idea of general schooling and education would have to be abandoned.

Third, the plaintiffs disputed one of the fundamental preconditions of a democratic political community, namely, the recognition of and the engagement with the positions of others, even if one rejects them. The capacity for 'critical judgement' is indispensable for democratic justification procedures – just as is the recognition of the equality of the sexes.[103]

Finally, these arguments exhibit an amalgamation of faith and knowledge which would lead, for example, to a privileging of 'creationism' in school

---

102. *Mozert* v. *Hawkins County Board of Education*, 1069. See also the discussions in Macedo, 'Liberal Civic Education and Religious Fundamentalism'.
103. This is why Gutmann and Thompson, *Democracy and Disagreement*, 65, reject the plaintiff's claims as a violation of the principle of reciprocity as they understand it.

instruction.[104] However, such an amalgamation of scientific and religious interpretations of the world cannot be justified because it conflicts with the interests of pupils in a reasonable education – which does not mean that religious interpretations of the world are therefore illegitimate: they are just that, *religious* interpretations of the world. Elevating them to the status of truths which can compete with scientific explanatory approaches is a violation of reason.[105]

Therefore, it is not the case that in such conflicts a 'liberal' comprehensive notion of truth and toleration opposes a different conception of truth, reason and respect and that between the two only an *ethical* decision remains possible, so that the 'liberal' standpoint would more or less coercively assimilate the other should it prevail by legal means – which, according to a certain criticism, reveals the true, partisan face of supposedly pluralistic toleration.[106] On the contrary, with this we clearly reach the threshold of reciprocity and generality, the limit of the criteria to which the complaint that this involves an unfair exclusion must *itself* appeal. The key point is that the aforementioned demands cannot be justified in reciprocal terms and they violate basic principles of practical and theoretical reason. They thereby lead to injustices, and primarily to injustices against the children concerned. To object to this kind of fundamentalism is not itself a form of fundamentalism. It does not substitute one particular truth with another – for instance, a pluralistic or an atheistic interpretation of the world – but instead calls for mutual respect.

7. Numerous conflicts in which a range of the viewpoints mentioned feature and in which opinions differ over what toleration requires – mere 'indulgence' or a particular form of legal recognition – also arise outside the education system. From among them I would like to select for discussion the controversy over whether the institution of marriage should also be extended to same-sex couples: is it enough just to 'put up with' such couples, as dictated by the permission conception, or can they demand legal recognition of or equal status for their partnership in accordance with the respect conception, so that refusing such recognition would constitute a form of intolerance?

---

104. In Kansas, for example, the theory of evolution was banned from the curriculum in 1999 (a move which has since been overturned). Many other cases could be cited.

105. Barry, *Culture and Equality*, 247, also rightly emphasises this and criticises half-hearted rejections of such educational claims when they remain confined to 'public' schools. Macedo, 'Liberal Civic Education and Religious Fundamentalism', 476, goes too far when he calls for 'religious' restraint on the part of schools on the issue of evolution versus creation. Scientific theories are not 'comprehensive doctrines'.

106. Thus Stolzenberg, '"He Drew a Circle That Shut Me Out"'; also, albeit with a different valuation, Fish, 'Mission Impossible'.

With the question of the toleration of homosexuality, we broach a problem area which, in the history of (in-)tolerance up to the present day, is marked by the connection between strong religious-ethical condemnation and a range of diverse forms of discrimination (extending to persecution and severe punishments). It will not be possible to address this in detail here. The important point in the present context is that, from a normative perspective, the call for equal legal treatment of same-sex couples in accordance with the criterion of *reciprocity of contents* as well as the criterion of *reciprocity of reasons* (see above §30.3) is justified. It is justified according to the former criterion because it does not involve any claims to rights which are denied to other couples, only a claim to equal rights; and it is justified according to the latter because no reciprocally rejectable ethical or religious arguments are presented, for example regarding the superiority or the special worth of such a particular form of life.

However, each of these justifications is contended in the discussion. Against the former it is objected that it *does* involve the denial of rights to other comparable forms of life, for example a long-term relationship of mutual care between brothers and sisters.[107] More importantly, it is claimed that here equality is demanded by an unequal partnership: a same-sex partnership cannot constitute a marriage or a marriage-like relationship and be recognised as such because it contradicts the usual understanding of marriage, which means a relationship between a man and a woman with the possibility (and for the purpose) of procreation. In justification, however, this latter argument often appeals to a higher truth which is not generally shared, for example to the God-given meaning of sexuality and wedlock.[108] Such ethical convictions can ground *ethical objections* but not *reciprocal and general rejections*. The law which holds equally for all citizens may with good reason protect certain forms of life based on generally shared values; but in an increasingly pluralistic society it cannot perpetuate one-sided ethical, non-shareable evaluative convictions in a discriminatory way.[109] Thus, the

---

107. Spaemann, 'Was nicht des Staates ist'.
108. As Cardinal Meisner, 'Der Bundeskanzler muß das Ehediskriminierungsgesetz aufhalten', argues, for example, in his critique of the law on registered lifetime partnerships which came into force on 1 August 2001 in Germany: 'With this, the policy of the federal government interferes directly in the Christian commitment to marriage and the family in this country by expressly promoting a form of behaviour which, according to the evidence of the Bible, the Occidental-Christian tradition and the teaching of the Church, is in contradiction with the order of creation.' Finnis, 'Law, Morality, and "Sexual Orientation"', presents a similar argument.
109. On this, see the exhaustive constitutional legal discussion in Huster, *Die ethische Neutralität des Staates*, ch. 6.

law has long since ceased to stipulate the 'indissolubility' of marriage, even though this corresponds to the traditional understanding. Therefore, reasons would have to be found which could show in what way extending the understanding of marriage or creating a new marriage-like legal institution would interfere with fundamental rights.

The aforementioned argument concerning discrimination against other 'mutually supportive communities' is not a candidate, because the similarity between communities of brothers and sisters who care for each other and a same-sex partnership is much less pronounced than that between such a partnership and a conventional marriage. Aside from the fact that family communities are already legally regulated, the parallel consists in the fact that an equalisation of status with regard to a legal institution is being demanded, an institution which protects a particular form of life that rests on intimacy, familiarity and loyalty founded on love, as a special kind of 'community of responsibility', which entails a series of negative and positive rights. The point of the aforementioned claim to equal treatment is to treat same-sex partnerships on an equal footing with marriage not just in a positive-legal but also in a symbolic sense, and thereby to document that such partnerships can exhibit the same relevant quality of intimacy and loyalty as heterosexual relationships.[110] For to deny this and argue on this basis for an unequal legal status is a form of discrimination.

Objections against such equal treatment in fact tend to appeal more to the fact that thereby the special 'worth' of marriage and the family – which, according to Article 6 (1) of the German Basic Law, for example, 'shall enjoy the special protection of the state' – would be undermined. But it is not clear how far such an extension of recognition would harm future or existing marriages, for equal status is manifestly not a devaluation but instead an enhancement of the existing institution. Therefore, there can be no fear of either legal or symbolic harm to marriage and the family.[111]

---

110. Sandel, 'Moral Argument and Liberal Toleration', 534, also emphasises this. However, in his view a same-sex partnership must generally exhibit the same virtues as a classical marriage if such partnerships are to be capable of being socially and legally tolerated, which amounts once again to imposing a particular identity on them. On the symbolic significance of the recognition of same-sex marriages, see also Galeotti, 'Toleration as Recognition', and Huster, *Die ethische Neutralität des Staates*, 613.

111. This is also the position taken by the Federal Constitutional Court in its judgment of 17 July 2002 (1 BvF 1/01) on the compatibility of the law on registered lifetime partnerships with the Basic Law. For a synopsis of the decision, see Russell Miller and Volker Röben, 'Constitutional Court Upholds Lifetime Partnership Act', *German Law Journal* 8 (2002): www.germanlawjournal.com/article.php?id=176 (accessed 19 September 2011).

Here it is often objected, however, that such 'marriages' cannot be marriages because in them one of the main functions, if not the essential function, of a marriage cannot be performed, namely, procreation and the rearing of children. This argument is questionable, however, given the large number of marriages in which procreation is either not desired or not possible; from the conjunction of the special protection of marriage and of the family one cannot conclude that only marriages that are families should enjoy protection. Moreover, it is also possible for same-sex couples to have children.

A final important argument connects up with this. The extension of marriage law, were it to include the right to rear children, would saddle the latter with unacceptable burdens, on the one hand, because such couples cannot provide a sufficient guarantee of a stable, identity-reinforcing education, which requires parents of different sexes and, on the other, because of the social exclusionary mechanisms which it can be expected to trigger. However, the latter must be rejected because it treats the existence of social discrimination as a reason for maintaining it. The former, by contrast, is an important objection because it appeals to the legitimate interests of children. This can assume three guises.[112] First, it is argued that such children could be confused in their identity, especially their sexual identity, and in all probability would themselves become homosexual. The latter is an inadequate objection based on a questionable value judgement, however, and the former is an empirical hypothesis in need of corroboration. The available studies, at any rate, do not substantiate it.[113] Second, the greater instability of same-sex relationships is cited as detrimental for children. However, this could be subjected to statistical examination only if the institution of same-sex marriages already existed and even then it would be questionable whether statistical findings should lead to general legal restrictions. Third, the importance of a classical heterosexual assignment of roles is cited as necessary for the development of identity. Here, too, it needs to be carefully examined which assignment of roles is necessary or productive and in what respects same-sex couples are unable to exhibit it – as are the advantages and disadvantages of the associated challenge to conventional role patterns. Mere conjectures or stereotypes do not justify any legal restrictions. In all of this, finally, we must bear in mind the plurality of forms of the family already existing in many societies which have deviated from the 'normal norms' called for here, while nevertheless enjoying legal protection.

112. On this, see Dees, *Trust and Toleration*, 148–50.
113. See Patterson, 'Children of Lesbian and Gay Parents', and Flaks *et al.*, 'Lesbians Choosing Motherhood'.

These considerations support the conclusion that reciprocal and general reasons against legally recognising same-sex marital relationships have yet to be offered. As long as this is the case, it follows that a 'mere toleration' of same-sex partnerships in accordance with the permission conception without equalisation of legal status draws the limits of toleration too narrowly, for it enshrines an ethical objection in law that is not reciprocally and generally sustainable. This is indeed a form of toleration, but an insufficient one, because it does not fulfil the democratic task of impartial justification of fundamental legal rules and defends a majoritarian understanding of law. This toleration not only enshrines ethical values in law; it also condemns the corresponding minorities to a condition of sociocultural, stigmatising 'deviance'. This involves a moment of disciplining permission toleration, whereas the call on those who are tolerated to recognise their inferior legal status involves a repressive moment. Goethe's dictum that toleration is a kind of insult holds for this form of toleration.

The alternative view of toleration in accordance with the respect conception, by contrast, does not require (unlike an esteem conception) that the corresponding forms of life should be regarded as ethically valuable or socially enriching; it only requires that the limits of toleration be drawn in accordance with principles of *justice*. Toleration is in this way grounded in the morally enjoined respect for persons, whose practices and convictions may nevertheless be objected to on ethical grounds. It is once again apparent how complex are the repercussions of the history of toleration, not only as regards the variant of 'Locke's fear' which fears that too extensive toleration could lead to the dissolution of political-moral ethical life, but especially when both sides to a conflict claim to have the correct understanding of toleration and accuse each other of intolerance. And we can also see that the concept of toleration is not sufficient of itself to settle this dispute, though it can be settled by a conception of toleration which defines the objection, acceptance and rejection components in the most defensible way, that is, with the aid of the principle of justification.

8. Let us consider one final conflict of this kind which leads back to one of the original problems concerning the concept of toleration, the *toleration of intolerance*. Based on the foregoing reflections, it is clear where the limits of the toleration of intolerance lie, namely, where (a) a particular community (even if it be the majority) *violates* the right to justification of another community or of persons and where (b) a person or group *denies* other persons or groups this right in principle. These represent two different forms of intolerance which call for different responses, but in neither case is such a

reaction itself a sign of 'intolerance', as asserted by the 'paradox of drawing the limits'. For taking measures against forms of intolerance which imply a violation of the right to justification should not itself be criticised as intolerant; instead it represents a morally legitimate and requisite underscoring of the limits of toleration. Persons or groups who ignore these limits do not have good reasons for complaining that these limits are unjustifiably brought to bear. For then they would have to recognise the principle of justification themselves, and hence that their actions and complaints lack legitimacy.[114]

Whereas violations of the criteria of justification in political procedures must be identified and corrected within these same procedures, within legal supervisory bodies and within the political public sphere, things are different when the fundamental rights of others are forcibly infringed or their legitimacy is rejected in principle. Then it is incumbent upon the citizens and the law to defend these fundamental rights. Where such infringements of rights occur in concrete cases – for example, in cases of physical assault or intimidation employing violent language – a legal intervention is necessary. But when such aggressive views become widespread in a society, toleration as a civic virtue of the citizens is called upon to become 'vigilant' in the sense that these views are exposed to unequivocal moral condemnation in the public arena and in private affairs. A democratic state is reliant upon the citizens actively defending their fundamental rights and those of others and in this sense assuming responsibility for each other. Racist and nationalistic resentments, for example, must be combated where they arise, namely, at the sociocultural level.

However, cases where parties and groups emerge within a democracy which make it their programme to abolish basic rights and democracy itself raise the question concerning 'militant democracy' (see above §27.3): when is it justified to place restrictions on the freedoms of establishment, communication,[115] assembly and association of such parties and groups and their rights to political participation? The aspects of legitimacy and of effectiveness must be distinguished in this regard. In a case in which a party had a clear National Socialist character, for example, and not just as regards its programme, but potentially represented a real threat[116] to the basic rights of the citizens and the foundations of democracy, a prohibition could be

114. See Rawls, *A Theory of Justice*, 190: 'A person's right to complain is limited to violations of principles he acknowledges himself.'
115. The important question of the prohibition of 'hate speech' belongs here; see the comparison between German and American regulations in Brugger, 'Verbot oder Schutz von Haßrede?'
116. Rawls, *A Theory of Justice*, 192, stresses the need for the existence of a real danger.

legitimate.[117] Although a particular form of democracy cannot be protected against autonomous political changes to this form, it can be protected against changes which are designed to restrict or prevent the exercise of political autonomy and which infringe upon basic rights (see above §25). The fundamental democratic justice of the right to justification is not subject to negotiation. A prohibition or other legal restriction is justifiable only as a last resort, however, when other social-political forms of 'militancy' prove to be inadequate, and a series of normatively important aspects must be borne in mind, for example the ramifications for the validity of basic rights in general. Finally, considerations of effectiveness are important, for under certain circumstances prohibitions fail to achieve their intended aims but give rise to unwelcome side effects. Thus, it may make more sense not to enforce the limits of toleration by legal means but in this respect to be 'indulgent' towards what is in principle intolerable on pragmatic grounds, an approach which may have positive, integrative effects.[118]

Against this it might be objected, however, that here, as it were at the margins of the respect conception, it becomes apparent to what extent a permission conception lies at its core after all. For, is it not true that, in the case in question, the supposedly tolerant side 'permits' the supposedly non-tolerable side to enjoy limited freedoms which the permission-granting side can determine as it sees fit? In a certain sense, this is true. The groups in question are granted areas of freedom because the costs of intervening would be too high, though on the condition that certain limits are observed. The key difference from the classical permission conception, however, is that these limits are laid down on the basis of the principle of justification, hence not on arbitrary, merely unilaterally justifiable grounds but on generally demonstrable grounds among persons who respect each other as free and equal. This is why this does not involve a regression to the permission conception but instead a contextual application of the principle of justification, though it should be noted that those who are 'tolerated' in this way do not have any claim to this toleration, which is instead granted to them on the basis of higher-level considerations.

117. See the extremely detailed discussion of this question in the motion of the German Bundestag to prohibit the National Democratic Party of Germany (NPD), drafted by G. Frankenberg and W. Löwer (29 March 2001). This attempts to show, in particular, that the NPD actively opposes fundamental principles of the democratic and liberal constitution of the Federal Republic of Germany and that it is similar in character to National Socialism. For the arguments pro and contra this prohibition, see the discussions in Leggewie and Meier (eds.), *Verbot der NPD oder Mit Rechtsradikalen leben?* The proceedings to ban the NPD were brought to a halt on procedural grounds by the decision of the Federal Constitutional Court of 18 March 2003 (2 BvB 1/01).
118. See Bobbio, 'Tolerance and Truth'; Rawls, *A Theory of Justice*, 192.

Finally, here again it becomes apparent that drawing the limits of tolerance with the aid of the principle of justification does not unmask those who defend such a form of toleration as 'preachers of tolerance' who, following Nietzsche, merely declare that their own partiality is impartiality (see above §29.33). For, although the claim to impartiality is itself a substantive, moral one, it is at the same time a higher-level claim which exposes all definitions of limits to scrutiny in reciprocal and general terms. Without such a foundation, which I have sought to reconstruct as a requirement of practical reason, it would not be possible to make a categorial and normative distinction between a form of intolerance which violates the principle of justification and resistance against such intolerance. In that case, studying the past and present of toleration and all of the struggles for freedom and justice would be only so much groping in the dark.

Despite this, toleration remains – as this survey of some contemporary toleration conflicts was intended to show – *in conflict*. For the present remains part of the history of toleration insofar as the very same differences between various conceptions and justifications of toleration which marked the historical discourse are to be found under altered conditions in contemporary controversies. In order to provide critical orientation in such conflicts, it is essential to have at one's disposal suitable categories for disentangling these threads.

§39 Limits

It is characteristic of the complex situation in a 'globalised' world that many of the conflicts which were analysed in the foregoing study as conflicts *within societies* are reappearing as conflicts *between societies*. And thus the question arises of whether in this global context of a veritably universal plurality of ethical conceptions and cultural self-understandings there can also be a reciprocally and generally non-rejectable basis for a form of *global* justice and a corresponding form of reciprocally grounded toleration. To provide an exhaustive explanation of why I think that the conception I have proposed, *mutatis mutandis*, does offer such a suitable basis, however, would require a more detailed analysis addressing the global context and its structures of rights, and of cultural – and, in particular, religious – values, though also of coercion and domination, which it is not possible to undertake here.[119]

Speaking in general terms, however, two questions must be kept apart, namely, the question concerning a global foundation of toleration *between*

119. On this, see Forst, 'Towards a Critical Theory of Transnational Justice'.

states (a 'global multiculturalism', so to speak), for which the respect conception is supposed to be a candidate, and the question of whether the respect
conception is generalisable *within* extremely diverse political communities
such as are found throughout the world. The two questions are connected,
though not only in such a way that a negative answer to the second also implies
a negative answer to the first. More importantly, answering the question of
intercultural toleration calls for a careful examination of the *intracultural* conflicts over toleration and the struggles for certain liberties. Thus, we can
see that the right to justification is appealed to not only by those who call
for more liberties and democratic self-determination, in whatever concrete
form, but also by those who call for 'respect for difference' of their political
communities in their ethical-cultural particularity at the intercultural level
and at the level of relations between states – specifically on the grounds
that these communities are ethically and politically integrated unities, so
that challenging their integrity and identity would amount to a violation
of the identity of their citizens. But, then, this respect for difference cannot
mean, conversely, that the suppression of difference and contradiction can be
legitimated and tolerated *within* such societies. The justified claim to external respect for ethical-cultural difference is incompatible with its internal
suppression.

Therefore, if one examines the toleration conflicts within the most
diverse societies, a similar dynamic emerges to the one I have described,
even though this is not to prescribe the European route of modernisation or
Western forms of political and economic organisation as obligatory. The key
issue is the possibility of an autonomous, political construction of the basic
structures of particular societies by the citizens themselves. This essentially
presupposes a moral construction of rights which, in a suitably abstract form,
count as *human rights* which cannot be denied to any person on account of
his or her right to justification.[120] these rights constitute the foundation of
internal *and* transnational toleration – and at the same time mark its limits.[121]
Without a deontological definition of what it means to be respected as a
'human being', however, these rights themselves lack a sufficient normative
basis; and, without a reciprocal and general definition of what can be justified
on this basis, they remain determinable in a one-sided and paternalistic way –
again both within and between states. How these rights are to be interpreted

120. See Forst, 'The Basic Right to Justification' and 'The Justification of Human Rights and the
Basic Right to Justification: A Reflexive Approach'.
121. Which, of course, by no means answers the question concerning the legitimacy of
interventions in 'non-tolerable' states.

must be exposed to critical discussion in intra- and intercultural discourses, in which contexts the right to justification must already be presupposed and to some extent secured.

That the history which I have reconstructed expresses something universal concerning this complex conflict situation within and between states follows from an analysis of this situation. Although the principle of justification and the norm of freedom from domination speak many languages in struggles against intolerance and false toleration, whether in national or in transnational contexts, nevertheless the voice of all those who demand their basic right not to have to live under conditions which cannot be justified towards them any longer remains unmistakable. This confirms once again what this study was intended to show, namely, that the conflicts over toleration were and are part of conflicts over justice, and hence that it is both a historical and a philosophical truth that just *one* justification of toleration can withstand these conflicts, namely, the one which makes the principle of justification itself its basis. It expresses what the champions of toleration have demanded at different times, that no ethical or religious truth is so preeminent that human beings should be subordinated to it by force, beyond reciprocal justification. Yet however true this may be in moral terms, it is equally true from a historical, legal and political perspective that people only *have* the rights which they have won through *struggles*.[122]

122. Bloch, *Natural Law and Human Dignity*, 188.

Bibliography

Abelard, Peter, *Dialogue between a Philosopher, a Jew, and a Christian*, in *Ethical Writings: His Ethics or 'Know Yourself' and his Dialogue between a Philosopher, a Jew, and a Christian*, trans. P. V. Spade, Indianapolis: Hackett, 1995.

    Ethics (or *Scito te Ipsum*), in *Abelard, Ethical Writings: His Ethics or 'Know Yourself' and his Dialogue between a Philosopher, a Jew, and a Christian*, trans. P. V. Spade, Indianapolis: Hackett, 1995.

Acontius, Jacobus, *Darkness Discovered: (Satan's Stratagems)* (Stratagemata Satanae) (1565), ed. R. E. Field, Delmar, NY: Scholars' Facsimiles and Reprints, 1978.

Adorno, Theodor W., *Studien zum autoritären Charakter*, trans. M. Weinbrenner, Frankfurt am Main: Suhrkamp, 1995.

Adorno, Theodor W. *et al.*, *The Authoritarian Personality*, New York: Harper, 1950.

Althusius, Johann, *Politica methodice digesta*, Herborn 1614, reprint Aalen: Scientia, 1961.

Anderson, Benedict, *Imagined Communities: Reflections on the Origins and Spread of Nationalism*, London and New York: Verso, 1991.

Anderson, Elisabeth, *Value in Ethics and Economics*, Cambridge, Mass.: Harvard University Press, 1993.

Anonymous, 'A Discourse concerning the True Understanding of the Pacification of Gent', cited from E. H. Kossmann and A. F. Mellink, *Texts concerning the Revolt of the Netherlands*: www.dbnl.org/tekst/koss002text01_01/koss002text01_01_0040.php (accessed June 2012).

Apel, Karl-Otto, 'Faktische Anerkennung oder einsehbar notwendige Anerkennung?', in *Auseinandersetzungen in Erprobung des transzendentalpragmatischen Ansatzes*, Frankfurt am Main: Suhrkamp, 1998, 221–80.

    'Plurality of the Good? The Problem of Affirmative Tolerance in a Multicultural Society from an Ethical Point of View', *Ratio Juris* 10, 1997, 199–212.

Araújo, Ana Christina *et al.*, 'The Historical and Philosophical Dimensions of the Concept of Tolerance', in G. Hálfdanarson (ed.), *Discrimination and Tolerance in Historical Perspective*, Pisa: Plus – Pisa University Press, 2008, 2–18.

Aristotle, *Nicomachean Ethics*, trans. T. Irwin, Indianapolis: Hackett, 1985.

Arnold, Gottfried, *Unpartheyische Kirchen- und Ketzerhistorie, vom Anfang des neuen Testaments bis auff das Jahr Christi 1688*, 2 vols., 1699/1700, n.d. (1729 edition) Hildesheim: Olms, 1967.

Assmann, Jan, 'Praktiken des Übersetzens und Konzepte von Toleranz im Alten Orient und in der hellenistisch-römischen Antike', in A. Wierlacher (ed.), *Kulturthema Toleranz*, Munich: Iudicium, 1996, 283–306.

Aubert, Roger, 'Das Problem der Religionsfreiheit in der Geschichte des Christentums', in H. Lutz (ed.), *Zur Geschichte der Toleranz und Religionsfreiheit*, Darmstadt: Wissenschaftliche Buchgesellschaft, 1977, 422–54.

Audi, Robert, *Religious Commitment and Secular Reason*, Cambridge University Press, 2000.

Augustine, *Contra epistulam Parmeniani*, in Patrologiae cursus completus, series latina, ed. P. G. Migne, vol. XLIII, Turnhout: Brepols, n.d. (English: 'Against the Letter of Parmenian', in *The Works of Saint Augustine: A Translation for the 21st Century*, vol. XVIII, ed. J. E. Rotelle, trans. E. Hill, New York: New City Press, 1990–2005).

De ordine, in Patrologiae cursus completus, series latina, ed. P. G. Migne, vol. XXXII, Turnhout: Brepols, n.d. (English: *On Order = De ordine*, trans. S. Borruso, South Bend, Ind.: St. Augustine's Press, 2007).

Expositions on the Book of Psalms, in Philip Schaff (ed.), *Nicene and Post-Nicene Fathers*, vol. VIII, Edinburgh: T. and T. Clark and Grand Rapids, Mich.: Wm. B. Erdmanns, 1989–94 (cited from www.newadvent.org/fathers/1801.htm (accessed May 2011)).

In Johannis Evangelium, in Patrologiae cursus completus, series latina, ed. P. G. Migne, vol. XXXV, Paris, 1845 (English: *Lectures or Tractates on the Gospel According to St. John*, trans. J. Gibb, in Philip Schaff (ed.), *Nicene and Post-Nicene Fathers*, vol. VII, Edinburgh: T. and T. Clark and Grand Rapids, Mich.: Wm. B. Erdmanns, 1989–94, 1–452 (cited from www.newadvent.org/fathers/1701.htm (accessed October 2008)).

Letters of St. Augustine, trans. J. G. Cunningham, in Philip Schaff (ed.), *Nicene and Post-Nicene Fathers*, vol. I, Edinburgh: T. and T. Clark and Grand Rapids, Mich.: Wm. B. Erdmanns, 1989–94, 209–596 (cited from www.newadvent.org/fathers/1102.htm (accessed October 2008)).

Letters Vol. II, trans. Sister W. Parsons, SND, Washington, DC: Catholic University Press of America, 1953.

Political Writings, ed. E. M. Atkins and R. Dodaro, trans. E. M. Atkins, Cambridge University Press, 2001.

Sermo Lambot, in Patrologiae cursus completus, series latina, ed. P. G. Migne, Suppl. vol. II, Paris: Éditions Garnier Frères, 1960.

The City of God against the Pagans, ed. and trans. R. W. Dyson, Cambridge University Press, 1998.

Averroes (Ibn Rushd), *On the Harmony of Religion and Philosophy (Kitab fasl al-maqal)*, trans. G. F. Hourani, London: Luzac and Co., 1976 (cited from www.muslimphilosophy.com/ir/fasl.htm (accessed November 2008)).

The Incoherence of the Incoherence (Tahafut al-Tahafut), trans. S. van den Bergh, vol. I, London: Luzac and Co., 1954 (www.muslimphilosophy.com/ir/tt/ (accessed November 2008)).

Bainton, Roland H., *Erasmus of Christendom*, New York: Scribner, 1969.

Balke, Friedrich *et al.* (eds.), *Schwierige Fremdheit: Über Integration und Ausgrenzung in Einwanderungsländern*, Frankfurt am Main: Fischer, 1993.

Barbers, Meinulf, *Toleranz bei Sebastian Franck*, Bonn: Ludwig Röhrscheid Verlag, 1964.

Barry, Brian, *Culture and Equality: An Egalitarian Critique of Multiculturalism*, Cambridge: Polity, 2001.

Justice as Impartiality, Oxford: Clarendon Press, 1995.

Barthou, Louis, *Mirabeau*, Freeport, NY: Books for Libraries Press, 1972.

Barton, Peter F., 'Das Toleranzpatent von 1781. Edition der wichtigsten Fassungen', in P. F. Barton (ed.), *Im Zeichen der Toleranz: Aufsätze zur Toleranzgesetzgebung des 18. Jahrhunderts im Reiche Joseph II.*, Vienna: Institut für protestantische Kirchengeschichte, 1981, 154–98.

Bartuschat, Wolfgang, 'Einleitung', in Spinoza, *Ethik in geometrischer Ordnung dargestellt*, trans. and ed. W. Bartuschat, Hamburg: Meiner, 1999, VII–XXIV.

Battenberg, Friedrich, *Das europäische Zeitalter der Juden: Zur Entwicklung einer Minderheit in der nichtjüdischen Umwelt Europas*, vol. I, Darmstadt: Wissenschaftliche Buchgesellschaft, 1990.

'Jews in Ecclesiastical Territories', in R. Po-Chia Hsia and H. Lehmann (eds.), *In and Out of the Ghetto*, Cambridge University Press, 1995, 247–74.

Bauberot, Jean, 'Liberté religieuse et la laïcité', in Mission du Bicentenaire de la Révolution Française, *Les catholiques français et l'héritage de 1798: 1889–1989*, Paris: Beauchesne, 1989, 93–104.

Bauböck, Rainer, 'Liberal Justifications for Ethnic Group Rights', in C. Joppke and S. Lukes (eds.), *Multicultural Questions*, Oxford University Press, 1999, 133–57.

Bauman, Zygmunt, *Modernity and Ambivalence*, Cambridge: Polity, 1991.

Bayle, Pierre, *Avis important aux refugiez sur leur prochain retour en France*, in *Œuvres diverses*, vol. II, The Hague 1727, reprint Hildesheim: Georg Olms, 1965.

Ce que c'est que la France toute catholique générale sous le règne de Louis Le Grand, in *Œuvres diverses*, vol. II, The Hague 1727, reprint Hildesheim: Georg Olms, 1965.

Commentaire philosophique sur ces paroles de Jesus-Christ 'Contrain-les d'entrer', in *Œuvres diverses*, vol. II, The Hague 1727, reprint Hildesheim: Georg Olms, 1965 (English translation of first two parts: *Philosophical Commentary on these Words of Jesus Christ, Compel Them to Come in*, ed. and trans. A. Godman Tannenbaum, New York: Peter Lang, 1987; English translation of complete text: *A Philosophical Commentary on These Words of the Gospel, Luke 14:23, 'Compel Them to Come In, That My House May Be Full'*, ed. J. Kilkullen and C. Kukathas, Indianapolis: Liberty Fund, 2005).

Continuation des Pensées diverses, in *Œuvres diverses*, vol. III, The Hague 1727, reprint Hildesheim: Georg Olms, 1966.

Critique générale de l'histoire du calvinisme du P. Maimbourg, in *Œuvres diverses*, vol. II, The Hague 1727, reprint Hildesheim: Georg Olms, 1965.

Entretiens de Maxime et de Themiste, in Œuvres diverses, vol. IV, The Hague 1731, reprint Hildesheim: Georg Olms, 1968.

Historical and Critical Dictionary: Selections, ed. and trans. R. Popkin, Indianapolis: Hackett, 1991 (French: *Choix d'articles tirés du Dictionnaire historique et critique, in*

Œuvres diverses, suppl. vol., ed. E. Labrousse, 2 vols., Hildesheim: Georg Olms, 1982).

Nouvelles lettres de l'auteur de la critique générale de l'histoire du calvinisme, in *Œuvres diverses*, vol. II, The Hague 1727, reprint Hildesheim: Georg Olms, 1965.

Various Thoughts on the Occasion of a Comet, trans. R. C. Bartlett, Albany, NY: SUNY Press, 2000 (French: *Pensées diverses écrites à un Docteur de Sorbonne*, in *Œuvres diverses*, vol. III, The Hague 1727, reprint Hildesheim: Georg Olms, 1966).

Becker, Werner, 'Nachdenken über Toleranz: Über einen vernachlässigten Grundwert unserer verfassungsmoralischen Orientierung', in S. Dietz *et al.* (eds.), *Sich im Denken orientieren*, Frankfurt am Main: Suhrkamp, 1996, 119–39.

'Toleranz: Grundwert der Demokratie?', *Ethik und Sozialwissenschaften* 8, 1997, 413–23.

Bejczy, Istvan, 'Tolerantia: A Medieval Concept', *Journal of the History of Ideas* 58, 1997, 365–84.

Benhabib, Seyla, 'On Reconciliation and Respect, Justice and the Good Life: Response to Herta Nagl-Docekal and Rainer Forst', *Philosophy and Social Criticism* 23/5, 1997, 97–114.

The Claims of Culture: Equality and Diversity in the Global Era, Princeton University Press, 2002.

Berghahn, Klaus L., *Grenzen der Toleranz: Juden und Christen im Zeitalter der Aufklärung*, Cologne, Weimar and Vienna: Böhlau, 2001.

Berlin, Isaiah, *Against the Current: Essays in the History of Ideas*, London and New York: Penguin, 1982.

'The Counter-Enlightenment', in *Against the Current*, London and New York: Penguin, 1982, 1–24.

'The Originality of Machiavelli', in *Against the Current*, London and New York: Penguin, 1982, 25–79.

'The Pursuit of the Ideal', in *The Crooked Timber of Humanity: Chapters in the History of Ideas*, New York: Vintage, 1992, 1–19.

'Two Concepts of Liberty', in *Four Essays on Liberty*, Oxford University Press, 1969, 118–72.

Vico and Herder: Two Studies in the History of Ideas, London and New York: Penguin, 1976.

Berman, Harold J., *Law and Revolution: The Formation of the Western Legal Tradition*, Cambridge, Mass.: Harvard University Press, 1983.

'Religious Freedom and the Challenge of the Modern State', in J. D. Hunter and O. Guinness (eds.), *Articles of Faith, Articles of Peace: The Religious Liberty Clauses and the American Public Philosophy*, Washington, DC: The Brookings Institution, 1990, 40–53.

Bermbach, Udo, 'Widerstandsrecht, Souveränität, Kirche und Staat: Frankreich und Spanien im 16. Jahrhundert', in I. Fetscher and H. Münkler (eds.), *Pipers Handbuch der politischen Ideen*, vol. III, Munich: Piper, 1985, 101–62.

Bernstein, Richard J., 'The Retrieval of the Democratic Ethos', in A. Arato and M. Rosenfeld (eds.), *Habermas on Law and Democracy*, Berkeley and Los Angeles: California University Press, 1998, 287–305.

Besier, Gerhard and Klaus Schreiner, 'Toleranz', in O. Brunner, W. Conze and R.
    Koselleck (eds.), *Geschichtliche Grundbegriffe*, vol. VI, Stuttgart: Klett-Cotta, 1990,
    445–605 (Schreiner: 445–94 and 524–605; Besier: 495–523).
Bethge, Herbert, 'Gewissensfreiheit', in J. Isensee and P. Kirchhof (eds.), *Handbuch
    des Staatsrechts der Bundesrepublik Deutschland*, Heidelberg: C. F. Müller, 1989,
    435–70.
Bielefeldt, Heiner and Wilhelm Heitmeyer (eds.), *Politisierte Religion: Ursachen und
    Erscheinungsformen des modernen Fundamentalismus*, Frankfurt am Main: Suhrkamp,
    1998.
Bien, David, *The Calas Affair*, Princeton University Press, 1960.
Bienert, Walther, *Martin Luther und die Juden*, Frankfurt am Main: Evangelisches
    Verlagswerk, 1982.
Blaschke, Lotte, 'Der Toleranzgedanke bei Sebastian Franck', in H. Lutz (ed.), *Zur
    Geschichte der Toleranz und Religionsfreiheit*, Darmstadt: Wissenschaftliche
    Buchgesellschaft, 1977, 42–63.
Bloch, Ernst, *Natural Law and Human Dignity*, trans. D. J. Schmidt, Cambridge, Mass.:
    MIT Press, 1986.
Blumenberg, Hans, *Säkularisierung und Selbstbehauptung*, Frankfurt am Main: Suhrkamp,
    1974.
    'Selbsterhaltung und Beharrung. Zur Konstitution der neuzeitlichen Rationalität', in
    H. Ebeling (ed.), *Subjektivität und Selbsterhaltung: Beiträge zur Diagnose der Moderne*,
    Frankfurt am Main: Suhrkamp, 1976, 144–207.
Bobbio, Norberto, 'Tolerance and Truth', in *In Praise of Meekness: Essays on Ethics and
    Politics*, trans. T. Chataway, Cambridge: Polity, 2000, 130–8.
Boccaccio, Giovanni, *The Decameron*, ed. and trans. G. H. McWilliam, London: Penguin,
    2003.
Böckenförde, Ernst-Wolfgang, 'Die Zukunft politischer Autonomie', in *Staat, Nation,
    Europa: Studien zur Staatslehre, Verfassungstheorie und Rechtsphilosophie*, Frankfurt am
    Main: Suhrkamp, 1999, 103–26.
    'Einleitung zur Textausgabe der "Erklärung über die Religionsfreiheit"', in H. Lutz
    (ed.), *Zur Geschichte der Toleranz und Religionsfreiheit*, Darmstadt: Wissenschaftliche
    Buchgesellschaft, 1977, 401–21.
    '"Kopftuchstreit" auf dem richtigen Weg?' *Neue Juristische Wochenschrift*, 2001, Heft
    10, 723–728.
    'Religion im säkularen Staat', *Universitas* 51, 1996, 990–8.
    'The Rise of the State as a Process of Secularisation', in *State, Society, and Liberty:
    Studies in Political Theory and Constitutional Law*, Oxford: Berg, 1991, 26–48.
    'Toleranz – Leidensgeschichte der christlichen Kirchen', in *Recht, Sittlichkeit, Toleranz*,
    Ulm: Humboldt-Studienzentrum, 2001.
Böckenförde, Ernst-Wolfgang and Robert Spaemann (eds.), *Menschenrechte und
    Menschenwürde: Historische Voraussetzungen – säkulare Gestalt – christliches Verständnis*,
    Stuttgart: Klett-Cotta, 1987.
Bodin, Jean, *Colloquium of the Seven about Secrets of the Sublime*, trans. M. L. D. Kuntz,
    Princeton University Press, 1975.
    On Sovereignty, trans. and ed. J. Franklin, Cambridge University Press, 1992.

On the Demon-Mania of Witches, trans. R. A. Scott, Toronto: Victoria University Press, 1995.

The Six Books of a Commonwealth, abridged and trans. M. J. Tooley, Oxford: Basil Blackwell, 1955 (www.constitution.org/bodin/bodin.htm).

Bohman, James, 'Reflexive Toleration in a Deliberative Democracy', in C. McKinnon and D. Castiglione (eds.), *The Culture of Toleration in Diverse Societies*, Manchester University Press, 2003, 111–31.

Bohn, Ursula, 'Moses Mendelssohn und die Toleranz', in P. van der Osten-Sacken (ed.), *Toleranz heute: 250 Jahre nach Mendelssohn und Lessing*, Berlin: Institut Kirche und Judentum, 1979, 26–36.

Bornkamm, Heinrich, 'Luthers Lehre von den zwei Reichen im Zusammenhang seiner Theologie', in H.-H. Schrey, *Reich Gottes und Welt: Die Lehre Luthers von den zwei Reichen*, Darmstadt: Wissenschaftliche Buchgesellschaft, 1969, 165–95.

Bosl, Karl, 'Reformorden, Ketzer und religiöse Bewegungen in der hochmittelalterlichen Gesellschaft', in I. Fetscher and H. Münkler (eds.), *Pipers Handbuch der politischen Ideen*, vol. ii, Munich: Piper, 1993, 243–310.

Bossuet, Jacques-Benigne, *Politics Drawn from the Very Words of Holy Scripture*, trans. P. Riley, Cambridge University Press, 1999.

Bossy, John, 'English Catholics after 1688', in O. P. Grell, J. I. Israel and N. Tyacke (eds.), *From Persecution to Toleration: The Glorious Revolution and Religion in England*, Oxford: Clarendon Press, 1991, 369–88.

Boyle, Kevin and Juliet Sheen (eds.), *Freedom of Religion and Belief: A World Report*, London and New York: Routledge, 1997.

Brandt, Reinhard, 'Freiheit, Gleichheit, Selbständigkeit bei Kant', in Forum für Philosophie Bad Homburg (ed.), *Die Ideen von 1789 in der deutschen Rezeption*, Frankfurt am Main: Suhrkamp, 1989, 90–127.

Broer, Ingo, 'Toleranz im Neuen Testament?', in I. Broer and R. Schlüter (eds.), *Christentum und Toleranz*, Darmstadt: Wissenschaftliche Buchgesellschaft, 1996, 57–82.

Brown, Peter, *Augustine of Hippo: A Biography*, Berkeley: University of California Press, 2000.

Brown, Wendy, 'Reflections on Tolerance in the Age of Identity', in A. Botwinick and W. E. Connolly (eds.), *Democracy and Vision: Sheldon Wolin and the Vicissitudes of the Political*, Princeton University Press, 2001, 99–117.

Regulating Aversion: Tolerance in the Age of Identity and Empire, Princeton University Press, 2008.

States of Injury: Power and Freedom in Late Modernity, Princeton University Press, 1995.

Brugger, Winfried, 'Rechtsvergleichende Beobachtungen zum deutschen und amerikanischen Verfassungsrecht', *Archiv des Öffentlichen Rechts* 128/3, 2003, 372–411.

Brugger, Winfried and Stefan Huster (eds.), *Der Streit um das Kreuz in der Schule: Zur religiös-weltanschaulichen Neutralität des Staates*, Baden-Baden: Nomos, 1998.

Brumlik, Micha, *Deutscher Geist und Judenhaß: Das Verhältnis des philosophischen Idealismus zum Judentum*, Munich: Luchterhand, 2000.

Brush, Craig B., *Montaigne and Bayle: Variations on the Theme of Skepticism*, The Hague: Nijhoff, 1966.

Brutus, Stephanus Junius (Pseudonym), *Vindiciae contra tyrannos, or, Concerning the legitimate power of a prince over the people, and of the people over a prince*, ed. G. Garnett, Cambridge University Press, 1994.

Bubner, Rüdiger, 'Zur Dialektik der Toleranz', in R. Forst (ed.), *Toleranz*, Frankfurt am Main: Campus, 2000, 45–59.

Burckhardt, Jacob, *The Civilization of the Renaissance in Italy: An Essay*, trans. S. G. C. Middlemore, Vienna: Phaidon, 1937.

Burgess, Glenn, 'Thomas Hobbes: Religious Toleration or Religious Indifference?', in C. J. Nederman and J. C. Laursen (eds.), *Difference and Dissent: Theories of Toleration in Medieval and Early Modern Europe*, Lanham, Md.: Rowman and Littlefield, 1996, 139–62.

Calvin, Jean, *Institutes of the Christian Religion* (Institutio Christianae Religionis), trans. J. Allen, Philadelphia: Presbyterian Board of Publication, 1844.

Campenhausen, Axel Freiherr von, 'Religionsfreiheit', in J. Isensee and P. Kirchhof (eds.), *Handbuch des Staatsrechts VI: Freiheitsrechte*, Heidelberg: C. F. Müller, 1989, 369–434.

Cancik, Hubert and Hildegard Cancik-Lindemaier, 'Moralische *tolerantia* – wissenschaftliche Wahrnehmung des Fremden – religiöse Freiheit und Repression', in A. Wierlacher (ed.), *Kulturthema Toleranz*, Munich: Iudicium, 1996, 263–82.

Cardinal Meisner, Joachim, 'Der Bundeskanzler muß das Ehediskriminierungsgesetz aufhalten', *Frankfurter Allgemeine Zeitung*, 16(9), 2000, 12.

Carens, Joseph H., *Culture, Citizenship, and Community: A Contextual Exploration of Justice as Evenhandedness*, Oxford University Press, 2000.

'Liberalism and Culture', *Constellations* 4, 1997, 35–47.

Carlin, Norah, 'Toleration for Catholics in the Puritan Revolution', in O. P. Grell and B. Scribner (eds.), *Tolerance and Intolerance in the European Reformation*, Cambridge University Press, 1996, 216–30.

Cassirer, Ernst, *The Philosophy of the Enlightenment*, Princeton University Press, 1951.

Castellion [Castellio], Sébastien, *Concerning Heretics*, ed. and trans. R. H. Bainton, New York: Octagon Books, 1965.

Counsel to France in Her Distress (1562), in Castellion, *Concerning Heretics: Whether They are to be Persecuted and How They Are to be Treated*, ed. and trans. R. Bainton, New York: Columbia University Press, 1935.

Chang, Ruth (ed.), *Incommensurability, Incomparability, and Practical Reason*, Cambridge, Mass.: Harvard University Press, 1997.

Chillingworth, William, *The Religion of Protestants: A Safe Way to Salvation*, Whitefish, Mont.: Kessinger Publishing, 2003.

Cicero, *On Moral Ends*, ed. J. Annas, trans. R. Woolf, Cambridge University Press, 2001.

Paradoxa stoicorum, in *De oratore*, Latin and English, trans. H. Rackham, Cambridge, Mass.: Harvard University Press, 1948.

Clairvaux, Bernard of, *In Praise of the New Knighthood*, trans. C. Greenia, from *Bernard of Clairvaux: Treatises III*, Washington, DC, Cistercian Publications, 1977, 127–45 (www.the-orb.net/encyclop/religion/monastic/bernard.html (accessed October 2008)).

The Letters of St. Bernard of Clairvaux, trans. B. S. James, New York, AMS Press, 1980.

Cohen, Joshua, 'Moral Pluralism and Political Consensus', in D. Copp, J. Hampton and J. Roemer (eds.), *The Idea of Democracy*, Cambridge University Press, 1993, 270–91.

Colomer, Eusebio, 'Die Vorgeschichte des Motivs vom Frieden im Glauben bei Raimund Lull', in R. Haubst (ed.), *Der Friede unter den Religionen nach Nikolaus von Kues*, Mainz: Matthias-Grünewald-Verlag, 1984, 82–112.

Conrad, Hermann, 'Religionsbann, Toleranz und Parität am Ende des alten Reiches', in H. Lutz (ed.), *Zur Geschichte der Toleranz und Religionsfreiheit*, Darmstadt: Wissenschaftliche Buchgesellschaft, 1977, 155–92.

Constant, Benjamin, 'The Liberty of the Ancients Compared with that of the Moderns', in Constant, *Political Writings*, ed. B. Fontana, Cambridge University Press, 1988, pp. 309–17.

Coornhert, Dirck Volckertszoon, *Proces van't ketter-dooden ende dwangh der conscientien (Trial of the Killing of Heretics)*, in Coornhert, *Wercken*, Amsterdam: Colom, 1630, 3 vols., vol. ii, fol. 60.

Cranston, Maurice, 'John Locke and the Case for Toleration', in J. Horton and S. Mendus (eds.), *A Letter Concerning Toleration in Focus*, London and New York: Routledge, 1991, 78–97.

Creppell, Ingrid, 'Locke on Toleration: The Transformation of Constraint', *Political Theory* 24, 1996, 200–40.

'Montaigne: The Embodiment of Identity as Grounds for Toleration', *Res Publica* 7, 2001, 247–71.

Crick, Bernard, 'Toleration and Tolerance in Theory and Practice', *Government and Opposition* 6, 1971, 144–71.

Crisp, Roger and Michael Slote (eds.), *Virtue Ethics*, Oxford University Press, 1997.

Cyprian, *Ad Demetrianum Apologeticus*, in Patrologiae cursus completus, series latina, ed. P. G. Migne, vol. iv, Paris, 1891 (English: *An Address to Demetrianus*, trans. Rev. E. Wallis, www.ewtn.com/library/PATRISTC/ANF5-13.TXT (accessed October 2008)).

De bono patientiae, in Patrologiae cursus completus, series latina, ed. P. G. Migne, vol. iv, Paris, 1891 (English: *On the Advantage of Patience*, trans. Rev. E. Wallis, www.ewtn.com/library/PATRISTC/ANF5-17.TXT (accessed October 2008)).

De lapsis, in Patrologiae cursus completus, series latina, ed. P. G. Migne, vol. iv, Paris, 1891 (English: *On the Lapsed*, trans. Rev. E. Wallis, www.ewtn.com/library/PATRISTC/ANF5-11.TXT (accessed October 2008)).

De moralitate, in Patrologiae cursus completus, series latina, ed. P. G. Migne, vol. 4, Paris, 1891 (English: *On the Mortality (or Plague)*, trans. Rev. E. Wallis, www.ewtn.com/library/PATRISTC/ANF5-15.TXT (accessed October 2008)).

Epistles of Cyprian of Carthage, in Ante-Nicene Fathers, vol. v, ed. A. Roberts, J. Donaldson and A. Cleveland Coxe, trans. R. E. Wallis, Buffalo, NY, Christian Literature Publishing Co., 1886; revised and ed. K. Knight. http://www.newadvent.org/fathers/0506.htm (accessed June 2012).

Davidson, Donald, *Expressing Evaluations*, Lindley Lecture, Department of Philosophy, University of Kansas, 1984.

'On the Very Idea of a Conceptual Scheme', in *Inquiries into Truth and Interpretation*, Oxford: Clarendon Press, 2001, 183–98.

Debus, Anne, *Das Verfassungsprinzip der Toleranz unter besonderer Berücksichtigung der Rechtsprechung des Bundesverfassungsgerichts*, Frankfurt am Main: Peter Lang, 1999.

Dees, Richard, 'The Justification of Tolerance', in G. Magill and M. Hoff (eds.), *Values and Public Life*, Lanham, Md.: University Press of America, 1995, 29–56.

'Trust and Toleration', unpublished manuscript, St. Louis, 2001.

Denck, Hans, 'Divine Order and the Work of His Creatures', in D. Liechty (ed.), *Early Anabaptist Spirituality*, trans. D. Liechty, New York: Paulist, 1994.

'Wer die Wahrheit wahrlich lieb hat', in *Schriften*, vol. ii, ed. W. Fellmann, Gütersloh: Bertelsmann, 1956.

Denninger, Erhard, 'Der Einzelne und das allgemeine Gesetz', *Kritische Justiz* 28, 1995, 425–38.

Dent, Nicholas, 'Rousseau and Respect for Others', in S. Mendus (ed.), *Justifying Toleration: Conceptual and Historical Perspectives*, Cambridge University Press, 1988, 115–36.

De Roover, Jankob, *A Kingdom of Another World: Christianity, Toleration and the History of Western Political Thought*, Universiteit Gent: Onderzoekscentrum Vergelijkende Cultuurwetenschap, 2005.

www.cultuurwetenschap.be/DOWNLOADS/AKingdomofAnotherWorld.pdf.

Detel, Wolfgang, 'Griechen und Barbaren. Zu den Anfängen des abendländischen Rassismus', *Deutsche Zeitschrift für Philosophie* 43, 1995, 1019–43.

Detering, Heinrich, 'Christian Wilhelm von Dohm und die Idee der Toleranz', in P. Freimark, F. Kopitzsch and H. Slessarev (eds.), *Lessing und die Toleranz*, Munich: edition text und kritik, 1986, 174–83.

Deveaux, Monique, *Cultural Pluralism and Dilemmas of Justice*, Ithaca, NY: Cornell University Press, 2000.

Devlin, Lord Patrick, *The Enforcement of Morals*, Oxford University Press, 1959.

D'Holbach, Paul Thiry, *The System of Nature, or, Laws of the Moral and Physical World*, 2 vols., trans. H. D. Robinson, Kitchener, Ontario: Batoche Books, 2001.

Dickmann, Fritz, 'Das Problem der Gleichberechtigung der Konfessionen im Reich im 16. und 17. Jahrhundert', in H. Lutz (ed.), *Zur Geschichte der Toleranz und Religionsfreiheit*, Darmstadt: Wissenschaftliche Buchgesellschaft, 1977, 203–51.

Diderot, Denis, *De la suffisance de la religion naturelle*, in *Œuvres complètes*, vol. i, ed. J. Assezat, Paris: Garnier Frères, 1875.

Philosophic Thoughts, in *Diderot's Early Philosohical Works*, trans. and ed. M. Jourdain, New York: ASM Press, 1916, 27–67.

Thoughts on Religion, trans. M. Abidor (www.marxists.org/reference/archive/diderot/1770/religion.htm (accessed June 2012)).

Diderot, Denis and Jacques le Rond d' Alembert (eds.), *The Encyclopedia of Diderot and d'Alembert* (http://quod.lib.umich.edu/d/did/ (accessed June 2012)).

Dilthey, Wilhelm, 'Auffassung und Analyse des Menschen im 15. und 16. Jahrhundert', in *Gesammelte Schriften*, vol. ii, Leipzig and Berlin: B. G. Teubner, 1921, 1–89.

'Das natürliche System der Geisteswissenschaften im 17. Jahrhundert', in *Gesammelte Schriften*, vol. II, Leipzig and Berlin: B. G. Teubner, 1921, 90–245.

'Die Autonomie des Denkens, der konstruktive Rationalismus und der pantheistische Monismus nach ihrem Zusammenhang im 17. Jahrhundert', in *Gesammelte Schriften*, vol. II, Leipzig and Berlin: B. G. Teubner, 1921, 246–390.

Dinzelbacher, Peter, 'Toleranz bei Bernard von Clairvaux?', *Humanistische Bildung* 19, 1996, 93–116.

Dippel, Horst, *Die amerikanische Revolution 1763–1787*, Frankfurt am Main: Suhrkamp, 1985.

Döring, Detlef, 'Samuel von Pufendorf and Toleration', in J. C. Laursen and C. J. Nederman (eds.), *Beyond the Persecuting Society: Religious Toleration before the Enlightenment*, Philadelphia: University of Pennsylvania Press, 1998, 178–96.

Dreitzel, Horst, 'Gewissensfreiheit und soziale Ordnung. Religionstoleranz als Problem der politischen Theorie am Ausgang des 17. Jahrhunderts', *Politische Vierteljahresschrift* 36, 1995, 3–34.

Du Bois, W. E. B., *The Souls of Black Folk*, New York: Penguin, 1995.

Dunn, John, 'The Claim to Freedom of Conscience: Freedom of Speech, Freedom of Thought, Freedom of Worship?', in O. P. Grell, J. I. Israel and N. Tyacke (eds.), *From Persecution to Toleration: The Glorious Revolution and Religion in England*, Oxford: Clarendon Press, 1991, 171–94.

The Political Thought of John Locke, Cambridge University Press, 1969.

Dworkin, Ronald, 'Foundations of Liberal Equality', *The Tanner Lectures on Human Values*, vol. XI, ed. G. B. Peterson, Salt Lake City: University of Utah Press, 1990, 1–119.

Life's Dominion: An Argument about Abortion, Euthanasia, and Individual Freedom, New York: Knopf, 1993.

Taking Rights Seriously, Cambridge, Mass.: Harvard University Press, 1977.

Ebbinghaus, Julius, 'Über die Idee der Toleranz. Eine staatsrechtliche und religionsphilosophische Untersuchung', *Archiv für Philosophie* 4, 1950, 1–34.

Eberhard, Winfried, 'Ansätze zur Bewältigung ideologischer Pluralität im 12. Jahrhundert: Pierre Abelard und Anselm von Havelberg', *Historisches Jahrbuch* 105, 1985, 353–87.

Ehler, Sidney Z. and John B. Morrall (eds.), *Church and State through the Centuries: A Collection of Historic Documents with Commentaries*, trans. S. Z. Ehler and J. B. Morrall, New York: Biblo and Tannen, 1988.

Emerson, Ralph Waldo, 'Self-Reliance', in *Selected Writings of Ralph Waldo Emerson*, ed. W. Gilman, New York: New American Library, 1983, 257–79.

Erasmus of Rotterdam, *Briefe*, trans. and ed. W. Köhler, Bremen: Schünemann, 1956.

Collected Works of Erasmus, 86 vols., Toronto: Toronto University Press, 1969–.

Concio in Psalmum, Quum invocarem, in *Desiderii Erasmi Opera Omnia*, vol. V (1704), Hildesheim: Olms, 1962.

De amabili ecclesiae concordia, in *Desiderii Erasmi Opera Omnia*, vol. V (1704), Hildesheim: Olms, 1962.

Ecclesiastes, sive De ratione concionandi, in *Desiderii Erasmi Opera Omnia*, vol. V (1704), Hildesheim: Olms, 1962.

'Erasmus' Letter to Carondolet: The Preface to His Edition of St. Hilary of Poitiers, 1523', in John C. Olin, *Six Essays on Erasmus and a Translation of Erasmus' Letter to Carondelet, 1523*, trans. J. C. Olin, New York: Fordham University Press, 1979, 93–120.

'Letter to Paul Volz' (Epistola ad Paulum Volzium), in *Christian Humanism and the Reformation: Selected Writings of Erasmus*, ed. J. C. Olin, New York: Fordham University Press, 1975, 109–30.

On the Freedom of the Will (De libero arbitrio), in E. Gordon Rupp (ed.), *Luther and Erasmus: Free Will and Salvation*, trans. E. G. Rupp and P. S. Watson, Louisville, Ky.: Westminster John Knox Press, 1978, 35–97.

Praise of Folly (Moriae encomium), trans. B. Radice, London: Penguin, 1993.

Supputatio errorum in censuris Beddae (Reckoning of the Errors in the Censure by [Noel] Beda), in *Desiderii Erasmi Opera Omnia*, vol. IX (1704), Hildesheim: Olms, 1962.

The Complaint of Peace (Querela pacis), New York: Cosimo Classics, 2004.

The Correspondence of Erasmus: Letters 842–992 (1518–1519), vol. VI, trans. R. A. B. Mynors and D. F. S. Thomson, Toronto University Press, 1982.

The Correspondence of Erasmus: Letters 1658–1801 (1526–1527), vol. XII, trans. A. Dalzell, Toronto University Press, 2003.

The Education of a Christian Prince, ed. L. Jardine, trans. N. M. Cheshire and M. J. Heath, Cambridge University Press, 1997.

The Julius Exclusus, trans. P. Pascal, Bloomington: Indiana University Press, 1968.

The Manual of the Christian Knight (Enchiridion militis christiani), London: Methuen, 1905.

Theologische Methodenlehre (Method of True Theology), in *Ausgewählte Schriften*, vol. III, trans. G. B. Winkler, Darmstadt: Wissenschaftliche Buchgesellschaft, 1995 (Latin: *Ratio seu Methodus compendio perveniendi ad veram theologiam*, in *Desiderius Erasmus Roterdamus: Ausgewählte Werke*, ed. H. Holborn and A. Holborn, Munich, 1933 (reprinted 1964), 175–305).

Fabry, Heinz-Josef, 'Toleranz im Alten Testament?', in I. Broer and R. Schlüter (eds.), *Christentum und Toleranz*, Darmstadt: Wissenschaftliche Buchgesellschaft, 1996, 9–34.

Faltenbacher, Karl Friedrich, *Das Colloquium Heptaplomeres, ein Religionsgespräch zwischen Scholastik und Aufklärung*, Frankfurt am Main: Lang, 1988.

(ed.), *Magie, Religion und Wissenschaft im Colloquium heptaplomeres*, Darmstadt: Wissenschaftliche Buchgesellschaft, 2002.

Feinberg, Joel, *The Moral Limits of the Criminal Law*, Oxford University Press, 1984 (vol. I: *Harm to Others*, vol. II: *Offense to Others*, vol. III: *Harm to Self*, vol. IV: *Harmless Wrongdoing*).

Fetscher, Iring, 'Politisches Denken im Frankreich des 18. Jahrhunderts vor der Revolution', in I. Fetscher and H. Münkler (eds.), *Pipers Handbuch der politischen Ideen*, vol. III, Munich: Piper, 1985, 423–528.

Rousseaus politische Philosophie, Neuwied: Luchterhand, 1960.

Toleranz: Von der Unentbehrlichkeit einer kleinen Tugend für die Demokratie, Stuttgart: Radius, 1990.

Feuerbach, Ludwig, *Pierre Bayle: Ein Beitrag zur Geschichte der Philosophie und Menschheit*, in *Gesammelte Werke*, vol. IV, ed. W. Schuffenhauer, Berlin: Akademie Verlag, 1967.

Ficino, Marsilio, *Commentary on Plato's Symposium on Love (De amore)*, trans. S. Jayne, Dallas, Tex.: Spring Publications, 1985.

De Christiana religione, in *Opera omnia*, vol. I, ed. P. O. Kristeller, Turin: Bottega d'Erasmo, 1959.

Platonic Theology (Theologia platonica), 6 vols., Latin and English, ed. J. Hankins and W. Bowen, trans. M. J. B. Allen and J. Warden, Cambridge, Mass.: Harvard University Press, 2001–6.

Finnis, John, 'Law, Morality, and "Sexual Orientation"', *Notre Dame Journal of Law, Ethics, and Public Policy* 9, 1995, 11–39.

Fish, Stanley, 'Mission Impossible: Settling the Just Bounds between Church and State', *Columbia Law Review* 97, 1997, 2255–333.

Fitzmaurice, Deborah, 'Autonomy as a Good: Liberalism, Autonomy and Toleration', *Journal of Political Philosophy* 1, 1993, 1–16.

Fitzpatrick, Martin, 'Toleration and the Enlightenment Movement', in O. P. Grell and R. Porter (eds.), *Toleration in Enlightenment Europe*, Cambridge University Press, 2000, 23–68.

Flaks, David K. *et al.*, 'Lesbians Choosing Motherhood: A Comparative Study of Lesbian and Homosexual Partners and Their Children', in A. Sullivan (ed.), *Same-Sex Marriage: Pro and Con*, New York: Random House, 1997, 246–9.

Fletcher, George, 'The Instability of Tolerance', in D. Heyd (ed.), *Toleration*, Princeton University Press, 1996, 158–72.

Forst, Rainer, *Contexts of Justice: Political Philosophy beyond Liberalism and Communitarianism*, trans. J. Farrell, Berkeley and Los Angeles: University of California Press, 2002.

'Einleitung', in R. Forst (ed.), *Toleranz: Philosophische Grundlagen und gesellschaftliche Praxis einer umstrittenen Tugend*, Frankfurt am Main: Campus, 2000, 7–25.

'Ethik und Moral', in L. Wingert and K. Günther (eds.), *Die Öffentlichkeit der Vernunft und die Vernunft der Öffentlichkeit* (Festschrift J. Habermas), Frankfurt am Main: Suhrkamp, 2001, 344–71.

'First Things First: Redistribution, Recognition and Justification', *European Journal of Political Theory* 6/3, 2007, 291–304.

'Foundations of a Theory of Multicultural Justice', *Constellations* 4, 1997, 63–71.

'Konstruktionen transnationaler Gerechtigkeit', in S. Gosepath and J.-C. Merle (eds.), *Weltrepublik: Globalisierung und Demokratie*, Munich: Beck, 2002, 181–94.

Justification and Critique, forthcoming.

'Political Liberty: Integrating Five Conceptions of Autonomy', in J. Christman and J. Anderson, *Autonomy and the Challenges to Liberalism: New Essays*, Cambridge University Press, 2005, 226–42.

'Praktische Vernunft und rechtfertigende Gründe. Zur Begründung der Moral', in S. Gosepath (ed.), *Motive, Gründe, Zwecke: Theorien praktischer Rationalität*, Frankfurt am Main: Fischer, 1999, 168–205.

'The Basic Right to Justification: Towards a Constructivist Conception of Human Rights', in Forst, *The Right to Justification*, ch. 2.

'The Justification of Human Rights and the Basic Right to Justification: A Reflexive Approach', *Ethics* 120, July 2010, 711–40.

'The Justification of Justice: Rawls and Habermas in Dialogue', trans. J. Anderson, in J. G. Finlayson and F. Freyenhagen (eds), *Disputing the Political: Habermas and Rawls*, London and New York: Routledge, 2011, 153–80 (with a response by Jürgen Habermas).

The Right to Justification: Elements of a Constructivist Theory of Justice, trans. J. Flynn, New York: Columbia University Press.

'The Rule of Reasons', *Ratio Juris* 14, 2001, 345–78.

'Towards a Critical Theory of Transnational Justice', in Forst, *The Right to Justification*, ch. 12.

'Utopia and Irony', *Constellations*, forthcoming.

Foucault, Michel, *Discipline and Punish: The Birth of the Prison*, trans. A. Sheridan, New York: Vintage, 1979.

'Governmentality', in *The Foucault Effect: Studies in Governmentality*, ed. G. Burchell, C. Gordon and P. Miller, University of Chicago Press, 1991, 87–104.

Madness and Civilization, trans. R. Howard, New York: Pantheon, 1965.

'Médecins, juges et sorciers au XVIIIe siècle', in Foucault, *Dits et écrits*, vol. I, Paris: Éditions Gallimard, 1994, 753–66.

'Omnes et singulatim. Towards a Criticism of "Political Reason"', in *Power: Essential Works of Michel Foucault 1954–84*, vol. III, ed. J. D. Faubion, trans. R. Hurley *et al.*, New York: New Press, 2000, 298–325.

The History of Sexuality, vol. I: *An Introduction*, trans. R. Hurley, New York: Vintage Books, 1990.

The History of Sexuality, vol. II: *The Use of Pleasure*, trans. R. Hurley, New York: Vintage, 1990.

The History of Sexuality, vol. III: *The Care of the Self*, trans. R. Hurley, New York: Vintage, 1988.

'The Subject and Power', in H. L. Dreyfus and P. Rabinow, *Michel Foucault: Beyond Structuralism and Hermeneutics*, University of Chicago Press, 1982, 208–26.

'What Is Enlightenment?', in P. Rabinow (ed.), *The Foucault Reader*, New York: Vintage, 1984, 32–50.

'What Is Critique?', trans. L. Hochroth, in S. Lothringer and L. Hochroth (eds.), *The Politics of Truth*, New York: Semiotext(e), 1997, 41–82.

Franck, Sebastian, *Chronica, Zeitbuch und Geschichtbibell* (1536 edn), Darmstadt: Wissenschaftliche Buchgesellschaft, 1969.

280 Paradoxes or Wondrous Sayings, trans. E. J. Furcha, Lewiston, NY: Edwin Mellen Press, 1986.

Frank, Martin, 'Probleme einer interkulturellen Gerechtigkeitstheorie: Minderheitenrechte und ihre Konsequenzen', Diss. phil., Frankfurt am Main, 1999.

Frankenberg, Günter, *Die Verfassung der Republik: Autorität und Solidarität in der Zivilgesellschaft*, Frankfurt am Main: Suhrkamp, 1997.

Frankfurt, Harry, 'Autonomy, Necessity, and Love', in *Necessity, Volition, and Love*, Cambridge University Press, 1999, 129–41.

'On the Necessity of Ideals', in *Necessity, Volition, and Love*, Cambridge University Press, 1999, 108–16.

Fraser, Nancy, 'From Redistribution to Recognition? Dilemmas of Justice in a "Postsocialist" Age', in *Justice Interruptus: Critical Reflections on the 'Post-socialist' Condition*, New York and London: Routledge, 1997, 11–40.

'Rethinking the Public Sphere: A Contribution to the Critique of Actually Existing Democracy', in *Justice Interruptus*, New York and London: Routledge, 1997, 69–98.

Fraser, Nancy and Axel Honneth, *Redistribution or Recognition? A Political-Philosophical Exchange*, trans. J. Golb *et al.*, London: Verso, 2003.

Frenkel-Brunswick, 'Intolerance of Ambiguity as an Emotional and Perceptual Variable', *Journal of Personality* 18, 1949, 108–43.

Freud, Sigmund, *Group Psychology and the Analysis of the Ego*, rev. edn, trans. and ed. J. Strachey, New York: Norton, 1990.

Friedrichs, Christopher R., 'Jews in the Imperial Cities: A Political Perspective', in R. Po-Chia Hsia and H. Lehmann (eds.), *In and Out of the Ghetto*, Cambridge University Press, 1995, 275–88.

Furcha, E. J., '"Turks and Heathen Are Our Kin": The Notion of Tolerance in the Works of Hans Denck and Sebastian Franck', in C. J. Nederman and C. Laursen (eds.), *Difference and Dissent: Theories of Toleration in Medieval and Early Modern Europe*, Lanham, Md.: Rowman and Littlefield, 1996, 83–98.

Gadamer, Hans-Georg, 'Herder und die geschichtliche Welt', in *Neuere Philosophie*, vol. II, Tübingen: Mohr (Siebeck), 1987, 318–35.

Truth and Method, 2nd rev. edn, trans. J. Weinsheimer and D. G. Marshall, New York: Continuum, 1993.

Galeotti, Anna Elisabetta, 'Citizenship and Equality: The Place for Toleration', *Political Theory* 21, 1993, 585–605.

'Toleration as Recognition: The Case for Same-Sex Marriage', in I. Creppell, R. Hardin and S. Macedo (eds.), *Toleration and Identity Conflict*, in preparation.

Gall, Lothar and Rainer Koch, 'Einleitung', in Gall and Koch (eds.), *Der europäische Liberalismus im 19. Jahrhundert: Texte zu seiner Entwicklung*, vol. I, Frankfurt am Main, Berlin and Vienna: Ullstein, 1981, IX–XXIV.

Gallie, W. B., 'Essentially Contested Concepts', *Proceedings of the Aristotelian Society* 56, 1955/56, 167–98.

Gandillac, Maurice de, 'Das Ziel der una religio in varietate rituum', in R. Haubst (ed.), *Der Friede unter den Religionen nach Nikolaus von Kues*, Mainz: Matthias-Grünewald-Verlag, 1984, 192–213.

Garnsey, Peter, 'Religious Toleration in Classical Antiquity', in W. J. Sheils (ed.), *Persecution and Toleration*, Oxford: Blackwell, 1984, 1–28.

Garzón Valdés, Ernesto, '"Nimm deine dreckigen Pfoten von meinem Mozart!" Überlegungen zum Begriff der Toleranz', in E. Garzón Valdes and R. Zimmerling (eds.), *Facetten der Wahrheit*, Freiburg and Munich: Alber, 1995, 469–94.

Gauchet, Marcel, *La Révolution des droits de l'homme*, Paris: Gallimard, 1989.

Gaus, Gerald, *Justificatory Liberalism: An Essay on Epistemology and Political Theory*, Oxford University Press, 1996.

Gawlick, Günter, 'Der Deismus im Colloquium heptaplomeres', in G. Gawlick and F. Niewöhner (eds.), *Jean Bodins Colloquium heptaplomeres*, Wiesbaden: Harrassowitz Verlag, 1996, 13–26.

'Einleitung', in Spinoza, *Theologisch-politischer Traktat*, ed. G. Gawlick, Hamburg: Meiner, 1994, xi–xxix.

Gehlen, Arnold, *Moral und Hypermoral*, Frankfurt am Main: Athenäum, 1969.

Geivett, R. Douglas and Brendan Sweetman (eds.), *Contemporary Perspectives on Religious Epistemology*, Oxford University Press, 1992.

Gelasius, 'Letter 1', in J. H. Robinson, *Readings in European History*, Boston: Ginn, 1905, 72–3 (www.fordham.edu/halsall/source/gelasius1.html (accessed Ocotober 2008)).

Gerhardt, Volker, *Selbstbestimmung: Das Prinzip der Individualität*, Stuttgart: Reclam, 1999.

Gessmann, Martin, *Montaigne und die Moderne: Zu den philosophischen Grundlagen einer Epochenwende*, Hamburg: Meiner, 1997.

Geuss, Raymond, *History and Illusion in Politics*, Cambridge University Press, 2001.

Geyer, Christian (ed.), *Biopolitik: Die Positionen*, Frankfurt am Main: Suhrkamp, 2001.

Goethe, Johann Wolfgang, *Maxims and Reflections*, trans. E. Stopp, ed. P. Hutchinson, London: Penguin, 1998.

Goeze, Johann Melchior, 'Lessings Schwächen (. . .)' 11, in Lessing, *Werke*, vol. viii, ed. H. G. Göpfert, Darmstadt: Wissenschaftliche Buchgesellschaft, 1996.

Goldie, Mark, 'Absolutismus, Parlamentarismus und Revolution in England', in I. Fetscher and H. Münkler (eds.), *Pipers Handbuch der politischen Ideen*, vol. iii, Munich: Piper Verlag, 1985, 275–352.

'Introduction', in John Locke, *Political Essays*, ed. M. Goldie, Cambridge University Press, 1997, xi–xxvii.

'The Theory of Religious Intolerance in Restoration England', in O. P. Grell, J. I. Israel and N. Tyacke (eds.), *From Persecution to Toleration: The Glorious Revolution and Religion in England*, Oxford: Clarendon Press, 1991, 331–68.

Goodwin, John, *Theomachia*, in W. Haller (ed.), *Tracts on Liberty in the Puritan Revolution*, vol. iii, New York: Octagon Books, 1965, 1–58.

Gough, J. W., 'The Development of Locke's Belief in Toleration', in J. Horton and S. Mendus (eds.), *A Letter Concerning Toleration in Focus*, London and New York: Routledge, 1991, 57–77.

Grasmück, Ernst Ludwig, *Coercitio: Staat und Kirche im Donatistenstreit*, Bonn: Röhrscheid, 1964.

Graus, Frantisek, 'Randgruppen der städtischen Gesellschaft im Spätmittelalter', *Zeitschrift Für historische Forschung* 8, 1981, 385–437.

Gray, John, *Two Faces of Liberalism*, New York: The New Press, 2000.

Grell, Ole Peter, Jonathan I. Israel and Nicholas Tyacke (eds.), *From Persecution to Toleration: The Glorious Revolution and Religion in England*, Oxford: Clarendon Press, 1991.

Großheim, Michael, 'Religion und Politik. Die Teile iii und iv des Leviathan', in W. Kersting (ed.), *Thomas Hobbes: Leviathan*, Berlin: Akademie Verlag, 1996, 283–316.

Grotius, Hugo, *The Rights of War and Peace*, trans. J. Morrice, ed. J. Barbeyrac and R. Tuck, Indianapolis, ind.: Liberty Fund, 2005.

Guggisberg, Hans (ed.), *Religiöse Toleranz: Dokumente zur Geschichte einer Forderung*, Stuttgart-Bad Cannstadt: frommann-holzboog, 1984.

  Sebastian Castellio, 1515–1563: Humanist and Defender of Religious Toleration in a Confessional Age, trans. and ed. B. Gordon, Burlington, Vt.: Ashgate, 2002.

Gutmann, Amy, 'The Challenge of Multiculturalism in Political Ethics', *Philosophy and Public Affairs* 22, 1993, 171–206.

Gutmann, Amy and Dennis Thompson, *Democracy and Disagreement*, Cambridge, Mass.: Harvard University Press, 1996.

Habermas, Jürgen, *Between Facts and Norms: Contributions to a Discourse Theory of Law and Democracy*, trans. W. Rehg, Cambridge, Mass.: MIT Press, 1996.

  Between Naturalism and Religion: Philosophical Essays, trans. C. Cronin, Cambridge: Polity, 2008.

  'Discourse Ethics: Notes on a Program of Philosophical Justification', in *Moral Consciousness and Communicative Action*, trans. C. Lenhardt and S. Weber Nicholsen, Cambridge, Mass.: MIT Press, 1990, 43–115.

  'Intolerance and Discrimination', *International Journal of Constitutional Law* 1, 2003, 1–12.

  'Natural Law and Revolution', in *Theory and Practice*, trans. J. Viertel, London: Heinemann, 1974, 82–120.

  'Norms and Values: on Hilary Putnam's Kantian Pragmatism', in *Truth and Justification*, trans. B. Fultner, Cambridge, Mass.: MIT Press, 2003, 237–76.

  'On the Pragmatic, the Ethical, and the Moral Employments of Practical Reason', in *Justification and Application: Remarks on Discourse Ethics*, trans. C. Cronin, Cambridge, Mass.: MIT Press, 1990, 1–17.

  'Popular Sovereignty as Procedure, *Between Facts and Norms*, Cambridge, Mass.: MIT Press, 1996, 463–90.

  'Remarks on Discourse Ethics', in *Justification and Application: Remarks on Discourse Ethics*, trans. C. Cronin, Cambridge, Mass.: MIT Press, 1990, 19–111.

  'Rightness versus Truth: On the Sense of Normative Validity in Moral Judgements and Norms', in *Truth and Justification*, trans. B. Fultner, Cambridge, Mass.: MIT Press, 2003, 237–76.

  'Some Further Clarifications of the Concept of Communicative Rationality', in *On the Pragmatics of Communication*, ed. M. Cooke, Cambridge, Mass.: MIT Press, 1998, 307–42.

  'Struggles for Recognition in the Democratic Constitutional State', in C. Taylor, *Multiculturalism: Examining the Politics of Recognition*, ed. A. Gutmann, Princeton University Press, 1994, 107–48.

  'The Classical Doctrine of Politics in Relation to Social Philosophy', in *Theory and Practice*, trans. J. Viertel, London: Heinemann, 1974, 41–81.

  The Future of Human Nature, trans. H. Beister, M. Pensky and W. Rehg, Cambridge: Polity, 2003.

  The Philosophical Discourse of Modernity, trans. F. Lawrence, Cambridge, Mass.: MIT Press, 1987.

  The Structural Transformation of the Public Sphere, trans. T. Burger and F. Lawrence, Cambridge, Mass.: MIT Press, 1991.

The Theory of Communicative Action, 2 vols., trans. T. McCarthy, Boston: Beacon, 1984
    and 1987.

'Versöhnung durch öffentlichen Vernunftgebrauch', in Philosophische Gesellschaft
    Bad Homburg and W. Hinsch (eds.), *Zur Idee des politischen Liberalismus*, Frankfurt
    am Main: Suhrkamp, 1997, 169–95.

Häfner, Ralph (ed.), *Bodinus Polymeres: Neue Studien zu Jean Bodins Spätwerk*
    (Wolfenbütteler Forschungen 87), Wiesbaden: Harrassowitz, 1999.

Halberstam, Joshua, 'The Paradox of Tolerance', *The Philosophical Forum* 14, 1982/83,
    190–207.

Hallauer, Hermann, 'Das Glaubensgespräch mit den Hussiten', in R. Haubst (ed.),
    Nikolaus von Kues als Promotor der Ökumene, Mainz: Matthias-Grünewald-Verlag,
    1971, 53–75.

Hampsher-Monk, Iain, 'Toleration, the Moral Will and the Justification of Liberalism',
    in J. Horton and S. Mendus (eds.), *Toleration, Identity and Difference*, Houndmills:
    Macmillan, 1999, 17–37.

Hampshire, Stuart, *Justice Is Conflict*, Princeton University Press, 2000.

Spinoza, London: Faber and Faber, 1956.

Hare, R. M., *Freedom and Reason*, Oxford: Clarendon Press, 1963.

Harrington, James, *The Commonwealth of Oceana, tog. with A System of Politics*, ed. J. G. A.
    Pocock, Cambridge University Press, 1992.

Hart, Herbert L. A., *Law, Liberty, and Morality*, Stanford: Stanford University Press, 1963.

The Concept of Law, Oxford: Clarendon Press, 1991.

Hartmann, Wilfried, 'Toleranz im Investiturstreit', in A. Patschovsky and H.
    Zimmermann (eds.), *Toleranz im Mittelalter*, Sigmaringen: Thorbecke, 1998, 27–52.

Hartney, Michael, 'Some Confusions Concerning Collective Rights', in W. Kymlicka
    (ed.), *The Rights of Minority Cultures*, Oxford University Press, 1995, 202–27.

Hassinger, Erich, *Religiöse Toleranz im 16. Jahrhundert*, Basel and Stuttgart: Helbing and
    Lichtenhahn, 1966.

'Wirtschaftliche Motive und Argumente für religiöse Duldsamkeit im 16. und 17.
    Jahrhundert', *Archiv für Reformationsgeschichte* 49, 1958, 226–44.

Haverkamp, Alfred (ed.), *Zur Geschichte der Juden im Deutschland des späten Mittelalters und
    der frühen Neuzeit*, Stuttgart: A. Hiersemann, 1981.

Hay, Johann Leopold, 'Hirtenbrief an den Klerus der Diözese Königgrätz', excerpts in
    H. Guggisberg (ed.), *Religiöse Toleranz*, Stuttgart-Bad Cannstadt: frommann-
    holzboog, 1984, 267–75.

Heckel, Martin, *Deutschland im konfessionellen Zeitalter*, Göttingen: Vandenhoeck und
    Ruprecht, 1983.

*Staat und Kirche nach den Lehren der evangelischen Juristen Deutschlands in der ersten Hälfte
    des 17. Jahrhunderts*, Munich: Claudius Verlag, 1968.

Hegel, Georg Wilhelm Friedrich, *Elements of the Philosophy of Right*, ed. A. Wood, trans.
    H. B. Nisbet, Cambridge University Press, 1991.

Lectures of the Philosophy of History, 1825–26, ed. R. F. Brown, trans. R. F. Brown and J.
    M. Stewart with the assistance of H. S. Harris, rev. edn, Oxford: Clarendon Press,
    2009.

Phenomenology of Spirit, trans. A. V. Miller, Oxford University Press, 1977.

The Positivity of the Christian Religion, in G. F. W. Hegel, *Early Theological Writings*, trans. T. M. Knox, University of Chicago Press, 1948, 67–181.

Heidegger, Martin, 'The Age of the Word Picture', in *The Question concerning Technology and Other Essays*, trans. W. Lovitt, New York: Harper Torch Books, 1977, 115–54.

Heilmann, Alfons, *Texte der Kirchenväter*, vol. III, Munich: Kösel, 1964.

Heine, Heinrich, *Religion and Philosophy in Germany: A Fragment*, ed. T. Pinkard, trans. H. Pollack-Milgate, Cambridge University Press, 2007.

Heitmeyer, Wilhelm and Rainer Dollase (eds.), *Die bedrängte Toleranz: Ethnisch-kulturelle Konflikte, religiöse Differenzen und die Gefahren politisierter Gewalt*, Frankfurt am Main: Suhrkamp, 1996.

Hellermann, Johannes, 'Der Grundrechtsschutz der Religionsfreiheit ethnisch-kultureller Minderheiten', in W. Heitmeyer and R. Dollase (eds.), *Die bedrängte Toleranz*, Frankfurt am Main: Suhrkamp, 1996, 382–400.

Helvetius, Claude Adrien, *Vom Menschen, seinen geistigen Fähigkeiten und seiner Erziehung*, trans. and ed. G. Mensching, Frankfurt am Main: Suhrkamp, 1972.

Henrich, Dieter, *Aesthetic Judgment and the Moral Image of the World*, Stanford University Press, 1992.

'Der Begriff der sittlichen Einsicht und Kants Lehre vom Faktum der Vernunft', in G. Prauss (ed.), *Kant: Zur Deutung seiner Theorie vom Erkennen und Handeln*, Cologne: Kiepenheuer und Witsch, 1973, 223–54.

'Die Grundstruktur der modernen Philosophie. Mit einer Nachschrift: Über Selbstbewußtsein und Selbsterhaltung', in H. Ebeling (ed.), *Subjektivität und Selbsterhaltung: Beiträge zur Diagnose der Moderne*, Frankfurt am Main: Suhrkamp, 1976, 97–143.

'Selbsterhaltung und Geschichtlichkeit', in H. Ebeling (ed.), *Subjektivität und Selbsterhaltung*, Frankfurt am Main: Suhrkamp, 1976, 303–13.

Herder, Johann Gottfried, *Another Philosophy of History for the Education of Mankind*, trans. I. D. Evrigenis and D. Pellerin, Indianapolis, ind.: Hackett, 2004, 3–98.

Outlines of a Philosophy of the History of Man, vols. I and II, trans. T. Churchill, London: Luke Hansard for J. Johnson, 1803. Eighteenth Century Collections Online. Gale. ECCO Consortium Germany (accessed 8 March, 2011).

Herdtle, Claudia and Thomas Leeb (eds.), *Toleranz: Texte zur Theorie und politischen Praxis*, Stuttgart: Reclam, 1987.

Hersch, I. H., 'The French Revolution and the Emancipation of the Jews', in *Jewish Quarterly Review* 19 (3), 1907, 540–65.

Heyd, David, 'Introduction', in Heyd (ed.), *Toleration: An Elusive Virtue*, Princeton University Press, 1996, 3–17.

Hick, John, 'Religious Pluralism', in M. Peterson, W. Hasker, B. Reichenbach and D. Basinger (eds.), *Philosophy of Religion*, Oxford University Press, 1996, 513–23.

'The Pluralistic Hypothesis', in *An Interpretation of Religion*, New Haven: Yale University Press, 2005, 233ff.

Himmelfarb, Gertrude, 'Editor's Introduction', in J. S. Mill, *On Liberty*, Harmondsworth: Penguin, 1974, 7–49.

Hinrichs, Ernst, *Fürstenlehre und politisches Handeln im Frankreich Heinrichs IV*, Göttingen: Vandenhoeck und Ruprecht, 1969.

Hirschman, Albert O., 'Social Conflicts as Pillars of Market Society', in *A Propensity to Self-Subversion*, Cambridge, Mass.: Harvard University Press, 1995, 231–48.

Hobbes, Thomas, *Behemoth or The Long Parliament*, ed. F. Tönnies, University of Chicago Press, 1990.

De cive, ed. R. Tuck and M. Silverthorne, Cambridge University Press, 1998.

Leviathan, ed. R. Tuck, Cambridge University Press, 1996.

Man and Citizen, trans. T. S. K. Scott-Craig *et al.*, ed. B. Gert, Indianapolis and Cambridge: Hackett, 1991.

The Elements of Law Natural and Politic, ed. F. Tönnies, London: Frank Cass, 1969.

Hobsbawm, Eric, *The Age of Extremes: A History of the World, 1914–1991*, New York: Vintage, 1994.

Höffe, Otfried, *Democracy in an Age of Globalisation*, trans. D. Haubrich and M. Ludwig, Dordrecht: Springer, 2007.

'Toleranz: Zur politischen Legitimation der Moderne', in R. Forst (ed.), *Toleranz*, Frankfurt am Main: Campus, 2000, 60–76.

Hollerbach, Alexander, 'Grundlagen des Staatskirchenrechts', in J. Isensee and P. Kirchhof (eds.), *Handbuch des Staatsrechts*, vol. vi: *Freiheitsrechte*, Heidelberg: C. F. Müller, 1989, 471–556.

Hollerbach, Alexander *et al.* (eds.), *Das Kreuz im Widerspruch*, Freiburg: Herder, 1996.

Holmes, Stephen, 'Gag Rules or the Politics of Omission', in J. Elster and R. Slagstad (eds.), *Constitutionalism and Democracy*, Cambridge University Press, 1988, 19–58.

'Jean Bodin: The Paradox of Sovereignty and the Privatization of Religion', in J. R. Pennock and J. W. Chapman (eds.), *Religion, Morality, and the Law*, Nomos xxx, New York University Press, 1988, 5–45.

Holzer, Harold (ed.), *The Lincoln–Douglas Debates*, New York: HarperCollins, 1993.

Honegger, Claudia, 'Die Hexen der Neuzeit. Analysen zur Anderen Seite der okzidentalen Rationalisierung', in *Die Hexen der Neuzeit*, 21–151.

(ed.), *Die Hexen der Neuzeit: Studien zur Sozialgeschichte eines kulturellen Deutungsmusters*, Frankfurt am Main: Suhrkamp, 1978.

Honneth, Axel, 'Between Hermeneutics and Hegelianism: John McDowell and the Challenge of Moral Realism', in N. Smith (ed.), *Reading McDowell: On Mind and World*, London and New York: Routledge, 2002, 246–65.

'Decentred Autonomy: The Subject after the Fall', in *The Fragmented World of the Social: Essays in Social and Political Philosophy*, ed. C. Wright, Albany, NY: SUNY Press, 1995, 261–72.

'Redistribution as Recognition', in N. Fraser and A. Honneth, *Redistribution or Recognition? A Political-Philosophical Exchange*, trans. J. Golb *et al.*, London: Verso, 2003, 110–96.

The Struggle for Recognition: The Moral Grammar of Social Conflicts, trans. J. Anderson, Polity, 1996.

'Unsichtbarkeit. Über die moralische Epistemologie von Anerkennung', in *Unsichtbarkeit: Stationen einer Theorie der Intersubjektivität*, Frankfurt am Main: Suhrkamp, 2003, 10–27.

Hood, F. C, *The Divine Politics of Thomas Hobbes*, Oxford: Clarendon Press, 1964.

Hooker, Richard, *Laws of Ecclesiastical Polity*, in *Works*, vols. i–iii, ed. W. S. Hill, Cambridge, Mass.: Harvard University Press, 1977–81.

Horkheimer, Max, 'Montaigne and the Function of Skepticism', in Horkheimer, *Between Philosophy and Social Science: Selected Early Writings*, trans. G. F. Hunter *et al.*, Cambridge, Mass.: MIT Press, 1995, 265–311.

'The End of Reason', *Studies in Philosophy and Social Science* 9, 1941, 316–89.

Horkheimer, Max and Theodor W. Adorno, *Dialectic of Enlightenment: Philosophical Fragments*, trans. E. Jephcott, Stanford University Press, 2002.

Horton, John, 'Three (Apparent) Paradoxes of Toleration', *Synthesis Philosophica* 17, 1994, 7–20.

'Toleration as a Virtue', in D. Heyd (ed.), *Toleration*, Princeton University Press, 1996, 28–43.

'Toleration, Morality and Harm', in J. Horton and S. Mendus (eds.), *Aspects of Toleration: Philosophical Studies*, London and New York: Methuen, 1985, 113–35.

Houston, Alan, 'Monopolizing Faith: The Levellers, Rights, and Religious Toleration', in A. Levine (ed.), *Early Modern Skepticism and the Origins of Toleration*, Lanham, Md.: Lexington Books, 1999, 147–64.

Hsia, R. Po-Chia, *Social Discipline in the Reformation: Central Europe 1550–1750*, London and New York: Routledge, 1989.

'The Usurious Jew: Economic Structure and Religious Representations in an Anti-Semitic Discourse', in R. Po-Chia Hsia and H. Lehmann (eds.), *In and Out of the Ghetto*, Cambridge University Press, 1995, 161–76.

Hsia, R. Po-Chia and Hartmut Lehmann (eds.), *In and Out of the Ghetto: Jewish–Gentile Relations in Late Medieval and Early Modern Germany*, Cambridge University Press, 1995.

Hubmaier, Balthasar, *Heretics and Those Who Burn Them*, in H. Wayne Pipkin (ed.), *Balthasar Hubmaier: Theologian of Anabaptism*, trans. H. W. Pipkin and J. H. Yoder, Scottdale, Pa.: Herald Press, 1989.

Humboldt, Wilhelm von, 'Ideen über Staatsverfassung, durch die neue französische Konstitution veranlaßt', in *Gesammelte Schriften*, vol. i, ed. Kgl. Preussischen Akademie der Wissenschaften, Berlin, 1903, and Berlin: de Gruyter, 1968.

The Sphere and Duties of Government, trans. J. Coulthard, London: John Chapman, 1854.

'Über Religion', in *Gesammelte Schriften*, vol. i, ed. Kgl. Preussischen Akademie der Wissenschaften, Berlin 1903, and Berlin: de Gruyter, 1968.

Hume, David, *Dialogues concerning Natural Religion*, ed. R. H. Popkin, Indianapolis, Ind.: Hackett, 1980.

Hunter, Ian, 'Kant's *Religion* and Prussian Religious Policy', in *Modern Intellectual History* 2(1), 2005, 1–27.

Huntington, Samuel P., *The Clash of Civilizations*, New York: Simon and Schuster, 1996.

Hurka, Thomas, *Perfectionism*, Oxford University Press, 1993.

Huster, Stefan, 'Bioethik im säkularen Staat', *Zeitschrift für Philosophische Forschung* 55, 2001, 258–76.

Die ethische Neutralität des Staates: Eine liberale Interpretation der Verfassung, Tübingen: Mohr Siebeck, 2003.

Ignatieff, Michael, 'Nationalism and Toleration', in S. Mendus (ed.), *The Politics of Toleration*, Edinburgh University Press, 1999, 77–106.

Israel, Jonathan I., 'William III and Toleration', in O. P. Grell, J. I. Israel and N. Tyacke (eds.), *From Persecution to Toleration: The Glorious Revolution and Religion in England*, Oxford: Clarendon Press, 1991, 129–70.

Jäckel, Eberhard, 'Nachwort', in T. Morus, *Utopia*, Stuttgart: Reclam, 1983, 169–78.

Jäger, Christoph (ed.), *Analytische Religionsphilosophie*, Paderborn: Schöningh (UTB), 1998.

Jefferson, Thomas, *Notes on the State of Virginia*, ed. W. Peden, Chapel Hill: University of North Carolina Press, 1955.

Jellinek, Georg, 'Die Erklärung der Menschen- und Bürgerrechte', in R. Schnur (ed.), *Zur Geschichte der Erklärung der Menschenrechte*, Darmstadt: Wissenschaftliche Buchgesellschaft, 1964, 1–77.

The Declaration of the Rights of Man and of Citizens: A Contribution to Modern Constitutional History, trans. M. Farrand, Westport, Conn.: Hyperion Press, 1979.

Jenkinson, Sally L., 'Two Concepts of Tolerance: Or Why Bayle Is Not Locke', *Journal of Political Philosophy* 4, 1996, 302–21.

Joas, Hans, *The Genesis of Values*, Chicago University Press, 2000.

Jordan, Wilbur K., *The Development of Religious Toleration in England*, 4 vols., London: George Allen and Unwin, 1932–40.

Jurieu, Pierre, *Traité des droits des deux souverains*, Rotterdam: DeGraef, 1687.

Kallscheuer, Otto (ed.), *Das Europa der Religionen: Ein Kontinent zwischen Säkularisierung und Fundamentalismus*, Frankfurt am Main: Fischer, 1996.

Kamen, Henry, *The Rise of Toleration*, New York: McGraw-Hill, 1967.

Kant, Immanuel, 'An Answer to the Question: What Is Enlightenment?', in Kant, *Practical Philosophy*, ed. and trans. Mary Gregor, Cambridge University Press, 1996, 11–22.

Critique of Practical Reason, ed. and trans. M. Gregor, Cambridge University Press, 1997.

Critique of Pure Reason, ed. and trans. P. Guyer and A. W. Wood, Cambridge University Press, 1998.

Critique of the Power of Judgement, ed. P. Guyer, trans. P. Guyer and E. Matthews, Cambridge University Press, 2000.

Groundwork of the Metaphysics of Morals, ed. and trans. M. Gregor, Cambridge University Press, 1998.

Letter to Moses Mendelssohn, August 16, 1783, in Kant, *Correspondence*, ed. and trans. A. Zweig, Cambridge University Press, 1999, 201–4.

'On the Common Saying: That May Be Correct in Theory, but It Is of no Use in Practice', in Kant, *Practical Philosophy*, ed. and trans. M. Gregor, Cambridge University Press, 1996, 279–309.

Religion within the Bounds of Mere Reason, ed. and trans. A. Wood and G. Di Giovanni, Cambridge University Press, 1998.

'Review of J. G. Herder's *Ideas for the Philosophy of the History of Humanity. Parts 1 and 2* (1785)', in Kant, *Anthropology, History, and Education*, ed. G. Zöller and R. B. Loudon, Cambridge University Press, 2007, 121–42.

The Conflict of the Faculties, in Kant, *Religion and Rational Theology*, ed. and trans. A. W. Wood and G. Di Giovanni, Cambridge University Press, 1996.

The Metaphysics of Morals, ed. and trans. M. Gregor, Cambridge University Press, 1996.

'Toward Perpetual Peace: A Philosophical Project', in Kant, *Practical Philosophy*, ed. and trans. Mary Gregor, Cambridge University Press, 1996, 317–51.

'What Does It Mean to Orient Oneself in Thinking?', in *Religion within the Bounds of Mere Reason*, ed. and trans. A. Wood and G. Di Giovanni, Cambridge University Press, 1998, 1–14.

Karniel, Joseph, *Die Toleranzpolitik Kaiser Josephs II.*, trans. L. Koppel, Gerlingen: Bleicher, 1985.

Katz, David S., 'The Jews of England and 1688', in O. P. Grell, J. I. Israel and N. Tyacke (eds.), *From Persecution to Toleration: The Glorious Revolution and Religion in England*, Oxford: Clarendon Press, 1991, 217–50.

Katz, Jacob, 'Aufklärung und Toleranz', in P. van der Osten-Sacken (ed.), *Toleranz heute: 250 Jahre nach Mendelssohn und Lessing*, Berlin: Institut Kirche und Judentum, 1979, 6–14.

Kelsen, Hans, 'On the Essence and Value of Democracy', in A. Jacobson and B. Schlink (eds.), *Weimar: A Jurisprudence of Crisis*, Berkeley and Los Angeles: University of California Press, 2000, 84–109.

'Verteidigung der Demokratie', in *Demokratie und Sozialismus*, ed. N. Leser, Darmstadt: Wissenschaftliche Buchgesellschaft, 1967, 60–8.

'What Is Justice?', in Kelsen, *What is Justice? Justice, Law, and Politics in the Mirror of Science: Collected Essays by Hans Kelsen*, Berkeley, Los Angeles and London: University of California Press, 1971, 1–24.

Kersting, Wolfgang, *Die politische Philosophie des Gesellschaftsvertrags*, Darmstadt: Wissenschaftliche Buchgesellschaft, 1994.

Thomas Hobbes zur Einführung, Hamburg: Junius, 1992.

Khoury, Adel Theodor, *Toleranz im Islam*, Altenberge: CIS, 1986.

Kierkegaard, Sören, 'Eine literarische Anzeige', trans. E. Hirsch, *Gesammelte Werke*, 17. Abteilung, Düsseldorf: Eugen Diederichs, 1954.

Kilkullen, John, *Sincerity and Truth: Essays on Arnauld, Bayle, and Toleration*, Oxford: Clarendon Press, 1988.

Kinder, Ernst, 'Gottesreich und Weltreich bei Augustinus und Luther', in H.-H. Schrey (ed.), *Reich Gottes und Welt: Die Lehre Luthers von den zwei Reichen*, Darmstadt: Wissenschaftliche Buchgesellschaft, 1969, 40–69.

King, Preston, *Thomas Hobbes: Critical Assessments*, vol. IV: *Religion*, London and New York: Routledge, 1993.

Toleration, New York: St. Martin's Press, 1976.

Kittsteiner, Heinz D., *Die Entstehung des modernen Gewissens*, Frankfurt am Main: Suhrkamp, 1995.

Klein, Richard, 'Das politische Denken des Christentums', in I. Fetscher and H. Münkler (eds.), *Pipers Handbuch der politischen Ideen*, vol. I, Munich: Piper, 1988, 595–634.

Kniffka, Hannes, 'Zur Kulturspezifik von Toleranzkonzepten. Linguistische Perspektiven', in A. Wierlacher (ed.), *Kulturthema Toleranz*, Munich: Iudicium, 1996, 205–60.

Kompridis, Nikolas, 'On World Disclosure: Heidegger, Habermas and Dewey', *Thesis Eleven* 37, 1994, 29–45.

Korsgaard, Christine, 'The Reasons We Can Share', in *Creating the Kingdom of Ends*, Cambridge University Press, 1996, 275–310.

The Sources of Normativity, Cambridge University Press, 1996.

Koselleck, Reinhart, 'Aufklärung und die Grenzen ihrer Toleranz', in T. Rendtorff (ed.), *Glaube und Toleranz: Das theologische Erbe der Aufklärung*, Gütersloh: Mohn, 1982, 256–71.

Critique and Crisis: Enlightenment and the Pathogenesis of Modern Society, Cambridge, Mass.: MIT Press, 1988.

'"Space of Experience" and "Horizon of Expectation": Two Historical Categories', in *Futures Past: On the Semantics of Historical Time*, trans. K. Tribe, Cambridge, Mass.: MIT Press, 1985, 267–88.

(ed.), *Studien zum Beginn der modernen Welt*, Stuttgart: Klett-Cotta, 1977.

Kötting, Bernhard, *Religionsfreiheit und Toleranz im Altertum*, Opladen: Westdeutscher Verlag, 1977.

Krämer, Werner, 'Der Beitrag des Nikolaus von Kues zum Unionskonzil mit der Ostkirche', in R. Haubst (ed.), *Nikolaus von Kues als Promotor der Ökumene*, Mainz: Matthias-Grünewald-Verlag, 1971, 34–52.

Kristeller, Paul Oskar, *The Philosophy of Marsilio Ficino*, trans. V. Conant, New York: Columbia University Press, 1943.

Kristeva, Julia, *Strangers to Ourselves*, trans. L. S. Roudiez, New York: Columbia University Press, 1991.

Kühn, Johannes, *Toleranz und Offenbarung*, Leipzig: Meiner, 1923.

Kukathas, Chandran, 'Are There Any Cultural Rights?', in W. Kymlicka (ed.), *The Rights of Minority Cultures*, Oxford University Press, 1995, 228–55.

'Cultural Toleration', in I. Shapiro and W. Kymlicka (eds.), *Ethnicity and Group Rights*, Nomos XXXIX, New York University Press, 1997, 69–104.

Küng, Hans, 'Vorwort', in G. Mensching, *Toleranz und Wahrheit in der Religion*, ed. U. Tworuschka, Weimar and Jena: Wartburg Verlag, 1996, 11–14.

Kuntz, Marion Leathers, 'The Concept of Toleration in the *Colloquium Heptaplomeres* of Jean Bodin', in J. C. Laursen and C. J. Nederman (eds.), *Beyond the Persecuting Society: Religious Toleration before the Enlightenment*, Philadelphia: University of Pennsylvania Press, 1998, 125–44.

Kymlicka, Will, 'Do We Need a Liberal Theory of Minority Rights? A Reply to Carens, Young, Parekh and Forst', *Constellations* 4, 1997, 72–87.

Finding Our Way: Rethinking Ethnocultural Relations in Canada, Oxford University Press, 1998.

Multicultural Citizenship, Oxford University Press, 1995.

Politics in the Vernacular: Nationalism, Multiculturalism, and Citizenship, Oxford University Press, 2001.

'Two Models of Pluralism and Tolerance', in D. Heyd (ed.), *Toleration*, Princeton University Press, 1996, 81–105.

Labrousse, Elisabeth, *Bayle*, trans. D. Potts, Oxford University Press, 1983.

Pierre Bayle, vol. I: *Du pays de foix à la cité d'Érasme*, The Hague: Martinus Nijhoff, 1963; vol. II: *Heterodoxie et rigorisme*, The Hague: Martinus Nijhoff, 1964.

'The Political Ideas of the Huguenot Diaspora (Bayle and Jurieu)', in R. M. Golden (ed.), *Church, State, and Society under the Bourbon Kings of France*, Lawrence: University of Kansas Press, 1982, 222–83.

Lactantius, *De institutionibus divinis*, in Patrologiae cursus completus, series latina, ed. P. G. Migne, vol. VI, Paris, 1844 (English: Lactantius, *The Divine Institutes*, trans. W. Fletcher (www.newadvent.org/fathers/0701.htm (accessed October 2008)).

De mortibus persecutorum, in Patrologiae cursus completus, series latina, ed. P. G. Migne, vol. VII, Paris, 1844.

Laden, Anthony Simon, *Reasonably Radical: Deliberative Liberalism and the Politics of Identity*, Ithaca, NY: Cornell University Press, 2001.

Lafont, Cristina, 'Realismus und Konstruktivismus in der kantianischen Moralphilosophie – das Beispiel der Diskursethik', *Deutsche Zeitschrift für Philosophie* 50, 2002, 39–52.

'World Disclosure and Reference', *Thesis Eleven* 37, 1994, 46–63.

Larmore, Charles, 'Denken und Handeln', *Deutsche Zeitschrift für Philosophie* 45, 1997, 183–95.

'Der Zwang des besseren Arguments', in L. Wingert and K. Günther (eds.), *Die Öffentlichkeit der Vernunft und die Vernunft der Öffentlichkeit* (Festschrift J. Habermas), Frankfurt am Main: Suhrkamp, 2001, 106–25.

'Moral Knowledge', in *The Morals of Modernity*, Cambridge University Press, 1996, 89–117.

'Pluralism and Reasonable Disagreement', in *The Morals of Modernity*, Cambridge University Press, 1996, 152–74.

'Political Liiberalism', in *Political Theory* 18 (3), 1990, 339–60.

'The Autonomy of Morality', in *The Autonomy of Morality*, Cambridge University Press, 2008, 87–136.

'The Moral Basis of Political Liberalism', *Journal of Philosophy* 96, 1999, 599–625.

The Romantic Legacy, New York: Columbia University Press, 1996.

Lea, Henry Charles, *A History of the Inquisition in the Middle Ages*, vol. I, New York: Russell and Russell, 1958.

Leaman, Oliver, *Averroes and his Philosophy*, Oxford: Clarendon Press, 1988.

Lecler, Joseph, 'Die Gewissensfreiheit', in H. Lutz (ed.), *Zur Geschichte der Toleranz und Religionsfreiheit*, Darmstadt: Wissenschaftliche Buchgesellschaft, 1977, 331–71.

Toleration and the Reformation, trans. T. L. Westow, New York: Association Press, 1960.

Leggewie, Claus and Horst Meier (eds.), *Verbot der NPD oder Mit Rechtsradikalen leben?*, Frankfurt am Main: Suhrkamp, 2002.

Leibholz, Gerhard, 'Vorwort', in L. Strauss, *Naturrecht und Geschichte*, Frankfurt am Main: Suhrkamp, 1977, VII–XI.

Leibniz, Gottfried Wilhelm, *Theodicy: Essays on the Goodness of God, the Freedom on Man and the Origin of Evil*, trans. E. M. Huggard, La Salle, Ill.: Open Court, 1985.

Lessing, Gotthold Ephraim, 'A Parabel', in *Philosophical and Theological Writings*, ed. and trans. H. B. Nisbet, Cambridge University Press, 2005, 110–19.

'Axioms (If There Are Any in Matters Such as This)', in *Philosophical and Theological Writings*, ed. and trans. H. B. Nisbet, Cambridge University Press, 2005, 120–47.

'Bemerkungen zu "Von Duldung der Deisten"' in *Werke*, vol. VII, ed. H. G. Göpfert, Darmstadt: Wissenschaftliche Buchgesellschaft, 1996, 313–30.

'Bibliolatrie', in *Werke*, vol. VII, ed. H. G. Göpfert, Darmstadt: Wissenschaftliche Buchgesellschaft, 1996, 667–72.

'Editorial Commentary on the "Fragments" of Reimarus', in *Philosophical and Theological Writings*, ed. and trans. H. B. Nisbet, Cambridge University Press, 2005, 61–82.

Nathan the Wise, in *Nathan the Wise, Minna von Barnhelm, and Other Plays and Writings*, ed. P. Demetz, New York: Continuum, 1991, 173–275.

Preface to *Nathan the Wise*, in *Nathan the Wise, with an Introduction and Notes*, trans. E. K. Corbett, London: Trench, 1833.

The Education of the Human Race, in *Philosophical and Theological Writings*, ed. and trans. H. B. Nisbet, Cambridge University Press, 2005, 217–40.

'Womit sich die geoffenbarte Religion am meisten weiß, macht sie mir gerade am verdächtigsten', in *Werke*, vol. VII, ed. H. G. Göpfert, Darmstadt: Wissenschaftliche Buchgesellschaft, 1996.

Levinas, Emmanuel, *Totality and Infinity: An Essay on Exteriority*, trans. A. Lingis, The Hague and Boston: Nijhoff, 1979.

Levine, Alan, 'Skepticism, Self, and Toleration in Montaigne's Political Thought', in A. Levine (ed.), *Early Modern Skepticism and the Origins of Toleration*, Lanham, Md.: Lexington Books, 1999, 51–76.

Lewis, Bernard and Friedrich Niewöhner (eds.), *Religionsgespräche im Mittelalter*, Wiesbaden: Otto Harrassowitz, 1992.

Lewis, David, 'Mill and Milquetoast', in *Papers in Ethics and Social Philosophy*, Cambridge University Press, 2000, 159–86.

L'Hôpital, Michel de, *Œuvres complètes*, ed. P. J. S. Dufay, 3 vols. (Paris, 1824–25), Geneva: Slatkine Reprints, 1968.

'Speech to the Estates-General of Orléans (December 13, 1560)', in De L'Hôpital, *Œuvres complètes*, vol. II, 399–402 (English excerpt: 'Speech to the Estates-General of Orléans (December 13, 1560)' in C. Lindberg (ed.), *The European Reformations Sourcebook*, Malden: Blackwell, 1991).

'Speech to the Assembly of Parliamentary Delegates at Saint-Germain, January 3, 1562', in De L'Hôpital, *Œuvres complètes*, vol. I, 435–58.

Lilburne, John, *Englands Birth-Right Justified*, in W. Haller (ed.), *Tracts on Liberty in the Puritan Revolution*, vol. III, New York: Octagon Books, 1965, 257–308.

Lindberg, Carter (ed.), *The European Reformations Sourcebook*, Malden, Blackwell, 2000.

Lipsius, Justus, *Politica: Six Books of Politics or Political Instruction*, ed. J. H. Waszink, Assen: Uitgeverij Van Gorcum, 2004.

Llull, Ramon, *Book of the Gentile and the Three Wise Men*, in *Selected Works of Ramon Llull*, ed. and trans. A. Bonner, 2 vols., Princeton University Press, 1985, vol. I, 91–304.

Disputatio Raymundi christiani et Hamar sarraceni, in *Raimundi Lulli Opera*, vol. IV, Mainz 1729, Frankfurt am Main: Minerva, 1965.

Doctor Illuminatus: A Ramón Llull Reader, ed. and trans. A. Bonner and E. Bonner, Princeton University Press, 1994.

Vita Coaetanea, in *Raimundi Lulli Opera Latina*, vol. VIII, Turnhout: Brepols, 1980 (English: Ramon Llull, *Contemporary Life*, in *Selected Works of Ramon Llull*, ed. and trans. A. Bonner, 2 vols., Princeton University Press, 1985, vol. I, 12–84).

Locke, John, *A Fourth Letter for Toleration*, in *The Works of John Locke*, vol. VI, 1823, reprint Aalen: Scientia, 1963.

A Letter Concerning Toleration, ed. J. Tully, Indianapolis, Ind.: Hackett, 1983 (Latin: *Epistola de tolerantia*, ed. M. Montuori, The Hague: Martinus Nijhoff, 1963).

An Essay Concerning Human Understanding, ed. P. H. Nidditch, Oxford: Clarendon Press, 1975.

'An Essay on Toleration', in *Political Essays*, ed. M. Goldie, Cambridge University Press, 1997, 134–59.

A Second Letter Concerning Toleration, in *The Works of John Locke*, vol. VI, 1823, reprint Aalen: Scientia, 1963.

A Third Letter for Toleration: to the Author of the Third Letter concerning Toleration, in *The Works of John Locke*, vol. VI, 1823, reprint Aalen: Scientia, 1963.

First Tract on Government, in *Political Essays*, ed. M. Goldie, Cambridge University Press, 1997.

Letter to Ph. v. Limborch, 6 June 1689, in *The Correspondence of John Locke*, vol. III, ed. E. S. de Beer, Oxford: Clarendon Press, 1978, 633–4.

Second Tract on Government, in *Political Essays*, ed. M. Goldie, Cambridge University Press, 1997.

The Reasonableness of Christianity, as delivered in the Scriptures, in *The Works of John Locke*, vol. VII, 1823, reprint Aalen: Scientia, 1963.

'Toleration D', in *Political Essays*, ed. M. Goldie, Cambridge University Press, 1997, 276–7.

Two Treatises of Government, ed. P. Laslett, Cambridge University Press, 1989.

Lohrmann, Klaus, 'Fürstenschutz als Grundlage jüdischer Existenz im Mittelalter', in A. Patschovsky and H. Zimmermann (eds.), *Toleranz im Mittelalter*, Sigmaringen: Thorbecke, 1998, 75–100.

Lohse, Bernhard (ed.), *Der Durchbruch der reformatorischen Erkenntnis bei Luther*, Darmstadt: Wissenschaftliche Buchgesellschaft, 1968.

Luhmann, Niklas, *Gesellschaftsstruktur und Semantik: Studien zur Wissenssoziologie der modernen Gesellschaft*, vol. III, Frankfurt am Main: Suhrkamp, 1993.

Lukes, Steven, 'Making Sense of Moral Conflict', in *Moral Conflict and Politics*, Oxford University Press, 1991, 3–20.

'Relativism: Cognitive and Moral', *Proceedings of the Aristotelian Society*, Suppl. 48, 1974, 165–89.

'Toleration and Recognition', *Ratio Juris* 10, 1997, 213–22.

Luther, Martin, *Address to the Nobility*, trans. R. S. Grignon, Charleston, SC: BiblioBazaar, 2008.

'Before the Diet at Worms (18 April 1521)' (orig. lat. in *WA* 7, 832–8), in W. J. Bryan (ed.), *The World's Famous Orations*, New York: Funk and Wagnalls, 1906 (www.bartleby.com/268/7/8.html (accessed December 2008)).

Brief an die Fürsten Johann und Georg von Anhalt (11 and 12 June 1541), *Luthers Werke (WA)*, *Briefe*, vol. IX, Weimar: Hermann Böhlaus Nachfolger, 1941, 436–45.

Brief an J. L. Metzsch (26 August 1529), *Luthers Werke (WA)*, *Briefe*, vol. V, Weimar: Hermann Böhlaus Nachfolger, 1934, 136–7.

Brief an Kurfürst Johann von Sachsen (9 February 1526), *Luthers Werke (WA)*, *Briefe*, vol. IV, Weimar: Hermann Böhlaus Nachfolger, 1933, 27–9.

Concerning Christian Liberty, trans. R. S. Grignon, vol. XXXVI, Pt 6, The Harvard Classics, New York: P. F. Collier and Son, 1909–14 (www.bartleby.com/36/6/ (accessed December 2008)) (cited by paragraph number of online edition) (German: *Von der Freiheit eines Christenmenschen*, in *Luthers Werke in Auswahl*, ed. O. Clemen, vol. II, Berlin: de Gruyter, 1959).

Heidelberg Disputation, in Gerhard O. Forde, *On Being a Theologian of the Cross: Reflections on Luther's Heidelberg Disputation, 1518*, Grand Rapids, Mich.: Wm. B. Eerdmans, 1997, 23–116 (Latin original in *WA* 1, 353–65).

Letter to George Spalatin (11 November 1525), quoted from, Preserved Smith, *The Life and Letters of Martin Luther*, London, Routledge, 1968, 217.

On Secular Authority, in Harro Höpfel (ed.), *Luther and Calvin on Secular Authority*, trans. H. Höpfel, Cambridge University Press, 1991, 1–43.

On the Bondage of the Will, in E. Gordon Rupp (ed.), *Luther and Erasmus: Free Will and Salvation*, trans. E. G. Rupp and P. S. Watson, Louisville, Ky.: Westminster John Knox Press, 1978, 101–334 (Latin: *De servo arbitrio*, in *Luthers Werke in Auswahl*, ed. O. Clemen, vol. III, Berlin: de Gruyter, 1959).

'Preface to the Complete Edition of Luther's Latin Works (1545)' (orig. lat. in *WA* 54, 179–87), trans. A. Thornton (www.iclnet.org/pub/resources/text/wittenberg/ luther/preflat-eng.txt (accessed December 2008)).

Sermons of Martin Luther: The Church Postils, ed. J. N. Lenker, Grand Rapids, Mich.: Baker Book House, 1995.

The Babylonian Captivity of the Church: A Prelude 1520 (orig. lat. in *WA* 6, 497–573) (www.lutherdansk.dk/Web-Babylonian%20Captivitate/Martin%20Luther.htm (accessed December 2008)).

Vermahnung zum Frieden auf die zwölf Artikel der Bauernschaft in Schwaben, in *Luthers Werke in Auswahl*, ed. O. Clemen, vol. III, Berlin: de Gruyter, 1959.

Vom Greuel der Stillmesse ('On the Abomination of the Low Mass'), in *Luthers Werke (WA)*, vol. XVIII, Weimar: Hermann Böhlaus Nachfolger, 1908.

Von den Juden und ihren Lügen, in *Luthers Werke (WA)*, vol. LIII, Weimar: Hermann Böhlaus Nachfolger, 1920.

'Whether Soldiers, Too, Can Be Saved', in *Luther's Works*, ed. J. Pelikan, H. C. Oswald and H. T. Lehmann, 55 vols., St. Louis: Concordia, 1955–86, vol. XLVI, 99–102.

Wider die räuberischen und mörderischen Rotten der Bauern, in *Luthers Werke in Auswahl*, ed. O. Clemen, vol. III, Berlin: de Gruyter, 1959.

Luther, Martin *et al.*, *Ob Christliche Fürsten schuldig sind, der Widerteuffer unchristlichen Sect mit leiblicher straffe, und mit dem schwert zu wehren* ('Should Christian princes use the sword and employ physical punishment angainst Anabaptists?'), in *Luthers Werke (WA)*, vol. L, Weimar: Hermann Böhlaus Nachfolger, 1914 (English: www.uni-duisburg.de/Institute/CollCart/es/sem/s6/txt08_2.htm (accessed December 2008)).

Macartney, C. A. (ed.), *The Habsburg and Hohenzollern Dynasties in the Seventeenth and Eighteenth Centuries*, New York: Walker, 1970.

McClain, Linda C., 'Toleration, Autonomy, and Governmental Promotion of Good Lives: Beyond "Empty" Toleration to Toleration as Respect', *Ohio State Law Journal* 59, 1998, 19–132.

McClure, K., 'Difference, Diversity, and the Limits of Toleration', *Political Theory* 18, 1990, 361–91.

McDowell, John, 'Might There Be External Reasons', in *Mind, Value, and Reality*, Cambridge, Mass.: Harvard University Press, 1998, 95–111.

Mind and World, Cambridge, Mass.: Harvard University Press, 1994.

'Two Sorts of Naturalism', in *Mind, Value, and Reality*, Cambridge, Mass.: Harvard University Press, 1998, 167–97.

'Virtue and Reason', in *Mind, Value, and Reality*, Cambridge, Mass.: Harvard University Press, 1998, 50–73.

Macedo, Stephen, 'Liberal Civic Education and Religious Fundamentalism: The Case of God v. John Rawls?', *Ethics* 105, 1995, 468–96.

Liberal Virtues, Oxford University Press, 1991.

'Toleration and Fundamentalism', in R. E. Goodin und P. Pettit (eds.), *A Companion to Contemporary Political Philosophy*, Oxford: Blackwell, 1993, 622–8.

Machiavelli, Niccolò, *The Discourses*, ed. B. Crick, trans. L. J. Walker and B. Rickardson, Harmondsworth: Penguin, 1983.

The Prince (Il principe), ed. Q. Skinner, trans. R. Price, Cambridge University Press, 1988.

MacIntyre, Alasdair, *After Virtue: A Study in Moral Theory*, vol. II, London: Duckworth, 1987.

'Toleration and the Goods of Conflict', in S. Mendus (ed.), *The Politics of Toleration*, Edinburgh University Press, 1999, 133–55.

Whose Justice? Which Rationality? London: Duckworth, 1988.

Macpherson, Crawford Brough, *The Political Theory of Possessive Individualism*, Oxford University Press, 1962.

Madison, James, Federalist Paper No. 51, in A. Hamilton, J. Madison, and J. Jay, *The Federalist Papers*, ed. C. Rossiter, New York: New American Library, 1961, 214–21.

Maihofer, Werner (ed.), *Naturrecht oder Positivismus?*, Darmstadt: Wissenschaftliche Buchgesellschaft, 1966.

Maimonides (Mose ben Maimon), *The Book of Knowledge (from the Mishnah Torah of Maimonides)*, trans. H. M. Russell and Rabbi J. Weinberg, Edinburgh: Royal College of Physicians of Edinburgh, 1981.

The Code of Maimonides (Mishneh Tora), New Haven: Yale University Press, 1949–.

The Guide for the Perplexed, trans. M. Friedländer, New York: E. P. Dutton, 1904 (quoted from: www.forgottenbooks.org (accessed November 2008)).

Mandt, Hella, 'Grenzen politischer Toleranz in der offenen Gesellschaft', *Aus Politik und Zeitgeschichte* 3, 1978, 3–16.

Mann, Thomas, *The Magic Mountain*, trans. J. E. Woods, New York: Knopf, 2005.

Marcuse, Herbert, 'Repressive Tolerance', in R. P. Wolff, B. Moore and H. Marcuse (eds.), *A Critique of Pure Tolerance*, Boston: Beacon Press, 1969, 81–117.

Margalit, Avishai, 'Der Ring: Über religiösen Pluralismus', trans. M. Iser, in R. Forst (ed.), *Toleranz*, Frankfurt am Main and New York: Campus, 2000, 162–76.

The Decent Society, trans. N. Goldblum, Cambridge, Mass.: Harvard University Press, 1996.

The Ethics of Memory, Cambridge, Mass.: Harvard University Press, 2002.

Marshall, John, *John Locke, Toleration and Early Enlightenment Culture*, Cambridge University Press, 2006.

Marsilius of Padua, *Defensor pacis*, ed. and trans. A. Gewirth, New York: Columbia University Press, 2001.

Martin, James G., *The Tolerant Personality*, Detroit, Mich.: Wayne State University Press, 1964.

Martinich, Aloysius P., *The Two Gods of Leviathan: Thomas Hobbes on Religion and Politics*, Cambridge University Press, 1992.

Marty, Martin E. and R. Scott Appleby, *The Glory and the Power: The Fundamentalist Challenge to the Modern World*, Boston: Beacon Press, 1992.

Marx, Karl, 'On the Jewish Question', in R. C. Tucker (ed.), *The Marx–Engels Reader*, 2nd edn, New York: W. W. Norton, 1978, 26–52.

Maus, Ingeborg, *Bürgerliche Rechtstheorie und Faschismus: Zur sozialen Funktion und aktuellen Wirkung der Theorie Carl Schmitts*, 2nd expanded edn, Munich: Fink, 1980.

Zur Aufklärung der Demokratietheorie, Frankfurt am Main: Suhrkamp, 1992.

Meinecke, Friedrich, *Machiavellism: The Doctrine of Raison d'État and its Place in Modern History*, trans. D. Scott, New Brunswick: Transaction Publishers, 1997.

Meinhardt, Helmut, 'Konjekturale Erkenntnis und religiöse Toleranz', in R. Haubst (ed.), *Der Friede unter den Religionen nach Nikolaus von Kues*, Mainz: Matthias-Grünewald-Verlag, 1984, 325–32.

Mendelssohn, Moses, *Jerusalem: A Treatise on Ecclesiastical Authority and Judaism*, trans. M. Samuels, 3 vols., London: Longman, Orme, Brown and Longmans, 1838.

'Open Letter to Deacon Lavater of Zurich', trans. R. Levy, in *German History in Documents and Images*, vol. II: *From Absolutism to Napoleon, 1648–1815*, http://germanhistorydocs.ghi-dc.org/sub_document_s.cfm?document_id=3646 (accessed 17 March 2010).

'Preface to Manasseh Ben Israel, *Vindiciae Judaeorum*', in Mendelssohn, *Jerusalem: A Treatise on Ecclesiastical Authority and Judaism*, vol. I, 77–116.

Mendus, Susan, 'Locke: Toleration, Morality and Rationality', in J. Horton and S. Mendus (eds.), *A Letter Concerning Toleration in Focus*, London and New York: Routledge, 1991, 147–62.

Toleration and the Limits of Liberalism, Atlantic Highlands, NJ: Humanities Press, 1989.

Menke, Christoph, *Spiegelungen der Gleichheit*, Berlin: Akademie Verlag, 2000.

Tragödie im Sittlichen: Gerechtigkeit und Freiheit nach Hegel, Frankfurt am Main: Suhrkamp, 1996.

Mensching, Gustav, *Tolerance and Truth in Religion*, trans. H.-J. Klimkeit, University of Alabama Press, 1971.

Meuthen, Erich, 'Der Fall von Konstantinopel und der lateinische Westen', in R.
    Haubst (ed.), *Der Friede unter den Religionen nach Nikolaus von Kues*, Mainz:
    Matthias-Grünewald-Verlag, 1984, 35–60.
'Nikolaus von Kues in der Entscheidung zwischen Konzil und Papst', in R. Haubst
    (ed.), *Nikolaus von Kues als Promotor der Ökumene*, Mainz: Matthias-
    Grünewald-Verlag, 1971, 19–33.
Miethke, Jürgen, 'Der Weltanspruch des Papstes im späteren Mittelalter. Die Politische
    Theorie der Traktate *De potestate papae*', in I. Fetscher and H. Münkler (eds.), *Pipers
    Handbuch der politischen Ideen*, vol. II, Munich: Piper, 1993, 351–445.
Mill, James, *The Principles of Toleration*, New York: Lenox Hill, 1837, reprint 1971.
Mill, John Stuart, *On Liberty*, in *Mill: Texts, Commentaries*, ed. A. Ryan, New York:
    Norton, 1975, 41–132.
Milton, John, *Areopagitica*, in *Complete Poems and Major Prose*, ed. M. Y. Hughes, New
    York: The Odyssey Press, 716–49.
A Treatise of Civil Power in Ecclesiastical Causes, in *Complete Poems and Major Prose*, ed. M.
    Y. Hughes, New York: The Odyssey Press, 1957, 839–55.
*Of True Religion, Heresy, Schism, Toleration; and what best means may be used against the
    growth of Popery*, in *The Prose Works of John Milton*, ed. R. W. Griswold, Philadelphia:
    John W. Moore, 1847, 343–9.
The Reason of Church Government Urged against Prelaty, in *Complete Poems and Major
    Prose*, ed. M. Y. Hughes, New York: The Odyssey Press, 640–89.
The Second Defense of the People of England, excerpts in *Complete Poems and Major Prose*,
    ed. M. Y. Hughes, New York: The Odyssey Press, 817–38.
The Tenure of Kings and Magistrates, in *Complete Poems and Major Prose*, ed. M. Y.
    Hughes, New York: The Odessey Press, 750–80.
Minois, Georges, *Histoire de l'athéisme: les incroyants dans le monde occidental des origines à
    nos jours*, Paris: Fayard, 1998.
Minow, Martha, *Making all the Difference: Inclusion, Exclusion, and American Law*, Ithaca,
    NY: Cornell University Press, 1990.
'Putting Up and Putting Down: Tolerance Reconsidered', in M. Tushnet (ed.),
    Comparative Constitutional Federalism: Europe and America, New York: Greenwood
    Press, 1990, 77–113.
Mirabeau, Honoré-Gabriel de Riquetti, Comte de, *Œuvres de Mirabeau*, vol. I, ed. J.
    Mérilhou, Paris: Lecointe et Pougin, 1834.
Mitscherlich, Alexander, 'Toleranz – Überprüfung eines Begriffs', in *Gesammelte
    Schriften*, vol. v, ed. H. Haase, Frankfurt am Main: Suhrkamp, 1983, 429–55.
'"Wie ich mir – so ich dir". Zur Psychologie der Toleranz', in *Gesammelte Schriften*,
    vol. v, ed. H. Haase, Frankfurt am Main: Suhrkamp, 1983, 410–28.
Möhring, Hannes, 'Die Kreuzfahrer, ihre muslimischen Untertanen und die heiligen
    Stätten des Islam', in A. Patschovsky and H. Zimmermann (eds.), *Toleranz im
    Mittelalter*, Sigmaringen: Thorbecke, 1998, 129–58.
Möller, Horst, *Vernunft und Kritik: Deutsche Aufklärung im 17. und 18. Jahrhundert*,
    Frankfurt am Main: Suhrkamp, 1986.
Moller Okin, Susan, *Is Multiculturalism Bad for Women?*, ed. J. Cohen, M. Howard and M.
    Nussbaum, Princeton University Press, 1999.

Montaigne, Michel de, *The Complete Essays of Montaigne*, trans. D. M. Frame, Stanford
    University Press, 1958 (French: *Essais*, 3 vols., Paris: Société les belles lettres, 1946).
Montesquieu, Charles-Louis de Secondat, *Persian Letters*, in *The Complete Works*, vol. III,
    London: T. Evans and W. Davis, 1777, 191–485.
    The Spirit of the Laws, 2 vols. in one, trans. T. Nugent, New York: Hafner, 1949.
Moody-Adams, Michele M., *Fieldwork in Familiar Places: Morality, Culture, and Philosophy*,
    Cambridge, Mass.: Harvard University Press, 1997.
Moon, J. Donald, *Constructing Community: Moral Pluralism and Tragic Conflicts*, Princeton
    University Press, 1993.
Moore, Robert Ian, *The Formation of a Persecuting Society: Power and Deviance in Western
    Europe, 950–1250*, Oxford: Blackwell, 1987.
More, Thomas, *Dialogue concerning Heretics*, in *The Works of Sir Thomas More*, London:
    Rastell, 1557.
    Utopia, ed. and trans. G. M. Logan and R. M. Adams, Cambridge University Press,
    1989.
Mori, Gianluca, 'Pierre Bayle, the Rights of the Conscience, the "Remedy" of
    Toleration', *Ratio Juris* 10, 1997, 45–60.
Morsy, Zaghloul (ed.), *Toleranz: Gedanken der Welt*, trans. M. u. Killisch-Horn, H. van
    Laak and D. Schetar-Köthe, Nuremberg: Verlag Das Andere, 1994.
Mousnier, Roland, *The Assassination of Henry IV: The Tyrannicide Problem and the
    Consolidation of the French Absolute Monarchy in the Early Seventeenth Century*, trans. J.
    Spencer (New York: Scribner, 1973).
Mulhall, Stephen and Adam Swift, *Liberals and Communitarians*, Oxford: Blackwell, 1992.
Münkler, Herfried, *Im Namen des Staates: Die Begründung der Staatsraison in der Frühen
    Neuzeit*, Frankfurt am Main: Fischer, 1987.
    *Machiavelli: Die Begründung des politischen Denkens der Neuzeit aus der Krise der Republik
    Florence*, Frankfurt am Main: Europäische Verlagsanstalt, 1982.
    'Politisches Denken in der Zeit der Reformation', in I. Fetscher and H. Münkler
    (eds.), *Pipers Handbuch der politischen Ideen*, vol. II, Munich: Piper, 1993, 615–83.
    Thomas Hobbes, Frankfurt am Main: Campus, 1993.
Nagel, Thomas, *Equality and Partiality*, Oxford University Press, 1991.
    'Moral Conflict and Political Legitimacy', *Philosophy and Public Affairs* 16, 1987,
    215–40.
    'The Fragmentation of Value', in *Mortal Questions*, Cambridge University Press, 1979,
    128–41.
Nederman, Cary, *Worlds of Difference: European Discourses of Toleration c. 1100 – c. 1550*,
    University Park: Pennsylvania State University Press, 2000.
Nestle, Wilhelm, 'Asebieprozesse', in *Reallexikon für Antike und Christentum*, vol. I, ed. T.
    Klauser, Stuttgart: Hiersemann, 1950, 735–40.
Neumann, Johannes, 'Toleranz als grundlegendes Verfassungsprinzip', in J. Neumann
    and M. W. Fischer (eds.), *Toleranz und Repression*, Frankfurt am Main: Campus,
    1987, 71–98.
Newey, Glen, *Virtue, Reason and Toleration: The Place of Toleration in Ethical and Political
    Philosophy*, Edinburgh University Press, 1999.

Nicholas of Cusa, *Cribratio Alchorani*, in *Philosophisch-Theologische Schriften*, vol. III,
    Latin–German, trans. D. and W. Dupre, Vienna: Herder, 1967 (English: *Cribratio
    Alchorani: Nicholas Cusanus's Criticism of the Koran in the Light of His Philosophy of
    Religion*, ed. and trans. F. H. Burgevin, New York: Vintage Press, 1969).
De coniecturis, in *Philosophisch-Theologische Schriften*, vol. II, Latin–German, trans. D.
    and W. Dupre, Vienna: Herder, 1966 (English: *On Surmises*, in *Complete Philosophical
    and Theological Treatises of Nicholas of Cusa*, trans. J. Hopkins, 2 vols., Minneapolis:
    Arthur J. Banning Press, 2001, vol. II, 162–297).
*Nicholas of Cusa on Learned Ignorance: A Translation and an Appraisal of De Docta
    Ignorantia*, 2nd edn, ed. and trans. J. Hopkins, Minneapolis: Arthur J. Banning
    Press, 1985.
On the Peace of Faith, in *Nicholas of Cusa on Interreligious Harmony: Text, Concordance and
    Translation of De pace fidei*, ed. and trans. J. E. Biechler and H. L. Bond, Lewiston:
    E. Mellen Press, 1990.
Nicholson, Peter, 'John Locke's Later Letters on Toleration', in J. Horton and S.
    Mendus (eds.), *A Letter Concerning Toleration in Focus*, London and New York:
    Routledge, 1991, 163–87.
'Toleration as a Moral Ideal', in J. Horton and S. Mendus (eds.), *Aspects of Toleration:
    Philosophical Studies*, London and New York: Methuen, 1985, 158–73.
Nickel, Rainer, *Gleichheit und Differenz in der vielfältigen Republik*, Baden-Baden: Nomos,
    1999.
Nietzsche, Friedrich, *Beyond Good and Evil*, eds. R.-P. Horstmann and J. Norman,
    Cambridge University Press, 2002.
Nachgelassene Fragmente 1880–1882, in *Kritische Studienausgabe*, vol. IX, ed. G. Colli
    and M. Montinari, Munich and Berlin: dtv/de Gruyter, 1988.
Nachgelassene Fragmente 1885–1887, in *Kritische Studienausgabe*, vol. XII, ed. G. Colli
    and M. Montinari, Munich and Berlin: dtv/de Gruyter, 1988.
On the Genealogy of Morals, trans. C. Diethe, ed. K. Ansell-Pearson, Cambridge
    University Press, 2007.
The Anti-Christ, in Nietzsche, *The Anti-Christ, Ecce Homo, Twilight of the Idols and Other
    Writings*, ed. A. Ridley and J. Norman, Cambridge University Press, 2005, 1–68.
The Gay Science, ed. B. Williams, Cambridge University Press, 2001.
Twilight of the Idols, in Nietzsche, *The Anti-Christ, Ecce Homo, Twilight of the Idols and
    Other Writings*, ed. A. Ridley and J. Norman, Cambridge University Press, 2005,
    153–229.
Untimely Meditations, trans. R. J. Hollingdale, ed. D. Breazeale, Cambridge University
    Press, 1997.
Niewöhner, Friedrich, 'Dialoge, die nicht stattgefunden haben: Judah ha-Levi und Peter
    Abailard', in W. Stegmaier (ed.), *Die philosophische Aktualität der jüdischen Tradition*,
    Frankfurt am Main: Suhrkamp, 2000, 225–48.
Maimonides: Aufklärung und Toleranz im Mittelalter, Heidelberg: Lambert Schneider,
    1988.
Veritas sive varietas: Lessings Toleranzparabel und das Buch von den drei Betrügern,
    Heidelberg: Lambert Schneider, 1988.

Nipperdey, Thomas, 'Thomas Morus', in H. Maier, H. Rausch and H. Denzer (eds.), *Klassiker des politischen Denkens*, vol. I, Munich: Beck, 1968, 222–43.

Nissen, Lowell A. and Abraham Anderson (eds.), *The Treatise of the Three Impostors and the Problem of Enlightenment*, trans. A. Anderson, Lanham, Md.: Rowman and Littlefield, 1997.

Nussbaum, Martha, 'Toleration, Compassion, and Mercy', in *Narrative, Self, and Social Practice*, ed. U. J. Jensen and C. F. Mattingly, Aarhus: Philosophia Press, 2009, 37–54.

Oberdiek, Hans, *Tolerance: Between Forbearance and Acceptance*, Lanham, Md.: Rowman and Littlefield, 2001.

Oberman, Heiko A., *Wurzeln des Antisemitismus: Christenangst und Judenplage im Zeitalter von Humanismus und Reformation*, Berlin: Severin and Siedler, 1981.

Oelmüller, Willi, *Die unbefriedigte Aufklärung: Beiträge zu einer Theorie der Moderne von Lessing, Kant und Hegel*, Neuausgabe, Frankfurt am Main: Suhrkamp, 1979.

Oestreich, Gerhard, *Antiker Geist und moderner Staat bei Justus Lipsius (1547–1606)*, ed. N. Mout, Göttingen: Vandenhoeck und Ruprecht, 1989.

'Justus Lipsius als Theoretiker des neuzeitlichen Machtstaates', in *Geist und Gestalt des frühmodernen Staates*, Berlin: Duncker und Humblot, 1969, 35–79.

'Strukturprobleme des europäischen Absolutismus', in *Geist und Gestalt des frühmodernen Staates*, Berlin: Duncker und Humblot, 1969, 179–97.

O'Neill, Onora, *Constructions of Reason: Explorations of Kant's Practical Philosophy*, Cambridge University Press, 1989.

'Practices of Toleration', in J. Lichtenberg (ed.), *Democracy and the Mass Media*, Cambridge University Press, 1990, 155–85.

Towards Justice and Virtue: A Constructive Account of Practical Reasoning, Cambridge University Press, 1996.

Overton, Richard, *The Arraignment of Mr. Persecution*, in W. Haller (ed.), *Tracts on Liberty in the Puritan Revolution*, New York: Octagon Books, 1965, 203–58.

Paine, Thomas, *Rights of Man, Common Sense, and Other Political Writings*, ed. M. Philp, Oxford: Oxford University Press, 1998.

Pappert, Peter (ed.), *Den Nerv getroffen: Engagierte Stimmen zum Kruzifix-Urteil von Karlsruhe*, Aachen: Bergmoser und Höller, 1995.

Parekh, Bhikhu, 'Dilemmas of a Multicultural Theory of Citizenship', *Constellations* 4, 1997, 54–62.

Rethinking Multiculturalism: Cultural Diversity and Political Theory, Cambridge, Mass.: Harvard University Press, 2000.

Pasquier, Étienne, *Écrits politiques*, ed. D. Thickett, Geneva: Droz, 1966.

Patterson, Charlotte, 'Children of Lesbian and Gay Parents: Summary of Research Findings', in A. Sullivan (ed.), *Same-Sex Marriage: Pro and Con*, New York: Random House, 1997, 240–5.

Paulus, Nikolaus, 'Religionsfreiheit und Augsburger Religionsfriede', in H. Lutz (ed.), *Zur Geschichte der Toleranz und Religionsfreiheit*, Darmstadt: Wissenschaftliche Buchgesellschaft, 1977, 17–41.

Penn, William, *The Great Case of Liberty of Conscience*, in *Select Works*, vol. II, London, 1825, reprint New York: Kraus, 1971.

Peters, Bernhard, *Die Integration moderner Gesellschaften*, Frankfurt am Main: Suhrkamp, 1993.

   'Understanding Multiculturalism', Working Paper 14/99 of the Institute for Intercultural and International Studies, Bremen, 1999 (www.iniis.uni-bremen.de/Welcome_en.php (accessed March 2012)).

Pico della Mirandola, Giovanni, *Ausgewählte Schriften*, trans. A. Liebert, Jena und Leipzig: Diederichs, 1905.

   Letter to Ermolao Barbaro, trans. W. A. Rebhorn, in *Renaissance Debates on Rhetoric*, ed. W. A. Rebhorn, Ithaca, NY: Cornell University Press, 2000, 58–67.

   On the Dignity of Man, trans. C. G. Wallis and P. J. W. Miller, Indianapolis, Ind.: Hackett, 1998.

Plantinga, Alvin and Nicholas Wolterstorff (eds.), *Faith and Rationality: Reason and Belief in God*, Notre Dame University Press, 1983.

Pogge, Thomas, 'Group Rights and Ethnicity', in I. Shapiro and W. Kymlicka (eds.), *Ethnicity and Group Rights*, Nomos xxxix, New York University Press, 1997, 187–221.

Popkin, Richard H., 'Pierre Bayle's Place in 17th Century Scepticism', in P. Dibon (ed.), *Pierre Bayle: le philosophe de Rotterdam*, Paris: Vrin, 1959, 1–19.

Popper, Karl, *The Open Society and Its Enemies*, vol. i: *The Spell of Plato*, New York: Routledge, 2003.

   'Toleration and Intellectual Responsibility (Stolen from Xenophanes and from Voltaire)', in *In Search of a Better World*, London and New York: Routledge, 1994, 188–203.

   'Toleration and Intellectual Responsibility', in S. Mendus and D. Edwards (eds.), *On Toleration*, Oxford: Clarendon, 1987, 17–34 (coincides in part with 'Toleration and Intellectual Responsibility (Stolen from Xenophanes and from Voltaire)').

Proast, Jonas, *The Argument of the Letter Concerning Toleration (1690) / A Third Letter Concerning Toleration (1691) / A Second Letter to the Author of the Three Letters for Toleration (1704)*, reprint New York and London: Garland, 1984.

Proß, Wolfgang, 'Herder und Vico: Wissenssoziologische Voraussetzungen des historischen Denkens', in G. Sauder (ed.), *Johann Gottfried Herder*, Hamburg: Meiner, 1987, 88–113.

Pufendorf, Samuel, *Of the Duty of Man and Citizen According to Natural Law*, trans. M. Silverthorne, ed. J. Tully, Cambridge University Press, 1991.

   Of the Nature and Qualification of Religion in Reference to Civil Society, trans. J. Crull, ed. S. Zurbuchen, Indianapolis, ind.: Liberty Fund, 2002.

Putnam, Hilary, *Reason, Truth and History*, Cambridge University Press, 1981.

Püttner, Günter, *Toleranz als Verfassungsprinzip*, Berlin: Duncker and Humblot, 1977.

Raphael, D. D., 'The Intolerable', in S. Mendus (ed.), *Justifying Toleration: Conceptual and Historical Perspectives*, Cambridge University Press, 1988, 137–54.

Rawls, John, *A Brief Inquiry into the Meaning of Sin and Faith*, ed. T. Nagel, Cambridge, Mass.: Harvard University Press, 2009.

   A Theory of Justice, rev. edn, Cambridge, Mass.: Harvard University Press, 1999.

   'Kantian Constructivism in Moral Theory', in *Collected Papers*, ed. S. Freeman, Cambridge, Mass.: Harvard University Press, 1999, 303–58.

Lectures on the History of Moral Philosophy, Cambridge, Mass.: Harvard University Press, 2000.

Political Liberalism, expanded edn, New York: Columbia University Press, 2005.

'Reply to Habermas', *Journal of Philosophy* 92, 1995, 132–80.

'The Basic Liberties and their Priority', in S. M. McMurrin (ed.), *The Tanner Lectures on Human Values*, vol. III, Salt Lake City: University of Utah Press, 1–87.

'The Domain of the Political and Overlapping Consensus', in *Collected Papers*, ed. S. Freeman, Cambridge, Mass.: Harvard University Press, 1999, 473–96.

'The Idea of an Overlapping Consensus, in *Collected Papers*, ed. S. Freeman, Cambridge, Mass.: Harvard University Press, 1999, 421–48.

'The Idea of Public Reason Revisited', *University of Chicago Law Review* 64, 1997, 765–807.

The Law of Peoples, Cambridge, Mass.: Harvard University Press, 1999.

Raz, Joseph, 'Facing Diversity: The Case of Epistemic Abstinence', *Philosophy and Public Affairs* 19, 1990, 3–46.

'Autonomy, Toleration and the Harm Principle', in S. Mendus (ed.), *Justifying Toleration: Conceptual and Historical Perspectives*, Cambridge University Press, 1988, 155–75.

'Multiculturalism: A Liberal Perspective', in *Ethics in the Public Domain*, rev. edn, Oxford: Clarendon Press, 1994, 170–91.

The Morality of Freedom, Oxford: Clarendon Press, 1986.

Reimarus, Hermann Samuel, *The Principal Truths of Natural Religion Defended and Illustrated*, London: B. Law, 1766.

'Von Duldung der Deisten. Fragment eines Ungenannten', ed. G. E. Lessing, in Lessing, *Luthers Werke*, vol. VII, ed. H. G. Göpfert, Darmstadt: Wissenschaftliche Buchgesellschaft, 1996.

Reinhard, Wolfgang, 'Zwang zur Konfessionalisierung? Prolegomena zu einer Theorie des konfessionellen Zeitalters', *Zeitschrift für historische Forschung* 10, 1983, 257–77.

Remer, Gary, *Humanism and the Rhetoric of Toleration*, University Park: Pennsylvania State University Press, 1996.

Renan, Ernest, *Averroès et l'Averroisme*, Paris, 1867, rev. edn ed. F. Sezgin, Frankfurt am Main: Institut für die Geschichte der arabisch-islamischen Wissenschaften, 1985.

Rescher, Nicholas, *Pluralism: Against the Demand for Consensus*, Oxford University Press, 1993.

Reuchlin, Johannes, *Augenspiegel*, reprint of Tübingen 1511 edn, Munich: Johann Froben, n.d.

Rex, Walter, *Essays on Pierre Bayle and Religious Controversy*, The Hague: Nijhoff, 1965.

Richards, David A. J., *Toleration and the Constitution*, Oxford University Press, 1986.

Ricoeur, Paul, 'The Erosion of Tolerance and the Resistance of the Intolerable', in Ricœur (ed.), *Tolerance between Intolerance and the Intolerable*, Providence, RI: Diogenes, 1996, 189–201.

Ries, Rotraud, 'German Territorial Princes and the Jews', in R. Po-Chia Hsia and H. Lehmann (eds.), *In and Out of the Ghetto*, Cambridge University Press, 1995, 215–46.

Rilinger, Rolf, 'Das politische Denken der Römer: Vom Prinzipat zum Dominat', in I. Fetscher and H. Münkler (eds.), *Pipers Handbuch der politischen Ideen*, vol. I, Munich: Piper, 1988, 521–93.

Robinson, Henry, *Liberty of Conscience*, in W. Haller (ed.), *Tracts on Liberty in the Puritan Revolution*, New York: Octagon Books, 1965, 105–78.

Rödel, Ulrich, Günter Frankenberg and Helmut Dubiel, *Die demokratische Frage*, Frankfurt am Main: Suhrkamp, 1989.

Roeck, Bernd, *Außenseiter, Randgruppen, Minderheiten: Fremde im Deutschland der frühen Neuzeit*, Göttingen: Vandenhoeck und Ruprecht, 1993.

Roellenbleck, Georg, 'Der Schluß des "Heptaplomeres" und die Begründung der Toleranz bei Bodin', in H. Denzer (ed.), *Jean Bodin: Verhandlungen der internationalen Bodin Tagung in Munich*, Munich: C. H. Beck, 1973, 53–68.

Rorty, Richard, *Contingency, Irony, and Solidarity*, Cambridge University Press, 1989.

  'Postmodernist Bourgeois Liberalism', in *Objectivity, Relativism, and Truth*, Cambridge University Press, 1991, 197–202.

  'Private Irony and Liberal Hope', in *Contingency, Irony, and Solidarity*, Cambridge University Press, 1989, 73–95.

Rotteck, Carl von, 'Duldung; Toleranz; Unduldung; Intoleranz', in C. von Rotteck and C. Welcker (eds.), *Staats-Lexikon oder Encyklopädie der Staatswissenschafien*, vol. IV, Altona: Verlag von Johann Friedrich Hammerich, 1839, 532–49.

Rousseau, Jean-Jacques, *Discourse on the Origin and Foundations of Inequality among Men*, in *The Discourses and Other Early Writings*, trans. and ed. V. Gourevitch, Cambridge University Press, 1997, 111–88.

  Discourse on the Sciences and Arts, in *The Discourses and Other Early Writings*, trans. and ed. V. Gourevitch, Cambridge University Press, 1997, 1–28.

  Emile or On Education, trans. and ed. A. Bloom, New York: Basic Books, 1979 (French: *Émile*, in *Œuvres complètes*, vol. IV, Paris: Bibliothèque de la Pleiade, 1969).

  Letter to Beaumont, trans. C. Kelly, in C. Kelly (ed.), *Rousseau on Philosophy, Morality and Religion*, Dartmouth, NH: Dartmouth College Press, 2007, 162–226.

  Letter to M. D'Alembert on the Theatre, in Rousseau, *Politics and the Arts*, trans. and ed. A. Bloom, New York: Free Press, 1960, 1–138.

  Letter to Voltaire, in *The Discourses and Other Early Writings*, trans. and ed. V. Gourevitch, Cambridge University Press, 1997, 232–46.

  Letters Written from the Mountain, in *Rousseau, Letter to Beaumont, Letters Written from the Mountain, and Related Writings*: vol. IX of *Collected Writings of Rousseau*, trans. C. Kelly, Dartmouth, NH: Dartmouth College Press, 2001.

  Observations [to Stanislas, King of Poland], in *The Discourses and Other Early Writings*, trans. and ed. V. Gourevitch, Cambridge University Press, 1997, 32–51.

  Outline of *Nouvelle Héloise*, in *Œuvres complètes*, vol. II, Paris: Bibliothèque de la Pleiade, 1969.

  The Social Contract, in *The Social Contract and Other Later Political Writings*, ed. and trans. V. Gourevitch, Cambridge University Press, 1977, 39–152 (French: *Du contrat social*, in *Œuvres complètes*, vol. III, Paris: Bibliothèque de la Pleiade, 1964).

Rudolph, Hartmut, 'Öffentliche Religion und Toleranz. Zur Parallelität preußischer Religionspolitik und josephinischer Reform im Lichte der Aufklärung', in P. F.

Barton (ed.), *Im Zeichen der Toleranz: Aufsätze zur Toleranzgesetzgebung des 18. Jahrhunderts im Reiche Joseph* ii, Vienna: Institut für protestantische Kirchengeschichte, 1981, 221–49.

Ryan, Alan, 'A More Tolerant Hobbes?', in S. Mendus (ed.), *Justifying Toleration: Conceptual and Historical Perspectives*, Cambridge University Press, 1988, 37–59.

Saage, Richard, *Herrschaft, Toleranz, Widerstand: Studien zur politischen Theorie der niederländischen und der englischen Revolution*, Frankfurt am Main: Suhrkamp, 1981.

Sandel, Michael, 'Judgemental Toleration', in R. P. George (ed.), *Natural Law, Liberalism, and Morality*, Oxford: Clarendon Press, 1996, 107–12.

'Moral Argument and Liberal Toleration: Abortion and Homosexuality', *California Law Review* 77, 1989, 521–38.

'Religious Liberty – Freedom of Conscience or Freedom of Choice?', *Utah Law Review* 3, 1989, 597–615.

'Tolerating the Tolerant', *The New Republic* 15 and 22 July 1996, 25.

Sandweg, Jürgen, *Rationales Naturrecht als revolutionäre Praxis*, Berlin: Duncker und Humblot, 1972.

Sartre, Jean-Paul, *Anti-Semite and Jew: An Exploration of the Etiology of Hate*, trans. G. J. Becker, New York: Schocken Books, 1995.

Scanlon, Thomas, 'Contractualism and Utilitarianism', in A. Sen and B. Williams (eds.), *Utilitarianism and Beyond*, Cambridge University Press, 1982, 103–28.

'The Difficulty of Tolerance', in D. Heyd (ed.), *Toleration*, Princeton University Press, 1996, 226–40.

What We Owe to Each Other, Cambridge, Mass.: Harvard University Press, 1998.

Schaber, Peter, 'Gründe für eine objektive Theorie des menschlichen Wohls', in H. Steinfath (ed.), *Was ist ein gutes Leben?*, Frankfurt am Main: Suhrkamp, 1998, 149–66.

Scheuner, Ulrich, 'Staatsräson und religiöse Einheit des Staates: Zur Religionspolitik in Deutschland im Zeitalter der Glaubensspaltung', in R. Schnur (ed.), *Staatsräson: Studien zur Geschichte eines politischen Begriffs*, Berlin: Duncker und Humblot, 1975, 363–405.

Schilling, Heinz, 'Die Konfessionalisierung im Reich: Religiöser und gesellschaftlicher Wandel in Deutschland zwischen 1555 und 1620', *Historische Zeitschrift* 246, 1988, 1–45.

Schleiermacher, Friedrich, *On Religion: Speeches to its Cultured Despisers*, trans. R. Crouter, Cambridge University Press, 1996.

Schleichert, Hubert, *Wie man mit Fundamentalisten diskutiert, ohne den Verstand zu verlieren: Anleitung zum subversiven Denken*, Munich: Beck, 1997.

Schlüter, Gisela, *Die französische Toleranzdebatte im Zeitalter der Aufklärung: Materiale und formale Aspekte*, Tübingen: Niemeyer, 1992.

Schmalz-Bruns, Rainer, *Reflexive Demokratie: Die demokratische Transformation moderner Politik*, Baden-Baden: Nomos, 1995.

Schmidt, Thomas, 'Glaubensüberzeugungen und säkulare Gründe. Zur Legitimität religiöser Argumente in einer pluralistischen Gesellschaft', *Zeitschrift für Evangelische Ethik* 45, 2001, 248–61.

Schmidt-Leukel, Perry, 'Ist das Christentum notwendig intolerant?', in R. Forst (ed.), *Toleranz: Philosophische Grundlagen und gesellschaftliche Praxis einer umstrittenen Tugend*, Frankfurt am Main: Campus, 2000, 177–213.

'Zur Klassifikation religionstheologischer Modelle', *Catholica* 46, 1993, 163–83.

Schmitt, Carl, *Political Theology: Four Chapters on the Concept of Sovereignty*, trans. G. Schwab, Cambridge, Mass.: MIT Press, 1985.

'State Ethics and the Pluralist State', in A. Jacobson and B. Schlink (eds.), *Weimar: A Jurisprudence of Crisis*, Berkeley and Los Angeles: University of California Press, 2000, 300–12.

The Leviathan in the State Theory of Thomas Hobbes, ed. and trans. G. Schwab and E. Hilfstein, Westport, Conn.: Greenwood Press, 1996.

'Übersicht über die verschiedenen Bedeutungen und Funktionen des Begriffes der innerpolitischen Neutralität des Staates', Corollarium zu *Der Begriff des Politischen*, Berlin: Duncker und Humblot, 1979.

'Weiterentwicklung des totalen Staates in Deutschland', in *Positionen und Begriffe im Kampf mit Weimar – Genf – Versailles 1923–1939*, Hamburg: Hanseatische Verlagsanstalt, 1940, 211–17.

'Wesen und Werden des faschistischen Staates', in *Positionen und Begriffe im Kampf mit Weimar – Genf – Versailles 1923–1939*, Hamburg: Hanseatische Verlagsanstalt, 1940, 124–31.

Schnapp, Friedrich E., 'Toleranzidee und Grundgesetz', in *Juristen-Zeitung* 40, 1985, 857–63.

Schneewind, Jerome B., 'Bayle, Locke, and the Concept of Toleration', in M. A. Razavi and D. Ambuel (eds.), *Philosophy, Religion, and the Question of Intolerance*, Albany: State University of New York Press, 1997, 3–15.

The Invention of Autonomy: A History of Modern Moral Philosophy, Cambridge University Press, 1998.

Schnur, Roman, *Die französischen Juristen im konfessionellen Bürgerkrieg des 16. Jahrhunderts: Ein Beitrag zur Entstehungsgeschichte des modernen Staates*, Berlin: Duncker und Humblot, 1962.

Schöfthaler, Traugott, 'Prinzipien der Toleranz – eine Deklaration der Unesco', in A. Wierlacher (ed.), *Kulturthema Toleranz*, Munich: Iudicium, 1996, 673–82.

Schöndorf, Kurt Erich, 'Judenhaß und Toleranz im Spiegel von Flugschriften und Einblattdrucken des 16. Jahrhunderts', in T. Sirges and K. E. Schöndorf (eds.), *Haß, Verfolgung und Toleranz: Beiträge zum Schicksal der Juden von der Reformation bis in die Gegenwart*, Frankfurt am Main.: Lang, 2000, 11–46.

Schreiner, Klaus, '"Duldsamkeit" (tolerantia) oder "Schrecken" (terror)', in D. Simon (ed.), *Religiose Devianz*, Frankfurt am Main: Klostermann, 1990, 159–210.

'"Tolerantia". Begriffs- und wirkungsgeschichtliche Studien zur Toleranzauffassung des Kirchenvaters Augustinus', in A. Patschovsky and H. Zimmermann (eds.), *Toleranz im Mittelalter*, Sigmaringen: Thorbecke, 1998, 335–89.

Schulte, Christoph, *Die jüdische Aufklärung: Philosophie, Religion, Geschichte*, Munich: C. H. Beck, 2002.

Schulze, Reinhard, 'Toleranzkonzepte in islamischer Tradition', in A. Wierlacher (ed.), *Kulturthema Toleranz*, Munich: Iudicium, 1996, 495–514.

Schulze, Winfried, 'Concordia, Discordia, Tolerantia. Deutsche Politik im konfessionellen Zeitalter', in *Zeitschrift für Historische Forschung*, Special Issue 3, ed. J. Kunisch, 1987, 43–79.
Deutsche Geschichte im 16. Jahrhundert, 1550–1618, Frankfurt am Main: Suhrkamp, 1987.
'Gerhard Oestreichs Begriff "Sozialdisziplinierung in der Frühen Neuzeit"', *Zeitschrift für historische Forschung* 14, 1987, 265–302.
Schultz, Uwe, *Die Erfindung der Toleranz: Michel de Montaigne und Henri Quatre*, Hamburg: EVA, 1998.
(ed.), *Toleranz: Die Krise der demokratischen Tugend und sechzehn Vorschläge zu ihrer Überwindung*, Reinbek: Rowohlt, 1974.
Schultze, Harald, *Lessings Toleranzbegriff: Eine theologische Studie*, Göttingen: Vandenhoeck und Ruprecht, 1969.
Schuster, Peter, *Das Frauenhaus: Städtische Bordelle in Deutschland, 1350–1600*, Paderborn: Schöningh, 1992.
Scribner, Bob, 'Preconditions of Tolerance and Intolerance in Sixteenth-Century Germany', in O. P. Grell and B. Scribner (eds.), *Tolerance and Intolerance in the European Reformation*, Cambridge University Press, 1996, 32–47.
Seel, Martin, 'On Rightness and Truth: Reflections on the Concept of World Disclosure', *Thesis Eleven* 37, 1994, 64–81.
Versuch über die Form des Glücks, Frankfurt am Main: Suhrkamp, 1995.
Seneca, L. Annaeus, *Seneca's Letters to Lucilius*, trans. E. P. Barker, Oxford: Clarendon Press, 1932.
Shackleton, R., 'Bayle and Montesquieu', in P. Dibon (ed.), *Pierre Bayle: le philosophe de Rotterdam*, Paris: Vrin, 1959, 142–9.
Sharp, Andrew (ed.), *The English Levellers*, Cambridge University Press, 1998.
Sher, George, *Beyond Neutrality: Perfectionism and Politics*, Cambridge University Press, 1997.
Shklar, Judith, 'The Liberalism of Fear', in N. Rosenblum (ed.), *Liberalism and the Moral Life*, Cambridge, Mass.: Harvard University Press, 1989, 21–38.
Skinner, Quentin, *Liberty before Liberalism*, Cambridge University Press, 1998.
The Foundations of Modern Political Thought, vol. I: *The Renaissance*, vol. II: *The Age of Reformation*, Cambridge University Press, 1978.
Smith, Steven B., 'Toleration and the Skepticism of Religion in Spinoza's *Tractatus Theologico-Politicus*', in A. Levine (ed.), *Early Modern Skepticism and the Origins of Toleration*, Lanham, Md.: Lexington Books, 1999, 127–46.
Sommerville, Johann P., *Thomas Hobbes: Political Ideas in Historical Context*, Houndmills: Macmillan, 1992.
Spaemann, Robert, 'Bemerkungen zum Begriff des Fundamentalismus', in K. Michalski (ed.), *Die liberale Gesellschaf*, Stuttgart: Klett-Cotta, 1993, 177–94.
'Bürgerliche Ethik und nichtteleologische Ontologie', in H. Ebeling (ed.), *Subjektivität und Selbsterhaltung: Beiträge zur Diagnose der Moderne*, Frankfurt am Main: Suhrkamp, 1976, 76–96.
'Über den Begriff der Menschenwürde', in E.-W. Böckenförde and R. Spaemann (eds.), *Menschenrechte und Menschenwürde*, Stuttgart: Klett-Cotta, 1987, 295–313.

'Was nicht des Staates its: Die Homosexuellenehe wäre ungerecht', *Frankfurter Allgemeine Zeitung*, 14 March 2000, 49.

Speyer, Wolfgang, 'Toleranz und Intoleranz in der alten Kirche', in I. Broer and R. Schlüter (eds.), *Christentum und Toleranz*, Darmstadt: Wissenschaftliche Buchgesellschaft 1996, 83–106.

Spinner, Jeff, *The Boundaries of Citizenship*, Baltimore, Md.: Johns Hopkins University Press, 1994.

Spinoza, Benedict de, *A Theological-Political Treatise*, in Spinoza, *Works of Spinoza*, vol. I: *A Theological-Political Treatise, A Political Treatise*, trans. R. H. M. Elwes, New York: Dover, 1951 (Latin: *Tractatus theologico-politicus*, ed. G. Gawlick and F. Niewöhner, Opera 1, Darmstadt: Wissenschaftliche Buchgesellschaft, 1979).

  The Correspondence of Spinoza, trans. and ed. A. Wolf, London: Cass, 1966.

  The Ethics, in Spinoza, *Works of Spinoza*, vol. II: *Of the Improvement of the Understanding, The Ethics, Correspondence*, trans. R. H. M. Elwes, New York: Dover, 1955.

Springborg, Patricia, 'Hobbes on Religion', in T. Sorell (ed.), *The Cambridge Companion to Hobbes*, Cambridge University Press, 1996, 346–80.

Starobinski, Jean, *Montaigne in Motion*, trans. A. Goldhammer, University of Chicago Press, 1985.

Steinacker, K., 'Emancipation der Juden', in C. von Rotteck and C. Welcker (eds.), *Staats-Lexikon oder Encyklopädie der Staatswissenschaf en*, vol. v, Altona: Verlag von Johann Friedrich Hammerich, 1839.

Steinfath, Holmer, *Orientierung am Guten: Praktisches Überlegen und die Konstitution von Personen*, Frankfurt am Main: Suhrkamp, 2001.

Stemmer, Peter, 'Was es heißt, ein gutes Leben zu leben', in H. Steinfath (ed.), *Was ist ein gutes Leben?*, Frankfurt am Main: Suhrkamp, 1998, 47–72.

Stenner, Karen, 'The Authoritarian Dynamic: Racism and Intolerance under Conditions of Societal Threat', in I. Creppell, R. Hardin and S. Macedo (eds.), *Toleration on Trial*, Lanham, Md.: Lexington Books, 2008.

Sternberger, Dolf, 'Toleranz als Leidenschaft für die Wahrheit', in *Gut und Böse*, Schriften IX, Frankfurt am Main: Insel, 1988, 141–66.

Stierle, Karlheinz, 'Montaigne und die Erfahrung der Vielheit', in W.-D. Stempel and K. Stierle (eds.), *Die Pluralität der Welten: Aspekte der Renaissance in der Romania*, Munich: Fink, 1987, 417–48.

Stocker, Michael, *Plural and Conflicting Values*, Oxford: Clarendon Press, 1990.

Stolzenberg, Nomi Maya, '"He Drew a Circle That Shut Me Out": Assimilation, indoctrination, and the Paradox of Liberal Education', *Harvard Law Review* 106, 1993, 581–667.

Stow, Kenneth R., *Alienated Minority: The Jews of Medieval Latin Europe*, Cambridge, Mass.: Harvard University Press, 1992.

Strauss, Leo, *Philosophy and Law: Contributions to Understanding Maimonides and his Predecessors* (1935), trans. E. Adler, Albany, NY: SUNY Press, 1995.

  Spinoza's Critique of Religion, trans. E. M. Sinclair, University of Chicago Press, 1997.

Strawson, Peter, 'Social Morality and Individual Ideal', in *Freedom and Resentment*, London: Methuen, 1974, 26–44.

Streithofen, Heinrich Basilius (ed.), *Das Kruzifixurteil: Deutschland vor einem neuen Kulturkampf*, Frankfurt am Main and Berlin: Ullstein, 1995.

Struve, Tilman, 'Regnum und Sacerdotium', in I. Fetscher and H. Münkler (eds.), *Pipers Handbuch der politischen Ideen*, vol. ii, Munich: Piper, 1993, 189–242.

Swanton, Christine, 'On the "Essential Contestedness" of Political Concepts', *Ethics* 95, 1985, 811–27.

Tamir, Yael, 'Against Collective Rights', in C. Joppke and S. Lukes (eds.), *Multicultural Questions*, Oxford University Press, 1999, 158–80.

Liberal Nationalism, Princeton University Press, 1993.

Taylor, Charles, 'Leading a Life', in R. Chang (ed.), *Incommensurability, incomparability and Practical Reason*, Cambridge, Mass.: Harvard University Press, 1997, 170–83.

Sources of the Self: The Making of the Modern Identity, Cambridge, Mass.: Harvard University Press, 1989.

'The Politics of Recognition', in *Multiculturalism: Examining the Politics of Recognition*, ed. A. Gutmann, Princeton University Press, 1994, 25–73.

Tertullian, *Ad Scapulam*, in Patrologiae cursus completus, series latina, ed. P. G. Migne, vol. i, Paris, 1879 (English: *To Scapula*, trans. S. Thelwall, www.newadvent.org/fathers/0305.htm (accessed March 2011)).

Apologeticus adversus gentes pro christianis, in Patrologiae cursus completus, series latina, ed. P. G. Migne, vol. i, Paris, 1879 (English: *Apology*, trans. S. Thelwall, www.newadvent.org/fathers/0301.htm (accessed October 2008)).

De fuga in persecutione, in Corpus christianorum seu nova patrum collectivo, series latina, vol. ii, Turnhout: Brepols, 1956 (English: *On Flight in Persecution*, trans. S. Thelwall, www.newadvent.org/fathers/0409.htm (accessed October 2008)).

Thom, Martina, 'Einleitung', in Moses Mendelssohn, *Schriften über Religion und Aufklärung*, ed. M. Thom, Darmstadt: Wissenschaftliche Buchgesellschaft, 1989.

Thomas Aquinas, *Commentum in quartum librum sententiarum*, in *Opera omnia*, vol. x, ed. S. E. Frette and P. Mare, Paris: Ludovicum Vives, 1873.

On Law, Morality, and Politics, 2nd edn, ed. W. P. Baumgarth and R. J. Regan, Indianapolis, ind.: Hackett, 2002.

Quaestiones Quodlibetales, in *Opera omnia*, vol. xv, ed. S. E. Frette, Paris: Ludovicum Vives, 1875.

Summa Theologiae, Volume 18, 1a2ae. 18–21: Principles of Morality, ed. T. Gilby, trans. Fathers of the English Dominican Province, Cambridge University Press, 2006.

Summa Theologiae, Volumes 31 and 32, 2a2ae. 1–7: Faith, ed. T. O'Brien, trans. Fathers of the English Dominican Province, Cambridge University Press, 2006.

Summa Theologiae, Volume 32, 2a2ae. 8–16: Consequences of Faith, ed. T. Gilby, trans. Fathers of the English Dominican Province, Cambridge University Press, 2006.

Tocqueville, Alexis de, *Democracy in America*, 2 vols., ed. P. Bradley, trans. H. Reeve, rev. F. Bowen, New York: Vintage Books, 1945.

Troeltsch, Ernst, *The Social Teaching of the Christian Churches*, 2 vols., trans. O. Wyon, Louisville, Ky.: Westminster John Knox Press, 1992.

Tuck, Richard, *Hobbes*, Oxford University Press, 1989.

Natural Rights Theories: Their Origin and Development, Cambridge University Press, 1979.

'Scepticism and Toleration in the Seventeenth Century', in S. Mendus (ed.), *Justifying Toleration: Conceptual and Historical Perspectives*, Cambridge University Press, 1988, 21–36.

Tully, James, 'An Introduction to Locke's Political Philosophy', in *An Approach to Political Philosophy: Locke in Contexts*, Cambridge University Press, 1993, 9–68.

'Governing Conduct: Locke on the Reform of Thought and Behaviour', in *An Approach to Political Philosophy: Locke in Contexts*, Cambridge University Press, 1993, 179–241.

Strange Multiplicity: Constitutionalism in an Age of Diversity, Cambridge University Press, 1995.

Van den Brink, Bert, *The Tragedy of Liberalism: An Alternative Defense of a Political Tradition*, Albany: State University of New York Press, 2000.

Van Dülmen, Richard, *Entstehung des frühneuzeitlichen Europa 1550–1648*, Frankfurt am Main: Fischer, 1982.

Vernon, Richard, *The Career of Toleration: John Locke, Jonas Proast, and After*, Montreal: McGill-Queen's University Press, 1997.

Vernon, Richard and Samuel V. LaSelva, 'Justifying Tolerance', *Canadian Journal of Political Science* 17, 1984, 3–23.

Vocelka, Karl, 'Enlightenment in the Habsburg Monarchy: History of a Belated and Short-Lived Phenomenon', in O. P. Grell and R. Porter (eds.), *Toleration in Enlightenment Europe*, Cambridge University Press, 2000, 196–211.

Volkmann, Uwe, 'Grund und Grenzen der Toleranz', *Der Staat* 39, 2000, 325–53.

Voltaire, 'An Address to the Public concerning the Parracides imputed to the Calas and Sirven Families', in Voltaire, *Treatise on Tolerance*, trans. B. Masters, trans. and ed. S. Harvey, Cambridge University Press, 2000, 117–37.

A Philosophical Dictionary: From the French of M. de Voltaire, 2 vols., London: W. Dugdale, 1843.

Candide, trans. R. M. Adams, New York: W. W. Norton and Company, 1991.

Dialogues chrétiens, ou préservatif contre l'Encyclopédie, Geneva and Lyons: Rigolet, 1760. *Œuvres completes de Voltaire: Mélanges* III *1753–1763*.

Die Toleranz-Affäre, ed. and trans. A. Gier and C. Paschold, Bremen: Manholt, 1993.

Proféssion de foi des théistes. Œuvres completes de Voltaire: Mélanges VI 1768–1769 (cited from: www.voltaire-integral.com/Html/27/05_Profession.html (accessed July 2011)).

Treatise on Tolerance, trans. B. Masters, trans. and ed. S. Harvey, Cambridge University Press, 2000.

von Oranien, Wilhelm, 'Denkschrift über den kritischen Zustand der Niederlande und über die Maßnahmen zu seiner Verbesserung', excerpts in Germanin H. Guggisberg (ed.), *Religiose Toleranz*, Stuttgart-Bad Cannstatt: frommann-holzboog, 1984, 123–30.

Wagener, Herrmann, 'Toleranz', in Wagener (ed.), *Staats- und Gesellschaftslexikon*, vol. xx, Berlin: Heinicke, 1865, 554–6.

Waldron, Jeremy, *Law and Disagreement*, Oxford: Clarendon Press, 1999.

'Locke: Toleration and the Rationality of Persecution', in J. Horton and S. Mendus (eds.), *A Letter Concerning Toleration in Focus*, London and New York: Routledge, 1991, 98–124.

'Theoretical Foundations of Liberalism', in *Liberal Rights: Collected Papers 1981–1991*, Cambridge University Press, 1993, 35–62.

Walwyn, William, *A Helpe to the Right Understanding of a Discourse Concerning Independency*, in *The Writings of William Walwyn*, ed. J. R. McMichel and B. Taft, Athens and London: University of Georgia Press, 1989, 131–42.

The Compassionate Samaritane, in *The Writings of William Walwyn*, ed. J. R. McMichel and B. Taft, Athens and London: University of Georgia Press, 1989, 97–124.

Tolleration Justified, and Persecution Condemned, in *The Writings of William Walwyn*, ed. J. R. McMichel and B. Taft, Athens and London: University of Georgia Press, 1989, 154–172.

Walzer, Michael, 'Liberalism and the Art of Separation', in *Zivile Gesellschaft und amerikanische Demokratie*, trans. C. Goldmann, ed. O. Kallscheuer, Berlin: Rotbuch, 1992, 38–63.

On Toleration, New Haven: Yale University Press, 1997.

The Revolution of the Saints: A Study in the Origins of Radical Politics, Cambridge, Mass.: Harvard University Press, 1965.

Warnock, Mary, 'The Limits of Toleration', in S. Mendus and D. Edwards (eds.), *On Toleration*, Oxford: Clarendon Press, 1987, 123–40.

Waters, Mary, *Ethnic Options: Choosing Identities in America*, Berkeley and Los Angeles: University of California Press, 1990.

Weale, Albert, 'Toleration, individual Differences, and Respect for Persons', in J. Horton and S. Mendus (eds.), *Aspects of Toleration*, London and New York: Methuen, 1985, 16–35.

Weber, Max, *Economy and Society*, 2 vols., ed. G. Roth and C. Wittich, Berkeley and Los Angeles: University of California Press, 1978.

Weischedel, Wilhelm, *Der Gott der Philosophen*, 2 vols., Darmstadt: Wissenschaftliche Buchgesellschaft, 1983.

Weithman, Paul J. (ed.), *Religion and Contemporary Liberalism*, University of Notre Dame Press, 1997.

Wellmer, Albrecht, 'Ethics and Dialogue', in Wellmer, *The Persistence of Modernity*, trans. D. Midgley, Cambridge, Mass.: MIT Press, 1991, 113–231.

Welsch, Wolfgang, 'Einleitung', in Welsch (ed.), *Wege aus der Moderne: Schlüsseltexte der Postmoderne-Diskussion*, vol. II, Berlin: Akademie Verlag, 1994.

Wenar, Leif, '*Political Liberalism*: An Internal Critique', *Ethics* 106, 1995, 32–62.

Werling, Hans Friedrich, *Die weltanschaulichen Grundlagen der Reunionsbemühungen von Leibniz im Briefwechsel mit Bossuet und Pellison*, Frankfurt am Main: Peter Lang, 1977.

White, B. R., 'The Twilight of Puritanism in the Years before and after 1688', in O. P. Grell, J. I. Israel and N. Tyacke (eds.), *From Persecution to Toleration: The Glorious Revolution and Religion in England*, Oxford: Clarendon Press, 1991, 307–30.

Wieland, Georg, 'Das Eigene und das Andere: Theoretische Elemente zum Begriff der Toleranz im hohen und späten Mittelalter', in A. Patschovsky and H. Zimmermann (eds.), *Toleranz im Mittelalter*, Sigmaringen: Thorbecke, 1998, 11–25.

Wierlacher, Alois (ed.), *Kulturthema Toleranz: Zur Grundlegung einer interdisziplinären und interkulturellen Toleranzforschung*, Munich: Iudicium, 1996.

'Toleranzdiskurse in Deutschland', in Wierlacher, *Kulturthema Toleranz*, Munich: Iudicium, 1996, 515–64.

'Zur Grundlegung einer interdisziplinären und interkulturellen Toleranzforschung', in Wierlacher, *Kulturthema Toleranz*, Munich: Iudicium, 1996, 11–27.

Wilbur, Earl Morse, *A History of Unitarianism: Socinianism and its Antecedents*, Boston: Beacon Press, 1946, 1972.

Williams, Bernard, *Ethics and the Limits of Philosophy*, Cambridge, Mass.: Harvard University Press, 1985.

'Deciding to Believe', in *Problems of the Self*, Cambridge University Press, 1976, 136–51.

'Persons, Character and Morality', in *Moral Luck*, Cambridge University Press, 1981, 1–19.

'Toleration, a Political or Moral Question?', in *In the Beginning Was the Deed: Realism and Moralism in Political Argument*, ed. G. Hawthorn, Princeton University Press, 2005, 128–38.

'Toleration: An Impossible Virtue?', in D. Heyd (ed.), *Toleration*, Princeton University Press, 1996, 18–27.

Williams, Melissa, *Voice, Trust and Memory: Marginalized Groups and the Failings of Liberal Representation*, Princeton University Press, 1998.

Williams, Roger, *The Bloudy Tenent of Persecution*, in *The Complete Writings of Roger Williams*, vol. III, ed. S. Caldwell, New York: Russell and Russell, 1963.

Wingert, Lutz, *Gemeinsinn und Moral*, Frankfurt am Main: Suhrkamp, 1993.

Wolf, Ernst, 'Toleranz nach evangelischem Verständnis', in H. Lutz (ed.), *Zur Geschichte der Toleranz und Religionsfreiheit*, Darmstadt: Wissenschaftliche Buchgesellschaft, 1977, 135–54.

Wolf, Ursula, 'Zur Struktur der Frage nach dem guten Leben', in H. Steinfath (ed.), *Was ist ein gutes Leben?*, Frankfurt am Main: Suhrkamp, 1998, 32–46.

Wollheim, Richard, *The Thread of Life*, New Haven, Conn.: Yale University Press, 1984.

Woodhouse, A. S. P. (ed.), *Puritanism and Liberty*, University of Chicago Press, 1951.

Wootton, David, 'Pierre Bayle, Libertine?', in M. A. Stewart (ed.), *Studies in Seventeenth-Century European Philosophy*, Oxford: Clarendon Press, 1997, 197–226.

Wurtenberger, Thomas, 'Zu den Voraussetzungen des freiheitlichen, säkularen Staates', in W. Brugger and S. Huster (eds.), *Der Streit um das Kreuz in der Schule*, Baden-Baden: Nomos, 1998, 277–96.

Young, Iris, 'A Multicultural Continuum: A Critique of Will Kymlicka's Ethnic-Nation Dichotomy', *Constellations* 4, 1997, 48–53.

Justice and the Politics of Difference, Princeton University Press, 1990.

Young, James P., *Reconsidering American Liberalism: The Troubled Odyssey of the Liberal Idea*, Boulder, Colo.: Westview, 1996.

Young-Bruehl, Elisabeth, *The Anatomy of Prejudices*, Cambridge, Mass.: Harvard University Press, 1996.

Yovel, Yirmiyahu, *Spinoza and Other Heretics*, vol. I: *The Marrano of Reason*, Princeton University Press, 1989.

'Tolerance as Grace and as Rightful Recognition', *Social Research* 65, 1998, 897–919.

Zurbuchen, Simone, *Naturrecht und natürliche Religion: Zur Geschichte des Toleranzbegriffs von Samuel Pufendorf bis Jean-Jacques Rousseau*, Würzburg: Königshausen und Neumann, 1991.

'Samuel Pufendorf's Concept of Toleration', in C. J. Nederman and C. Laursen (eds.), *Difference and Dissent: Theories of Toleration in Medieval and Early Modern Europe*, Lanham, Md.: Rowman and Littlefield, 1996, 163–84.

Index

IDEAS IN CONTEXT

Edited by David Armitage, Jennifer Pitts, Quentin Skinner and
James Tully